**Ordnance Survey**

STREET ATLAS
West Essex

Contents

IV   *Key to maps*

VI   *Administrative boundaries*

1   *Street maps*

196   *Index explanation and abbreviations*

197   *Index of towns, villages and rural localities*

198   *Index of street names*

PHILIP'S

First edition published 1990
Second edition published 1994
Reprinted 1997 by

Ordnance Survey®   and George Philip Ltd.
Romsey Road   an imprint of Reed Books
Maybush   Michelin House, 81 Fulham Road, London, SW3 6RB
Southampton SO16 4GU   and Auckland, Melbourne, Singapore and Toronto

ISBN 0-540-05849-1 (hardback)
ISBN 0-540-05867-X (softback)

To the best of the Publishers' knowledge, the information in this atlas was correct at
the time of going to press. No responsibility can be accepted for any errors or their
consequences.

The representation in this atlas of a road, track or path is no evidence of the
existence of a right of way.

The mapping between pages 1 and 194 (inclusive) in this atlas is derived from
Ordnance Survey® Land-Line® data and Landranger® mapping.

Ordnance Survey, Land-Line and Landranger are registered trade marks of
Ordnance Survey, the National Mapping Agency of Great Britain.

Printed and bound in Great Britain by Bath Press, Bath

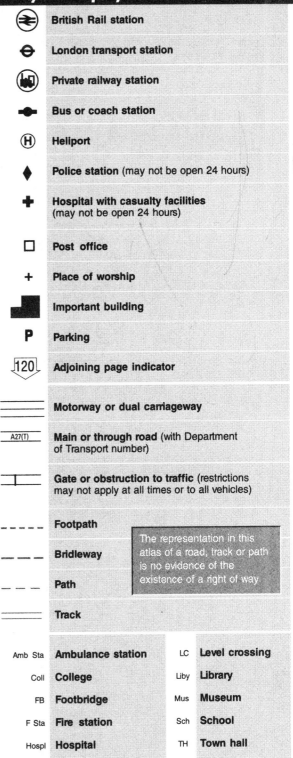

	British Rail station
	London transport station
	Private railway station
	Bus or coach station
(H)	Heliport
♦	**Police station** (may not be open 24 hours)
✚	**Hospital with casualty facilities** (may not be open 24 hours)
☐	Post office
✛	Place of worship
	Important building
P	Parking
120	Adjoining page indicator

	Motorway or dual carriageway
A27(T)	**Main or through road** (with Department of Transport number)
	Gate or obstruction to traffic (restrictions may not apply at all times or to all vehicles)
	Footpath
	Bridleway
	Path
	Track

The representation in this atlas of a road, track or path is no evidence of the existence of a right of way

Amb Sta	Ambulance station	LC	Level crossing
Coll	College	Liby	Library
FB	Footbridge	Mus	Museum
F Sta	Fire station	Sch	School
Hospl	Hospital	TH	Town hall

| 0 | ¼ | ½ | ¾ | 1 mile |
| 0 | 250m | 500m | 250m | 1 Kilometre |

The scale of the maps is 3½ inches to 1 mile (1:18103)

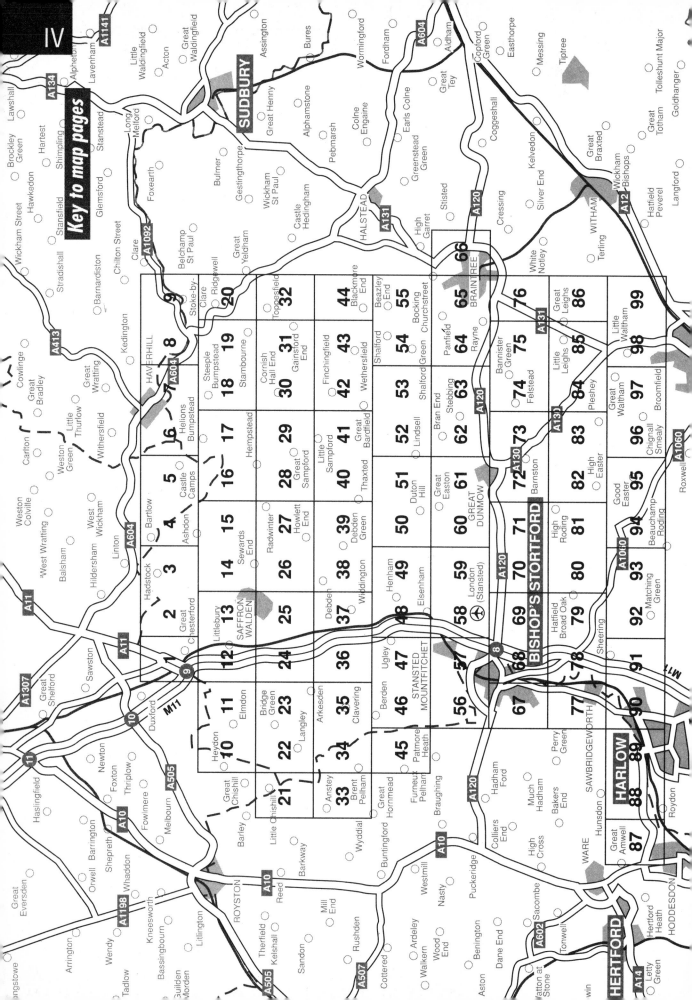

Key to map pages

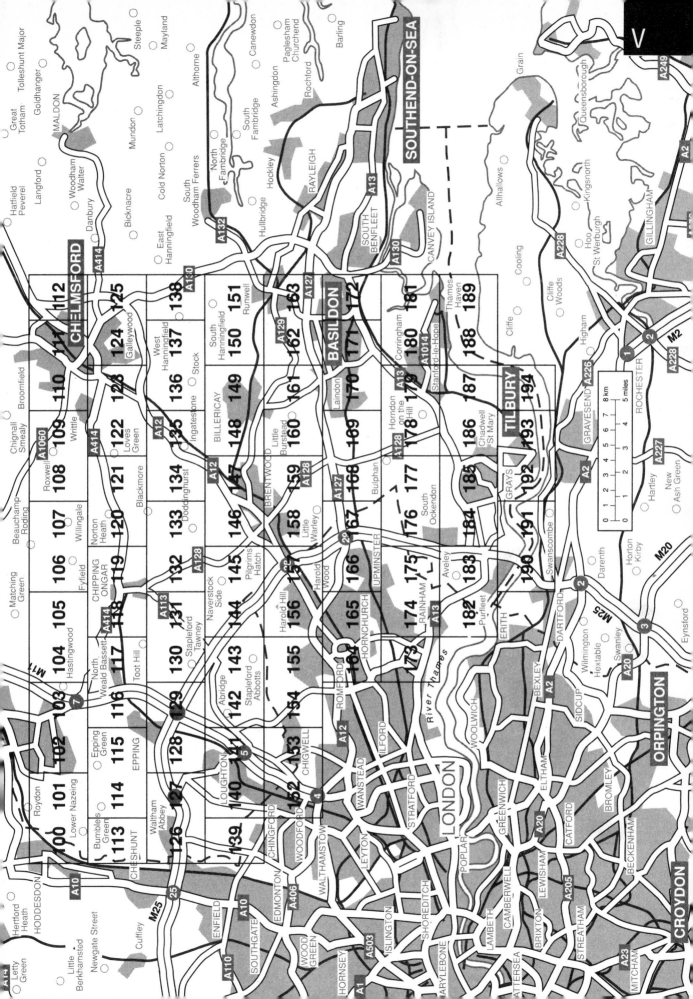

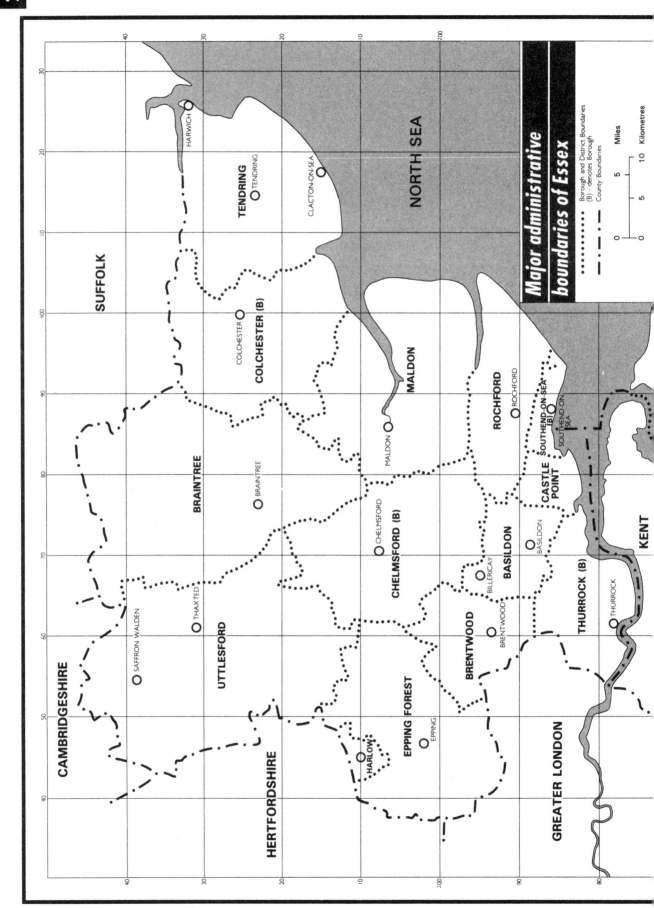

Major administrative boundaries of Essex

Borough and District Boundaries
(B) - denotes Borough
County Boundaries

Miles
0   5   10
0   5   10   Kilometres

SUFFOLK

NORTH SEA

CAMBRIDGESHIRE

HERTFORDSHIRE

GREATER LONDON

KENT

HARWICH

TENDRING

CLACTON-ON-SEA

COLCHESTER (B)

MALDON

ROCHFORD

SOUTHEND-ON-SEA (B)

CASTLE POINT

BRAINTREE

BASILDON

BILLERICAY

CHELMSFORD (B)

THURROCK (B)

BRENTWOOD

SAFFRON WALDEN

THAXTED

UTTLESFORD

EPPING FOREST

EPPING

HARLOW

not continued, see key diagram

A B C

4

A1301

NORTH END RD

DUXFORD RD

Ford

HUNTS LA

MILL LA

Hall
Farm

HIGH ST

Hinxton

CHURCH GREEN

The
Manor

Red Lion
(PH)

NEW RD

ICKLETON RD

Hinxton
Hall

The Bungalow

Park
Cottages

LC

BROOKHAMPTON ST

Cemy

The New Inn
(PH)

LC

MILL LA

BUTCHER'S HILL

ST JS

CHURCH

River Cam or Granta

FROGGE ST

ABBEY ST

PH

BIRDS CL

BACK LA

SOUTHFIELD

Ickleton

PRIORY CL

ICKFIELD CL

M11

M11

COPLOE RD

Strip
Lynchets

Field
Farm

Field Farm
Cottages

Field Farm
Cottages

ROMAN ROAD

45

Park Farm
Cottages

Park Road
Farm

PARK RD

3

A1301

A11(T)

M11

B1184

Stump
Cross

Sewage
Works

Luckfield

Mill House
Farm

Dell's
Farm

44

B1383

Fairacre

NEWMARKET RD

CARMEN ST

JACKSON'S LA

HYLL CL

MANOR

SPENCERS

THE
WILLOWS

BRANLEY
CLOSE
ROWELL

Chesterford
House

COW LA

2

Granta
Cottages

CARMEL ST

SCHOOL ST

Sch

PILGRIMS

HIGH ST

ROSE LA

WALDEN RD

43

CHURCH ST

South ST

FB

LC

ICKLETON
RD

WHITEWAYS

LONDON RD

GRANTA CL

Great
Chesterford

PH

MANOR LA

Manor
Farm

1

Smock Mill
House

Great Chesterford
Station

B1383

Highfield
House

Rectory
Farm

B1184

49 50 51 42

A B C

12

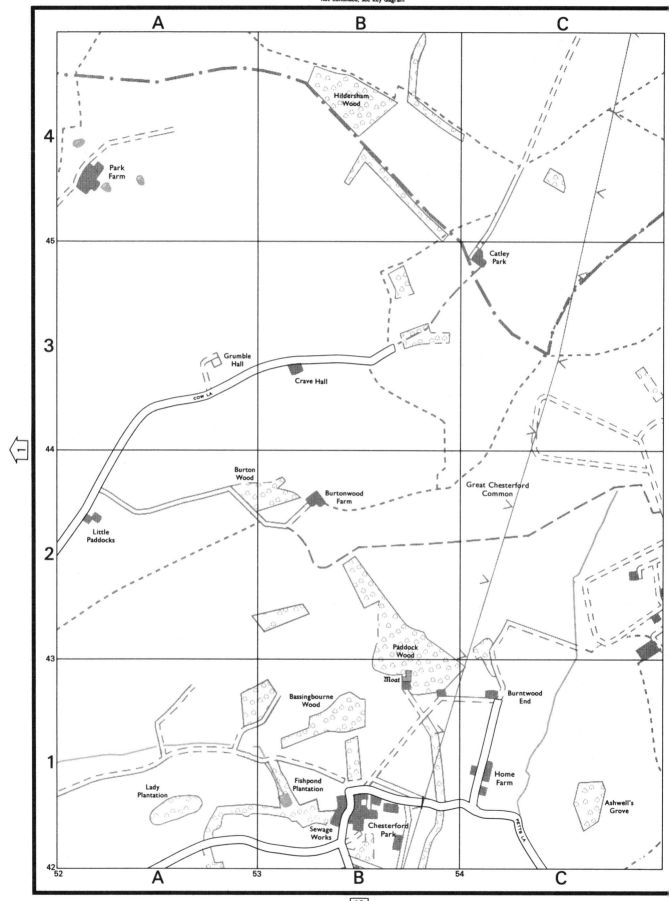

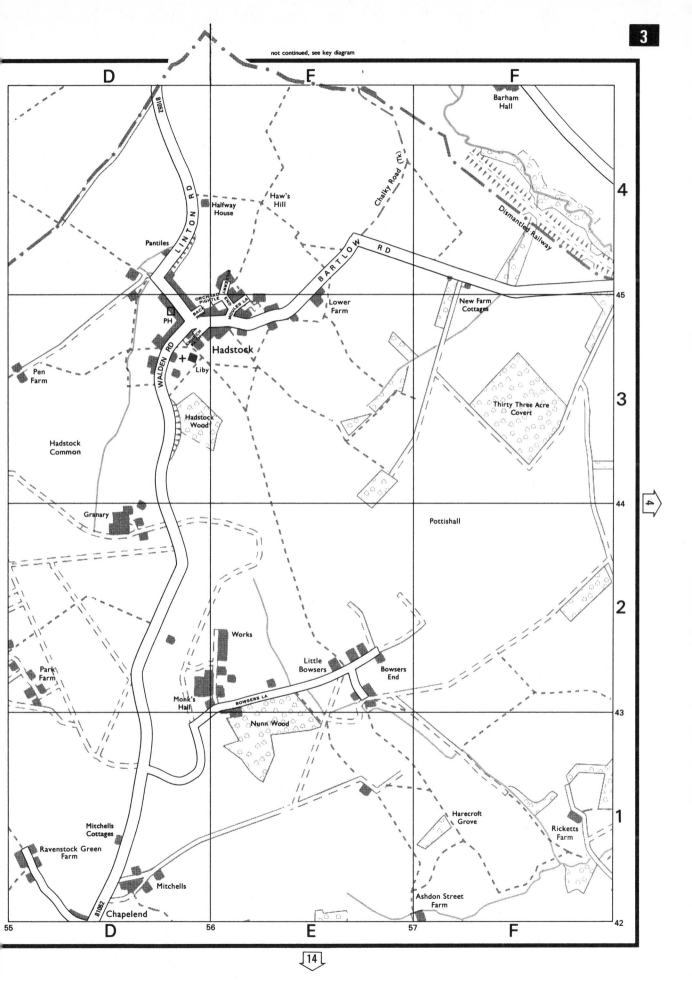

not continued, see key diagram

D

E

F

Barham
Hall

B1052

Haw's
Hill

Halfway
House

4

Chalky Road (Tk)

Dismantled Railway

Pantiles

BARTLOW   RD

LINTON RD

45

New Farm
Cottages

Lower
Farm

ORCHARD
PIGHTLE

MOULES LA

ABBEYS END

BACK
LANE

PH

Hadstock

CHURCH PATH

Liby

WALDEN RD

3

Pen
Farm

Thirty Three Acre
Covert

Hadstock
Wood

Hadstock
Common

44

Granary

Pottishall

4

2

Works

Park
Farm

Little
Bowsers

Bowsers
End

Monk's
Hall

BOWSERS LA

43

Nunn Wood

1

Mitchells
Cottages

Harecroft
Grove

Ricketts
Farm

Ravenstock Green
Farm

Mitchells

B1052

Ashdon Street
Farm

Chapelend

55   D   56   E   57   F   42

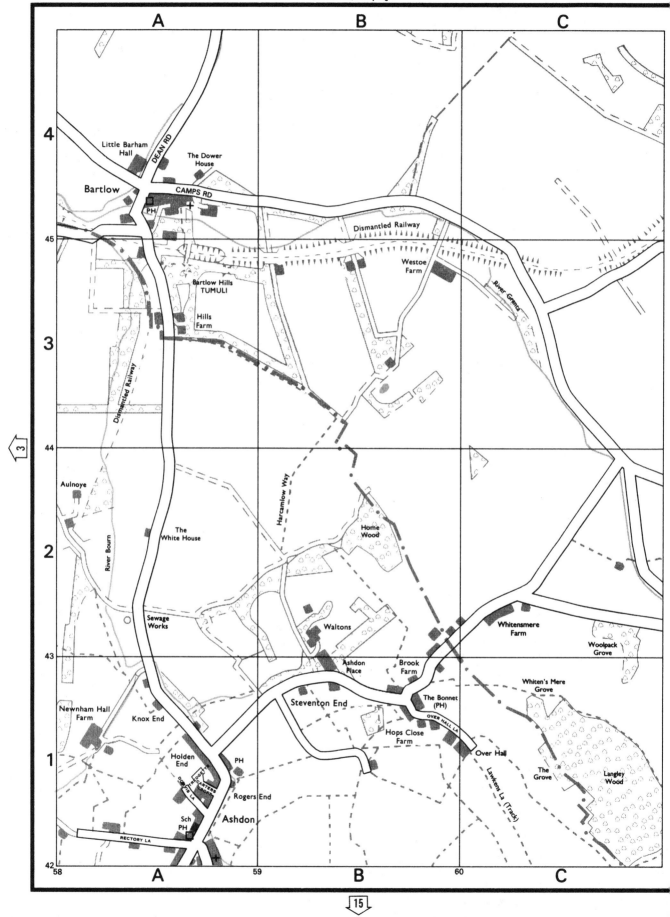

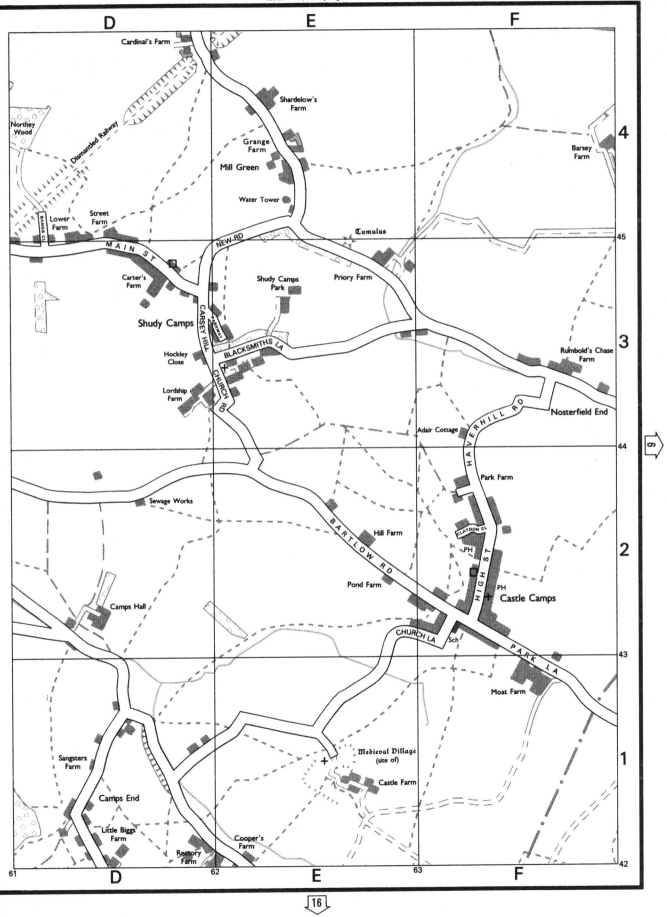

D

E

F

Cardinal's Farm

Northey Wood

Dismantled Railway

Shardelow's Farm

Grange Farm

Mill Green

4

Barsey Farm

Water Tower

Cumulus

45

Lower Farm

BANGS CL

Street Farm

MAIN ST

NEW RD

Carter's Farm

Shudy Camps Park

Priory Farm

Shudy Camps

CARSEY HILL

PARKWAY

BLACKSMITHS LA

Rumbold's Chase Farm

3

Hockley Close

CHURCH RD

Lordship Farm

Nosterfield End

Adair Cottage

HAVERHILL RD

44

6

Park Farm

Sewage Works

BARTLOW RD

Hill Farm

CLAYDON CL

PH

HIGH ST

2

Pond Farm

Camps Hall

PH

Castle Camps

CHURCH LA

Sch

PARK LA

43

Moat Farm

Sangsters Farm

1

Medieval Village (site of)

Camps End

Castle Farm

Little Biggs Farm

Cooper's Farm

Rectory Farm

61

D

62

E

63

F

42

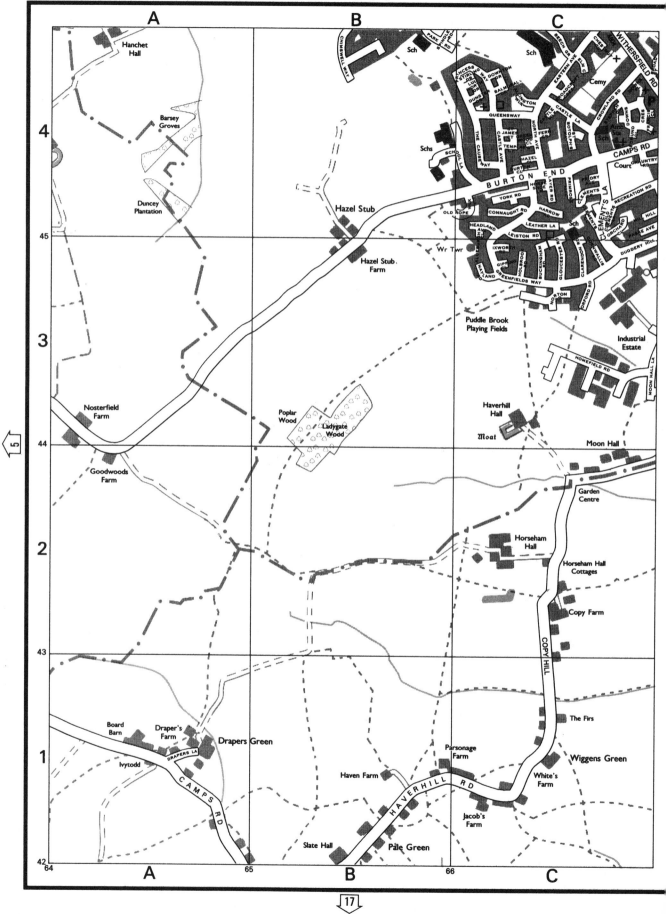

A | B | C

Hanchet Hall

Barsey Groves

Duncey Plantation

4

45

Nosterfield Farm

Goodwoods Farm

5

44

43

Board Barn

Draper's Farm

Drapers Green

Ivytodd

DRAPERS LA

CAMPS RD

42
64

Sch

CHISWELL WAY

PARK HOLE RD

Hazel Stub

Hazel Stub Farm

Wr Twr

Poplar Wood

Ladygate Wood

3

Puddle Brook Playing Fields

Haverhill Hall

Moat

Horseham Hall

2

Slate Hall

Haven Farm

HAVERHILL RD

Pale Green

65

Sch

Sch

Cemy

PRINCESS STIRLING WAY DOWNTON DR
LUI WAY SORREL SALMAN
DUNG WINGTON
QUEENSWAY
ST JAMES ST TEMPLE
URFIELD
HAZEL
SCHOOL LA
THE CAUSEWAY
NORTH AVE
FERN

BEECH GR ELM GR
EASTERN AVE ELK CL
BOAD YE CL
ISLE CASTLE LA
CASTLE ST CROWLAND RD
ARMS STA
DOWNS

CAMPS RD

BURTON END

Court COUNTRY RD

Schs

OLD ROPE

YORK RD
CONNAUGHT RD
LEATHER LA
HEADLAND AVE
LEISTON RD
IXWORTH
GIP

HARROW

CLEMENT'S LA
Sch
ORCHARD

RECREATION RD

HILL
PAGE AVE

DUDDERY HILL

GLOUCESTER RD
CLARENDON RD
NORTON
GREENFIELDS WAY
HAYLAND
WYBERTON
BUCKING

Industrial Estate

HOMEFIELD RD
MOON HALL LA

Moon Hall

Garden Centre

Horseham Hall Cottages

Copy Farm

COPY HILL

The Firs

Parsonage Farm

Wiggens Green

White's Farm

Jacob's Farm

Board Barn

B | C
66

WITHERSFIELD RD

P

17
5

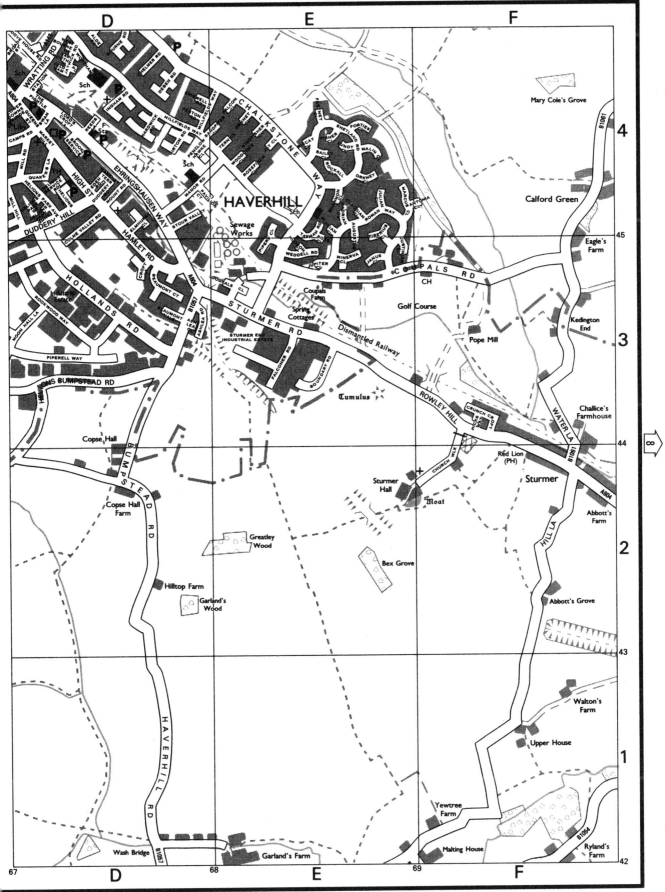

HAVERHILL

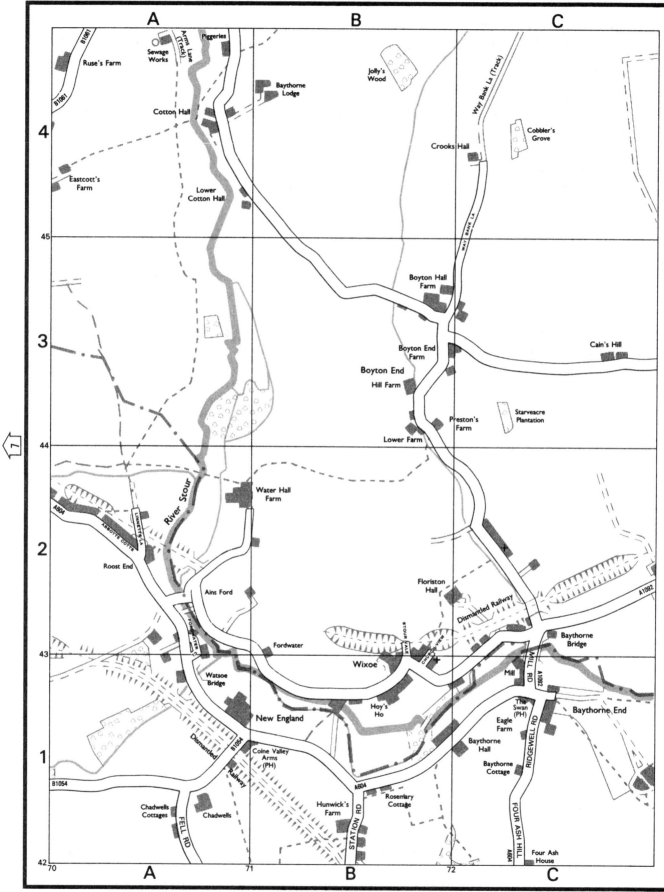

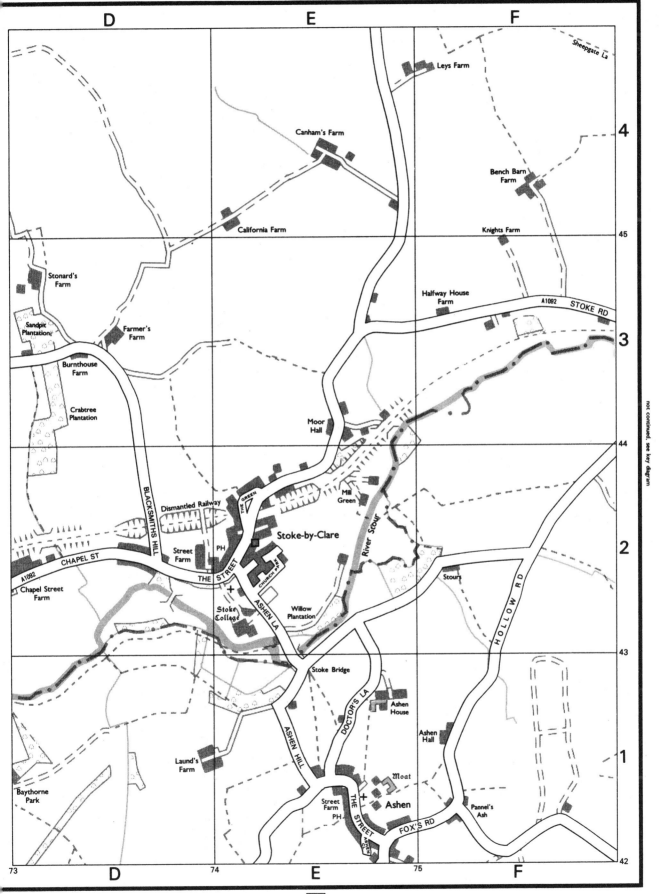

D   E   F

Sheepgate La

Leys Farm

4

Canham's Farm

Bench Barn
Farm

California Farm

Knights Farm

45

Stonard's
Farm

Halfway House
Farm

A1092   STOKE RD

Sandpit
Plantation

Farmer's
Farm

3

Burnthouse
Farm

Crabtree
Plantation

Moor
Hall

44

Dismantled Railway

THE GREEN

Mill
Green

River Stour

BLACKSMITHS HILL

Street
Farm

Stoke-by-Clare

CHAPEL ST

PH

Stours

2

A1092

THE STREET

CHURCH WALK

Chapel Street
Farm

Stoke
College

ASHEN LA

Willow
Plantation

HOLLOW RD

43

Stoke Bridge

Ashen
House

DOCTORS LA

Ashen
Hall

ASHEN HILL

Laund's
Farm

Moat

1

Baythorne
Park

Street
Farm

THE STREET

Ashen

Pannel's
Ash

PH

ASHEN

FOX'S RD

42

73   D   74   E   75   F

not continued, see key diagram

not continued, see key diagram

A   B   C

not continued, see key diagram

ROYSTON LA

The Belt

Redlands

Anthonyhill
Plantation

4

Anthony Hill

Reservoir

Heydon
Valley

41

Valley
Plantation

Reeve
Hill

FOWLMERE RD

3

High
Park

HERTFORD LA

MILL CAUSEWAY

Lane
Farm

Hillside
Farm

Mill
House

HIGH CL

Crawley
End

PINKNEYS

ENGLARIC

Dark Lane
(Path)

Moat

40

Hill
Farm

Heydon

CHISHILL RD

ABRAM'S LA

Wire
Farm

Cane's
Walks

HEYDON LA

Elmdon
Lodge

William the Fourth
(PH)

Arrow
Plantation

Broad
Green

King's
Grove

2

Broad Green
Farm

PALMERS LA

Chrishall

Parkhouse Lane

Dewberry
Grove

Sch

Wisdom's
Grove

The Red Cow
(PH)

HOG'S LA

BRICKS

HIGH ST

CHURCH RD

Park
Wood

39

Home Farm

Parsonage
Farm

CHALKY LA

Barnard's
Wood

Moat

HOLLOW RD

BURY LA

The
Vicarage

1

B1039

New
Farm

BUILDING END RD

White
Bridge

B1039

38
43   44   45

A   B   C

22

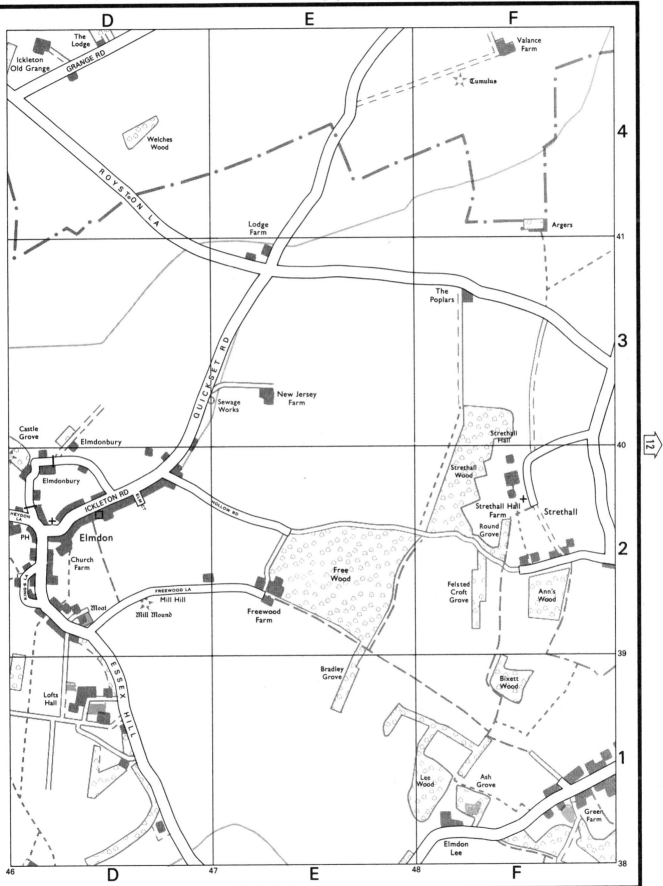

D

E

F

The Lodge

Ickleton
Old Grange

GRANGE RD

Welches
Wood

Valance
Farm

Tumulus

4

ROYSTON LA

Lodge
Farm

Argers

41

The
Poplars

QUICKSET RD

3

Sewage
Works

New Jersey
Farm

Strethall
Hall

Castle
Grove

Elmdonbury

Strethall
Wood

40

Elmdonbury

ICKLETON RD

HOLLOW RD

Strethall Hall
Farm

Strethall

ELM ST

HEYDON LA

Elmdon

Round
Grove

2

PH

Church
Farm

Free
Wood

Felsted
Croft
Grove

Ann's
Wood

KING'S LA

Moat

Mill Hill

FREEWOOD LA

Mill Mound

Freewood
Farm

ESSEX HILL

Bradley
Grove

39

Bixett
Wood

Lofts
Hall

1

Lee
Wood

Ash
Grove

Green
Farm

Elmdon
Lee

38

46

D

47

E

48

F

12

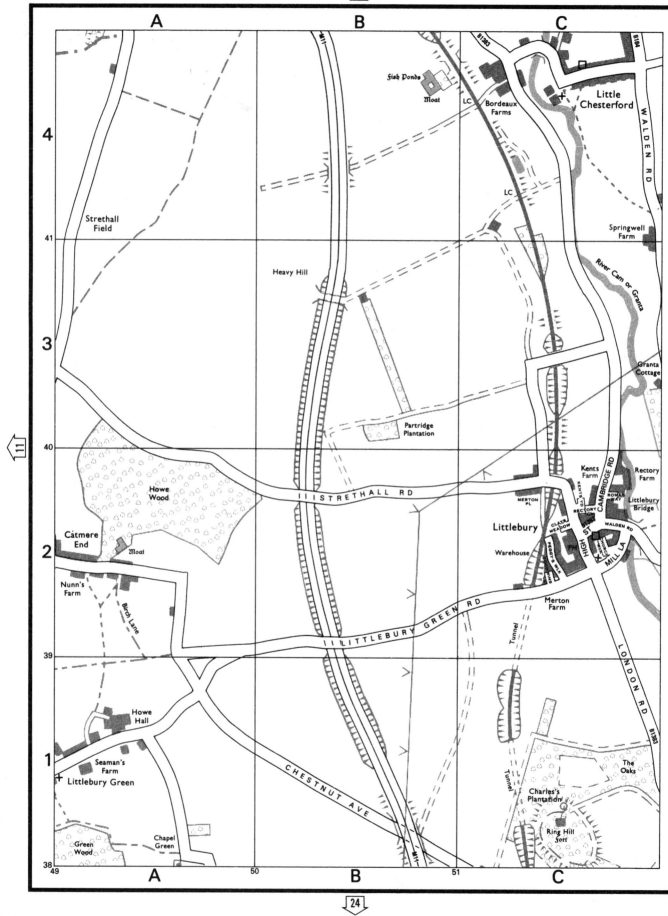

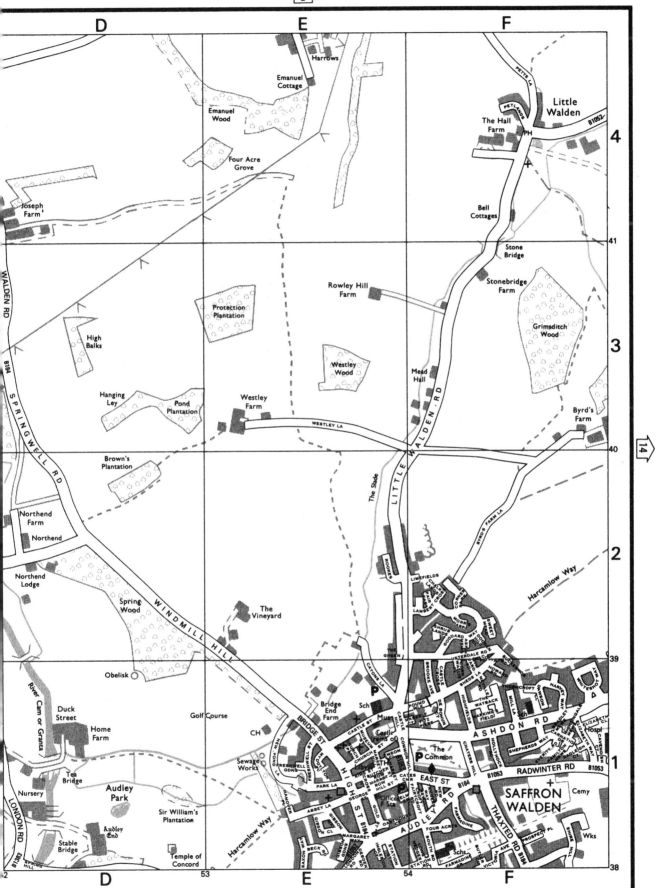

2

D   E   F

Harrows

Emanuel
Cottage

Emanuel
Wood

Little
Walden

PETTS LA

PETLANDS

B1052

The Hall
Farm

PH

4

Four Acre
Grove

Bell
Cottages

Joseph
Farm'

41

WALDEN RD

Stone
Bridge

Rowley Hill
Farm

Stonebridge
Farm

Protection
Plantation

High
Balks

Grimsditch
Wood

3

B184

Westley
Wood

Mead
Hall

Hanging
Ley

Pond
Plantation

Westley
Farm

Byrd's
Farm

SPRINGWELL RD

Brown's
Plantation

WESTLEY LA

LITTLE WALDEN RD

40

14

The Slade

Northend
Farm

Northend

BYRD'S FARM LA

2

Harcamlow Way

LIMEFIELDS

Northend
Lodge

Spring
Wood

WINDMILL HILL

The
Vineyard

THE
GREEN

39

Obelisk

Golf Course

Bridge
End
Farm

Sch

P

ASHDON RD

River Cam or Granta

Duck
Street

Home
Farm

CH

BRIDGE ST

Castle
Mus

Castle

HIGH ST

The
Common

P

RADWINTER RD

B1053

B1053

1

Tea
Bridge

Sewage
Works

EAST ST

B184

Nursery

Audley
Park

Sir William's
Plantation

SAFFRON
WALDEN

Cemy

THAXTED RD B184

Wks

LONDON RD

Audley
End

Stable
Bridge

B1383

SPRING HILL

Temple of
Concord

Schs

PROSPECT PL

Shire Hill

38

D   53   E   54   F

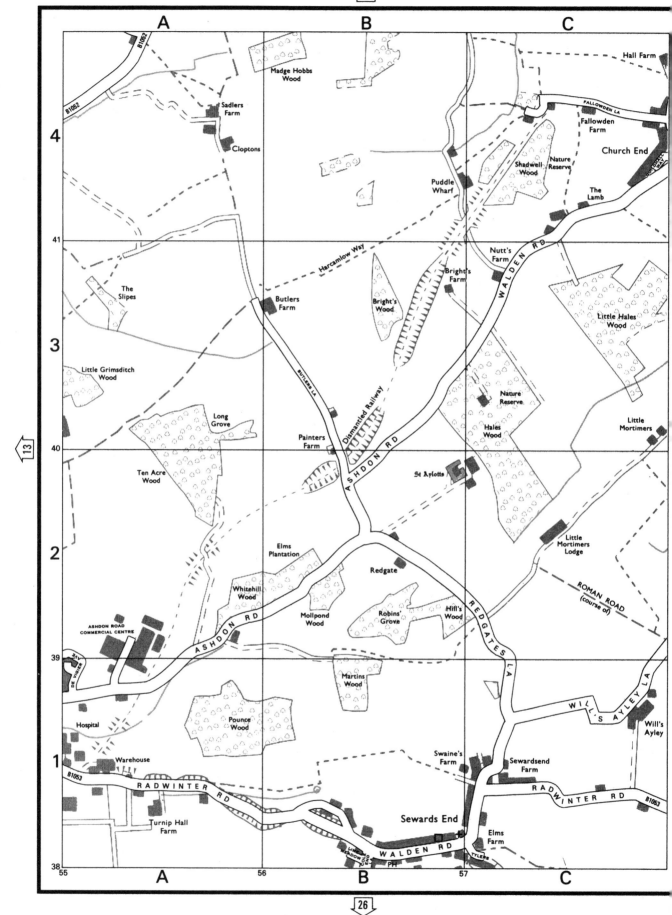

A   **B**   **C**

Hall Farm

B1052

Madge Hobbs Wood

FALLOWDEN LA

Sadlers Farm

Fallowden Farm

Church End

B1052

Cloptons

Shadwell Wood

Nature Reserve

Puddle Wharf

The Lamb

4

WALDEN RD

Nutt's Farm

41

Harcamlow Way

Bright's Farm

The Slipes

Butlers Farm

Bright's Wood

Little Hales Wood

Little Grimsditch Wood

BUTLERS LA

3

Dismantled Railway

Nature Reserve

Long Grove

ASHDON RD

Little Mortimers

Painters Farm

Hales Wood

40

St Aylotts

Ten Acre Wood

Little Mortimers Lodge

Elms Plantation

Redgate

ROMAN ROAD (course of)

2

Whitehill Wood

Robins' Grove

Hill's Wood

REDGATES LA

Mollpond Wood

ASHDON RD

ASHDON ROAD COMMERCIAL CENTRE

WILL'S AYLEY LA

39

DE VIGIER AV

Martins Wood

Hospital

Pounce Wood

Will's Ayley

Warehouse

Swaine's Farm

Sewardsend Farm

1

B1053

RADWINTER RD

RADWINTER RD

B1053

Turnip Hall Farm

Sewards End

Elms Farm

LINDSEL MEADOW ROAD

WALDEN RD

TYLERS

PH

38

55   **A**   56   **B**   57   **C**

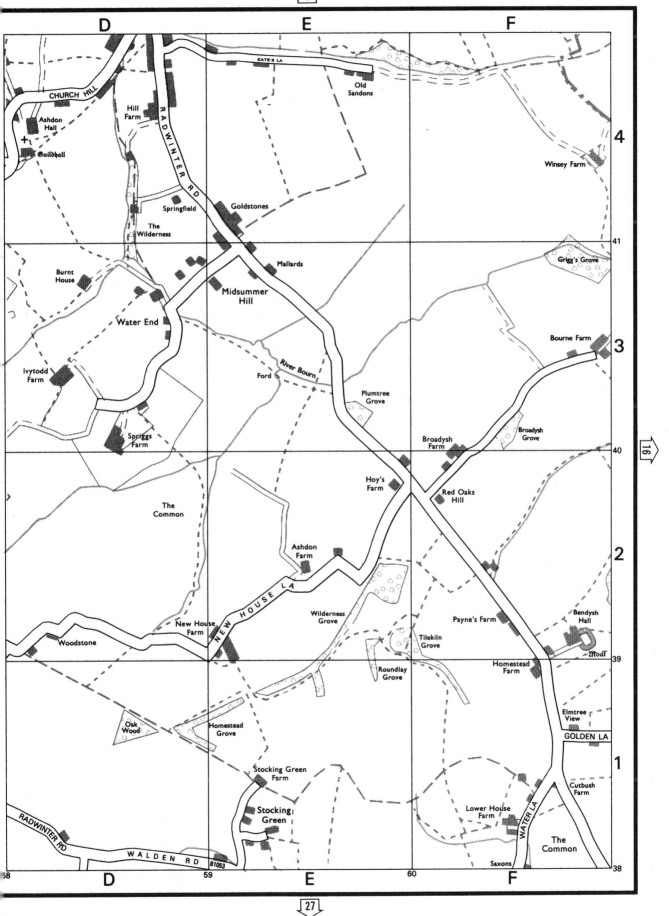

D   E   F

KATE'S LA

Old Sandons

CHURCH HILL

Hill Farm

Ashdon Hall

RADWINTER RD

+ Guildhall

Winsey Farm

4

Springfield

Goldstones

The Wilderness

Mallards

41

Burnt House

Midsummer Hill

Grigg's Grove

Water End

River Bourn

Bourne Farm

3

Ford

Plumtree Grove

Ivytodd Farm

Broadysh Grove

Spriggs Farm

Broadysh Farm

40

16

The Common

Hoy's Farm

Red Oaks Hill

2

Ashdon Farm

Wilderness Grove

Payne's Farm

Bendysh Hall

NEW HOUSE LA

Tilekiln Grove

Moat

New House Farm

Homestead Farm

39

Woodstone

Roundlay Grove

Elmtree View

Oak Wood

Homestead Grove

GOLDEN LA

1

Stocking Green Farm

Cutbush Farm

RADWINTER RD

Stocking Green

Lower House Farm

WATER LA

The Common

WALDEN RD

B1053

Saxons

38

58   D   59   E   60   F   38

15

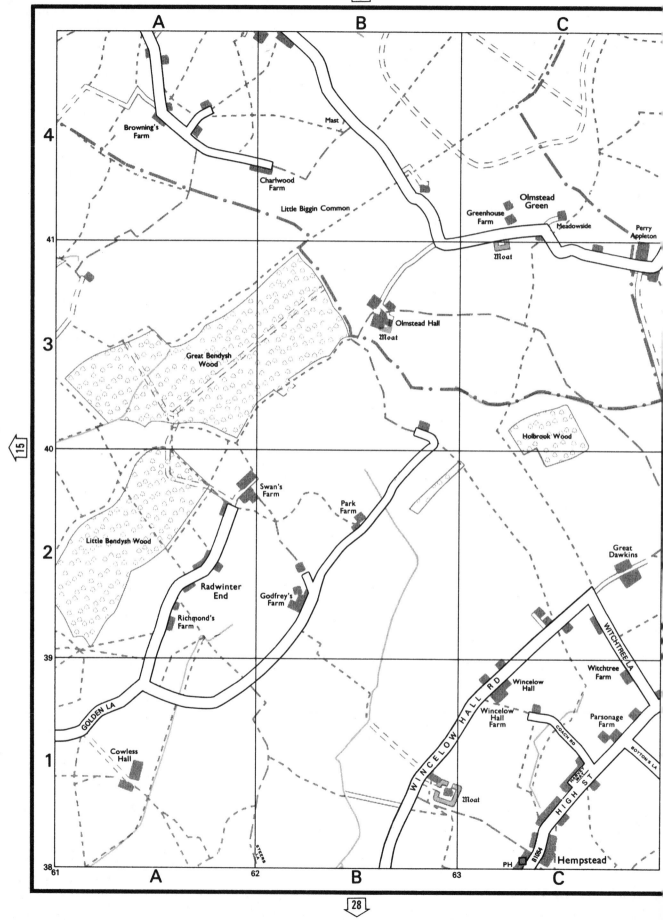

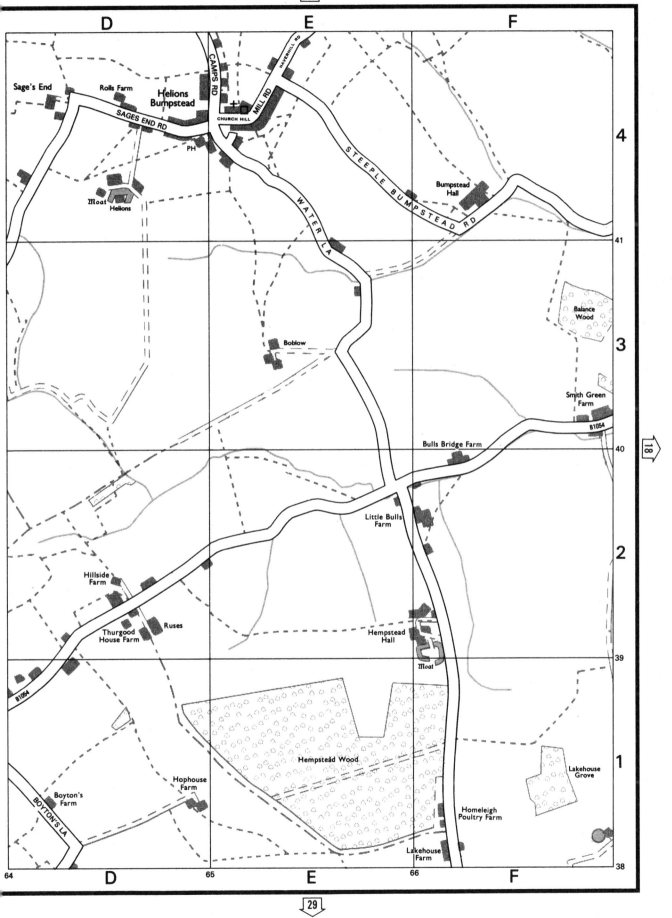

D　　　　　　　　　　　E　　　　　　　　　　　F

Sage's End

Rolls Farm

Helions
Bumpstead

CAMPS RD

HAVERHILL RD

MILL RD

SAGES END RD

CHURCH HILL

PH

4

Moat
Helions

WATER LA

STEEPLE BUMPSTEAD RD

Bumpstead
Hall

41

Balance
Wood

Boblow

3

Smith Green
Farm

B1054

Bulls Bridge Farm

40

18

Little Bulls
Farm

2

Hillside
Farm

Ruses

Thurgood
House Farm

Hempstead
Hall

39

Moat

B1054

Hempstead Wood

1

Lakehouse
Grove

Boyton's
Farm

Hophouse
Farm

BOYTON'S LA

Homeleigh
Poultry Farm

Lakehouse
Farm

64　　　　　　D　　　　　65　　　　　E　　　　　66　　　　　F　　　　38

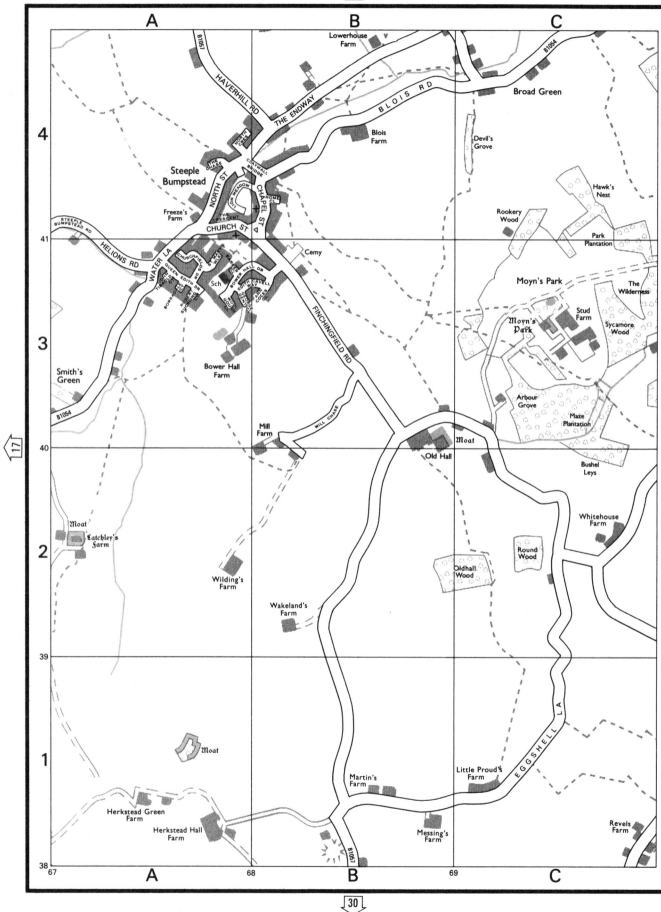

17

A   B   C

4

Lowerhouse Farm

B1057

HAVERHILL RD

THE ENDWAY

BLOIS RD

B1054

Broad Green

Blois Farm

Devil's Grove

Hawk's Nest

Steeple Bumpstead

NORTH COLES

THE CHASE

COLTWALL BRIDGE

HOME CL

Rookery Wood

Park Plantation

NORTH ST

THE CRESCENT

LON MEADOW

Freeze's Farm

CHAPEL ST

CHURCH ST

41

STEEPLE BUMPSTEAD RD

HELIONS RD

WATER LA

Cemy

Moyn's Park

The Wilderness

SCHOOL

CHURCH

QUEEN EDITH DR

ST MARY WAY

BOWER HALL DR

SOUTH COLES

Sch

EDITH WAY

CAVELL WAY

Stud Farm

Sycamore Wood

Moyn's Park

3

Smith's Green

Bower Hall Farm

FINCHINGFIELD RD

Arbour Grove

Maze Plantation

B1054

Mill Farm

MILL CHASE

Moat

Bushel Leys

40

Old Hall

Moat

Latchley's Farm

Whitehouse Farm

2

Round Wood

Wilding's Farm

Oldhall Wood

Wakeland's Farm

39

1

Moat

EGGSHELL LA

Martin's Farm

Little Proud's Farm

Revels Farm

Herkstead Green Farm

Herkstead Hall Farm

B1057

Messing's Farm

38

67   A   68   B   69   C

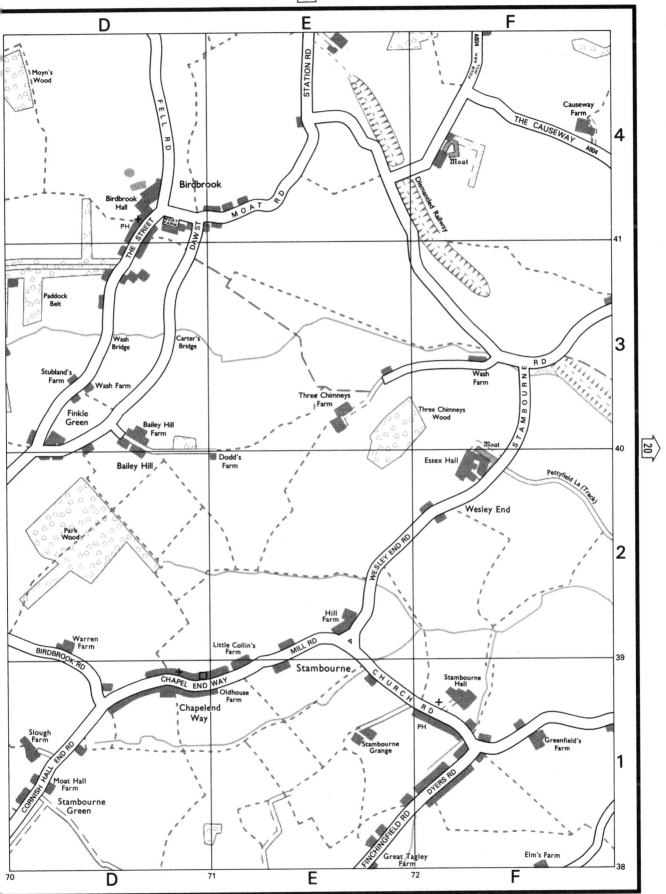

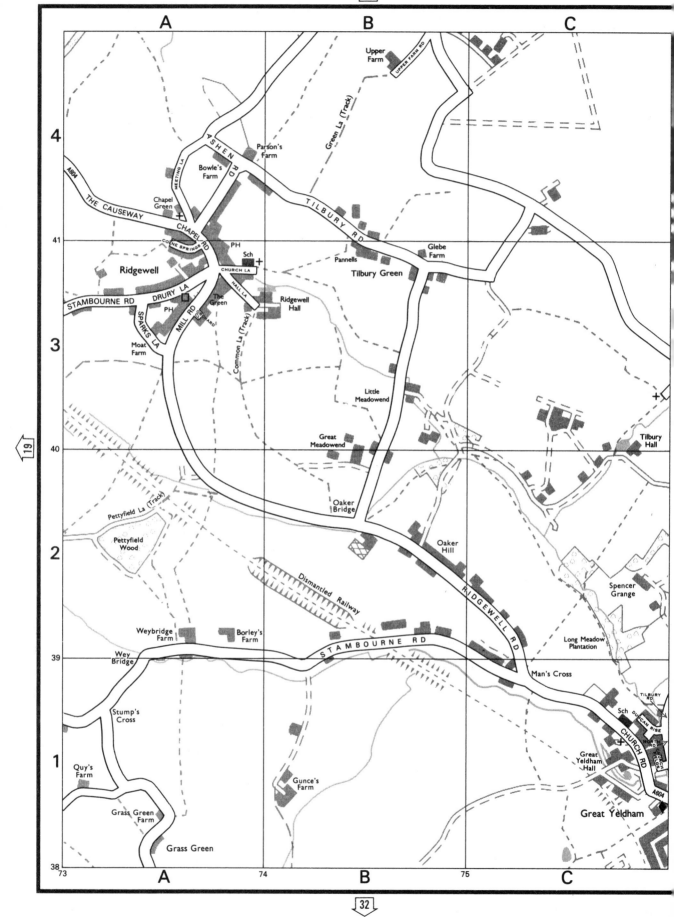

A   B   C

Upper Farm

UPPER FARM RD

Green La (Track)

ASHEND RD

MEETING LA

Parson's Farm

Bowle's Farm

THE CAUSEWAY

A604

Chapel Green

TILBURY RD

CHAPEL RD

COLNE SPRINGS RD

PH

Sch

Glebe Farm

Pannells

Tilbury Green

Ridgewell

CHURCH LA

HALL LA

STAMBOURNE RD

DRURY LA

MILL RD

The Green

PH

SPARKS LA

Ridgewell Hall

Moat Farm

Common La (Track)

Little Meadowend

Great Meadowend

Tilbury Hall

Pettyfield La (Track)

Pettyfield Wood

Oaker Bridge

Oaker Hill

RIDGEWELL RD

Spencer Grange

Dismantled Railway

Weybridge Farm

Borley's Farm

STAMBOURNE RD

Long Meadow Plantation

Wey Bridge

Man's Cross

Stump's Cross

TILBURY RD

Sch

DUNCAN RISE

Quy's Farm

CHURCH RD

NORTH RD

HIGH ST

Great Yeldham Hall

Gunce's Farm

A604

Grass Green Farm

Great Yeldham

Grass Green

73   A   74   B   75   C

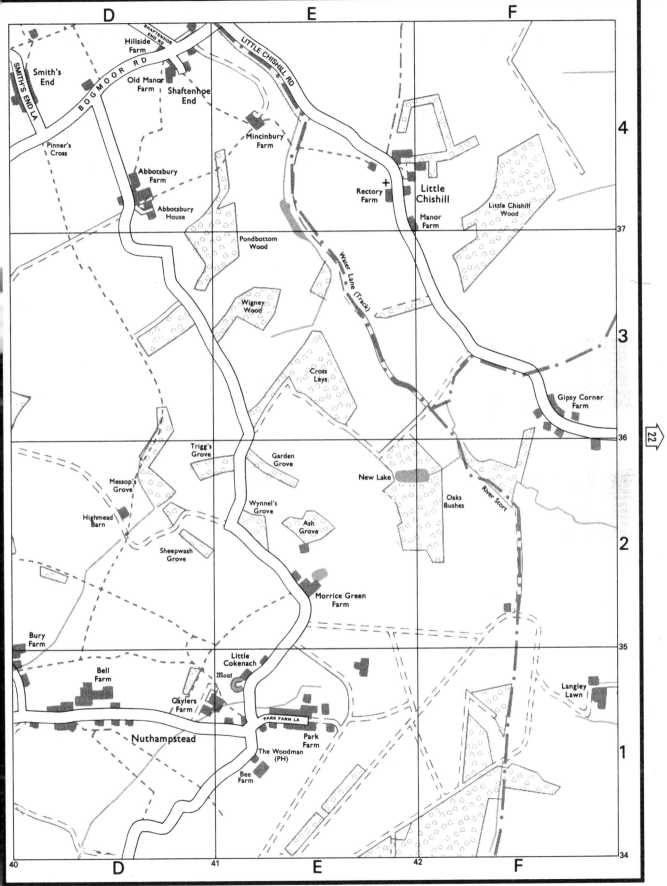

D · E · F

22

Smith's End
Hillside Farm
SHAFTENHOE END RD
BOGMOOR RD
Old Manor Farm
Shaftenhoe End
LITTLE CHISHILL RD
Pinner's Cross
SMITH'S END LA
Mincinbury Farm
Rectory Farm
Little Chishill
Little Chishill Wood
4
Abbotsbury Farm
Manor Farm
Abbotsbury House
Pondbottom Wood
37
Wigney Wood
Water Lane (Track)
3
Cross Leys
Gipsy Corner Farm
Trigg's Grove
Garden Grove
36
Messop's Grove
New Lake
River Stort
Highmead Barn
Wynnel's Grove
Ash Grove
Oaks Bushes
2
Sheepwash Grove
Morrice Green Farm
Bury Farm
35
Little Cokenach
Bell Farm
Moat
Langley Lawn
Gaylers Farm
PARK FARM LA
Nuthampstead
Park Farm
The Woodman (PH)
1
Bee Farm
34
40 · 41 · 42

21

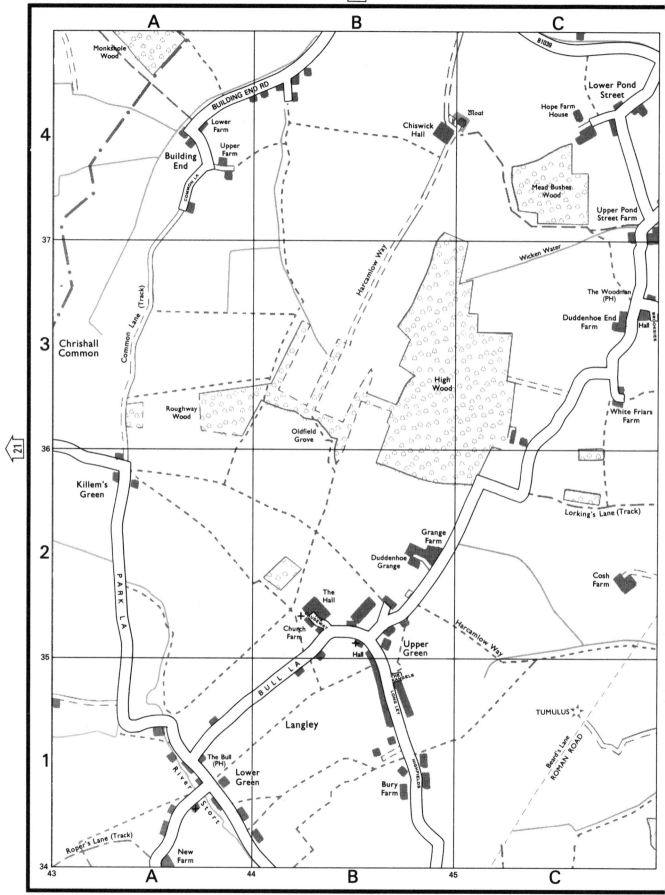

A   B   C

Monkshole Wood

BUILDING END RD

Lower Farm

Building End

Upper Farm

COMMON LA

Chiswick Hall

Moat

Lower Pond Street

Hope Farm House

Mead Bushes Wood

Upper Pond Street Farm

Harcamlow Way

Wicken Water

The Woodman (PH)

Chrishall Common

Common Lane (Track)

Duddenhoe End Farm

Hall

BROOKSIES

B1039

High Wood

Roughway Wood

Oldfield Grove

White Friars Farm

Killem's Green

Lorking's Lane (Track)

PARK LA

Grange Farm

Duddenhoe Grange

Cosh Farm

The Hall

CAUSEWAY

Church Farm

Upper Green

Harcamlow Way

Hall

TUMULUS

BULL LA

THE RANGELS

LONG LEY

Langley

Beard's Lane

ROMAN ROAD

The Bull (PH)

Lower Green

HIGHFIELDS

Bury Farm

River Stort

Roper's Lane (Track)

New Farm

34

43 A   44   B   45   C

37

36

35

34

3

2

1

4

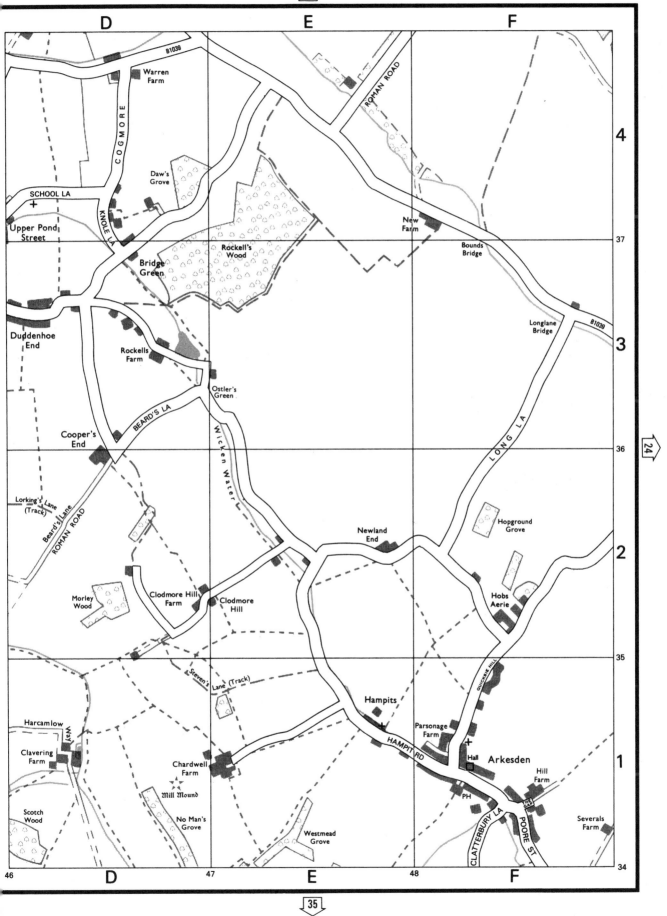

24

D   E   F

B1039

Warren Farm

COGMORE

Daw's Grove

SCHOOL LA

Upper Pond Street

KNOLE LA

Bridge Green

Rockell's Wood

New Farm

Bounds Bridge

4

37

Duddenhoe End

Rockells Farm

Ostler's Green

Longlane Bridge

B1039

3

BEARD'S LA

Cooper's End

Wicken Water

LONG LA

36

Lorking's Lane (Track)

Beard's Lane

ROMAN ROAD

Newland End

Hopground Grove

2

Morley Wood

Clodmore Hill Farm

Clodmore Hill

Hobs Aerie

35

Steven's Lane (Track)

Hampits

QUICKSIE HILL

Harcamlow Way

Parsonage Farm

Clavering Farm

Chardwell Farm

Hall

Arkesden

Hill Farm

1

Mill Mound

HAMPIT RD

PH

Scotch Wood

No Man's Grove

Westmead Grove

CLATTERBURY LA

POORE ST

Severals Farm

34

46   D   47   E   48   F

ROMAN ROAD

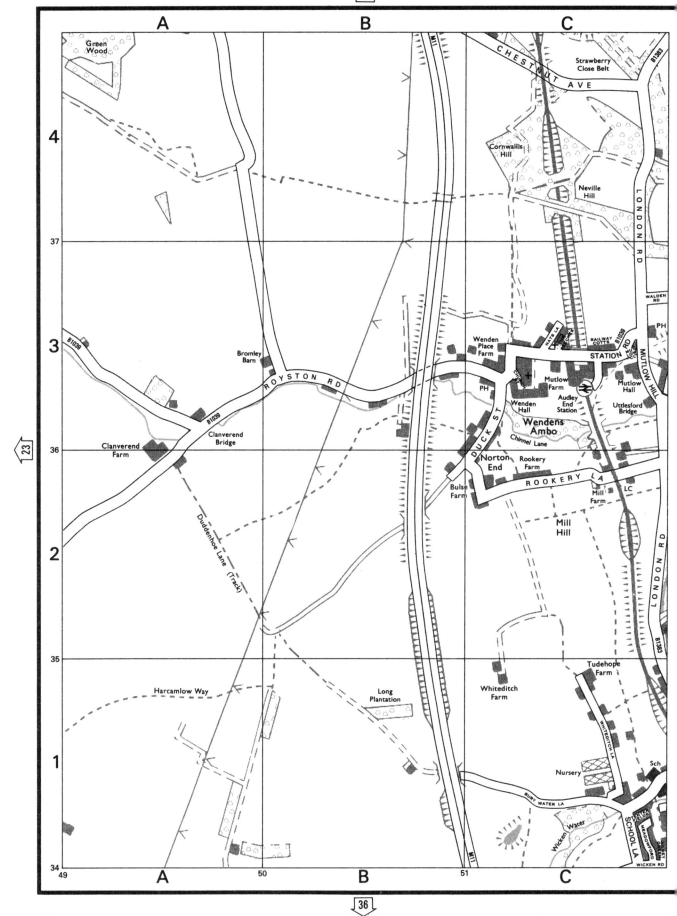

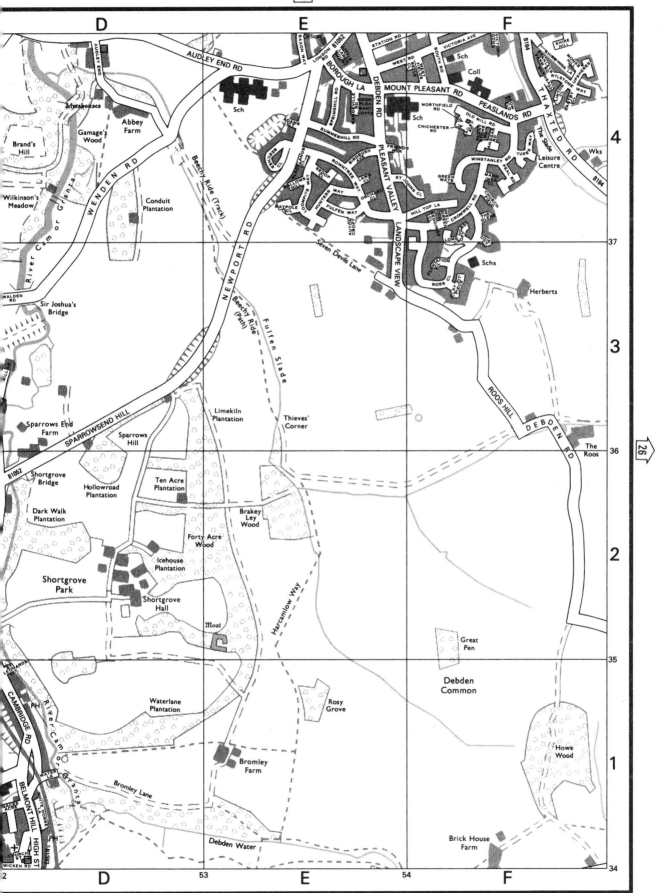

D

E

F

AUDLEY END RD

Offices

SAXON WAY

STATION RD

VICTORIA AVE

SHIRE HILL

B1184

BOROUGH LA

B1052

WEST RD

SOUTH RD

Sch

Coll

MOUNT PLEASANT RD

PEASLANDS RD

DEBDEN RD

RYLSTONE WAY

SHIREHILL LA

UPPSGEE

THAXTED RD

Almshouses

Gamage's Wood

Abbey Farm

Sch

ADAMS

SUMMERHILL RD

MOUNT PLEASANT COTT

NORTHFIELD RD

Sch

CHICHESTER RD

OLD MILL RD

The Slade

Leisure Centre

B1184

Wks

4

Brand's Hill

WENDEN RD

Conduit Plantation

Beechy Ride (Track)

NEWPORT RD

SUMMERHILL RD

BIRDBUSH WAY

ROWNTREE WAY

Sch

PLEASANT VALLEY

St JOHNS CL

WINSTANLEY RD

GREEN WAYS

MAHAI INGS

CHURCH

37

Wilkinson's Meadow

River Cam or Granta

MELLOW

COMPITS WAY

BEECH

MAYPOLE CL

HUNTERS WAY

PULFEN WAY

AUTUMN

ORCHARD

HILL TOP LA

CROMWELL RD

LONG

LANDSCAPE VIEW

Sir Joshua's Bridge

WALDEN RD

Seven Devils Lane

Schs

3

Beechy Ride (Path)

Fulfen Slade

ROSS

Herberts

ROOS HILL

Limekiln Plantation

Thieves' Corner

DEBDEN RD

36

26

Sparrows End Farm

SPARROWSEND HILL

Sparrows Hill

The Roos

B1052

Shortgrove Bridge

Hollowroad Plantation

Ten Acre Plantation

Dark Walk Plantation

Brakey Ley Wood

2

Forty Acre Wood

Icehouse Plantation

Harcamlow Way

Great Pen

Shortgrove Park

Shortgrove Hall

Moat

35

Debden Common

CAMBRIDGE RD

LEONARDS

PH

River Cam or Granta

Waterlane Plantation

Rosy Grove

1

BELMONT HILL

WATER

WHITE HORSE

Bromley Farm

Howe Wood

Bromley Lane

CHURCH ST

HIGH ST

PH

B1088

WICKEN RD

Debden Water

Brick House Farm

34

D

53

E

54

F

14

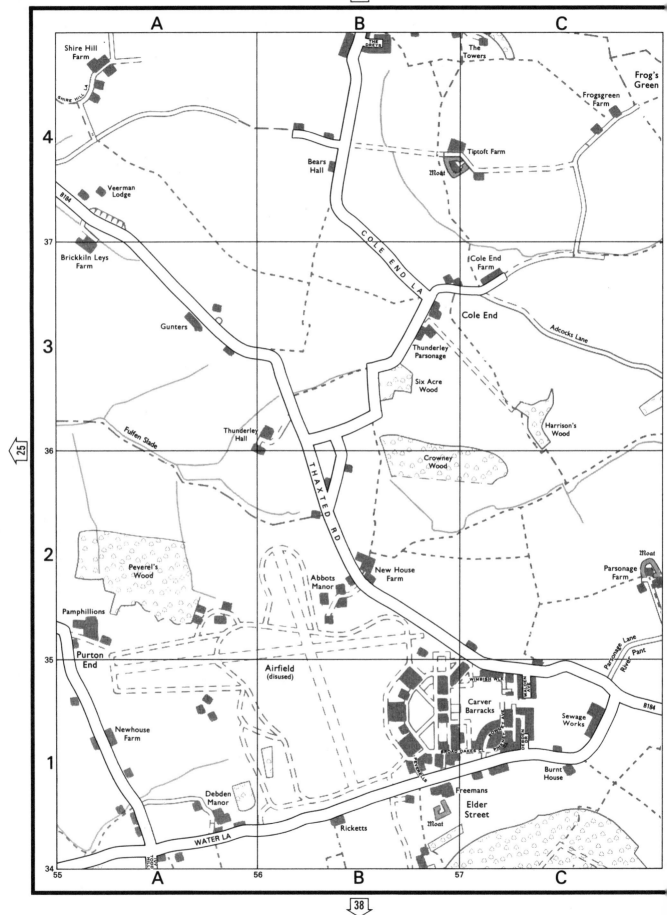

25

A **B** **C**

Shire Hill
Farm

SHIRE HILL LA

THE DREYS

The
Towers

Frog's
Green

Frogsgreen
Farm

Bears
Hall

Tiptoft Farm

Moat

B184

Veerman
Lodge

COLE END LA

37

Brickkiln Leys
Farm

Cole End
Farm

Gunters

Cole End

Adcocks Lane

3

Thunderley
Parsonage

Six Acre
Wood

Harrison's
Wood

Fulfen Slade

Thunderley
Hall

36

THAXTED RD

Crowney
Wood

2

Peverel's
Wood

Abbots
Manor

New House
Farm

Moat

Parsonage
Farm

Pamphillions

Parsonage Lane

River Pant

Purton
End

35

Airfield
(disused)

WIMBISH WK

WALDEN AVE

B184

Carver
Barracks

Sewage
Works

Newhouse
Farm

TOWER RD

BIRCHLEY AVE

DEBDEN

BROAD OAKES LA

PEVERELLS

Burnt
House

1

Freemans

Elder
Street

Debden
Manor

Moat

TODD HILL

WATER LA

Ricketts

34

55   56   57

A **B** **C**

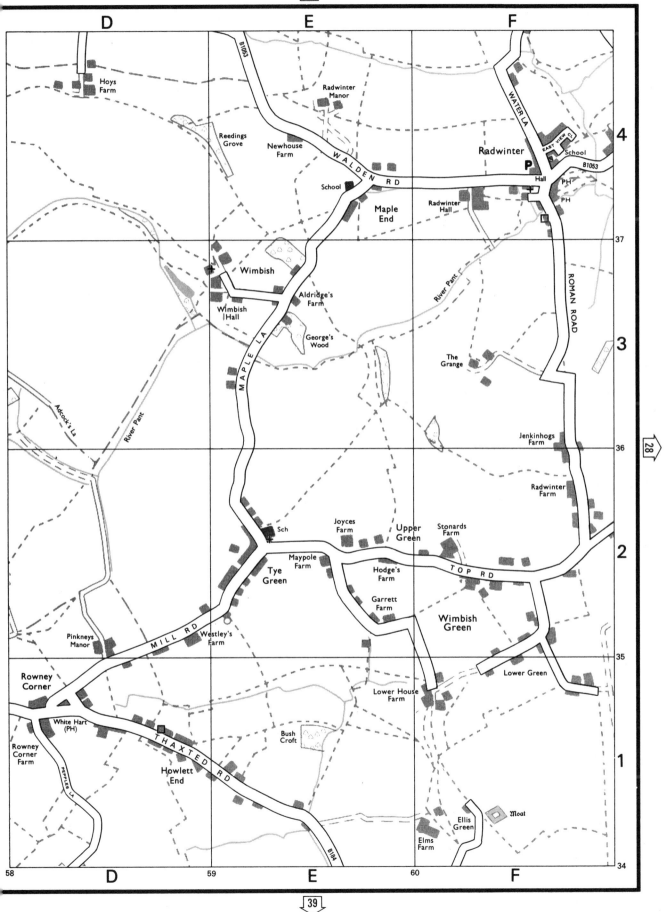

D E F

Hoys Farm

Reedings Grove

Radwinter Manor

B1053

WALDEN RD

Newhouse Farm

School

Maple End

WATER LA

Radwinter

EAST VIEW CL

School

P

Hall

B1053

PH

PH

Radwinter Hall

4

37

Wimbish

Aldridge's Farm

George's Wood

River Pant

River Pant

ROMAN ROAD

The Grange

Wimbish Hall

MAPLE LA

3

Adcock's La

River Pant

Jenkinhogs Farm

36

28

Radwinter Farm

Sch

Joyces Farm

Upper Green

Stonards Farm

Maypole Farm

Tye Green

Hodge's Farm

TOP RD

2

Garrett Farm

Wimbish Green

MILL RD

Pinkneys Manor

Westley's Farm

Lower Green

35

Rowney Corner

Lower House Farm

White Hart (PH)

THAXTED RD

Bush Croft

Rowney Corner Farm

PEPPLES LA

1

Howlett End

Moat

Ellis Green

B184

Elms Farm

34

58 D 59 E 60 F

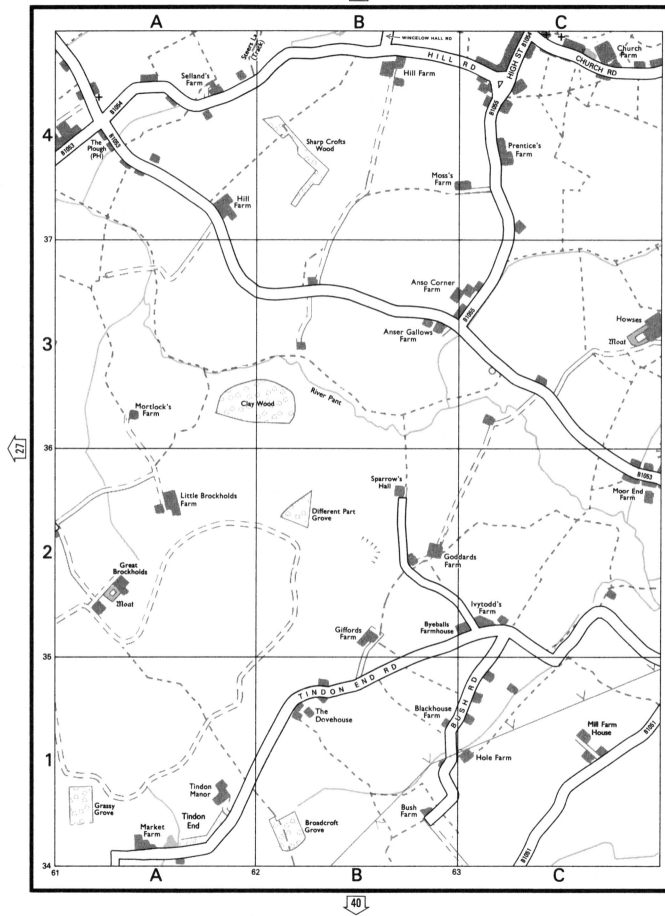

A B C

Seers La. (Track)

WINCELOW HALL RD

HILL RD

HIGH ST B1054

CHURCH RD

Church Farm

Selland's Farm

Hill Farm

B1054

B1055

The Plough (PH)

B1053

B1053

Sharp Crofts Wood

Prentice's Farm

4

Moss's Farm

Hill Farm

37

Anso Corner Farm

B1055

3

Anser Gallows Farm

Howses

Moat

Mortlock's Farm

Clay Wood

River Pant

36

B1053

Sparrow's Hall

Moor End Farm

Little Brockholds Farm

Different Part Grove

2

Goddards Farm

Great Brockholds

Ivytodd's Farm

Moat

Byeballs Farmhouse

Giffords Farm

35

TINDON END RD

BUSH RD

The Dovehouse

Blackhouse Farm

Mill Farm House

B1051

1

Hole Farm

Grassy Grove

Tindon Manor

Tindon End

Broadcroft Grove

Bush Farm

Market Farm

B1051

34

61 A 62 B 63 C

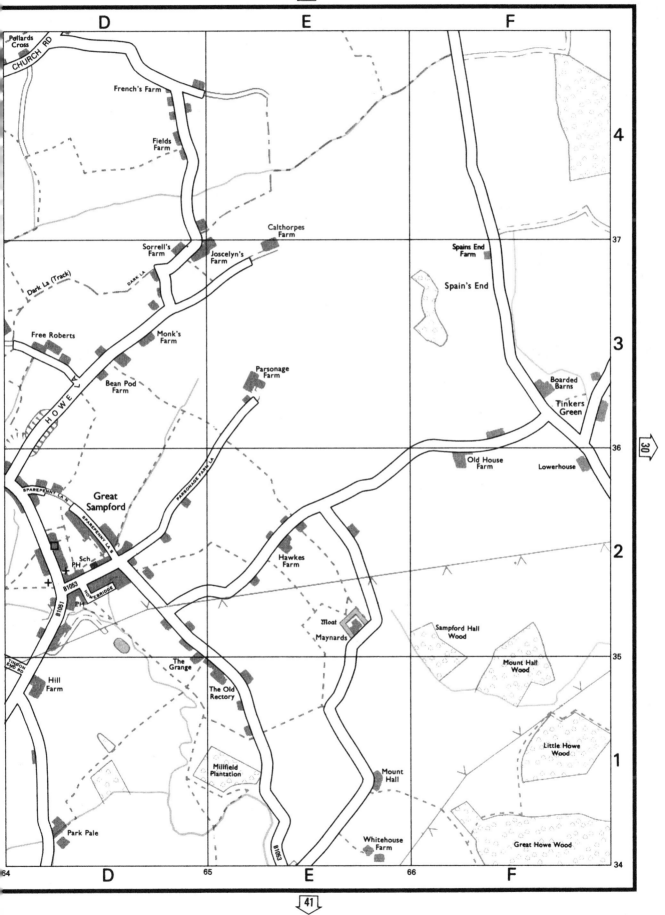

D   E   F

Pollards Cross

CHURCH RD

French's Farm

Fields Farm

Calthorpes Farm

Sorrell's Farm

Joscelyn's Farm

Dark La (Track)

DARK LA

Free Roberts

Monk's Farm

Bean Pod Farm

HOWE LA

Parsonage Farm

Spains End Farm

Spain's End

Boarded Barns

Tinkers Green

SPAREPENNY LA N

Great Sampford

PARSONAGE FARM LA

Old House Farm

Lowerhouse

Sch

PH

B1053

SPAREPENNY LA S

Hawkes Farm

HOWEBRIDGE

PH

B1051

Moat

Maynards

Sampford Hall Wood

Mount Hall Wood

The Grange

TINDON END RD

Hill Farm

The Old Rectory

Millfield Plantation

Mount Hall

Little Howe Wood

Park Pale

B1053

Whitehouse Farm

Great Howe Wood

64   D   65   E   66   F

4

37

3

36

30

2

35

1

34

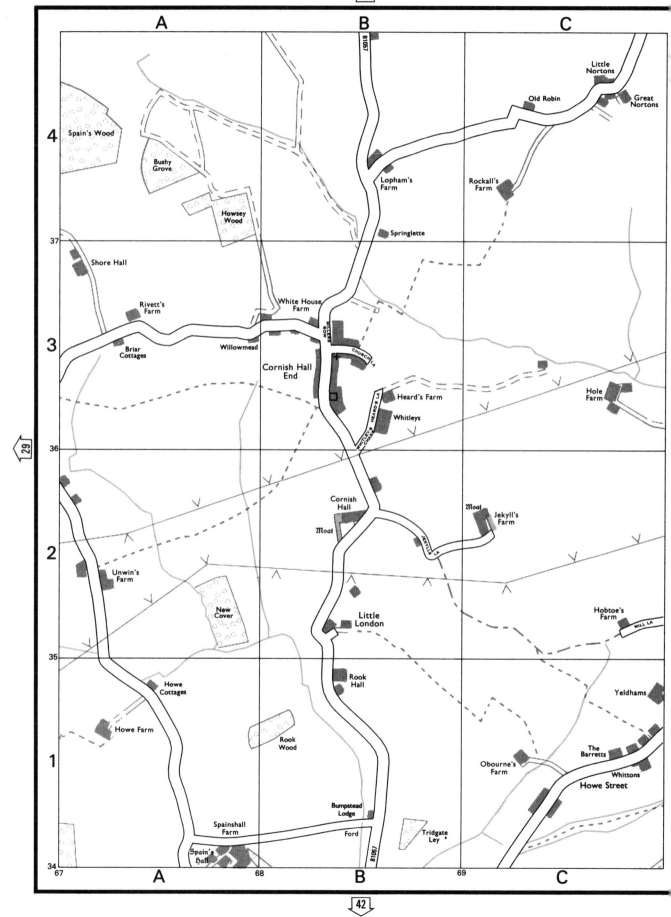

29

A   B   C

4

Spain's Wood

Bushy Grove

Howsey Wood

B1057

Little Nortons

Old Robin

Great Nortons

Lopham's Farm

Rockall's Farm

Springlette

37

Shore Hall

3

Rivett's Farm

White House Farm

Briar Cottages

Willowmead

MILLERS ROW

Cornish Hall End

CHURCH LA

Heard's Farm

Whitleys

Hole Farm

WHITLEYS CHASE

HEARD'S LA

36

Cornish Hall

Moat

Moat

Jekyll's Farm

JEKYLLS LA

2

Unwin's Farm

New Cover

Little London

Hobtoe's Farm

MILL LA

35

Howe Cottages

Rook Hall

Yeldhams

Howe Farm

Rook Wood

Obourne's Farm

The Barretts

Whittons

1

Howe Street

Bumpstead Lodge

Spainshall Farm

Ford

B1057

Tridgate Ley

34

67   A   68   B   69   C

Spain's Hall

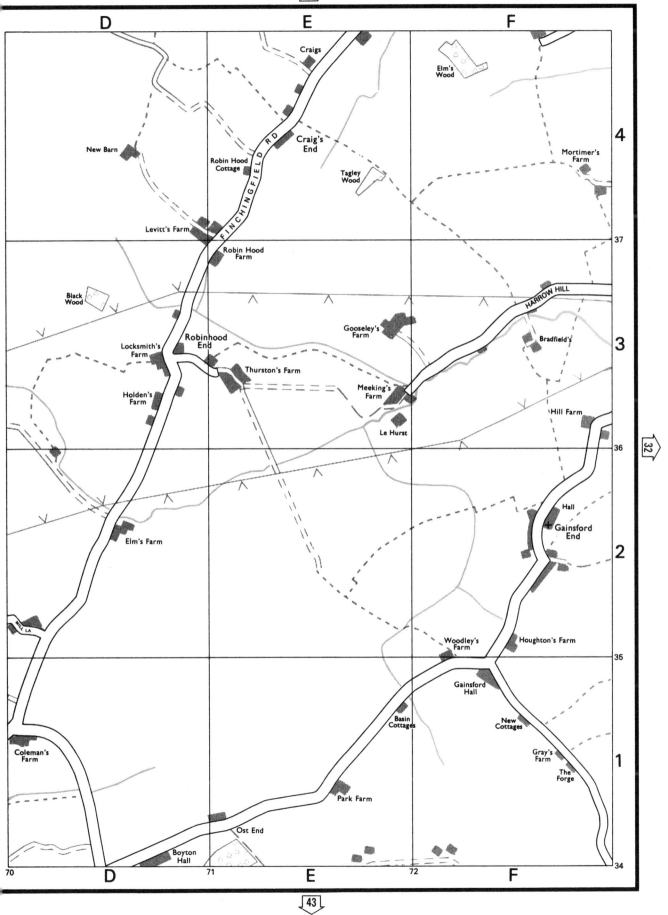

D
E
F

Craigs

New Barn

Robin Hood
Cottage

Craig's
End

Tagley
Wood

Elm's
Wood

Mortimer's
Farm

4

FINCHINGFIELD RD

Levitt's Farm

37

Robin Hood
Farm

HARROW HILL

Black
Wood

Gooseley's
Farm

Bradfield's

3

Locksmith's
Farm

Robinhood
End

Thurston's Farm

Meeking's
Farm

Hill Farm

Holden's
Farm

Le Hurst

36

Hall

Elm's Farm

Gainsford
End

2

MILL LA

Woodley's
Farm

Houghton's Farm

35

Gainsford
Hall

Coleman's
Farm

Basin
Cottages

New
Cottages

Gray's
Farm

1

The
Forge

Park Farm

Ost End

Boyton
Hall

70
D
71
E
72
F
34

32

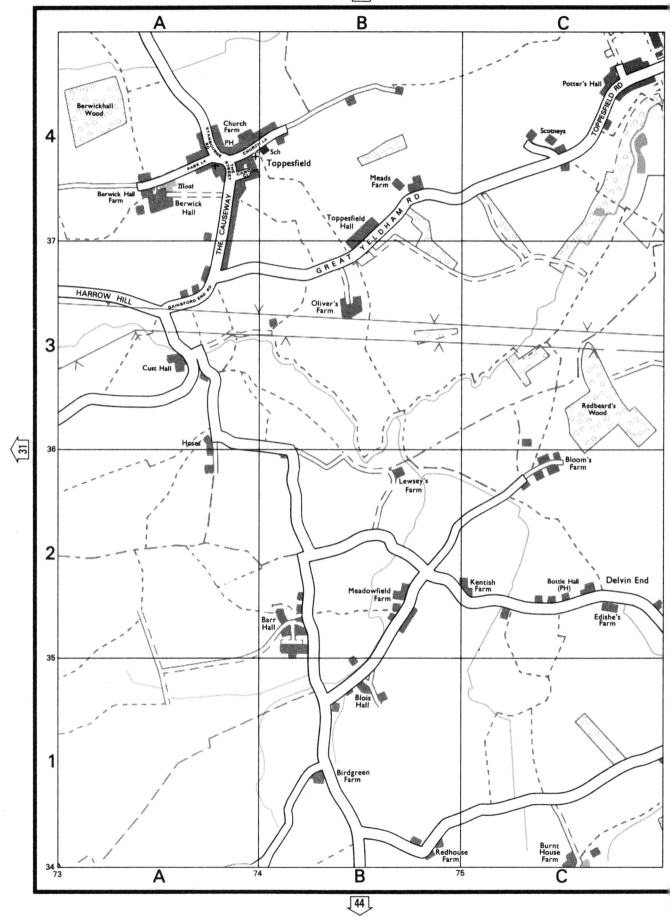

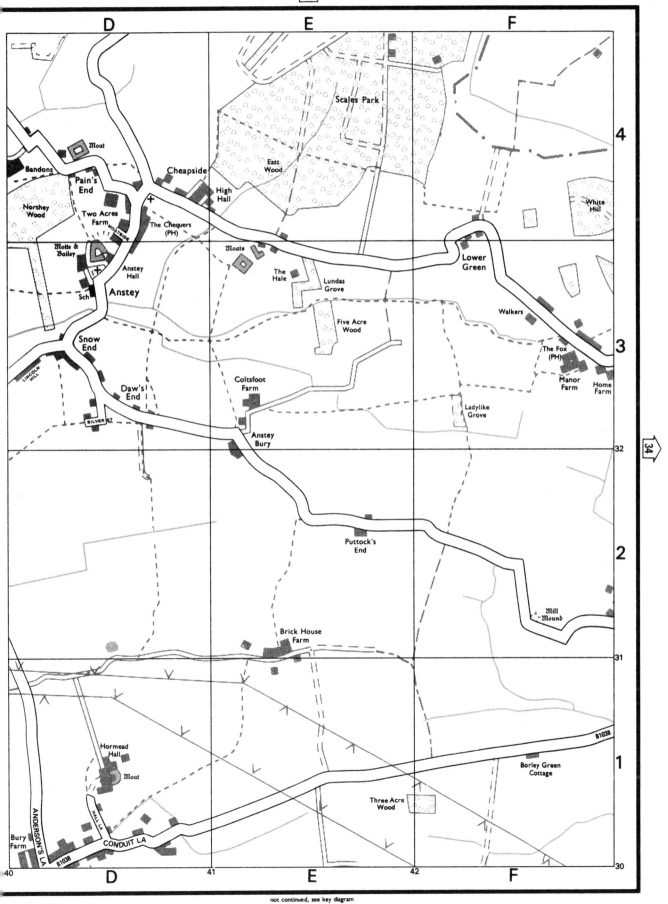

D   E   F

Moat

Bandons

Pain's End

Cheapside

High Hall

Scales Park

East Wood

Northey Wood

Two Acres Farm

The Chequers (PH)

Moats

The Hale

Lundas Grove

Lower Green

White Hill

4

Motte & Bailey

Anstey Hall

Sch

Anstey

Five Acre Wood

Walkers

The Fox (PH)

3

Snow End

LINCOLM HILL

Daw's End

SILVER ST

Coltsfoot Farm

Anstey Bury

Ladylike Grove

Manor Farm

Home Farm

32

Puttock's End

Mill Mound

2

Brick House Farm

31

B1038

Hormead Hall

Moat

Borley Green Cottage

1

ANDERSON'S LA

HALL LA

Bury Farm

B1038

CONDUIT LA

Three Acre Wood

30

D   E   F

40   41   42

not continued, see key diagram

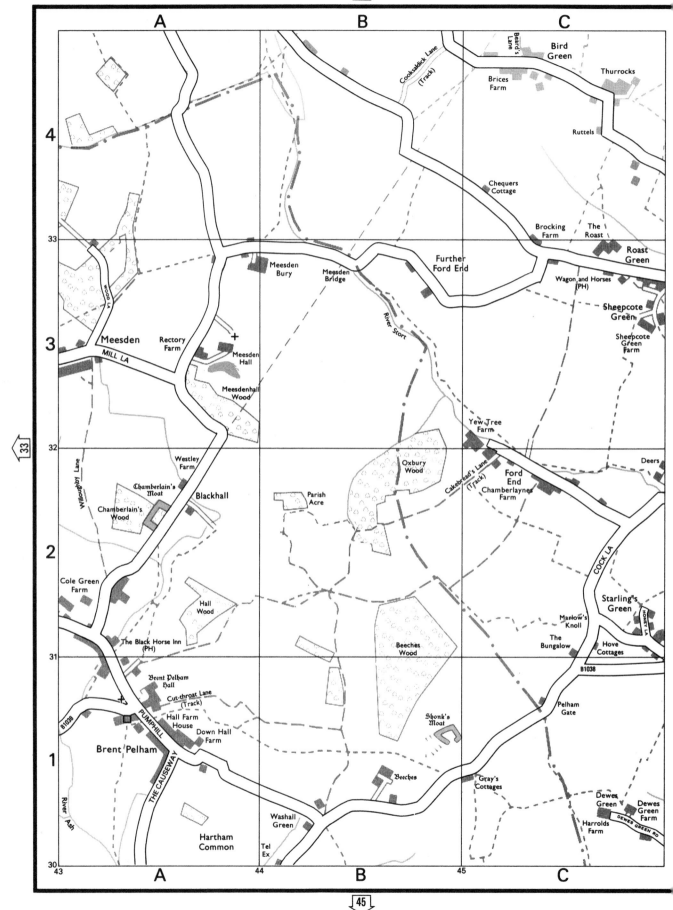

Bird Green

Thurrocks

Cooksdick Lane (Track)

Brices Farm

Beard's Lane

Ruttels

Chequers Cottage

Brocking Farm

The Roast

Roast Green

Further Ford End

Wagon and Horses (PH)

Sheepcote Green

Meesden Bury

Meesden Bridge

River Stort

Sheepcote Green Farm

Meesden

Rectory Farm

Meesden Hall

MILL LA

WOOD LA

Meesdenhall Wood

Yew Tree Farm

Westley Farm

Willoughby Lane

Chamberlain's Moat

Chamberlain's Wood

Blackhall

Parish Acre

Oxbury Wood

Cakebread's Lane (Track)

Ford End Chamberlaynes Farm

Deers

COCK LA

Cole Green Farm

Hall Wood

Beeches Wood

Starling's Green

Marlow's Knoll

The Bungalow

Hove Cottages

HONEY LA

The Black Horse Inn (PH)

B1038

Brent Pelham Hall

Cut-throat Lane (Track)

Hall Farm House

PUMPHILL

Down Hall Farm

Shonk's Moat

Pelham Gate

B1038

Brent Pelham

B1038

THE CAUSEWAY

River Ash

Beeches

Gray's Cottages

Dewes Green

Dewes Green Farm

DEWES GREEN RD

Harrolds Farm

Washall Green

Tel Ex

Hartham Common

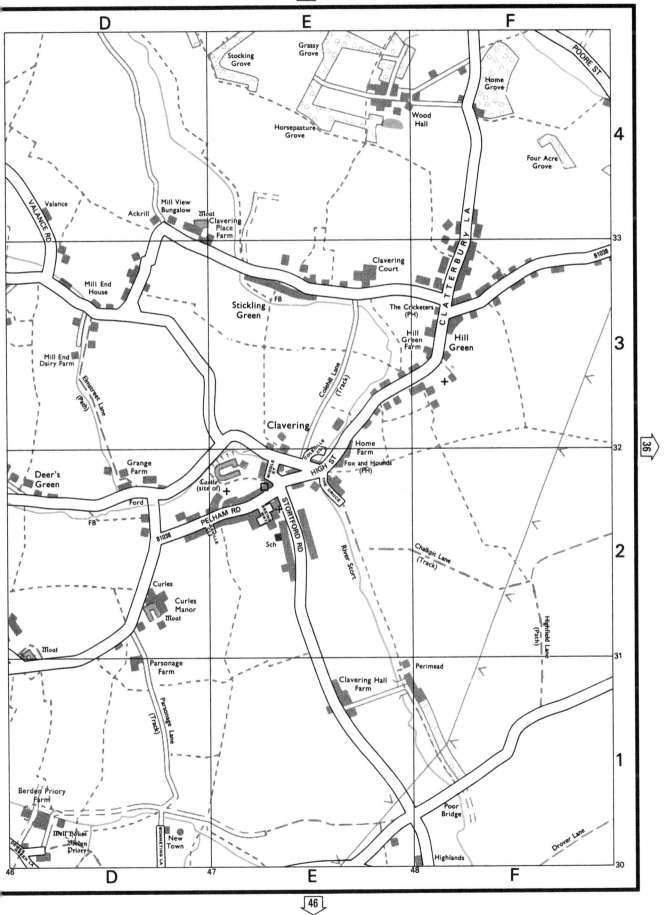

D   E   F

POORE ST

Grassy Grove

Stocking Grove

Home Grove

Wood Hall

Horsepasture Grove

Four Acre Grove

4

VALANCE RD

Valance

Ackrill

Mill View Bungalow

Moat
Clavering Place Farm

CLATTERBURY LA

B1038

33

Mill End House

Clavering Court

Stickling Green

FB

The Cricketers (PH)

Hill Green Farm

Hill Green

3

Mill End Dairy Farm

Elmstreet Lane (Path)

Colehill Lane (Track)

Clavering

Home Farm

Fox and Hounds (PH)

32

Deer's Green

Grange Farm

Castle (site of)

MIDDLE ST

HIGH ST

COLEHILL CH

THE DRUCE

Ford

FB

B1038

PELHAM RD

SEVILLE

STORTFORD RD

Sch

River Stort

Chalkpit Lane (Track)

Highfield Lane (Path)

2

Curles

Curles Manor
Moat

Moat

Parsonage Farm

Parsonage Lane (Track)

Clavering Hall Farm

Perimead

31

Berden Priory Farm

Clatterbury La

Poor Bridge

Highlands

Drover Lane

1

Well House
Berden Priory

BONNETING LA

New Town

30

46   D   47   E   48   F

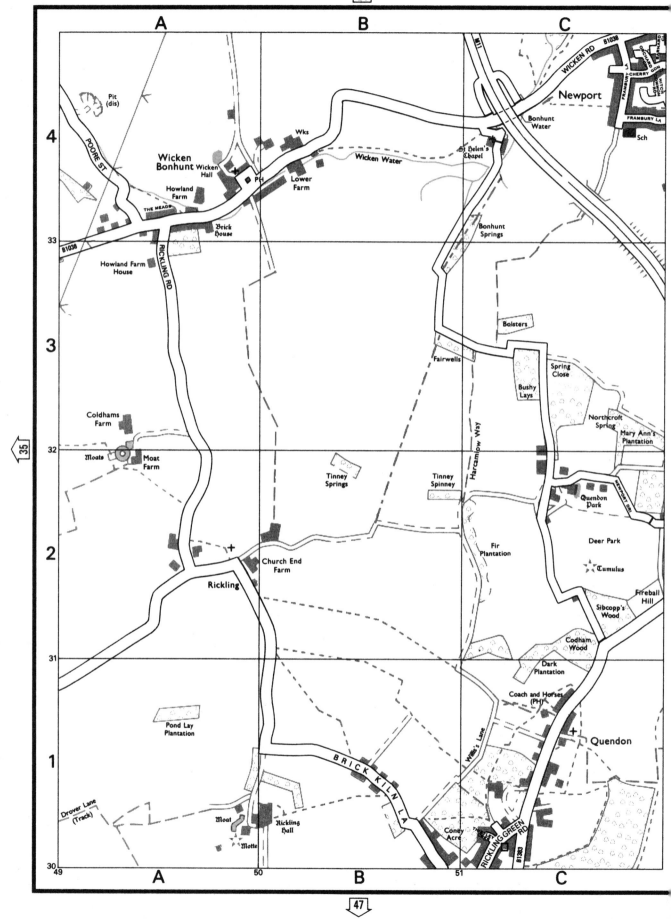

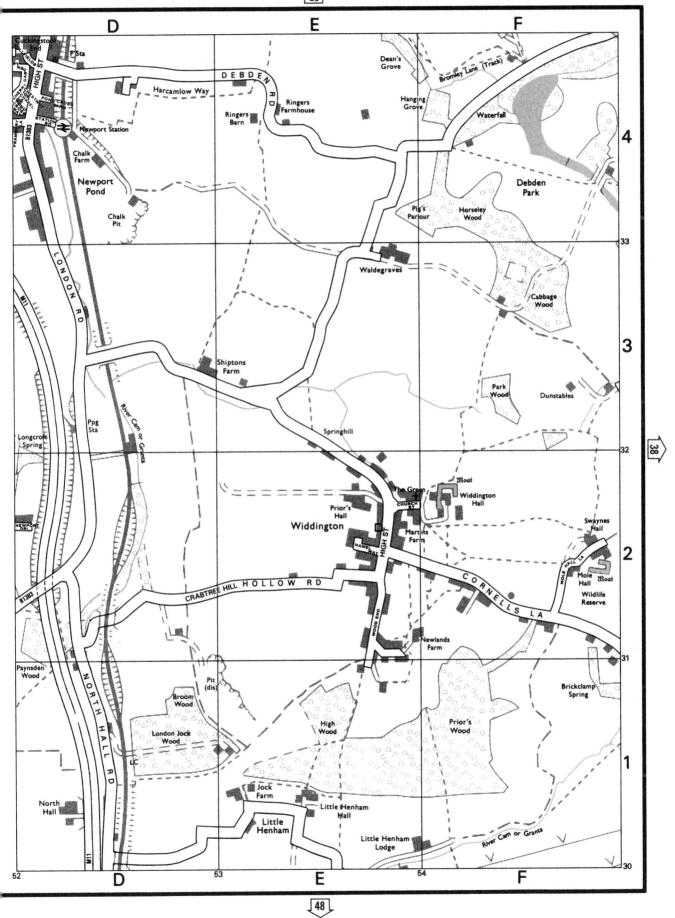

D E F

Cuckingstool End
F Sta
HIGH ST
Harcamlow Way
DEBDEN RD
Dean's Grove
Bromley Lane (Track)
Ringers Farmhouse
Hanging Grove
Ringers Barn
Waterfall
Newport Station
4
Chalk Farm
Debden Park
Newport Pond
Pig's Parlour
Horseley Wood
Chalk Pit
33
LONDON RD
Waldegraves
Cabbage Wood
3
M11
Shiptons Farm
Park Wood
Dunstables
River Cam or Granta
Springhill
32
38
Longcroft Spring
Ppg Sta
Moat
Widdington Hall
The Green
NEWPORT GRI
CHURCH ST
Prior's Hall
Swaynes Hall
Widdington
Martins Farm
HIGH ST
2
B1383
HAMEL WAY
CORNELLS LA
Mole Hall
Moat
MOLE HALL LA
CRABTREE HILL HOLLOW RD
Wildlife Reserve
WOOD END
Newlands Farm
31
Paynsden Wood
NORTH HALL RD
Pit (dis)
Broom Wood
Brickclamp Spring
High Wood
Prior's Wood
London Jock Wood
LC
1
North Hall
Jock Farm
Little Henham Hall
Little Henham
River Cam or Granta
M11
Little Henham Lodge
30

52 D 53 E 54 F

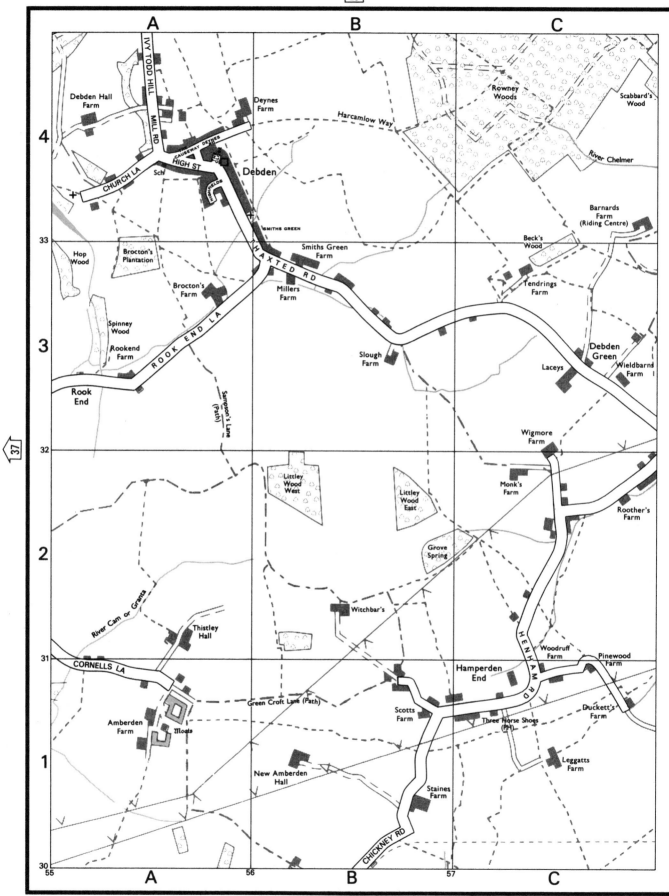

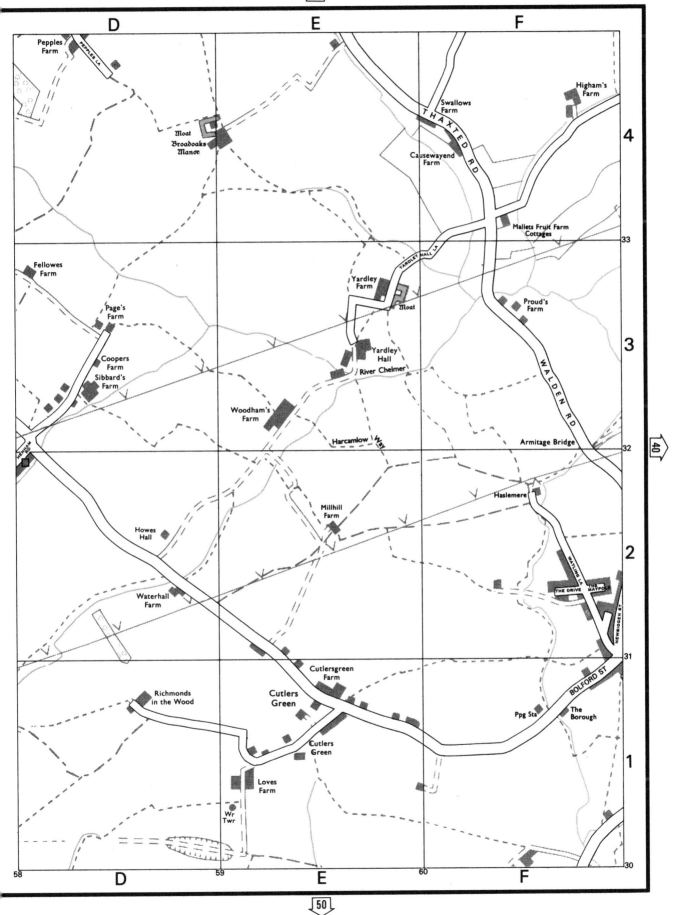

D   E   F

Pepples Farm

PEPPLES LA

Moat
Broadoaks Manor

Swallows Farm

THAXTED RD

Higham's Farm

Causewayend Farm

Mallets Fruit Farm Cottages

4

33

Fellowes Farm

Page's Farm

Coopers Farm

Sibbard's Farm

Yardley Farm

YARDLEY HALL LA

Moat

Yardley Hall

River Chelmer

Proud's Farm

3

Woodham's Farm

Harcamlow Way

WALDEN RD

Armitage Bridge

32

40

Millhill Farm

Haslemere

Howes Hall

WATLING LA

THE DRIVE

THE MAYPOLE

NEWBIGGEN ST

2

Waterhall Farm

31

BOLFORD ST

Richmonds in the Wood

Cutlersgreen Farm

Cutlers Green

Ppg Sta

The Borough

Cutlers Green

1

Loves Farm

Wr Twr

58   D   59   E   60   F   30

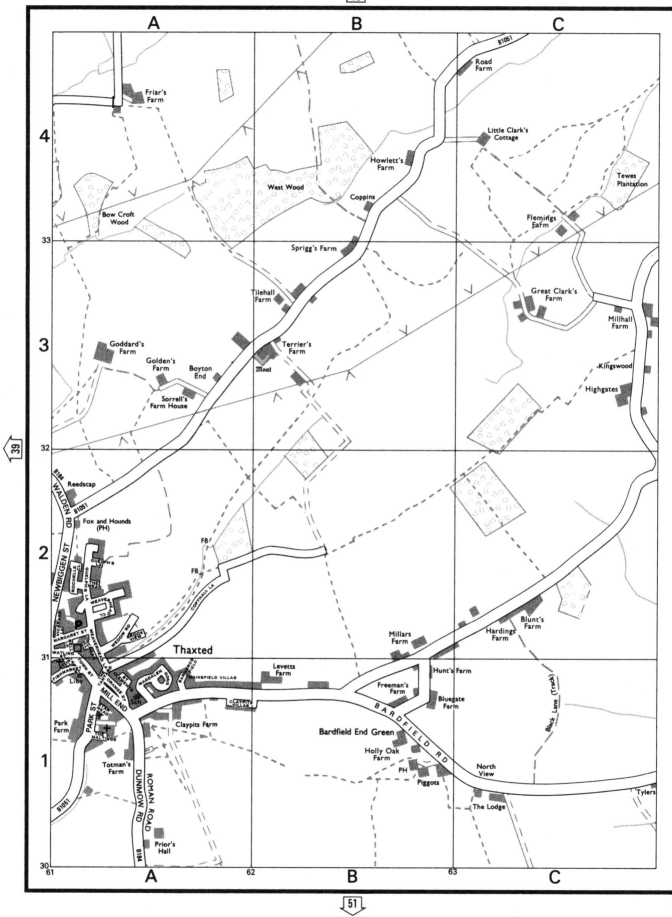

A   B   C

4

33

3

32

2

31

1

30

39

Friar's Farm

Road Farm

B1051

Little Clark's Cottage

Tewes Plantation

Howlett's Farm

West Wood

Coppins

Flemings Farm

Bow Croft Wood

Sprigg's Farm

Tilehall Farm

Great Clark's Farm

Millhall Farm

Goddard's Farm

Golden's Farm

Boyton End

Terrier's Farm

Moat

Sorrell's Farm House

Kingswood

Highgates

Reedscap

B184 WALDEN RD

B1051

Fox and Hounds (PH)

FB

FB

NEWBIGGEN ST

GUELPH'S

ROCHELLE

THE SQUARE

WEAVERS

WEDOW RD

BROOK VIEW

COPTHALL LA

P

VICARAGE

MARGARET ST

WATLING

Thaxted

FISHMARKET

Liby

Sch

WEAVERHEAD LA

ORANGE ST

TOWN ST

CLARENCE

MAGDALEN

GONG

BAINSFIELD

Levetts Farm

RAINSFIELD VILLAS

Millars Farm

Hardings Farm

Blunt's Farm

Hunt's Farm

Freeman's Farm

Bluegate Farm

Black Lane (Track)

PARK ST

MILL END

Park Farm

CLAYPIT VILLAS

Claypits Farm

Bardfield End Green

BARDFIELD RD

Holly Oak Farm

PH

Piggots

North View

Tylers

Totman's Farm

The MALTINGS

DUNMOW RD

ROMAN ROAD

B184

B1051

Prior's Hall

The Lodge

61   62   63

A   B   C

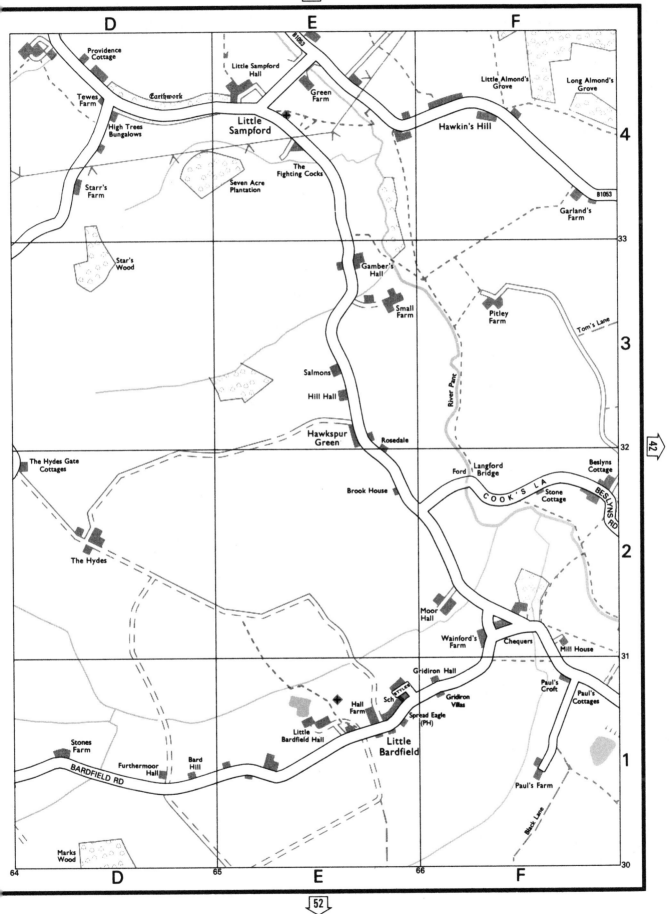

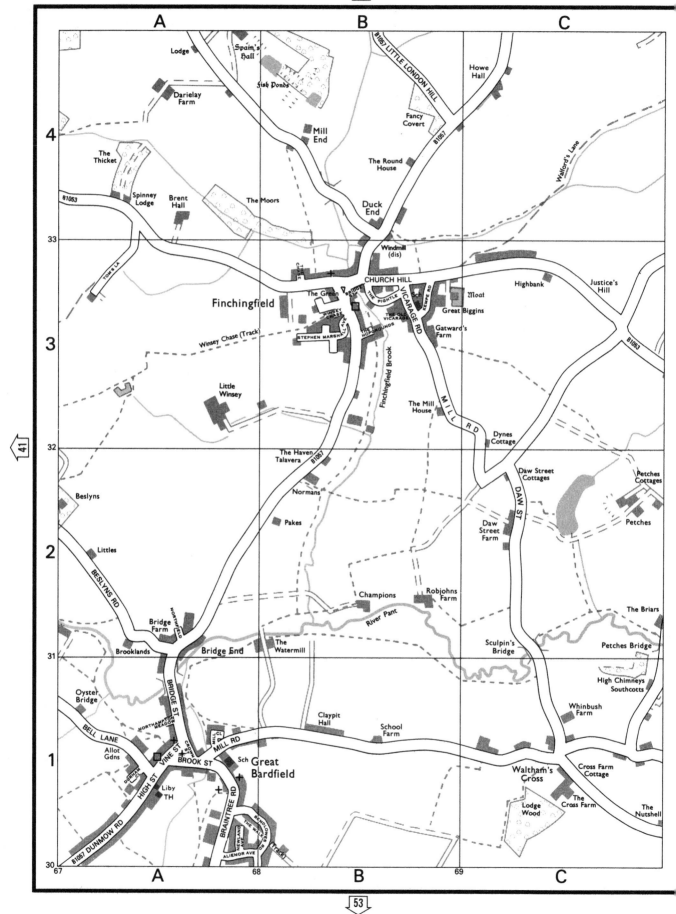

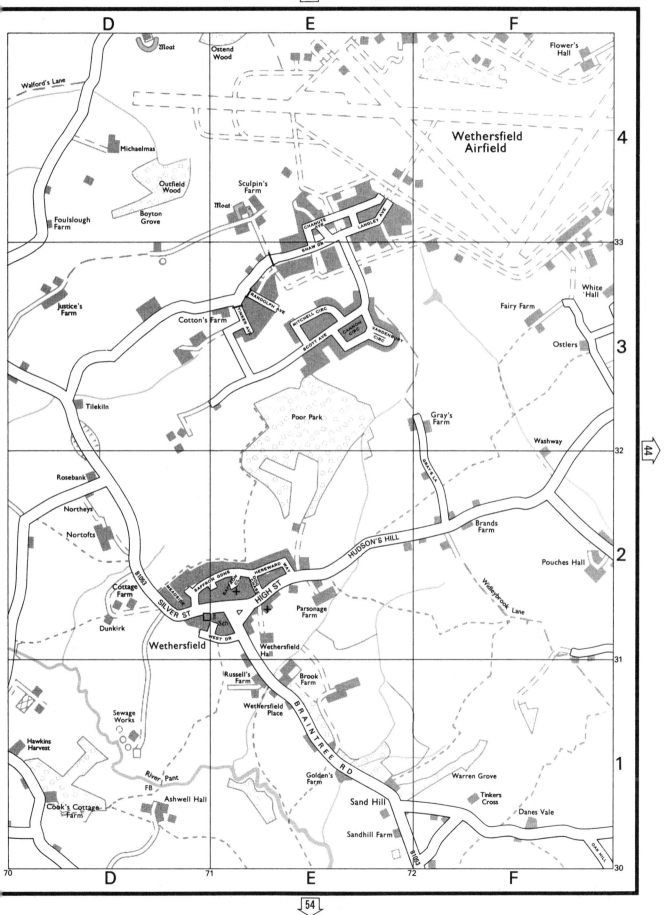

D E F

4

3

2

1

33

32

31

30

44

Walford's Lane

Moat

Ostend Wood

Flower's Hall

Wethersfield Airfield

Michaelmas

Sculpin's Farm

Outfield Wood

Moat

Boyton Grove

Foulslough Farm

CHANUTE AVE

LANGLEY AVE

SHAW DR

White Hall

Justice's Farm

RANDOLPH AVE

TINKER AVE

Cotton's Farm

MITCHELL CIRC

SCOTT AVE

CANNON CIRC

VANDENBURY CIRC

Fairy Farm

Ostlers

Tilekiln

Poor Park

Gray's Farm

Washway

Rosebank

GRAY'S LA

Northeys

Nortofts

Brands Farm

HUDSON'S HILL

Pouches Hall

Cottage Farm

MEADSIDE

SILVER ST

B1053

SAFFRON GDNS

SAFFRON CLOSE

HEREWARD WAY

HIGH ST

Widleybrook Lane

Dunkirk

Sch

WEST DR

Parsonage Farm

Wethersfield

Wethersfield Hall

Russell's Farm

Brook Farm

Sewage Works

Wethersfield Place

BRAINTREE RD

Hawkins Harvest

River Pant

FB

Golden's Farm

Warren Grove

Tinkers Cross

Danes Vale

Cook's Cottage Farm

Ashwell Hall

Sand Hill

B1053

Sandhill Farm

OAK HILL

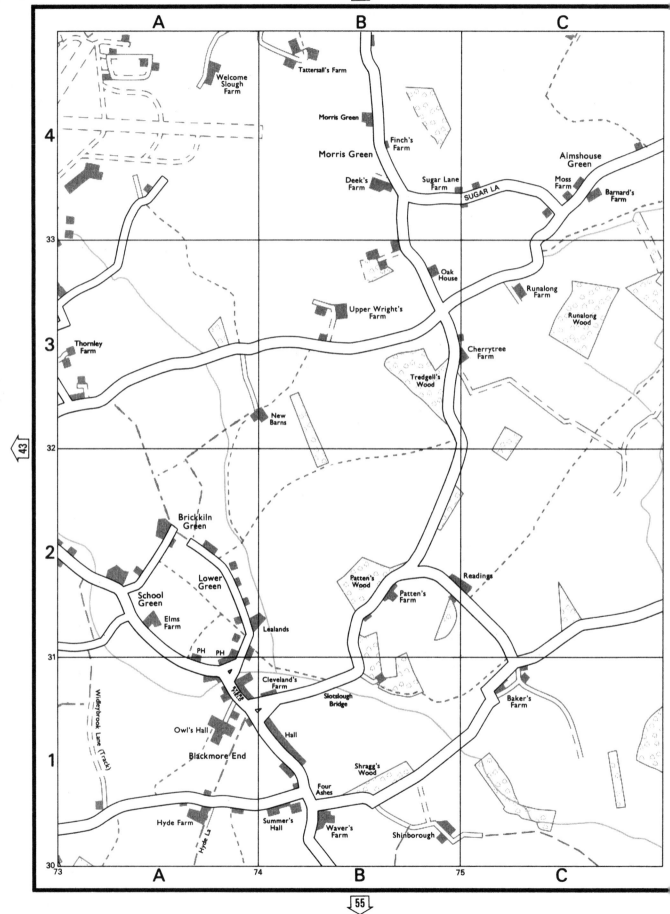

43

A B C

4

33

3

32

2

31

1

30

Welcome Slough Farm

Tattersall's Farm

Morris Green

Morris Green

Finch's Farm

Aimshouse Green

Deek's Farm

Sugar Lane Farm

SUGAR LA

Moss Farm

Barnard's Farm

Oak House

Runalong Farm

Upper Wright's Farm

Runalong Wood

Thornley Farm

Cherrytree Farm

Tredgell's Wood

New Barns

Brickkiln Green

Lower Green

School Green

Elms Farm

Patten's Wood

Patten's Farm

Readings

Lealands

PH PH

Cleveland's Farm

Slotslough Bridge

Baker's Farm

Widleybrook Lane (Track)

Owl's Hall

Hall

Blackmore End

Shragg's Wood

Four Ashes

Hyde Farm

Hyde La

Summer's Hall

Waver's Farm

Shinborough

73 A 74 B 75 C

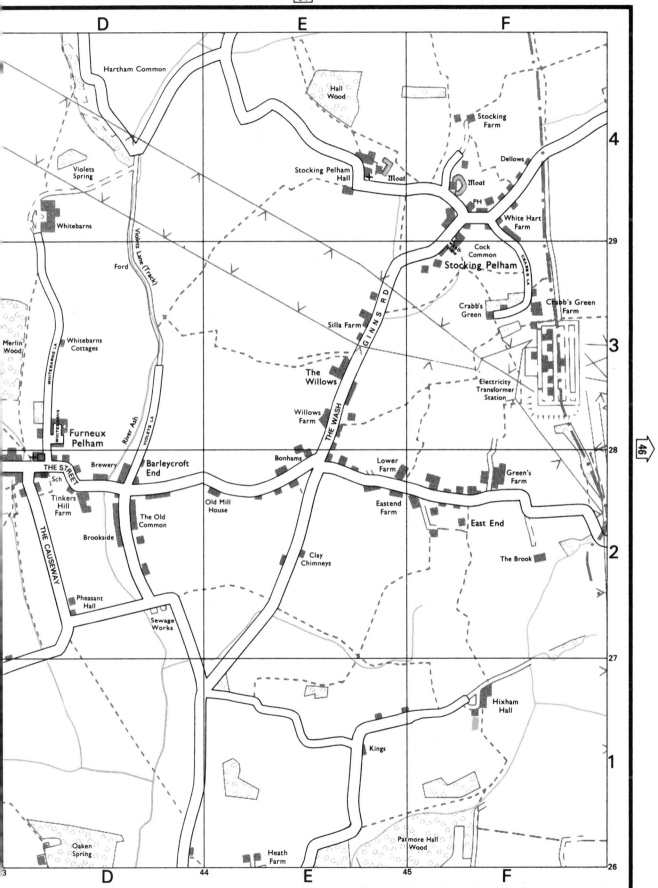

D   E   F

Hartham Common

Hall
Wood

Stocking
Farm

4

Violets
Spring

Stocking Pelham
Hall

Moat

Dellows

Moat

PH

White Hart
Farm

Whitebarns

29

Violets Lane (Track)

Cock
Common

Ford

Stocking Pelham

Crabb's Green
Farm

Silla Farm

GINNS RD

Crabb's
Green

CRABB'S LA

Merlin
Wood

Whitebarns
Cottages

The Willows

3

Electricity
Transformer
Station

River Ash

Willows
Farm

THE WASH

VIOLETS LA

WHITEBARNS LA

Furneux
Pelham

28

46

Brewery

Barleycroft
End

Bonhams

Lower
Farm

Green's
Farm

THE STREET

Sch

Tinkers
Hill
Farm

The Old
Common

Old Mill
House

Eastend
Farm

East End

Brookside

The Brook

2

THE CAUSEWAY

Clay
Chimneys

Pheasant
Hall

Sewage
Works

27

Hixham
Hall

Kings

1

Oaken
Spring

Patmore Hall
Wood

Heath
Farm

26

3   D   44   E   45   F

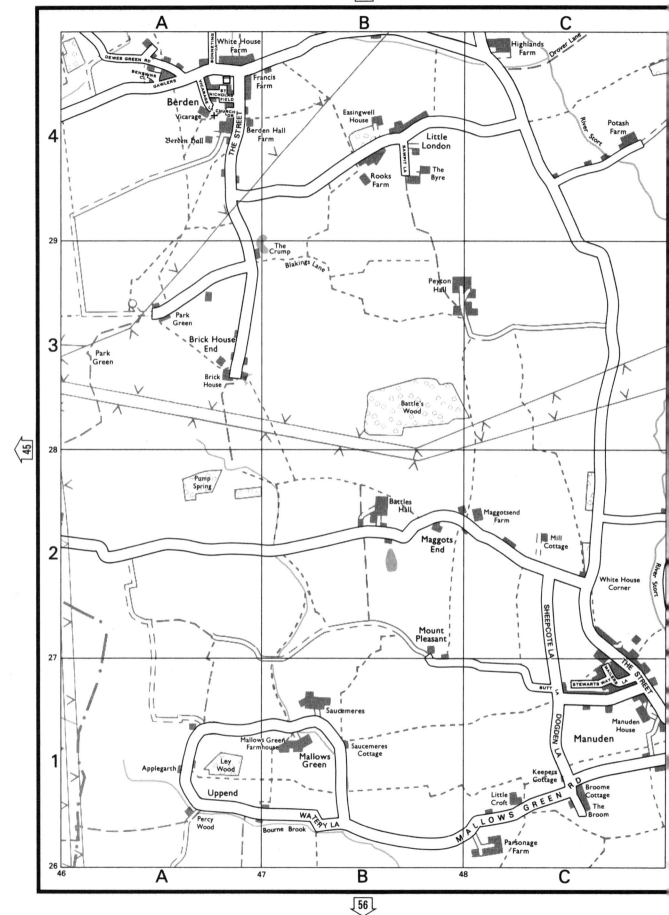

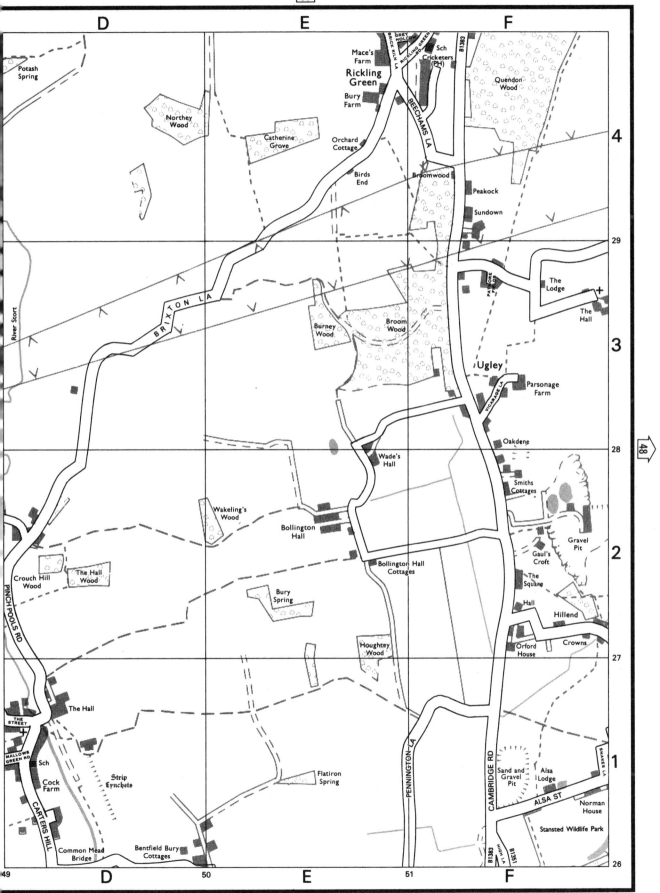

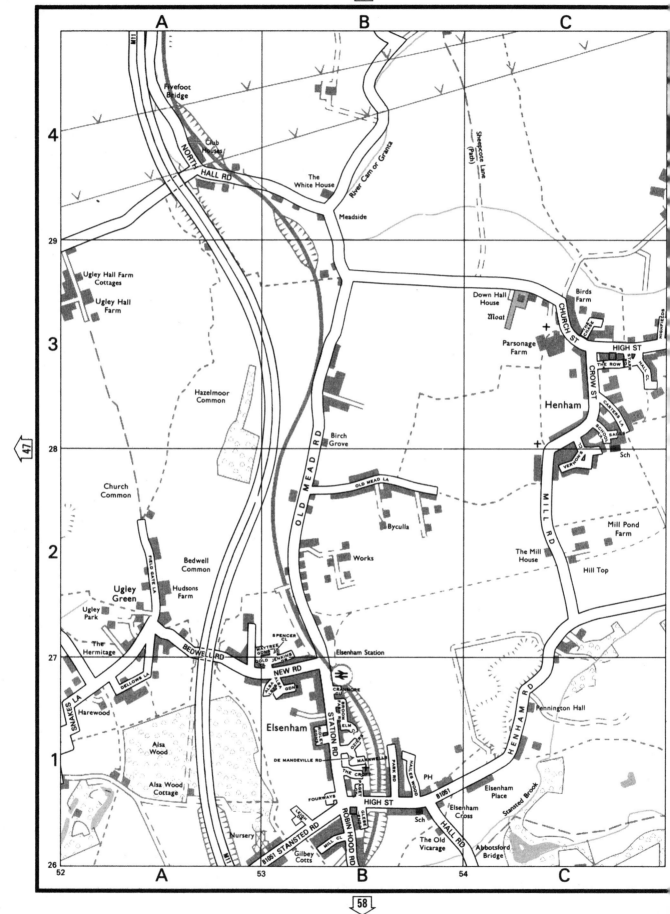

47

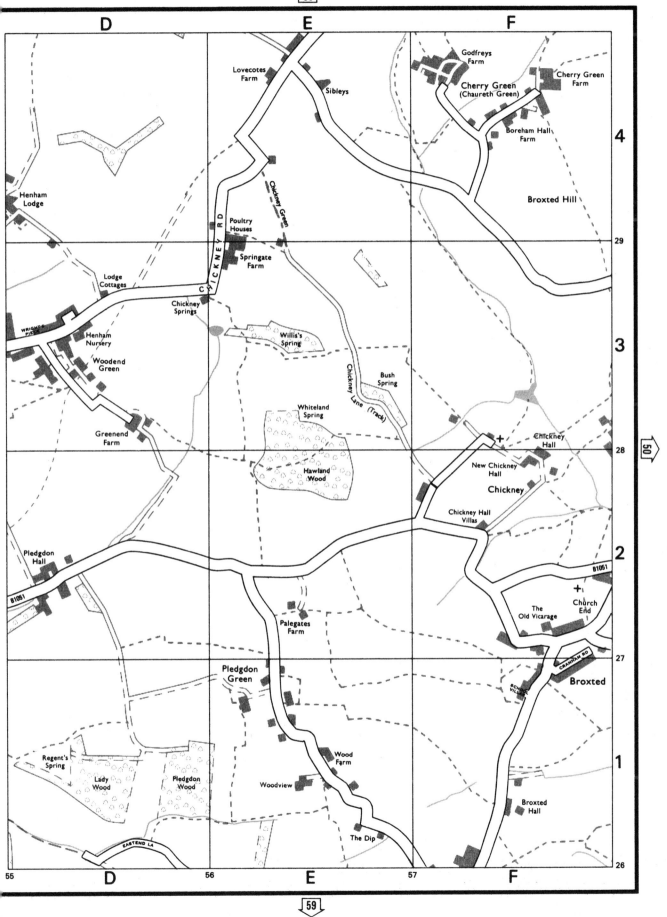

D   E   F

Godfreys Farm

Lovecotes Farm

Sibleys

Cherry Green (Chaureth Green)

Cherry Green Farm

Boreham Hall Farm

Henham Lodge

4

Broxted Hill

Chickney Green

CHICKNEY RD

Poultry Houses

29

Springate Farm

Lodge Cottages

Chickney Springs

C

Willis's Spring

WRIGHT'S PIECE

Henham Nursery

Woodend Green

Bush Spring

Chickney Lane (Track)

3

Whiteland Spring

New Chickney Hall

Chickney Hall

50

Greenend Farm

Hawland Wood

28

Chickney

Chickney Hall Villas

Pledgdon Hall

2

B1051

B1051

Palegates Farm

The Old Vicarage

Church End

Pledgdon Green

27

GRAHHAM RD

SCHOOL VILLA

Broxted

Regent's Spring

Lady Wood

Pledgdon Wood

Wood Farm

1

Woodview

Broxted Hall

EASTEND LA

The Dip

26

55   D   56   E   57   F

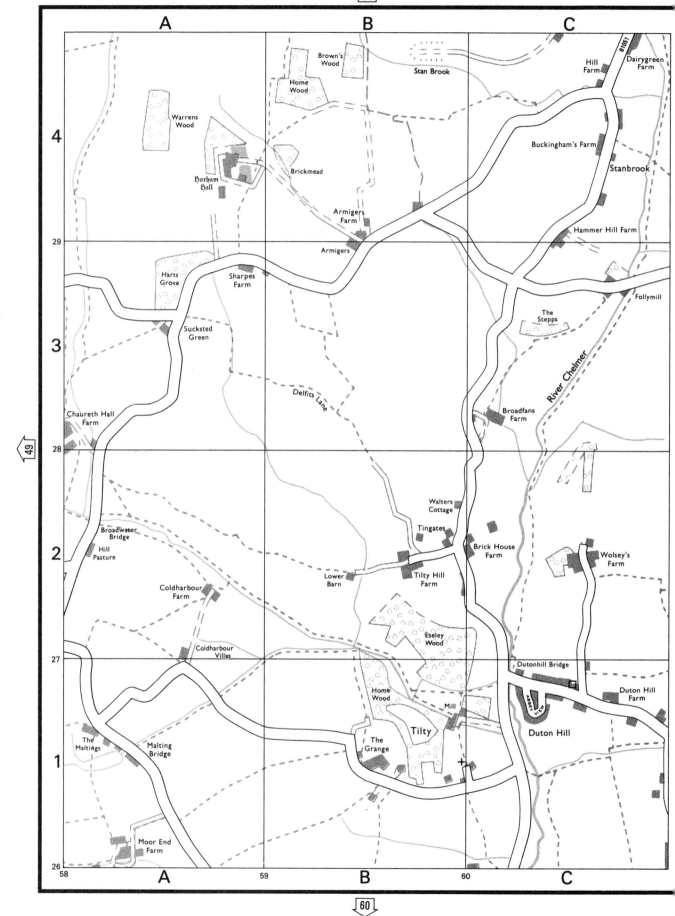

A   B   C

Brown's Wood

Home Wood

Stan Brook

Hill Farm

Dairygreen Farm

Warrens Wood

Buckingham's Farm

Stanbrook

4

Horham Hall

Brickmead

Armigers Farm

Hammer Hill Farm

29

Armigers

Harts Grove

Sharpes Farm

Follymill

The Stepps

3

Sucksted Green

Delfits Lane

River Chelmer

Chaureth Hall Farm

Broadfans Farm

28

Walters Cottage

Broadwater Bridge

Tingates

Brick House Farm

Wolsey's Farm

2

Hill Pasture

Lower Barn

Tilty Hill Farm

Coldharbour Farm

Eseley Wood

Coldharbour Villas

27

Dutonhill Bridge

Duton Hill Farm

Home Wood

Mill

The Maltings

Malting Bridge

Tilty

ABBEY VIEW

Duton Hill

1

The Grange

Moor End Farm

26

58   A   59   B   60   C

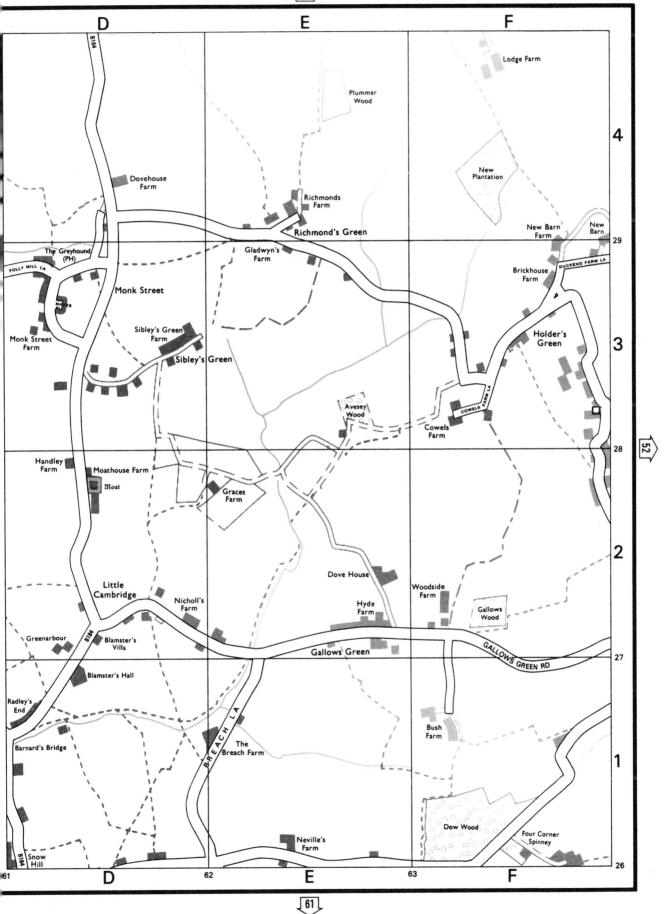

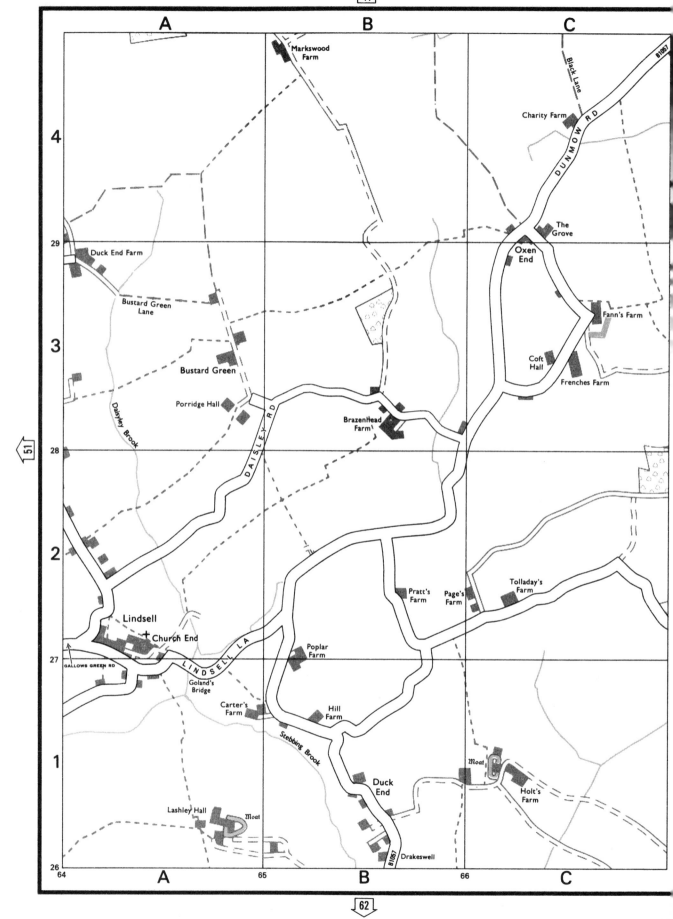

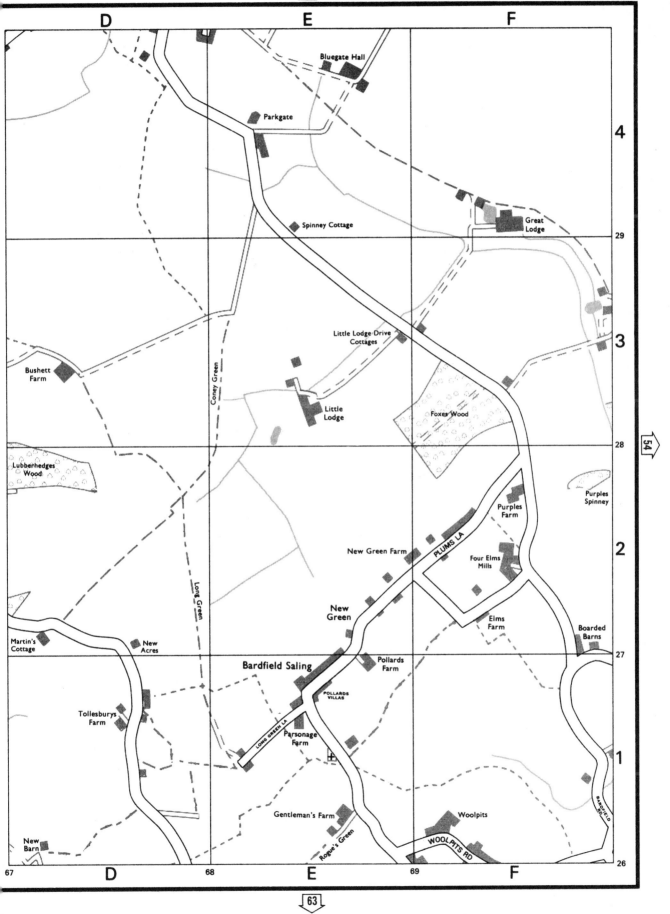

42
54
63

43

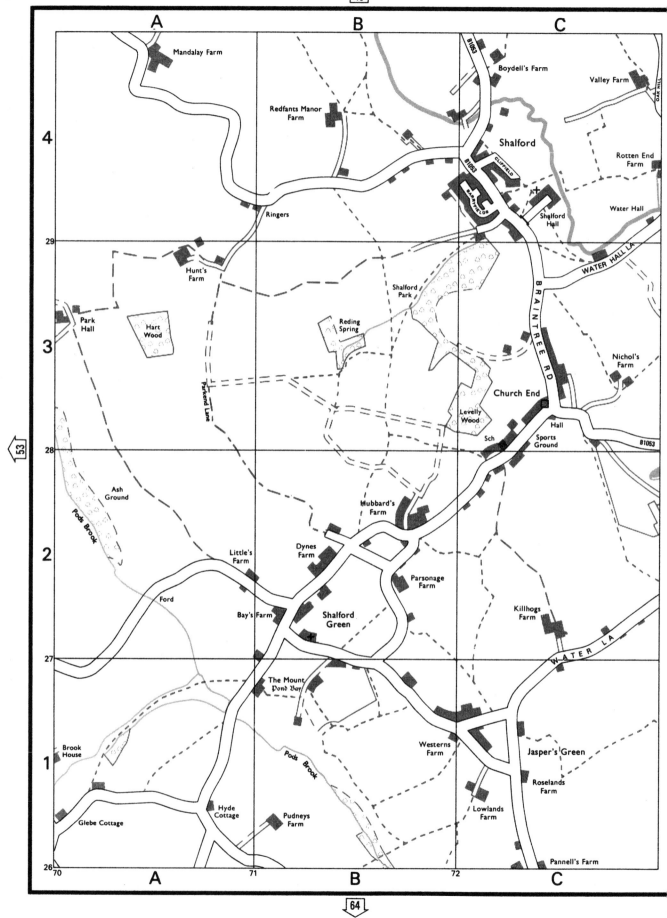

53

64

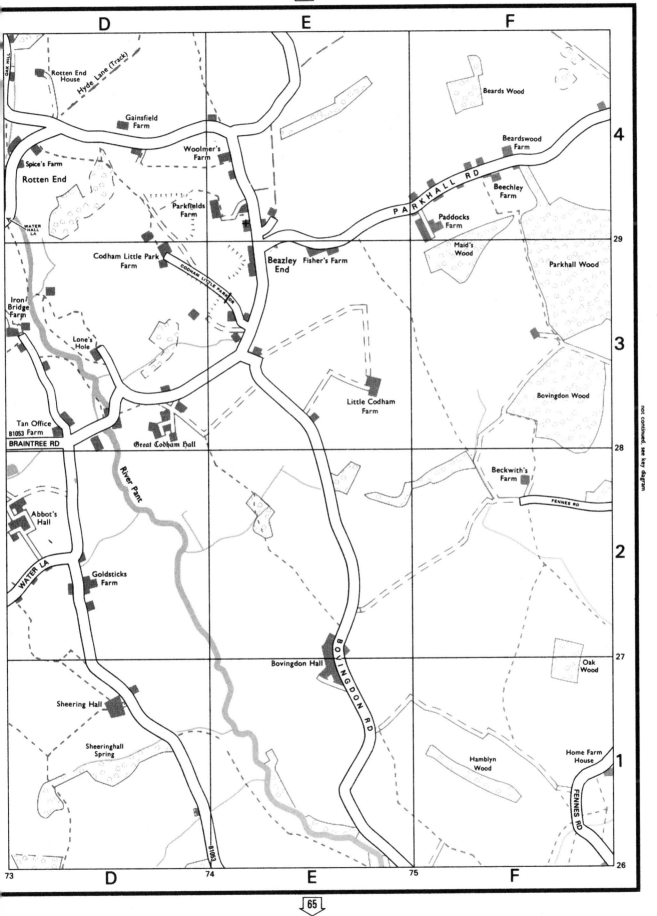

D   E   F

OAK HILL

Rotten End House

Hyde Lane (Track)

Gainsfield Farm

Woolmer's Farm

Spice's Farm

Rotten End

Beards Wood

Beardswood Farm

PARKHALL RD

Beechley Farm

Paddocks Farm

4

WATER HALL LA

Parkfields Farm

29

Codham Little Park Farm

Beazley End

Fisher's Farm

Maid's Wood

Parkhall Wood

CODHAM LITTLE PARK DR

Iron Bridge Farm

Lone's Hole

3

Little Codham Farm

Bovingdon Wood

Tan Office Farm

B1053

BRAINTREE RD

Great Codham Hall

28

River Pant

Abbot's Hall

Beckwith's Farm

FENNES RD

2

WATER LA

Goldsticks Farm

27

Oak Wood

Bovingdon Hall

BOVINGDON RD

Sheering Hall

Sheeringhall Spring

Hamblyn Wood

Home Farm House

1

FENNES RD

B1053

73   D   74   E   75   F   26

not continued, see key diagram

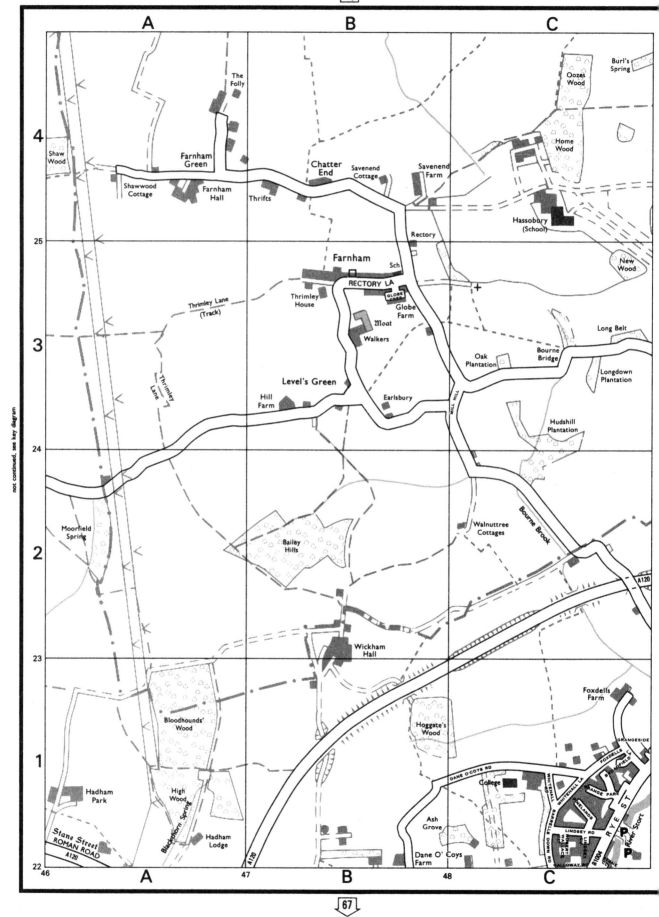

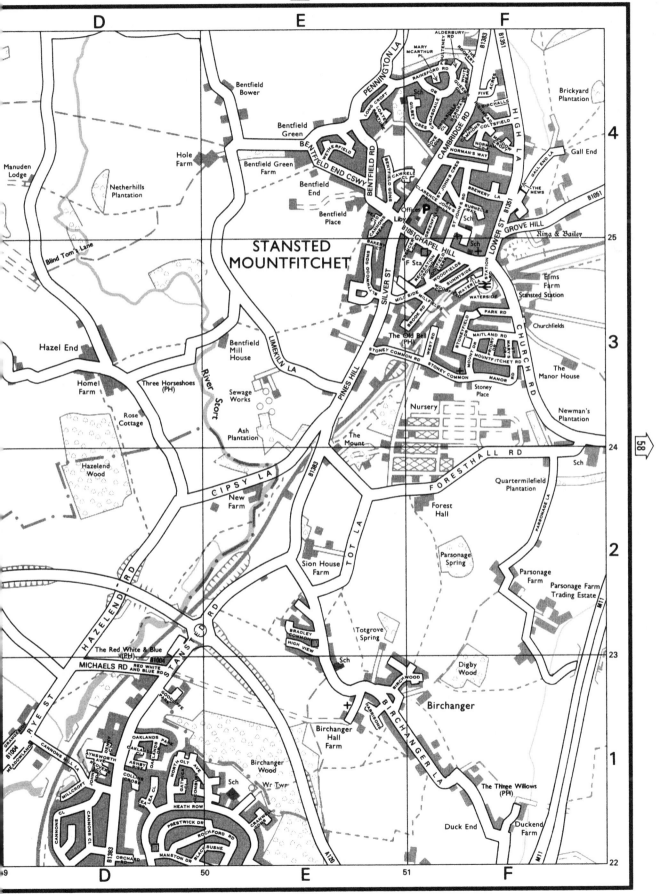

D   E   F

Bentfield
Bower

Manuden
Lodge

Netherhills
Plantation

Hole
Farm

Bentfield
Green

Bentfield Green
Farm

Bentfield
End

Bentfield
Place

ALDERBURY
RD
MARY
MCARTHUR
PL
RAINSFORD RD
POUTENEY
RD

Brickyard
Plantation

4

PENNINGTON LA

Sch

CAMBRIDGE RD

NORMAN'S WAY

HIGH LA

Gall End

GALL END LA

THE
MEWS

B1051

BENTFIELD RD

BENTFIELD END CSWY

Cawkell

BREWERY LA

Ring & Bailey

B1051

LOWER ST

GROVE HILL

25

STANSTED
MOUNTFITCHET

Blind Tom's Lane

SILVER ST

CHAPEL HILL

F Sta

WOODFIELDS

SUNNYSIDE

WATERSIDE

Elms
Farm

Stansted Station

Churchfields

3

Hazel End

Bentfield
Mill
House

LIMEKILN LA

Sewage
Works

The Old Bell
(PH)

STONEY COMMON RD

STONEY COMMON

PARK RD

MAITLAND RD

MOUNTFITCHET RD

Stoney
Place

CHURCH RD

The
Manor House

Homel
Farm

Three Horseshoes
(PH)

River Stort

Rose
Cottage

Ash
Plantation

PINES HILL

WEST RD

Nursery

Newman's
Plantation

24

58

Hazelend
Wood

CIPSY LA

New
Farm

B1383

The
Mount

FORESTHALL RD

Quartermilefield
Plantation

Sch

PARSONAGE LA

Forest
Hall

Parsonage
Spring

Parsonage
Farm

Parsonage Farm
Trading Estate

2

TOT LA

Sion House
Farm

Totgrove
Spring

M11

HAZELEND RD

STANSTED RD

The Red White & Blue
(PH)

B1004

MICHAELS RD

RED WHITE
AND BLUE RD

BRADLEY
COMMON

HIGH VIEW

Sch

Digby
Wood

Birchanger

23

RYE ST

B1004

GRANGE

MEADOWLANDS

CANNONS HILL LA

GODDUPPE

PARK

OAKLANDS PARK

LYNSWORTH

ASHBY

OAKLANDS

DENNY

COLLINS CROSS

NORTHOLT

GATWICK

BIRCHWOOD

HARRISONS

BIRCHANGER LA

Birchanger
Hall
Farm

Birchanger
Wood

Sch

Wr Twr

MILLCROFT

CANNONS
CL

CANNONS CL

B1383

HEATH ROW

PRESTWICK DR

ROCHFORD RD

MANSTON DR

ORCHARD
RD

CRANWELL

The Three Willows
(PH)

Duck End

Duckend
Farm

1

A120

M11

22

D   E   F
49   50   51

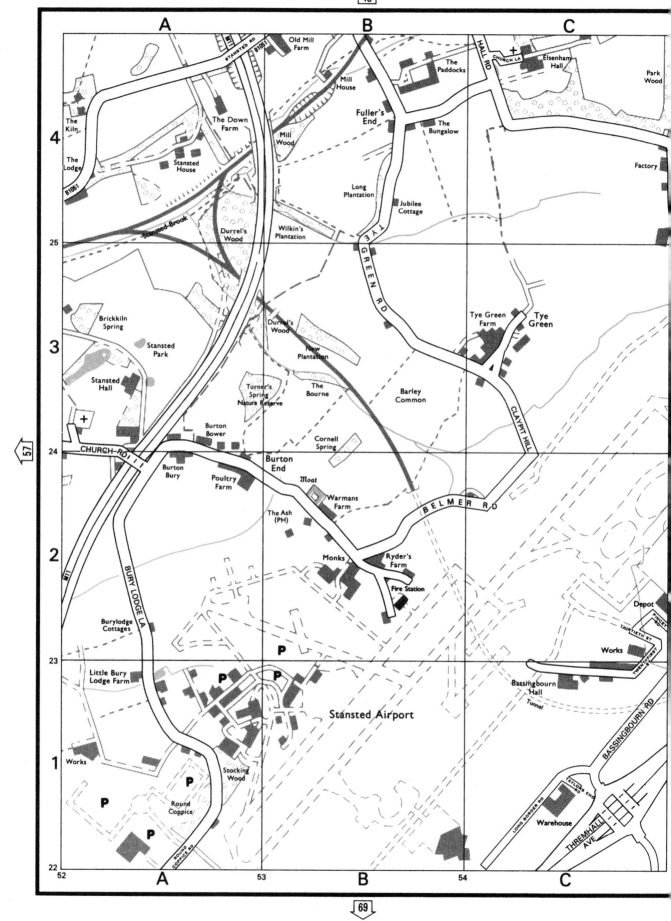

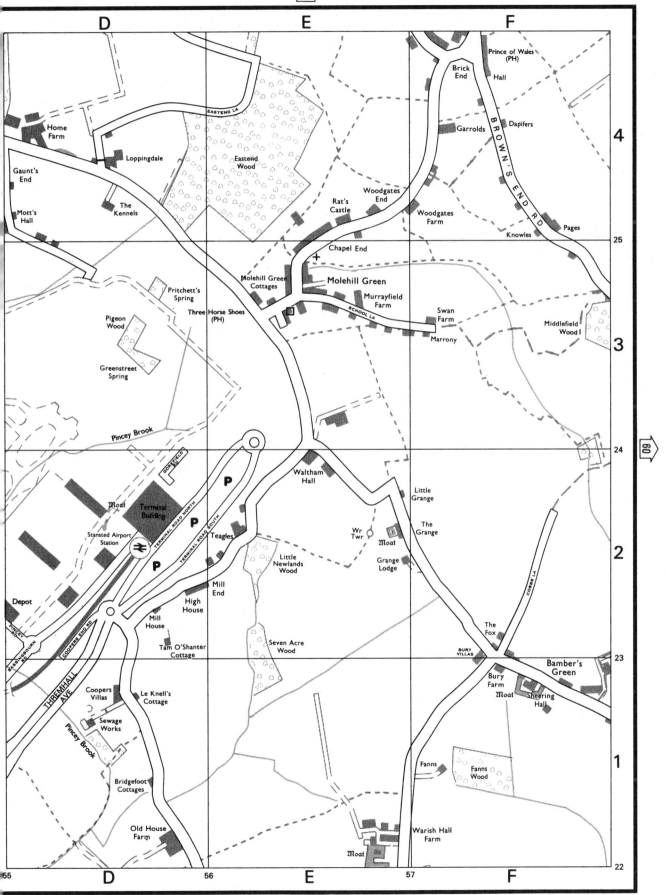

D   E   F

60

Prince of Wales (PH)

Brick End

Hall

Dapifers

Garrolds

BROWN'S END RD

Home Farm

EASTEND LA

Loppingdale

Eastend Wood

Woodgates End

Woodgates Farm

Pages

Gaunt's End

The Kennels

Rat's Castle

Knowles

Mott's Hall

25

Chapel End

Molehill Green Cottages

Molehill Green

Pritchett's Spring

Three Horse Shoes (PH)

Murrayfield Farm

Swan Farm

Middlefield Wood

Pigeon Wood

SCHOOL LA

Marrony

Greenstreet Spring

3

Pincey Brook

24

GORFIELD RD

Waltham Hall

Little Grange

Moat

Terminal Building

P

The Grange

Wr Twr

Moat

Stansted Airport Station

TERMINAL ROAD NORTH

TERMINAL ROAD SOUTH

P

Teagles

Little Newlands Wood

Grange Lodge

2

Depot

Mill End

High House

Seven Acre Wood

The Fox

Mill House

P

Tam O'Shanter Cottage

BURY VILLAS

Bamber's Green

COOPERS END RD

THREMHALL AVE

Coopers Villas

Le Knell's Cottage

Bury Farm

Moat

Sheering Hall

23

Sewage Works

Pincey Brook

Fanns

Fanns Wood

1

Bridgefoot Cottages

Old House Farm

Warish Hall Farm

Moat

22

55   D   56   E   57   F

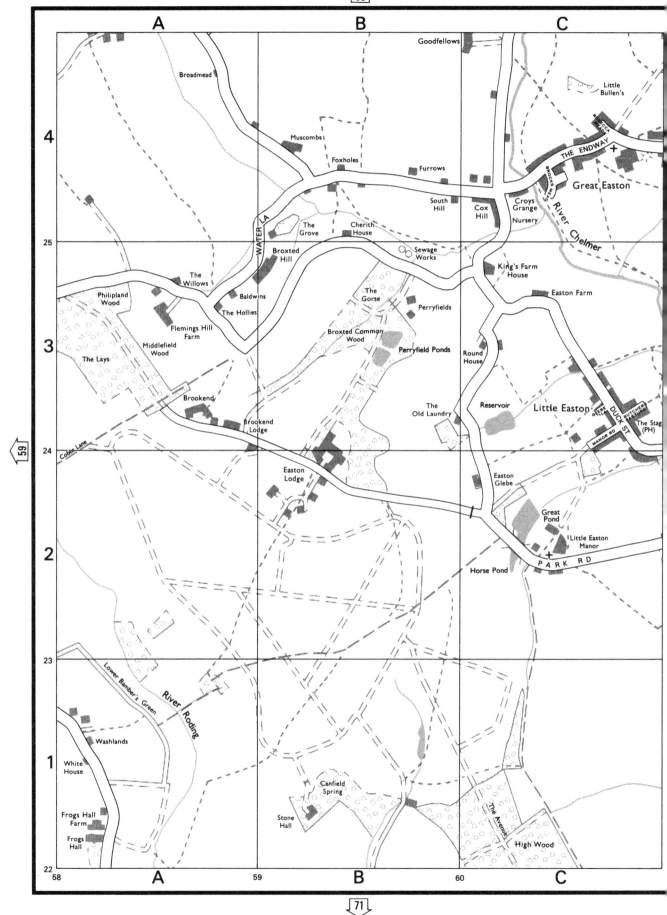

59

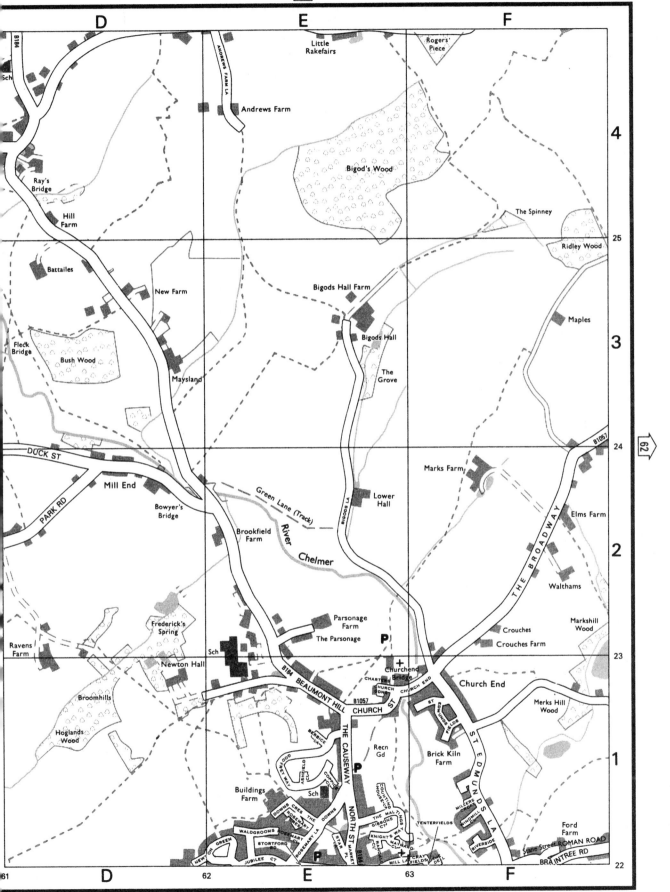

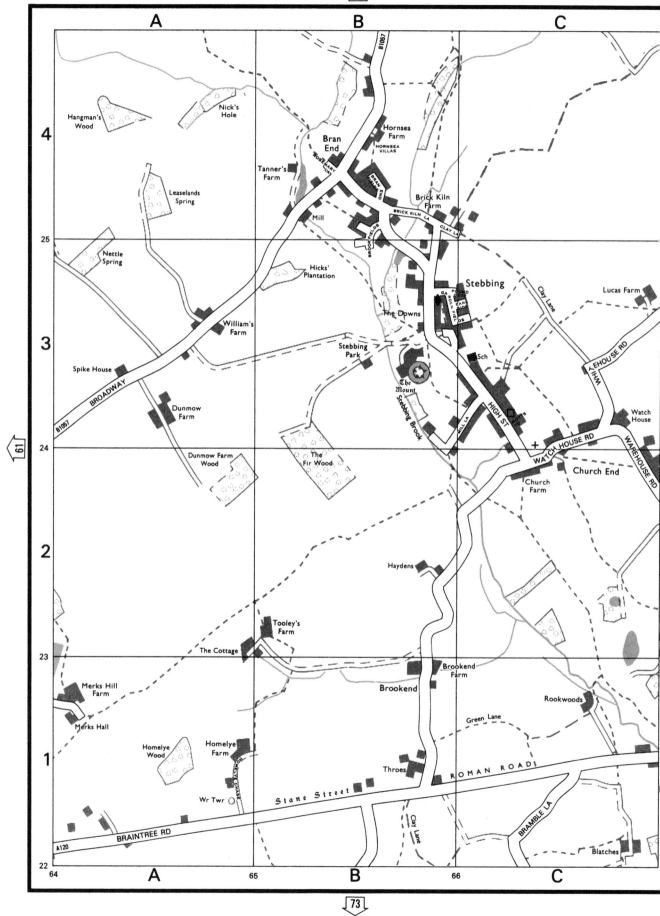

61

A   B   C

4

Hangman's Wood

Nick's Hole

Bran End

Hornsea Farm

HORNSEA VILLAS

Tanner's Farm

Brick Kiln Farm

Leaselands Spring

BRICK KILN LA

CLAY LA

Mill

25

Nettle Spring

Hicks' Plantation

Stebbing

The Downs

GARDEN FIELDS

PARK SIDE

POUND

Clay Lane

Lucas Farm

3

William's Farm

Stebbing Park

Sch

WHYEHOUSE RD

Spike House

BROADWAY

B1057

Dunmow Farm

The Mount

Stebbing Brook

HIGH ST

MILL LA

BOOTS

Watch House

24

Dunmow Farm Wood

The Fir Wood

WATCH HOUSE RD

WAREHOUSE RD

Church Farm

Church End

2

Haydens

Tooley's Farm

The Cottage

Brookend Farm

23

Merks Hill Farm

Brookend

Rookwoods

Merks Hall

Green Lane

Homelye Wood

Homelye Farm

1

MILKY CHASE

Throes

ROMAN ROAD

Stane Street

Clay Lane

BRAMBLE LA

Wr Twr

Blatches

BRAINTREE RD

A120

22

64   A   65   B   66   C

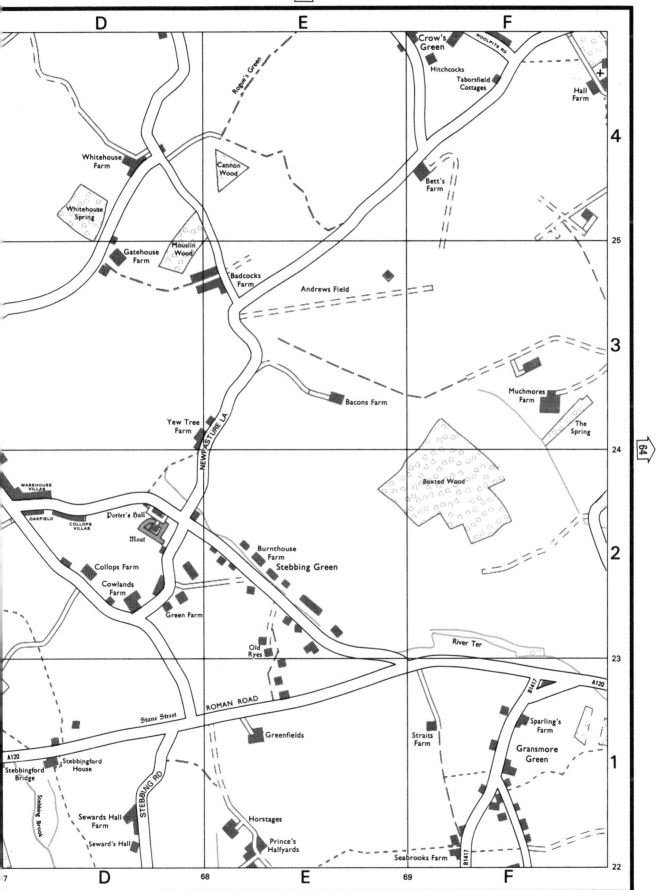

D   E   F

Crow's
Green

WOOLPITS RD

Hitchcocks

Taborsfield
Cottages

Hall
Farm

4

Whitehouse
Farm

Cannon
Wood

Bett's
Farm

Whitehouse
Spring

Gatehouse
Farm

Mouslin
Wood

25

Badcocks
Farm

Andrews Field

3

Muchmores
Farm

Bacons Farm

The
Spring

Yew Tree
Farm

NEWFASTURE LA

24

WAREHOUSE
VILLAS

Boxted Wood

OAKFIELD

COLLOPS
VILLAS

Porter's Hall

Moat

Burnthouse
Farm

2

Collops Farm

Stebbing Green

Cowlands
Farm

Green Farm

River Ter

Old
Ryes

23

Stane Street

ROMAN ROAD

Greenfields

Straits
Farm

B1417

A120

Sparling's
Farm

A120

Stebbingford
House

Gransmore
Green

1

Stebbingford
Bridge

STEBBING RD

Stebbing Brook

Sewards Hall
Farm

Horstages

Seward's Hall

Prince's
Halfyards

Seabrooks Farm

B1417

22

D   68   E   69   F

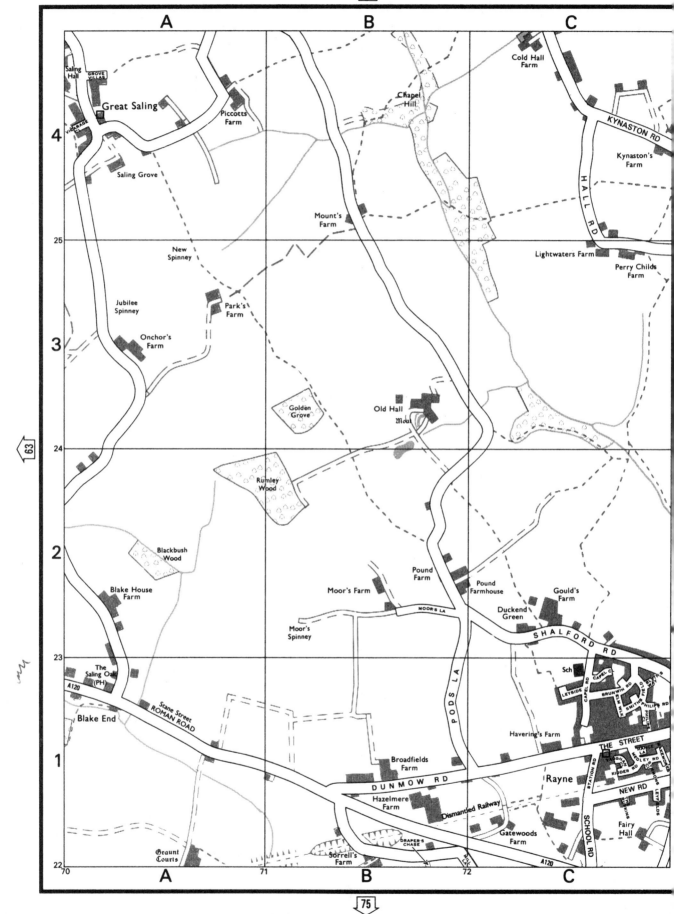

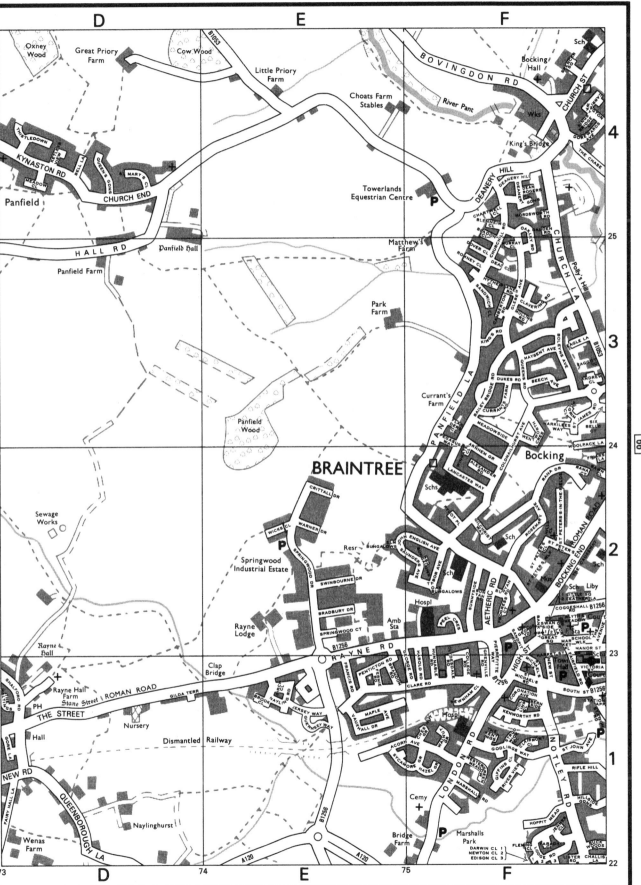

55

66

76

BRAINTREE

Bocking

Panfield

D   E   F

Oxney Wood

Great Priory Farm

Cow Wood

Little Priory Farm

Choats Farm Stables

River Pant

BOVINGDON RD

Bocking Hall

Sch

CHURCH ST

King's Bridge

THE CHASE

DEANERY HILL

Deanery Hill

Dean Rogers

WORDSWORTH RD

CHARTWELL

BLENHEIM CL

CHURCH LA

Towerlands Equestrian Centre

P

Matthew's Farm

DOVER CL

DEAL RD

ROMNEY CL

HYTHE CL

CLAVERING RD

SANDWICH CL

KING'S RD

MAYSENT AVE

BOLEYNE AVE

EAGLE LA

B1053

ANDREW CL

BAGGOT RD

DUKES RD

BEECH AVE

QUEENS RD

BAILEY BRIDGE RD

Currant's Farm

Currans Farm

MEADOWSIDE

COLDNAILHURST AVE

SIX BELLS CT

MARKILEES WAY

WOOLPACK LA

PANFIELD LA

4

25

3

24

Park Farm

Panfield Wood

LANCASTER WAY

ALEXANDER

Schs

RANA DR

RANA

St PETERS-IN-THE-FIELD

BOCKING END

ROMAN ROAD

Sch

Liby

Mus

Sch

Sewage Works

Springwood Industrial Estate

CRITTALL DR

WARNER DR

WICKS CL

P

SPRINGWOOD DR

Resr

Bungalows

JOHN ENGLISH AVE

SAUNDERS

SWINBOURNE DR

BRADBURY DR

SPRINGWOOD CT

B1256

Rayne Lodge

Amb Sta

Hospl

AETHERIC RD

SUNNYSIDE RD

COGGESHALL B1256

P

P

GREAT BRADFORDS

MANOR ST

2

23

1

22

Rayne Hall

Clap Bridge

RAYNE RD

Rayne Hall Farm

ROMAN ROAD

Stane Street

GILDA TERR

THE STREET

PH

Hall

SINALFORD RD

GORE LA

Nursery

Dismantled Railway

NAYLING RD

JERSEY WAY

GUERNSEY WAY

BROOM RD

VAUXHALL DR

FRANCIS RD

PENTICTON RD

GEORGE RD

HAROLD RD

CLARE RD

MAPLE DR

ACORN AVE

SYCAMORE GR

HAZEL GR

LONDON RD

B1256

WYNHAM CL

Hosp

KENWORTHY RD

GODLINGS WAY

CLAIRMONT RD

HIGH ST

St MICHAEL'S

Town Hall

SOUTH ST B1256

Victoria

P

P

COURT

MICHAEL'S

GREVILLE RD

PIERREFITTE WAY

COLLEGE RD

CLOVERDALE

ST JOHN AVE

RIFLE HILL

HILLSIDE GDNS

HOPPIT MEAD

RIVER VIEW

GIFFINS

JENKS RD

WICK WOODS

CHALLIS

LISTER RD

Cemy

Bridge Farm

P

Marshalls Park

MARSHALLS RD

NEW RD

QUEENBOROUGH LA

Wenas Farm

Naylinghurst

FAIRY HALL LA

A120

B1256

A120

DARWIN CL 1
NEWTON CL 2
EDISON CL 3

73   D   74   E   75   F

KYNASTON RD

CHURCH END

HALL RD

Panfield Hall

Panfield Farm

THISTLEDOWN

MEADOW CL

BELL LA

QUEEN'S GDNS

MARY'S CL

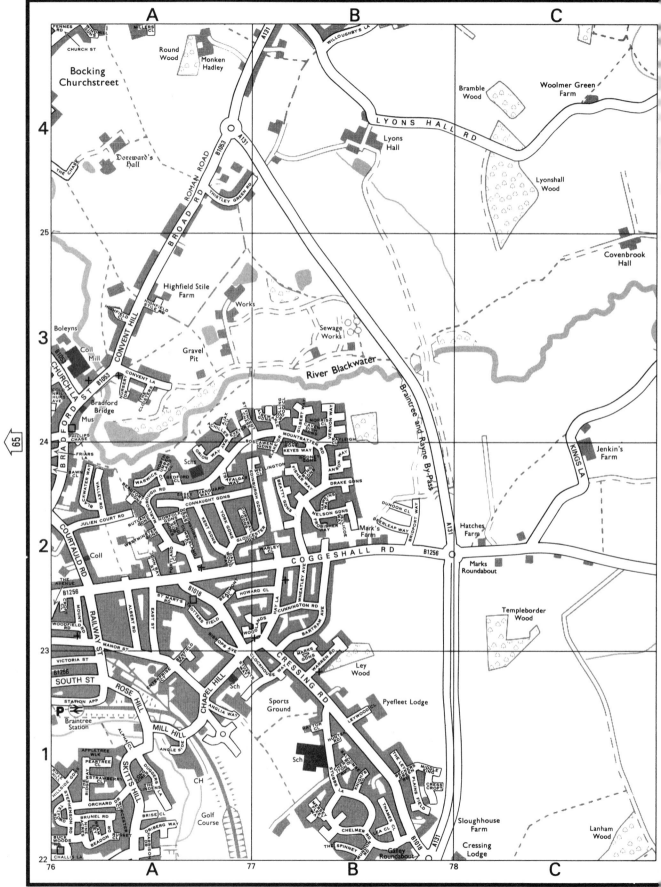

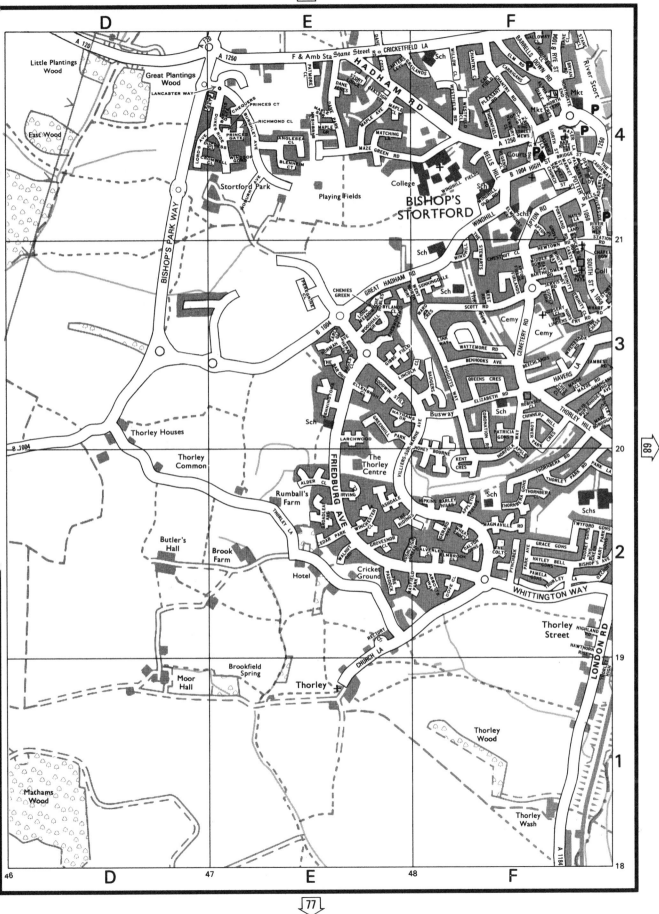

BISHOP'S STORTFORD

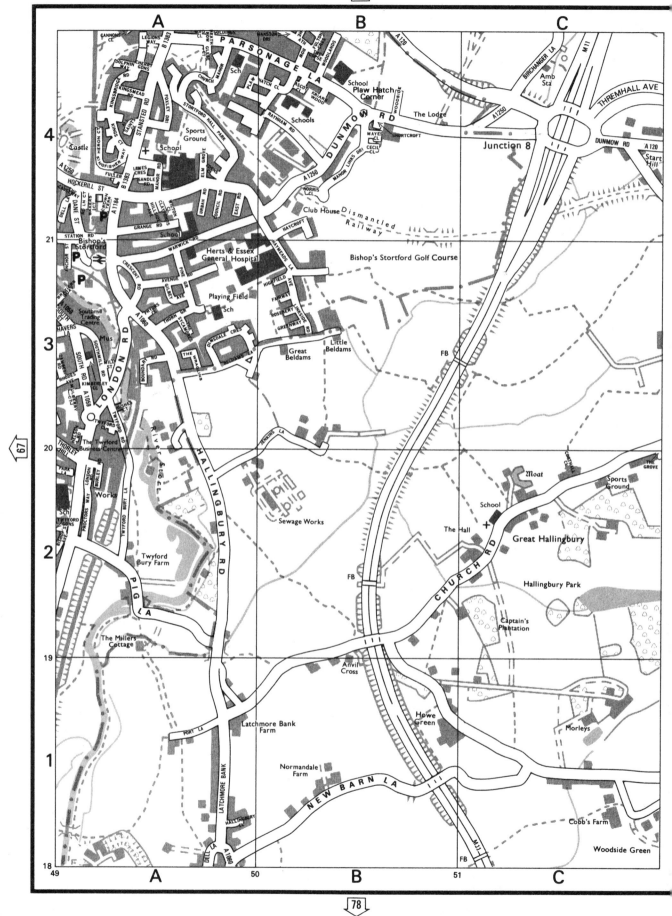

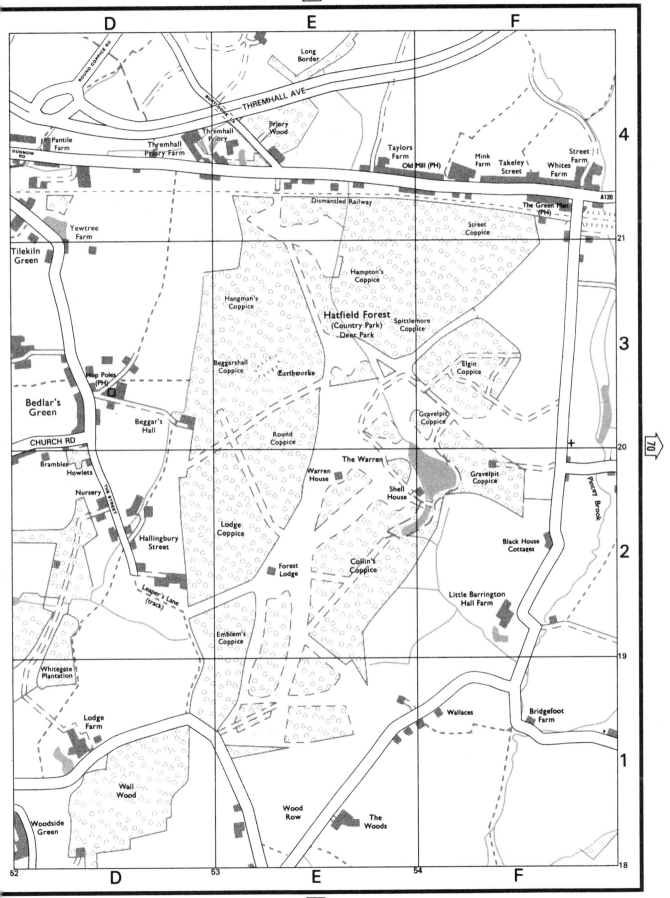

D E F

ROUND COPPICE RD

THREMHALL AVE

Long Border

Priory Wood

Thremhall Priory

DUNMOW RD

Pantile Farm

Thremhall Priory Farm

Taylors Farm

Old Mill (PH)

Mink Farm

Takeley Street

Whites Farm

Street Farm

4

A120

Dismantled Railway

The Green Man (PH)

Yewtree Farm

Street Coppice

21

Tilekiln Green

Hampton's Coppice

Hangman's Coppice

Hatfield Forest
(Country Park)
Deer Park

Spittlemore Coppice

3

Beggarshall Coppice

Earthworks

Elgin Coppice

Hop Poles (PH)

Bedlar's Green

Gravelpit Coppice

CHURCH RD

Beggar's Hall

Round Coppice

20

The Warren

Brambles

Howlets

Warren House

Gravelpit Coppice

Nursery

THE STREET

Shell House

Black House Cottages

Hallingbury Street

Lodge Coppice

2

Forest Lodge

Collin's Coppice

Little Barrington Hall Farm

Leaper's Lane (track)

Emblem's Coppice

19

Whitegate Plantation

Lodge Farm

Wallaces

Bridgefoot Farm

1

Wall Wood

Woodside Green

Wood Row

The Woods

52 D 53 E 54 F 18

70

Pincey Brook

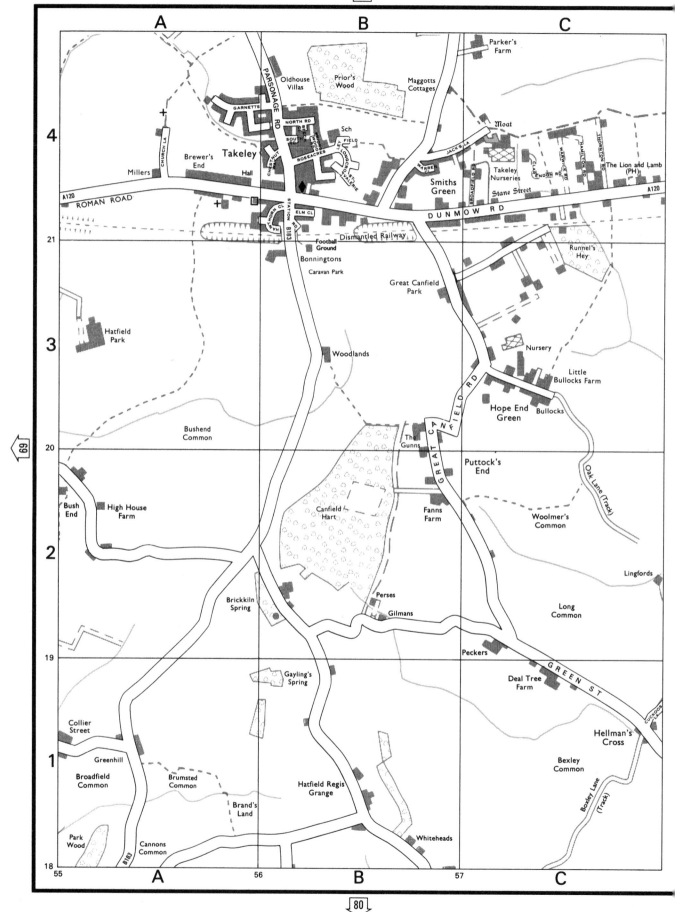

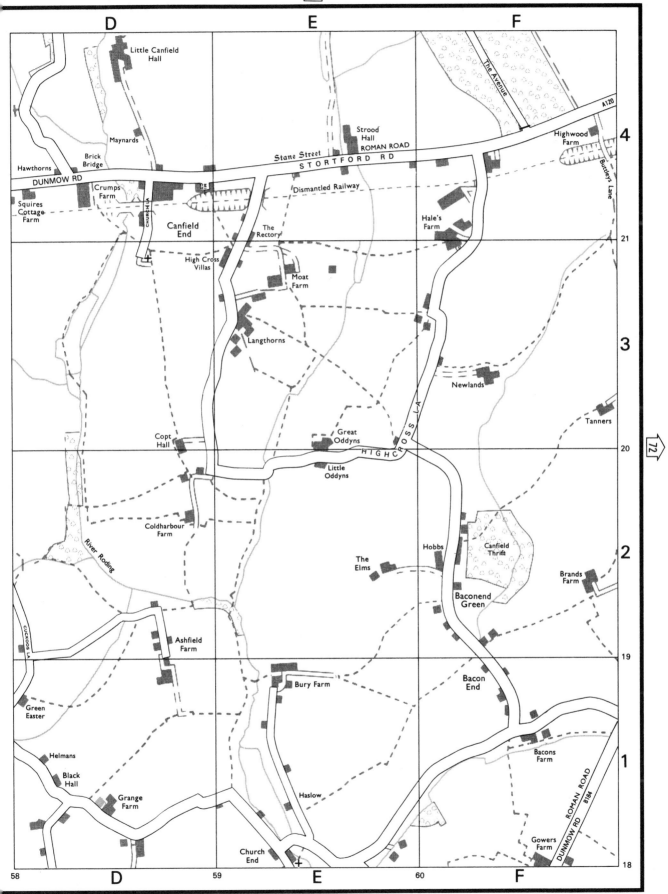

D   E   F

Little Canfield Hall

The Avenue

A120

Maynards

Strood Hall
ROMAN ROAD

Highwood Farm

4

Hawthorns

Brick Bridge

Stane Street
STORTFORD RD

Buttleys Lane

DUNMOW RD

Crumps Farm

Dismantled Railway

Squires Cottage Farm

CHURCH LA

Canfield End

The Rectory

Hale's Farm

21

High Cross Villas

Moat Farm

Langthorns

Newlands

3

Copt Hall

Great Oddyns

HIGHCROSS LA

Tanners

72

Little Oddyns

20

River Roding

Coldharbour Farm

The Elms

Hobbs

Canfield Thrift

2

CUCKOOS LA

Ashfield Farm

Baconend Green

Brands Farm

19

Green Easter

Bury Farm

Bacon End

Helmans

Bacons Farm

1

Black Hall

Grange Farm

Haslow

ROMAN ROAD
B184

Church End

Gowers Farm

DUNMOW RD

18

58   D   59   E   60   F

71

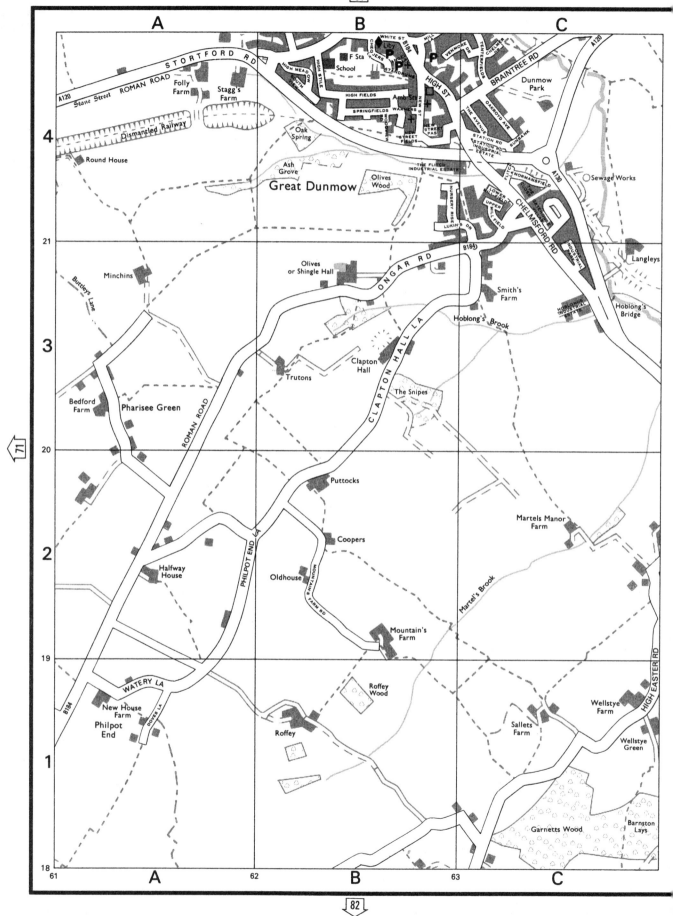

A **B** **C**

STORTFORD RD

A120 Stane Street ROMAN ROAD

WHITE ST B184
MILL
CHEQUERS
Library
P
P
VENMORE DR
TENTERFIELDS
CHELMER DR
BRAINTREE RD
A120

F Sta
School
STANDRUMS
HIGH ST
Dunmow Park

HIGH MEADOW
HIGH STILE
SOUTH FARM
NEW ST
Amb Stn
WARNERS
HIGH FIELDS
SPRINGFIELDS
STATION RD
THE AVENUE
OAKROYD AVE
SUNBANK
STATION RD INDUSTRIAL ESTATE

Folly Farm
Stagg's Farm

Dismantled Railway

4

Round House

Oak Spring

Ash Grove

Great Dunmow

Olives Wood

STREET FIELDS

THE FLITCH INDUSTRIAL ESTATE
NORMANSFIELD
A130
Sewage Works

NURSERY RISE
LOWER MILL FIELD
UPPER MILL FIELD
LUKIN'S DR
CHELMSFORD RD
FLITCH WAY

21

B184
Langleys

Minchins

Olives or Shingle Hall

ONGAR RD

Smith's Farm

HOBLONG INDUSTRIAL ESTATE
Hoblong's Bridge

Burtleys Lane

Hoblong's Brook

3

Bedford Farm
Pharisee Green

Trutons

CLAPTON HALL LA

Clapton Hall

The Snipes

ROMAN ROAD

20

Puttocks

Martels Manor Farm

2

Halfway House

PHILPOT END LA

Coopers

Oldhouse

MOUNTAINS FARM RD

Martel's Brook

Mountain's Farm

HIGH EASTER RD

19

WATERY LA

B184
DOVES LA
New House Farm
Philpot End

Roffey Wood

Roffey

Sallets Farm

Wellstye Farm

Wellstye Green

1

Barnston Lays

Garnetts Wood

18

A 62 **B** 63 **C**

61

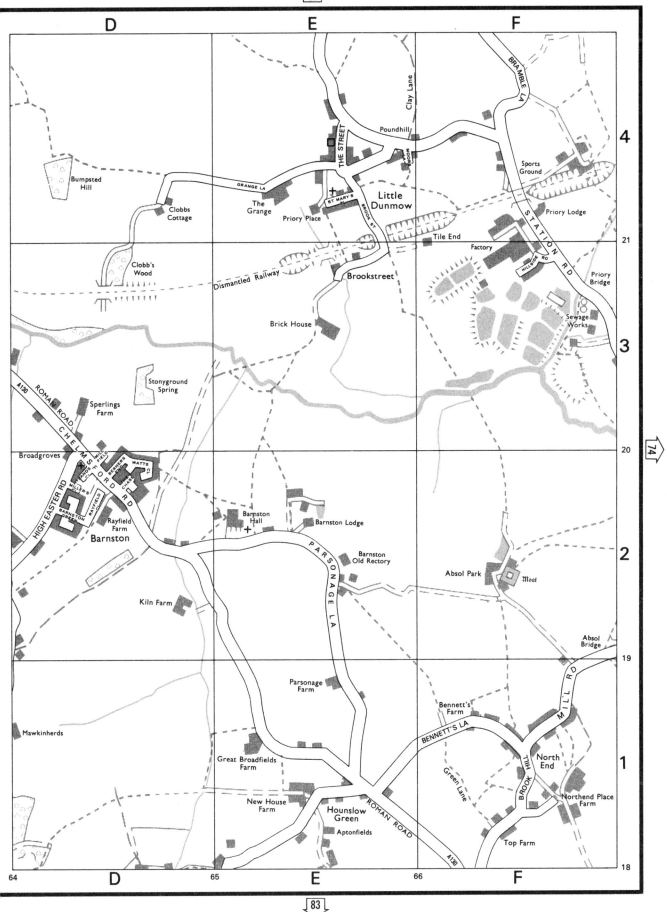

74

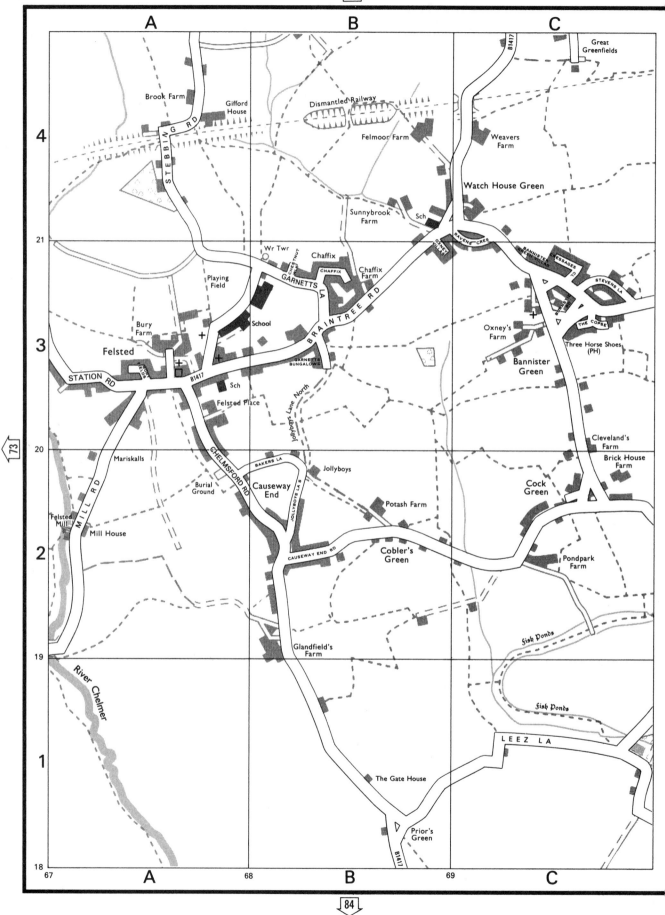

73

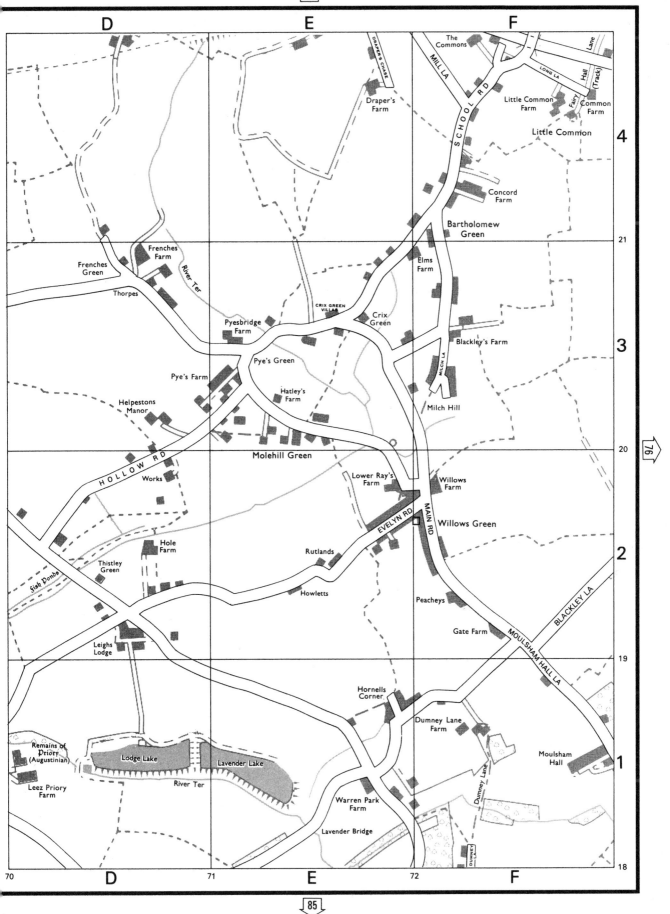

D   E   F

The Commons

Lane

Draper's Farm

DRAPER'S CHASE

MILL LA

SCHOOL RD

LONG LA

Hall

Fairy

(Track)

Little Common Farm

Common Farm

Little Common

4

Concord Farm

Bartholomew Green

21

Frenches Farm

Frenches Green

River Ter

Thorpes

Pyesbridge Farm

Elms Farm

MILCH LA

Blackley's Farm

Pye's Green

CRIX GREEN VILLAS

Crix Green

Pye's Farm

Hatley's Farm

Milch Hill

3

Helpestons Manor

Molehill Green

76

HOLLOW RD

Works

Lower Ray's Farm

Willows Farm

20

EVELYN RD

MAIN RD

Willows Green

Hole Farm

Thistley Green

Rutlands

Howletts

Peacheys

2

Fish Ponds

Gate Farm

MOULSHAM HALL LA

BLACKLEY LA

Leighs Lodge

19

Hornells Corner

Dumney Lane Farm

Remains of Priory (Augustinian)

Lodge Lake

Lavender Lake

River Ter

DUMNEY LANE

Moulsham Hall

1

Leez Priory Farm

Warren Park Farm

Lavender Bridge

DUMNEY LANE

18

70   D   71   E   72   F

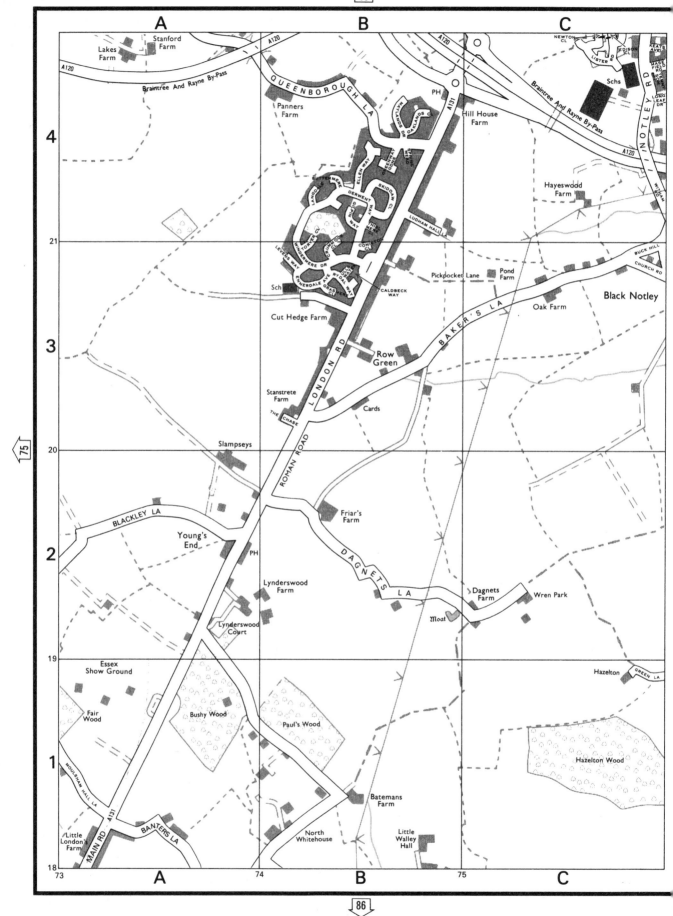

A   B   C

Stanford Farm

Lakes Farm

A120

Braintree And Rayne By-Pass

QUEENBOROUGH LA

A120

Panners Farm

A131

PH

Hill House Farm

Braintree And Rayne By-Pass

NOTLEY RD

NEWTON CL

LISTER RD

EDISON CL

KEATS AVE

MASEFIELD RD

LONG LEAF DR

Schs

4

HAYLANDS DR

OAKLANDS CL

ASKEW SQ

BECKFORD

ELLEN WAY

SKIDDAW CL

BUTTERMERE

LANGDALE

DERWENT

HIGH MERE

BORROWDALE

LUDHAM HALL LA

Hayeswodd Farm

WIGAN ROAD

21

LEVENS WAY

WINDERMERE DR

CRUMMOCK

CONISTON

RYDAL WAY

BUCK HILL

CHURCH RD

Sch

ENNERDALE AVE

GRASMERE

CALDBECK WAY

Pickpocket Lane

Pond Farm

Oak Farm

Black Notley

Cut Hedge Farm

LONDON RD

BAKER'S LA

3

Stanstrete Farm

Row Green

Cards

THE CHASE

Slampseys

20

ROMAN ROAD

Friar's Farm

DAGNETS LA

BLACKLEY LA

Young's End

PH

Dagnets Farm

Wren Park

2

Lynderswood Farm

Moat

Lynderswood Court

19

Essex Show Ground

Hazelton

GREEN LA

Fair Wood

Bushy Wood

Paul's Wood

Hazelton Wood

1

MOULSHAM HALL LA

MAIN RD A131

BANTERS LA

Batemans Farm

Little London's Farm

North Whitehouse

Little Walley Hall

18

73   A   74   B   75   C

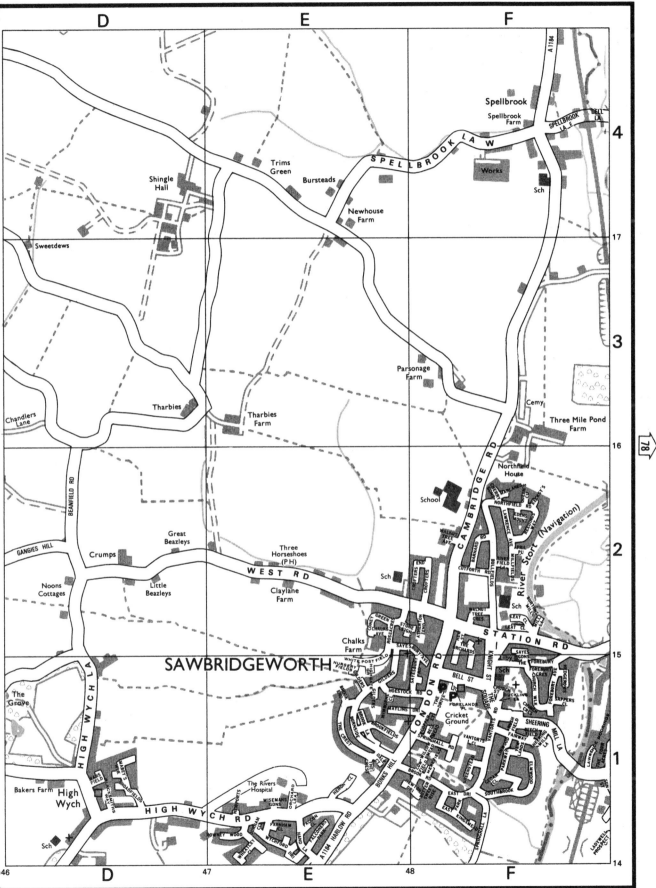

D   E   F

Spellbrook

Spellbrook
Farm

SPELLBROOK LA W

Works

Sch

DELL
LA

SPELLBROOK LA. F.

A1184

4

Trims
Green

Bursteads

Shingle
Hall

Newhouse
Farm

17

Sweetdews

3

Parsonage
Farm

Cemy

Chandlers
Lane

Tharbies

Tharbies
Farm

Three Mile Pond
Farm

16

78

BEANFIELD RD

Northfield
House

School

CAMBRIDGE RD

River Stort (Navigation)

NORTHFIELD
RD

EDENS
MOUNT

APRIL
PL

GANGIES HILL

Great
Beazleys

Crumps

Three
Horseshoes
(P H)

WEST RD

Sch

WALNUT
TREE AVE

BARNARD RD

LAWRENCE
AVE

MILLFIELDS

RIVER
FIELD

CUTFORTH

BULLFIELDS

2

Noons
Cottages

Little
Beazleys

Claylane
Farm

END

CROFTERS

WALNUT
TREE
CRES

Sch

Chalks
Farm

SAWBRIDGEWORTH

White Post Field

Sch

STATION RD

15

HIGH WYCH LA

The
Grove

BELL ST

THE
SQUARE

Liby

Sch

THE FOREBURY

FOREBURY

P

Cricket
Ground

LONDON RD

Bakers Farm

High
Wych

HIGH WYCH RD

The Rivers
Hospital

A1184 HARLOW RD

SHEERING MILL LA

1

EAST DRI

SOUTHBROOK

14

46   D   47   E   48   F

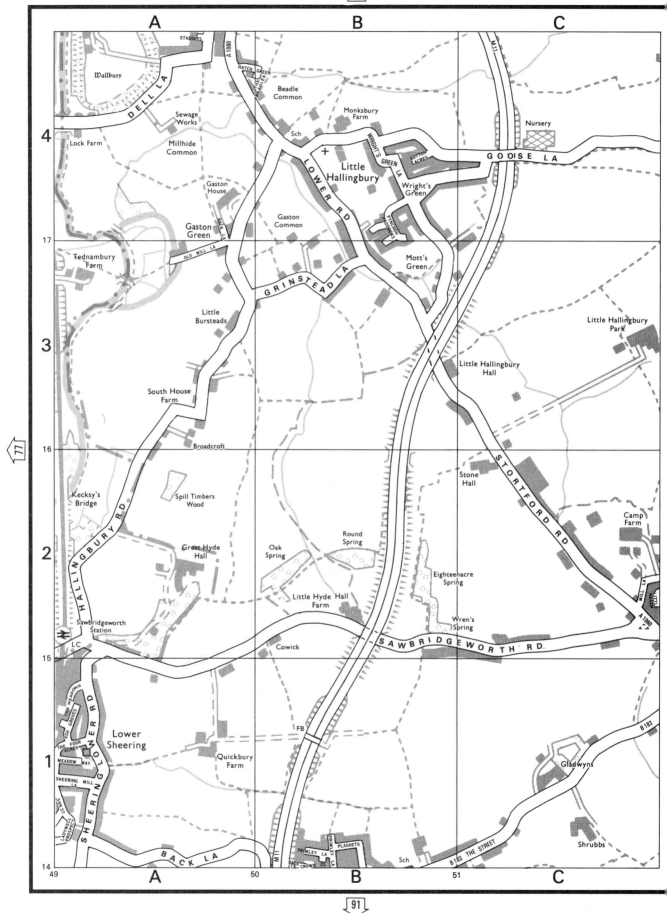

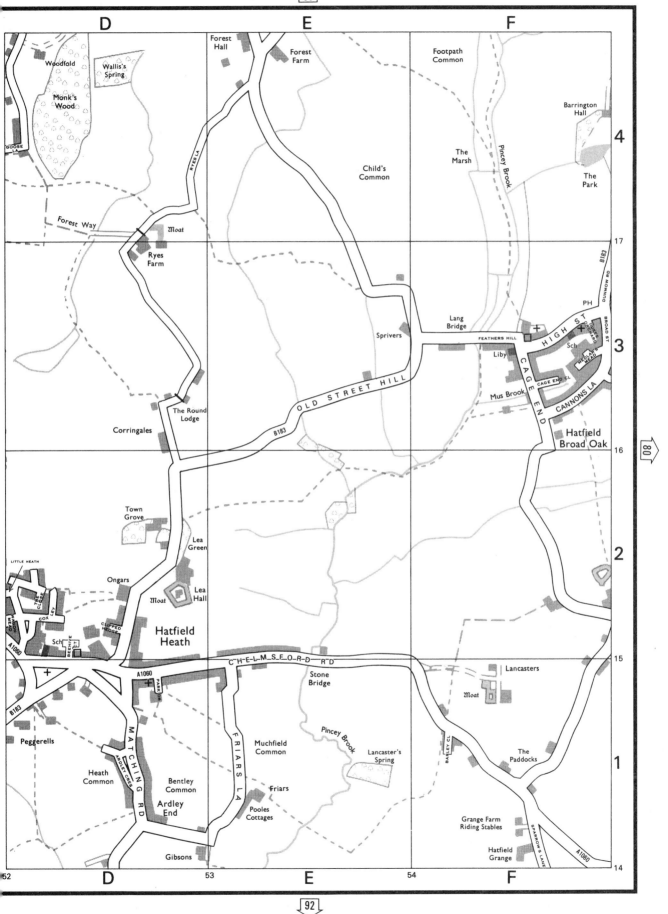

D   E   F

Woodfold

Wallis's Spring

Monk's Wood

GOOSE LA

Forest Hall

Forest Farm

Child's Common

Footpath Common

The Marsh

Pincey Brook

Barrington Hall

The Park

4

RYES LA

Forest Way

Moat

Ryes Farm

17

Lang Bridge

Sprivers

Feathers Hill

Medlars Head

HIGH ST

B183

DUNMOW RD

PH

Sch

BROAD ST

3

Liby

OLD STREET HILL

B183

The Round Lodge

Corringales

Mus Brook

CAGE END

CAGE END CL

CANNONS LA

Hatfield Broad Oak

16

Town Grove

Lea Green

2

LITTLE HEATH

Ongars

Moat

Lea Hall

TREE CLOSE

COX LEY

CLIPPED HEDGE

A1060

Sch

BEEHIVE

Hatfield Heath

Lancasters

Moat

C H E L M S F O R D R D

15

Stone Bridge

B183

A1060

PARK DR

MATCHING RD

FRIARS LA

Muchfield Common

Pincey Brook

Lancaster's Spring

BARLEY CL

The Paddocks

Peggerells

ARDLEY CRES

Heath Common

Bentley Common

Friars

Ardley End

Pooles Cottages

Grange Farm Riding Stables

SPARROWS LANE

A1060

1

Gibsons

Hatfield Grange

52   D   53   E   54   F   14

80

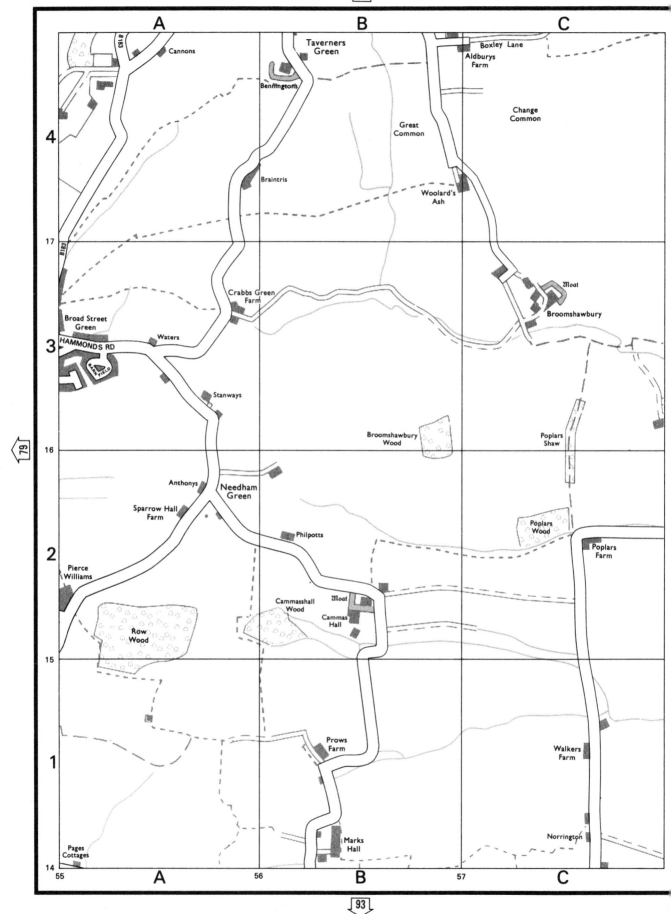

79

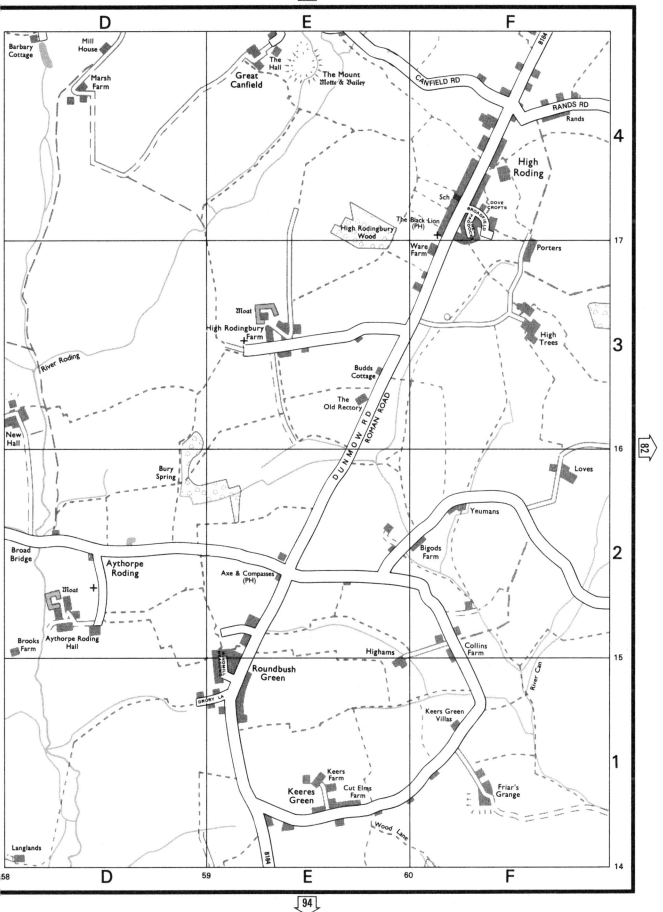

D E F

Barbary
Cottage

Mill
House

Marsh
Farm

The
Hall

Great
Canfield

The Mount
Motte & Bailey

CANFIELD RD

B184

RANDS RD

Rands

4

High
Roding

Sch

DOVE
CROFTS

BROADFIELD
PADDOCK

The Black Lion
(PH)

High Rodingbury
Wood

Ware
Farm

Porters

17

River Roding

Moat

High Rodingbury
Farm

Budds
Cottage

High
Trees

3

The
Old Rectory

DUNMOW RD

ROMAN ROAD

New
Hall

Bury
Spring

16

Loves

Yeumans

Broad
Bridge

Aythorpe
Roding

Axe & Compasses
(PH)

Bigods
Farm

2

Moat

Brooks
Farm

Aythorpe Roding
Hall

WINDMILL

DRURY LA

Roundbush
Green

Highams

Collins
Farm

River Can

15

Keers Green
Villas

1

Keers
Farm

Keeres
Green

Cut Elms
Farm

Friar's
Grange

Langlands

Wood Lane

B184

14

58 D 59 E 60 F

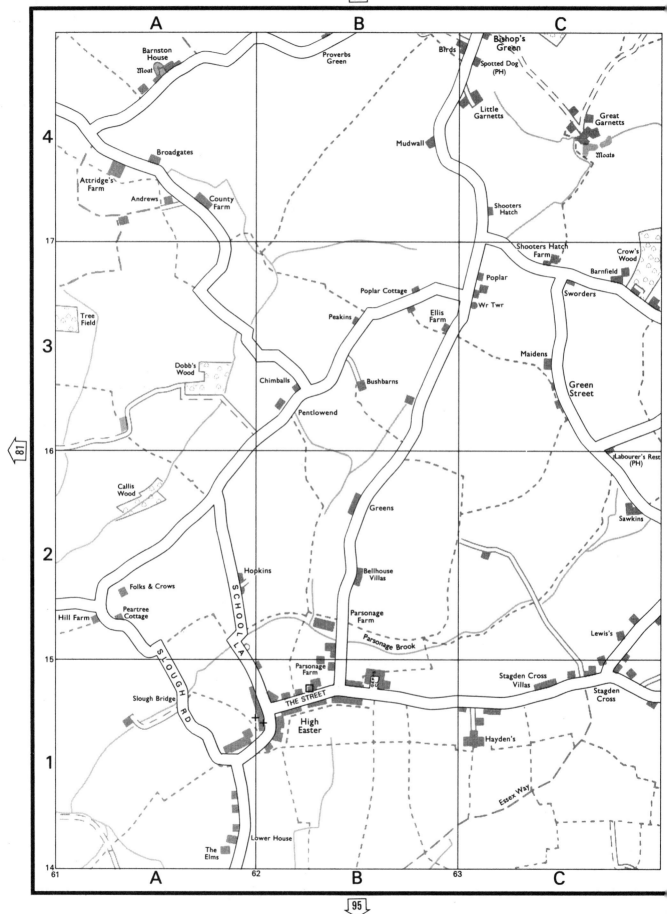

A

B

C

Barnston House
Moat
Broadgates
Attridge's Farm
Andrews
County Farm

Proverbs Green

Birds
Bishop's Green
Spotted Dog (PH)
Little Garnetts
Mudwall
Great Garnetts
Moats
Shooters Hatch

4

17

Shooters Hatch Farm
Crow's Wood
Poplar
Barnfield
Poplar Cottage
Sworders

Tree Field

Peakins
Ellis Farm
Wr Twr

Maidens

3

Dobb's Wood
Chimballs
Bushbarns
Green Street
Pentlowend

16

Labourer's Rest (PH)

Callis Wood

Greens
Sawkins

2

Hopkins
Folks & Crows
Bellhouse Villas

Peartree Cottage
Parsonage Farm
Lewis's

Hill Farm
Parsonage Brook

SCHOOL LA

15

SLOUGH RD
Parsonage Farm
Stagden Cross Villas
Stagden Cross

Slough Bridge
THE STREET
High Easter
Hayden's

1

Essex Way

Lower House
The Elms

14

61
A
62
B
63
C

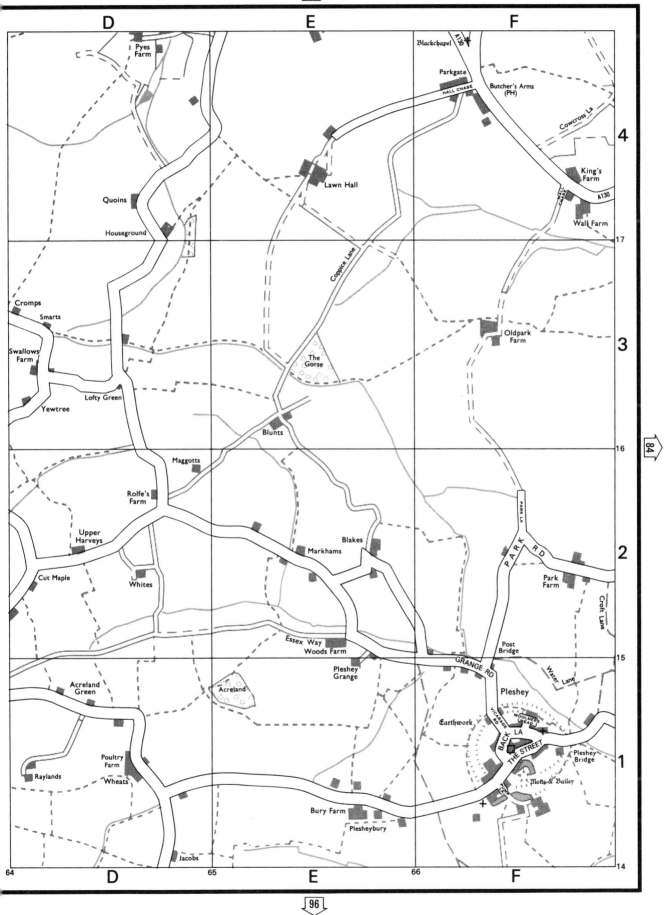

84

D   E   F

Pyes Farm

Blackchapel

Parkgate

HALL CHASE

Butcher's Arms (PH)

Cowcross La

4

Lawn Hall

King's Farm

Quoins

A130

Wall Farm

Houseground

17

Coppice Lane

Cromps

Smarts

Oldpark Farm

3

Swallows Farm

The Gorse

Lofty Green

Yewtree

Blunts

16

Maggotts

Rolfe's Farm

PARK LA

Upper Harveys

Blakes

PARK RD

2

Markhams

Park Farm

Cut Maple

Whites

Croft Lane

Essex Way Woods Farm

Post Bridge

15

GRANGE RD

Water Lane

Pleshey Grange

Pleshey

Acreland Green

Acreland

Earthwork

VICARAGE RD

WOOLMER'S HEAD

BACK LA

+

Poultry Farm

THE STREET

Pleshey Bridge

1

Raylands

Wheats

Motte & Bailey

Bury Farm

+

Pleshøybury

Jacobs

64   D   65   E   66   F   14

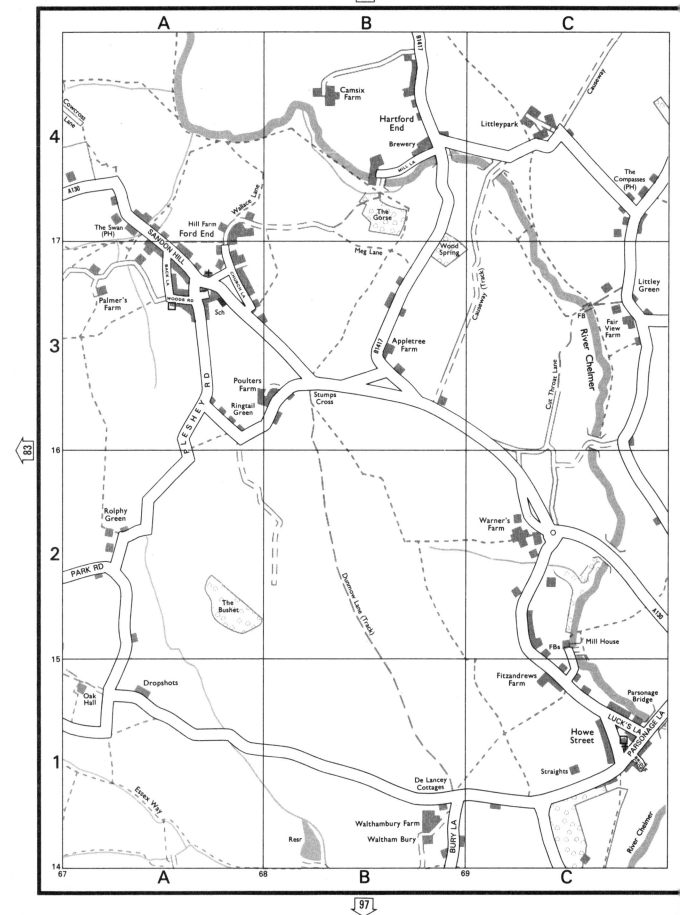

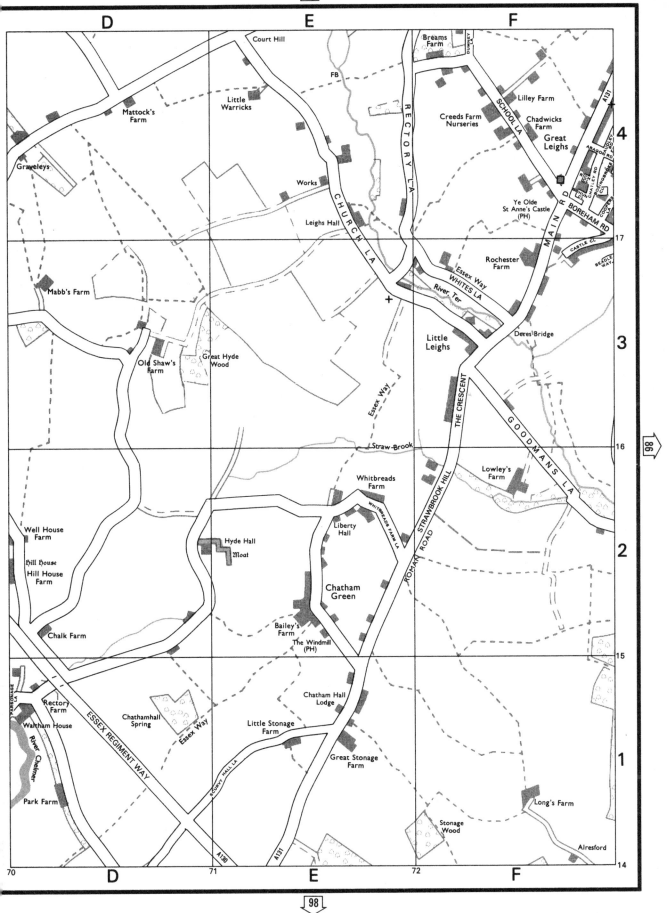

D E F

Court Hill

Breams Farm

Mattock's Farm

Little Warricks

Lilley Farm

Creeds Farm Nurseries

SCHOOL LA

Chadwicks Farm

Great Leighs

4

Graveleys

Works

RECTORY LA

Ye Olde St Anne's Castle (PH)

MAIN RD

BOREHAM RD

Leighs Hall

CHURCH LA

17

Mabb's Farm

Rochester Farm

Essex Way

WHITES LA

CASTLE CL

BEADLE WAY

Deres Bridge

3

Old Shaw's Farm

Great Hyde Wood

River Ter

Little Leighs

Essex Way

THE CRESCENT

GOODMANS LA

86

Straw Brook

16

Whitbreads Farm

Lowley's Farm

STRAWBROOK HILL

Well House Farm

Hyde Hall

Moat

Liberty Hall

WHITBREADS FARM LA

ROMAN ROAD

2

Hill House

Hill House Farm

Chatham Green

Chalk Farm

Bailey's Farm

The Windmill (PH)

15

PARSONAGE LA

Rectory Farm

ESSEX REGIMENT WAY

Chathamhall Spring

Chatham Hall Lodge

Waltham House

River Chelmer

Essex Way

Little Stonage Farm

SLUNNY HALL LA

Great Stonage Farm

1

Park Farm

Long's Farm

Stonage Wood

A130

A131

Alresford

70 D 71 E 72 F 14

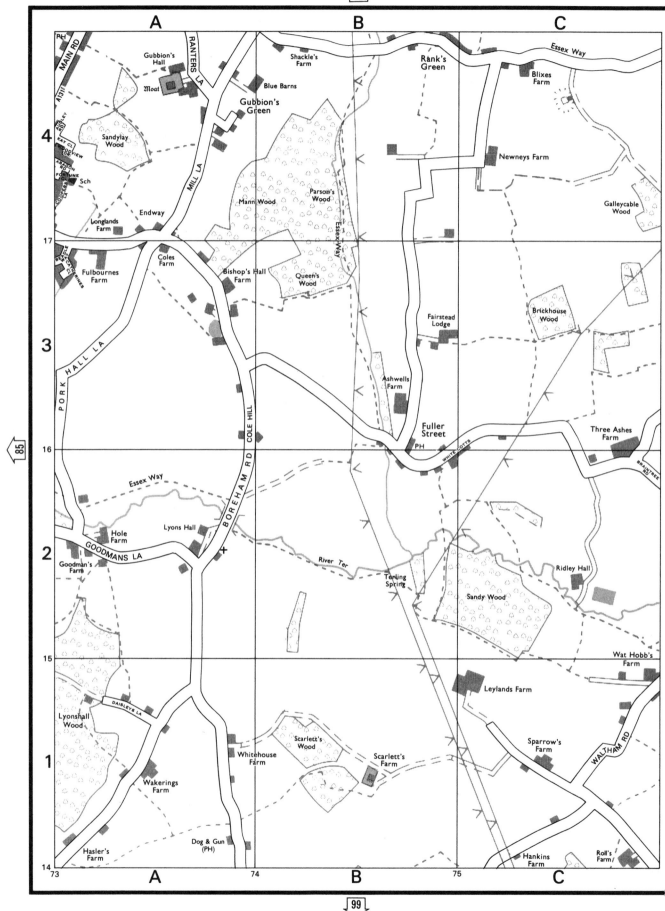

not continued, see key diagram

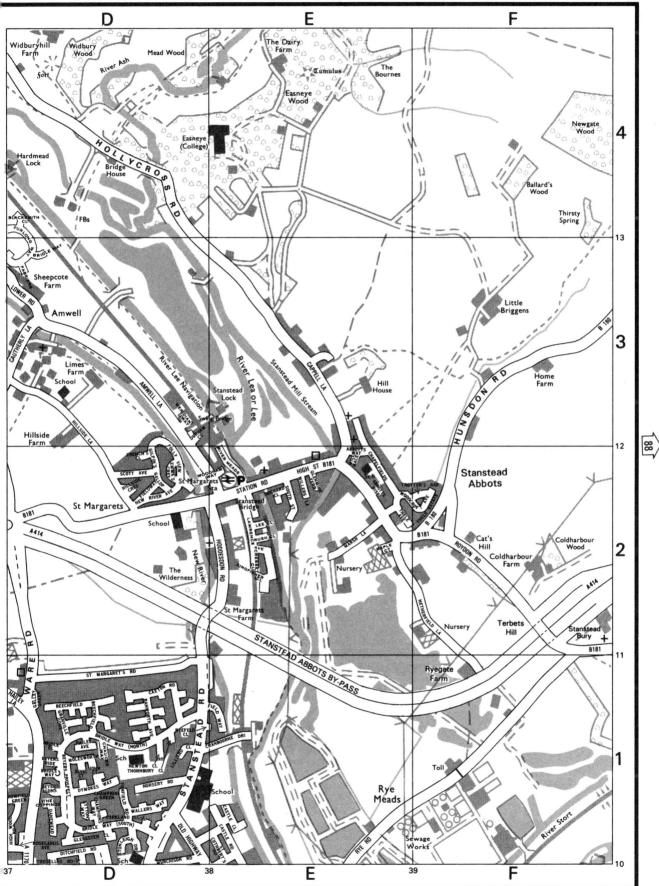

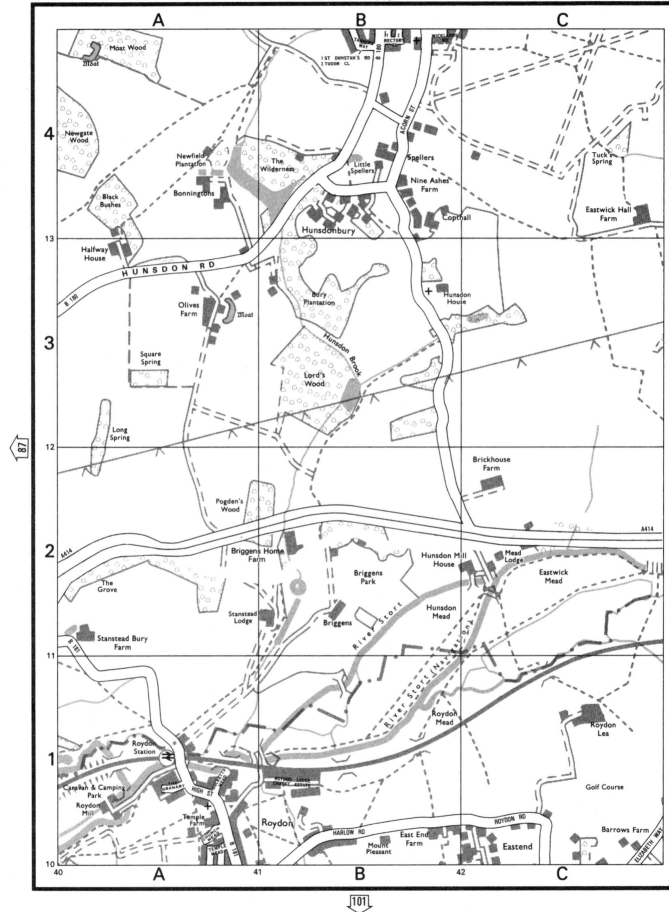

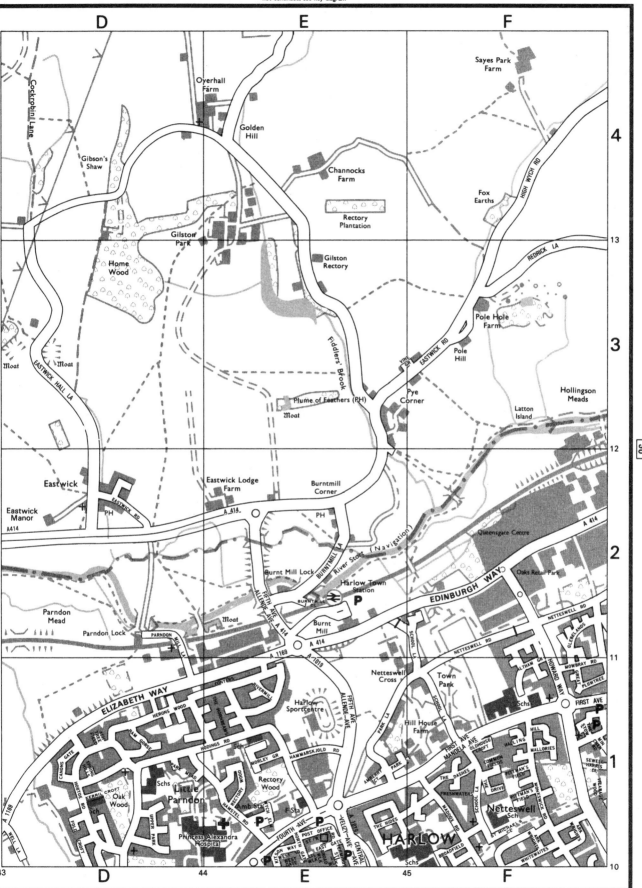

90

102

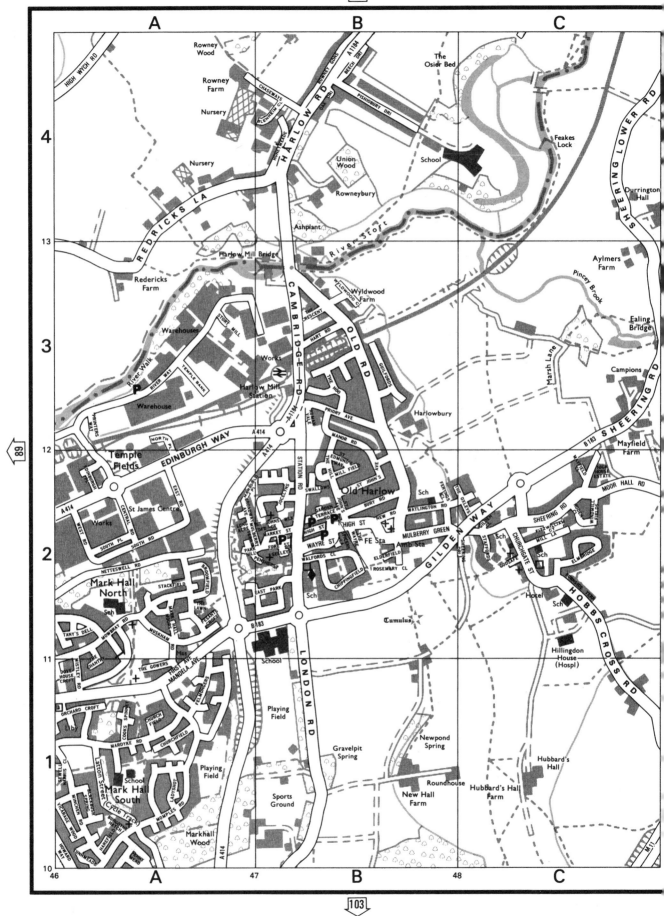

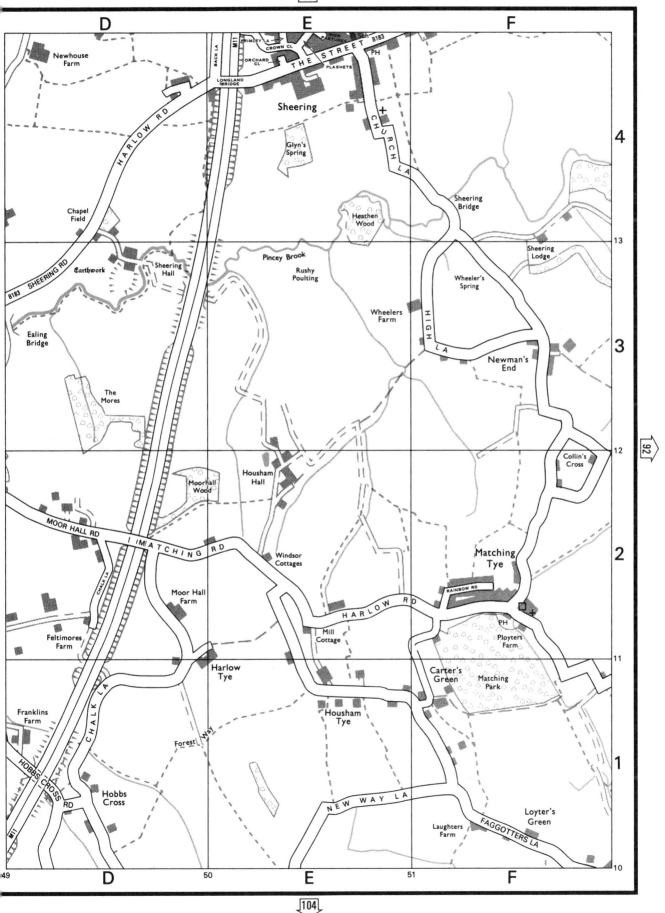

92

D   E   F

Newhouse Farm

Sheering

Glyn's Spring

4

Chapel Field

Sheering Bridge

Heathen Wood

13

Earthwork

Sheering Hall

Pincey Brook

Rushy Poulting

Sheering Lodge

Ealing Bridge

Wheelers Farm

Wheeler's Spring

3

Newman's End

The Mores

12

Housham Hall

Moorhall Wood

Collin's Cross

MOOR HALL RD

MATCHING RD

Matching Tye

2

Moor Hall Farm

Windsor Cottages

RAINBOW RD

Feltimores Farm

Mill Cottage

HARLOW RD

PH

Ployters Farm

CHALK LA

Harlow Tye

11

Carter's Green

Matching Park

Franklins Farm

Housham Tye

Forest Way

HOBBS CROSS

Hobbs Cross

1

NEW WAY LA

Loyter's Green

Laughters Farm

FAGGOTTERS LA

49   D   50   E   51   F   10

SHEERING RD

HARLOW RD

BACK LA

LONGLAND BRIDGE

M11

PRIMLEY LA

CROWN CL

ORCHARD CL

THE STREET

B183

PLASHETS

CHURCH LA

HIGH LA

PH

79

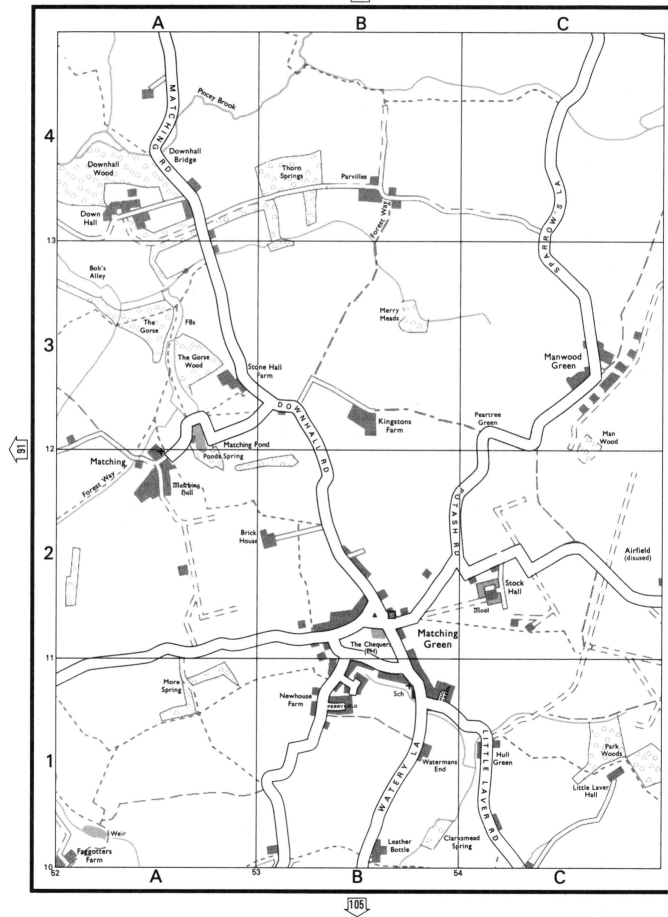

91

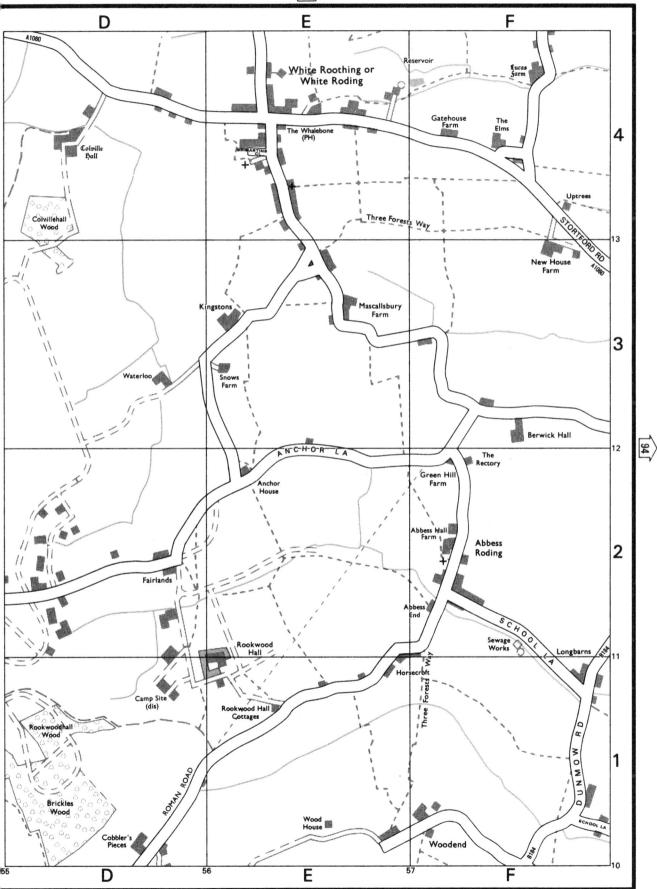

80

D   E   F

A1060

White Roothing or
White Roding

Reservoir

Lucas
Farm

Gatehouse
Farm

The
Elms

4

Colville
Hall

The Whalebone
(PH)

ST MARTINS
C of E

Uptrees

STORTFORD RD

Three Forests Way

A1060

Colvillehall
Wood

New House
Farm

13

Kingstons

Mascallsbury
Farm

3

Waterloo

Snows
Farm

Berwick Hall

A N C H O R   L A

12

The Rectory

Anchor
House

Green Hill
Farm

94

Abbess Hall
Farm

Abbess
Roding

2

Fairlands

Abbess
End

SCHOOL LA

Sewage
Works

Longbarns

B184

Rookwood
Hall

11

Horsecroft

Camp Site
(dis)

Rookwood Hall
Cottages

Three Forestd Way

DUNMOW RD

SCHOOL LA

Rookwoodhall
Wood

1

Brickles
Wood

ROMAN ROAD

Wood
House

Woodend

B184

Cobbler's
Pieces

55   D   56   E   57   F   10

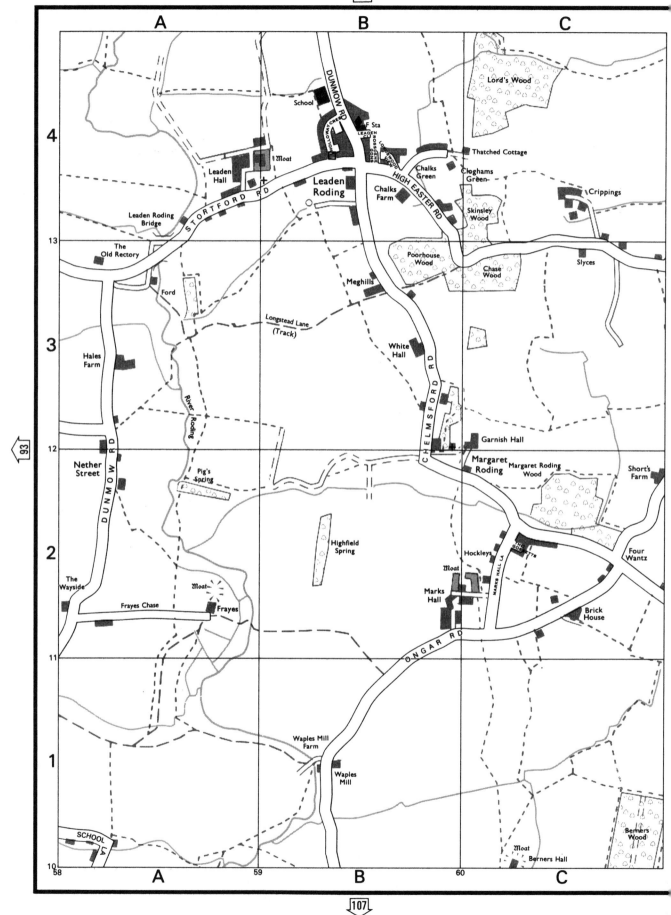

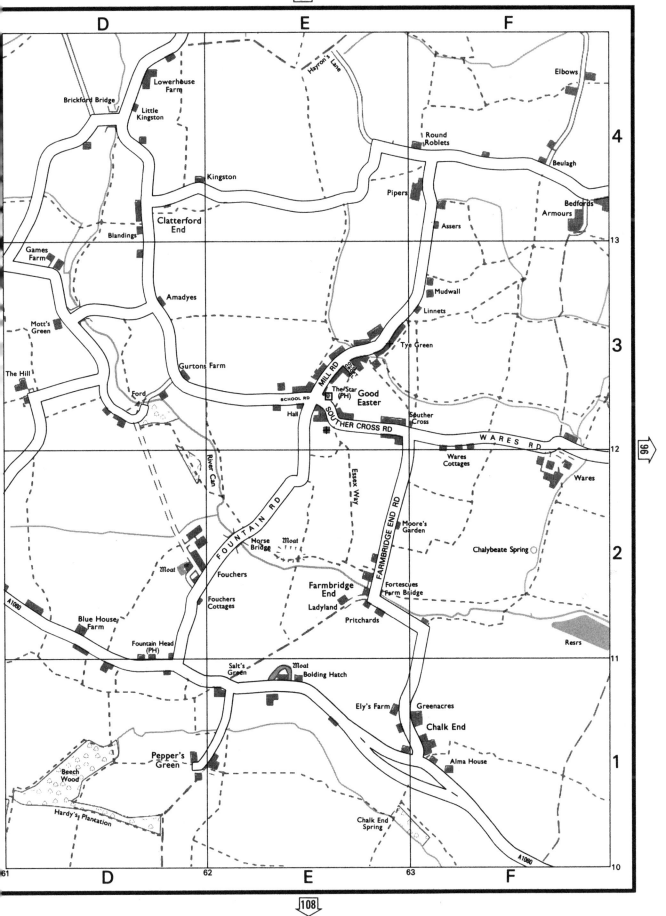

D   E   F

Elbows

4

Lowerhouse Farm

Brickford Bridge

Little Kingston

Round Roblets

Beulagh

Kingston

Pipers

Bedfords

Clatterford End

Assers

Armours

13

Blandings

Games Farm

Amadyes

Mudwall

Linnets

3

Mott's Green

Gurtons Farm

Tye Green

The Hill

MILL RD

The Star (PH)

Good Easter

Ford

SCHOOL RD

Hall

SOUTHER CROSS RD

Souther Cross

WARES RD

12

River Can

Wares Cottages

Wares

FOUNTAIN RD

Essex Way

Moore's Garden

Chalybeate Spring

2

Horse Bridge

Moat

FARMBRIDGE END RD

Moat

Fouchers

Farmbridge End

Fortescues Farm Bridge

Fouchers Cottages

Ladyland

Pritchards

A1060

Blue House Farm

Resrs

Fountain Head (PH)

11

Salt's Green

Moat

Bolding Hatch

Ely's Farm

Greenacres

Chalk End

Beech Wood

Pepper's Green

Alma House

1

Hardy's Plantation

Chalk End Spring

A1060

61   D   62   E   63   F   10

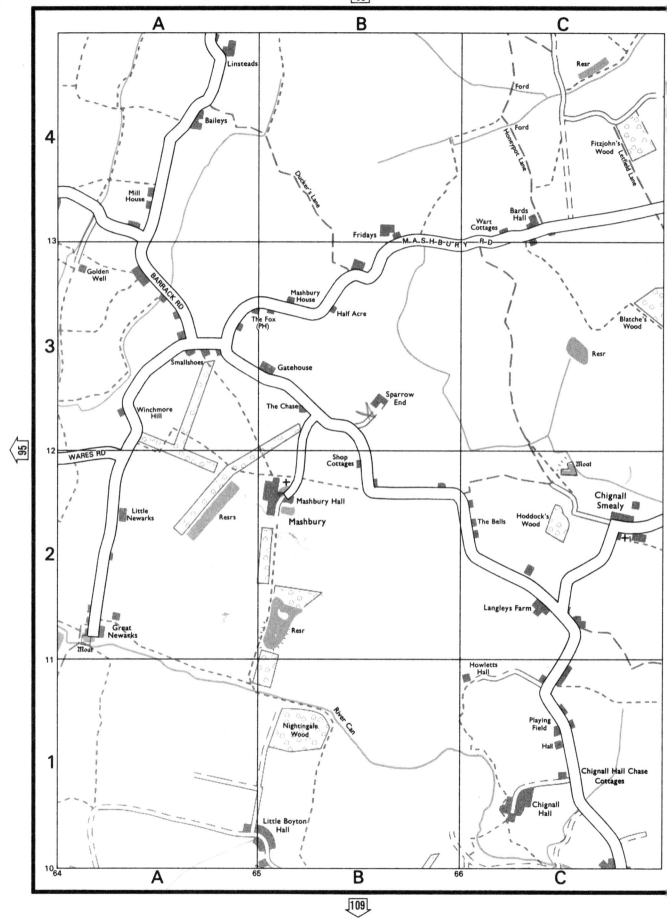

95

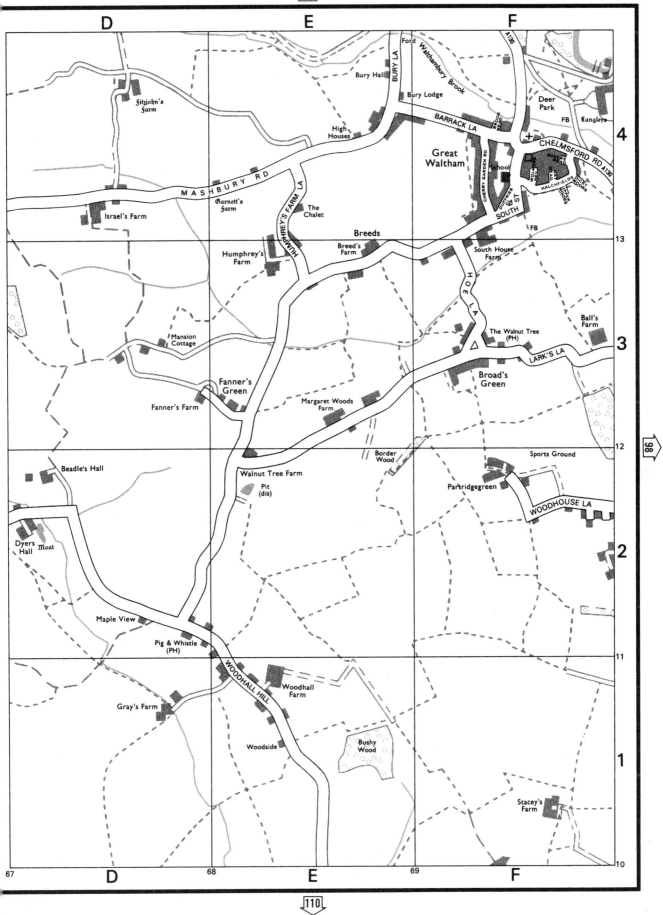

D   E   F

Fitzjohn's Farm

Bury Hall

Ford

Walthambury Brook

Bury Lodge

Deer Park

FB

Langleys

BURY LA

High Houses

BARRACK LA

Great Waltham

School

CHELMSFORD RD A130

4

MASHBURY RD

Garnett's Farm

The Chalet

Breeds

SOUTH ST

FB

13

Israel's Farm

HUMPHREY'S FARM LA

Humphrey's Farm

Breed's Farm

South House Farm

HOE LA

Ball's Farm

Mansion Cottage

The Walnut Tree (PH)

LARK'S LA

3

Fanner's Green

Margaret Woods Farm

Broad's Green

Fanner's Farm

Border Wood

Sports Ground

98

12

Beadle's Hall

Walnut Tree Farm

Pit (dis)

Partridgegreen

WOODHOUSE LA

Dyers Hall

Moat

2

Maple View

Pig & Whistle (PH)

11

WOODHALL HILL

Woodhall Farm

Gray's Farm

Woodside

Bushy Wood

1

Stacey's Farm

10

67   D   68   E   69   F

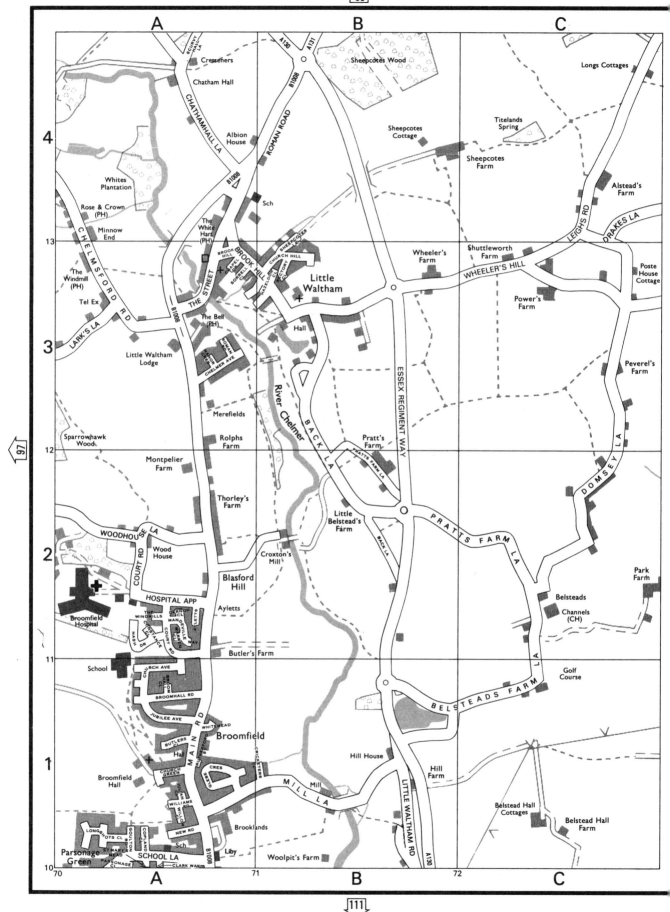

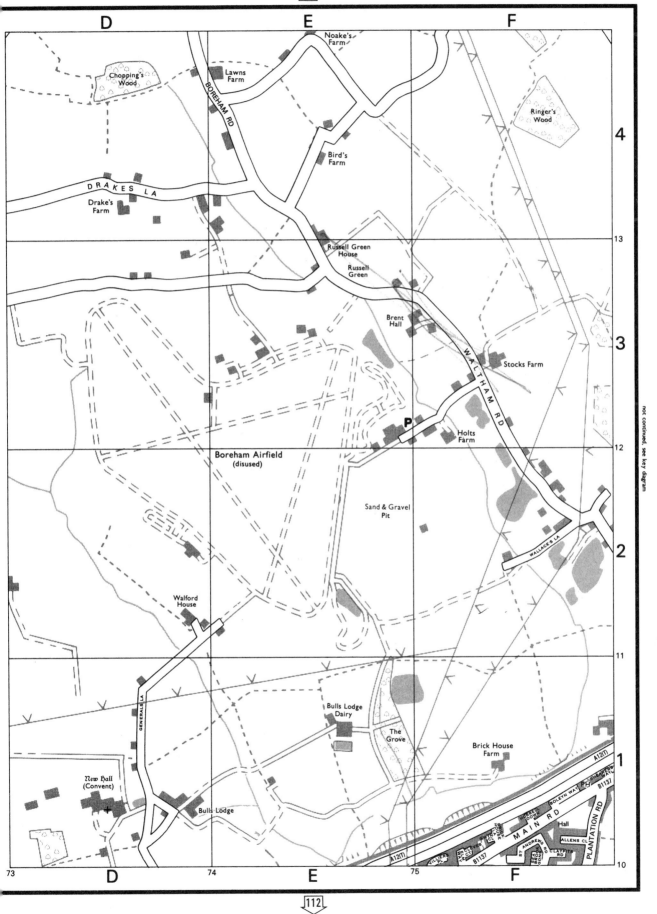

D   E   F

Noake's Farm

Chopping's Wood

Lawns Farm

BOREHAM RD

Ringer's Wood

4

Bird's Farm

DRAKES LA

Drake's Farm

13

Russell Green House

Russell Green

Brent Hall

3

WALTHAM RD

Stocks Farm

P

Holts Farm

12

Boreham Airfield (disused)

Sand & Gravel Pit

WALLACE'S LA

2

Walford House

11

GENERALS LA

Bulls Lodge Dairy

The Grove

Brick House Farm

1

New Hall (Convent)

Bulls Lodge

A12(T)

MAIN RD

PLANTATION RD

BOLEYN WAY

B1137

Hall

ALLENS CL

CLAYPITS RD

ST ANDREWS RD

B1137

A12(T)

10

73   D   74   E   75   F

not continued, see key diagram

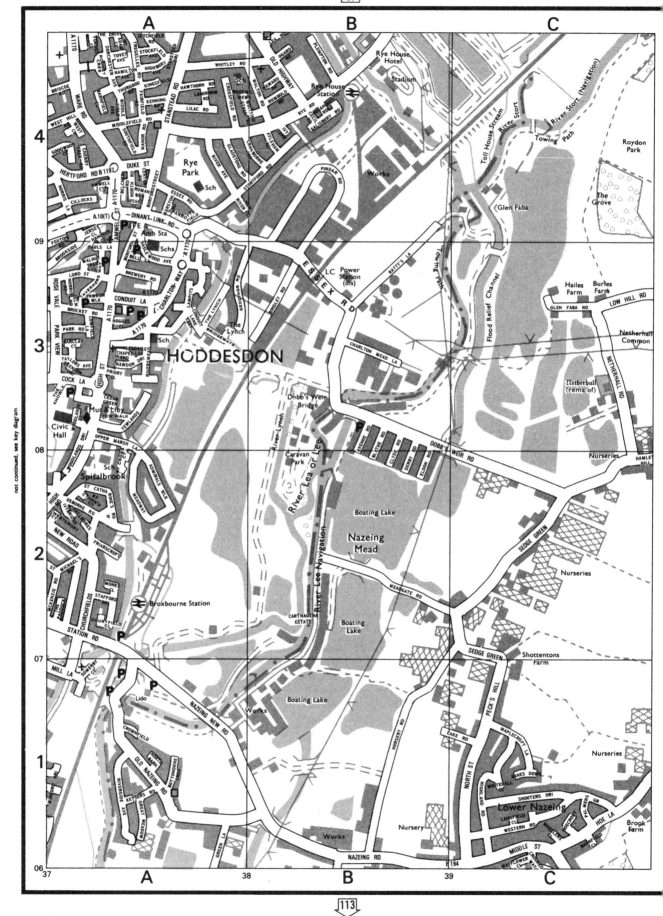

A   B   C

THE DRIVE
TREGELLES
DITCHFIELD RD
TOVET AVE
STOCKFIELD AVE
STANSFIELD RD
A 1170
DORCHESTER AVE
HAMILTON CRES
HIGHBURY
WHITLEY RD
WARE RD
BRISCOE RD
THURGOOD AVE
KENNING
HAWTHORN RD
LABURNUM RD
CROSSFIELD RD
OGARD RD
Rye House
Hotel

Old Highway
PLUMPTON RD

Stadium

Rye House
Station

WEST RD
WEST CL
CHERRY RD
MIDDLEFIELD
SOUTHFIELD
LILAC RD
RUMBOLD RD
WALTON RD
WOODHAM
HENTERTON
ATLMAR

Toll House Stream
River Stort (Navigation)
River Stort

GOODWOOD RD
HERTFORD RD B 1197
DUKE ST
NORRIS LA
Rye
Park
Sch
RIVER AVE
GLADSTONE RD
STORTFORD RD
GRAYBORNE RD
RIVER CL
SALISBURY RD
CHANDLERS
ESSEX
Works

Towing Path
Roydon
Park

ANWELL CT
CILLOCKS
A 1170
DINANT LINK RD
AMWELL ST
A 10(T)
FIRE &
Amb Sta
NORTH RD
BELCROM
PRESTON
ANNOFIELD
ESSEX
PINDAR
RD

Glen Faba
The
Grove

FOXTON
BROOKSIDE
JERSEY
PAULS LA
WALNUT TREE
WOOD AVE
Schs
A 1170
LC Power
Station
(dis)
BATTY'S LA
Town Path

Hailes
Farm
Burtes
Farm

ROSE VALE
NORRIS
LORD ST
TAWKIN WLK
CONDUIT LA
BREWERY RD
BROCKET
A 1170
HOGGES CL
CHARLTON WAY
LAMPITS
THE LYNCH
GEORGES RD
BINGLEY RD
Flood Relief Channel

GLEN FABA RD
LOW HILL RD
Netherhall
Common
NETHERHALL RD

PARK VIEW
PARK CT
BARCLAY CT
TAYLORS AVE
PRIORY CL
CHAPEL LA
RAWDON DRI
LOWFIELD
POWNALL
COCK LA
Sch
BRIDGEWAYS
The
Lynch
CHARLTON MEAD LA

Netherhall
(rems of)

HODDESDON

THE KNOLLE
CEDAR GREEN
NEW WALK
VIEW WALK
Mus & Lby
NEWLANDS
Civic
Hall
Dobb's Weir
Bridge

River Lynch
Dobb's Weir Rd

Nurseries

UPPER MARSH LA
WOODLANDS DRI
ADMIRALS WLK
Caravan
Park

AVENUE RD
HILTONE RD
CLYDE RD
DERBY RD
ELDON RD

HAMLET

Sch
Spitalbrook

River Lea or Lee

HIGH RD
ST CATHA
TIME'S CL
OSBORNE RD
DELAMORES
ST CATHER'S RD
MEADWAY
Boating
Lake

SEDGE GREEN

NEW ROAD
HYBRIDGE
WESTCROFT
FRIARSCROFT
Nazeing
Mead
Nurseries

ST MICHAEL'S RD
MCKENZIE RD
THE PADDOCK
MONKS CL
STAFFORD
COUNTFIELD
Broxbourne Station

River Lee Navigation

SEDGE GREEN

CHURCHFIELDS
STATION RD
CARTHAGENA
ESTATE
MEADGATE RD
Boating
Lake
Shottentons
Farm

MILL LA
SOMERBY CL
Lido
NAZEING NEW RD
Works
Boating Lake

SEDGE GREEN
PECK'S HILL
LAKE RD
MAPLECROFT LA
Nurseries

CROWNFIELD
NURSERY RD

NORTH ST
NORTH MAR
OLD NAZEING RD
BUTTONDENE
RIVERSIDE
KETSERS
GREAT MEADOW
GREEN LA
Nursery
HIGHLAND RD
NORTH ST
WHITEHALL GT
BANES DOWN
LANGFIELD CL
SHOOTERS DRI
PALMERS GR
HOE LA
Lower Nazeing
Brook
Farm

Works
NAZEING RD
B 194
MIDDLE ST
MAYFLOWER WAY

not continued, see key diagram

06
07
08
09
1
2
3
4

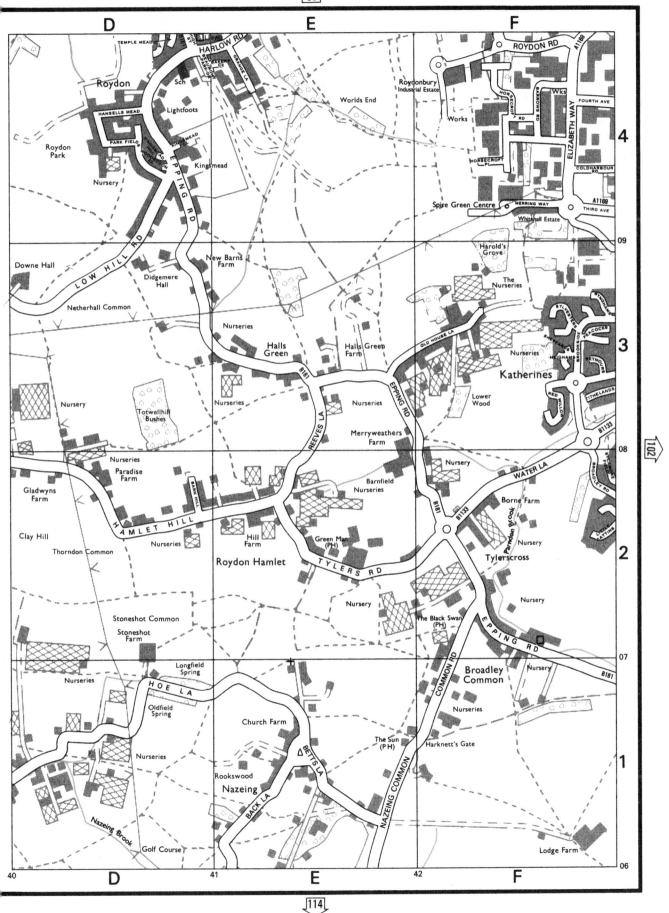

D   E   F

TEMPLE MEAD

HARLOW RD

Roydon

Sch

Lightfoots

HANSELLS MEAD

PARK FIELD

Roydon Park

Nursery

Kingsmead

GRANGE LA

EPPING RD

LOW HILL RD

Downe Hall

Netherhall Common

Didgemere Hall

New Barns Farm

Worlds End

ROYDON RD

A1169

Roydonbury
Industrial Estate

Works

Wks

FOURTH AVE

ELIZABETH WAY

COLDHARBOUR RD

HORSECROFT RD

BARROWS RD

HORSECROFT PL

Spire Green Centre

MERRING WAY

THIRD AVE

A1169

Whitehall Estate

Harold's Grove

The Nurseries

SYNGHAMS

SYLVESTERS

SHEPPARDS

HEIGHAMS

BROOKSIDE

PEACOCKS

SEYMOURS

RED WILLOW

TITHELANDS

Katherines

09

Nurseries

Halls Green

Halls Green Farm

Nursery

Totwellhill Bushes

Nurseries

REEVES LA

B181

Nurseries

EPPING RD

Old House La

Lower Wood

Nurseries

B1133

08

Nurseries

Paradise Farm

Gladwyns Farm

Clay Hill

Thorndon Common

HAMLET HILL

BARN HILL

Nurseries

Nurseries

Hill Farm

Roydon Hamlet

Merryweathers Farm

Barnfield Nurseries

Green Man (PH)

TYLERS RD

Nursery

Nursery

B181

B1133

Paradon Brook

Borne Farm

Nursery

Tylerscross

WATER LA

STONARD RD

BROADLEY RD

LONG CATLINS

3

2

Stoneshot Common

Stoneshot Farm

Nurseries

Longfield Spring

HOE LA

Oldfield Spring

Nurseries

Church Farm

Rookswood

Nazeing

BACK LA

BETTS LA

Nazeing Brook

Golf Course

The Sun (PH)

NAZEING COMMON

COMMON RD

The Black Swan (PH)

EPPING RD

Broadley Common

Nursery

Nurseries

Harknett's Gate

Lodge Farm

B181

07

1

06

40   D   41   E   42   F

89

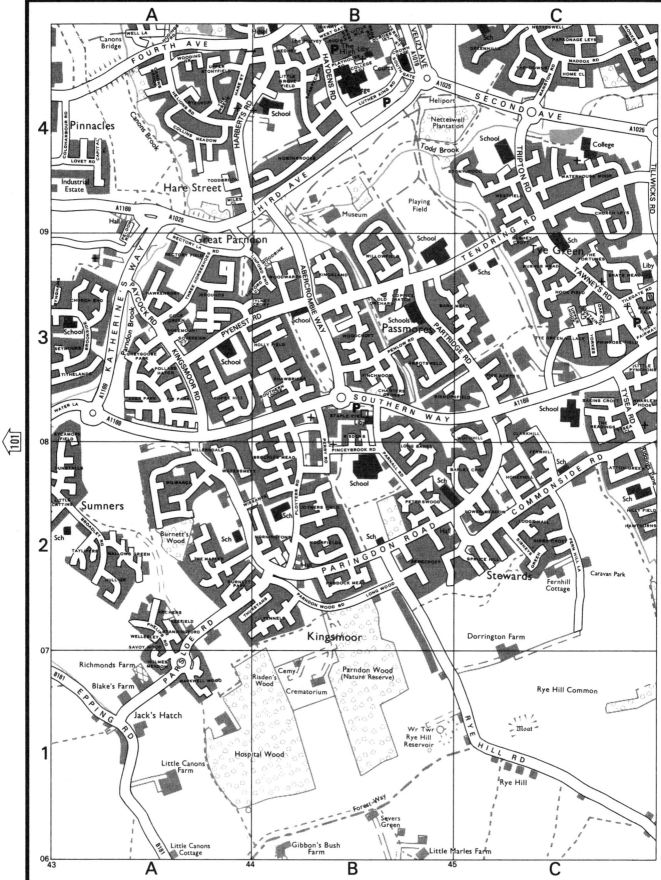

101

115

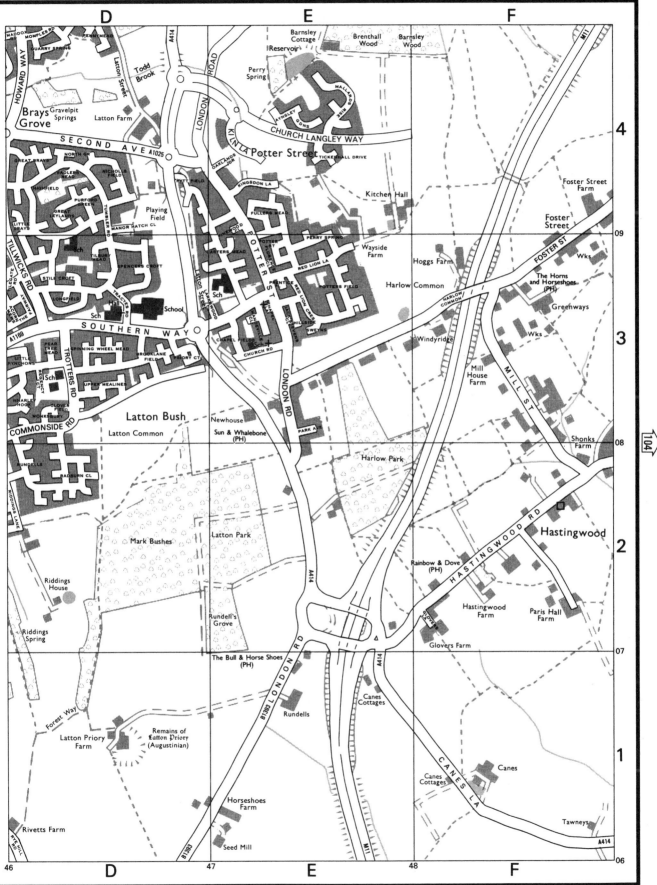

D E F

4

09

3

104

08

Hastingwood

2

07

1

46 47 E 48 F 06

D

Brays Grove
HOWARD WAY
MADDOX RD
MOMPLES RD
QUARRY SPRING
PENNYMEAD
Latton Street
Todd Brook
Gravelpit Springs
Latton Farm
SECOND AVE A1025
A414
LONDON ROAD
Reservoir
Barnsley Cottage
Perry Spring
Brenthall Wood
Barnsley Wood
CHURCH LANGLEY WAY
MALLARDS
AYNSLEY GDNS
SISKIN
KILN LA
Potter Street
OAKLANDS JNR
Tickenhall Drive
Kitchen Hall
Foster Street Farm
Foster Street
FOSTER ST
Wks
The Horns and Horseshoes (PH)
Greenways
Wks
NORTH GR
GREAT BRAYS RD
SADLERS MEAD
NICHOLLS FIELD
HIGHFIELD
PURFORD GREEN
GREAT LEYLANDS
LITTLE BRAYS
TUMBLERS RD
PYTT FIELD
KINGSDON LA
FULLERS MEAD
Playing Field
MANOR HATCH CL
CARTERS MEAD
Perry Spring
Wayside Farm
Hoggs Farm
Harlow Common
TILLWICKS RD
RYE CROFT
Sch
TILBURY MEAD
STILE CROFT
SPENCERS CROFT
LONGFIELD
TRACIES RD
Hall
Sch
School
POTTER STREET
RED LION LA
PRENTICE
RED LION CRES
POTTERS FIELD
HILLSIDE
SWEYNS
Harlow Common
Windyridge
HARLOW COMMON
MILL ST
Mill House Farm
A1169
SOUTHERN WAY
PEAR TREE MEAD
SPINNING WHEEL MEAD
BROOKLANE FIELD
PRIORY CT
CHAPEL FIELD
Sch
CHURCH RD
LONDON RD
SHARPECROFT
HOOKFIELD
LITTLE RYNCHONS
Sch
REGENCY
WHARLEY HOOK
CLOVER FIELD
MONKBURY
UPPER MEALINES
Latton Bush
Latton Common
Newhouse
Sun & Whalebone (PH)
PARK AVE
Harlow Park
Shonks Farm
COMMONSIDE RD
RUNDELLS
RADBURN CL
Mark Bushes
Latton Park
Riddings House
Riddings Spring
Rundell's Grove
A414
Rainbow & Dove (PH)
HASTINGWOOD RD
Hastingwood Farm
Paris Hall Farm
GLOVERS
Glovers Farm
RIDDINGS LANE
The Bull & Horse Shoes (PH)
Forest Way
Latton Priory Farm
Remains of Latton Priory (Augustinian)
B1393 LONDON RD
Rundells
Canes Cottages
A414 M11
Canes Cottages
Canes
CANES LA
Horseshoes Farm
Rivetts Farm
RYE HILL RD
Seed Mill
B1393
M11
A414
Tawneys

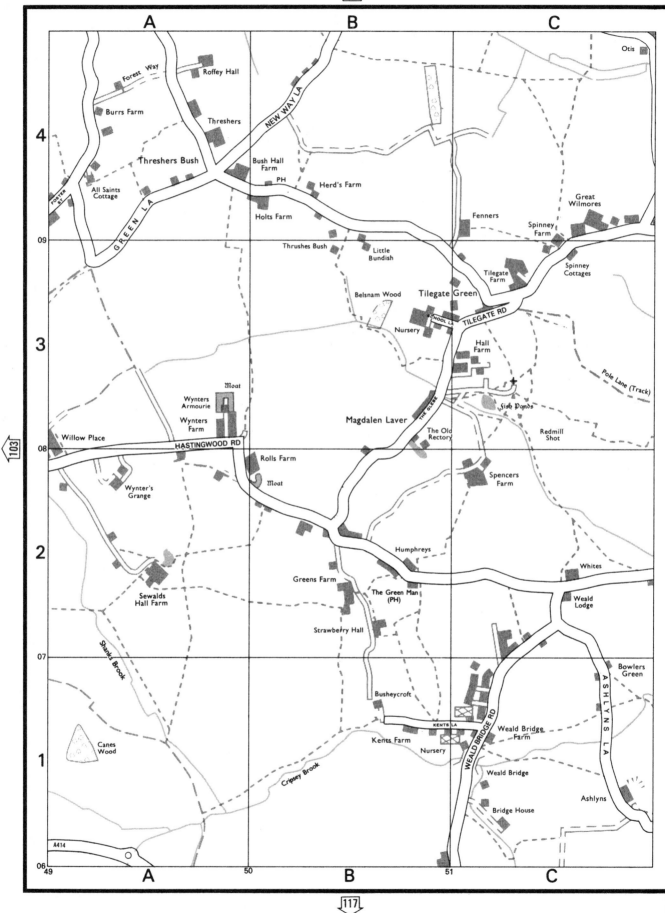

A　　　　B　　　　C

Forest Way
Roffey Hall
Burrs Farm
Threshers
Threshers Bush
All Saints Cottage
FOSTER ST
GREEN LA
NEW WAY LA
Bush Hall Farm
PH
Herd's Farm
Holts Farm
Thrushes Bush
Little Bundish
Belsnam Wood
Tilegate Green
SCHOOL LA
Nursery
TILEGATE RD
Fenners
Great Wilmores
Spinney Farm
Tilegate Farm
Spinney Cottages
Otis

4

09

3

Moat
Wynters Armourie
Wynters Farm
Willow Place
Magdalen Laver
THE GLEBE
Hall Farm
Pole Lane (Track)
Fish Ponds
The Old Rectory
Redmill Shot

HASTINGWOOD RD
08
Rolls Farm
Moat
Wynter's Grange
Spencers Farm

2

Sewalds Hall Farm
Greens Farm
Strawberry Hall
Humphreys
The Green Man (PH)
Whites
Weald Lodge

Shanks Brook
07

Busheycroft
Bowlers Green
ASHLYNS LA
WEALD BRIDGE RD
KENTS LA
Kents Farm
Nursery
Weald Bridge Farm

1

Canes Wood
Cripsey Brook
Weald Bridge
Ashlyns
Bridge House

A414
06
49　　　A　　　50　　　B　　　51　　　C

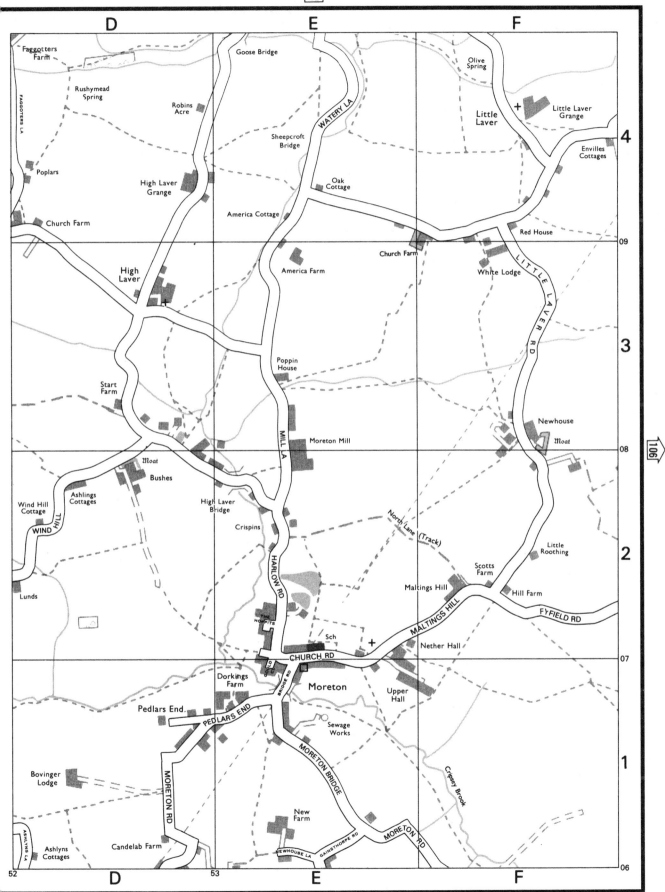

92

D   E   F

Faggotters Farm

Goose Bridge

Olive Spring

Rushymead Spring

FAGGOTERS LA

Robins Acre

WATERY LA

Little Laver

Little Laver Grange

4

Sheepcroft Bridge

Poplars

Oak Cottage

Envilles Cottages

High Laver Grange

America Cottage

Red House

Church Farm

Church Farm

LITTLE LAVER RD

09

High Laver

America Farm

White Lodge

3

Poppin House

Start Farm

Newhouse

Moat

08

Moat

MILL LA

Moreton Mill

Bushes

Wind Hill Cottage

Ashlings Cottages

High Laver Bridge

North Lane (Track)

Little Roothing

WIND HILL

Crispins

Scotts Farm

2

Lunds

HARLOW RD

Maltings Hill

Hill Farm

FYFIELD RD

THE HOWPITS

MALTINGS HILL

Sch

Nether Hall

07

CHURCH RD

BRIDGE RD

GDG. CL.

Dorkings Farm

Moreton

Upper Hall

Pedlars End.

PEDLARS END

Sewage Works

MORETON RD

MORETON BRIDGE

1

Bovinger Lodge

Cripsey Brook

New Farm

Candelab Farm

NEWHOUSE LA

GAINSTHORPE RD

MORETON RD

ASHLYNS LA

Ashlyns Cottages

52   D   53   E   F   06

106

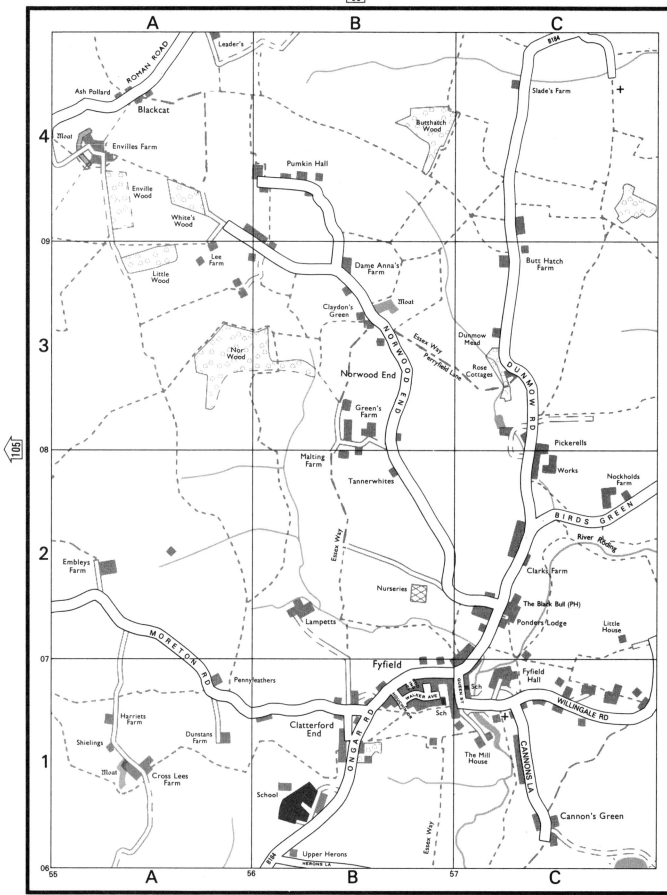

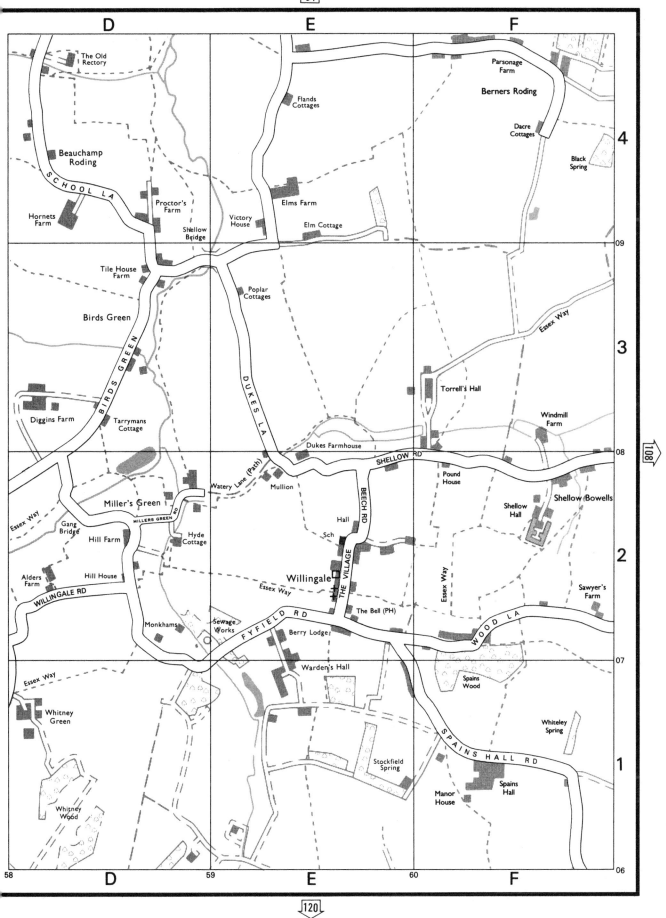

D
E
F

The Old
Rectory

Parsonage
Farm

Berners Roding

Flands
Cottages

Dacre
Cottages

Beauchamp
Roding

Black
Spring

4

SCHOOL LA

Proctor's
Farm

Elms Farm

Hornets
Farm

Shellow
Bridge

Victory
House

Elm Cottage

09

Tile House
Farm

Poplar
Cottages

Essex Way

Birds Green

BIRDS GREEN

DUKES LA

Torrell's Hall

3

Windmill
Farm

Diggins Farm

Tarrymans
Cottage

Dukes Farmhouse

SHELLOW RD

08

108

Essex Way

Watery Lane (Path)

Mullion

Pound
House

Shellow Bowells

Miller's Green

MILLERS GREEN RD

Hyde
Cottage

Hall

BEECH RD

Shellow
Hall

Gang
Bridge

Hill Farm

Sch

THE VILLAGE

2

Alders
Farm

Hill House

Willingale

Essex Way

Essex Way

Sawyer's
Farm

WILLINGALE RD

Monkhams

Sewage
Works

FYFIELD RD

The Bell (PH)

WOOD LA

Berry Lodge

07

Essex Way

Warden's Hall

Spains
Wood

Whitney
Green

Whiteley
Spring

SPAINS HALL RD

Stockfield
Spring

1

Whitney
Wood

Manor
House

Spains
Hall

06

58
D
59
E
60
F

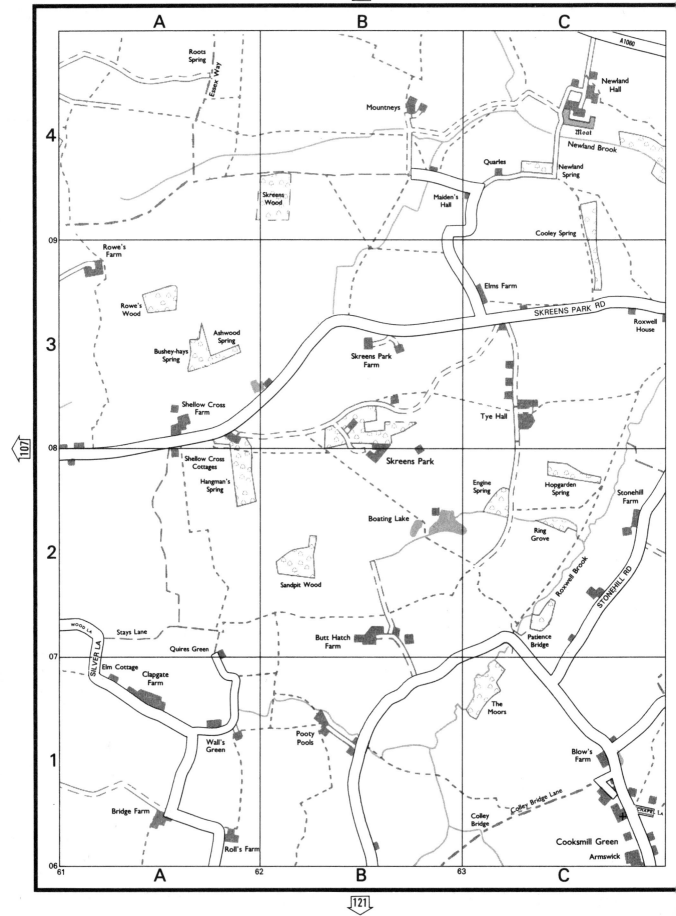

A
B
C

Roots Spring
Essex Way

Mountneys

Newland Hall

Moat
Newland Brook

Skreens Wood

Quarles
Newland Spring

Maiden's Hall

Cooley Spring

4

09

Rowe's Farm

Elms Farm

SKREENS PARK RD

Roxwell House

Rowe's Wood

Ashwood Spring

Skreens Park Farm

Bushey-hays Spring

3

Shellow Cross Farm

Tye Hall

08

Shellow Cross Cottages

Skreens Park

Hangman's Spring

Engine Spring

Hopgarden Spring

Stonehill Farm

Boating Lake

Ring Grove

Sandpit Wood

Roxwell Brook

STONEHILL RD

2

WOOD LA

Stays Lane

Patience Bridge

SILVER LA

Quires Green

07

Elm Cottage

Clapgate Farm

Butt Hatch Farm

The Moors

Wall's Green

Pooty Pools

Blow's Farm

1

Colley Bridge Lane

CHAPEL LA

Bridge Farm

Colley Bridge

Cooksmill Green

Roll's Farm

Armswick

06

61
62
63

A
B
C

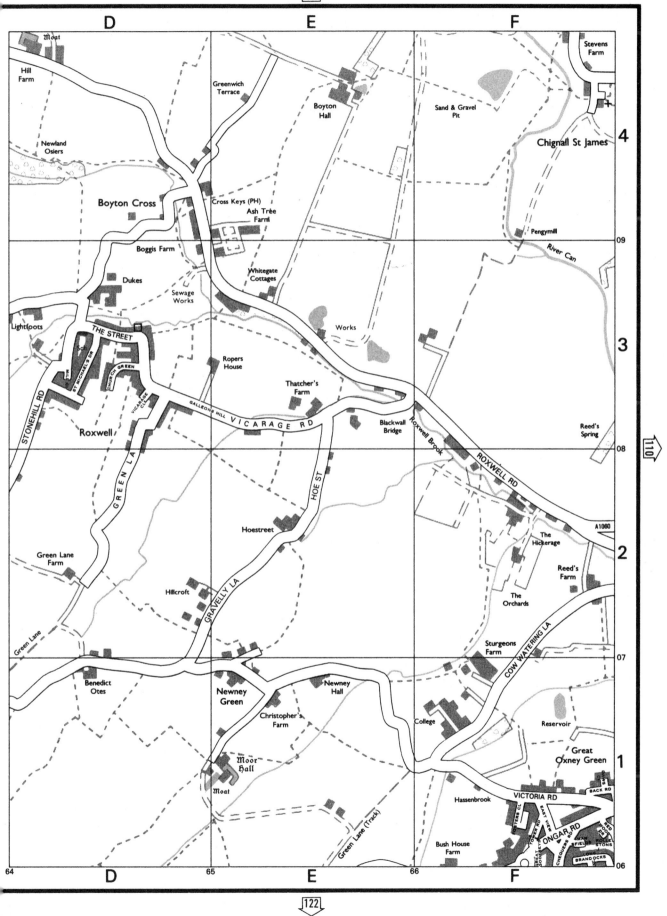

D

E

F

Moat

Hill Farm

Greenwich Terrace

Stevens Farm

Boyton Hall

Sand & Gravel Pit

Chignall St James

4

Newland Osiers

Boyton Cross

Cross Keys (PH)

Ash Tree Farm

Pengymill

09

River Can

Boggis Farm

Whitegate Cottages

Dukes

Sewage Works

Works

110

Lightfoots

THE STREET

Sch

MILL

ST MICHAEL'S DR

CHURCH GREEN

Ropers House

Thatcher's Farm

Reed's Spring

3

VICARAGE CL

GALLEONS HILL

VICARAGE RD

Blackwall Bridge

Roxwell Brook

ROXWELL RD

Roxwell

GREEN LA

HOE ST

08

STONEHILL RD

A1060

Green Lane Farm

The Hickerage

2

Hoestreet

Reed's Farm

Hillcroft

GRAVELLY LA

The Orchards

Green Lane

Sturgeons Farm

COW WATERING LA

07

Benedict Otes

Newney Green

Newney Hall

College

Reservoir

Christopher's Farm

Great Oxney Green

1

Moor Hall

Moat

Green Lane (Track)

VICTORIA RD

BACK RD

Hassenbrook

ONGAR RD

Bush House Farm

BRANDOCKS

64

D

65

E

66

F

06

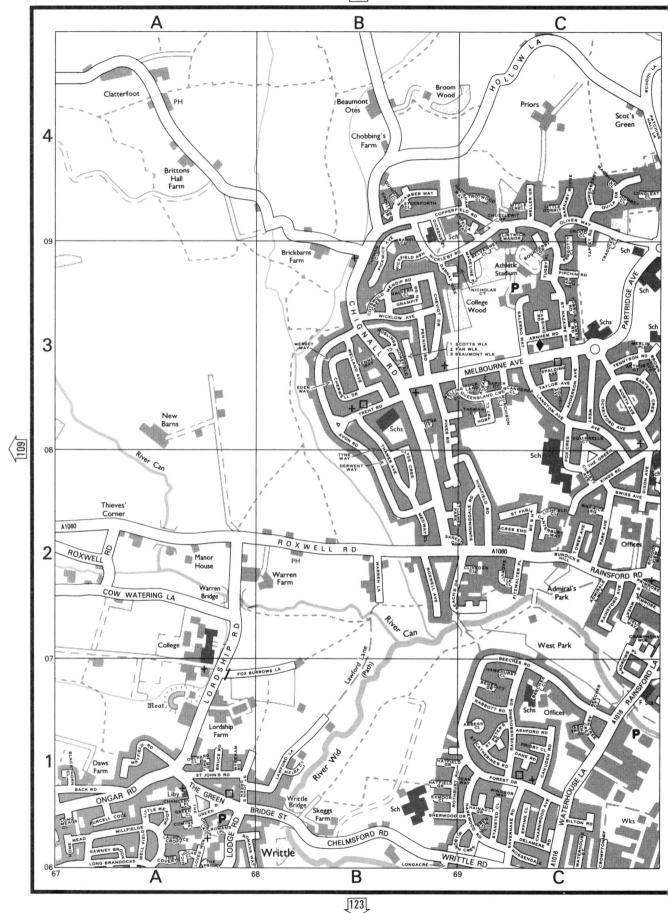

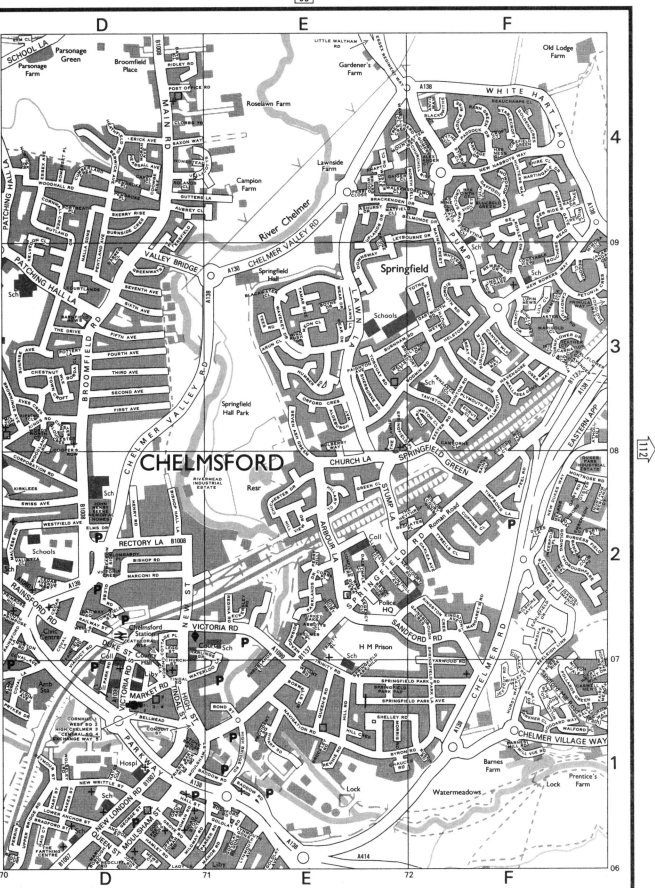

112

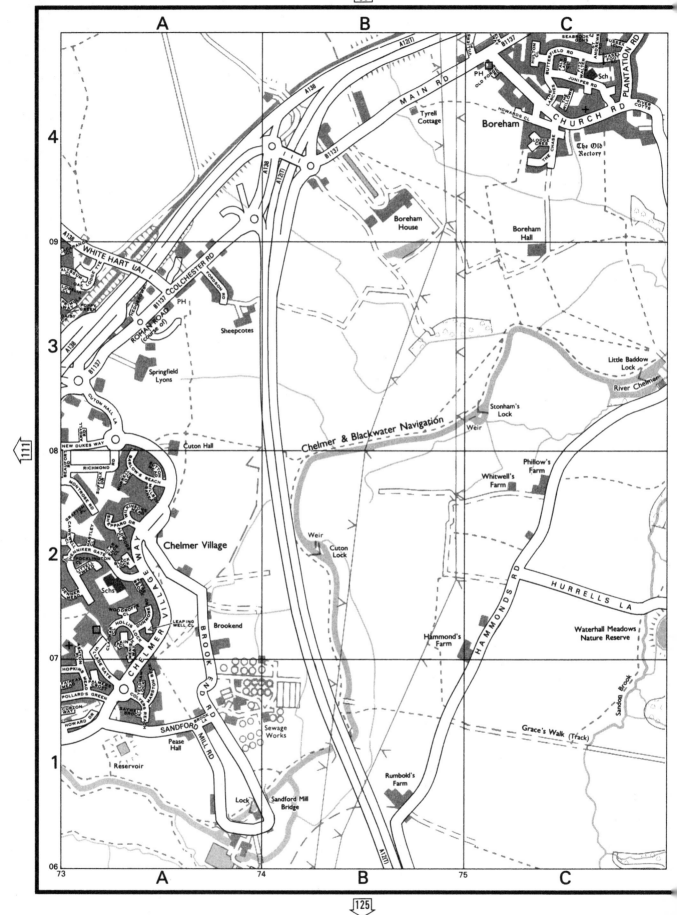

111

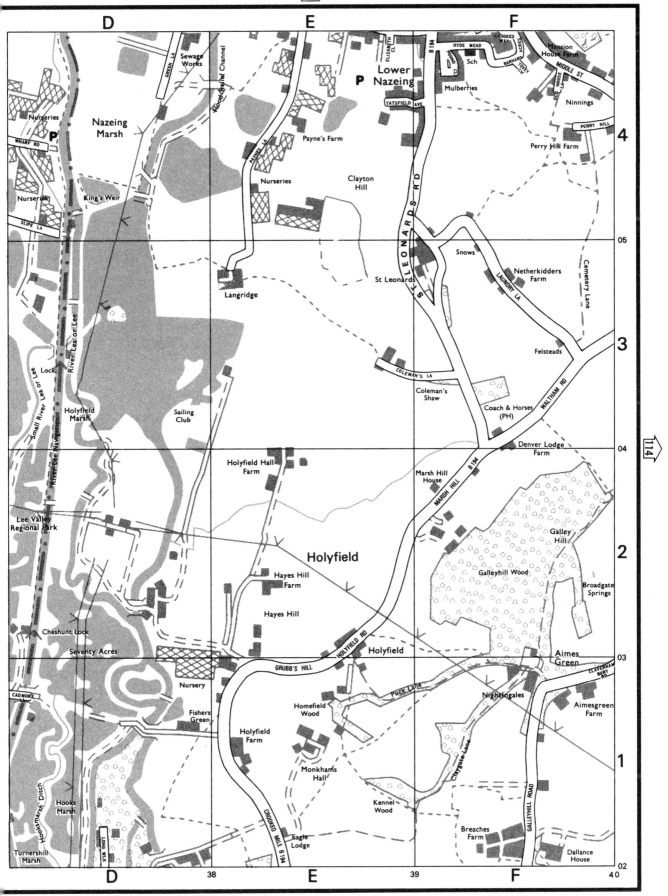

D E F

Sewage Works

GREEN LA

Nazeing Marsh

Nurseries

WHARF RD

P

Nurseries

SLIPE LA

King's Weir

Flood Relief Channel

PAYNE'S LA

Nurseries

Payne's Farm

Clayton Hill

Lower Nazeing

P

TATSFIELD AVE

ELIZABETH CL

B 194

HYDE MEAD

POUND CL

Sch

BARNARD ACRES

TOVEY CL

CROOKED WAY

OLD HOUSE LA

MIDDLE ST

Mansion House Farm

Ninnings

PERRY HILL

Perry Hill Farm

4

ST LEONARDS RD

05

Langridge

River Lea or Lee

St Leonards

COLEMAN'S LA

Coleman's Shaw

Snows

LAUNDRY LA

Netherkidders Farm

Cemetery Lane

Felsteads

WALTHAM RD

Coach & Horses (PH)

3

Lock

Small River Lea or Lee

River Lee Navigation

Holyfield Marsh

Sailing Club

Holyfield Hall Farm

Marsh Hill House

MARSH HILL B 194

Denver Lodge Farm

04

Lee Valley Regional Park

Holyfield

Hayes Hill Farm

Hayes Hill

Galleyhill Wood

Galley Hill

Broadgate Springs

2

Cheshunt Lock

Seventy Acres

Nursery

GRUBB'S HILL

HOLYFIELD RD

Holyfield

Puck Lane

Aimes Green

CLAVERHAMBURY RD

Nightingales

CADMORE

Fishers Green

Homefield Wood

Holyfield Farm

Monkhams Hall

Chrysler Lane

Kennel Wood

Aimesgreen Farm

1

Hooksmarsh Ditch

LONG WLK

Hooks Marsh

CROOKED MILE B 194

Eagle Lodge

Breaches Farm

GALLEYHILL ROAD

Dallance House

Turnershill Marsh

D 38 E 39 F 40

02

114

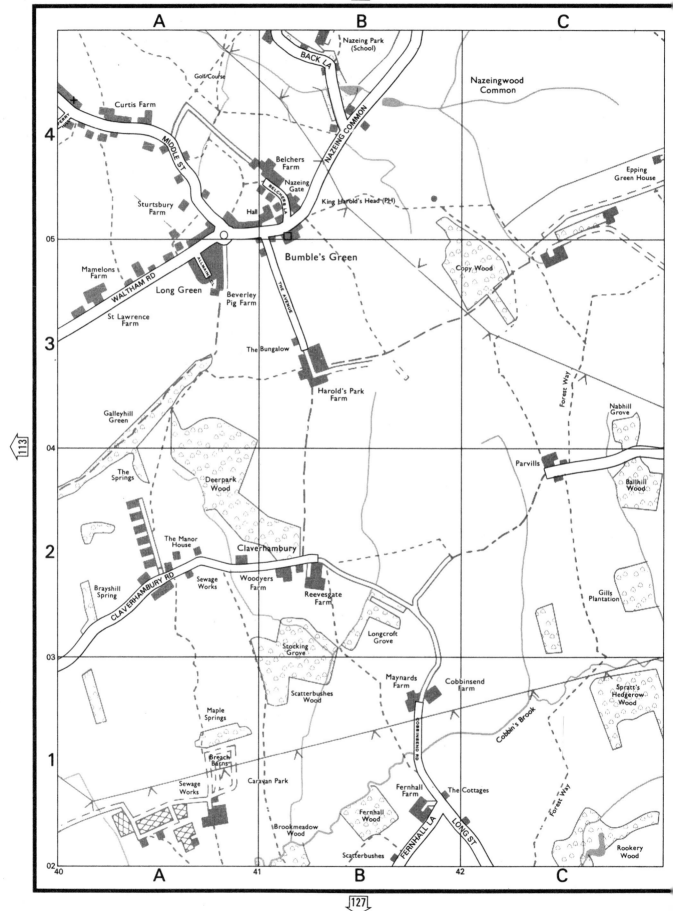

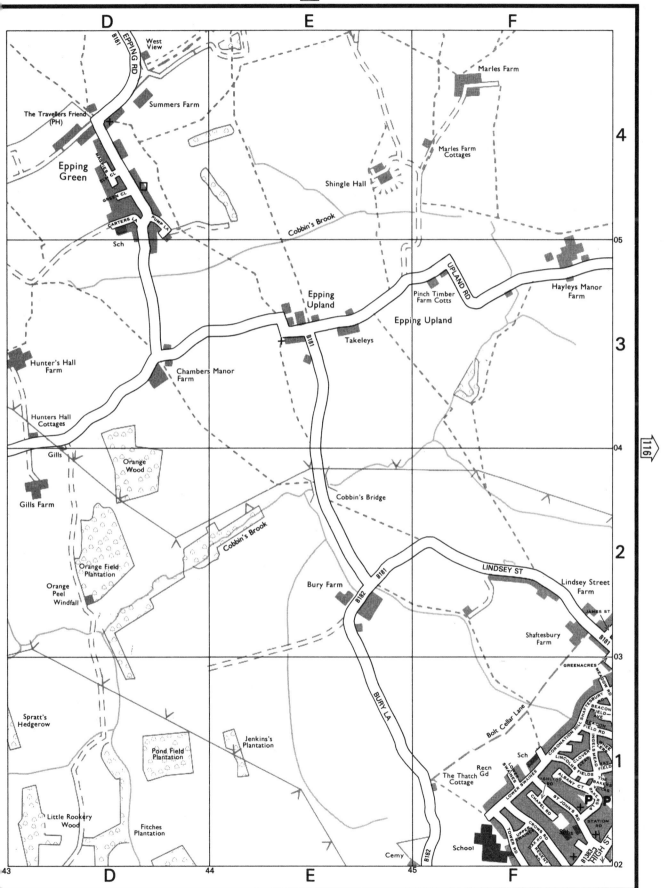

D   E   F

West View

The Travellers Friend (PH)

Summers Farm

Marles Farm

4

Epping Green

Marles Farm Cottages

Shingle Hall

Sch

Cobbin's Brook

05

UPLAND RD

Epping Upland

Pinch Timber Farm Cotts

Hayleys Manor Farm

Epping Upland

Hunter's Hall Farm

Chambers Manor Farm

B181

Takeleys

3

Hunters Hall Cottages

Gills

04

116

Orange Wood

Gills Farm

Cobbin's Bridge

Cobbin's Brook

2

LINDSEY ST

Lindsey Street Farm

Orange Field Plantation

Bury Farm

B181

James St

B181

Orange Peel Windfall

B182

Shaftesbury Farm

03

GREENACRES

MEADOW RD

Spratt's Hedgerow

BURY LA

Bolt Cellar Lane

BEACON FIELD AVE

BEACON FIELD RD

CORONATION HILL

SHAFTESBURY

LINCOLN FIELDS

Jenkins's Plantation

Pond Field Plantation

Sch

Recn Gd

The Thatch Cottage

ALBANY CT

LOWER SWAINES

ASHLYNE RD

P P

1

Little Rookery Wood

Fitches Plantation

CHAPEL RD

ST JOHN'S RD

UPPER SWAINES

STATION RD

Cemy

B182

School

HIGH ST

B1393

02

43   D   44   E   45   F

103
115
129

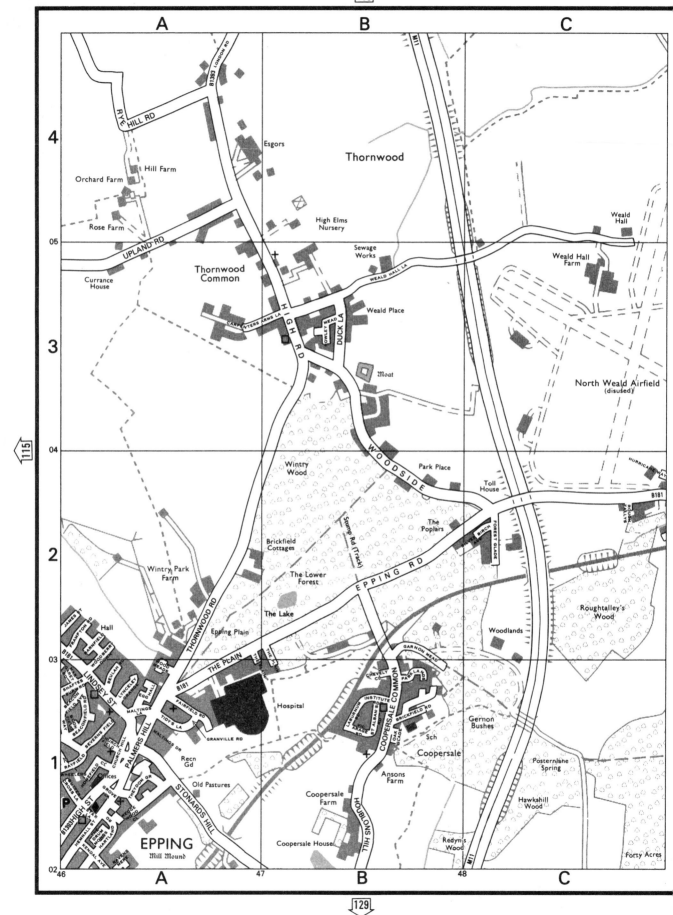

A B C

4
Thornwood

Esgors

Hill Farm

Orchard Farm

High Elms
Nursery

Rose Farm

Weald
Hall

05
UPLAND RD

Currance
House

Thornwood
Common

Sewage
Works

Weald Hall
Farm

CARPENTERS ARMS LA

Weald Place

OWLEY MEAD

DUCK LA

WEALD HALL LA

HIGH RD

3
Moat

North Weald Airfield
(disused)

RYE HILL RD

LONDON RD

B1393

M11

04
Wintry
Wood

WOODSIDE

Park Place

Toll
House

HURRICANE WAY

Stump Rd (Track)

The
Poplars

BIRCH

FOREST GLADE

B181

ROUGH
TALLYS

2
Wintry Park
Farm

Brickfield
Cottages

The Lower
Forest

EPPING RD

Woodlands

Roughtalley's
Wood

The Lake

THORNWOOD RD

Epping Plain

Hall

James St

Fairstead Rd

Garnfield

Woodberry

B181

Shaftes

Lindsey St

Lynceley

Egg Hall

Maltinges

Hood
Reads

Beulah

Granby

GARNON MEAD

The Plain

THE PLAIN

03
Chevely
Cl

Coopersale Common

Park La

02 46

Hospital

Fairfield Rd

Tidy's La

Granville Rd

Maltings Dr

Institute

Labtration

St Alban
Rd

Oak
Glade

Brickfield Rd

Gernon
Bushes

Sch

Postern lane
Spring

1
Rayfield

Sevena Field

Beaconfield Way

Palmers Hill

Church Hill

Theydon Gr

Recn
Gd

Old Pastures

Coopersale

Hawkshill
Wood

Offices

P

B1393 HIGH ST

Hernall St

Grove

Stonards Hill

Ansons
Farm

Houblons Hill

Coopersale
Farm

Coopersale House

Redyn's
Wood

Forty Acres

EPPING
Mill Mound

M11

A 47 B 48 C

104

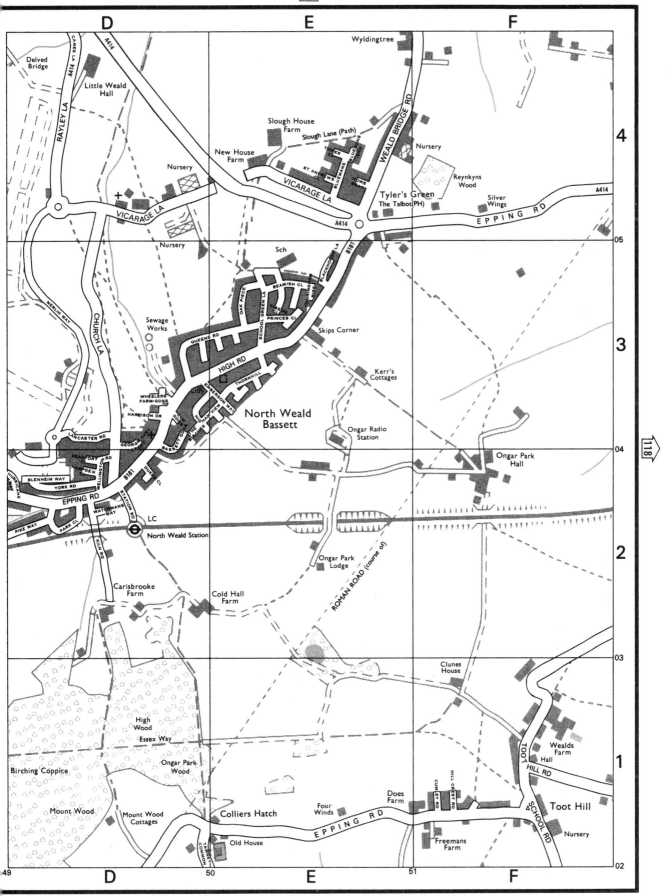

105

117

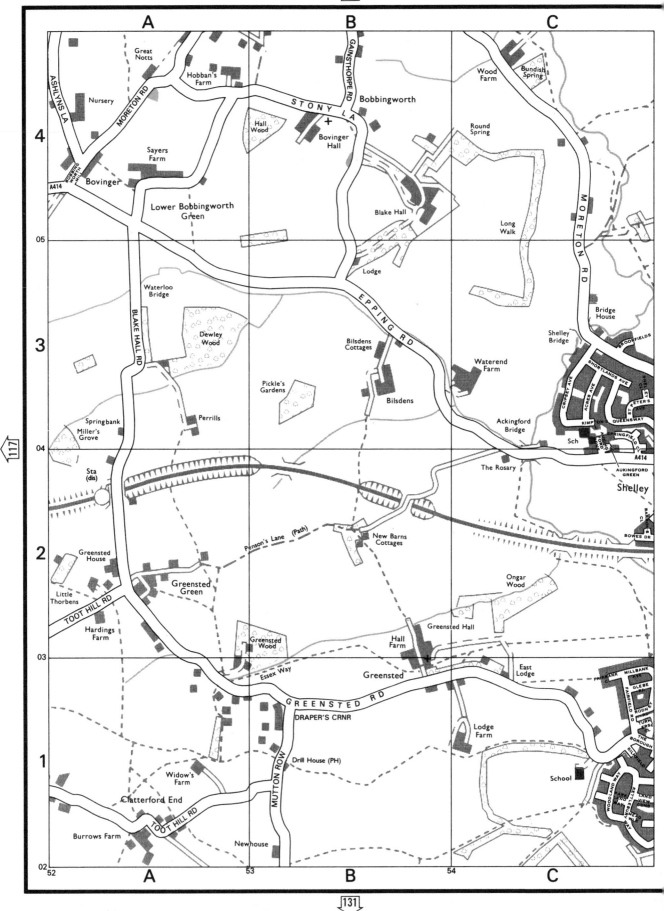

131

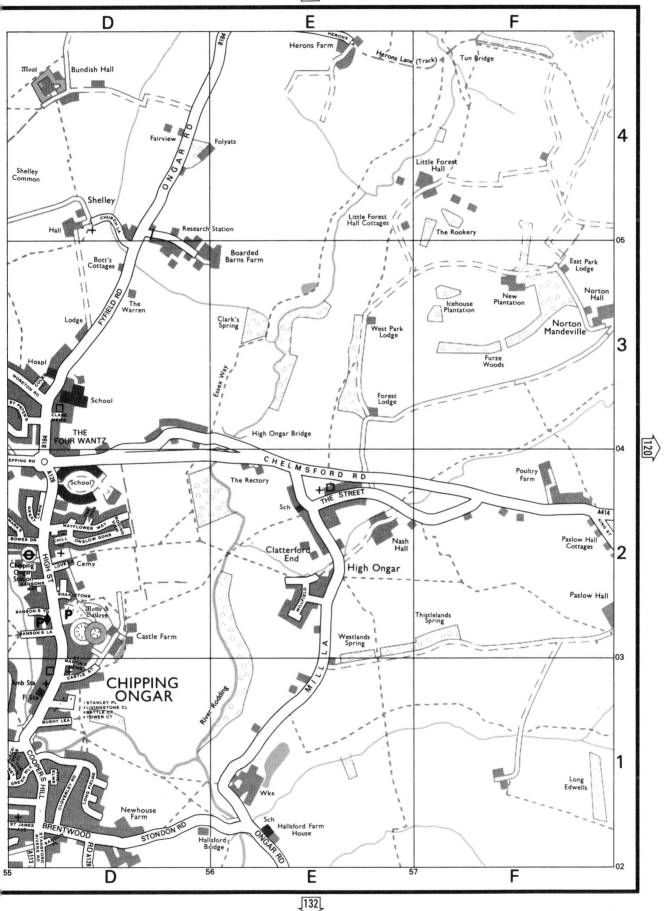

106

D   **E**   **F**

Moat

Bundish Hall

Herons Farm

Herons Lane (Track)

Tun Bridge

Fairview

Folyats

4

Little Forest Hall

Shelley Common

Shelley

Hall

CHURCH LA

Research Station

Little Forest Hall Cottages

The Rookery

ONGAR RD

B184

05

Bott's Cottages

Boarded Barns Farm

East Park Lodge

Norton Hall

FYFIELD RD

The Warren

Clark's Spring

Icehouse Plantation

New Plantation

Lodge

West Park Lodge

Norton Mandeville

Hospl

Essex Way

Furze Woods

3

MORETON RD

COLE

School

Forest Lodge

ST PETER'S

CLARE MEWS

THE FOUR WANTZ

High Ongar Bridge

04

B184

EPPING RD

CHELMSFORD RD

120

A128

School

The Rectory

Poultry Farm

MAY 1

GREAT

MAYFLOWER WAY

The Street

Sch

A414

KING ST

BOWES DR

CHILL

ONSLOW GDNS

Clatterford End

Nash Hall

Paslow Hall Cottages

Chipping Ongar Station

LOVE

Cemy

High Ongar

2

SANSONS WAY

SHAKLETONS

MILLFIELD

Thistlelands Spring

Paslow Hall

BANSON'S YD

P

Motte & Baileys

MILL LA

BANSON'S LA

Castle Farm

Westlands Spring

03

ST MARTIN'S MEWS

CASTLE ST

Amb Sta

F Sta

CHIPPING ONGAR

River Rodding

BUSHY LEA

1 STANLEY PL

2 LIVINGSTONE CL

3 BATTLE CT

4 TOWER CT

COOPERS HILL

Long Edwells

1

KING

THE ELMS

GREY

CLOVERLEY RD

LONG FIELDS

Newhouse Farm

Wks

ST JAMES AVE

A113

BRENTWOOD

RD A128

STONDON RD

Hallsford Bridge

ONGAR RD

Sch

Hallsford Farm House

STANSFORD RIVERS RD

02

D   **E**   **F**

55   56   57

132

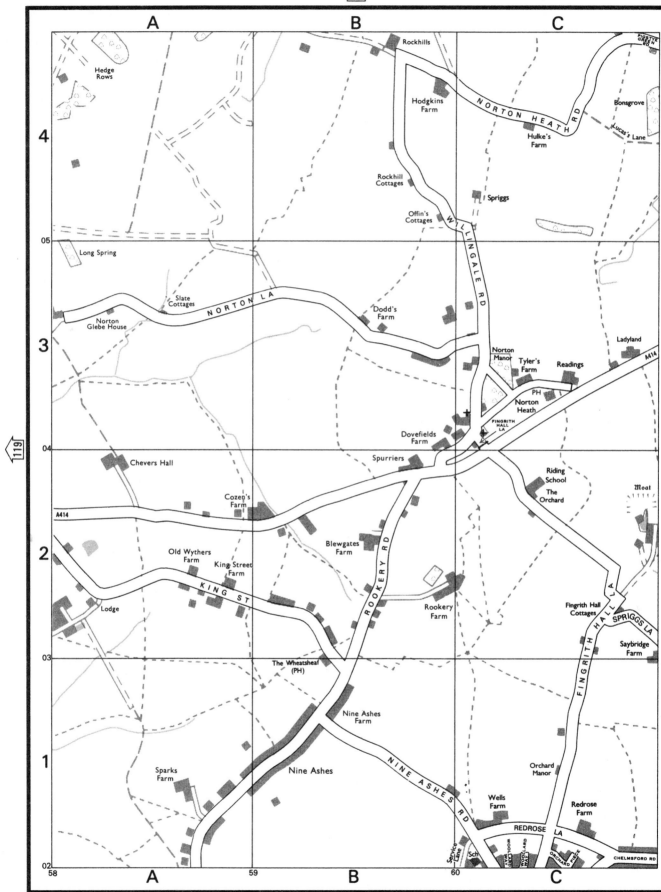

A   B   C

Hedge Rows

Long Spring

Slate Cottages

Norton Glebe House

NORTON LA

Rockhills

Hodgkins Farm

NORTON HEATH RD

Bonsgrove

Lucas's Lane

Hulke's Farm

Rockhill Cottages

Spriggs

Offin's Cottages

WILLINGALE RD

Dodd's Farm

Norton Manor

Tyler's Farm

Readings

Ladyland

A414

PH

Norton Heath

FINGRITH HALL LA

Chevers Hall

Dovefields Farm

Spurriers

Riding School

The Orchard

Moat

Cozen's Farm

A414

Old Wythers Farm

King Street Farm

KING ST

Blewgates Farm

ROOKERY RD

Rookery Farm

Fingrith Hall Cottages

SPRIGGS LA

FINGRITH HALL LA

Saybridge Farm

Lodge

The Wheatsheaf (PH)

Nine Ashes Farm

Nine Ashes

NINE ASHES RD

Orchard Manor

Sparks Farm

Wells Farm

Redrose Farm

REDROSE LA

Service Lane

Sch

WOODLAND WAY

ORCHARD PIECE

CHELMSFORD RD

05   04   03   02

4   3   2   1

58   59   60

A   B   C

108

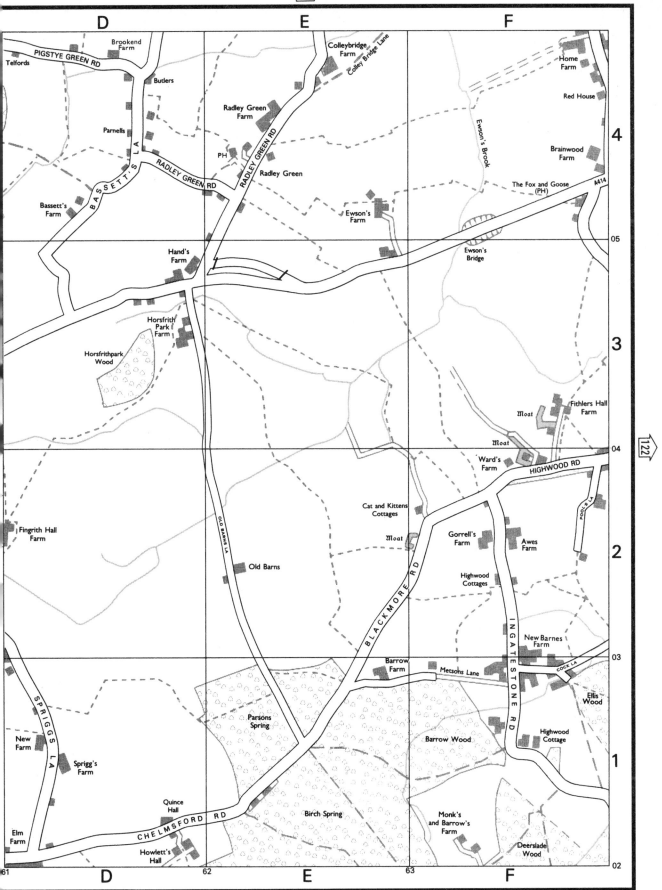

134
122

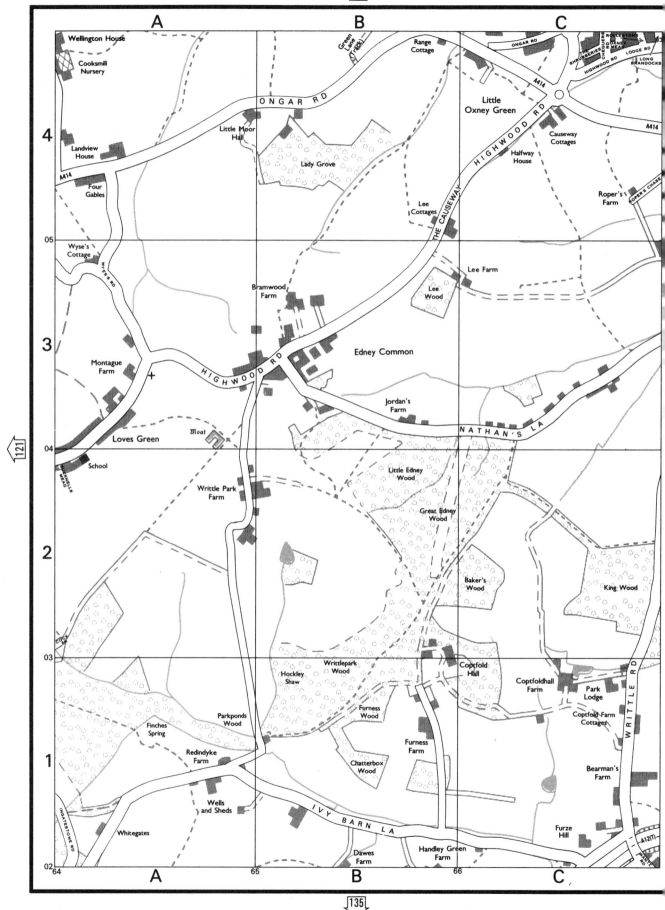

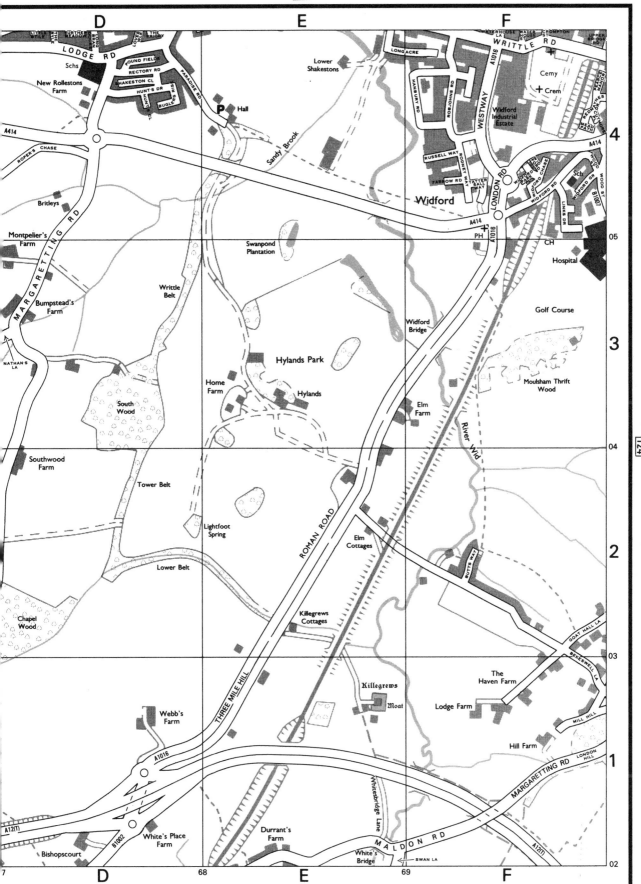

D

E

F

LODGE RD

Schs

New Rollestons Farm

HAKESTON CL

RECTORY RD

HUNT'S DR

PARADISE RD

BUGLE

Lower Shakestons

LONGACRE

WRITTLE RD

CROMPTON

WATERHOUSE WATER

Cemy

Crem

Widford Industrial Estate

A1016

WESTWAY

HANBURY RD

ROBSONS RD

RUSSELL WAY

RODNEY WAY

FARROW RD

TATTER BALL WAY

Hall

P

A414

ROPER'S CHASE

Bridleys

Widford

LONDON RD

Sch

B1007

WOOD ST

WIDFORD CHASE

WIDFORD RD

LINKS DR

A414

Montpelier's Farm

A1016

PH

CH

05

MARGARETTING RD

Bumpstead's Farm

Swanpond Plantation

Hospital

Sandy Brook

Writtle Belt

Widford Bridge

Golf Course

NATHAN'S LA

Hylands Park

Home Farm

Hylands

Elm Farm

Moulsham Thrift Wood

3

South Wood

River Wild

Southwood Farm

04

Tower Belt

124

Lightfoot Spring

ROMAN ROAD

Elm Cottages

BUTTS WAY

2

Lower Belt

Killegrews Cottages

GOAT HALL LA

Chapel Wood

BEKESWELL LA

The Haven Farm

03

Killegrews

Moat

Lodge Farm

MILL HILL

Webb's Farm

THREE MILE HILL

Hill Farm

A1016

LONDON HILL

MARGARETTING RD

1

A12(T)

B1002

White's Place Farm

Whitesbridge Lane

MALDON RD

A12(T)

Bishopscourt

Durrant's Farm

White's Bridge

SWAN LA

02

7

D

68

E

69

F

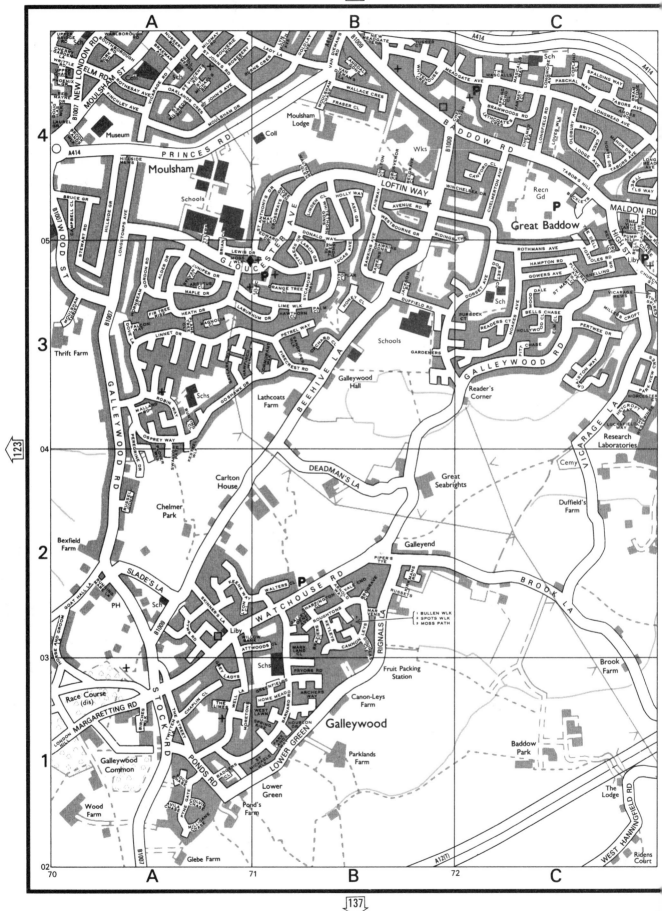

112

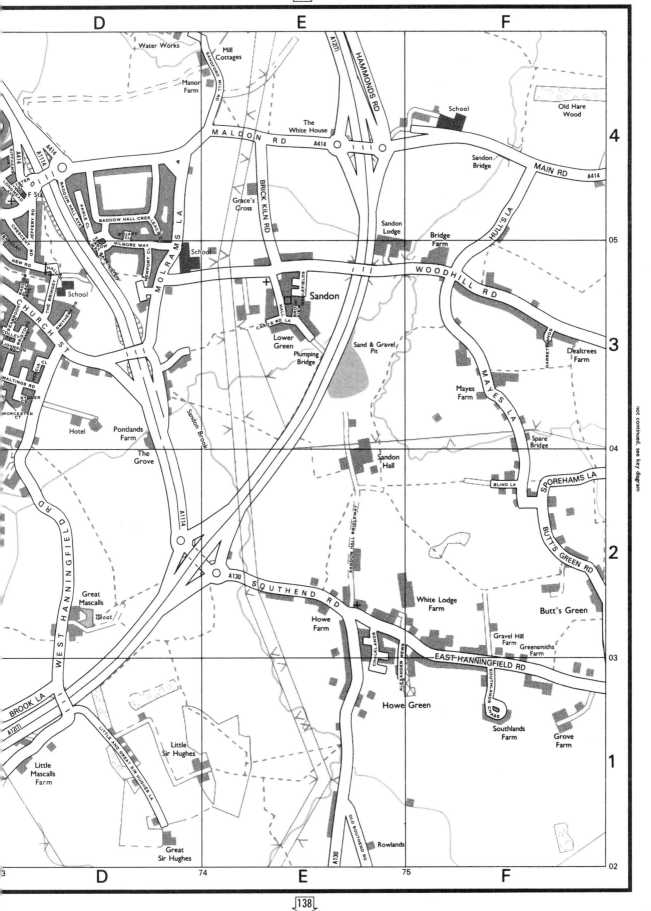

138

D · E · F

4 · 05 · 3 · 04 · 2 · 03 · 1 · 02

Water Works
Mill Cottages
Manor Farm
The White House
MALDON RD · A414
Grace's Cross
School
Sandon Bridge
MAIN RD · A414
Old Hare Wood
School
HAMMONDS RD · A12(T)
BRICK KILN RD
SANDFORD MILL RD
Sandon Lodge
Bridge Farm
HULL'S LA
WOODHILL RD
Sandon
Lower Green
Plumping Bridge
GABLEFIELDS
CARD'S RD LA
HALL LA
BIRCH LA
Sand & Gravel Pit
MAYES LA
Mayes Farm
GARRET LANDS
Dealtrees Farm
Spare Bridge
BADDOW HALL CRES · LEACH C
GILMORE WAY
MOLRAMS LA
School
Sandon Brook
A1114
Pontlands Farm
The Grove
Sandon Hall
BLIND LA
SPOREHAMS LA
BUTT'S GREEN RD
WEST HANNINGFIELD RD
Great Mascalls
Moat
A130
SOUTHEND RD
SANDON HALL BRIDLEWAY
Howe Farm
White Lodge Farm
Butt's Green
Gravel Hill Farm
Greensmiths Farm
CHALKLANDS
ALEXANDER MEWS
EAST HANNINGFIELD RD
SOUTHLANDS CHASE
BROOK LA
A12(T)
Little Sir Hughes
LITTLE AND GREAT SIR HUGHES LA
Howe Green
Southlands Farm
Grove Farm
Little Mascalls Farm
Great Sir Hughes
A130
OLD SOUTHEND RD
Rowlands
CHURCH ST
Hotel

not continued, see key diagram

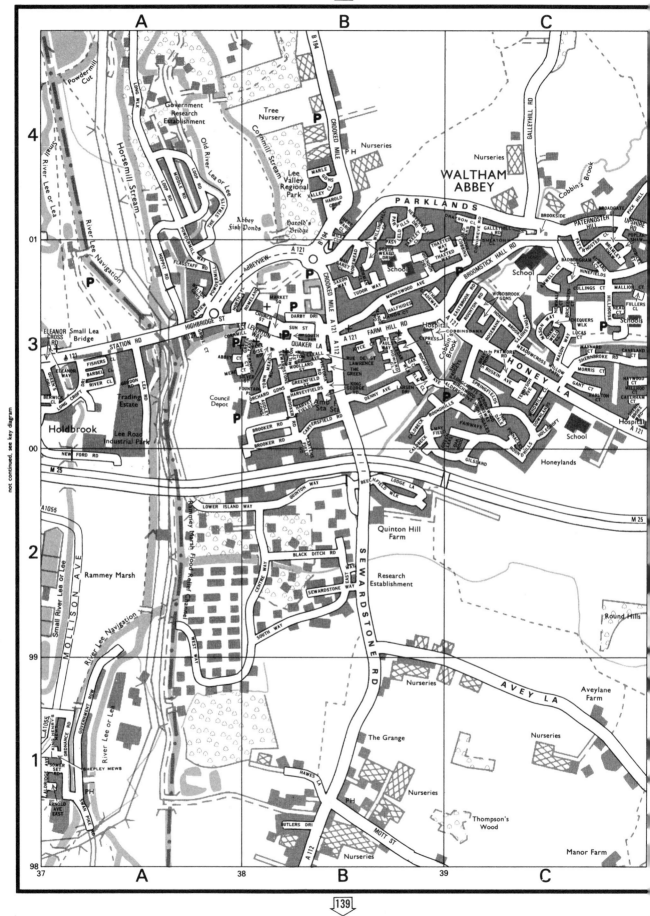

A   **B**   **C**

4

01

3

00

2

99

1

98

not continued, see key diagram

WALTHAM ABBEY

PARKLANDS

HONEY LA

Holdbrook

Rammey Marsh

Mollison Ave

River Lee or Lea

Lee Valley Regional Park

Council Depot

Trading Estate

Lee Road Industrial Park

Government Research Establishment

Tree Nursery

Nurseries

Nurseries

Quinton Hill Farm

Research Establishment

Round Hills

Aveylane Farm

The Grange

Nurseries

Nurseries

Thompson's Wood

Manor Farm

Honeylands

School

Hospital

AVEY LA

M 25

SEWARDSTONE RD

37   **A**   **38**   **B**   **39**   **C**

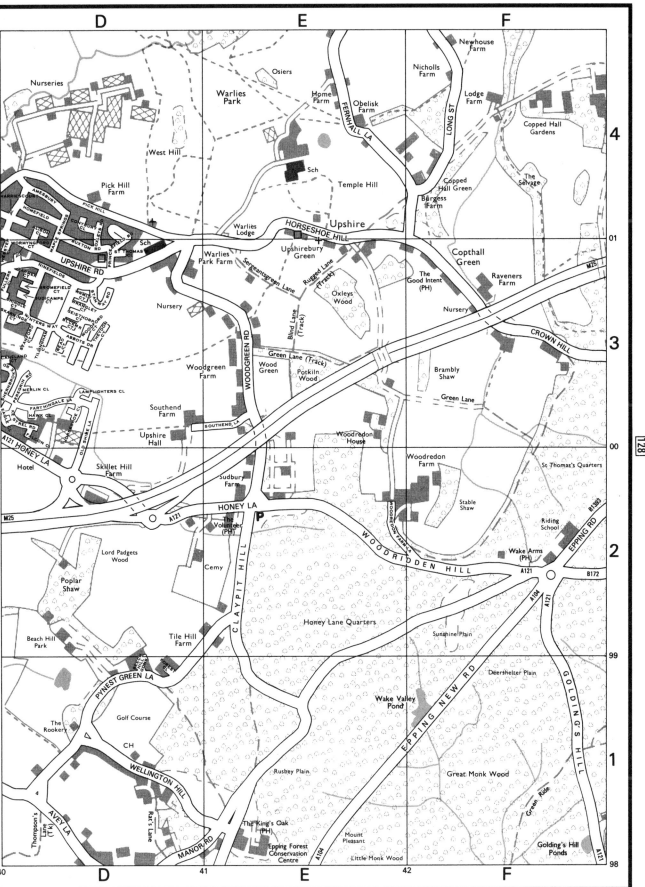

D   E   F

Nurseries

Warlies Park

Osiers

Home Farm

Nicholls Farm

Newhouse Farm

Lodge Farm

Copped Hall Gardens

4

West Hill

Obelisk Farm

Pick Hill Farm

FERNHALL LA

LONG ST

Temple Hill

Copped Hall Green

The Selvage

HARRIESCOURT
AMESBURY
HONEFIELD
Pick Hill
COVEYHURT
CL
ALLISON
CT
WORMYNGFORD
CT
MAPLE SPRINGS
BUXTON RD
OXLEYS RD
PRINCE FIELD RD
Sch
ST THOMAS

UPSHIRE RD

NINEFIELDS
FULLERS
BROMEFIELD CT
ALDER
SUDICAMPS CT
SWIGGS CT
WRANGLE
GEIST THORPD
WINTERS WAY
WOODCROFT
BLOMAR
TRETTON
RELLD
ABBOTS DR
BRABNERS WAY
ST ACHORD
TILLBROOK
CANELAND CT
SHERNINGTON RD
PERGWIRN CL
MERLIN CL
FARTHINGALE LA
HAWK CL
KESTREL RD
FALCON CT
LAMPLIGHTERS CL
OLD SHIRE LA

Warlies Lodge

HORSESHOE HILL

Upshire

Burgess Farm

Copthall Green

01

Warlies Park Farm

Sergeantsgreen Lane

Upshirebury Green

Rugged Lane (Track)

The Good Intent (PH)

Raveners Farm

M25

Nursery

Blind Lane (Track)

Oxleys Wood

Nursery

CROWN HILL

3

WOODGREEN RD

Green Lane (Track)

Wood Green

Potkiln Wood

Brambly Shaw

Woodgreen Farm

Green Lane

Southend Farm

SOUTHEND LA

Woodredon House

A121 HONEY LA

Upshire Hall

Woodredon Farm

St Thomas's Quarters

00

Hotel

Skillet Hill Farm

Sudbury Farm

HONEY LA

Stable Shaw

Riding School

B1393

EPPING RD

M25

A121

The Volunteer (PH)

P

Wake Arms (PH)

B172

2

Lord Padgets Wood

Cemy

WOODRIDDEN HILL

A121

A104

A121

Poplar Shaw

CLAYPIT HILL

Honey Lane Quarters

Sunshine Plain

Beach Hill Park

Tile Hill Farm

99

PYNEST GREEN LA

Deershelter Plain

EPPING NEW RD

GOLDING'S HILL

The Rookery

Golf Course

Wake Valley Pond

CH

1

WELLINGTON HILL

Rushey Plain

Great Monk Wood

Green Ride

AVEY LA

Rat's Lane

Thompson's Lane (Tk)

MANOR RD

The King's Oak (PH)

Epping Forest Conservation Centre

A104

Mount Pleasant

Little Monk Wood

Golding's Hill Ponds

A121

98

40   D   41   E   42   F

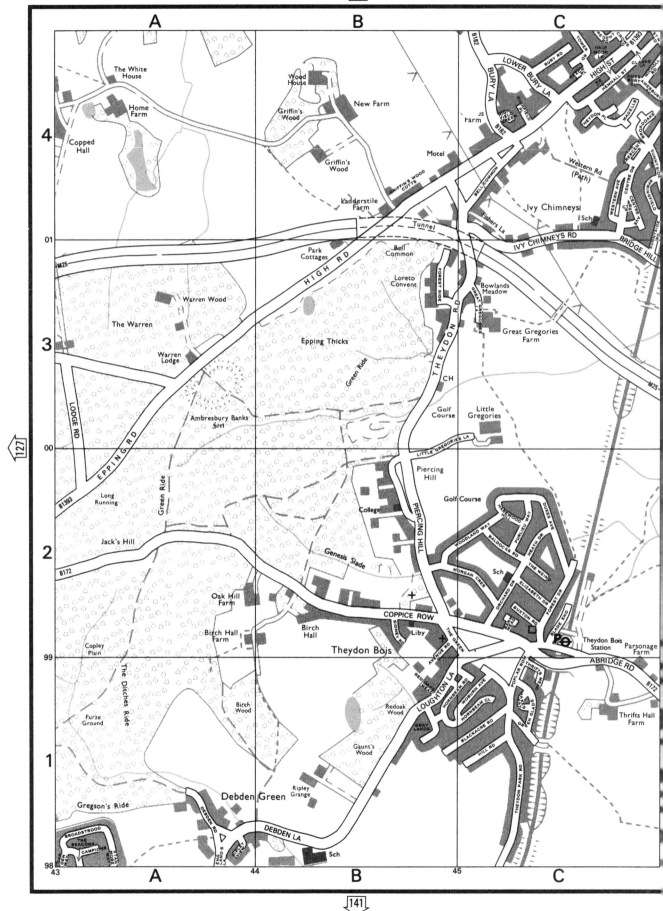

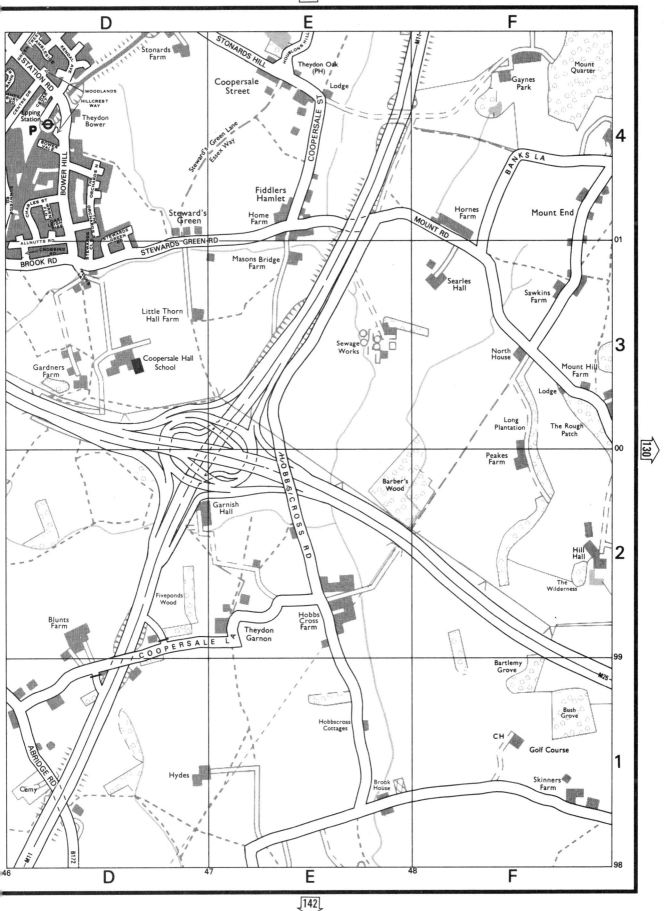

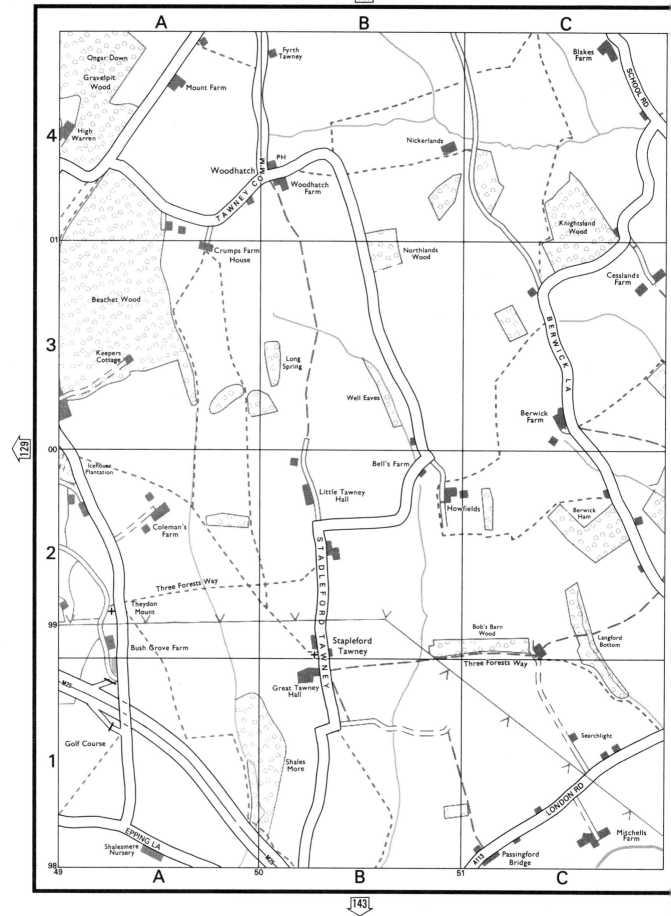

A   B   C

Ongar Down
Gravelpit Wood
Mount Farm
High Warren
Fyrth Tawney
Blakes Farm
SCHOOL RD
4
PH
Woodhatch
Nickerlands
Woodhatch Farm
TAWNEY COMM
Knightsland Wood
01
Crumps Farm House
Northlands Wood
Cesslands Farm
Beachet Wood
BERWICK LA
3
Keepers Cottage
Long Spring
Well Eaves
Berwick Farm
00
Icehouse Plantation
Bell's Farm
Little Tawney Hall
Howfields
Berwick Ham
Coleman's Farm
STADLEFORD TAWNEY
2
Three Forests Way
Theydon Mount
Bob's Barn Wood
Langford Bottom
99
Bush Grove Farm
Stapleford Tawney
Three Forests Way
M25
Great Tawney Hall
Searchlight
Golf Course
1
Shales More
LONDON RD
EPPING LA
Shalesmere Nursery
M25
Mitchells Farm
A113
Passingford Bridge
98
49   50   51

A   B   C

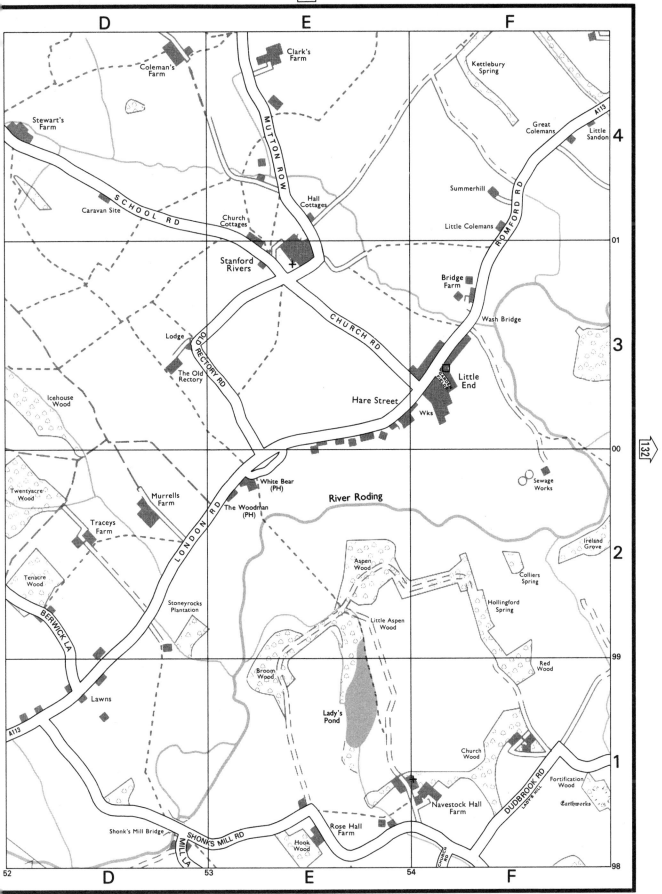

D   E   F

Coleman's Farm

Clark's Farm

Kettlebury Spring

Stewart's Farm

A113

Great Colemans

Little Sandon

4

SCHOOL RD

Caravan Site

MUTTON ROW

Church Cottages

Hall Cottages

Summerhill

ROMFORD RD

Little Colemans

01

Stanford Rivers

CHURCH RD

Bridge Farm

Wash Bridge

Lodge

OLD RECTORY RD

3

The Old Rectory

Hare Street

Little End

Wks

Icehouse Wood

00

Twentyacre Wood

Murrells Farm

LONDON RD

White Bear (PH)

The Woodman (PH)

River Roding

Sewage Works

Traceys Farm

Aspen Wood

Ireland Grove

2

Tenacre Wood

Stoneyrocks Plantation

Little Aspen Wood

Colliers Spring

Hollingford Spring

BERWICK LA

99

A113

Lawns

Broom Wood

Red Wood

Lady's Pond

Church Wood

DUDBROOK RD

1

Fortification Wood

LADY'S HILL

Earthworks

Navestock Hall Farm

Shonk's Mill Bridge

MILL LA

SHONKS MILL RD

Hook Wood

Rose Hall Farm

CHURCH RD

98

52   D   53   E   54   F

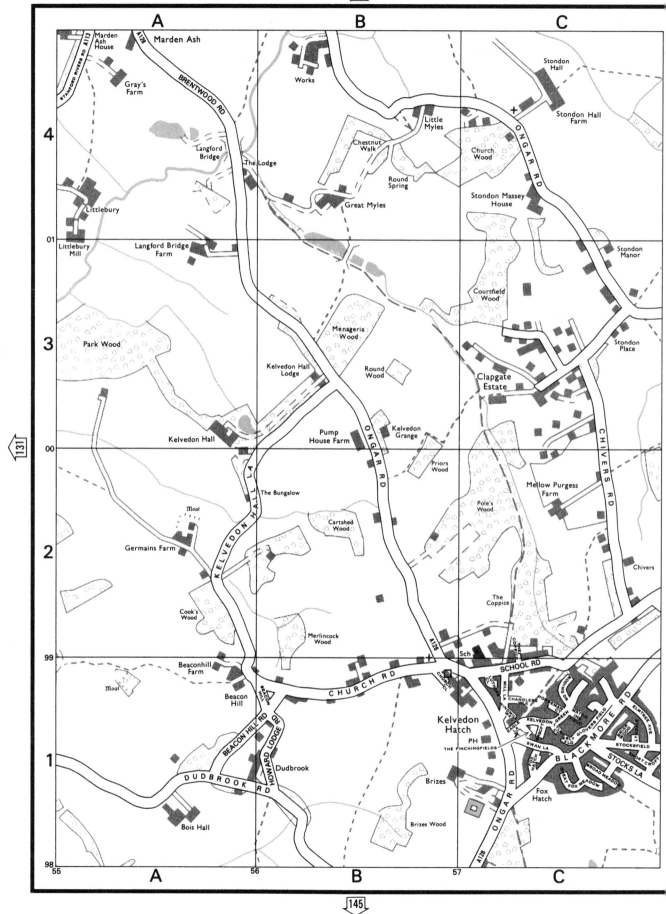

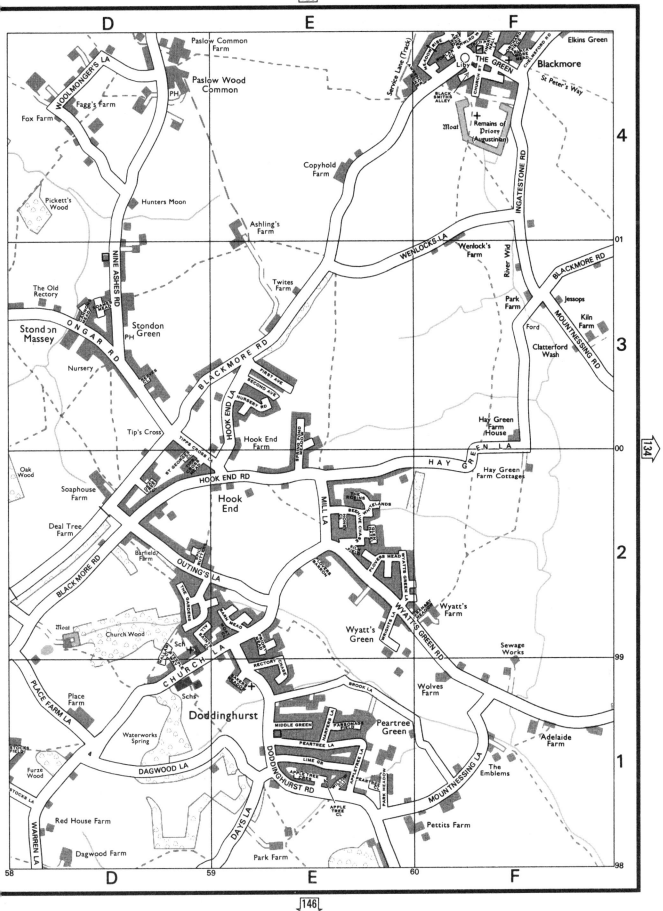

120
134

D
E
F

4
3
2
1

Paslow Common Farm
Paslow Wood Common
WOOLMONGER'S LA
Fagg's Farm
PH
Fox Farm
Pickett's Wood
Hunters Moon
Ashling's Farm
Copyhold Farm
Service Lane (Track)
MEADOW RISE
THE GREEN
Library
BLACK SMITHS ALLEY
CHURCH ST
Elkins Green
Blackmore
St Peter's Way
CHELMSFORD RD
ORCHARD MEAD
Moat
Remains of Priory (Augustinian)
INGATESTONE RD

The Old Rectory
NINE ASHES RD
Stondon Green
PH
Twites Farm
WENLOCKS LA
Wenlock's Farm
River Wid
01
BLACKMORE RD
MOUNTNESSING RD
Jessops
Kiln Farm

Stondon Massey
ONGAR RD
Nursery
BLACKMORE RD
FIRST AVE
SECOND AVE
NURSERY RD
HOOK END LA
Park Farm
Ford
Clatterford Wash
3

Tip's Cross
TIPPS CROSS LA
Hook End Farm
SPRING POND MEADOW
Hay Green Farm House
HAY GREEN LA
00

Oak Wood
Soaphouse Farm
ST GEORGE'S
HOOK END RD
Hook End
MILL LA
THE ROBINS
BEEHIVE CHASE
WHITELANDS
Hay Green Farm Cottages

Deal Tree Farm
BLACK MORE RD
Barfield Farm
OUTING'S LA
THE GARDENS
BARN MEAD
FLOVERS MEAD
CLOVERS BARROW
WYATT'S GREEN LA
GRANARY MEADOW
Wyatt's Farm
2

Moat
Church Wood
Sch
BARN MEAD
WRIGHT'S LA
Wyatt's Green
WYATT'S GREEN RD
Sewage Works
99

Place Farm
PLACE FARM LA
CHURCH LA
Schs
RECTORY CHASE
Wolves Farm
Adelaide Farm

STOCKS FIELD
Furze Wood
Waterworks Spring
Doddinghurst
DAGWOOD LA
MIDDLE GREEN
PARSONAGE FIELD
HARPERS LA
PEARTREE LA
LIME GR
Peartree Green
BROOK LA
PARK MEADOW
MOUNTNESSING LA
The Emblems
1

STOCKS LA
WARREN LA
Red House Farm
Dagwood Farm
DODDINGHURST RD
DAYS LA
APPLE TREE GREEN
APPLE TREE CL
Park Farm
Pettits Farm

58
59
60
98

D
E
F

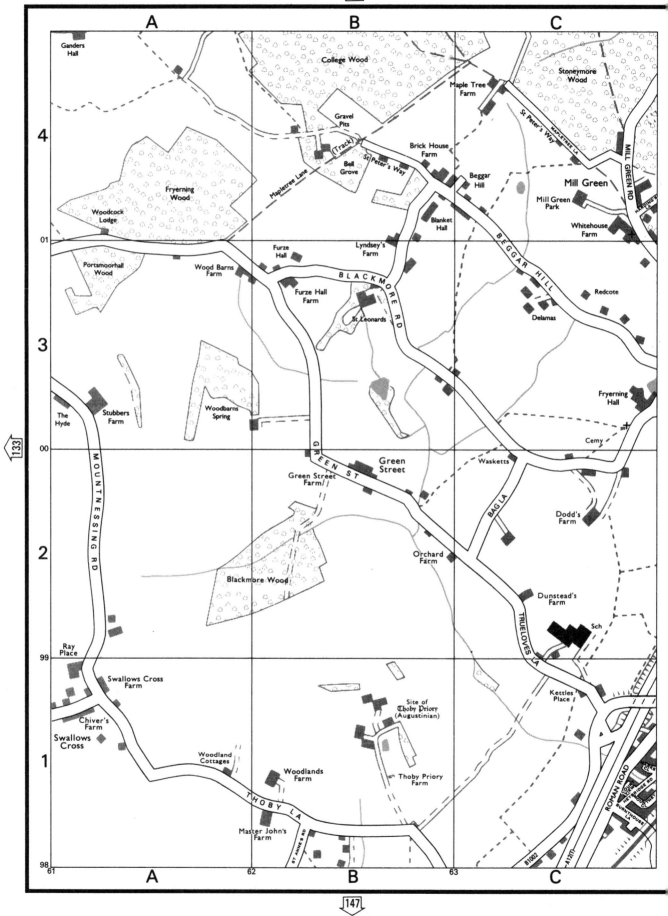

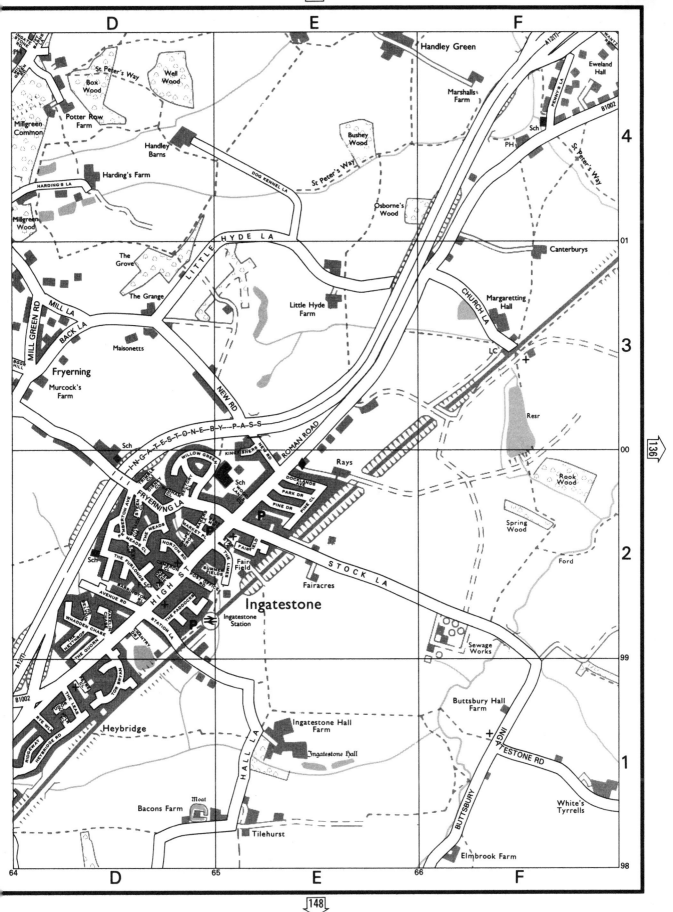

D   **E**   **F**

Handley Green

Eweland Hall

St Peter's Way

Well Wood

Box Wood

Marshalls Farm

Sch

PH

St Peter's Way

B1002

Potter Row Farm

Millgreen Common

Handley Barns

Bushey Wood

St Peter's Way

4

Harding's Farm

HARDING'S LA

DOG KENNEL LA

Osborne's Wood

Canterburys

01

Millgreen Wood

LITTLE HYDE LA

The Grove

CHURCH LA

Margaretting Hall

MILL GREEN RD

MILL LA

The Grange

Little Hyde Farm

LC

3

BACK LA

Maisonetts

NEW RD

Resr

Fryerning

Murcock's Farm

00

INGATESTONE-BY-PASS

ROMAN ROAD

Sch

WILLOW GREEN

Rays

Rook Wood

KINGFISHERS NEW RD

Sch

DOCKLANDS AVE

Spring Wood

2

FRYERNING LA

PARK DR

PINE DR

PINE CL

Ford

Sch

MARKET PL

FAIRFIELD

STOCK LA

Fair Field

Fairacres

Ingatestone

HIGH ST

STATION LA

Ingatestone Station

Sewage Works

99

AVENUE RD

THE PADDOCKS

B1002

HEYBRIDGE RD

Buttsbury Hall Farm

Heybridge

HALL LA

Ingatestone Hall Farm

INGATESTONE RD

Ingatestone Hall

BUTTSBURY

1

RIDGEWAY

RYE WLK

Bacons Farm

Moat

White's Tyrrells

Tilehurst

Elmbrook Farm

98

D   **E**   **F**

64   65   66

123

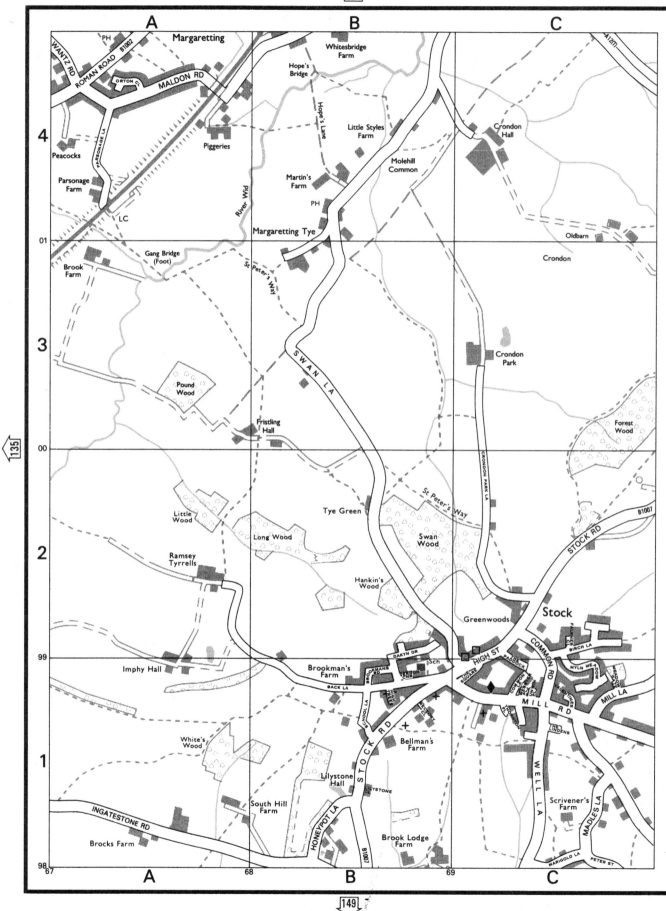

135

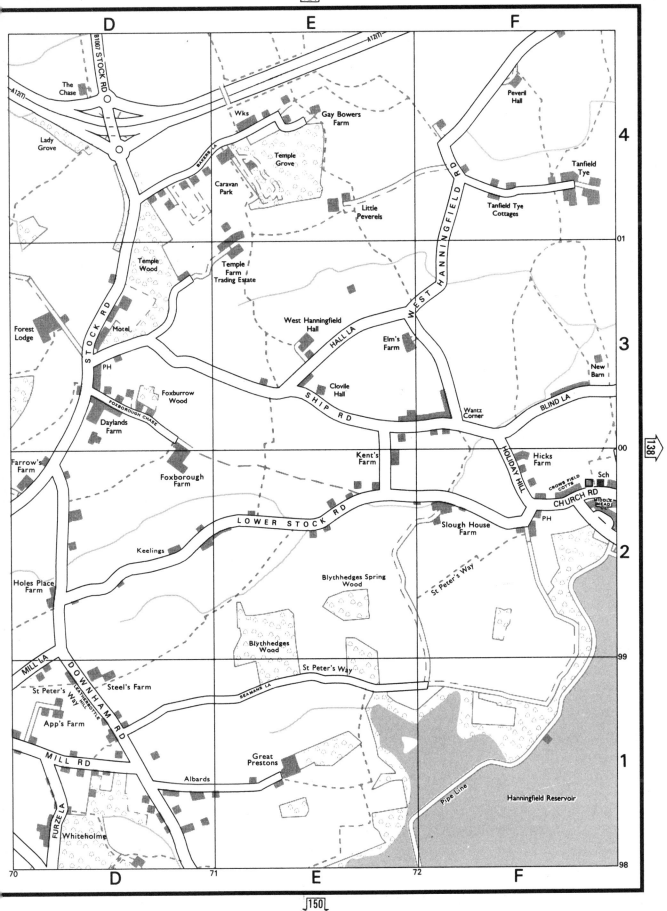

D

E

F

The Chase

B1007 STOCK RD

A12(T)

Wks

Gay Bowers Farm

Peveril Hall

BAKERS LA

Lady Grove

Temple Grove

Tanfield Tye

4

Caravan Park

Little Peverels

Tanfield Tye Cottages

WEST HANNINGFIELD RD

01

Temple Wood

Temple Farm Trading Estate

West Hanningfield Hall

HALL LA

Elm's Farm

New Barn

Forest Lodge

STOCK RD

Motel

PH

Clovile Hall

Wantz Corner

BLIND LA

3

Foxburrow Wood

SHIP RD

Hicks Farm

FOXBOROUGH CHASE

Daylands Farm

HOLIDAY HILL

00

Farrow's Farm

Kent's Farm

CROWS FIELD COTTS

Sch

Foxborough Farm

CHURCH RD

MIDDLE MEAD

Holes Place Farm

LOWER STOCK RD

Slough House Farm

PH

2

Keelings

Blythhedges Spring Wood

St Peter's Way

99

MILL LA

DOWNHAM RD

Blythhedges Wood

St Peter's Way

St Peter's Way

LEATHERBOTTLE HILL

Steel's Farm

SEAMANS LA

App's Farm

MILL RD

Great Prestons

1

Albards

FURZE LA

Pipe Line

Hanningfield Reservoir

Whiteholme

70

71

72

98

D

E

F

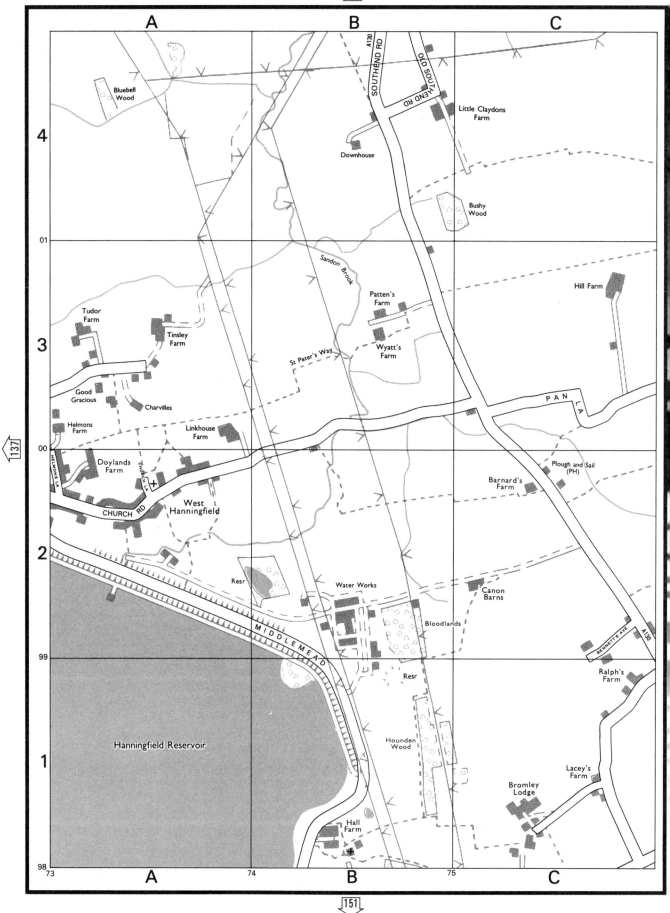

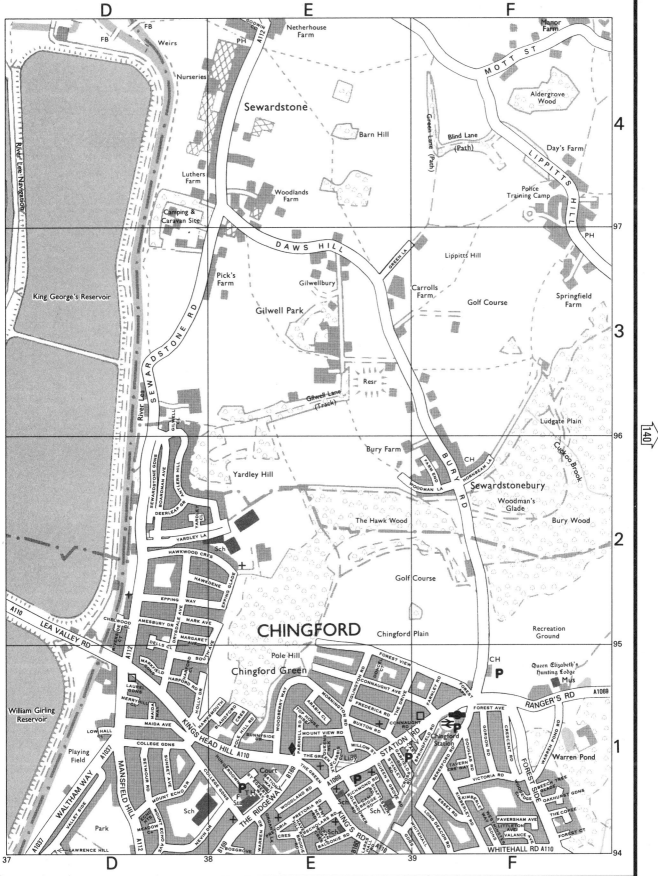

127

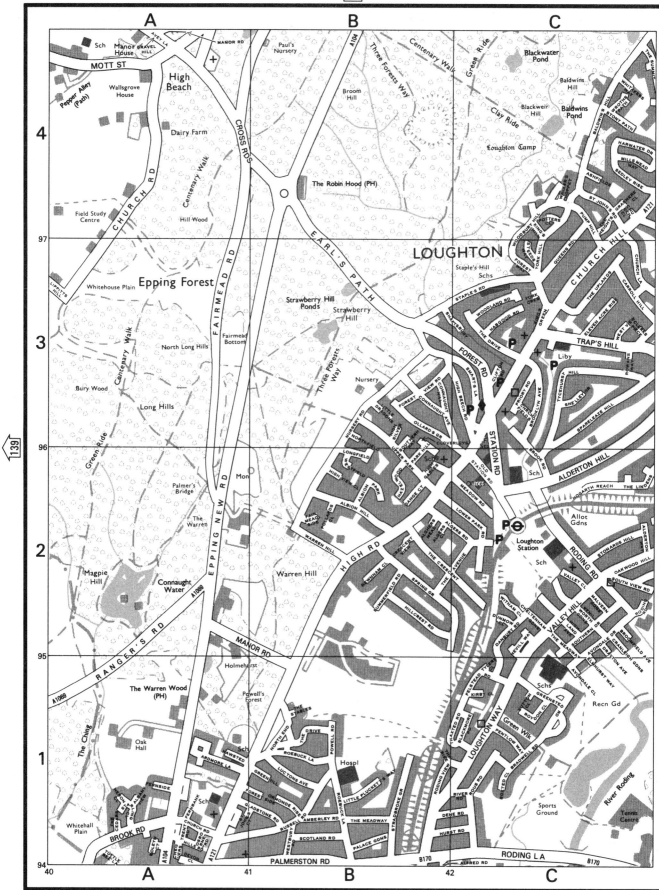

139

152

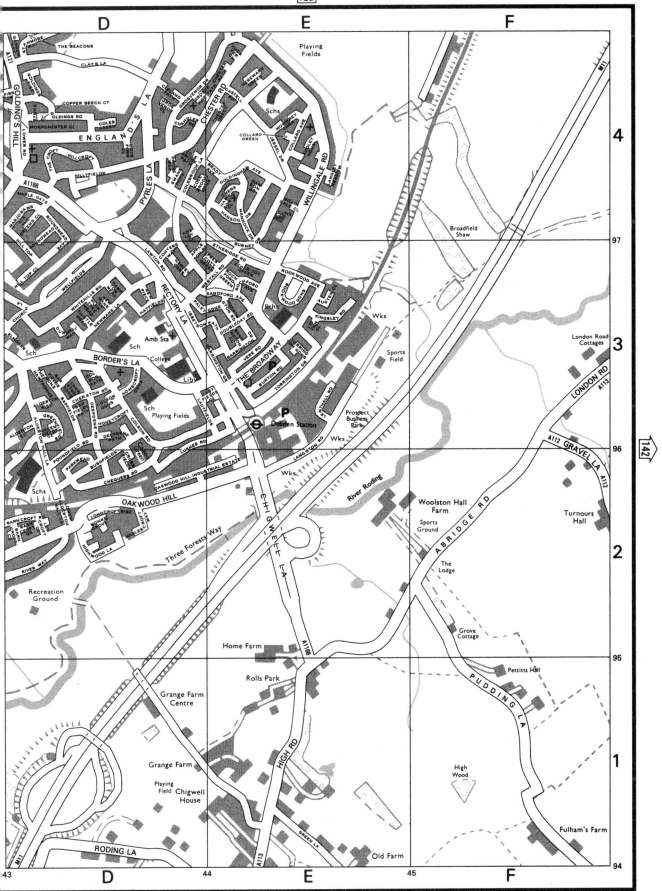

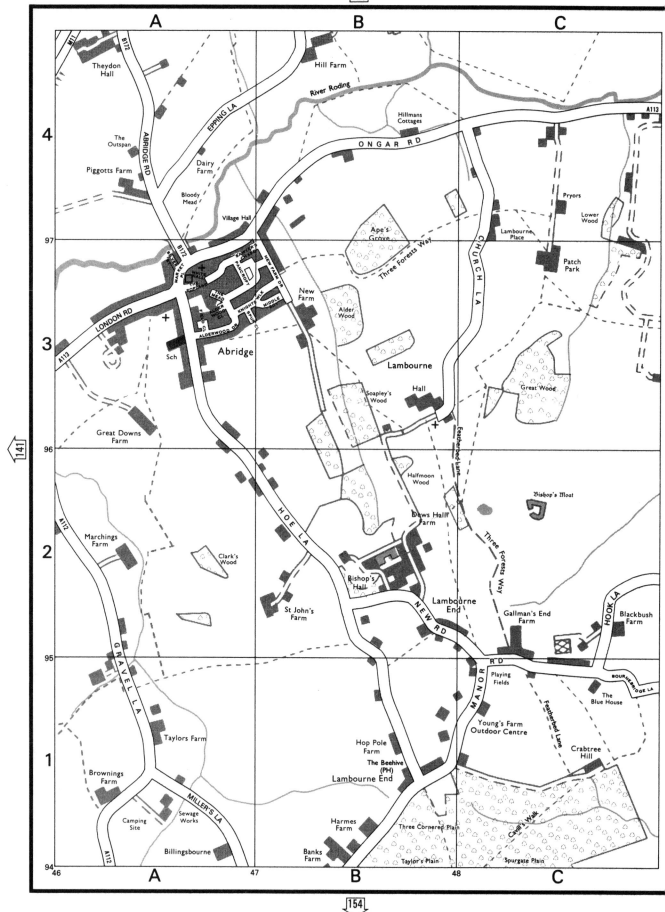

A B C

4

97

3

96

2

95

1

94

46 A 47 B 48 C

M11
B172
Theydon Hall
The Outspan
Piggotts Farm
ABRIDGE RD
EPPING LA
Dairy Farm
Bloody Mead
Village Hall
Hill Farm
River Roding
Hillmans Cottages
ONGAR RD
A113
Pryors
Lower Wood
Lambourne Place
CHURCH LA
Patch Park
Ape's Grove
Three Forests Way
B172
MARKET PL
WHITE HART
THE MEAD
KNIGHTS WLK
ALDERWOOD DR
MIDDLE
NEW FARM DR
New Farm
Alder Wood
LONDON RD
A113
Sch
Abridge
Lambourne
Hall
Soapley's Wood
Great Wood
Featherbed Lane
Great Downs Farm
Halfmoon Wood
Bishop's Moat
HOE LA
Marchings Farm
Clark's Wood
Dews Hall Farm
Three Forests Way
A112
St John's Farm
Bishop's Hall
Lambourne End
Gallman's End Farm
HOOK LA
Blackbush Farm
NEW RD
MANOR RD
Playing Fields
BOURNEBRIDGE LA
The Blue House
GRAVEL LA
Taylors Farm
Young's Farm Outdoor Centre
Featherbed Lane
Crabtree Hill
Brownings Farm
Hop Pole Farm
The Beehive (PH)
Lambourne End
MILLER'S LA
Camping Site
Sewage Works
Harmes Farm
Cavill's Walk
Three Cornered Plain
A112
Billingsbourne
Banks Farm
Taylor's Plain
Spurgate Plain

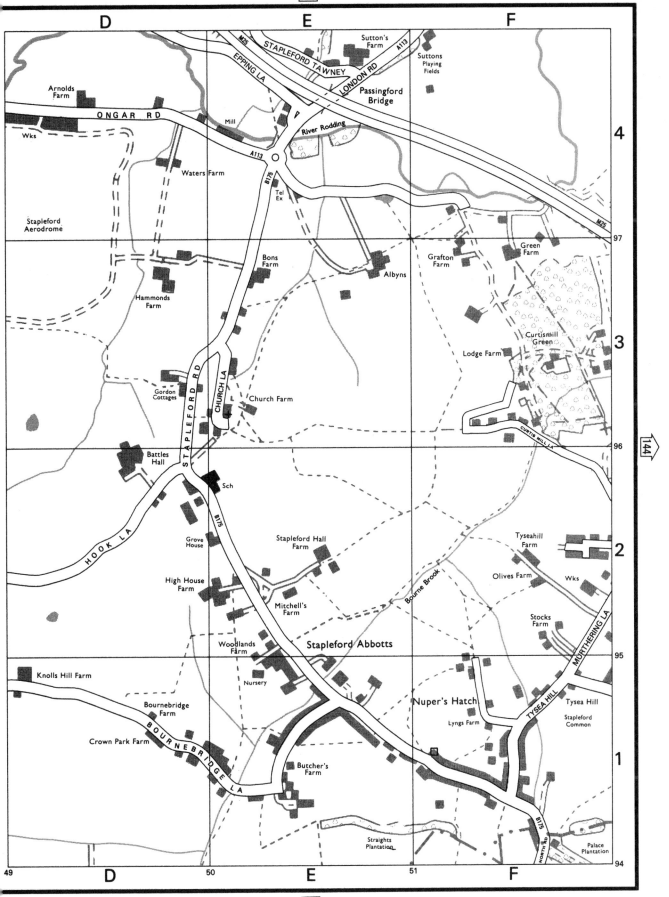

D E F

Arnolds Farm

ONGAR RD

Wks

Waters Farm

M25

STAPLEFORD TAWNEY

EPPING LA

LONDON RD

A113

Sutton's Farm

Suttons Playing Fields

Passingford Bridge

Mill

River Rodding

4

A113

B175

Tel Ex

Stapleford Aerodrome

Bons Farm

Albyns

Grafton Farm

Green Farm

97

Hammonds Farm

Curtismill Green

3

Gordon Cottages

STAPLEFORD RD

CHURCH LA

Church Farm

Lodge Farm

CURTIS MILL LA

144

Battles Hall

Sch

96

HOOK LA

B175

Grove House

Stapleford Hall Farm

Tyseahill Farm

2

High House Farm

Mitchell's Farm

Bourne Brook

Olives Farm

Wks

Stocks Farm

MURTHERING LA

Woodlands Farm

Stapleford Abbotts

95

Knolls Hill Farm

Nursery

Nuper's Hatch

Lyngs Farm

TYSEA HILL

Tysea Hill

Stapleford Common

Bournebridge Farm

Crown Park Farm

BOURNEBRIDGE LA

Butcher's Farm

1

B175

NORTH RD

Straights Plantation

Palace Plantation

94

49 D 50 E 51 F

131

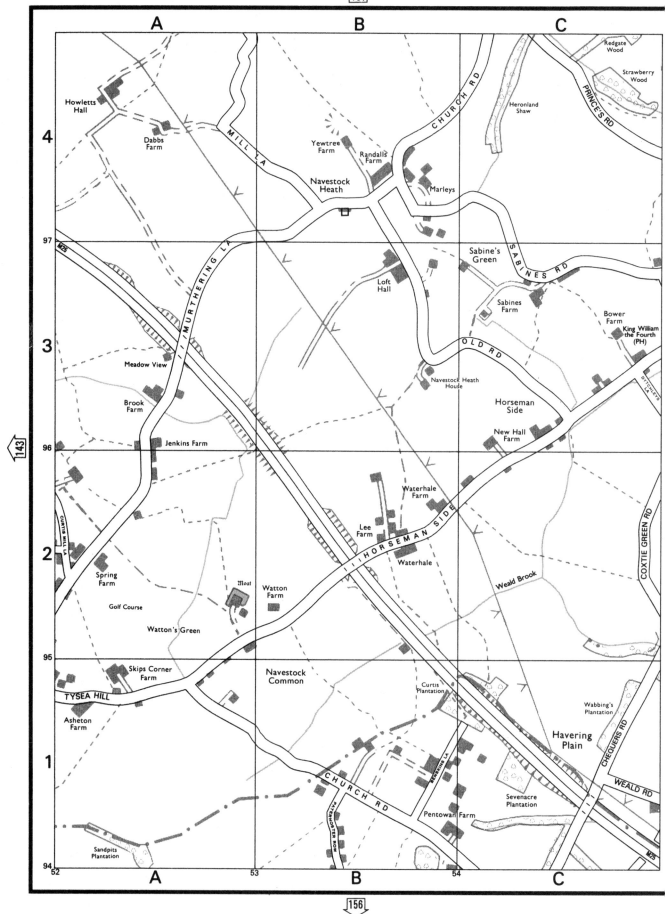

143

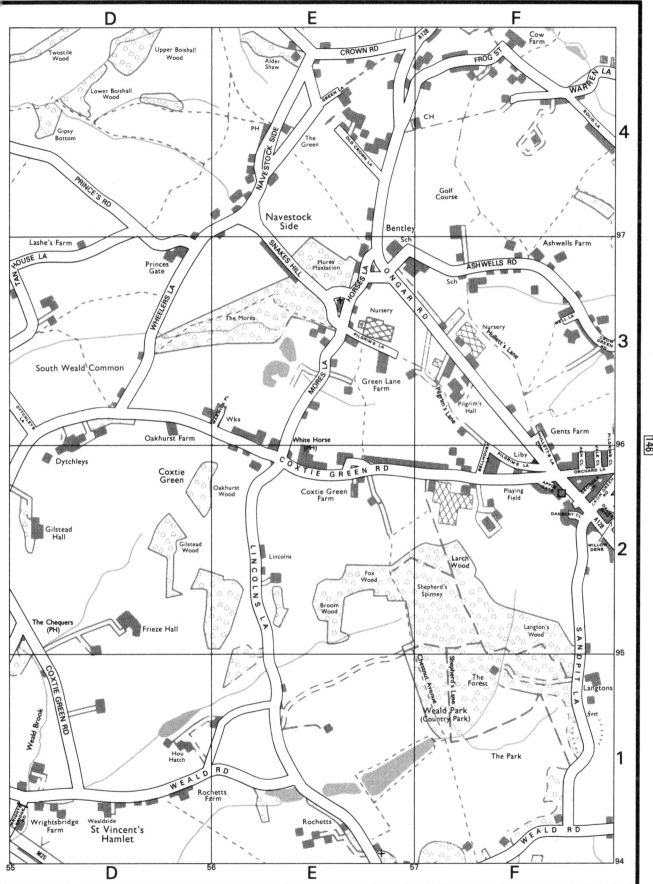

D E F

Twostile Wood

Upper Boishall Wood

Lower Boishall Wood

Gipsy Bottom

Alder Shaw

CROWN RD

A128

FROG ST

Cow Farm

WARREN LA

GREEN LA

4

PH

The Green

OLD CROWN LA

CH

SOLID LA

PRINCE'S RD

NAVESTOCK SIDE

Golf Course

Navestock Side

Bentley

Sch

97

Lashe's Farm

TAN HOUSE LA

Princes Gate

WHEELERS LA

SNAKES HILL

Mores Plantation

HORSES LA

ONGAR RD

ASHWELLS RD

Ashwells Farm

Sch

WELL LA

3

The Mores

Nursery

Nursery

Hulett's Lane

CROW GREEN RD

South Weald Common

PILGRIM'S LA

Green Lane Farm

Pilgrim's Lane

Pilgrim's Hall

DYTCHLEYS LA

MORES LA

WANTZ PL

Wks

White Horse (PH)

Gents Farm

HULETT'S LA

PILGRIMS CL

Oakhurst Farm

COXTIE GREEN RD

BELLHOUSE

PILGRIM'S LA

Liby

ASH CL

VALE CL

ORCHARD LA

96

Dytchleys

Coxtie Green

Oakhurst Wood

Coxtie Green Farm

Playing Field

APPLE

GEORGE

CROW GREEN RD

DANBURY CL

A128

2

Gilstead Hall

Gilstead Wood

Lincolns

Larch Wood

WILLOW DENE

SANDPIT LA

Fox Wood

Shepherd's Spinney

The Chequers (PH)

Frieze Hall

LINCOLNS LA

Broom Wood

Langton's Wood

95

Weald Brook

COXTIE GREEN RD

Chestnut Avenue

Shepherd's Lane

The Forest

Langtons

Fort

Hou Hatch

Weald Park (Country Park)

The Park

1

WEALD RD

Rochetts Farm

WRIGHT'S

M25

Wrightsbridge Farm

Wealdside

St Vincent's Hamlet

Rochetts Farm

Rochetts

WEALD RD

94

D E F

55 56 57

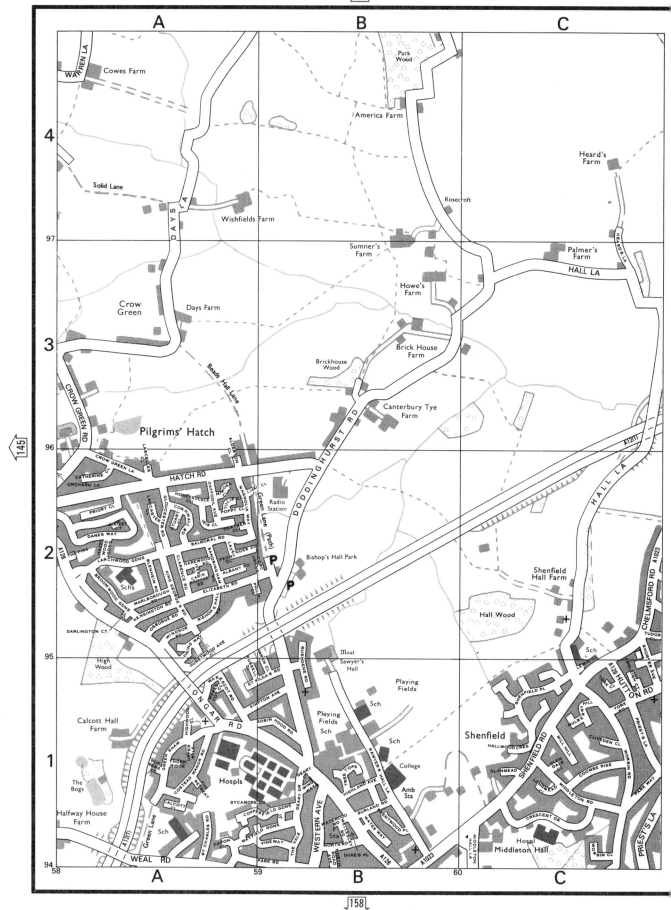

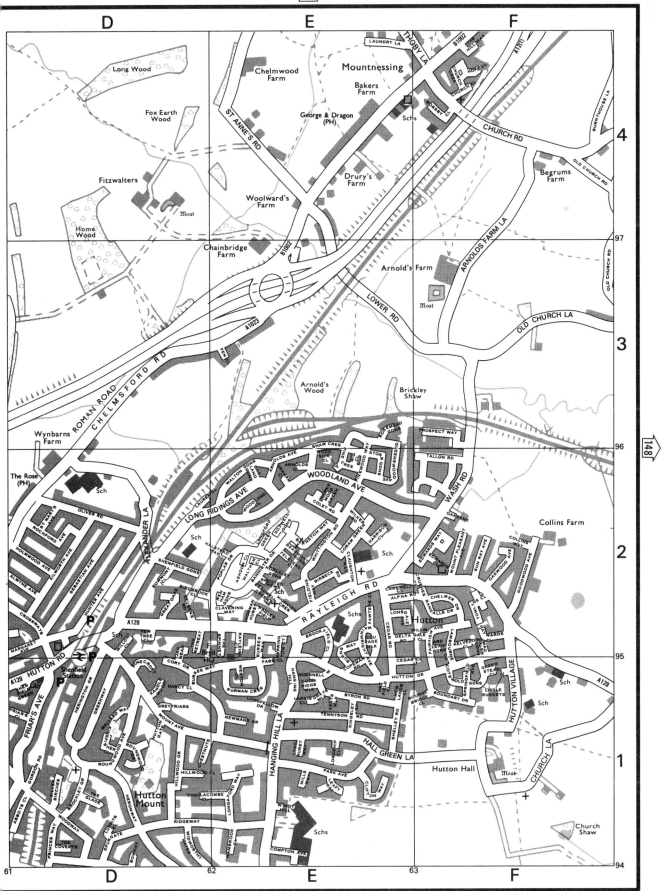

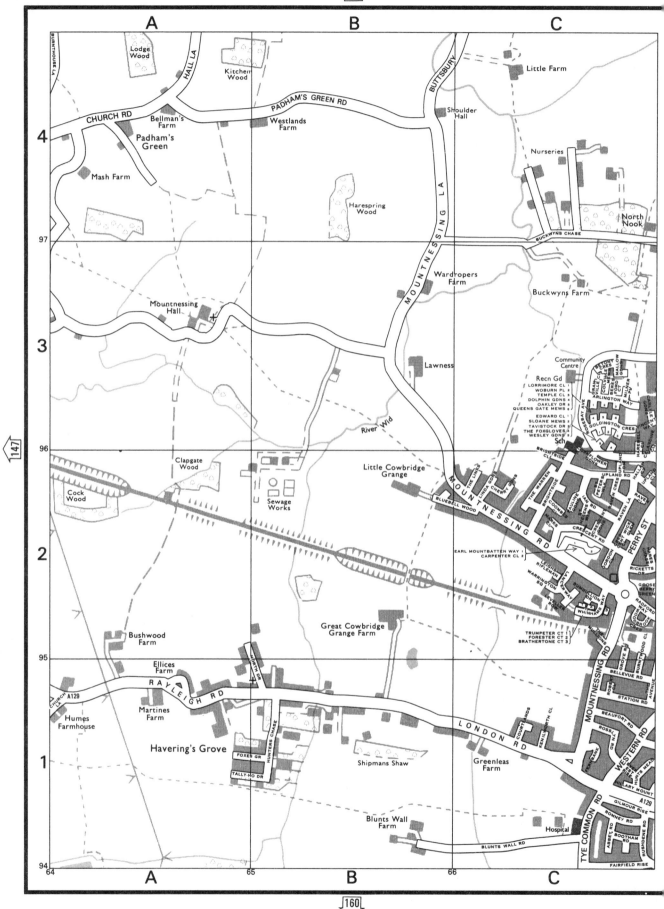

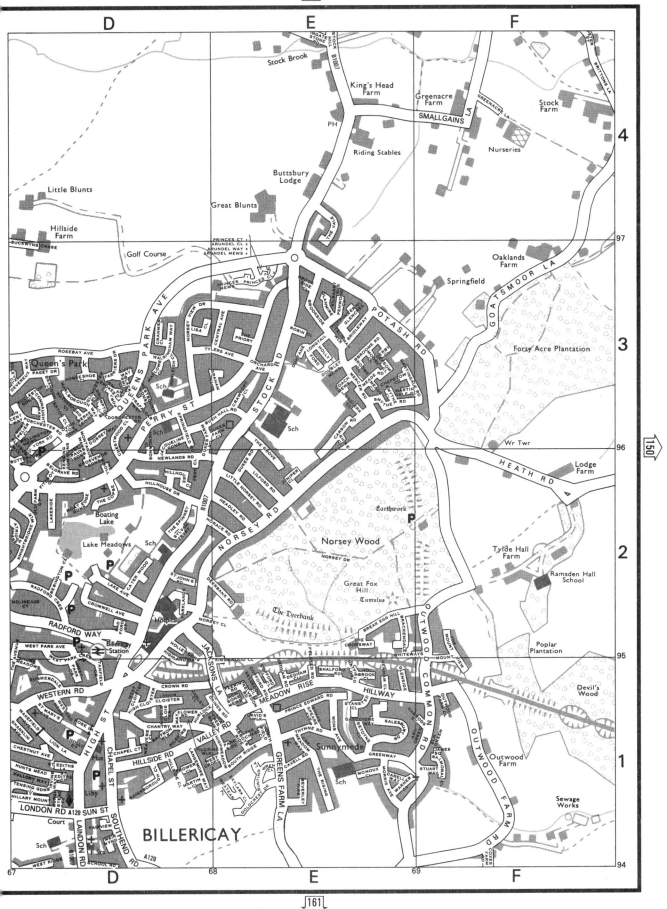

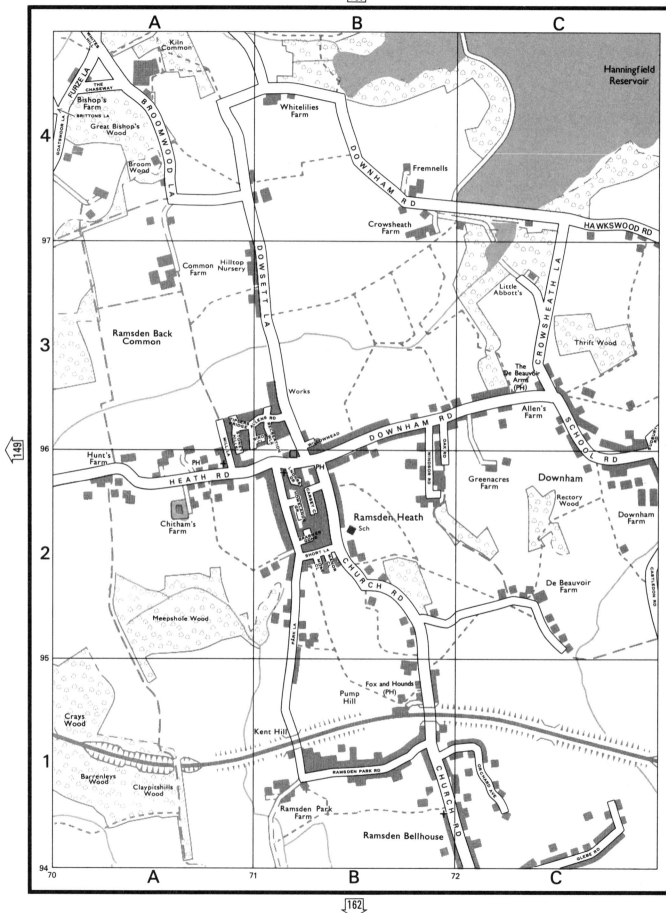

A B C

4

3

2

1

97

96

95

94

70 71 72

Hanningfield
Reservoir

Kiln
Common

WHITES HILL
FURZE LA
THE
CHASEWAY
Bishop's
Farm
GOATSDOOR LA
BRITTONS LA
Great Bishop's
Wood
Broom
Wood

BROOMWOOD LA

Whitelilies
Farm

DOWNHAM RD

Fremnells

HAWKSWOOD RD

Crowsheath
Farm

Common
Farm
Hilltop
Nursery

DOWSETT LA

Little
Abbott's

CROWSHEATH LA

Thrift Wood

Ramsden Back
Common

The
De Beauvoir
Arms
(PH)

Works

Allen's
Farm

SCHOOL RD

Hunt's
Farm

HEATH RD

TIPLER'S
BRIDGE
STONEY
HILL
MILL LA
ALLENS RD
SHOP
RECREATION
WILLOWMEAD
DOWNHAM RD
OAK RD
WINDSOR RD

PH

PH

Greenacres
Farm

Downham

Rectory
Wood

Downham
Farm

CASTLEDON RD

Chitham's
Farm

LINDSEY
HOPEFIELD
CARBEY C
BRASHER
CLOSE
SHORT LA
MOORS
WINDSOR

Ramsden Heath

Sch

De Beauvoir
Farm

Meepshole Wood

PARK LA

CHURCH RD

Crays
Wood

Kent Hill

Pump
Hill

Fox and Hounds
(PH)

Barrenleys
Wood
Claypitshills
Wood

RAMSDEN PARK RD

CHURCH RD

ORCHARD AVE

Ramsden Park
Farm

Ramsden Bellhouse

GLEBE RD

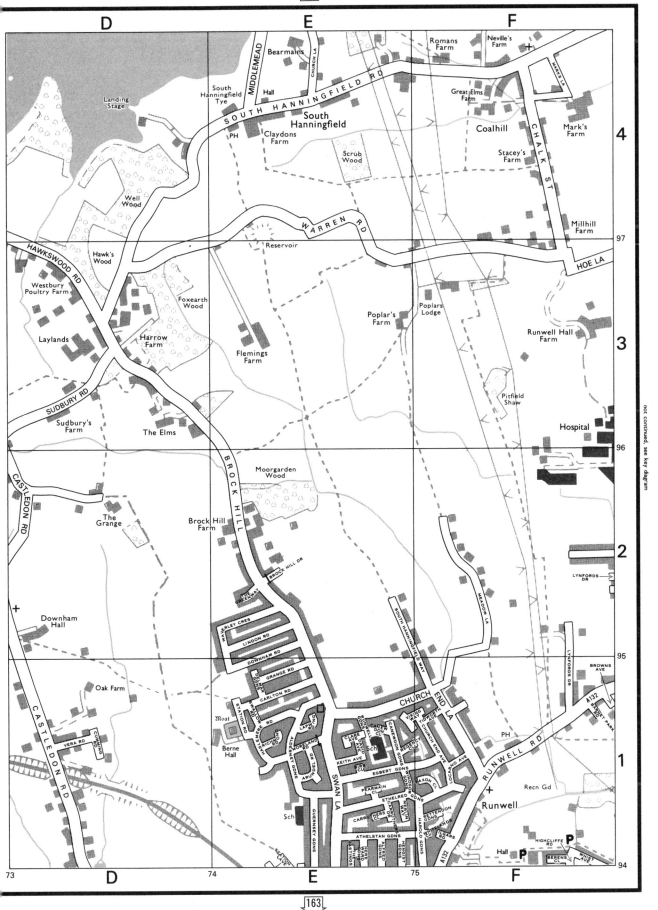

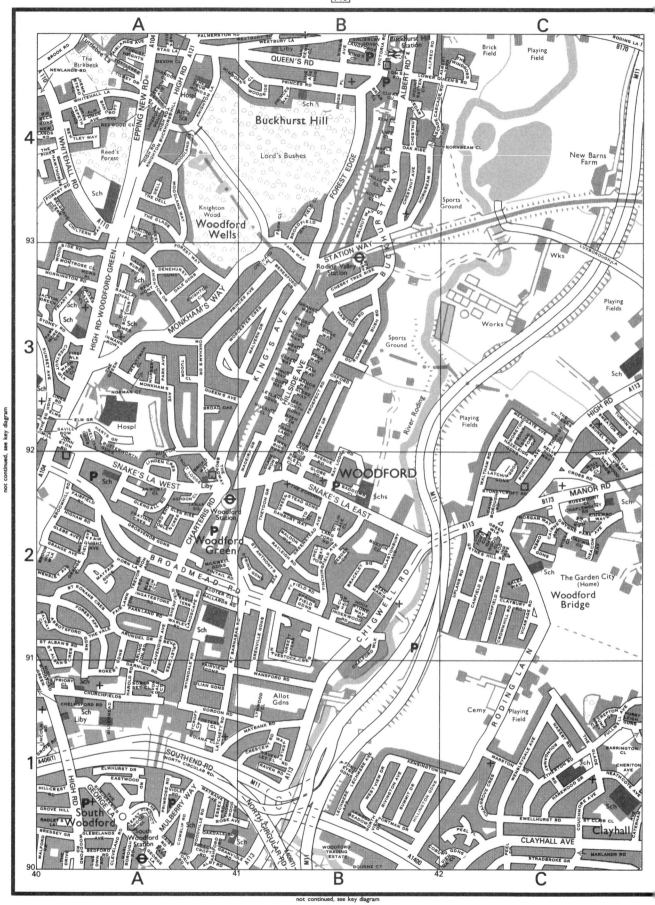

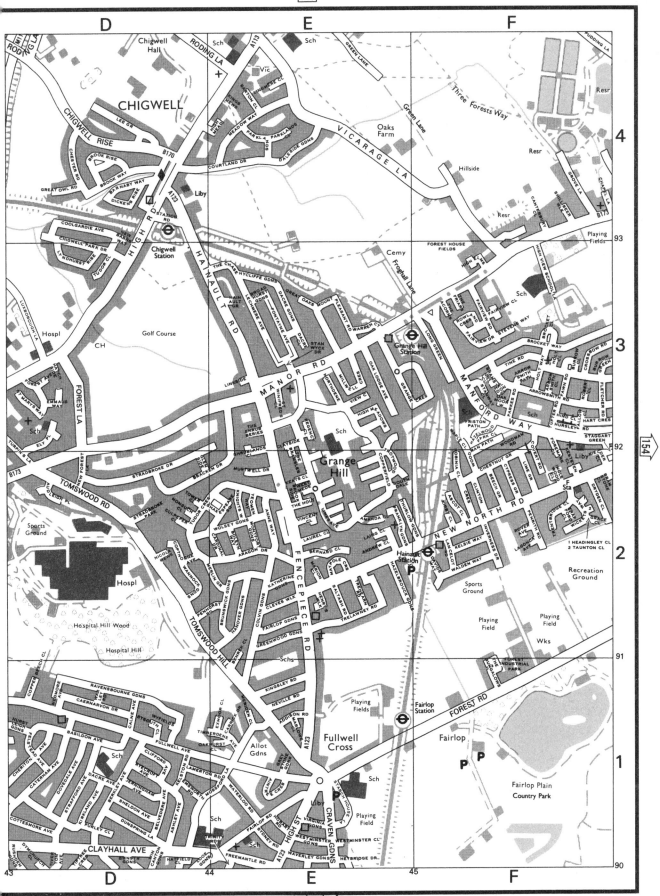

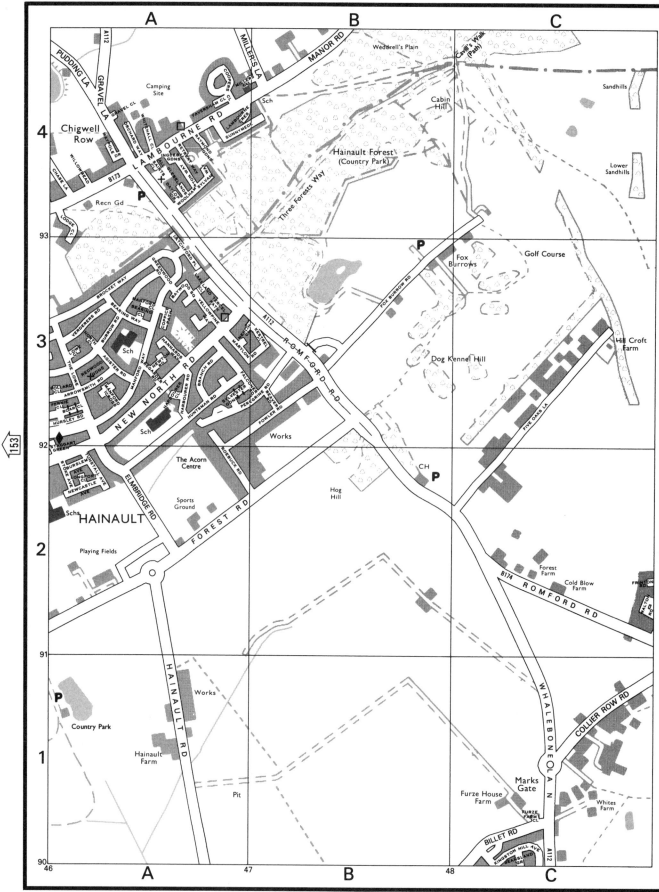

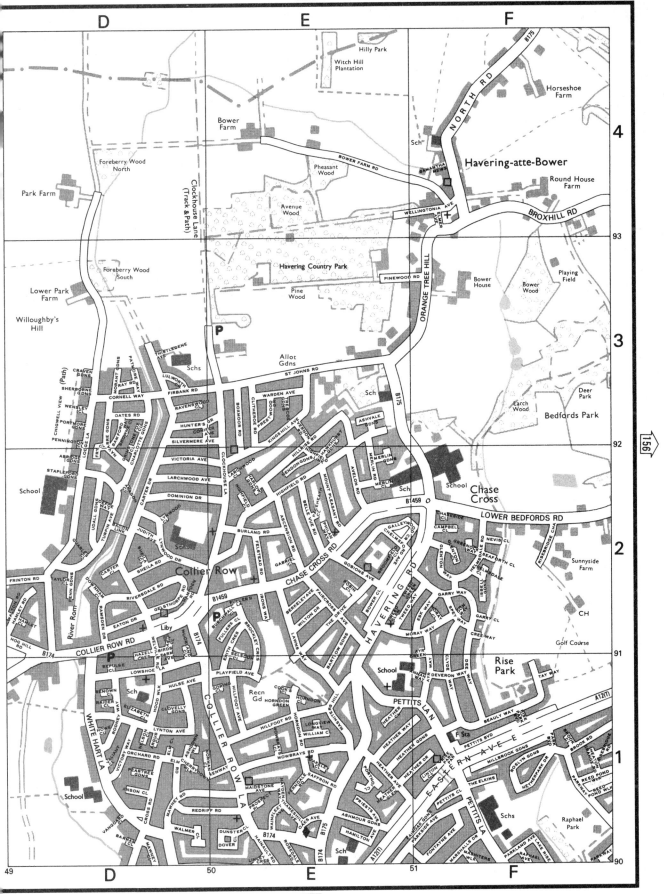

D   E   F

Hilly Park

Witch Hill Plantation

NORTH RD

B175

Horseshoe Farm

Bower Farm

Sch

4

Foreberry Wood North

Park Farm

Bower Farm Rd

Pheasant Wood

SAMANTHA NEWS

Havering-atte-Bower

Round House Farm

Clockhouse Lane (Track & Path)

Avenue Wood

WELLINGTONIA AVE

BROXHILL RD

93

Foreberry Wood South

Havering Country Park

PINEWOOD RD

ORANGE TREE HILL

Bower House

Bower Wood

Playing Field

Lower Park Farm

Pine Wood

B175

Willoughby's Hill

P

Allot Gdns

Larch Wood

Deer Park

3

THISTLEDENE AVE

Schs

St Johns Rd

Sch

Bedfords Park

CRAVEN GDNS

LULWORTH RD

WARDEN AVE

CHISWELL VIEW (Path)

FIRBANK RD

RAVENSWOOD CL

CLITHEROE RD

Sch

SHERBORNE GDNS

MORANT GDNS

PATRICKS WAY

CORNELL WAY

HUNTER'S DR

KINGS HILL AVE

92

156

WENSLEY RD

OATES RD

CONIFER AVE

SILVERMERE AVE

ASHVALE GDNS

MERLIN GDNS

PORTMORE GDNS

PENNINGTON RD

VICTORIA AVE

CLOCKHOUSE LA

HIGHFIELD RD

MERLIN CL

Sch

School

Chase Cross

STAPLEFORD GDNS

LARCHWOOD AVE

DOMINION DR

School

LOWER BEDFORDS RD

School

UDALL GDNS

TURPIN AVE

JUDITH AVE

LYNWOOD DR

BURLAND RD

ASCENSION RD

FELSTEAD RD

CHASE CROSS RD

BELLE VUE RD

MOUNT PLEASANT RD

GALLEYWOOD

CHELMSFORD RD

HAVERING RD

CAMPBELL CL

NEVIS CL

2

Frinton Rd

TAYLORS

CARTER

SHEILA RD

RIVERSDALE RD

Collier Row

GABRIEL

GOBIONS AVE

BOWER CL

TWEED WAY

TOBIN

GARRY WAY

SPEY WAY

CREE WAY

Sunnyside Farm

HAMLET RD

DOWNHAM DR

RAMSDEN DR

EATON DR

B1459

PULLERS CL

BROCKLEY CRES

BERKELEY AVE

FAIRCROSS AVE

WILTON DR

LAWNS WAY

BARTLOW GDNS

THE BRIDE

MORAY WAY

GARRY CL

CH

HOG HILL RD

B174

COLLIER ROW RD

Liby

P

ERITH CRES

SELSDON

IRONS WAY

School

AYR GREEN

DEE WAY

Golf Course

91

REPULSE CL

LOWSHOE

HAZELL CRES

MELVILLE RD

PLAYFIELD AVE

COOK'S

Rise Park

TAY WAY

Sch

RENOWN

RAIDER CL

HOOD WLK

HULSE AVE

CLOVELLY GDNS

GORING

Recn Gd

HORNDON GREEN

HILLFOOT AVE

HORNDON RD

PETTITS LAN

DEVERON WAY

BEAULY WAY

A12(T)

WHITE HART LA

ELIZABETH CL

LYNTON AVE

COLLIER ROW LA

HILLFOOT RD

LONGVIEW WAY

WILLIAM C

HEATHER WAY

PETTITS BVD

EASTERN AVE

MILLBROOK GDNS

BROOK WAY

HOWARD

VICTORY WAY

RODNEY WAY

NELSON

ORCHARD RD

ELM

CHURCH

KENWAY

MOWBRAYS RD

HEATHER AVE

HEATHER DR

HEATHER GLEN

THE ELKINS

ROSLYN GDNS

NETHERPARK DR

PARKWAY

1

School

PEARTREE GDNS

ANSON CL

MANNEY RD

REDRIFF RD

BERNDALE

SAFFRON RD

PRIESTS LAN

ASHMOUR GDNS

PETTITS CL

PETTITS LA

Schs

Raphael Park

VANGUARD

BARRA CL

MANNEY

WALMER RD

DUNSTER CL

DOVER

B174

HANNAH CL

LINLEY CRES

OAKS AVE

ROSEDALE

B175

HAMILTON

A12(T)

Sch

TOMTAYNE AVE

MARSHALLS DR

MASBUTERS

PARKLAND AVE

RAPHAEL AVE

LAKE RISE

PARKWAY

90

49   D   50   E   51   F

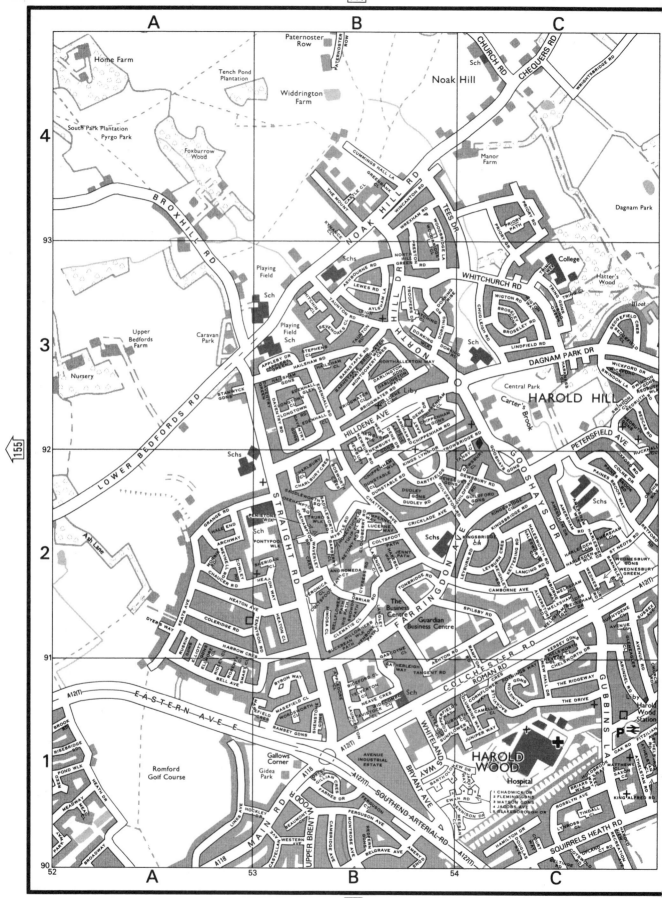

145
158
166

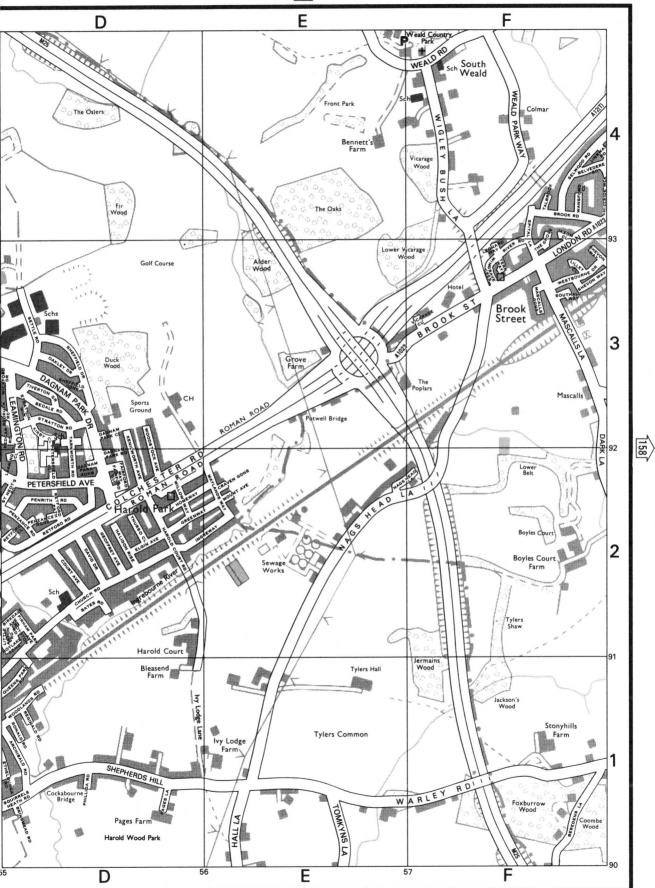

D E F

4

3

2

1

M25

The Osiers

Fir Wood

Golf Course

Schs

SETTLE RD

DAGNAM PARK DR

OAKLEY RD
SHEFFIELD DR
TIVERTON DR
BEDALE RD
STRATTON RD

LEAMINGTON RD

PETERSFIELD AVE

PENRITH RD

ST NEOTS RD
PENZANCE RD
RETFORD RD

COLCHESTER RD
ROMAN ROAD

Harold Park

CH

Duck Wood

Sports Ground

KENILWORTH AVE
DAGNAM PARK SQ
DAGNAM PARK CL

WOODS OCK AVE

CRAVEN GDNS
MAYLANDS WAY
MOUNT AVE

WILLOW WAY
HONEYWAY
GREENWAY
INGREWAY

Sch

COURT AVE
DAVID DR
GEOFFREY AVE
CHURCH RD
BATES RD
THURBO CL
ELGIN AVE
HALLION RISE

HAROLD COURT RD

Ingrebourne River

Harold Court

Bleasend Farm

Ivy Lodge Lane

Ivy Lodge Farm

WOODLANDS RD
REGINALD RD
RONALD RD
ARCHIBALD RD
ETHELBURGA RD

QUEENS PARK

SHEPHERDS HILL

Cockabourne Bridge

PHILLIPA RD
PAGES LA

Pages Farm

Harold Wood Park

SQUIRRELS HEATH RD
BRIDGEHEAD RD

HALL LA

TOMKYNS LA

Front Park

Bennett's Farm

The Oaks

Alder Wood

Grove Farm

Putwell Bridge

ROMAN ROAD

Sewage Works

NAGS HEAD LA

Tylers Hall

Tylers Common

WARLEY RD

Weald Country Park

WEALD RD

South Weald

Sch

Sch

WIGLEY BUSH LA

Vicarage Wood

Lower Vicarage Wood

Hotel

VICARAGE CL

BROOK ST

The Poplars

Colmar

WEALD PARK WAY

A1171

SELWOOD RD
BELVEDERE RD
WANSFORD CL
SPITAL LA
TALBROOK
THE DRIVE

LONDON RD A1023

River Rd
LEONARD WAY
DITCHFIELD WAY

NAGS HEAD LA

Brook Street

MASCALLS LA
MASCALLS GDNS

WESTBOURNE DR
SHEVON WAY
SOUTHALL WAY
LILLEY

DARK LA

Mascalls

Lower Belt

Boyles Court

Boyles Court Farm

Tylers Shaw

Jermains Wood

Jackson's Wood

Stonyhills Farm

Foxburrow Wood

Coombe Wood

BERDENS LA

M25

90

91

92

93

65 D 56 E 57 F

146

157

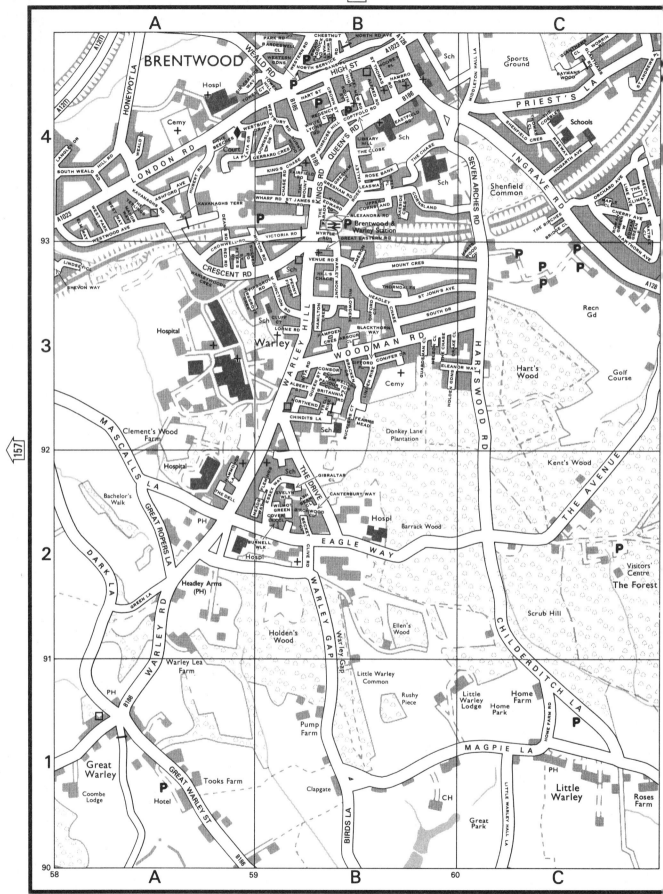

167

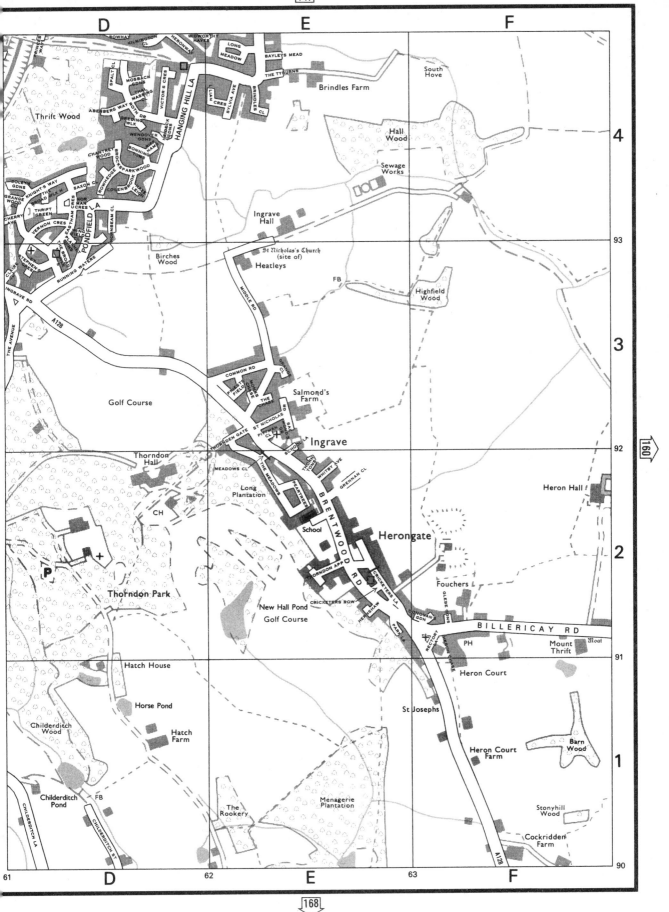

D   E   F

BOWHAY
KILMINGTON CL
HERONWAY
WIDWORTH HAYES
LONG MEADOW
BAYLEYS MEAD
THE TYBURNS

4

South Hove

Brindles Farm

Thrift Wood

SPALT CL
MOSBACH GDNS
SPRAT MASSING
VICTOR'S CRES
HANGING HILL LA
ABENBERG WAY
ROTH DR
BREDING WLK
WENDOVER GDNS
MERROCK GDNS
BONNINGHAM GDNS
CHANTREY WOOD
BROCK'S PARK WOOD
ROWREDGE

BRINDLES CL
SYLVIA AVE
LYTTI CRES

Hall Wood

Sewage Works

BOLEYN GDNS
KNIGHT'S WAY
GRANGE WOOD
BROAD WLK N
CHERRY LANE
THRIFT GREEN
VERNON CRES
THE BROAD
PONDFIELD LA
EASTHAM CRES
SAXON CL
NORMAN CRES
HORNBEAM CL
RUNNING WATERS

Ingrave Hall

Birches Wood

Heatleys

St Nicholas's Church (site of)

FB

Highfield Wood

93

INGRAVE RD

A128

THE AVENUE

Golf Course

MIDDLE RD

3

COMMON RD
PINNETTE FIELD
LUCAS CHASE
THE CHASE
ST NICHOLAS
PITMANS
THORNDEN GATE
HOOK LA
SCHOOL LA

Salmond's Farm

Ingrave

92

Thorndon Hall

MEADOWS CL
THE MEADOWS
HEARTREES
THORN POND
WHITBY AVE
GRENNAN CL
SA

Long Plantation

BRENTWOOD RD

Heron Hall

CH

School

Herongate

2

P

Thorndon Park

THORNDON APP
CRICKETERS LA
CRICKETERS ROW
HERONSHAW
PART LA

Fouchers

DONOVAN GDN
GLEBE GDNS

New Hall Pond Golf Course

RECTORY
HERON WAY
PH

BILLERICAY RD

Mount Thrift
Moat

91

Heron Court

Hatch House

Horse Pond

St Josephs

Childerditch Wood

Hatch Farm

Heron Court Farm

Barn Wood

1

CHILDERDITCH LA

Childerditch Pond

FB

CHILDERDITCH ST

The Rookery

Menagerie Plantation

Stonyhill Wood

Cockridden Farm

A128

90

61   D   62   E   63   F

148

159

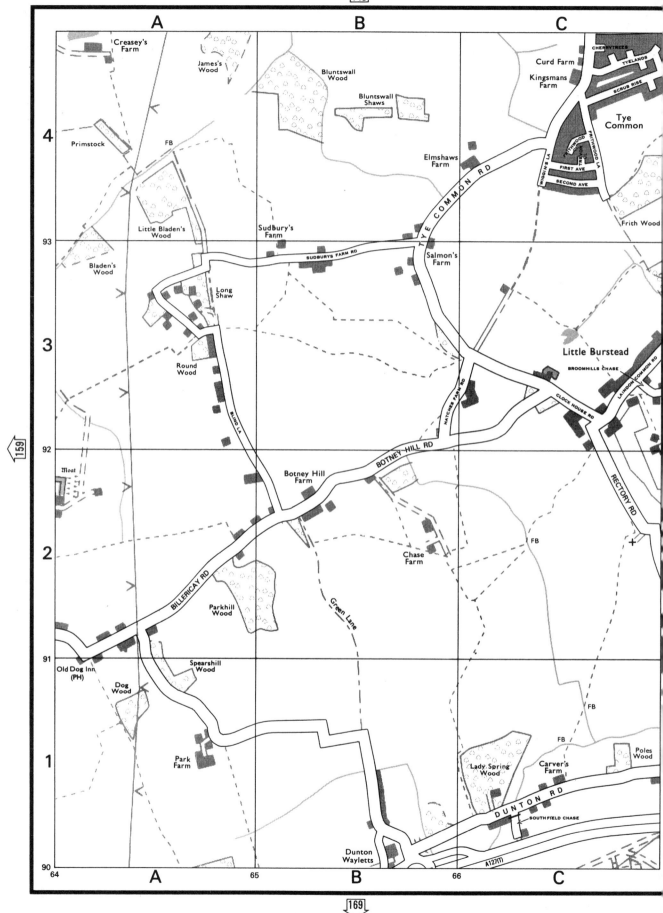

A   B   C

Creasey's Farm

James's Wood

Bluntswall Wood

Bluntswall Shaws

Curd Farm

Kingsmans Farm

CHERRYTREES

TYELANDS

SCRUB RISE

Tye Common

4

Primstock

FB

Elmshaws Farm

TITANWOOD

FRITHWOOD LA

FIRST AVE

SECOND AVE

WIGGINS LA

Frith Wood

Little Bladen's Wood

Sudbury's Farm

TYE COMMON RD

93

Bladen's Wood

SUDBURYS FARM RD

Salmon's Farm

Long Shaw

Little Burstead

BROOMHILLS CHASE

LAINDON COMMON RD

3

Round Wood

CLOCK HOUSE RD

BLIND LA

HATCHES FARM RD

92

Moat

BOTNEY HILL RD

RECTORY RD

Botney Hill Farm

FB

X

2

BILLERICAY RD

Chase Farm

FB

Parkhill Wood

Green Lane

91

Old Dog Inn (PH)

Spearshill Wood

Dog Wood

FB

FB

1

Park Farm

Lady Spring Wood

Carver's Farm

Poles Wood

DUNTON RD

SOUTHFIELD CHASE

Dunton Wayletts

A127(T)

90

64   A   65   B   66   C

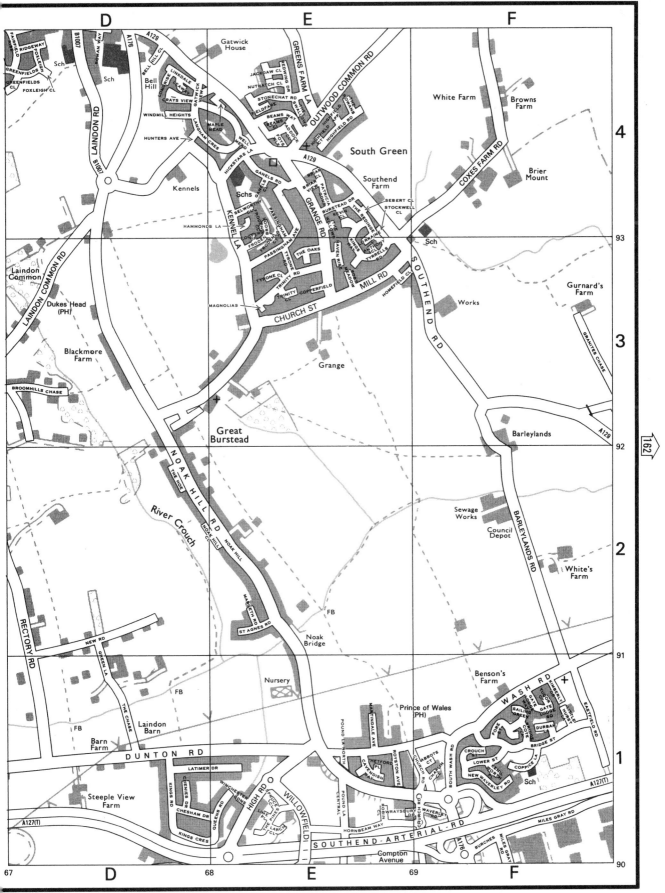

D
E
F

4

White Farm
Browns Farm

Gatwick House

Greens Farm La
Outwood Common Rd

Bell Hill

Jackdaw Cl
Redwing Dr
Stonechat Rd
Swallow
Nuthatch Cl
Feldfare
Beams Way
Beams

Windmill Heights
Maple Head

Hunters Ave

Langham Cres

Hickstars La

South Green

A129

Southend Farm

Coxes Farm Rd

Brier Mount

Kennels

Schs

Selworthy
Hammonds La

Kennel La

Ganels Rd

Grange Rd

Sebert Cl
Stockwell Cl

Sch

93

Laindon Common

Laindon Common Rd

The Oaks
Passingham Ave
Tyrone
Tyrone Cl
Trinity Rd
Trinity
Copperfield
Magnolias

Church St

Aven Rise
Kings
Meadow
Tyrells

Mill Rd

Homefield Rd

Works

Southend Rd

Gurnard's Farm

Granites Chase

3

Dukes Head (PH)

Blackmore Farm

Grange

Broomhills Chase

Great Burstead

Barleylands

A129

92

162

River Crouch

Noak Hill Rd
The Hob

Noak Hill

Sewage Works

Council Depot

Barleylands Rd

White's Farm

2

Rectory Rd

Margeth Rd
St Agnes Rd

New Rd

Green La

FB

Noak Bridge

FB

91

Benson's Farm

Wash Rd

Kimberley

Sailing Green
Fore St
Tulip
Gate
Dodge
Gate
Cotts

Eastfield Rd

Durban

The Chase

Laindon Barn

FB

Nursery

Prince of Wales (PH)

Martingale Ave

Pound La North

Crouch
Lower St
Kenil
New Waverley Rd
Coppice La

Bridge St

Sch

Barn Farm

Dunton Rd

Latimer Dr

Winchester Gdns

High Rd

Willowfield

Pound La Central

Thetford
Royston Ave
Clavendish
Cavendish
Pl
Abbots Ct
Church Rd
Chafua
South Wash Rd

Waverley Rd

1

Steeple View Farm

Kings Rd
Chesham Dr
Glenties Dr
Queens Rd
Kings Cres

The Pines
The Larch Cl

Hornbeam Way

Southend-Arterial-Rd

Wraysbury Dr
Robin

A176
Burches Rd
Miles Gray Rd

A127(T)

Compton Avenue

A127(T)

90

67
D
68
E
69
F

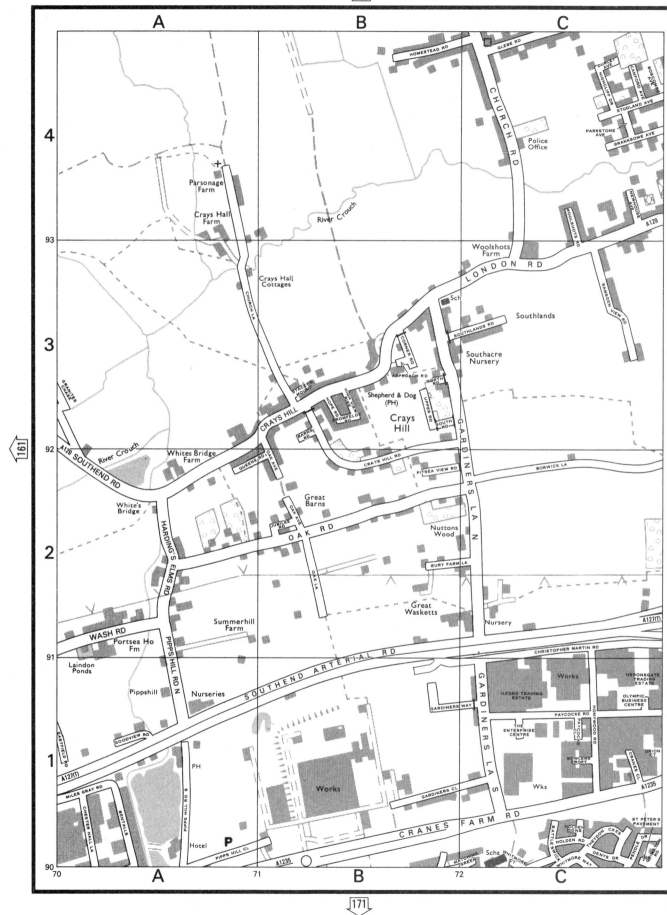

A   B   C

4

Parsonage Farm

Crays Hall Farm

River Crouch

93

Crays Hall Cottages

HOMESTEAD RD

GLEBE RD

CHURCH RD

Police Office

DURLEY AVE

HIGHCLIFF DR

CANFORD AVE

BOSCOMBE

STUDLAND AVE

PARKSTONE AVE

BRANKSOME AVE

NEWHOUSE

A129

WOOLSHOTS RD

Woolshots Farm

LONDON RD

RAMSDEN VIEW RD

Sch

Southlands

SOUTHLANDS RD

Southacre Nursery

3

CHURCH LA

GRANGE FARM

CRAYS HILL

STACEYS MOUNT

CORNER RD

APPROACH RD

NORTH RD

Shepherd & Dog (PH)

HIGH VIEW

UPPER RD

SOUTH RD

Crays Hill

GARDINERS LAN

161

92

A129 SOUTHEND RD

River Crouch

Whites Bridge Farm

HOPE RD

BROMFELD

BARNS RD

QUEENS RD

OAK AVE

Crays Hill Rd

CRAYS HILL RD

PITSEA VIEW RD

BORWICK LA

White's Bridge

Great Barns

JUBILEE RD

OAK AVE

OAK RD

Nuttons Wood

2

HARDING'S ELMS RD

OAK LA

BURY FARM LA

Summerhill Farm

Great Wasketts

Nursery

A127(T)

WASH RD

Portsea Ho Fm

PIPPS HILL RD N

91

Laindon Ponds

Pippshill

Nurseries

SOUTHEND ARTERIAL RD

CHRISTOPHER MARTIN RD

GARDINERS LANS

ILFORD TRADING ESTATE

Works

HERONSGATE TRADING ESTATE

OLYMPIC BUSINESS CENTRE

GARDINERS WAY

THE ENTERPRISE CENTRE

PAYCOCKE RD

HONYWOOD RD

PAYCOCKE

GOODVIEW RD

EASTFIELD RD

1

A127(T)

PH

BOWLERS CROFT

CRANES CL

ORION CT

A1235

MILES GRAY RD

CHESTER HALL LA

BENTALLS

PIPPS HILL RD S

Works

GARDINERS CL

Wks

CRANES FARM RD

Hotel

P

PIPPS HILL CL

A1235

Schs

MATCHING GREEN

WHITMORE CT

ST PETER'S PAVEMENT

HOLDEN GDNS

BATTLE SWICK

HOLDEN RD

THEYDON CRES

DENYS DR

PENDLE DR

WHITMORE WAY

90

70   A   71   B   72   C

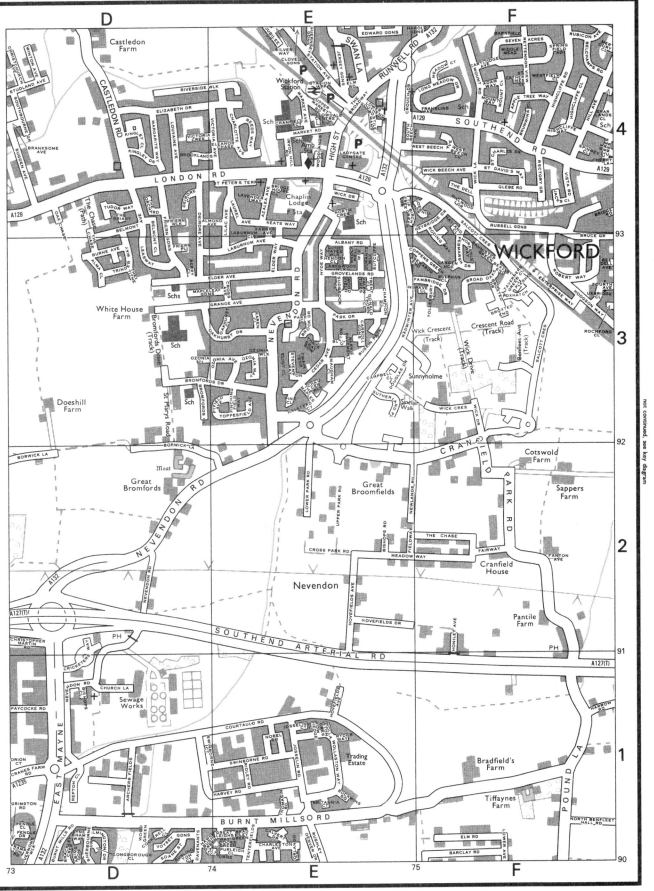

WICKFORD

not continued, see key diagram

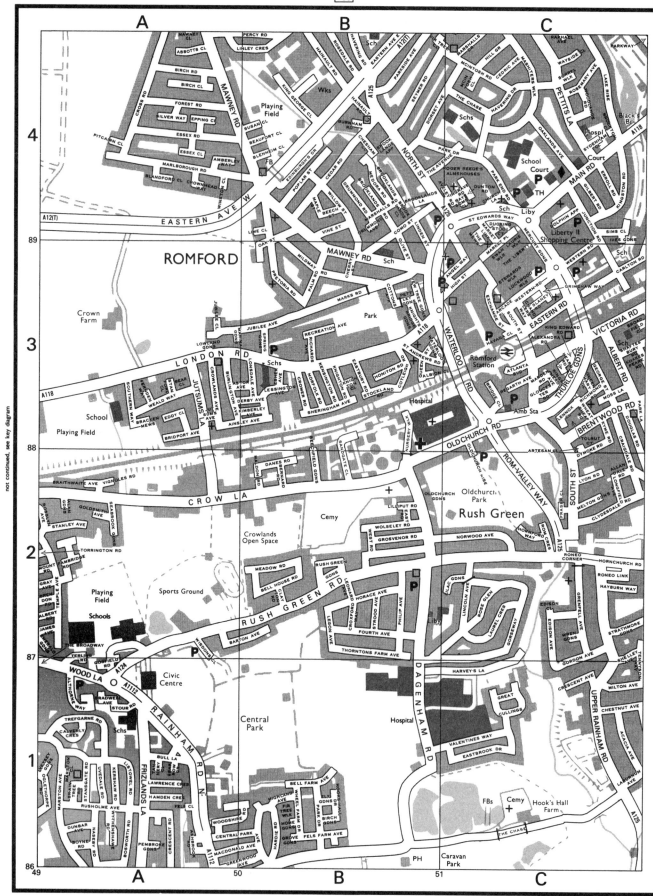

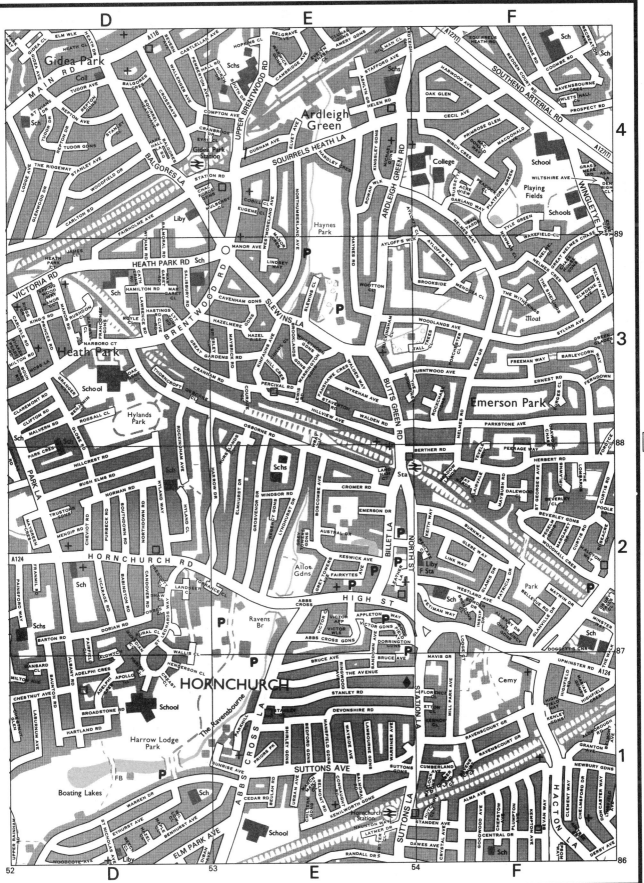

157

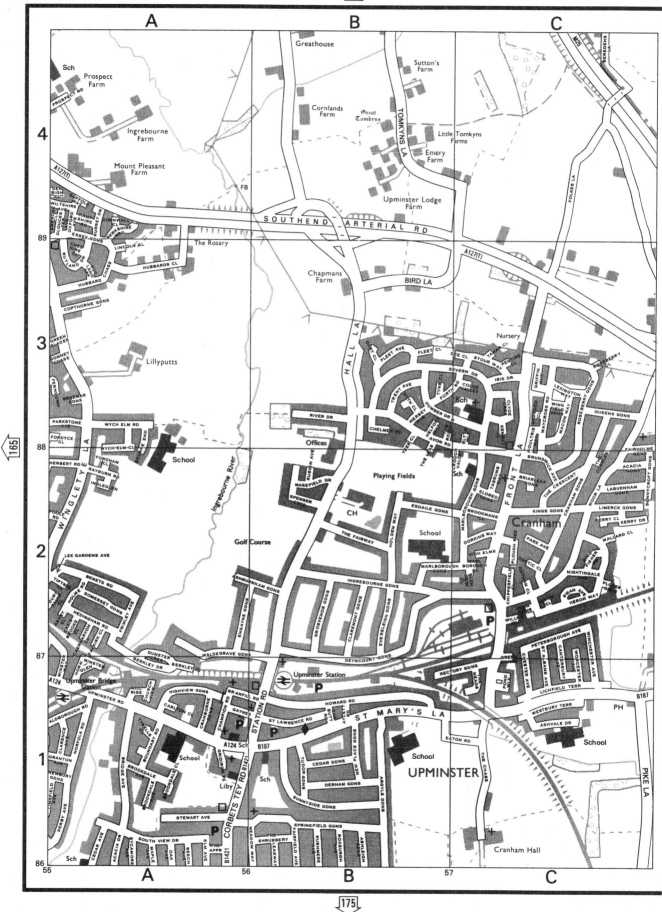

165

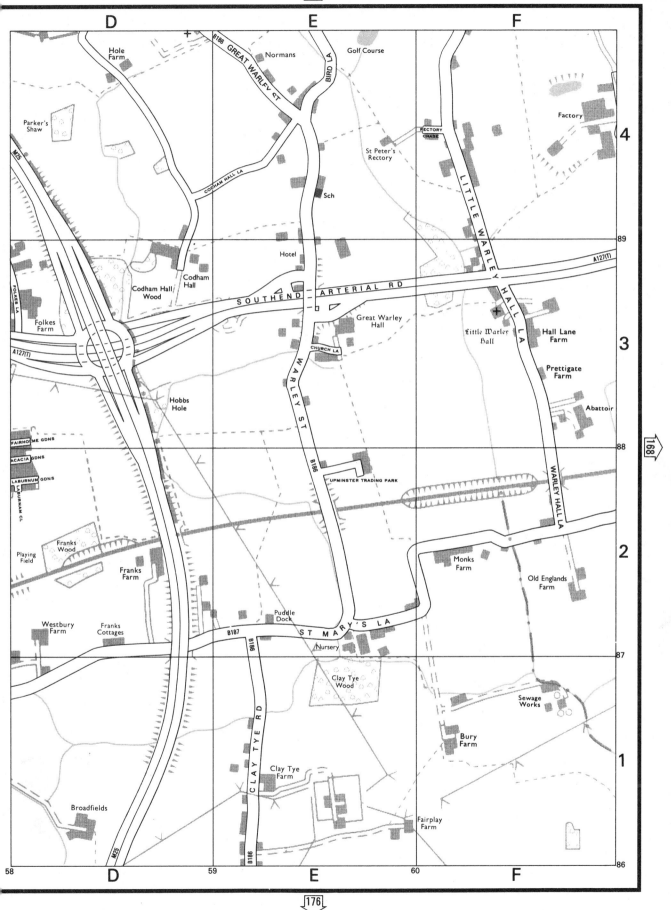

D E F

Hole Farm

Normans

B186

GREAT WARLEY ST

BIRD LA

Golf Course

Parker's Shaw

RECTORY CHASE

Factory

4

St Peter's Rectory

Sch

LITTLE WARLEY HALL LA

89

M25

Hotel

SOUTHEND ARTERIAL RD

A127(T)

168

Codham Hall Wood

Codham Hall

Great Warley Hall

Little Warley Hall

Hall Lane Farm

FOLKES LA

Folkes Farm

CHURCH LA

WARLEY ST

WARLEY HALL LA

Prettigate Farm

3

A127(T)

Hobbs Hole

Abattoir

FAIRHOLME GDNS

88

ACACIA GDNS

B186

LABURNUM GDNS

UPMINSTER TRADING PARK

LABURNAM CL

Playing Field

Franks Wood

Monks Farm

2

Franks Farm

Old Englands Farm

Westbury Farm

Franks Cottages

Puddle Dock

B187

B186

ST MARY'S LA

Nursery

87

Clay Tye Wood

Sewage Works

CLAY TYE RD

Bury Farm

1

Clay Tye Farm

Broadfields

Fairplay Farm

M25

B186

86

58 D 59 E 60 F

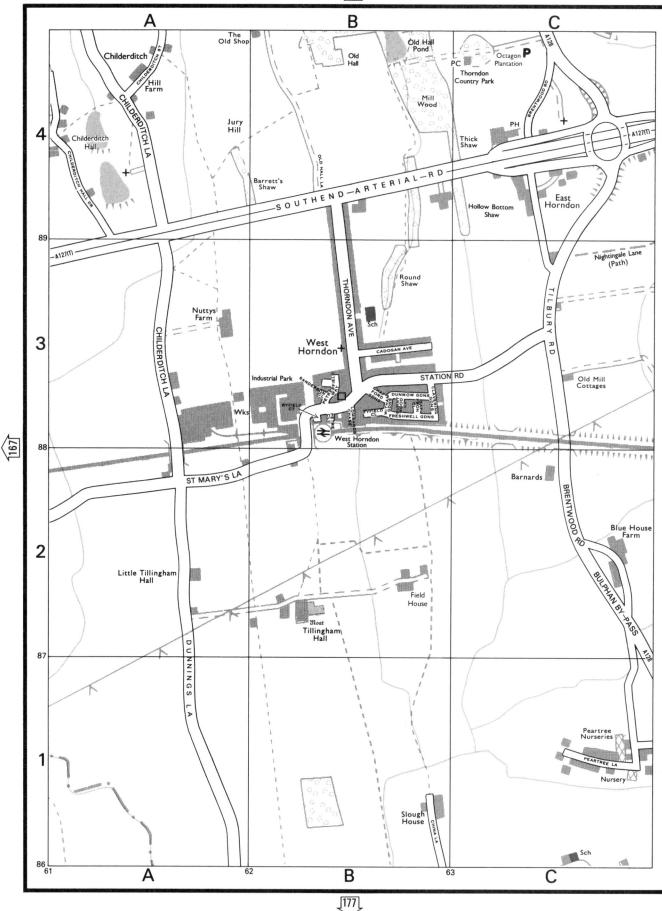

A · B · C

Childerditch

CHILDERDITCH ST

Hill Farm

The Old Shop

Old Hall

Old Hall Pond

PC

Octagon Plantation

P

A128

Thorndon Country Park

Mill Wood

Jury Hill

Childerditch Hall

CHILDERDITCH LA

CHILDERDITCH HALL DR

Thick Shaw

PH

BRENTWOOD RD

A127(T)

4

Barrett's Shaw

OLD HALL LA

SOUTHEND—ARTERIAL—RD

Hollow Bottom Shaw

East Horndon

89

A127(T)

Nightingale Lane (Path)

THORNDON AVE

Round Shaw

TILBURY RD

Nuttys Farm

CHILDERDITCH LA

West Horndon

Sch

CADOGAN AVE

3

Industrial Park

STATION RD

Old Mill Cottages

SANDERSON

PETREFIELD

BYFIELD CT

CHAPEL LODGE

DUNMOW GDNS

CLAYTON GDNS

Wks

OLD PARK CRES

FRESHWELL GDNS

West Horndon Station

88

ST MARY'S LA

Barnards

BRENTWOOD RD

Blue House Farm

2

Little Tillingham Hall

DUNNINGS LA

Field House

Moat

Tillingham Hall

BULPHAN BY-PASS

A128

87

Peartree Nurseries

PEARTREE LA

1

Nursery

Slough House

CHINA LA

Sch

86

61 · A · 62 · B · 63 · C

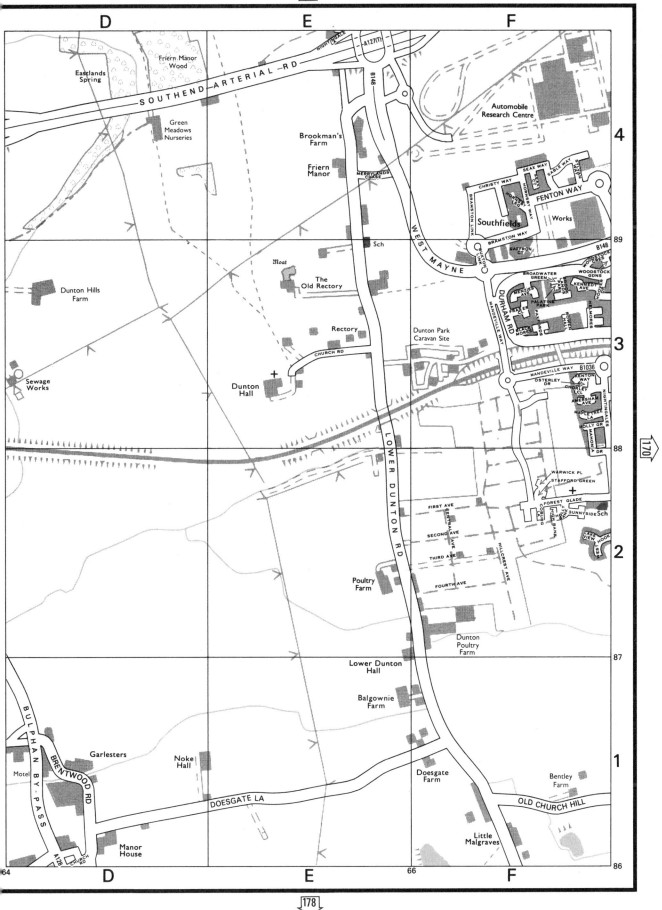

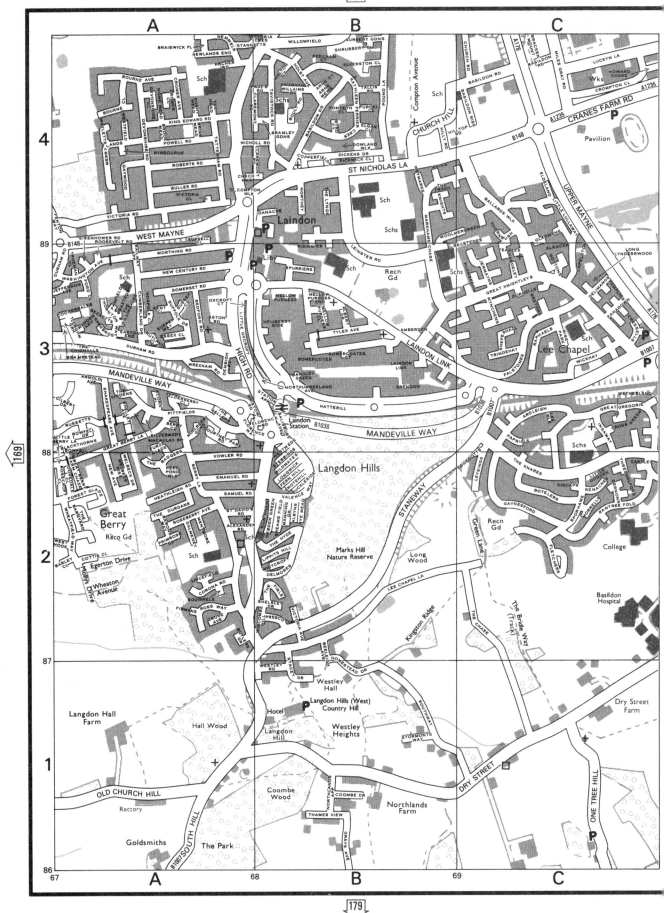

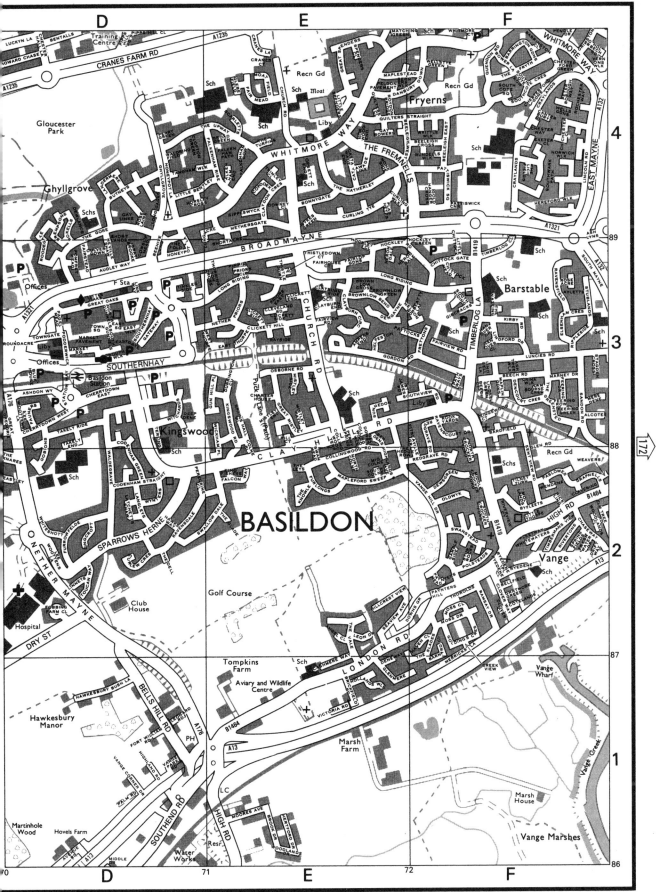

BASILDON

171

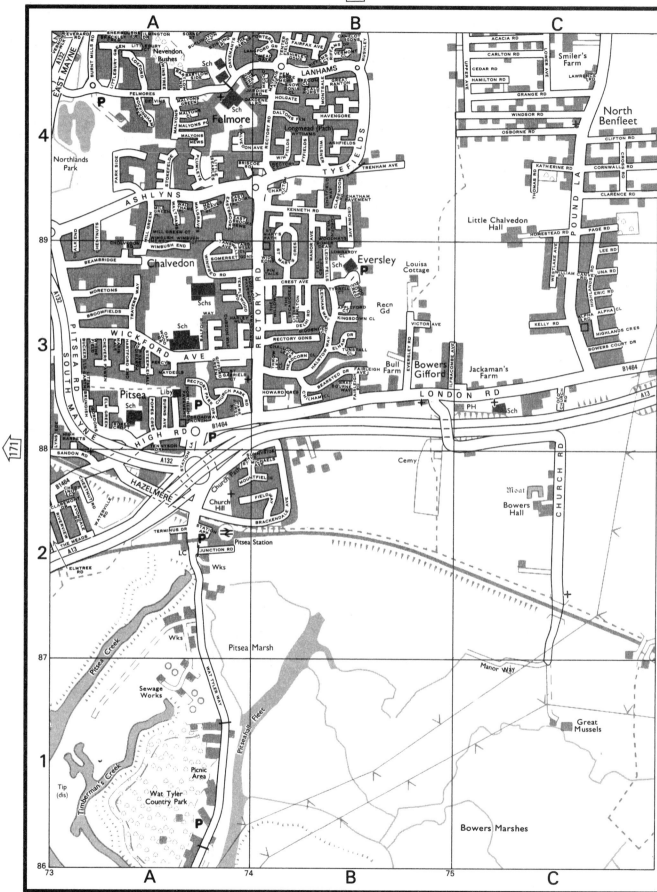

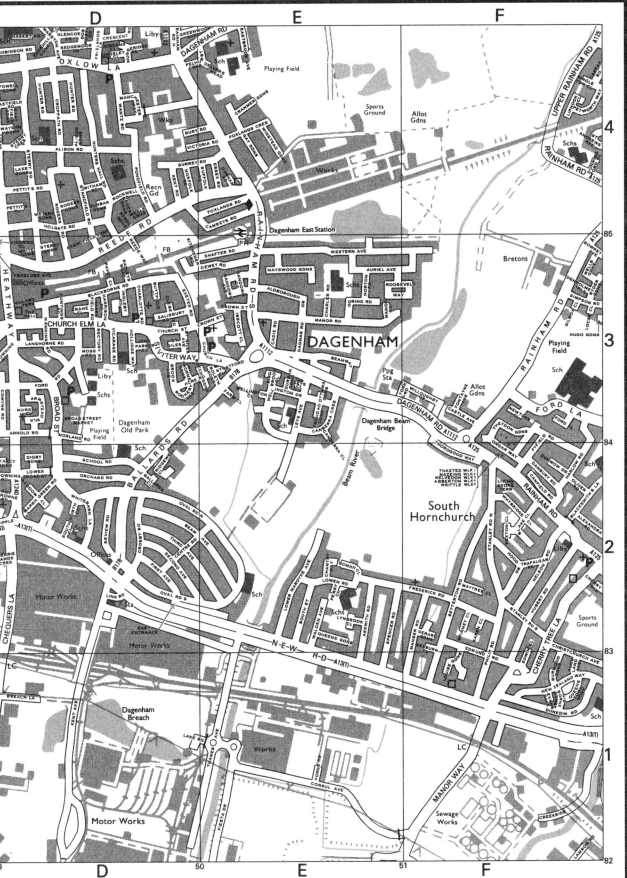

D E F

4

85

3

174

84

2

83

1

82

9 D 50 E 51 F

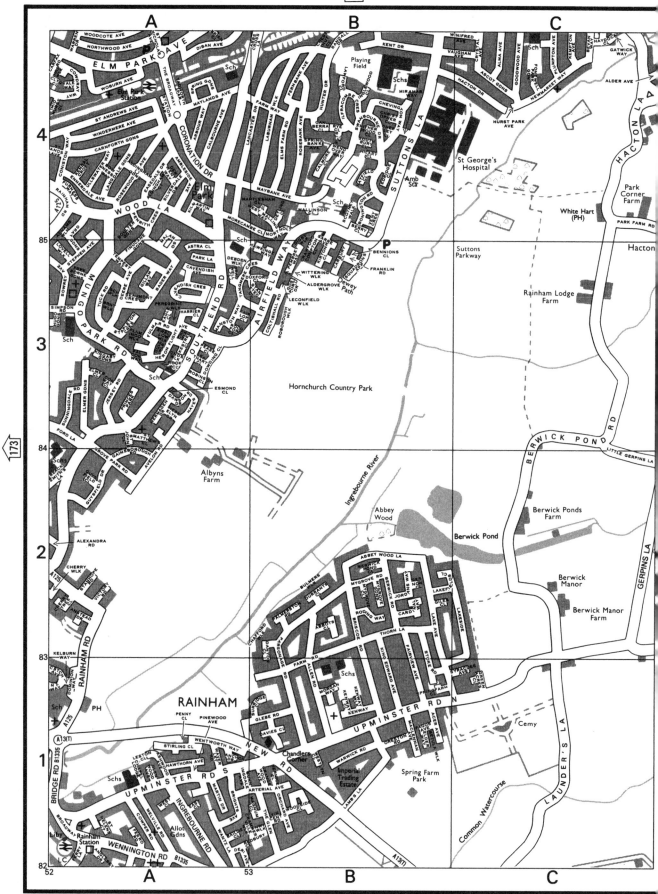

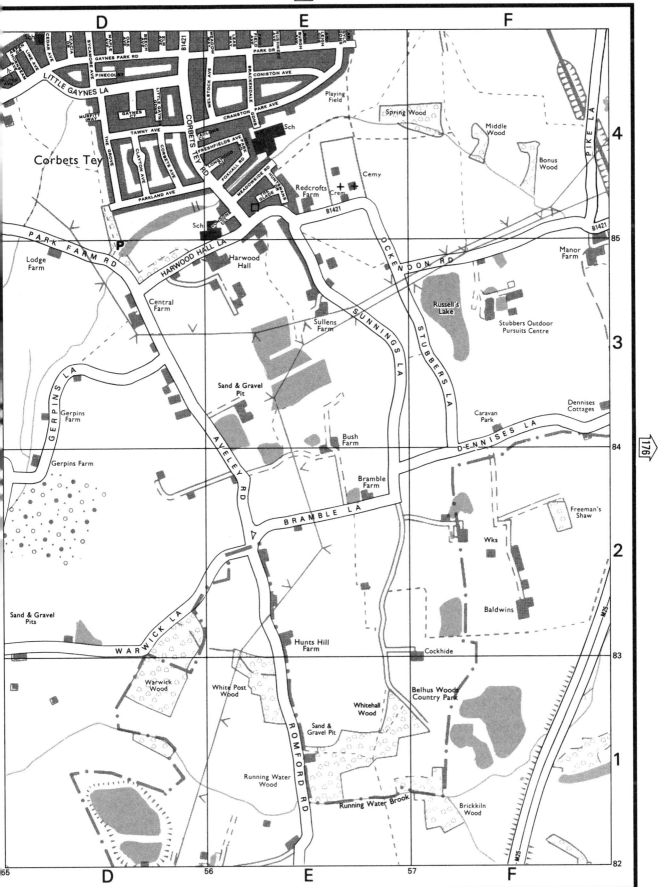

D E F

4

Little Gaynes La

Corbets Tey

Spring Wood

Middle Wood

Bonus Wood

Pike La

Playing Field

Sch

Cemy

Redcrofts Farm

Crem

B1421

Manor Farm

B1421

85

Park Farm Rd

Lodge Farm

Harwood Hall La

Harwood Hall

Ockendon Rd

Russell's Lake

Stubbers Outdoor Pursuits Centre

3

Central Farm

Sullens Farm

Sunnings La

Stubbers La

Gerpins La

Gerpins Farm

Sand & Gravel Pit

Caravan Park

Dennises Cottages

Dennises La

84

1176

Gerpins Farm

Aveley Rd

Bush Farm

Bramble Farm

Freeman's Shaw

Wks

2

Sand & Gravel Pits

Warwick La

Bramble La

Baldwins

M25

Warwick Wood

Hunts Hill Farm

Cockhide

83

White Post Wood

Whitehall Wood

Belhus Woods Country Park

Romford Rd

Sand & Gravel Pit

1

Running Water Wood

Running Water Brook

Brickkiln Wood

M25

82

D E F

55 56 57

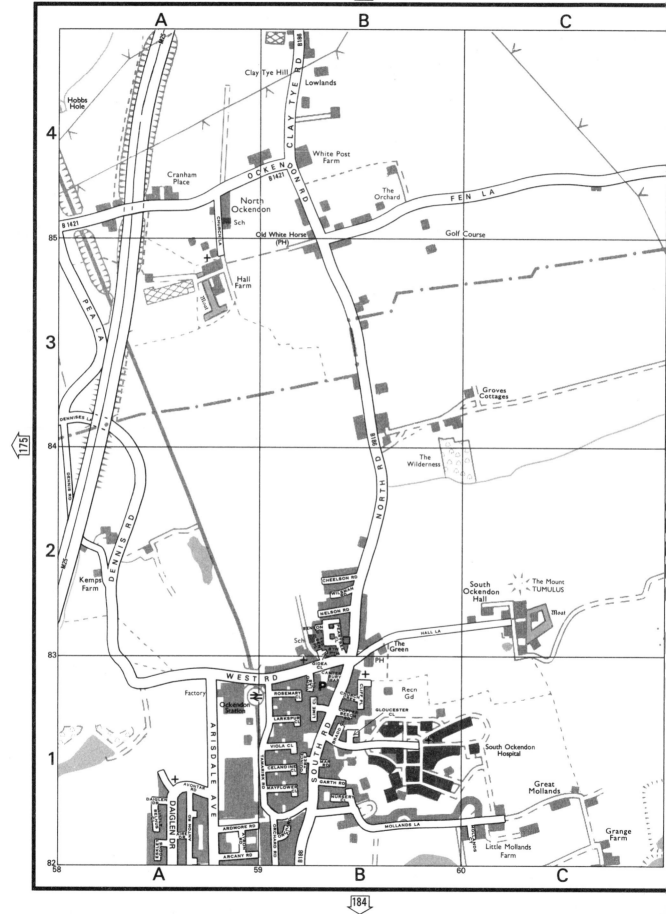

A B C

Hobbs Hole

Clay Tye Hill

Lowlands

B186

CLAY TYE RD

Cranham Place

OCKENDON RD

White Post Farm

B1421

North Ockendon

Sch

The Orchard

FEN LA

B 1421

Old White Horse (PH)

Golf Course

PEA LA

Hall Farm

Moat

DENNISES LA

The Wilderness

Groves Cottages

DENNIS RD

NORTH RD

B186

M25

Kemps Farm

DENNIS RD

CHEELSON RD

WILSMAN

South Ockendon Hall

The Mount TUMULUS

Moat

NELSON RD

BENTON

PEA CL

Sch

HALL LA

The Green

PH

GIDEA CL

WEST RD

CANTER BURY RD

Factory

ARISDALE AVE

Ockendon Station

ROSEMARY

P

CLIFF PL

Recn Gd

Cl

LIME CL

COPPER BEECH

CHURCH CRES

LARKSPUR

BRADO

GLOUCESTER CL

South Ockendon Hospital

VIOLA CL

SOUTH RD

TAMARISK RD

CELANDINE

QUINCE RD

MAR RD

Great Mollands

DAIGLEN DR

AVONTAR RD

MAYFLOWER CL

GARTH RD

DAIGLEN DR

NOLAN RD

ORCHARD RD

NURSERY RD

ESSEX GDNS

BELHUS

ARDMORE RD

AXON RD

B186

MOLLANDS LA

MOLLANDS CL

Little Mollands Farm

Grange Farm

ARCANY RD

A B C

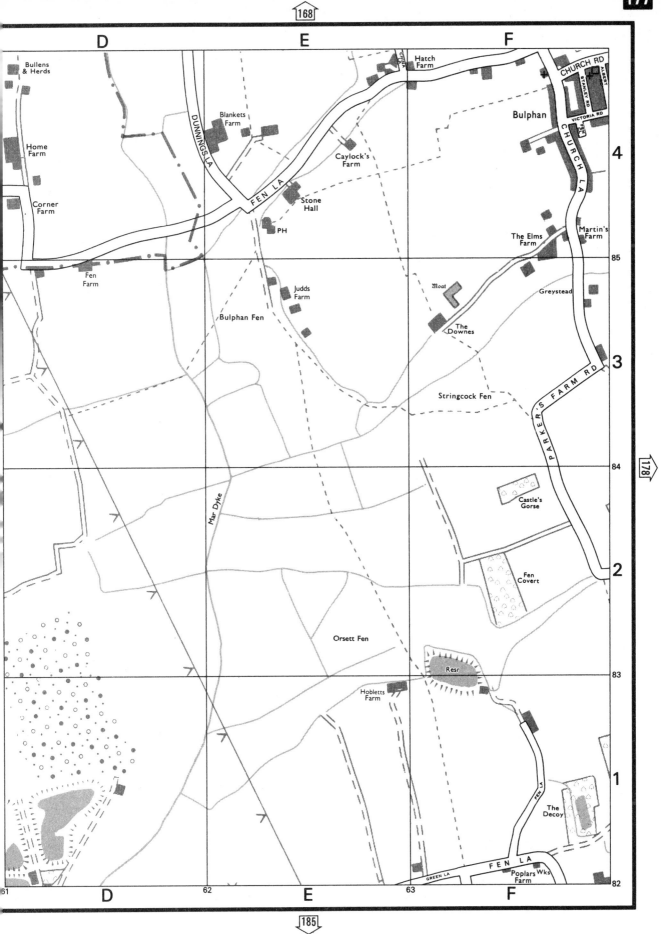

D E F

Bullens & Herds

Home Farm

Corner Farm

DUNNINGS LA

Blankets Farm

FEN LA

Caylock's Farm

Stone Hall

PH

Fen Farm

Judds Farm

Bulphan Fen

Hatch Farm

CHURCH RD

STANLEY RD

ALBERT RD

VICTORIA RD

Bulphan

FEN

CHURCH LA

The Elms Farm

Martin's Farm

Moat

Greystead

The Downes

Stringcock Fen

PARKER'S FARM RD

4

85

3

84

Mar Dyke

Castle's Gorse

Fen Covert

2

Orsett Fen

Resr

83

Hobletts Farm

1

FEN LA

The Decoy

82

FEN LA

GREEN LA

Poplars Farm

Wks

61 62 63

D E F

178

169
177

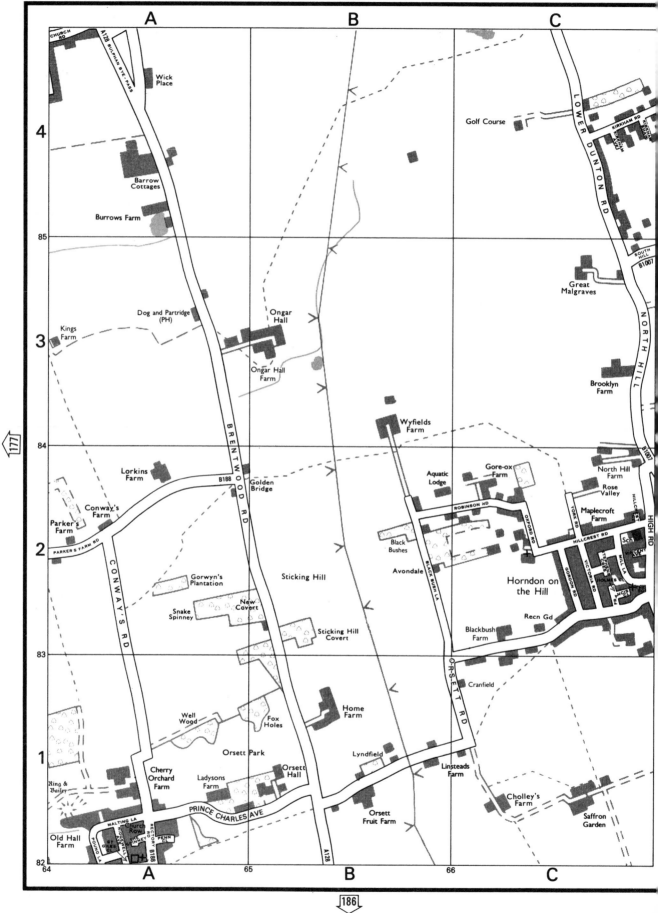

CHURCH RD

A128 BULPHAN BYE-PASS

Wick Place

A

B

C

4

Barrow Cottages

Burrows Farm

Golf Course

LOWER DUNTON RD

KIRKHAM RD

85

SOUTH HILL

B1007

Kings Farm

Dog and Partridge (PH)

Ongar Hall

Great Malgraves

3

Ongar Hall Farm

Brooklyn Farm

NORTH HILL

B1007

Lorkins Farm

BRENTWOOD RD

Wyfields Farm

84

Conway's Farm

B188

Golden Bridge

Aquatic Lodge

Gore-ox Farm

North Hill Farm

Rose Valley

Parker's Farm

PARKER'S FARM RD

ROBINSON RD

Maplecroft Farm

HILLCREST RD

HIGH RD

Sch

2

CONWAY'S RD

Gorwyn's Plantation

Sticking Hill

Black Bushes

Avondale

BLACK BUSH LA

OXFORD RD

YORK RD

Horndon on the Hill

HILL LA

GORDON RD

VICTORIA RD

HOLMES

Snake Spinney

New Covert

Sticking Hill Covert

Blackbush Farm

Recn Gd

83

ORSETT RD

Cranfield

Well Wood

Fox Holes

Home Farm

Lyndfield

Linsteads Farm

Cholley's Farm

1

Orsett Park

Cherry Orchard Farm

Ladysons Farm

Orsett Hall

Orsett Fruit Farm

Saffron Garden

Ring & Bailey

PRINCE CHARLES AVE

MALTING LA

Church Row

RIDGEWELL

ST GILES LA

RECTORY B188

PENN

POUND LA

Old Hall Farm

82

64

A

65

B

A128

66

C

186

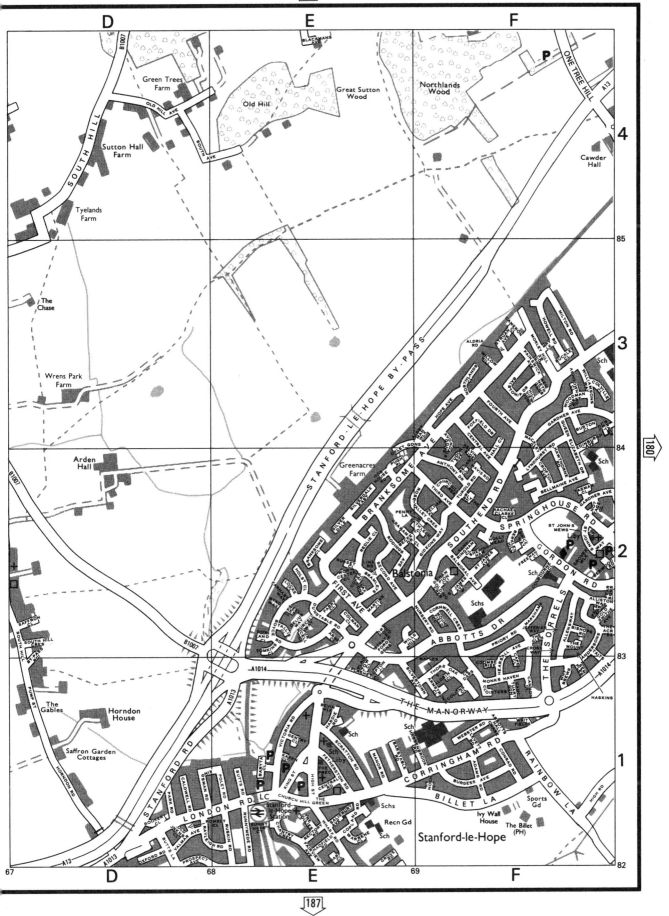

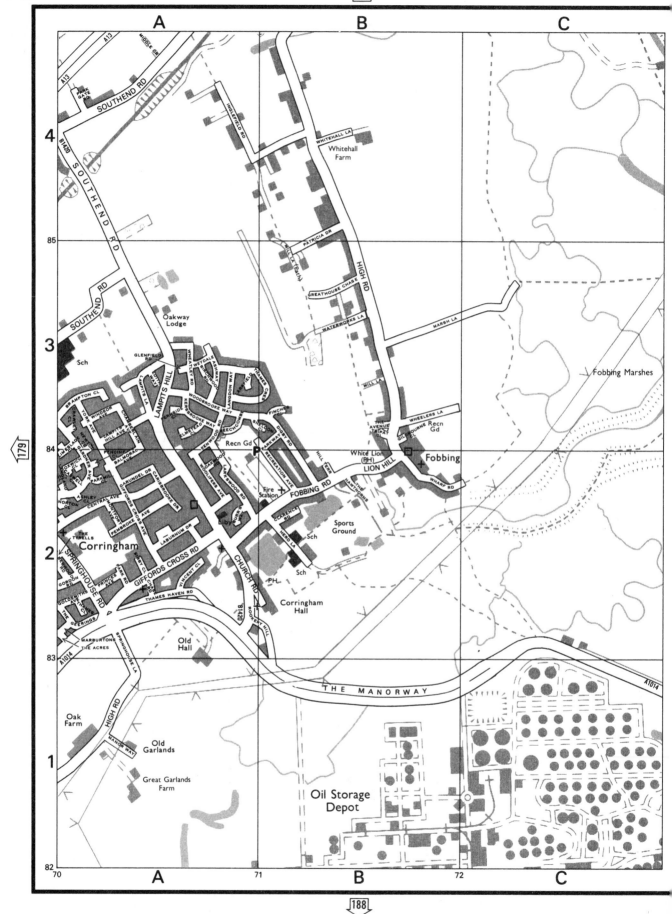

171

A   B   C

A13
MIDDLE RD
PARK GATE RD
SOUTHEND RD

INGLEFIELD RD

WHITEHALL LA

Whitehall
Farm

4

B1420

SOUTHEND RD

PATRICIA DR

MILL LA (Path)

HIGH RD

85

SOUTHEND RD

GREATHOUSE CHASE

WATERWORKS LA

MARSH LA

Oakway
Lodge

MILL LA

Fobbing Marshes

3

Sch

GLENFIELD RD

LAMPITS HILL
WHEATLEY RD
ASHWOOD WAY
LANGDON AVE
THAMES DR
WEYDALE

BRAMPTON CL
CRAMEL WAY
WINDSOR RD
CHURCHILL RD
WOODBROOKE WAY
LAMPITS LA
KELVEDON WAY
BEECHCOMBE
FINCHES

WHEELERS LA

Recn
Gd

THE
AVENUE

4

IMPERIAL
YORK AVE
WOOSTER AVE
LAMPITS HILL
PENDING RD
ELMSTEAD
KENWOOD RD
DIGBY RD
PARKWAY
SHELDON
CROSS

Recn Gd
P

RECREATION AVE

GILLOURNE
CL

White Lion
(PH)
LION HILL
Fobbing

NORWICH
IPSWICH
AVE
PARK HILL
BALMORAL
BARUNDEL DR
CHRISTOPHER DR
WOODFORD
CARLSWOOD RD
CRESBROOKE DR

HILL TERR

THE HAWTHORNS

WHARF RD

ASHLEY
NORTON RD
CENTRAL AVE
CLIFFORD AVE
PEMBROKE AVE
LABURNUM DR

Fire
Station

FOBBING RD

Sports
Ground

THE TYRELLS

Liby

CLARENCE RD
NERO LA

Sch

Corringham

2

SPRINGHOUSE RD
GORDON
GOLDSMITHS AVE
VISTA
PRINCES AVE
PARK AVE
WEST CL
VINCENT CL
GIFFORDS CROSS RD

CHURCH RD
B1420

Sch

PH

THE
GEERINGS

THAMES HAVEN RD

ROOKERY HILL

Corringham
Hall

WARBURTONS
THE ACRES

SPRINGHOUSE LA

Old
Hall

83

A1014

THE MANORWAY

A1014

Oak
Farm

HIGH RD

MANOR WAY

Old
Garlands

1

Great Garlands
Farm

Oil Storage
Depot

82

70   A   71   B   72   C

179

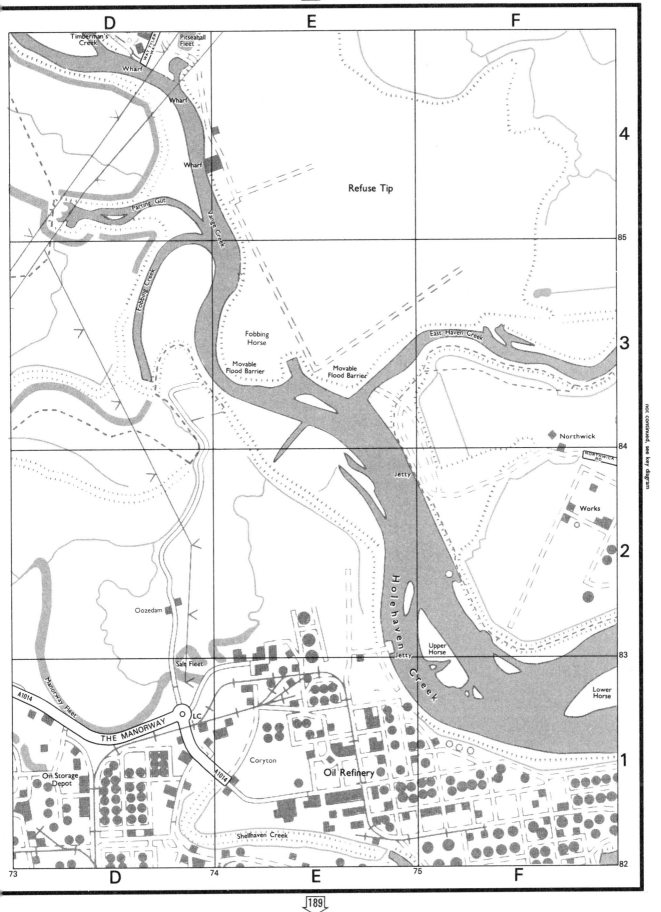

D   E   F

Timberman's Creek

Pitseahall Fleet

WAT TYLER

Wharf

Wharf

Wharf

Parting Gut

Vange Creek

Fobbing Creek

Refuse Tip

4

85

Fobbing Horse

Movable Flood Barrier

Movable Flood Barrier

East Haven Creek

3

84

Northwick

NORTHWICK RD

Jetty

Works

2

Holehaven Creek

Upper Horse

83

Jetty

Oozedam

Lower Horse

Salt Fleet

Manorway Fleet

A1014

THE MANORWAY

LC

A1014

Coryton

Oil Refinery

1

Oil Storage Depot

Shellhaven Creek

82

73   D   74   E   75   F

not continued, see key diagram

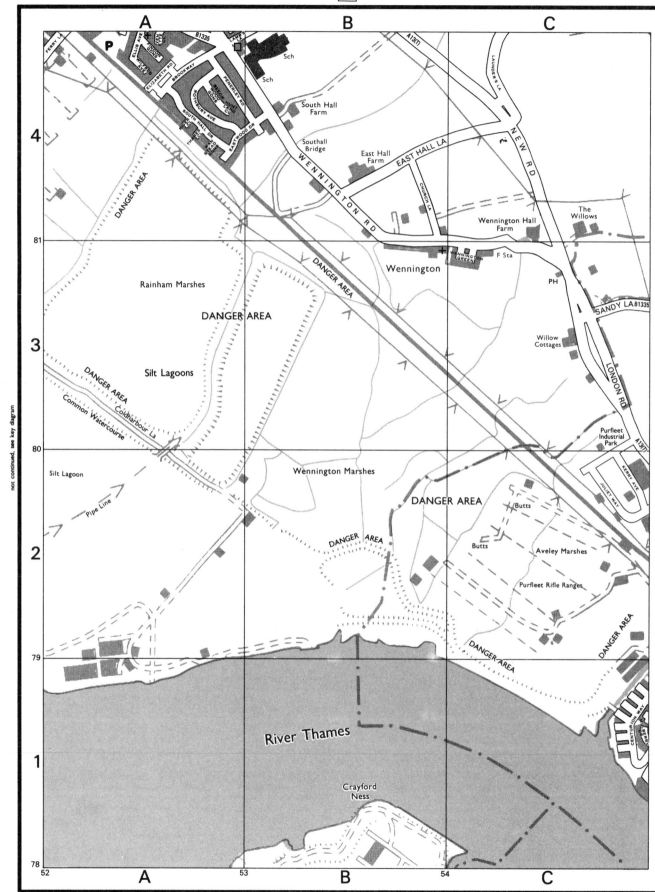

A B C

not continued, see key diagram

FERRY LA
ELLIS AVE
ELIZABETH RD
VEN BELL
CHURCH GONG
BROOKWAY
PENERLEY RD
ROTHBURY AVE
SOUTH HALL DRO
EASTWOOD DR
B1335
LAWRS
P
Sch
Sch

South Hall
Farm

A13(T)

LAUNDER'S LA

NEW RD

4

Southall
Bridge

East Hall
Farm

EAST HALL LA

CHURCH LA

Wennington Hall
Farm

The
Willows

WENNINGTON RD

DANGER AREA

81

Rainham Marshes

DANGER AREA

Wennington

WENNINGTON GREEN

F Sta

PH

SANDY LA B1335

DANGER AREA

Willow
Cottages

LONDON RD

3

Silt Lagoons

DANGER AREA

Coldharbour La

Common Watercourse

Purfleet
Industrial
Park

A13(T)

80

Silt Lagoon

Wennington Marshes

DANGER AREA

Butts

KERRY AVE

JULIET WAY

Pipe Line

DANGER AREA

Butts

Aveley Marshes

2

Purfleet Rifle Ranges

DANGER AREA

DANGER AREA

79

CENTURION WAY

River Thames

1

Crayford
Ness

78
52 A 53 B 54 C

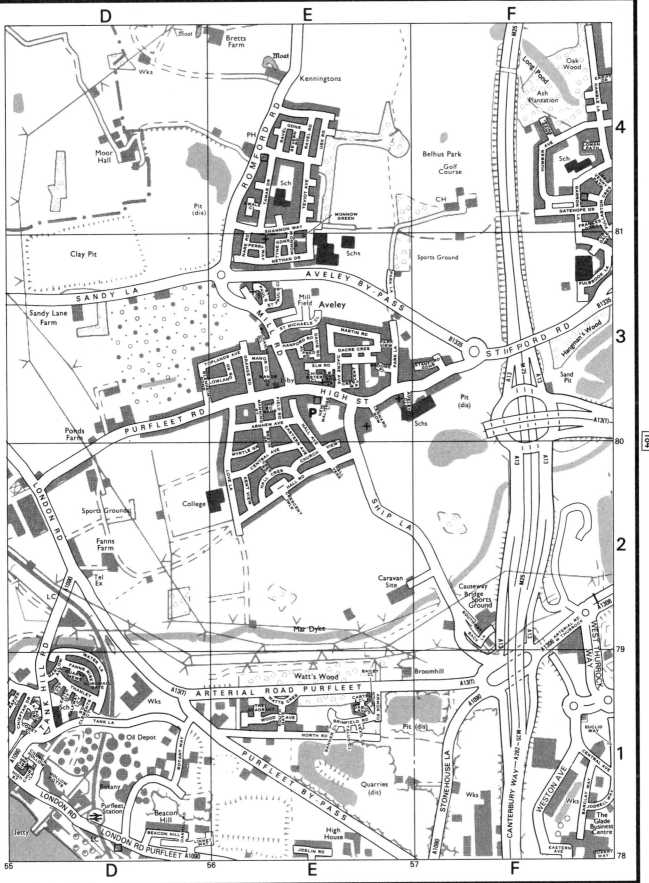

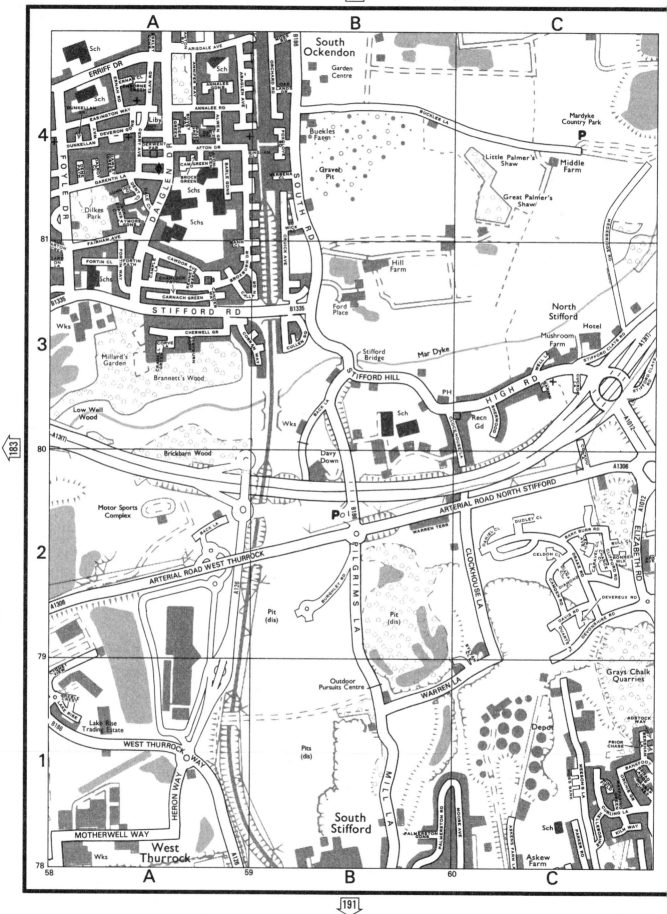

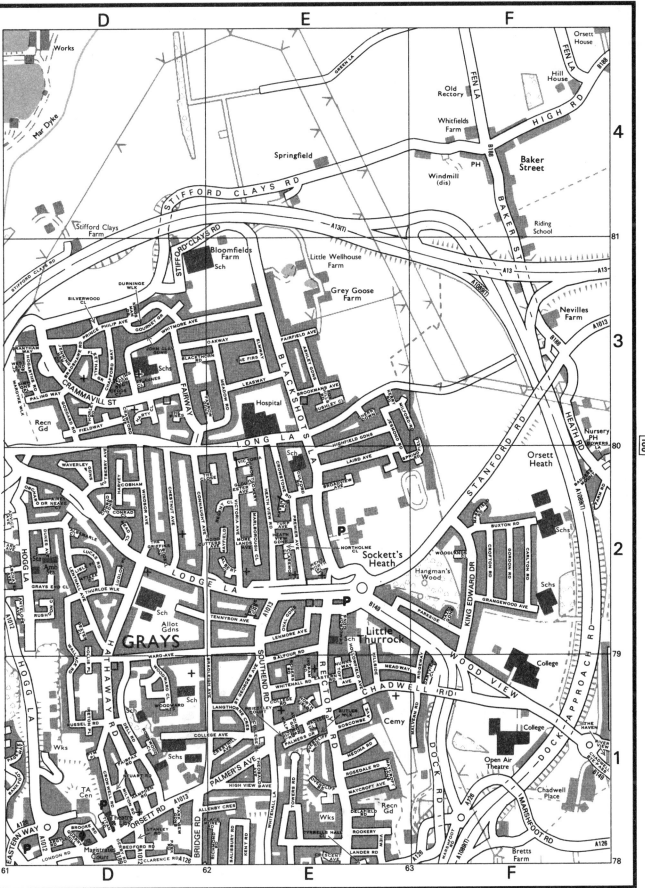

186

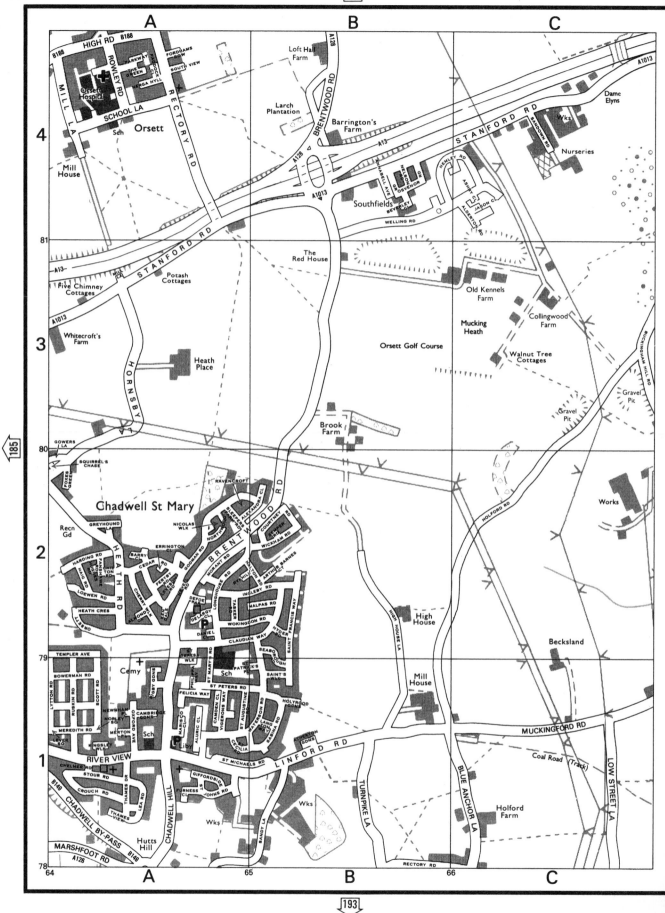

185

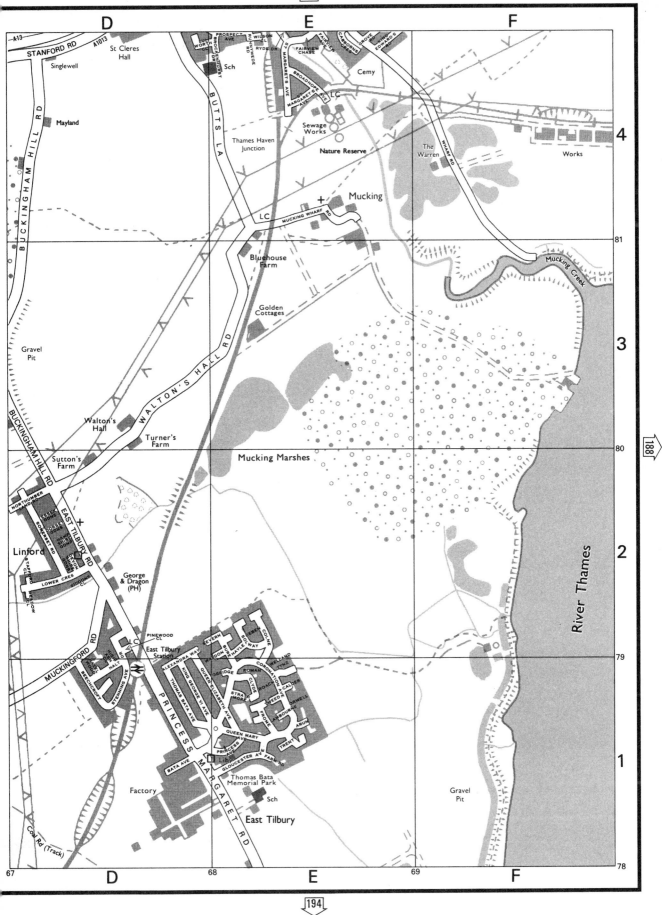

179

D　　　　　　　　E　　　　　　　　F

A13　STANFORD RD　A1013

St Cleres Hall

Singlewell

Mayland

BUCKINGHAM HILL RD

BUTTS LA

PROSPECT AVE

WORTH

BROCKENHURST

WILSON CL

RUNNYMEDE RD

RYDE DR

ST MARGARET'S AVE

MARGARET'S AVE

BROADHOPE AVE

FAIRVIEW CHASE

FAIRVIEW

CABORNE

GROVE

EDWARD'S RD

Sch

Cemy

4

Thames Haven Junction

Sewage Works

LC

The Warren

WHARF RD

Works

Nature Reserve

Mucking

LC

MUCKING WHARF RD

Mucking Creek

81

Bluehouse Farm

Golden Cottages

Gravel Pit

WALTON'S HALL RD

3

Walton's Hall

Turner's Farm

Sutton's Farm

BUCKINGHAM HILL RD

Mucking Marshes

80

188

EAST TILBURY RD

NORTHUMBER LAND RD

ESSEX GDNS

DORSET GDNS

SOMERSET RD

HAMPSHIRE GDNS

DEVON

LOWER CRES

CHILTERN

GIDDINGS CL

Linford

George & Dragon (PH)

2

River Thames

MUCKINGFORD RD

PRINCESS MARGARET RD

PINEWOOD CL

LC

STENNING AVE

East Tilbury Station

ALEXANDRA WAY

KING GEORGE VI AVE

THOMAS BATA AVE

QUEEN ELIZABETH AVE

STRATHMORE

SEVERN

WANDON

URE

BURE

HAYLE

ORRBRIDGE

DEBEN

COLNE

SOLWAY

ROMAN

ROACH

WELLAND

CORONATION AVE

LYN?

CALDER

FROME

WEED R

ORWELL

TAMBOURNE

ARUN

79

BRECKCROFT

HALL DR

PRINCESS

Queen Mary AVE

TRENT

BATA AVE

Library

GLOUCESTER AV

PARK RD

Thomas Bata Memorial Park

1

Factory

Sch

Gravel Pit

East Tilbury

Coal Rd (Track)

67　　　　　D　　　　　68　　　　　E　　　　　69　　　　　F　　78

194

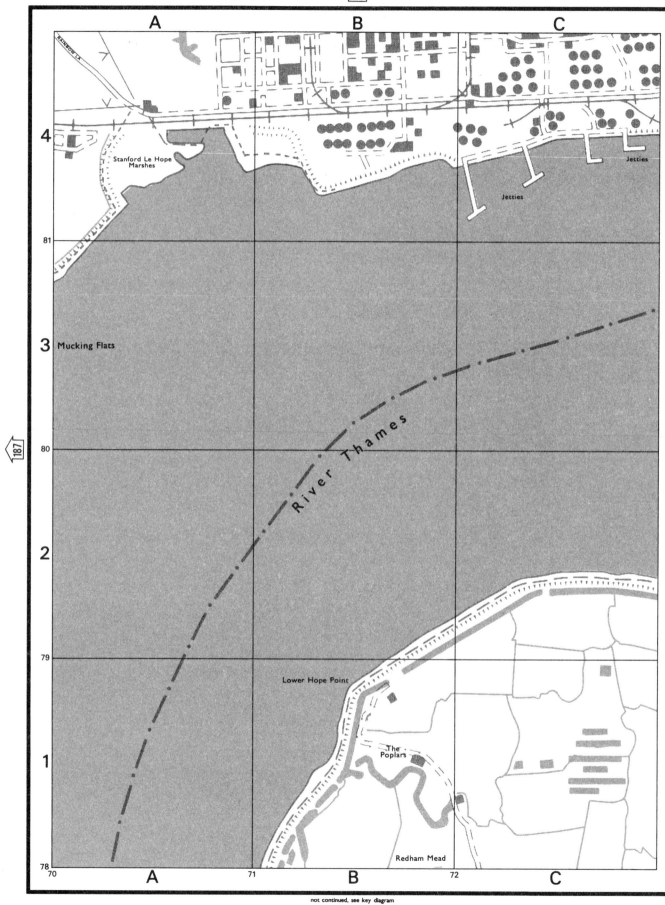

180

187

A

B

C

4

Stanford Le Hope
Marshes

Jetties

Jetties

81

3 Mucking Flats

River Thames

80

2

79

Lower Hope Point

The
Poplars

1

Redham Mead

78

70

A

71

B

72

C

RAINBOW LA

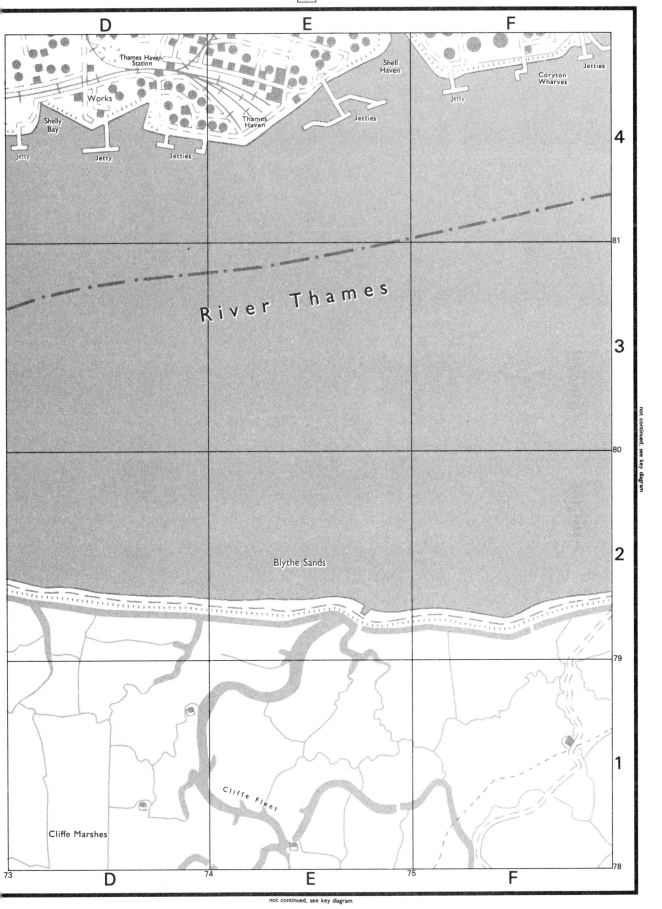

D

E

F

Thames Haven
Station

Shell
Haven

Coryton
Wharves

Jetties

Works

Jetty

Shelly
Bay

Thames
Haven

Jetties

4

Jetty

Jetty

Jetties

81

R i v e r   T h a m e s

3

80

Blythe Sands

2

79

Cliffe Fleet

1

Cliffe Marshes

D

E

F

not continued, see key diagram

not continued, see key diagram

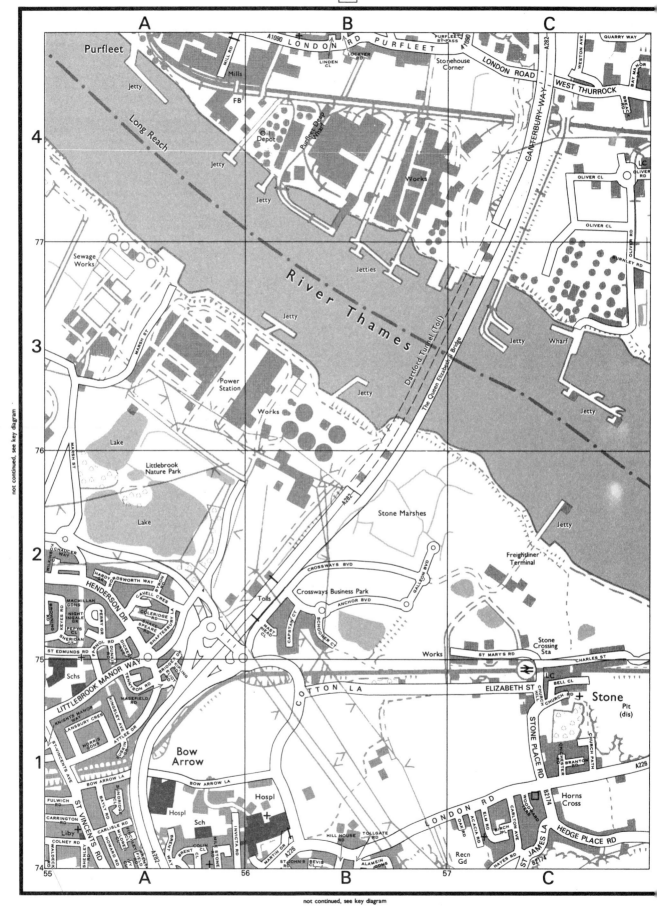

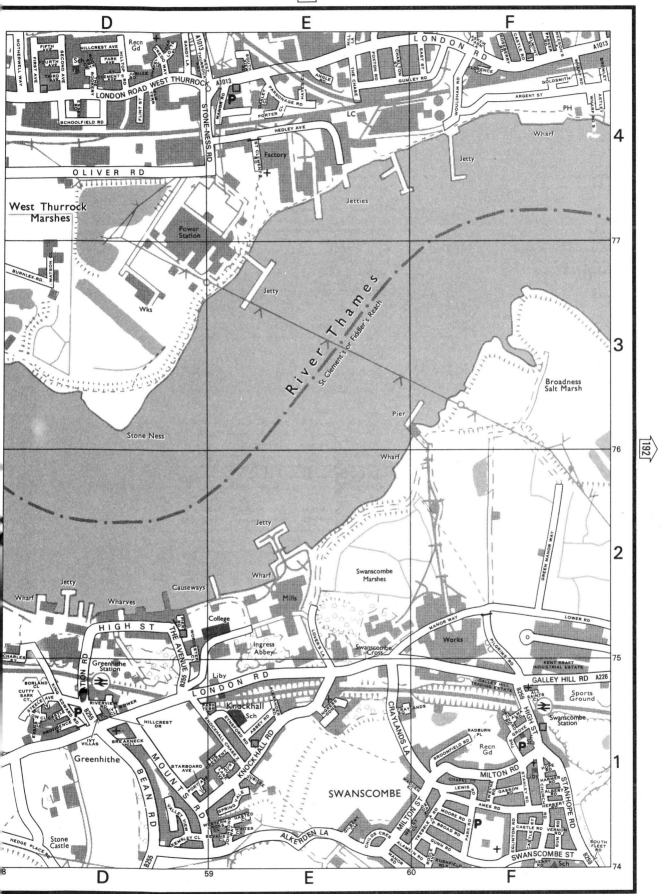

184

192

D

E

F

London Rd
A1013
London Road West Thurrock
A1013
Schoolfield Rd
Hillcrest Ave
Recn Gd
Motherwell Way
First Ave
Second Ave
Third Ave
Fifth Ave
Park Ave
Hilltop Rd
Jubilee Rd
Clement's Rd
Rookery
Sandy La
Flint St
Year Terr
Stone-Ness Rd
Manor Rd
Parsonage Rd
Porter Cl
Oxley Cl
Hayes Cl
South
Angle
The Chase
Foxton Rd
Charlton
East St
Gumley Rd
Mouldham Rd
Lorence Cl
Castle Rd
Belmont
Parker
Weston's
Sack Farm
Rosebery
Bromley
Wharf Rd S.
Astley
Wharf Rd
Argent St
Goldsmith
PH
LC
Hedley Ave
St Clement's
Factory
4

Oliver Rd

West Thurrock
Marshes

Power
Station
Burnley Rd
Watson Cl
Wks

Jetties
Wharf
Jetty
77

Jetty
Wks

River Thames

St Clement's or Fiddler's Reach

Stone Ness
3

Pier
Broadness
Salt Marsh

76

Wharf

Jetty

Wharf
2

Swanscombe
Marshes

Green Manor Way

Jetty
Wharf
Causeways

Jetty
Wharves
Wharf
Mills

College
Works
Manor Way
Lower Rd
Kent Kraft
Industrial Estate

HIGH ST
THE AVENUE
WORCESTER
PIER RD
Ingress
Abbey
Swanscombe
Cross
Lower La
Pilgrims Rd

CHARLES
Greenhithe
Station
Liby
London Rd
Galley Hills
Trading Estate
GALLEY HILL RD A226
B259
Sports
Ground
75

Borland Cl
Cutty
Sark
Ct
Low Cl
East
King Edward Rd
Bower
Providence Rd
Riverview
Mount Cl
Park
Terr
Knockhall
Sch
Abbey Rd
Eynsford Rd
Ingress
Bower
Crayfields
Craylands
Manor Way
All Saints Rd
Swanscombe
Station
Radburn
Pl
Broomfield Rd
Recn
Gd
The Grove
HIGH ST
Liby
Sch
STANHOPE RD

Greenhithe
Ivy
Villas
Breakneck
Hill
Hillcrest
Dr
Starboard
Ave
Knockhall Chase
Portal
Vale
Jubilee
MOUNTS RD
BEAN RD
Stone
Castle
Hedge Place Rd
Valley
View
Kemsley Cl
Spring
Vale
Hasted
Cross
Western
Whites
Bevans
ALKERDEN LA
Childs Cres
MILTON ST
SWANSCOMBE
Alamein Rd
Manor Rd
Bushfield
Way
Gunn Rd
Broad Rd
Moore Rd
Park Rd
Ames Rd
Gasson Rd
Lewis Rd
Chapel Cl
Stanley Rd
Herbert
Albert
Castle Rd
Eglinton Rd
Vernon Rd
Church Rd
Harmer Rd
Hope Rd
MILTON RD
Keary Rd
Sch
SWANSCOMBE ST
South
Fleet
Rd
B259
1

58

D

59

E

60

F

74

185

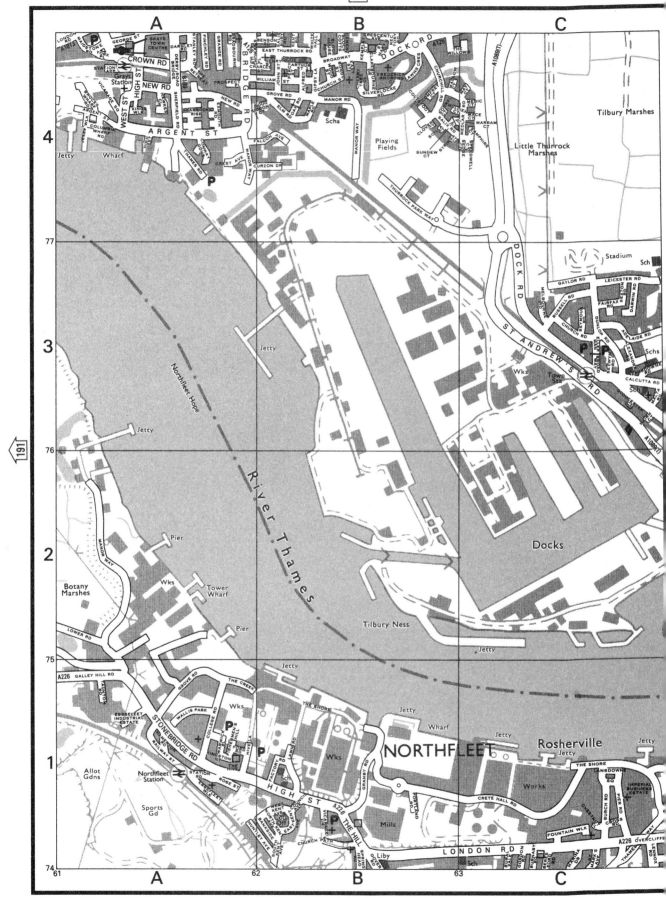

191

A   **B**   **C**

4

3

2

1

77

76

75

74

61   62   63

A   **B**   **C**

River Thames

NORTHFLEET

Rosherville

Docks

Tilbury Marshes

Little Thurrock Marshes

Tilbury Ness

Botany Marshes

Grays Station

CROWN RD

ARGENT ST

Northfleet Station

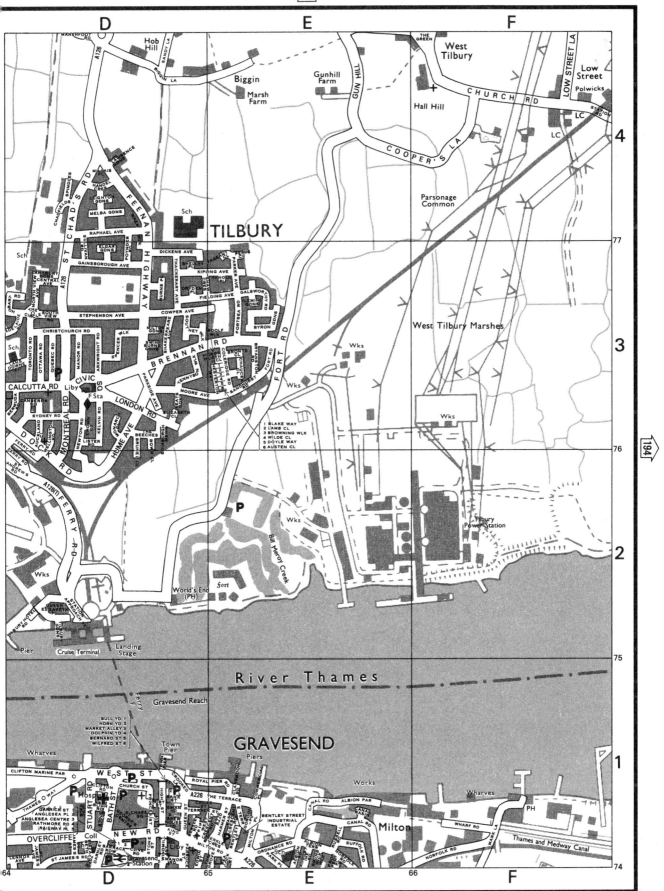

D · **E** · **F**

Hob Hill

SANDY LA

BIGGIN LA

MXRSHFOOT

A126

Biggin

Marsh Farm

Gunhill Farm

GUN HILL

THE GREEN

West Tilbury

CHURCH RD

Low Street LA

Low Street

Polwicks

STATION RD

LC

LC

4

Hall Hill

+

COOPER'S LA

Parsonage Common

LAWRENCE

MILLAIS

HANDEL

LEIGHTON GDNS

MELBA GDNS

CHAPELFIELDS

SPINDLES

ST CHAD'S RD

RAPHAEL AVE

HYATTS

ELGAR GDNS

POYNDER

GAINSBOROUGH AVE

Sch

Sch

FEENAN HIGHWAY

TILBURY

77

DICKENS AVE

SHELLEY

KIPLING AVE

THACKERAY AVE

PARKER AVE

FERRY

ARNOLD AVE

DRYDEN PL

FIELDING AVE

GALSWORTHY

GOMS

FLEMING GDNS

BYRON GDNS

West Tilbury Marshes

SANSBURY

NORTH VIEW

CENTRAL AVE

A126

Sch

ADELAIDE

SOUTH VIEW

CIRCLE VIEW

BURNS

STEPHENSON AVE

COWPER AVE

HEY

DUDOLF

SHAKESPEARE WLK

SPENCER WLK

BRENNAN RD

SWINBURNE

KEATS

KENNYSON

CHAUCER

TENNYSON

FORT RD

Wks

Wks

3

CHRISTCHURCH RD

MANOR RD

ARKWRIGHT RD

TORONTO RD

QUEBEC RD

Sch

CALCUTTA RD

CIVIC

Liby

F Sta

PARKSIDE AVE

MOORE AVE

BERMUDA

CANBERRA

SYDNEY RD

AUCKLAND

WELLINGTON

NEWTON RD

KELVIN RD

LISTER RD

LONDON RD

ELIZABETH CL

SANDHURST

BRON

CERISIDE RD

1 BLAKE WAY
2 LAMB CL
3 BROWNING WLK
4 WILDE CL
5 DOYLE WAY
6 AUSTEN CL

Wks

LANSDOWNE

DOCK RD

MONTREAL RD

HUME AVE

THE BEECHES

Wks

Wks

76

FERRY RD

A126(T)

ST ANDREW'S

P

Wks

Bill Meroy Creek

Tilbury Power Station

Wks

World's End (PH)

Fort

2

Wks

QUEEN ELIZABETH RD

TILBURY HOTEL RD

STATION APPROACH

Pier

Cruise Terminal

Landing Stage

75

Ferry

River Thames

Gravesend Reach

BULL YD 1
HORN YD 2
MARKET ALLEY 3
DOLPHIN YD 4
BERNARD ST 5
WILFRED ST 6

Town Pier

Piers

GRAVESEND

Wharves

Works

Wharves

1

CLIFTON MARINE PAR

WEST ST

CLIFTON RD

ROYAL PIER RD

CANAL RD

ALBION PAR

PH

THAMES O WAY

P

HOSPIR

P

STUART RD

BATH ST

CHURCH ST

A226

THE TERRACE

Milton

CANAL RD

WHARF RD

GARRICK ST

ANGLESEA PL

ANGLESEA CENTRE

RATHMORE RD

RAILWAY PL

NEW RD

QUEEN ST

BENTLEY STREET INDUSTRIAL ESTATE

Sch

OVERCLIFFE

Coll

P

ORDNANCE RD

MILTON RD

NORFOLK RD

Thames and Medway Canal

LENNOX AVE

ST JAMES'S RD

P

Gravesend Station

A226

PARK ST

SUFFOLK RD

MARK LA

74

D · 65 · **E** · 66 · **F**

64

194

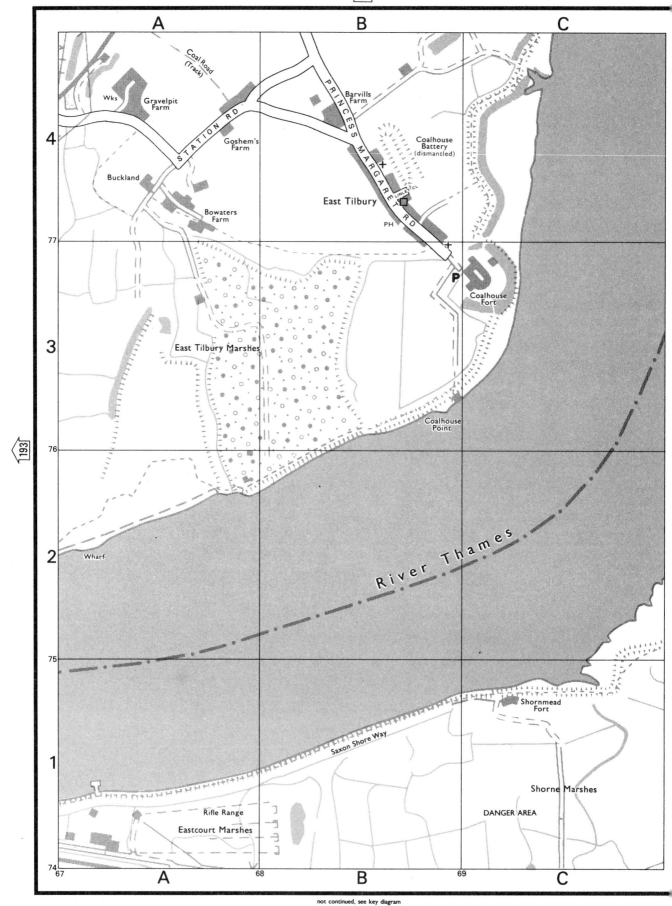

A B C

193

Coal Road
(Track)

Wks

Gravelpit
Farm

Barvills
Farm

Coalhouse
Battery
(dismantled)

4

STATION RD

Goshem's
Farm

Buckland

Bowaters
Farm

East Tilbury

PRINCESS MARGARET RD

LINLEY CL

PH

77

P

Coalhouse
Fort

East Tilbury Marshes

3

Coalhouse
Point

76

River Thames

2

Wharf

75

Shornmead
Fort

Saxon Shore Way

1

Shorne Marshes

Rifle Range

Eastcourt Marshes

DANGER AREA

74

67 A 68 B 69 C

USER'S NOTES

EXPLANATION OF THE STREET INDEX REFERENCE SYSTEM

Street names are listed alphabetically and show the locality, the page number and a reference to the square in which the name falls on the map page.

Example:	Dellows La. Ugl...48 A1

Dellows La.	This is the full street name, which may have been abbreviated on the map.
Ugl.	This is the abbreviation for the town, village or locality in which the street falls.
48	This is the page number of the map on which the street name appears.
A1	The letter and figure indicate the square on the map in which the centre of the street falls. The square can be found at the junction of the vertical column carrying the appropriate letter and the horizontal row carrying the appropriate figure.

ABBREVIATIONS USED IN THE INDEX
Road Names

Approach	App	Lane	La
Avenue	Ave	North	N
Boulevard	Bvd	Orchard	Orch
Broadway	Bwy	Parade	Par
By-Pass	By-Ps	Passage	Pas
Causeway	Cswy	Place	Pl
Common	Comm	Pleasant	Plea
Corner	Cnr	Precinct	Prec
Cottages	Cotts	Promenade	Prom
Court	Ct	Road	Rd
Crescent	Cres	South	S
Drive	Dr	Square	Sq
Drove	Dro	Street,Saint	St
East	E	Terrace	Terr
Gardens	Gdns	Walk	Wlk
Grove	Gr	West	W
Heights	Hts	Yard	Yd

Towns, Villages and Rural Localities

Abbess Roding .... Abb Rod 93 F2
Abridge .... Abr 142 A3
Anstey .... Ans 33 D3
Arkesden .... Arkes 23 F1
Ashdon .... Ash 4 A1
Ashen .... Ashe 9 E1
Aveley .... Ave 183 E3
Aythorpe Roding .... Ay Rod 81 D2
Bardfield Saling .... Ba Sal 53 E1
Barnston .... Barn 73 D2
Bartlow .... Bart 4 A4
Basildon .... Basil 171 E2
Berden .... Berd 46 A4
Billericay .... Bill 149 D1
Birchanger .... Birhr 57 F1
Birdbrook .... Bird 19 D4
Bishop's Stortford .... Bis St 68 A3
Black Notley .... Bl Not 76 C3
Blackmore .... Bla 133 F4
Bobbingworth .... Bobb 118 B4
Boreham .... Bore 112 C4
Braintree .... Brain 65 E2
Brent Pelham .... Br Pl 34 A1
Brentwood .... Brent 158 A4
Broomfield .... Broom 98 A1
Broxted .... Brox 49 F1
Canfield End .... Can E 71 D4
Chadwell St Mary ..... Cha S M 186 A2
Chelmsford .... Chelm 111 D2
Chigwell .... Chig 153 D4
Chingforth .... Ching 139 E2
Chipping Ongar .... Ch Ong 119 D1
Chrishall .... Chris 10 B2
Clare .... Cla 9 F4
Clavering .... Clav 35 E3
Corringham .... Corr 180 A2
Dagenham .... Dag 173 E3
Debden .... Deb 38 A4
Doddinghurst .... Dodd 133 E1
East Hanningfield .... E Han 138 C3
Eastwick .... East 89 D2
Elmdon .... Elm 11 D2
Elsenham .... Els 48 B1
Enfield .... Enf 126 A2

Epping .... Epp 116 A1
Epping Green .... Ep Gr 115 D4
Fairstead .... Fair 86 C3
Farnham .... Far 56 B3
Felstead .... Felst 74 A3
Finchingfield .... Finch 42 B3
Furneaux Pelham .... Fu Pel 45 D3
Fyfield .... Fyf 106 B1
Good Easter .... G Ea 95 E3
Gravesend .... Grave 193 E1
Grays .... Grays 185 D2
Great Baddow .... Gt Bad 124 C4
Great Bardfield .... Gt Ba 42 A1
Great Canfield .... Gt Can 81 E4
Great Chesterford .... Gt C 1 B1
Great Dunmow .... Gt Dun 72 B4
Great Easton .... Gt Ea 60 C4
Great Hallingbury .... Gt Ha 68 C2
Great Leighs .... Gt Le 85 F4
Great Saling .... Gt Sal 64 A4
Great Sampford ....Gt Sam 29 D2
Great Waltham .... Gt Wal 97 F4
Great Yeldham .... Gt Y 20 C1
Hadstock .... Had 3 E3
Harlow .... Harl 89 E1
Hatfield Broad Oak .... Hat B O 79 F3
Haverhill .... Hav 7 E4
Havering-atte-Bower .... Hav B 155 F4
Helions Bumpstead .... Hel B 17 D4
Hempstead .... Hemp 16 C1
Henham .... Hen 48 C3
Heydon .... Hey 10 A2
High Easter .... H Ea 8 B1
High Laver .... H Lav 105 D3
High Ongar .... H Ong 119 E2
High Roding .... H Rod 81 F4
High Wych .... H Wy 77 D1
Hinxton .... Hinxt 1 A4
Hoddesdon .... Hod 100 A3
Hordon on the Hill .... Horn H 178 C2
Hornchurch .... Hornc 165 D1
Ingatestone .... Ing 135 E2
Kelvedon Hatch .... Kelv H 132 C1
Langley .... Langl 22 B1

Leadon Roding .... Lea Rod 94 B4
Lindsell .... Lind 52 A2
Little Baddow .... Lit Bad 112 C2
Little Bardfield .... Lit Ba 41 E1
Little Chesterford .... Lit C 12 C4
Little Chishill .... Lit Chis 21 F4
Little Dunmow .... Lit Dun 73 E4
Little Easton .... Lit Ea 60 C3
Little Hallingbury .... L Hal 78 B4
Little Laver .... Lit Lav 105 F4
Little Sampford .... Lit Sam 41 E4
Little Waltham .... Lit Wal 98 B3
Littlebury .... Litt 12 C2
Loughton .... Lou 140 C3
Lower Nazeing .... Lo Naz 113 E4
Magdalen Laver .... Mag Lav 104 D3
Manuden .... Man 46 C1
Margaret Roding .... Mar Rod 94 C2
Margaretting .... Marg 136 A4
Matching Green .... Match 92 B2
Meesden .... Mee 34 A3
Moreton .... More 105 E1
Mountnessing .... Mtssg 147 E4
Navestock Heath .... Nave H 144 B4
Newport .... New 36 C4
North Weald
    Bassett .... N W Bas 117 E3
Nuthampstead .... Nut 21 D1
Panfield .... Pan 65 D4
Pleshey .... Ple 83 F1
Purfleet .... Pur 183 A4
Quendon .... Quen 36 C1
Radwinter .... Rad 27 F4
Rainham .... Rain 174 A1
Rayne .... Ray 64 C1
Rettendon .... Rett 151 F4
Ridgewell .... Ridge 20 A3
Romford .... Romf 164 B3
Roxwell .... Rox 109 D3
Royden .... Roy 101 D4
Runwell .... Runw 151 F1
Saffron Walden .... Saff W 13 F1
Sandon .... Sand 125 E3
Sawbridgeworth .... Saw 77 E1

Shalford .... Shal 54 C4
Sheering .... Sheer 91 E4
South Hanningfield .... S Han 151 E4
South Ockendon .... S Ock 184 B4
Springfield .... Sprin 112 F3
Stambourne .... Stam 19 E1
Stanford le Hope .... Sta L H 179 F1
Stanford Rivers .... Sta R 131 E3
Stanstead Abbots ...... Sta Ab 87 F2
Stanstead
    Mountfitchet .... Stan M 57 E3
Stapleford Abbotts .... Sta Abb 143 E2
Stapleford Tawney ...... Sta T 130 B2
Stebbing .... Steb 62 C3
Steeple Bumpstead ...... Ste B 18 A4
Stock .... Stock 136 C2
Stocking Pelham .... St Pel 45 F3
Stondon Massey .... Sto M 133 D3
Stone .... Stone 190 C1
Strethall .... Stret 11 F2
Sturmer .... Stur 7 F2
Swanscombe .... Swan 191 E1
Takeley .... Take 70 A4
Terling .... Terl 86 C1
Thaxted .... Thax 40 A2
Theydon Bois .... The B 128 B2
Thorley .... Thor 67 E1
Tilbury .... Tilb 193 E4
Toppesfield .... Topp 32 B4
Ugley .... Ugl 47 F3
Upminster .... Upm 166 B1
Waltham Abbey .... Wa Aby 126 C4
Wendens Ambo .... Wen A 24 C3
West Hanningfield .... W Han 138 A2
West Thurrock .... W Thu 184 A1
Wethersfield .... Weth 43 D2
White Roothing .... Wh Rot 93 E4
Wicken Bonhunt .... Wic Bon 36 A4
Wickford .... Wick 163 F3
Widdington .... Widd 37 E2
Willingale .... Will 107 E2
Wimbush .... Wim 27 E3
Woodford .... Woodf 152 B2
Writtle .... Writ 110 B1

Abberton Wlk. Rain 173 F2
Abbess Cl. Chelm 110 C1
Abbey Ct. Wa Aby 126 A3
Abbey La. Saff W 13 E1
Abbey Rd. Bill 148 C1
Abbey Rd. Swan 191 E1
Abbey St. Hinx 1 A2
Abbey View. Gt Ea 50 C1
Abbey Wood La. Rain 174 B2
Abbeyview. Wa Aby 126 B3
Abbots Cl. Brent 147 D1
Abbots Cl. Rain 174 B2
Abbots Cl. Bill 161 F1
Abbots Dr. Wa Aby 127 D3
Abbots Ride. Bill 149 E1
Abbotsford Gdns. Woodf 152 A2
Abbotsweld. Harl 102 B3
Abbotts Cl. Chelm 111 E2
Abbotts Cl. Romf 164 A4
Abbotts Cotts. Stur 8 A2
Abbotts Dr. Corr 179 F2
Abbotts Hall Chase. Sta L H . 179 F1
Abbotts Rise. Sta Ab 87 E2
Abbotts Way. Bis St 67 F2
Abbotts Way. Sta Ab 87 E2
Abbs Cross. Hornc 165 E2
Abbs Cross Gdns. Hornc 165 E2
Abbs Cross La. Hornc 165 E1
Abenberg Way. Brent 159 D4
Abercrombie Way. Harl 102 B3
Abingdon Ct. Basil 163 D1
Abram's La. Chris 10 B2
Abridge Gdns. Romf 155 D2
Abridge Rd. Chig 141 F2
Abridge Rd. The B 142 A4
Acacia Ave. Hornc 164 C1
Acacia Dr. Upm 175 D4
Acacia Gdns. Upm 166 C2
Acacia Rd. Basil 172 C4
Acacia Rd. Stone 190 C1
Acer Ave. Rain 174 B1
Achilles Way. Brain 66 A3
Acorn Ave. Brain 65 E1
Acorn Mews. Harl 103 D3
Acorn Pl. Basil 170 A3
Acorn St. Hun 88 B4
Acorns The. Chig 153 F3
Acre Rd. Dag 173 D3
Acre View. Hornc 165 F4
Acres Ave. Ch Ong 118 C3
Acres End. Chelm 110 C2
Acres The. Corr 179 F2
Adam Way. Wick 163 F4
Adams Ct. Saff W 25 E4
Adams Rd. Sta L H 179 F1
Adderley Rd. Bis St 67 F4
Addison Gdns. Grays 185 E1
Addison Pavement. Basil 172 A3
Addison Rd. Woodf 153 E1
Adelaide Rd. Tilb 192 C3
Adelphi Cres. Hornc 165 D1
Admirals Wlk. Chelm 110 C2
Admirals Wlk. Hod 100 A2
Adnams Wlk. Hornc 174 A4
Adstock Way. Grays 184 C1
Advice Ave. Grays 185 D2
Aethelric Rd. Brain 65 F2
Afton Dr. S Ock 184 A4
Agister Rd. Chig 154 A3
Ainsley Ave. Romf 164 B3
Aintree Cres. Woodf 153 E1
Aintree Gr. Upm 165 F1
Aire Dr. S Ock 176 A1
Airey Neave Ct. Grays 185 D2
Airfield Way. Hornc 174 B3
Ajax Cl. Brain 66 A3
Alamein Gdns. Stone 190 B1
Alamein Rd. Chelm 110 C3
Alamein Rd. Swan 191 E1
Alan Gdns. Romf 164 A2
Albany Cl. Chelm 110 C3
Albany Rd. Epp 115 F1
Albany Rd. Brent 146 A2
Albany Rd. Hornc 165 D1
Albany Rd. Wick 163 E3
Albany View. Lou 140 A1
Albemarle Gdns. Grays 185 D2
Albemarle Gdns. Brain 66 B3
Albert Cl. Grays 185 E2
Albert Dr. Basil 170 B3
Albert Rd. Brain 66 A2
Albert Rd. Dag 164 A2
Albert Rd. Horn H 177 F4
Albert Rd. Lou 152 B4
Albert Rd. Romf 164 C3
Albert Rd. Swan 191 F1
Albert Rd. Woodf 152 A1
Albert St. Brent 158 B3
Albert Terr. Lou 152 C4
Albion Cl. Romf 164 B3
Albion Hill. Lou 140 B2
Albion Par. Grave 193 E1
Albion Park. Lou 140 B2
Albion Rd. Grave 193 E1
Albion Terr. Grave 193 E1
Albyns. Basil 170 B2
Alconbury. Bis St 57 D1
Alcotes. Basil 171 F3
Aldborough Rd. Dag 173 E3

Aldborough Rd. Upm 165 F1
Alde Rd. Hav 7 D4
Aldeburgh Cl. Hav 6 C4
Aldeburgh Pl. Woodf 152 A3
Aldeburgh Way. Sprin 111 E3
Alder Ave. Upm 175 D4
Alder Cl. Bis St 67 E2
Alder Dr. Chelm 124 A3
Alderbury Rd. Stan M 57 F4
Aldergrove Wlk. Hornc 174 B3
Alderman Wlk. Corr 179 F3
Alderney Gdns. Runw 151 E1
Aldersgrove. Wa Aby 126 C3
Alderton Cl. Brent 146 A2
Alderton Hall La. Lou 141 D3
Alderton Hill. Lou 140 C2
Alderton Rd. Grays 186 C4
Alderton Rise. Lou 141 D3
Alderton Way. Lou 140 C2
Alderwood Cl. Abr 142 A3
Alderwood Dr. Abr 142 A3
Aldingham Ct. Hornc 174 A4
Aldingham Gdns. Hornc 174 A4
Aldria Rd. Corr 179 F3
Aldridge Ave. Enf 126 A1
Aldridge Cl. Sprin 112 A2
Aldrin Cl. Corr 179 F1
Aldwych Cl. Hornc 165 D1
Alexander Cl. Sprin 111 F4
Alexander La. Brent 147 D2
Alexander Mews. Sand 125 E1
Alexander Rd. Basil 170 A2
Alexander Rd. Hav 65 F2
Alexander Rd. Swan 191 E1
Alexandra Cl. Grays 186 B2
Alexandra Rd. Brent 158 B4
Alexandra Rd. Rain 173 F2
Alexandra Rd. Romf 164 C3
Alexandra Rd. Tilb 192 C3
Alexandra Way. Grays 187 D2
Alf Lowne Ct. Grays 186 A2
Alfred Gdns. Runw 151 E1
Alfred Rd. Ave 183 E3
Alfred Rd. Brent 158 B4
Alfred Rd. Lou 152 B4
Alfred St. Grays 192 B4
Algers Cl. Lou 140 B2
Algers Rd. Lou 140 B2
Alghers Mead. Lou 140 B2
Alibon Gdns. Dag 173 D4
Alibon Rd. Dag 173 D4
Alienor Ave. Gt Ba 42 A1
Alison Cl. Wa Aby 127 D4
Alkerden La. Swan 191 E1
All Saints Cl. Bis St 68 A4
All Saints Cl. Chig 154 A4
All Saints Cl. Dodd 133 D2
All Saints Cl. Sprin 111 F2
All Saints Cl. Swan 191 F1
Allandale Rd. Hornc 164 C2
Allen Rd. Rain 174 B1
Allenby Cres. Grays 185 E1
Allenby Dr. Hornc 165 F2
Allende Ave. Harl 89 E1
Allens Cl. Bore 99 F1
Allens Rd. S Han 150 B3
Allensway. Corr 179 F2
Allington Wlk. Hav 6 C4
Allistonway. Corr 179 F2
Allmains Cl. Lo Naz 114 A3
Allnutts Rd. Epp 129 D3
Allysum Wlk. Bill 149 D2
Alma Ave. Hornc 165 F1
Alma Cl. Wick 163 D3
Alma Dr. Chelm 111 D1
Alma Rd. Swan 191 F1
Almond Ave. Wick 163 E4
Almond Cl. Grays 186 A2
Almonds Ave. Woodf 152 A4
Alpha Cl. Basil 172 C3
Alpha Cl. Brain 66 A1
Alpha Pl. Bis St 67 F4
Alpha Rd. Basil 172 C3
Alpha Rd. Brent 147 E2
Alracks. Basil 170 C3
Alsa Gdns. Els 48 B1
Alsa Leys. Els 48 B1
Alsa St. Stan M 47 F1
Altham Gr. Harl 89 F1
Althorne Cl. Basil 163 D1
Althorne Way. Dag 164 A1
Aluric Cl. Grays 186 A1
Alverstoke Rd. Romf 156 C2
Alwen Gr. S Ock 184 A4
Alwyne Ave. Brent 147 D2
Alyssum Cl. Brain 112 A3
Amanda Cl. Chig 153 E2
Amberden. Basil 170 B3
Amberley Rd. Lou 140 B1
Amberley Way. Romf 164 A4
Amberry Ct. Harl 89 E1
Ambleside. Epp 129 D4
Ambleside Ave. Hornc 174 A4
Amersham Ave. Basil 169 F3
Amersham Cl. Romf 156 C2
Amersham Dr. Romf 156 C2
Amersham Rd. Romf 156 C2
Amersham Wlk. Romf 156 C2

Amery Gdns. Romf 165 E4
Ames Rd. Swan 191 F1
Amesbury. Wa Aby 127 D4
Amesbury Cl. Epp 128 C4
Amesbury Dr. Ching 139 D2
Amesbury Rd. Epp 128 C4
Amoss Rd. Gt Bad 124 C4
Ampers End. Basil 171 E3
Amwell Ct. Hod 100 A4
Amwell Ct. Wa Aby 126 C3
Amwell La. Sta Ab 87 D3
Amwell St. Hod 100 A4
Anan Way. Romf 155 F1
Anchor Bvd. Stone 190 B2
Anchor Dr. Rain 174 A1
Anchor La. Abb Rod 93 E2
Anchor St. Bis St 68 A3
Anchor St. Chelm 111 D1
Anderson Ave. Chelm 110 C3
Anderson's La. Br Pel 33 D1
Andersons. Corr 179 F2
Andrew Cl. Brain 65 F3
Andrew Cl. Chig 153 E2
Andrews Cl. Lou 152 B4
Andrews Farm La. Gt Ea 61 E4
Andrews Pl. Chelm 110 C2
Andromeda Ct. Romf 156 B2
Angel Cl. Basil 171 E2
Angel La. Gt Dun 72 B4
Angel Way. Romf 164 C3
Angle Rd. Grays 191 E4
Angle Side. Brain 66 A1
Anglesea Centre. Grave 193 D1
Anglesea Pl. Grave 193 D1
Anglesey Cl. Bis St 67 E4
Anglesey Dr. Rain 174 A1
Anglia Way. Brain 66 A1
Ann Coles Cl. Ste B 18 B3
Annabell Ave. Grays 186 B4
Annalee Gdns. S Ock 184 A4
Annalee Rd. S Ock 184 A4
Annifer Way. S Ock 184 A4
Ansgar Rd. Saff W 25 E4
Anson Cl. Romf 155 D1
Anson Way. Brain 66 B2
Anstead Dr. Rain 174 A2
Antelope Ave. Grays 185 D2
Anthony Cl. Bill 161 E3
Anthony Dr. Corr 179 F2
Antlers Hill. Ching 139 D2
Anton Rd. S Ock 176 A1
Antonia Cl. Hav 7 F4
Anvil Way. Bill 149 D3
Anvil Way. Sprin 111 F4
Anworth Cl. Woodf 152 A2
Apollo Cl. Hornc 165 D1
Apple Tree Cl. Dodd 133 E1
Apple Tree Cres. Dodd 133 E1
Apple Tree La. Dodd 133 E1
Apple Tree Way. Wick 163 F4
Appleby Dr. Romf 156 B3
Appleby Green. Romf 156 B3
Appledore Cl. Romf 156 B1
Appleford Ct. Basil 172 B3
Appleton Fields. Bis St 67 F2
Appleton Rd. Lou 141 D3
Appleton Way. Hornc 165 D2
Appletree Wlk. Brain 66 A1
Approach Rd. Bill 162 B3
Approach The. Upm 166 A1
April Pl. Saw 77 F2
Apsley Pl. Bis St 67 F2
Apton Cl. Bis St 67 F4
Apton Fields. Bis St 67 F3
Apton Rd. Bis St 67 F4
Arabia Cl. Ching 139 E1
Araglen Ave. S Ock 184 A4
Aragon Cl. Romf 155 D2
Aragon Dr. Woodf 153 E2
Aragon Rd. Gt Le 85 F4
Arbour Cl. Brent 158 B3
Arbour La. Sprin 111 E2
Arbour Way. Hornc 174 A4
Arbutus Cl. Chelm 124 A3
Arcade Pl. Romf 164 C3
Arcade The. Romf 156 B3
Arcany Rd. S Ock 176 A1
Archate Ave. Grays 185 D2
Archer Rd. Basil 170 A4
Archers. Harl 102 A2
Archers Fields. Basil 163 D1
Archers Way. Chelm 124 B1
Archibald Rd. Romf 157 D1
Archway. Romf 156 A2
Ardleigh. Basil 170 C3
Ardleigh Cl. Hornc 165 E4
Ardleigh Ct. Brent 146 C1
Ardleigh Gdns. Brent 147 F2
Ardleigh Green Rd. Hornc 165 E4
Ardley Cres. Hat B O 79 D1
Ardmore La. Lou 140 A1
Ardmore Rd. S Ock 176 A1
Argent St. Grays 191 F4
Argent St. Grays 192 A4
Argus Cl. Romf 155 D1
Argyle Gdns. Upm 166 B1
Argyll Rd. Bore 112 A3
Argyll Rd. Grays 185 D1

Arisdale Ave. S Ock 176 A1
Ark Ave. Grays 185 D2
Arkwright Rd. Tilb 193 D3
Arkwrights. Harl 89 F1
Arlington Gdns. Romf 156 C1
Arlington Rd. Woodf 152 A2
Arlington Way. Bill 148 C3
Armor Rd. W Thu 183 E1
Armstead Wlk. Dag 173 D3
Armstrong Cl. Corr 179 F1
Arne Cl. Corr 179 E2
Arne Ct. Basil 170 B4
Arne Mews. Basil 170 B4
Arnhem Ave. Ave 183 E3
Arnhem Gr. Brain 65 F2
Arnhem Rd. Chelm 110 C3
Arnold Ave. Basil 170 A3
Arnold Ave East. Enf 126 A1
Arnold Pl. Tilb 193 E3
Arnold Rd. Dag 173 D3
Arnold Way. Chelm 124 B2
Arnolds Ave. Brent 147 E2
Arnolds Cl. Brent 147 E2
Arnolds Farm La. Mtssg 147 F3
Arrowsmith Cl. Chig 153 F3
Arrowsmith Path. Chig 153 F3
Arrowsmith Rd. Chig 153 F3
Arterial Ave. Rain 174 B1
Arterial Rd N Stifford. Grays . 184 C2
Arterial Rd Purfleet. Pur 183 E1
Arterial Rd Purfleet. W Thu 183 E1
Arterial Rd W Thurrock. Grays184 A2
Arterial Rd W Thurrock. W Thu184 A2
Artesan Cl. Hornc 164 C2
Arthur Barnes Ct. Grays 186 B2
Arthur Ct. Chelm 110 C3
Arthur St. Grays 192 B4
Arun. Grays 187 E1
Arun Cl. Sprin 111 E3
Arundel Cl. Bill 149 E3
Arundel Dr. Woodf 152 A2
Arundel Mews. Bill 149 E3
Arundel Rd. Romf 156 C1
Arundel Rd. Runw 151 E1
Arundel Way. Bill 149 E3
Ascension Rd. Romf 155 E2
Ascot Cl. Bis St 68 B4
Ascot Cl. Chig 153 F2
Ascot Gdns. Hornc 174 C4
Ash Bungalows. Brain 65 F2
Ash Cl. Brent 145 F2
Ash Gr. Chelm 124 B4
Ash Green. Bill 149 F1
Ash Groves. Saw 78 A1
Ash La. Hornc 165 F4
Ash Tree Cl. Chelm 110 C1
Ash Tree Cres. Chelm 110 C1
Ash Tree Field. Harl 89 D1
Ash Tree Wlk. Basil 171 F3
Ashbeam Cl. Brent 158 B2
Ashbourne Rd. Romf 156 B3
Ashbrook Rd. Dag 164 A1
Ashby Cl. Grays 186 C4
Ashby Cl. Hornc 164 A2
Ashby Rise. Bis St 57 D1
Ashdale. Bis St 67 E2
Ashdon Cl. Brent 147 E2
Ashdon Cl. Woodf 152 A2
Ashdon Rd. Saff W 14 B2
Ashdon Rd Comm Cntre.
  Saff W 14 A2
Ashdon Way. Basil 171 D3
Ashdown Cl. Corr 179 F3
Ashdown Wlk. Romf 155 D1
Ashen Cl. Ashe 9 E1
Ashen Hill. Ashe 9 E1
Ashen La. Cla 9 E2
Ashen Rd. Ashe 20 A4
Ashfield Cl. Gt Dun 61 E1
Ashfields. Basil 172 B4
Ashfields. Lou 140 C4
Ashford Ave. Brent 158 A4
Ashford Rd. Chelm 110 C1
Ashford Rd. Woodf 152 A1
Ashlea Cl. Hav 7 D3
Ashlea Rd. Hav 7 D3
Ashleigh Gdns. Upm 166 B1
Ashley Ave. Woodf 153 D1
Ashley Cl. Corr 180 A2
Ashley Gdns. Grays 185 E3
Ashlyn Gr. Hornc 165 E4
Ashlyns. Basil 172 A4
Ashlyns La. Bobb 104 C1
Ashlyns La. Mag Lav 104 C1
Ashlyns Rd. Epp 115 F1
Ashmour Gdns. Romf 155 E1
Ashton Pl. Sprin 112 A2
Ashton Rd. Romf 156 B1
Ashurst Dr. Sprin 111 E4
Ashvale Dr. Upm 166 C1
Ashvale Gdns. Romf 155 E3
Ashvale Gdns. Upm 166 C1
Ashway. Corr 180 A3
Ashwells Rd. Dodd 145 F3
Ashwood Ave. Rain 174 A1
Askew Farm La. Grays 184 C1
Askwith Rd. Rain 173 E2

Aspen Gr. Upm 175 D4
Aspin Mews. Saff W 13 F2
Aster Ct. Sprin 111 F3
Astley. Grays 191 F4
Aston Rd. Basil 170 A3
Astor Ave. Romf 164 B3
Astra Cl. Hornc 174 A3
Athelstan Cl. Romf 156 C1
Athelstan Gdns. Runw 151 E1
Athelstan Rd. Romf 156 C1
Atherton End. Saw 77 F2
Atherton Gdns. Grays 186 B1
Atherton Rd. Woodf 152 C1
Atholl Rd. Sprin 111 F3
Atlanta Blvd. Romf 164 C3
Atridge Chase. Bill 149 D2
Attlee Ct. Grays 185 D2
Attlee Dr. Stone 190 A1
Attwoods Cl. Chelm 124 B2
Aubrey Cl. Chelm 111 D4
Aubrietia Cl. Romf 156 B1
Auckland Ave. Rain 173 F1
Auckland Cl. Chelm 110 C3
Auckland Cl. Tilb 193 D3
Audleigh Pl. Chig 153 D2
Audley End. Romf 156 C4
Audley End Rd. Saff W 25 E4
Audley Gdns. Lou 141 E4
Audley Rd. Gt Le 85 F4
Audley Rd. Saff W 13 F1
Audley Way. Basil 171 D3
Audrey Gdns. Bis St 67 F2
Augustine Rd. Grave 193 E1
Augustus Cl. Hav 7 E4
Aukingford Gdns. Ch Ong 118 C3
Aukingford Green. Ch Ong 118 C2
Auriel Ave. Dag 173 E3
Austen Cl. Lou 141 E3
Austen Cl. Swan 191 E1
Austen Cl. Tilb 193 E3
Austral Dr. Hornc 165 E2
Auton Croft. Saff W 25 E4
Aveley By-Ps. Ave 183 E3
Aveley Rd. Ave 183 E3
Aveley Rd. Ave 175 E2
Aveley Rd. Romf 164 C4
Aveley Rd. Upm 175 E2
Avelon Rd. Rain 174 A2
Avelon Rd. Romf 155 E2
Avenue Cl. Romf 156 C2
Avenue Ind Est. Romf 156 B1
Avenue Rd. Bis St 68 A3
Avenue Rd. Corr 171 D1
Avenue Rd. Gt Bad 124 B4
Avenue Rd. Ing 135 D2
Avenue Rd. Romf 156 C2
Avenue Rd. Roy 100 B3
Avenue Rd. The B 128 B2
Avenue Rd. Woodf 152 B2
Avenue The. Bill 149 D1
Avenue The. Brain 65 F2
Avenue The. Brent 158 C2
Avenue The. Corr 180 B3
Avenue The. Gt Dun 72 C4
Avenue The. Hornc 165 E1
Avenue The. Lo Naz 114 C1
Avenue The. Lou 140 C2
Avenue The. Lou 152 B4
Avenue The. Romf 164 B4
Avenue The. Swan 191 D2
Avey La. Wa Aby 126 C1
Avila Chase. Chelm 124 A1
Avon Green. S Ock 184 A4
Avon Rd. Chelm 110 B3
Avon Rd. Upm 166 B3
Avondale Cl. Lou 140 C1
Avondale Ct. Woodf 152 A1
Avondale Dr. Lou 140 C2
Avondale Gdns. Corr 179 F3
Avondale Rd. Basil 172 A2
Avontar Rd. S Ock 176 A1
Aylett Rd. Upm 166 B1
Ayletts. Basil 171 F3
Ayletts. Broom 98 A2
Ayloff's Wlk. Hornc 165 F3
Ayloffs Cl. Hornc 165 F4
Aylsham La. Romf 156 B3
Aylsham Rd. Hod 100 B4
Aynsley Gdns. Harl 103 E4
Aynsworth Ave. Bis St 57 D1
Ayr Green. Romf 155 F1
Ayr Way. Romf 155 F1
Ayron Rd. S Ock 176 A1
Azalea Ave. Wick 163 E4

Babington Rd. Hornc 165 D2
Back Hill. Had 3 D3
Back La. Gt Wal 84 A3
Back La. Hal 78 A4
Back La. Hinx 1 A2
Back La. Ing 135 D3
Back La. Lit Wal 98 B2
Back La. Lo Naz 101 E1
Back La. Ple 83 F1
Back La. Saw 78 A1
Back La. Stock 136 B1
Back La. W Thu 184 A2
Back Rd. Writ 110 A1

Bacon Link. Romf 155 D2
Badburgham Ct. Wa Aby 126 C3
Baddow Cl. Dag 173 D2
Baddow Hall Ave. Gt Bad 125 D4
Baddow Hall Cres. Gt Bad 125 D4
Baddow Place Ave. Gt Bad ... 125 D3
Baddow Rd. Chelm 111 E1
Baddow Rd. Chelm 124 C4
Baddow Rd. Gt Bad 124 C4
Baddows Cl. Woodf 152 B2
Bader Way. Rain 174 A3
Badgers. Bis St 67 F3
Badgers Cl. Chelm 124 A1
Badgers Mount. Grays 185 D2
Badgers The. Basil 170 A2
Bag La. Ing 134 C2
Bailey Bridge Rd. Brain 65 F3
Bailey Cl. Hav 7 E4
Bailey Cl. W Thu 183 E1
Baillie Cl. Rain 174 A1
Baker St. Chelm 111 D1
Baker St. Grays 185 F3
Baker St. Grays 76 B3
Bakers Ct. Bis St 68 A4
Bakers La. Epp 115 F1
Bakers La. Felst 74 A3
Bakers La. Ing 135 D2
Bakers La. Stock 137 D4
Bakers Mead. Gt Wal 97 F4
Bakers Meadow. Dodd 133 E1
Bakers Mews. Ing 135 D2
Bakers Villas The. Epp 115 F1
Bakery Cl. Roy 101 E4
Bakery Ct. Stan M 57 E3
Baldocks Rd. The B 128 C2
Baldwin's Hill. Lou 140 C4
Balfour Rd. Grays 185 E1
Balfour Way. Basil 172 A3
Balgonie Rd. Ching 139 E1
Balgores Cres. Romf 165 D4
Balgores La. Romf 165 D4
Balgores Sq. Romf 165 D4
Ballards Cl. Dag 173 D2
Ballards Rd. Dag 173 D3
Ballards Wlk. Basil 170 C4
Balmoral Ave. Corr 179 F2
Balmoral Ave. Corr 180 A2
Balmoral Cl. Bill 149 F1
Balmoral Dr. Hav 6 C4
Balmoral Rd. Brent 146 A2
Balmoral Rd. Hornc 165 E1
Balmoral Rd. Hornc 165 E1
Balstonia Dr. Corr 179 F3
Bamford Way. Romf 155 D3
Bampton Rd. Romf 156 C2
Bancroft Ave. Woodf 152 A4
Banes Down. Lo Naz 100 C1
Bangs Ct. Bart 5 D4
Bank Pl. Brent 158 B4
Bank St. Brain 65 F2
Bank St. Grave 193 D1
Bankart La. Sprin 111 F2
Bankfoot. Grays 185 D1
Banks La. Sta T 129 F4
Bankside. Grave 192 B1
Bann Cl. S Ock 184 A3
Banner Cl. W Thu 183 E1
Bannister Dr. Brent 147 E2
Bannister Green. Wick 163 F3
Bannister Green Villas. Felst .. 74 C3
Banson's La. Ch Ong 119 D2
Banson's Yd. Ch Ong 119 D2
Bansons Way. Ch Ong 119 D2
Banters La. Gt Le 76 A1
Banyards. Hornc 165 F4
Barbel Cl. Ches 126 A3
Barberry Cl. Romf 156 B2
Barclay Cl. Gt Bad 125 D3
Barclay Ct. Hod 100 A3
Barclay Oval. Woodf 152 A3
Barclay Rd. Basil 163 F1
Barclay Way. W Thu 183 F1
Bardeswell Cl. Brent 158 B4
Bardfield. Basil 171 F3
Bardfield Rd. Gt Sal 53 F1
Bardfield Rd. Thax 40 B1
Barfields. Lou 141 D3
Barfields Gdns. Lou 141 D3
Barfields Path. Lou 141 D3
Barham Ct. Romf 155 D1
Bark Burr Rd. Grays 184 C2
Barker Cl. Ste B 18 A3
Barkis Cl. Chelm 110 B4
Barkers Reach. Sprin 112 A2
Barle Gdns. S Ock 184 A4
Barley Cl. Basil 170 A2
Barley Cl. Hat B O 79 F1
Barley Croft. Harl 102 C2
Barley Field. Kelv H 132 C1
Barley Hills. Bis St 67 F2
Barleycorn Way. Hornc 165 F3
Barleylands Rd. Bill 161 F2
Barlow's Reach. Sprin 112 A2
Barn Green. Sprin 111 F4
Barn Hill. Harl 101 D2
Barn Mead. Bla 133 D4
Barn Mead. Harl 102 B3
Barn Mead. The B 128 C2
Barnaby Rudge. Chelm 110 C4
Barnaby Way. Chig 153 D4

Barnard Acres. Lo Naz 113 F4
Barnard Cl. Basil 171 F1
Barnard Cl. New 36 C4
Barnard Rd. Chelm 124 B1
Barnard Rd. Saw 77 F2
Barnards Field. Thax 40 A1
Barncroft Cl. Lou 141 D2
Barncroft Green. Lou 141 D2
Barncroft Rd. Lou 141 D2
Barnet Park Rd. Runw 151 F1
Barnfield. Epp 116 C3
Barnfield. Hat B O 80 A3
Barnfield. Wick 163 F4
Barnfield Cl. Hod 100 A4
Barnfield Cl. Lo Naz 100 C1
Barnfield Mews. Chelm 111 D3
Barns Rd. Bill 162 B3
Barnsley Rd. Romf 156 C2
Barnstaple Path. Romf 156 B3
Barnstaple Rd. Romf 156 B3
Barnston Green. Barn 73 D2
Barnston Way. Brent 147 E2
Barnyard The. Basil 170 A2
Barons Gate. Bis St 67 E4
Barons The. Bis St 67 E3
Barons Way. Basil 170 A2
Barrack La. Gt Wal 97 F4
Barrack Rd. G Ea 96 A3
Barrack Row. Grave 193 D1
Barrack Sq. Chelm 111 D1
Barrells Down Rd. Bis St 56 C1
Barrett La. Bis St 67 F4
Barrington Cl. Basil 171 F4
Barrington Cl. Gt Bad 125 D3
Barrington Cl. Lou 141 E3
Barrington Cl. Woodf 152 C1
Barrington Ct. Brent 147 E2
Barrington Gdns. Basil 171 F4
Barrington Green. Lou 141 E3
Barrington Pl. Ing 135 D2
Barrington Rd. Lou 141 E3
Barron's Cl. Ch Ong 118 C2
Barrows Rd. Harl 101 F4
Barry Cl. Grays 186 A2
Barryfields. Shal 54 C4
Barstable Rd. Corr 179 E1
Bartholomew Cl. Gt C 1 C4
Bartholomew Dr. Romf 156 B1
Bartholomew Rd. Bis St 67 F3
Bartlow End. Basil 172 A4
Bartlow Gdns. Romf 155 E1
Bartlow Rd. Bart 5 E2
Bartlow Rd. Had 3 E4
Bartlow Side. Basil 172 A4
Barton Ave. Romf 164 A2
Barton Cl. Chig 153 E4
Barton Rd. Hornc 165 D2
Bartram Ave. Brain 66 B2
Baryta Cl. Sta L H 179 E1
Basbow La. Bis St 67 F4
Basildon Ave. Woodf 153 D1
Basildon Dr. Basil 170 B4
Basildon Rd. Basil 170 C4
Basildon Rise. Basil 170 C4
Bassett Gdns. N W Bas 117 D3
Bassett's La. Will 121 D4
Bassingbourn Rd. Take 58 C1
Bata Ave. Grays 187 D1
Bates Rd. Romf 157 D2
Bath St. Grave 193 D1
Battle Ct. Ch Ong 119 D1
Battleswick. Basil 162 C1
Bawn Cl. Brain 66 A2
Bay Manor La. W Thu 190 C4
Bayleys Mead. Brent 159 E4
Bayly Rd. Stone 190 A1
Baymans Wood. Brent 158 C4
Baywood Sq. Chig 154 A3
Beach's Dr. Chelm 110 B2
Beacon Hill. Nave H 132 B1
Beacon Hill. Pur 183 D1
Beacon Hill Rd. Nave H 132 A1
Beaconfield Ave. Epp 116 A1
Beaconfield Rd. Epp 116 A1
Beaconfield Way. Epp 116 A1
Beacons The. Lou 128 A1
Beadle Way. Gt Le 86 A3
Beadles The. Lit Hal 78 A4
Beadon Dr. Brain 66 A1
Beam Ave. Dag 173 D2
Beambridge. Basil 172 A3
Beaminster Gdns. Woodf 153 D1
Beamish Cl. N W Bas 117 E3
Beams Cl. Bill 161 E4
Beams Way. Bill 161 E4
Beamway. Dag 173 E3
Bean Rd. Swan 191 D1
Beanfield Rd. H Wy 77 D2
Beansland Gr. Romf 154 C1
Bear Cl. Romf 164 A3
Beard's La. Elm 23 D3
Beardsley Dr. Sprin 111 F4
Bearing Cl. Chig 154 A3
Bearing Way. Chig 154 A3
Bearsted Dr. Basil 172 B3
Beatty Gdns. Brain 66 B2
Beatty La. Basil 171 F3
Beauchamps Cl. Spring 111 F4

Beaufort Cl. N W Bas 117 D2
Beaufort Cl. Romf 164 B4
Beaufort Gdns. Brain 66 A2
Beaufort Rd. Bill 148 C1
Beaufort Rd. Sprin 112 A2
Beauly Way. Romf 155 F1
Beaumaris. Woodf 152 B2
Beaumont Cl. Romf 156 B1
Beaumont Cres. Rain 174 A3
Beaumont Ct. Hav 7 D3
Beaumont Gdns. Brent 147 E2
Beaumont Hill. Gt Dun 61 E1
Beaumont Park Dr. Roy 101 D4
Beaumont Pl. Brain 66 A2
Beaumont Vale. Hav 7 D3
Beaumont Wlk. Chelm 110 B3
Beaver Rd. Chig 154 B3
Beazley End. Wick 163 F3
Bebington Cl. Bill 149 D2
Beckers Green Rd. Brain 66 B1
Becket Cl. Brent 158 B2
Beckett Dr. Corr 179 E2
Becketts. Basil 170 A3
Bedale Rd. Romf 157 D3
Bedford Cl. Brain 66 A2
Bedford Gdns. Hornc 165 E1
Bedford Rd. Brain 170 A3
Bedford Rd. Grays 185 D1
Bedford Rd. Woodf 152 A1
Bedwell Rd. Ugl 48 A2
Beech Ave. Brain 65 F3
Beech Ave. Brent 158 C4
Beech Ave. Lou 152 A4
Beech Ave. Upm 175 D4
Beech Cl. Hornc 165 D1
Beech Cl. Take 70 B4
Beech Ct. Basil 171 F3
Beech Dri. Saw 90 B4
Beech Gdns. Dag 173 E3
Beech Gr. Ave 183 E2
Beech Gr. Chig 153 F2
Beech Gr. Hav 6 C4
Beech Hill Gdns. Wa Aby 127 D1
Beech La. Woodf 152 A4
Beech Pl. Epp 128 C4
Beech Rd. Basil 171 F3
Beech Rd. Will 107 E2
Beech St. Romf 164 B4
Beech Tree Glade. Ching 139 F1
Beecham Ct. Basil 170 B4
Beechams La. Quen 47 D3
Beechcombe. Corr 180 A3
Beechcroft. Sta L H 187 D1
Beechcroft Rd. Woodf 152 A1
Beeches Cl. Chelm 110 C1
Beeches Cl. Chelm 110 C1
Beeches Rd. Chelm 110 C1
Beeches The. Brent 158 A4
Beeches The. Tilb 193 D3
Beeches The. Wen A 24 C3
Beechfield. Hod 87 D1
Beechfield. Saw 77 F1
Beechfield Gdns. Romf 164 B2
Beechfield Wlk. Wa Aby 126 B2
Beechlands. Bis St 67 F3
Beechwood Gdns. Rain 182 A4
Beedell Ave. Wick 163 F3
Beehive Chase. Bla 133 D2
Beehive Ct. Hat B O 79 D2
Beehive La. Basil 171 D3
Beehive La. Chelm 124 B3
Beehive La. Gt Bad 124 B3
Beeleigh Ave. Basil 170 B2
Beeleigh Cross. Basil 171 F4
Beeleigh East. Basil 171 F4
Beeleigh Link. Sprin 111 F2
Beeleigh West. Basil 171 E4
Beggarhill. Ing 134 C3
Begonia Cl. Sprin 111 F3
Bekeswell La. Chelm 123 F1
Belchamps Rd. Wick 163 F4
Belcher Rd. Hod 100 A4
Belchers La. Lo Naz 114 B4
Beldams La. Bis St 68 A3
Beldowes. Basil 171 E3
Belgrave Ave. Romf 156 B1
Belgrave Cl. Gt Bad 124 B4
Belgrave Rd. Bill 149 D2
Belgrave Terr. Woodf 152 A4
Bell Ave. Romf 156 A1
Bell Cl. Stone 190 C1
Bell Comm. Epp 128 C4
Bell Farm Ave. Dag 164 B1
Bell Hill Cl. Bill 161 D4
Bell House Rd. Romf 164 B2
Bell La. Hod 100 A3
Bell La. Pan 65 D4
Bell La. Thax 40 A2
Bell Lane. Gt Ba 42 A1
Bell Mead. Saw 77 F1
Bell St. Gt Bad 124 C3
Bell St. Saw 77 F1
Belle Vue. Chelm 111 D1
Belle Vue Rd. Romf 155 E2
Bellevue Rd. Bill 148 C1
Bellevue Rd. Hornc 165 F2
Bellfield. Basil 171 E3
Bellflower Path. Romf 156 B2

Bellhouse La. Dodd 145 F2
Bellmaine Ave. Corr 179 F2
Bellmead. Chelm 111 D1
Bells Chase. Gt Bad 124 C3
Bells Hill. Bis St 67 F4
Bells Hill Rd. Basil 171 D1
Belmer Rd. Stan M 58 B2
Belmonde Dr. Sprin 111 F4
Belmont Ave. Upm 165 F1
Belmont Ave. Wick 163 D4
Belmont Cl. Sprin 111 F4
Belmont Cl. Wick 163 D4
Belmont Dr. Woodf 152 A3
Belmont Hill. New 25 D1
Belmont Rd. Grays 191 F4
Belmont Rd. Hornc 165 E1
Belsteads Farm La. Broom 98 C1
Belstedes. Basil 170 C3
Belsyns Rd. Gt Ba 42 A2
Beltinge Rd. Romf 165 F4
Belvawney Cl. Chelm 110 C3
Belvedere Ave. Woodf 153 D1
Belvedere Rd. Brent 157 F4
Belvoir The. Ing 135 C2
Bendlowes Rd. Gt Ba 42 B1
Benedict Dr. Chelm 110 C1
Benets Rd. Hornc 166 A2
Benfalls. Basil 162 A1
Benfield Way. Brain 66 A1
Benhurst Ave. Hornc 165 D1
Benjamin Cl. Hornc 165 D3
Bennett's Ave. E Han 138 C2
Bennett's La. Gt Wal 73 F1
Bennions Cl. Hornc 174 B3
Bennison Dr. Romf 156 C1
Benrek Cl. Woodf 153 E1
Benskins Cl. Berd 46 A4
Benskins La. Hav B 144 B1
Benson Rd. Grays 192 B4
Bentalls The. Bas 57 E4
Bentfield End Cswy. Stan M 57 E4
Bentfield Gdns. Stan M 57 E4
Bentfield Rd. Stan M 57 E4
Bentley Cl. Bis St 67 F3
Bentley St. Grave 193 E1
Bentley Way. Woodf 152 A4
Benton Gdns. Corr 179 F3
Benyon Cl. S Ock 176 B2
Benyon Path. S Ock 176 B2
Beran Way. Hornc 165 F1
Berbice La. Gt Dun 61 E1
Berdens. Basil 171 E3
Berecroft. Harl 102 B2
Beredens La. Romf 157 F1
Berens Cl. Runw 151 F1
Beresford Ct. Bill 148 C3
Beresford Dr. Woodf 152 B3
Beresford Rd. Ching 139 F1
Beresford Rd. Grave 192 C1
Berkeley Ave. Romf 155 E2
Berkley Ave. Woodf 153 D1
Berkley Cl. Hornc 166 A1
Berkley Cres. Grave 193 E1
Berkley Dr. Hornc 166 A1
Berkley Hill. Corr 179 F2
Berkley Rd. Grave 193 D1
Berkshire Way. Hornc 166 A4
Bermuda Rd. Tilb 193 D3
Bernard Cl. Chig 153 E2
Bernard Rd. Romf 164 B2
Bernard St. Grave 193 D1
Berners End. Barn 73 D2
Berners Wlk. Basil 171 E4
Bernice Cl. Rain 174 B1
Bernside. Brain 65 F1
Berry Cl. Basil 170 A3
Berry Cl. Hornc 174 B4
Berry Cl. Wick 163 D3
Berry La. Basil 170 A2
Bersham La. Grays 184 C1
Berther Rd. Hornc 165 F2
Berwick Ave. Chelm 111 D4
Berwick Cl. Ches 126 A3
Berwick La. Sta R 130 C3
Berwick Pond Cl. Rain 174 B2
Berwick Pond Rd. Upm 174 C3
Berwick Rd. Rain 174 B2
Berwood Rd. Corr 179 F2
Betony Cres. Bill 148 C3
Betony Rd. Romf 156 B2
Betoyne Cl. Bill 149 E1
Betterton Rd. Rain 173 F2
Betts La. Lo Naz 101 E3
Betula Wlk. Rain 174 B1
Beulah Rd. Epp 116 A1
Beulah Rd. Hornc 165 E1
Bevans Cl. Swan 191 E1
Beverley Cl. Grays 186 B4
Beverley Cl. Hornc 165 F2
Beverley Cres. Woodf 152 A2
Beverley Gdns. Hornc 165 F2
Beverley Rise. Bill 149 E1
Bevil Ct. Hod 87 D1
Bevin Wlk. Sta L H 179 E1
Bevis Cl. Stone 190 B1
Beyers Gdns. Hod 87 D1

Beyers Prospect. Hod 87 D1
Beyers Ride. Hod 87 D1
Bibby Cl. Corr 180 A2
Biddenden Ct. Basil 172 B3
Bideford Rd. Romf 156 B1
Biggin La. Grays 193 D4
Bigods La. Gt Dun 61 E2
Bilberry End. Had 3 E3
Billericay Rd. Brent 160 A2
Billet La. Hornc 165 E2
Billet La. Sta L H 179 F1
Billet Rd. Romf 154 C1
Bilton Rd. Chelm 110 C1
Bingham Cl. S Ock 184 A4
Bingley Rd. Hod 100 B3
Binley Rd. Sprin 111 F1
Birbeck Gdns. Woodf 152 A4
Birbeck Rd. Brent 147 E2
Birch Cl. Brain 65 E1
Birch Cl. Lou 152 B4
Birch Cl. Romf 164 A4
Birch Cres. Hornc 165 F4
Birch Gdns. Dag 164 B1
Birch La. Stock 136 C2
Birch Pl. Stone 190 C1
Birch Rd. Romf 164 A4
Birchalls. Stan M 57 F4
Birchanger La. Birhr 57 F1
Birches The. Brent 158 C4
Birches The. N W Bas 117 D3
Birches Wlk. Chelm 124 A1
Birchwood. Birhr 57 E1
Birchwood. Wa Aby 126 C3
Birchwood Cl. Brent 158 B2
Birchwood Rd. Corr 180 A3
Bird La. Brent 167 E4
Bird La. Upm 166 B3
Birdbrook Cl. Brent 147 D2
Birdbrook Cl. Dag 173 E3
Birdbrook Rd. Stan 19 D2
Birdbush Ave. Saff W 25 E4
Birds Cl. Hinx 1 A2
Birds Farm Ave. Romf 155 D2
Birds Green. Will 107 D3
Birkdale Ave. Romf 157 D2
Biros Cl. S Han 150 B3
Birs Cl. Runw 151 E1
Biscay Cl. Hav 7 E4
Bishop Hall La. Chelm 111 D2
Bishop Rd. Chelm 111 D2
Bishop's Ave. Bis St 67 F2
Bishop's Hall Rd. Brent 146 A2
Bishop's Park Way. Bis St 67 D4
Bishops Ave. Brain 66 A2
Bishops Cl. Basil 163 D1
Bishops Rd. Corr 179 F2
Bishops Rd. Wick 163 E2
Bishopscourt Gdns. Sprin 111 F2
Bishopsfield. Harl 102 B3
Black Bush La. Horn H 178 B2
Black Ditch Rd. Wa Aby 126 B2
Black La. Lit Ba 41 F1
Blackacre Rd. The B 128 C4
Blackborne Rd. Dag 173 D3
Blackbush Spring. Harl 90 A1
Blackbushe. Bis St 57 E1
Blackhorse La. N W Bas 117 E3
Blacklands Cl. Saff W 25 E4
Blackley La. Gt Le 76 A2
Blacklock. Sprin 112 A2
Blackmans Ave. Corr 179 E4
Blackmore Ct. Wa Aby 127 D3
Blackmore Mead. Bla 133 F4
Blackmore Rd. Bla 134 B3
Blackmore Rd. Dodd 133 D2
Blackmore Rd. Grays 185 E1
Blackmore Rd. Ing 121 E2
Blackmore Rd. Ing 134 B3
Blackmore Rd. Kelv H 133 D2
Blackmore Rd. Lou 140 C1
Blackmores. Basil 169 F3
Blackshots La. Grays 185 E2
Blacksmith Cl. Bill 149 D3
Blacksmith Cl. Sprin 111 F4
Blacksmith Cl. Sta Ab 87 D4
Blacksmith's La. Rain 173 F2
Blacksmiths Alley. Bla 133 F4
Blacksmiths Hill. Cla 9 D2
Blacksmiths La. Bart 5 E3
Blacksmiths Way. H Wy 77 D1
Blackthorn Cl. Writ 110 A1
Blackthorn Rd. Grays 185 D3
Blackthorn Way. Brent 158 B3
Blackthorns. Basil 170 A2
Blackwater Cl. Sprin 111 E3
Blackwater Way. Brain 66 A2
Blade End. The B 128 C2
Bladon Cl. Brain 65 F4
Blake Cl. Rain 173 F2
Blake Dr. Brain 66 B2
Blake Hall Rd. Bobb 118 A3
Blake Way. Tilb 193 E3
Blakeborough Dr. Romf 156 C1
Blandford Cl. Romf 164 A4
Blandford Cres. Ching 139 E1
Blenheim Cl. Romf 164 B4
Blenheim Cl. Saw 90 B4
Blenheim Cl. Upm 166 C2

Blenheim Ct. Woodf 152 A2
Blenheim Gdns. Ave 183 D3
Blenheim Rd. Brent 146 A2
Blenheim Way. N W Bas 117 D2
Blenheim Cl. Brain 65 F4
Bligh Rd. Grave 193 D1
Blind La. Bill 160 A3
Blind La. Sand 125 F2
Blind La. W Han 137 F3
Blockhouse Rd. Grays 192 B4
Blois Cl. Bis St 18 B4
Blue Anchor La. Grays 186 C1
Bluebell Green. Sprin 111 F4
Bluebell Wood. Bill 148 C2
Bluehouse. Basil 171 D3
Bluemans. N W Bas 117 E4
Bluemans End. N W Bas 117 E4
Blunts Wall Rd. Bill 148 C1
Blyth Wlk. Upm 166 C3
Blyth's Meadow. Brain 65 F2
Blyth's Way. Ray 64 C1
Blythe Rd. Corr 179 F2
Blythe Rd. Roy 100 B3
Blythwood Gdns. Stan M 57 E3
Blyton Cl. Wick 163 E3
Boar Cl. Chig 154 A3
Boardman Ave. Ching 139 D2
Bobbingworth Mill. Bobb 118 A4
Bocking End. Brain 65 F2
Bockingham Green. Basil 172 A4
Bodell Cl. Grays 185 D2
Bodle Ave. Swan 191 F1
Bodmin Rd. Sprin 111 F3
Bogmoor Rd. Nut 21 D4
Bohun Cl. Gt Le 85 F4
Boleyn Cl. Bill 149 D3
Boleyn Ct. Lou 140 A1
Boleyn Gdns. Brent 159 D4
Boleyn Gdns. Dag 173 E3
Boleyn Way. Bore 99 F1
Boleyn Way. Woodf 153 E2
Boleyns Ave. Brain 65 F3
Bolford St. Thax 39 F1
Bolingbroke Cl. Gt Le 85 F4
Boltons The. Woodf 152 A3
Bond St. Chelm 111 E1
Bond St. Grays 192 B4
Bonington Chase. Sprin 111 F3
Bonington Rd. Hornc 174 B4
Bonks Hill. Saw 77 E1
Bonner Wlk. Grays 184 C2
Bonneting La. Clav 35 D1
Bonningtons. Brent 159 D4
Bonnygate. Basil 171 E4
Bootham Cl. Bill 148 C1
Bootham Rd. Bill 148 C1
Borda Cl. Chelm 111 D3
Border's La. Lou 141 D3
Boreham Rd. Gt Le 86 A2
Borland Cl. Stone 191 D1
Borough La. Saff W 25 E4
Borough The. Ch Ong 118 C1
Borradale Cl. Ste B 18 A3
Borwick La. Bill 162 C2
Bosanquet Rd. Hod 100 B4
Boscawen Gdns. Brain 66 B2
Boscombe Ave. Grays 185 E1
Boscombe Ave. Hornc 165 E2
Boscombe Ave. Wick 162 C4
Bosgrove. Ching 139 E1
Boswells Dr. Chelm 111 E1
Bosworth Cres. Romf 156 B2
Bosworth Rd. Dag 164 A1
Botany Way. Pur 183 D1
Botelers. Basil 170 C2
Botney Hill Rd. Bill 160 B2
Bouchers Mead. Sprin 111 F4
Bouchier Wlk. Rain 174 A3
Boult Rd. Basil 170 B4
Boulter Gdns. Hornc 174 A4
Boundary Dr. Brent 147 F1
Boundary Rd. Bis St 68 A3
Boundary Rd. Hav 7 E3
Boundary Rd. Romf 165 D3
Boundary Rd. Upm 166 A1
Bounderby Gr. Chelm 110 C3
Bourne Ave. Basil 170 A4
Bourne Cl. Basil 170 A4
Bourne Ct. Woodf 152 B1
Bourne End. Hornc 166 A2
Bourne Rd. Hav 7 D4
Bournebridge Cl. Brent 147 F1
Bournebridge La. Abr 143 D1
Bournebridge La. Sta Abb 143 D1
Bouverie Rd. Chelm 124 A4
Bovey Way. S Ock 184 A4
Bovingdon Rd. Brain 55 E1
Bow Arrow La. Stone 190 A1
Bowden Dr. Hornc 165 F2
Bower Cl. Romf 155 E2
Bower Farm Rd. Hav B 155 E4
Bower Hall Dr. Ste B 18 A3
Bower Hill. Epp 129 D4
Bower La. Basil 171 F4
Bower Vale. Epp 129 D4
Bowerman Rd. Grays 186 A1
Bowers Court Dr. Basil 172 C3
Bowers Dr. Ch Ong 119 D2
Bowfell Ct. Basil 170 A2

Bowfell Dr. Basil 170 A3
Bowhay. Brent 159 D4
Bowland Rd. Woodf 152 B2
Bowlers Croft. Basil 162 C1
Bowmont Cl. Brent 147 D2
Bown Cl. Tilb 193 D3
Bowness Way. Hornc 174 A4
Bowsers La. Ash 3 E2
Bowsers La. Saff W 3 E2
Boxmoor Rd. Romf 155 E3
Boxted Cl. Lou 140 C1
Boyce Rd. Corr 179 E2
Boyd Cl. Bis St 68 A4
Boyne Dr. Sprin 111 E3
Boyne Rd. Dag 164 A1
Boyton's La. Hemp 17 D1
Boytons. Basil 170 C3
Brabner Gdns. S Han 150 B2
Bracelet Cl. Corr 179 F3
Bracken Dr. Brent 158 B3
Bracken Dr. Chig 153 F2
Bracken Mews. Romf 164 A3
Bracken Mount. Basil 170 C4
Brackendale. Bill 149 E2
Brackendale Ave. Basil 172 B2
Brackendale Gdns. Upm 175 E4
Brackenden Dr. Sprin 111 E4
Brackley Cres. Basil 163 D1
Brackley Sq. Woodf 152 B2
Bradbourne Rd. Grays 192 A4
Bradbourne Way. Basil 172 B3
Bradbury Dr. Brain 65 E2
Bradd Cl. S Ock 176 B1
Bradford St. Brain 66 A3
Bradford St. Chelm 111 D1
Bradleigh Ave. Grays 185 E1
Bradley Common. Birhr 57 E2
Bradley Green. Basil 163 E1
Bradley Mews. Saff W 13 F1
Bradshawe Rd. Grays 185 D3
Bradwell Ave. Dag 164 A1
Bradwell Cl. Hornc 174 A3
Bradwell Green. Brent 147 E2
Bradwell Rd. Lou 140 C1
Brady Ave. Lou 141 E4
Braemar Ave. Chelm 124 A4
Braemar Gdns. Hornc 166 A3
Braintree Rd. Dag 164 A1
Braintree Rd. Felst 74 B3
Braintree Rd. Gt Ba 42 A1
Braintree Rd. Gt Dun 61 F1
Braintree Rd. Shal 54 C3
Braintree Rd. Weth 43 E1
Braiswick Pl. Basil 170 A4
Braithwaite Ave. Romf 164 A2
Bramble La. Lit Dun 62 C1
Bramble La. Upm 175 E2
Brambles The. Chig 153 E2
Bramley Cl. Brain 66 A1
Bramley Gdns. Basil 170 B4
Bramley Shaw. Wa Aby 126 C3
Bramleys. Corr 179 E2
Brampstead. Basil 170 A3
Brampton Cl. Corr 180 A3
Bramshill Cl. Chig 153 F3
Bramston Link. Basil 169 F4
Bramston Way. Basil 169 F3
Bramstone Cl. Chig 153 F2
Bramstone Cl. Gt Bad 124 C4
Bramwoods Rd. Gt Bad 124 C4
Bran End Fields. Steb 62 B4
Brancepeth Gdns. Woodf 152 A4
Branch Rd. Chig 154 A3
Brandon Cl. Bill 149 D3
Brandon Rd. Brain 65 E1
Branfill Rd. Upm 166 A1
Branksome Ave. Corr 179 F2
Branksome Ave. Wick 162 C4
Branksome Cl. Corr 179 E2
Branton Rd. Stone 190 C1
Bratherstone Ct. Bill 148 C2
Braxteds. Basil 170 A3
Braybrooke. Basil 171 D3
Brays Mead. Harl 102 C3
Brays Springs. Wa Aby 126 C3
Brazier Quay. Bis St 68 A3
Braziers Cl. Chelm 124 B2
Breach La. Dag 173 D1
Breach La. Gt Ea 51 E1
Breach Rd. W Thu 190 C4
Break Egg Hill. Bill 149 E2
Breakneck Hill. Swan 191 D1
Breams Field. Basil 170 B2
Brecon Cl. Basil 172 B4
Brempsons. Basil 171 D4
Brendans Cl. Hornc 165 F2
Brendon. Basil 170 B3
Brendon Pl. Chelm 110 C1
Brendon Rd. Dag 164 A2
Brennan Rd. Tilb 193 D3
Brent Cl. Stone 190 A1
Brent Way. Stone 190 A1
Brentfield Rd. Stone 190 A1
Brentwood Pl. Brent 146 B1
Brentwood Rd. Brent 159 E2
Brentwood Rd. Ch Ong 132 A4
Brentwood Rd. Horn H 178 A2
Brentwood Rd. Romf 165 D3

Bressey Gr. Woodf 152 A1
Bretons. Basil 170 C3
Brewery La. Stan M 57 F4
Brewery Rd. Hod 100 A3
Brewhouse Yd. Grave 193 D1
Brian Cl. Chelm 124 A3
Brian Cl. Hornc 174 A4
Briar Cl. Bill 161 E4
Briar Cl. Lou 152 B4
Briar Mead. Basil 170 A4
Briar Rd. Romf 156 B2
Briar View. Bill 161 E4
Briarleas Gdns. Upm 166 C2
Briars Wlk. Romf 156 C1
Briarswood. Sprin 111 E4
Briarwood. Kelv H 132 C1
Briary The. Wick 163 D4
Briceway. Corr 179 F2
Brick House La. Bore 99 F1
Brick Kiln La. Quen 36 B1
Brick Kiln La. Steb 62 B4
Brick Kiln Rd. Sand 125 E4
Brick Row. Chris 10 B2
Brickenden Ct. Wa Aby 126 C3
Brickfield Rd. Basil 171 E1
Brickfield Rd. Epp 116 B1
Bridge Ave. Upm 166 A1
Bridge Cl. Brent 158 C4
Bridge Cl. Romf 164 C3
Bridge Croft. Gt Wal 84 C1
Bridge Hill. Epp 128 C3
Bridge House Cl. Wick 163 E4
Bridge Rd. Grays 192 A4
Bridge Rd. More 105 E4
Bridge Rd. Rain 174 A1
Bridge St. Bill 161 F1
Bridge St. Bis St 67 F4
Bridge St. Finch 42 B3
Bridge St. Gt Ba 42 A1
Bridge St. Saff W 13 E1
Bridge St. Writ 110 B1
Bridgecote La. Bill 161 F1
Bridges Dr. Stone 190 A1
Bridgeways. Hod 100 A3
Bridgwater Cl. Romf 156 B3
Bridgwater Rd. Romf 156 B3
Bridgwater Wlk. Romf 156 B3
Bridle Cl. Hod 87 D1
Bridle Way. Hod 87 D1
Bridle Way. Sta Ab 87 D3
Bridle Way (N). Hod 87 D1
Bridle Way (S). Hod 87 D1
Bridleway. Bill 149 E3
Bridport Ave. Romf 164 A3
Bridport Rd. Sprin 111 E3
Bridport Way. Brain 66 B2
Brierley Cl. Hornc 165 E3
Brights Ave. Rain 174 A1
Brightside. Bill 148 C2
Brightside Cl. Bill 148 C2
Brimfield Rd. W Thu 183 E1
Brindles Cl. Brent 159 E4
Bringey The. Gt Bad 125 D3
Brinsmead Rd. Romf 157 D1
Briscoe Rd. Basil 172 A4
Briscoe Rd. Rain 174 B2
Brise Cl. Brain 66 A1
Bristow Rd. Basil 170 B3
Bristowe Ave. Gt Bad 125 D3
Britannia Ct. Basil 163 E1
Britannia Rd. Brent 158 B3
Britten Cres. Gt Bad 124 C4
Brittons La. S Han 149 F4
Brixton La. Man 47 E3
Brixton La. Quen 47 E3
Brixton La. Ugl 47 E3
Broad Green. Basil 171 E4
Broad Meadow. Kelv H 132 C1
Broad Oak. Woodf 152 A3
Broad Oakes Cl. Wim 26 C1
Broad Oaks. Wick 163 F3
Broad Rd. Brain 66 A4
Broad Rd. Swan 191 F1
Broad St. Dag 173 D3
Broad St. Hat B O 79 F3
Broad St. Hav 6 C4
Broad Street Market. Dag 173 D3
Broad Wlk. Harl 89 E1
Broad Wlk (N) The. Brent 159 D4
Broad Wlk (S) The. Brent 159 D3
Broadcroft Cres. Hav 6 C4
Broadfield. Bis St 56 C1
Broadfield. H Rod 81 F4
Broadfield. Harl 89 F1
Broadfield Cl. Romf 164 C3
Broadfield Rd. Take 70 C4
Broadfield Way. Lou 152 B4
Broadfields. H Wy 77 D1
Broadgate. Wa Aby 126 C3
Broadhope Ave. Sta L H 187 E4
Broadhurst Gdns. Chig 153 E3
Broadhurst Wlk. Rain 174 A3
Broadlands. Grays 184 C1
Broadleaf Ave. Bis St 67 E2
Broadley Rd. Harl 102 A2
Broadmayne. Basil 171 E3
Broadmead Rd. Woodf 152 A3
Broadoaks. Epp 128 C4
Broadstone Rd. Hornc 165 D1

Broadstrood. Lou 128 A1
Broadview Ave. Grays 185 E2
Broadwater Green. Basil 169 F3
Broadway. Grays 192 B4
Broadway. Gt Dun 62 A3
Broadway. Rain 174 A1
Broadway. Romf 156 A1
Broadway. Tilb 192 C3
Broadway Ave. Harl 90 A2
Broadway Cl. Woodf 152 A2
Broadway North. Basil 172 A3
Broadway The. Dag 164 A1
Broadway The. Gt Dun 61 F2
Broadway The. Hornc 174 A4
Broadway The. Lou 141 E3
Broadway The. Runw 163 E4
Broadway The. Woodf 152 A2
Brock Green. S Ock 184 A4
Brock Hill. Runw 151 E2
Brock Hill Dr. Runw 151 E2
Brockenhurst Dr. Sta L H 187 E4
Brocket Cl. Chig 153 F3
Brocket Rd. Hod 100 A3
Brocket Way. Chig 153 F3
Brockles Mead. Harl 102 B2
Brockley Cres. Romf 155 E2
Brockley Gr. Brent 147 D1
Brockley Rd. Chelm 111 E1
Brocks Mead. Gt Ea 60 C4
Brocksparkwood. Brent 159 D4
Brockton Cl. Romf 164 C4
Brockwell Wlk. Wick 163 E3
Brodie Rd. Ching 139 E1
Brograve Cl. Sprin 124 B2
Bromefield Ct. Wa Aby 127 D3
Bromfield. Saff W 25 F4
Bromfords Cl. Wick 163 D3
Bromfords Dr. Wick 163 E3
Bromley. Grays 191 F4
Brompton Cl. Bill 149 D3
Bronfelde Rd. Bill 162 B3
Bronte Cl. Tilb 193 E3
Brook Ave. Dag 173 D3
Brook Cl. Brain 65 E1
Brook Cl. Romf 155 F1
Brook Dr. Basil 171 E1
Brook Dr. Wick 163 E3
Brook End. Saw 77 E1
Brook End Rd. Sprin 112 A2
Brook Hill. Gt Wal 73 F1
Brook Hill. Lt Wal 98 B3
Brook La. Chelm 124 C2
Brook La. Dodd 133 E1
Brook La. Saw 77 E1
Brook La. Sprin 112 A1
Brook La. W Han 124 C2
Brook Mead. Basil 170 A4
Brook Mead. Gt Wal 97 F4
Brook Rd. Brent 157 F4
Brook Rd. Lou 140 A1
Brook Rd. Lou 140 C2
Brook Rd. Romf 155 F1
Brook Rd. Saw 77 F1
Brook Rd. Sta T 129 D3
Brook Rd. Sta M 57 F3
Brook Rise. Chig 153 D4
Brook Service Rd. Hav 7 D4
Brook St. Brent 157 F3
Brook St. Gt Ba 42 A1
Brook St. Lit Dun 73 E4
Brook View. Sand 125 E3
Brook View. Thax 40 A2
Brook Way. Chig 153 D4
Brookdale Ave. Upm 166 A1
Brookdale Cl. Upm 166 A1
Brooke Ave. Saff W 13 F1
Brooke Rd. Grays 185 D1
Brooker Rd. Wa Aby 126 B3
Brookfield Cl. Brent 147 E2
Brookfields. Ch Ong 118 C3
Brookfields. Saw 77 E1
Brookfields. Steb 62 B4
Brookhampton St. Hinx 1 A3
Brookhurst Cl. Sprin 111 E2
Brooklands. Wick 163 D4
Brooklands App. Romf 164 B4
Brooklands Cl. Romf 164 B4
Brooklands Gdns. Hornc 165 E3
Brooklands La. Romf 164 B4
Brooklands Park. Basil 169 F3
Brooklands Rd. Romf 164 B4
Brooklands Wlk. Chelm 124 A4
Brooklane Field. Harl 103 D3
Brooklyn Ave. Lou 140 C3
Brookmans Ave. Grays 185 E3
Brookmans Cl. Upm 166 C2
Brookmans Rd. Stock 136 B1
Brookside. Bill 149 E3
Brookside. Chig 153 E2
Brookside. Harl 101 F3
Brookside. Hod 100 A3
Brookside. Hornc 165 F3
Brookside. Wa Aby 126 C4
Brookside Cl. Bill 149 E3
Brooksies. Elm 22 C3
Brookway. Rain 182 A4
Broom Farm Rd. Els 48 B1
Broome Cl. Bill 149 E1
Broome Pl. Ave 183 E3

Broome Rd. Bill 149 E3
Broomfield. Harl 90 A2
Broomfield Ave. Lou 140 C2
Broomfield Cl. Romf 155 E2
Broomfield Rd. Chelm 111 D3
Broomfield Rd. Swan 191 F1
Broomfields. Basil 172 A3
Broomhall Cl. Broom 98 A1
Broomhall Rd. Broom 98 A1
Broomhill Rd. Woodf 152 A2
Broomhill Wlk. Woodf 152 A2
Broomhills Chase. Bill 161 E3
Broomstick Hall Rd. Wa Aby .. 126 C3
Broomwood Gdns. Brent 146 A2
Broomwood La. S Han 150 A4
Broseley Gdns. Romf 156 C3
Broseley Rd. Romf 156 C3
Brown's End Rd. Brox 59 F4
Browne Cl. Romf 155 D3
Browning Rd. Stone 190 A2
Browning Wlk. Tilb 193 E3
Brownings Ave. Chelm 111 D3
Brownlow Bend. Basil 171 E3
Brownlow Cross. Basil 171 E3
Brownlow Green. Basil 171 E3
Browns Ave. Runw 151 F1
Broxburn Dr. S Ock 184 A3
Broxhill Rd. Hav B 156 A4
Broxted Dr. Wick 163 F3
Broxted End. Wick 163 F3
Broxted Mews. Brent 147 F2
Bruce Ave. Hornc 165 E1
Bruce Gr. Chelm 124 A4
Bruce Rd. Writ 110 A1
Bruces Wharf Rd. Grays 192 A4
Brundish. Basil 172 A3
Brunel Cl. Tilb 193 D3
Brunel Rd. Brain 66 A1
Brunel Rd. Chig 152 C3
Brunswick Ave. Upm 166 C2
Brunswick Gdns. Woodf 153 E2
Brunswick Wlk. Grave 193 E1
Brunwin Rd. Ray 64 C1
Brunwins Cl. Wick 163 F4
Bryan Rd. Bis St 67 F4
Bryanston Rd. Tilb 193 E3
Bryant Ave. Romf 156 B1
Bryce Way. Basil 172 B3
Buchanan Cl. Ave 183 E3
Buck Hill. Bl Not 76 C3
Buckbean Path. Romf 156 B2
Buckenhoe Rd. Saff W 13 F1
Buckerills. Basil 172 A3
Buckhurst Way. Lou 152 B4
Buckingham Cl. Hornc 165 E3
Buckingham Hill Rd. Sta L H .. 187 D3
Buckingham Rd. Hav 6 C3
Bucklers Ct. Brent 158 B3
Buckles La. S Ock 184 B4
Buckley Cl. Corr 179 F3
Buckleys. Gt Bad 124 C4
Bucknells Mead. Ing 122 A2
Buckwins Sq. Basil 163 E1
Buckwoods Rd. Brain 66 A1
Buckwyns Chase. Bill 148 C3
Buckwyns Chase. Mtssg 148 C3
Buglers Rise. Writ 123 D4
Building End Rd. Chris 22 A4
Bull Cl. Grays 184 C2
Bull La. Dag 164 A1
Bull La. Langl 22 B1
Bull Yd. Grave 193 D1
Bullen Wlk. Chelm 124 B2
Buller Rd. Basil 170 A4
Bullfields. New 37 D4
Bullfields. Saw 77 F2
Bulmers Wlk. Rain 174 B2
Bulphan By-Ps. Horn H 169 D1
Bulphan Cl. Wick 163 F3
Bumpstead Rd. Hav 7 D2
Bumpstead Rd. Hel B 7 D2
Bundick's Hill. Chelm 110 C2
Bungalows The. Chig 153 F1
Bunting Cl. Chelm 124 A3
Bunting La. Bill 149 E1
Bunyan Rd. Brain 65 F2
Burch Rd. Grave 192 C1
Burches. Basil 161 F1
Burchwall Cl. Romf 155 E2
Bure. Grays 187 E2
Burford St. Hod 100 A3
Burford Cl. Romf 165 F3
Burges Cl. Hornc 165 F3
Burgess Field. Sprin 111 F2
Burghley Ave. Bis St 67 E4
Burghley Rd. Grays 184 B2
Burghstead Cl. Bill 149 D1
Burgoyne Hatch. Harl 90 A1
Burgundy Gdns. Basil 172 A4
Burland Gdns. Brent 146 B1
Burland Rd. Brent 155 E2
Burleigh Cl. Bill 149 D3
Burley Rd. Bis St 68 A2
Burlington Ave. Romf 164 A3
Burlington Ct. Basil 163 D1
Burlington Pl. Woodf 153 F1
Burnaby Rd. Grave 192 C1
Burne Ave. Wick 163 D3

Burnell Wlk. Brent 158 B2
Burnells Way. Stan M 57 F4
Burnett Park. Harl 102 A2
Burney Dr. Lou 141 E3
Burnham Rd. Romf 164 B4
Burnham Rd. Sprin 111 E3
Burnley Rd. W Thu 191 D3
Burns Ave. Basil 172 A3
Burns Cres. Chelm 124 B4
Burns Way. Brent 147 E2
Burnsall Cl. Saff W 25 F4
Burnside. Saw 77 E1
Burnside Cres. Chelm 111 D4
Burnside Terr. Harl 90 C2
Burnstie Rd. Felst 74 C3
Burnt Mill Cl. Harl 89 E2
Burnt Mills Rd. Basil 163 E1
Burnt Wood. Brent 158 B4
Burnthouse La. Mtssg 148 A4
Burntmill Cl. Harl 89 E2
Burntmill La. H Wy 89 E2
Burntwood Ave. Hornc 165 F3
Burntwood Cl. Bill 148 C1
Burntwood Cl. Horn H 168 B3
Burnway. Hornc 165 F2
Burr's Way. Corr 180 A2
Burrow Cl. Chig 153 F3
Burrow Green. Chig 153 F3
Burrow Rd. Chig 154 A3
Burses Way. Brent 147 D1
Burses Way. Brent 147 E2
Burslem Ave. Chig 154 A2
Burstead Dr. Bill 161 E4
Burton Cl. Corr 179 F3
Burton Cl. Hav 6 C4
Burton End. Hav 6 C4
Burton Pl. Sprin 111 F2
Burton Rd. Lou 141 E3
Burtons Mill. Saw 77 F2
Burwood Gdns. Rain 173 F1
Bury Farm La. Bill 162 B2
Bury Fields. Felst 74 A3
Bury La. Chris 10 B1
Bury La. Epp 115 E1
Bury La. Gt Wal 97 E4
Bury Lodge La. Stan M 58 A4
Bury Lodge La. Stan M 69 E4
Bury Rd. Ching 139 F2
Bury Rd. Dag 173 D4
Bury Rd. Epp 128 C4
Bury Rd. Harl 90 B2
Bury Rd. Wa Aby 139 F2
Bury Villas. Take 59 F2
Bury Water La. New 24 C1
Bush Elms Rd. Hornc 165 D2
Bush Fair. Harl 102 C3
Bush Hall Rd. Bill 149 E3
Bush Rd. Lit Sam 28 B1
Bush Rd. Woodf 152 B3
Bushey Croft. Harl 102 C3
Butterfield Wlk. Swan 191 F1
Bushfields. Lou 141 D2
Bushy Lea. Ch Ong 119 D1
Bushy Mead. Basil 170 A4
Butcher Row. Saff W 13 E1
Butcher's Hill. Hinx 1 A2
Butchers Pasture. Lit Ea 60 C3
Butler Cl. Saff W 13 F1
Butler Wlk. Grays 185 E1
Butlers Cl. Broom 98 A1
Butlers Dri. Wa Aby 126 B1
Butlers Gr. Basil 170 A2
Butlers La. Saff W 14 B3
Butneys. Basil 171 D4
Butt La. Man 46 C1
Butt's Green Rd. Sand 125 F2
Buttercross La. Epp 116 A1
Buttercup Cl. Bill 149 D2
Buttercup Cl. Romf 156 B1
Butterfield Rd. Bore 112 C4
Buttermere. Bl Not 76 B4
Buttersweet Rise. Saw 77 F1
Butterworth Gdns. Woodf 152 A3
Buttfield Cl. Dag 173 D3
Buttondene Cres. Lo Naz 100 A1
Butts Green Rd. Hornc 165 E3
Butts Green Rd. Harl 187 E4
Butts Rd. Sta L H 179 E1
Butts Way. Chelm 123 F2
Buttsbury. Stock 135 F1
Buxton Cl. Woodf 152 B2
Buxton Link. Basil 169 F3
Buxton Rd. Ching 139 E1
Buxton Rd. Grays 185 F2
Buxton Rd. The B 128 C2
Buxton Rd. Wa Aby 127 D3
By-Pass Rd. Horn H 179 F2
Byfield Cl. Horn H 168 B3
Byfleets. Basil 171 F2
Bylands Cl. Bis St 67 E3
Byng Gdns. Brain 66 B2
Byngham. Harl 101 F3
Bynghams. Harl 102 A3
Byrd Ct. Basil 170 B4
Byrd Way. Corr 179 E2
Byrd's Farm La. Saff W 13 F2
Byron Gdns. Tilb 193 E3
Byron Rd. Brent 147 E1

Byron Rd. Chelm 111 E1
Byron Rd. Stone 190 A2
Byron Way. Romf 156 B1
Bysouth Cl. Woodf 153 D1

Cabborns Cres. Sta L H 187 E4
Cadiz Rd. Dag 173 E3
Cadogan Way. Horn H 168 B3
Caernarvon Cl. Hornc 166 A2
Caernarvon Dr. Woodf 153 D1
Cage End. Hat B O 79 F3
Cage End Cl. Hat B O 79 F3
Cairns Way. Brent 152 C2
Calbourne Ave. Hornc 174 A4
Calcott Cl. Brent 146 A1
Calcutta Rd. Tilb 193 D3
Caldbeck. Wa Aby 126 B3
Caldbeck Way. Bl Not 76 B3
Calder. Grays 187 E1
Caldwell Rd. Sta L H 179 D1
Calf St. Gt C 1 B2
Calmore Cl. Hornc 174 B4
Calne Ave. Woodf 153 D1
Calverley Cl. Bis St 67 F2
Calverly Cres. Dag 164 A1
Calvert Dr. Basil 163 E1
Cam Green. S Ock 184 A4
Camberton Rd. Brain 65 F3
Cambeys Rd. Dag 173 E4
Camborne Ave. Romf 156 C2
Camborne Cl. Sprin 111 F3
Camborne Way. Romf 156 C2
Cambridge Ave. Romf 165 E4
Cambridge Gdns. Grays 186 A1
Cambridge Rd. Ching 139 E1
Cambridge Rd. Harl 90 B3
Cambridge Rd. Litt 12 C2
Cambridge Rd. New 25 D1
Cambridge Rd. Saw 77 F2
Cambridge Rd. Stan M 57 F4
Camden Cl. Grays 186 A1
Camden Rd. Grays 184 C2
Camellia Cl. Romf 156 C1
Camellia Cl. Sprin 111 F3
Camelot Gdns. Basil 172 B4
Cameron Cl. Brent 158 B3
Cameron Cl. Corr 179 F3
Cameron Cl. Ing 135 D2
Camoise Cl. Topp 32 A4
Campbell Cl. Chelm 124 A4
Campbell Cl. Romf 155 F2
Campbell Cl. Wick 163 E3
Campions. Lou 128 A1
Campions The. Stan M 57 F4
Cample La. S Ock 184 A3
Camps Rd. Bart 4 A4
Camps Rd. Hav 6 C4
Camps Rd. Hel B 6 A1
Canal Basin. Grave 193 E1
Canal Rd. Grave 193 E1
Canberra Cl. Chelm 110 C3
Canberra Cl. Dag 173 E3
Canberra Cl. Hornc 174 B4
Canberra Cres. Dag 173 E3
Canberra Sq. Tilb 193 D3
Cander Way. S Ock 184 A3
Candover Rd. Hornc 165 D2
Candytuft Rd. Sprin 111 F3
Caneland Ct. Wa Aby 126 C3
Canes La. N W Bas 103 F1
Canewdon Cl. Runw 151 E1
Canewdon Gdns. Runw 151 E1
Canfield. Bis St 67 F4
Canfield Rd. H Rod 81 F4
Canfield Rd. Rain 173 F2
Canfield Rd. Woodf 152 C2
Canford Ave. Wick 162 C4
Canford Cl. Gt Bad 124 C4
Cannon Circ. Finch 43 E3
Cannon Cl. Corr 179 F1
Cannon Leys. Chelm 124 B2
Cannons Cl. Bis St 57 D1
Cannons La. Fyf 106 C1
Cannons La. Hat B O 79 F3
Cannons Mead. Stan M 57 E4
Cannons Mead. Sto M 133 D3
Cannons Mill La. Bis St 57 D1
Canons Brook. Harl 102 A4
Canons Gate. Harl 89 D1
Canterbury Ave. Upm 166 C1
Canterbury Cl. Basil 171 F4
Canterbury Cl. Chig 153 F4
Canterbury Par. S Ock 176 B1
Canterbury Way. Brent 158 B2
Canterbury Way. Chelm 110 C2
Canterbury Way. W Thu 183 F1
Canuden Rd. Chelm 110 C1
Canvey Rd. Basil 172 C3
Canvey Wlk. Sprin 111 F3
Capel Cl. Chelm 111 D4
Capel Cl. Ray 64 C1
Capel Rd. Ray 64 C1
Capelston. Basil 170 C3
Capital Pl. Harl 102 A4
Capon Cl. Brent 146 A1
Cappell La. Sta Ab 87 E3
Capstan Cl. Stone 190 B2
Caravel Cl. Grays 184 C2
Carbis Cl. Ching 139 E1

Carbury Cl. Hornc 174 B3
Card's Rd. Sand 125 E3
Cardinal Dr. Woodf 153 E2
Cardinal Way. Rain 174 B2
Carfax Rd. Hornc 173 F4
Carisbrooke Cl. Hornc 166 A2
Carisbrooke Dr. Corr 180 A2
Carisbrooke Rd. Brent 146 A2
Carlisle Rd. Romf 165 D3
Carlisle Rd. Stone 190 A1
Carlton Ave. Stone 190 C1
Carlton Cl. Upm 166 A1
Carlton Rd. Basil 172 C4
Carlton Rd. Grays 185 F2
Carlton Rd. Romf 165 D4
Carlton Rd. Runw 151 E1
Carlyle Gdns. Bill 148 C3
Carmen St. Gt C 1 B2
Carnach Green. S Ock 184 A3
Carnation Cl. Sprin 111 F3
Carnation Dr. Saff W 13 F1
Carnel St. Gt C 1 B1
Carnforth Gdns. Hornc 174 A4
Carpenter Cl. Bill 148 C2
Carpenters Arms La. N W Bas 116 B3
Carriage Dr. Sprin 111 F4
Carrick Dr. Woodf 153 E1
Carrigans. Bis St 67 F4
Carrington Rd. Stone 190 A1
Carrington Way. Brain 65 F4
Carroll Gdns. Wick 163 E3
Carroll Hill. Lou 140 C3
Carruthers Cl. Runw 151 E1
Carruthers Dr. Runw 151 E1
Carsey Cl. S Han 150 B2
Carsey Hill. Bart 5 D3
Carson Rd. Bill 149 E3
Carswell Cl. Brent 147 E2
Cart La. Ching 139 F1
Cartel Cl 183 E1
Carter Cl. Romf 155 D2
Carter Dr. Romf 155 D2
Carters Croft. Ash 4 A1
Carters Hill. Man 47 D1
Carters La. Ep Gr 115 D4
Carters La. Hen 48 C3
Carters Leys. Bis St 67 E4
Carters Mead. Harl 103 E3
Cartersfield Rd. Wa Aby 126 B3
Carthagena Estate. Lo Naz ... 100 B2
Cartlodge Ave. Wick 163 F4
Cartwright Wlk. Sprin 111 F1
Cascade Cl. Lou 152 B4
Cascade Rd. Lou 152 B4
Cashmere Way. Basil 171 E1
Cassino Rd. Chelm 110 C3
Castell Rd. Lou 141 E4
Castle Ave. Hav 6 C4
Castle Ave. Rain 173 F3
Castle Cl. Gt Le 85 F3
Castle Cl. Hod 87 E1
Castle Cl. Romf 156 B4
Castle Cross. Saff W 13 E1
Castle Hill. Saff W 13 E1
Castle La. Hav 6 C4
Castle Rd. Grays 191 F4
Castle Rd. Hod 87 E1
Castle Rd. Swan 191 F1
Castle St. Bis St 67 F3
Castle St. Ch Ong 119 D1
Castle St. Saff W 13 E1
Castle St. Stone 191 D1
Castle St. Swan 191 F1
Castle Wlk. Hav 6 C4
Castledon Rd. S Han 151 D1
Castlellan Ave. Romf 165 D4
Caswell Cl. Corr 180 A2
Caswell Mews. Sprin 111 F1
Cater Wood. Bill 149 D2
Caterham Ave. Woodf 153 D1
Caterham Ct. Wa Aby 126 C3
Cates Cnr. Saff W 13 E1
Cathedral Wlk. Chelm 111 D2
Catherine Cl. Brent 146 A2
Catherine Rd. Romf 165 D3
Catherines Cl. Gt Le 86 A3
Catons La. Saff W 13 E1
Cattawade End. Basil 171 E4
Cattawade Link. Basil 171 E4
Causeway End Rd. Felst 74 B2
Causeway The. Bis St 67 F2
Causeway The. Br Pel 34 A1
Causeway The. Brain 65 F2
Causeway The. Deb 38 A4
Causeway The. Fu Pel 45 D2
Causeway The. Gt Bad 124 C4
Causeway The. Gt Dun 61 E1
Causeway The. Hav 6 C4
Causeway The. Langl 22 B2
Causeway The. Ridge 20 A4
Causeway The. Topp 32 A4
Causeway The. Writ 122 B4
Cautherly La. Sta Ab 87 D3
Cavell Cres. Stone 190 A2
Cavell Rd. Bill 149 E1
Cavendish Ave. Hornc 174 A3
Cavendish Ave. Woodf 152 A2
Cavendish Cres. Hornc 174 A3
Cavendish Ct. Saff W 13 F1

Cavendish Gdns. Brain 66 B3
Cavendish Way. Bill 161 E1
Cavenham Gdns. Hornc 165 E3
Cawdor Ave. S Ock 184 A3
Cawkell Cl. Stan M 57 E4
Cawkwell Cl. Sprin 112 A2
Caxton Rd. Hod 87 D1
Cecil Ave. Grays 184 C2
Cecil Ave. Hornc 165 F4
Cecil Cl. Bis St 68 B4
Cecil Rd. Hod 100 B4
Cedar Ave. Chelm 111 D2
Cedar Ave. Upm 175 D4
Cedar Ave. Wick 163 E3
Cedar Ave W. Chelm 111 D2
Cedar Cl. Lou 152 B4
Cedar Cl. Saw 77 F1
Cedar Ct. Epp 129 D4
Cedar Gdns. Upm 166 B1
Cedar Green. Hod 100 A3
Cedar Park. Bis St 67 E2
Cedar Rd. Basil 172 C4
Cedar Rd. Brent 147 E2
Cedar Rd. Grays 186 A2
Cedar Rd. Hornc 165 E1
Cedar Rd. Romf 164 B4
Cedar Wlk. Wa Aby 126 B3
Cedars. Corr 179 F1
Cedars The. Lou 140 A1
Cedric Ave. Romf 159 E2
Celandine Cl. Bill 148 C2
Celandine Cl. S Ock 176 B1
Celedon Cl. Grays 184 C2
Cement Block Cotts. Grays .. 192 B4
Cemetery Rd. Bis St 67 F3
Central Ave. Ave 183 E1
Central Ave. Basil 169 F2
Central Ave. Bill 149 E3
Central Ave. Corr 180 A2
Central Ave. Harl 89 E1
Central Ave. Tilb 193 D3
Central Ave. W Thu 183 F1
Central Dr. Hornc 165 F1
Central Park Ave. Dag 164 A1
Central Rd. Harl 90 A2
Central Rd. Sta L H 179 E1
Central Sq. Chelm 111 D1
Centre Ave. Epp 128 C4
Centre Dr. Epp 128 C4
Centre Green. Epp 128 C4
Centre Rd. Dag 173 D2
Centre Way. Wa Aby 126 B2
Centurion Way. Pur 182 C1
Century Rd. Hod 100 A4
Chadfields. Tilb 193 D4
Chadwell By-Ps. Grays 186 A1
Chadwell Hill. Grays 186 A1
Chadwell Rd. Grays 185 F1
Chadwick Dr. Romf 156 B1
Chaffix. Felst 74 B3
Chafford Gdns. Horn H 168 B3
Chafford Way. Grays 185 D3
Chafford Wlk. Rain 174 B2
Chalford Wlk. Woodf 152 B2
Chalforde Gdns. Romf 165 D4
Chalgrove Cres. Woodf 152 C1
Chalk End. Basil 172 A3
Chalk La. Match 91 D1
Chalklands. Saff W 13 F2
Chalklands. Sand 125 E2
Chalks Ave. Saw 77 E2
Chalkstone Way. Hav 7 E4
Chalky La. Chris 10 B1
Challacombe Cl. Brent 147 E1
Challis La. Brain 65 F1
Challock Lees. Basil 172 B3
Chalvedon Ave. Basil 172 A4
Chamberlain Ave. Corr 180 A3
Champion Cl. Corr 179 F2
Champion Cl. Wick 163 E3
Champion Rd. Upm 166 A1
Champions Green. Hod 87 D1
Champions Way. Hod 87 D1
Chance Cl. Grays 184 C2
Chancery Pl. Writ 110 A1
Chandler Rd. Lou 141 D4
Chandlers Way. Romf 164 C3
Chandlers Wlk. Kelv H 132 C1
Chandos Cl. Lou 152 A4
Chanlock Path. S Ock 184 A3
Chantreywood. Brent 159 D4
Chantry Cl. Bis St 67 F4
Chantry Cres. Sta L H 179 E1
Chantry Dr. Ing 135 D2
Chantry Rd. Bis St 67 F4
Chantry The. Harl 90 A1
Chantry Way. Bill 149 D1
Chantry Way. Rain 173 E2
Chanute Ave. Finch 43 E4
Chapel Cl. W Thu 191 D1
Chapel Ct. Bill 149 D1
Chapel Ct. Swan 191 F1
Chapel Dr. Lit Wal 98 A3
Chapel End. Hod 100 A4
Chapel End Way. Stam 19 E1
Chapel Fields. Harl 103 E3

Chapel High. Brent 158 B4
Chapel Hill. Brain 66 A1
Chapel Hill. Stan M 57 E3
Chapel La. Chig 153 F4
Chapel La. Harl 103 E3
Chapel La. New 37 D4
Chapel La. Rox 108 C1
Chapel Lodge. Rain 174 A1
Chapel Rd. Epp 115 F1
Chapel Rd. Ridge 20 A4
Chapel Row. Bis St 67 F3
Chapel St. Bill 149 D1
Chapel St. Cla 9 D2
Chapel St. Ste B 18 B4
Chapelfields. Sta Ab 87 E2
Chaplaincy Gdns. Hornc 165 F2
Chaplemount Rd. Woodf 152 C2
Chaplin Cl. Bill 161 F1
Chaplin Cl. Chelm 124 A1
Charlbury Cl. Romf 156 B2
Charlbury Cres. Romf 156 B2
Charles Rd. Dag 173 E3
Charles St. Epp 129 D4
Charles St. Grays 192 B4
Charles St. Stone 191 D1
Charleston Ave. Basil 163 E1
Charlotte Ave. Wick 163 E4
Charlotte Gdns. Romf 155 D2
Charlotte Pl. W Thu 191 D4
Charlotte Rd. Dag 173 D3
Charlton Cl. Basil 172 B4
Charlton Mead La. Hod 100 B3
Charlton St. Grays 191 E4
Charlton Way. Hod 100 A3
Charnwood Ave. Chelm 110 C1
Charterhouse. Basil 171 E3
Charteris Rd. Woodf 152 A2
Charters. Gt Dun 61 E1
Charters Cross. Harl 102 B3
Chartwell Cl. Brain 65 F4
Chartwell Cl. Wa Aby 126 C3
Chase Cross Rd. Romf 155 E2
Chase House Gdns. Hornc ... 165 F2
Chase La. Chig 154 A4
Chase Rd. Brent 158 B4
Chase Rd. Corr 180 A2
Chase Sq. Grave 193 D1
Chase The. Barn 73 D2
Chase The. Basil 170 C2
Chase The. Bill 149 E1
Chase The. Bill 161 D1
Chase The. Bis St 67 F3
Chase The. Bl Not 76 B3
Chase The. Bore 112 C4
Chase The. Brain 65 F4
Chase The. Brent 158 B4
Chase The. Brent 159 E3
Chase The. Chig 153 E3
Chase The. Finch 42 B3
Chase The. Grays 191 E4
Chase The. Gt Bad 124 C3
Chase The. Hen 48 C3
Chase The. Hornc 164 C1
Chase The. Romf 164 C1
Chase The. Romf 164 C4
Chase The. Ste B 18 A4
Chase The. Upm 166 C1
Chase The. Wick 163 D3
Chase The. Wick 163 F2
Chaseside Cl. Romf 155 F2
Chaseway. Basil 171 F2
Chaseway The. S Han 150 A4
Chaseways. Saw 90 B4
Chaters Hill. Saff W 13 F1
Chatfield Way. Basil 172 B4
Chatham Pavement. Basil ... 172 B4
Chathamhall La. Lit Wal 98 A4
Chatley Rd. Gt Le 85 F4
Chatteris Ave. Romf 156 B2
Chaucer Cl. Tilb 193 E3
Chaucer Rd. Chelm 111 E1
Chaucer Rd. Romf 156 A2
Chaucer Way. Hod 87 D1
Chaucer Way. Stone 190 A2
Chaucer Wlk. Hod 163 E3
Chauntry Rd. Hav 6 C4
Cheelson Rd. S Ock 176 B2
Chelmer Ave. Lit Wal 98 A3
Chelmer Dr. Brent 147 F2
Chelmer Dr. Gt Dun 72 C4
Chelmer Lea. Gt Bad 124 C4
Chelmer Pl. Chelm 111 E2
Chelmer Rd. Brain 66 B1
Chelmer Rd. Grays 186 A1
Chelmer Rd. Hav 7 D4
Chelmer Rd. Sprin 111 F2
Chelmer Rd. Upm 166 B3
Chelmer Valley Rd. Chelm .. 111 E3
Chelmer Village Way. Sprin . 112 A2
Chelmerton Ave. Gt Bad 124 C4
Chelmsford Ave. Romf 155 E2
Chelmsford Dr. Upm 165 F1
Chelmsford Rd. Barn 73 D2
Chelmsford Rd. Bla 121 D1
Chelmsford Rd. BO 79 E2
Chelmsford Rd. Brent 147 D3
Chelmsford Rd. Ch Ong 119 E2
Chelmsford Rd. Chelm 110 B1
Chelmsford Rd. Felst 74 A2

Chelmsford Rd. Gt Wal 98 A3
Chelmsford Rd. H Ong 119 E2
Chelmsford Rd. Mar Rod 94 B2
Chelmsford Rd. Woodf 152 A1
Chelsworth Cl. Romf 156 C2
Chelsworth Dr. Romf 156 C1
Cheltenham Gdns. Lou 140 C2
Chelwater. Bal 124 B4
Chelwood Cl. Ching 139 D2
Chenies Dr. Bill 161 D1
Chenies Green. Bis St 67 E3
Chepstow Ave. Hornc 165 F1
Chepstow Cl. Bill 149 E3
Chequers. Bis St 67 E4
Chequers. Lou 140 A1
Chequers La. Dag 173 D2
Chequers La. Gt Dun 72 B4
Chequers Rd. Brent 144 C1
Chequers Rd. Lou 141 D2
Chequers Rd. Writ 109 F1
Chequers Wlk. Wa Aby 126 C3
Cheriton Ave. Woodf 153 D1
Cheriton Rd. Brain 66 B1
Cherry Ave. Brent 158 C4
Cherry Garden La. New 37 D4
Cherry Garden Rd. Gt Wal 97 F4
Cherry Gdns. Bill 148 C2
Cherry Gdns. Bis St 68 A4
Cherry Gdns. Saw 77 F2
Cherry St. Romf 164 B3
Cherry Tree Cl. Grays 192 B4
Cherry Tree Cl. Rain 174 A2
Cherry Tree La. Rain 173 F2
Cherry Tree Rd. Hod 100 A4
Cherry Tree Rise. Woodf 152 B3
Cherry Wlk. Grays 186 A2
Cherry Wlk. Rain 174 A2
Cherrydown. Grays 185 E3
Cherrydown East. Basil 171 D3
Cherrydown West. Basil 171 D3
Cherrydown Wlk. Romf 155 D1
Cherrygarden La. Chelm 124 A4
Cherrytrees. Bill 160 C4
Cherston Gdns. Lou 141 D3
Cherston Rd. Lou 141 D3
Cherwell Dr. Chelm 110 B3
Cherwell Gr. S Ock 184 A3
Chesfield Cl. Bis St 67 F3
Chesham Cl. Romf 164 B4
Chesham Dr. Bill 161 C1
Cheshire Cl. Hornc 166 A3
Chester Ave. Upm 166 C1
Chester Cl. Lou 141 E4
Chester Green. Lou 141 E4
Chester Hall La. Basil 162 A1
Chester Path. Lou 141 E4
Chester Pl. Chelm 111 D3
Chester Rd. Chig 153 D4
Chester Rd. Lou 141 D4
Chester Way. Basil 171 F4
Chesterford Gdns. Basil 171 F4
Chesterford Green. Basil 171 F4
Chesterton Way. Tilb 193 E3
Chestnut Ave. Bill 149 D1
Chestnut Ave. Grays 185 D2
Chestnut Ave. Hornc 165 D1
Chestnut Ave. Litt 12 B1
Chestnut Ave. Lou 152 B4
Chestnut Cl. Bis St 67 F3
Chestnut Cl. Grave 192 C1
Chestnut Cl. Hav 6 C4
Chestnut Cl. Hornc 174 B4
Chestnut Cl. Lou 152 B4
Chestnut Ct. Basil 172 A2
Chestnut Ct. New 37 D4
Chestnut Glen. Hornc 165 D1
Chestnut Gr. Brain 65 F1
Chestnut Gr. Brent 158 A4
Chestnut Gr. Chig 153 F2
Chestnut Rd. Basil 172 A2
Chestnut Way. Take 70 B4
Chestnut Wlk. Chelm 111 D3
Chestnut Wlk. Felst 74 B3
Chestnut Wlk. Woodf 152 A3
Chestnuts. Basil 172 A4
Chestnuts. Brent 147 D1
Chestwood Cl. Bill 149 D3
Cheveley Cl. Romf 156 C1
Chevely Cl. Epp 116 B1
Chevers Pawen. Basil 172 A3
Chevington Way. Hornc 174 B4
Cheviot Dr. Chelm 110 B3
Cheviot Rd. Hornc 165 D2
Chichester. Cl. Ave 183 E3
Chichester Cl. Basil 171 F4
Chichester Dr. Sprin 111 E2
Chichester Rd. Saff W 25 F4
Chichester Rd. Stone 190 C1
Chickney Rd. Brox 49 E3
Chickney Rd. Hen 49 E3
Chieftan Dr. Pur 183 D1
Chignall Rd. Chelm 110 B3
Chignalls The. Basil 170 A3
Chigwell La. Chig 141 E2
Chigwell Park Dr. Chig 153 D3
Chigwell Rd. Woodf 152 B2
Chigwell Rise. Chig 153 D4
Chigwell View. Romf 155 D3
Childerditch Hall Dr. Brent 168 A4

Childerditch La. Brent 158 C1
Childerditch St. Brent 168 A4
Childers The. Woodf 152 C3
Childs Cl. Hornc 165 E3
Childs Cres. Swan 191 E1
Chilham Cl. Basil 172 B3
Chiltern Gdns. Hornc 165 E1
Chiltern Way. Woodf 152 A4
Chilton Cl. Gt Bad 124 B4
Chilton Rd. Grays 186 A2
Chimswell Way. Hav 6 B4
China La. Horn H 168 B1
Chindits La. Brent 158 B3
Chinnery Hill. Bis St 67 F3
Chippenham Cl. Romf 156 B3
Chippenham Gdns. Romf 156 B3
Chippenham Rd. Romf 156 B3
Chippenham Wlk. Romf 156 B2
Chipperfield Cl. Upm 166 C2
Chippingfield. Harl 90 B2
Chishill Rd. Hey 10 A2
Chittock Gate. Basil 171 F3
Chittock Mead. Basil 171 F3
Chivers Rd. Sto M 132 C2
Cholvedon Sq. Basil 172 A3
Chorley Cl. Basil 169 F3
Christchurch Ave. Rain 173 F1
Christchurch Ave. Wick 163 D4
Christchurch Rd. Tilb 193 D3
Christopher Cl. Hornc 174 B4
Christopher Martin Rd. Basil . 162 C2
Christy Ave. Chelm 110 C2
Christy Way. Basil 169 F4
Chudleigh Rd. Romf 156 C3
Church Ave. Broom 98 A1
Church Cl. Kelv H 132 B1
Church Cl. Lou 140 C4
Church Cl. Mtssg 147 F4
Church Cres. Mtssg 147 F4
Church Cres. S Ock 176 B1
Church Cres. Saw 77 F1
Church Dr. Berd 46 A4
Church Elm La. Dag 173 D3
Church End. Gt Dun 61 F1
Church End. Harl 102 A3
Church End. Pan 65 D4
Church End Ave. Runw 151 F1
Church End La. Runw 151 F1
Church Field. Epp 116 A1
Church Field. Saff W 25 F4
Church Fields. Gt Y 20 C1
Church Gdns. Gt Dun 61 E1
Church Green. Broom 98 A1
Church Green. Hinx 1 A4
Church Green. Rox 109 D3
Church Hill. Ash 15 D4
Church Hill. Basil 170 B4
Church Hill. Epp 116 A1
Church Hill. Finch 42 B3
Church Hill. Hel B 17 E4
Church Hill. Lit Wal 98 B3
Church Hill. Lou 140 C3
Church Hill. Sta L H 179 E1
Church Hill. Stone 190 C1
Church Hollow. Pur 183 D1
Church La. Abr 142 C3
Church La. Bart 5 F2
Church La. Basil 163 D1
Church La. Bill 162 A3
Church La. Brain 65 F3
Church La. Brent 147 F1
Church La. Brent 167 E3
Church La. Can E 71 D4
Church La. Ch Ong 119 D4
Church La. Chelm 111 D1
Church La. Dag 173 E3
Church La. Deb 38 A4
Church La. Dodd 133 D1
Church La. Els 58 C4
Church La. Gt Le 85 E4
Church La. Gt Wal 84 A3
Church La. Horn H 177 F4
Church La. Kelv H 133 D1
Church La. Lou 140 C3
Church La. Marg 135 F3
Church La. N W Bas 117 D3
Church La. Pur 183 D1
Church La. Rain 182 B4
Church La. Ridge 20 A3
Church La. Romf 164 C4
Church La. S Han 151 E4
Church La. Sheer 91 E4
Church La. Sprin 111 E2
Church La. Sta Abb 143 E3
Church La. Take 70 A4
Church La. Thor 67 E2
Church La. Topp 32 A4
Church La. Upm 176 A4
Church La. W Han 138 A2
Church La. Writ 110 A1
Church Langley Way. Harl 103 E4
Church Leys. Harl 102 C4
Church Manor. Bis St 68 A4
Church Mead. Roy 88 A1
Church Mews. Basil 170 A4
Church Park. Cla 9 E2
Church Park Rd. Basil 172 A3
Church Path. Grave 192 B1
Church Path. Gt Am 87 D3

Church Path. Had 3 D3
Church Path. Saff W 13 E1
Church Path. Stone 190 C1
Church Rd. Bart 5 D3
Church Rd. Basil 169 E3
Church Rd. Bill 171 E3
Church Rd. Bill 161 F1
Church Rd. Chris 10 B2
Church Rd. Corr 180 A2
Church Rd. Grays 193 F4
Church Rd. Gt Ha 68 C2
Church Rd. Gt Ha 69 D3
Church Rd. Gt Y 20 C1
Church Rd. Harl 103 E3
Church Rd. Hav B 144 B1
Church Rd. Hemp 28 C4
Church Rd. Horn H 178 A4
Church Rd. Kelv H 132 B1
Church Rd. L Hal 68 A1
Church Rd. Lou 140 A1
Church Rd. More 105 E1
Church Rd. Mtssg 147 F4
Church Rd. Nave H 144 B1
Church Rd. Nave H 144 C4
Church Rd. Romf 157 D2
Church Rd. S Han 150 B2
Church Rd. Sta R 131 E3
Church Rd. Stam 19 E1
Church Rd. Stan M 57 E3
Church Rd. Stone 190 C1
Church Rd. Swan 191 F1
Church Rd. Tilb 192 C3
Church Rd. W Han 138 A2
Church Rd. Wa Aby 140 A4
Church Rd. Wick 150 B1
Church St. Bill 161 E3
Church St. Bis St 67 F4
Church St. Bla 133 F4
Church St. Chelm 111 D1
Church St. Dag 173 D3
Church St. Grave 193 D1
Church St. Grays 192 B4
Church St. Gt Bad 125 D3
Church St. Gt C 1 B1
Church St. Gt Dun 61 E1
Church St. Hinx 1 A2
Church St. New 25 D1
Church St. Pan 65 F4
Church St. Saff W 13 E1
Church St. Saw 77 F1
Church St. Ste B 18 A4
Church St. Wa Aby 126 B3
Church St. Wen A 24 C3
Church St. Widd 37 E2
Church View. Ave 183 E2
Church View. Cla 8 B1
Church View. Upm 166 A1
Church Wlk. Litt 12 C2
Church Wlk. Saw 77 F1
Church Wlk. Stur 7 F2
Churchfield. Hod 100 A1
Churchfields. Hod 100 A2
Churchfields. Lou 140 C3
Churchfields. Woodf 152 A1
Churchfields Dr. Ste B 18 A3
Churchgate St. Harl 90 C2
Churchill Cl. Ch Ong 119 D2
Churchill Cres. Corr 179 F2
Churchill Rd. Brain 65 F4
Churchill Rd. Grays 192 B4
Churchill Rise. Sprin 111 F4
Chuzzlewit Dr. Chelm 110 C4
Cillocks Cl. Hod 100 A4
Circle The. Tilb 193 D3
Civic Sq. Tilb 193 D3
Clachar Cl. Sprin 112 A2
Claire Cl. Brent 159 D3
Clairmont Cl. Brain 65 F1
Clairvale. Hornc 165 F2
Clapton Hall La. Gt Dun 72 B3
Clare Ave. Runw 151 E1
Clare Mews. Ch Ong 119 D3
Clare Rd. Brain 65 F1
Claremont. Basil 170 B4
Claremont Cl. Grays 185 E2
Claremont Dr. Basil 172 A2
Claremont Gdns. Upm 166 B2
Claremont Gr. Woodf 152 B2
Claremont Rd. Hornc 165 D3
Clarence Ave. Upm 166 A1
Clarence Cl. Sprin 112 A2
Clarence Rd. Basil 172 C4
Clarence Rd. Brent 146 A2
Clarence Rd. Corr 180 B2
Clarence Rd. Grays 185 D1
Clarence Rd. Stan M 57 F4
Clarendon Rd. Basil 172 B4
Clarendon Rd. Grave 193 E1
Clarendon Rd. Hav 6 C3
Clarendon Rd. Take 70 C4
Clark Way. Broom 98 A1
Clarkbourne Dr. Grays 192 B4
Clarkhill. Harl 102 C3
Clarks La. Epp 128 C4
Clatterbury La. Clav 35 F3
Claudian Cl. Hav 7 E4
Claudian Way. Grays 186 A2
Claughton Way. Brent 147 E2

Claverhambury Rd. Wa Aby . 114 A2
Clavering. Basil 171 F2
Clavering Gdns. Horn H 168 B3
Clavering Rd. Brain 65 F3
Clavering Way. Brent 147 E2
Clay Hill Rd. Basil 171 E3
Clay Pit Piece. Saff W 25 F3
Clay Tye Rd. Upm 167 E1
Clay's La. Lou 141 D4
Clayburn Circ. Basil 171 E3
Clayburn End. Basil 171 E3
Clayburn Gdns. S Ock 184 A3
Clayburn Side. Basil 171 E3
Claybury Rd. Woodf 152 C2
Claydon Cl. Bart 5 F2
Claydon Cres. Basil 171 E4
Claygate Cl. Hornc 174 A4
Clayhall Ave. Woodf 152 C1
Claypit Hill. Els 58 C3
Claypit Hill. Wa Aby 127 E2
Claypits Rd. Bore 99 F1
Claypits Villas. Thax 40 A1
Clayponds. Bis St 68 A4
Clays Meadow. Litt 12 C2
Clayside. Chig 153 E3
Clayton Ave. Upm 175 D4
Clayton Cl. Romf 164 B2
Claywall Bridge. Ste B 18 B4
Cleall Ave. Wa Aby 126 B3
Cleland Path. Lou 141 D4
Clematis Cl. Romf 156 B2
Clematis Tye. Sprin 111 F4
Clement Way. Upm 165 F1
Clement's La. Hav 6 C4
Clements Cl. Hav 6 C4
Clements Dr. Hav 6 C4
Clerks Piece. Lou 140 C3
Cleveland Rd. Basil 171 E3
Cleveland Rd. Woodf 152 A1
Cleves Ct. Bore 99 F1
Cleves Wlk. Woodf 153 E2
Clickett End. Basil 171 E3
Clickett Hill. Basil 171 E3
Clickett Side. Basil 171 E3
Cliff Pl. S Ock 176 B1
Cliffield. Shal 54 C4
Clifford Ave. Woodf 153 D1
Clifford Rd. Grays 184 C2
Clifton Marine Par. Grave 193 D1
Clifton Rd. Basil 172 C4
Clifton Rd. Grave 193 D1
Clifton Rd. Hornc 165 D3
Clifton Rd. Lou 140 C3
Clifton Way. Brent 147 E1
Clinton Cres. Chig 153 F2
Clipped Hedge. Hat B O 79 D2
Clitheroe Rd. Romf 155 E3
Clive Rd. Brent 158 B2
Clive Rd. Grave 193 D1
Clive Rd. Romf 165 D3
Cliveden Cl. Brent 146 C1
Cliveden Cl. Chelm 110 C2
Clobbs Yd. Chelm 111 D4
Clock House La. Grays 184 C2
Clockhouse La. Hav B 155 E2
Clockhouse La. Romf 155 E2
Clockhouse Way. Brain 66 B1
Cloisters. Corr 179 F1
Cloisters The. Brain 66 A3
Clopton Green. Basil 171 D4
Close The. Brent 158 B4
Close The. Deb 38 A4
Close The. Grays 185 E2
Close The. Gt Dun 72 C4
Close The. Hat B O 79 D2
Cloudberry Rd. Romf 156 B2
Clovelly Gdns. Romf 155 D1
Clovelly Gdns. Runw 163 E4
Clover Cl. Basil 171 F2
Clover Ct. Grays 192 B4
Clover Field. Harl 103 D3
Clover Leas. Epp 115 F1
Clover Way. Basil 171 F2
Cloverley Rd. Ch Ong 119 D1
Cloverleys. Lou 140 B3
Cluff Ct. Brent 158 B3
Clunas Gdns. Romf 165 E4
Clyde. Grays 187 E1
Clyde Cres. Chelm 110 B2
Clyde Cres. Upm 166 C3
Clyde Rd. Roy 100 B2
Clyde Way. Romf 155 F1
Clydesdale Rd. Brain 65 F1
Clydesdale Rd. Hornc 164 C2
Coach Mews. Bill 149 E3
Coach Rd. Hemp 16 C1
Coates Cl. Brain 7 D4
Cobbins The. Wa Aby 126 C3
Cobbinsbank. Wa Aby 126 B3
Cobbinsend Rd. Wa Aby 114 B1
Cobbles The. Brent 158 C4
Cobbles The. Upm 166 C2
Cobbs La. Take 59 F2
Cobbs Pl. Sprin 111 E2
Cobden Wlk. Basil 172 B4
Cobham. Grays 185 D2
Cobill Cl. Hornc 165 E4
Coburg Gdns. Woodf 152 C1

Coburg La. Basil 169 F2
Cock Green. Harl 102 A3
Cock La. Clav 34 C2
Cock La. Ing 121 F1
Cockerell Cl. Basil 163 D1
Codenham Green. Basil 171 D2
Codenham Straight. Basil 171 D2
Codham Hall La. Brent 167 D4
Codham Little Park Dr. Weth .. 55 E3
Coggeshall Rd. Brain 66 B3
Coggeshall Rd. Stis 66 B2
Cogmore. Elm 23 D4
Colbourne Cl. Corr 179 F2
Colchester Rd. Bore 112 A3
Colchester Rd. Romf 156 C1
Coldharbour Rd. Harl 102 A4
Coldnailhurst Ave. Brain 65 F3
Cole End La. Saff W 26 B3
Cole End La. Wim 26 B3
Cole Hill. Gt Le 86 A3
Colebrook Gdns. Lou 141 D4
Colebrook La. Lou 141 D4
Colebrook Path. Lou 141 D4
Colehills Cl. Clav 35 E3
Coleman's La. Lo Naz 113 F3
Coleridge Cl. Romf 156 A4
Coleridge Rd. Stone 190 A2
Coleridge Rd. Tilb 193 E3
Coleridge Wlk. Brent 147 E1
Coles Cl. Gt Ong 119 D4
Coles Green. Lou 141 D4
Colet Rd. Brent 147 F1
Colin Cl. Stone 190 A1
Collard Ave. Lou 141 E4
Collard Green. Lou 141 E4
College Ave. Grays 185 E1
College Cl. Grays 185 F1
College Gdns. Ching 139 E1
College Rd. Brain 65 F1
College Rd. Grave 192 A1
College Rd. Grays 185 E1
College Sq. Harl 102 B4
Colley Rd. Gt Bad 125 D3
Collier Row La. Romf 155 E1
Collier Row Rd. Romf 155 D2
Collingwood Cl. Brain 66 B3
Collingwood Rd. Basil 171 E2
Collingwood Terr. Basil 171 E3
Collingwood Wlk. Basil 171 E3
Collins Cl. Brain 65 F1
Collins Cl. Corr 179 F1
Collins Cross. Bis St 57 F3
Collins Meadow. Harl 102 A4
Collins Way. Brent 147 F2
Collops Villas. Steb 63 D2
Colman Cl. Corr 179 E2
Colne. Grays 187 E2
Colne Cl. Corr 179 F3
Colne Pl. Basil 171 E2
Colne Springs. Ridge 20 A3
Colne Valley. Upm 166 C3
Colne Valley Rd. Hav 7 D4
Colney Rd. Stone 190 A1
Colson Gdns. Lou 141 D3
Colson Green. Lou 141 D2
Colson Path. Lou 141 D3
Colson Rd. Lou 141 D3
Coltishall Rd. Hornc 174 B3
Colts The. Bis St 67 F2
Coltsfield. Stan M 57 F4
Coltsfoot Ct. Grays 192 B4
Coltsfoot Path. Romf 156 B2
Columbia Wharf Rd. Grays .. 192 A4
Columbine Way. Romf 156 C1
Colville Cl. Corr 179 F3
Colville Mews. Bill 148 C3
Colvin Chase. Chelm 124 A1
Colvin Gdns. Woodf 153 E2
Colyers Reach. Sprin 112 A1
Colyn Pl. Saff W 13 F2
Comet Cl. Pur 183 D1
Comfrey Ct. Grays 192 B4
Commercial Pl. Grave 193 E1
Common Hill. Saff W 13 E1
Common La. Chris 22 A4
Common La. Stock 136 C1
Common Rd. Brent 159 D3
Common Rd. Lo Naz 101 F1
Common Rd. Stock 136 C1
Commonfields. Harl 89 F1
Commonside Rd. Harl 102 C2
Como St. Romf 164 B4
Compton Ave. Brent 147 E1
Compton Ave. Romf 165 E4
Compton Wlk. Basil 170 A4
Comyns Pl. Writ 109 F4
Comyns Rd. Dag 173 D3
Condor Wlk. Rain 155 D3
Congreve Rd. Wa Aby 126 C4
Conifer Ave. Romf 155 D3
Conifer Dr. Brent 158 B3
Coniston Ave. Upm 175 D4
Coniston Cl. Bl Not 76 B3
Coniston Way. Hornc 174 A4

nnaught Ave. Ching 139 E1
nnaught Ave. Grays 185 D2
nnaught Ave. Lou 140 B3
nnaught Gdns. Brain 66 A2
nnaught Hill. Lou 140 B3
nnaught Rd. Ching 139 F1
nnaught Rd. Hav 6 C4
nnaught Rd. Hornc 165 C1
nnaught Way. Bill 149 D3
nrad Cl. Grays 185 D2
nrad Gdns. Grays 185 D2
nrad Rd. Sta L H 179 F1
nsort Cl. Brent 158 B3
nstable View. Sprin 111 F3
nstance Cl. Broom 98 A1
nsul Ave. Rain 173 E1
nvent Hill. Brain 66 A3
nvent La. Brain 66 A3
nway Cl. Rain 174 A3
nway Gdns. Grays 192 A4
nway's Rd. Grays 178 A1
nway's Rd. Horn H 178 A1
nybury Cl. Wa Aby 127 D4
nyers. Harl 89 E1
nyers Way. Lou 141 D3
ok Pl. Sprin 111 F2
ok's Cl. Romf 155 E1
ok's La. Gt Ba 41 F2
oks Green. Basil 163 E1
oks Spinney. Harl 90 A1
olgardie Ave. Chig 153 D4
ombe Dr. Basil 170 B1
ombe Rd. Romf 165 F4
ombe Rise. Brent 146 C1
ombe Rise. Chelm 111 D4
ombe Rise. Corr 179 F1
ombes Cl. Bill 148 C2
oper's La. Grays 193 F4
oper's Row. Chelm 111 D3
opers Cl. Chig 154 A4
opers Dr. Bill 161 E4
opers End Rd. Take 59 D2
opers Hill. Ch ong 119 D1
opers La. Gt Le 85 F4
opersale Common. Epp 116 B1
opersale La. The B 129 D2
opersale St. Epp 129 E4
opersales. Basil 170 A3
opdoek. Basil 171 E4
opeman Rd. Brent 147 E1
opford Cl. Bill 149 E1
opford Cl. Woodf 152 C1
opford Rd. Bill 149 E1
opland Cl. Broom 98 A1
opland Rd. Gt Bad 124 C4
opland Rd. Sta L H 179 E1
ople Rd. Hinx 1 A1
oppens Green. Wick 163 F3
opper Beech Cl. Woodf 153 D1
opper Beech Ct. Lou 141 D4
opper Beech Rd. S Ock 176 B1
opper Ct. Saw 77 F1
opperfield. Bill 161 E3
opperfield. Chig 153 E2
opperfield Gdns. Brent 146 B1
opperfield Rd. Chelm 110 C4
opperfields. Basil 170 B4
opperfields Way. Romf 156 B1
oppice Hatch. Harl 102 B3
oppice La. Bill 161 F1
oppice Path. Chig 154 A3
oppice Row. The B 128 B2
oppice The. Kelv H 132 C1
oppings The. Hod 87 D1
oppins Cl. Sprin 111 F2
opse Hill. Harl 102 A3
opse The. Bill 149 D2
opse The. Bis St 68 B4
opse The. Ching 139 F1
opse The. Felst 74 C3
optfold Rd. Brent 158 B4
opthall La. Thax 40 A2
opthorne Ave. Woodf 153 D2
opthorne Gdns. Hornc 166 A3
opy Hill. Hel B 6 C1
oram Green. Brent 147 E2
orbets Ave. Upm 175 D4
orbets Tey Rd. Upm 175 D4
orcorans. Brent 146 B2
ormorant Wlk. Chelm 124 B3
ormorant Wlk. Rain 174 A3
ornell Way. Romf 155 D3
ornells La. Widd 37 F2
orner Park. Saff W 13 F2
orner Rd. Bill 162 B3
ornflower Dr. Sprin 111 F3
ornflower Gdns. Bill 148 C2
ornflower Way. Romf 156 C1
ornhill. Chelm 111 D1
ornish Hall End Rd. Stam ... 19 D1
ornmill. Wa Aby 126 A3
ornsland. Brent 158 B4
ornwall Cl. Hornc 166 A4
ornwall Cres. Chelm 111 D4
ornwall Gdns. Brent 66 A2
ornwall Gate. Pur 183 D1
ornwall Rd. Basil 172 C4
ornwall Rd. Brent 146 A2

Cornwallis Pl. Saff W 13 F1
Cornwallis Rd. Hav 6 C3
Cornwell Cres. Corr 179 F2
Corona Rd. Basil 170 A2
Coronation Ave. Brain 65 F1
Coronation Ave. Grays 187 E1
Coronation Dr. Hornc 174 A4
Coronation Hill. Epp 115 F1
Coronation Rd. Bis St 67 F3
Corporation Rd. Chelm 111 D2
Corran Way. S Ock 184 B3
Corringham Rd. Sta L H 179 F1
Corve La. S Ock 184 A3
Cory Dr. Brent 147 D1
Costead Manor Rd. Brent ... 146 A1
Coteford Cl. Lou 141 D4
Cotelands. Basil 171 F2
Cotleigh Rd. Romf 164 B3
Cotswold Cres. Chelm 110 B3
Cotswold Gdns. Brent 147 F1
Cotswold Rd. Romf 156 C1
Cottage Pl. Chelm 111 D2
Cottesmore Ave. Woodf 153 D1
Cottis Cl. Basil 170 A2
Cotton La. Stone 190 B1
Cottons App. Romf 164 B3
Couchmore Ave. Woodf 152 C1
Council Ave. Grave 192 B1
Council Rd. Bis St 68 A4
Counting House La. Gt Dun ... 61 E1
Coupals Cl. Hav 7 E3
Coupals Rd. Hav 7 F3
Courage Cl. Hornc 165 E3
Courage Wlk. Brent 147 E2
Court Ave. Romf 157 D2
Court Rd. Broom 98 A2
Court Rd. Broom 98 A2
Court View. Ing 134 C1
Court Way. Romf 156 C1
Courtauld Rd. Basil 163 E1
Courtauld Rd. Brain 66 A2
Courtfield Cl. Hod 100 A2
Courtland Dr. Chig 153 E4
Courtlands. Bill 148 C1
Courtlands. Chelm 111 D3
Courtney Park Rd. Basil 170 A3
Courtney Rd. Grays 186 B2
Courtway. Woodf 152 B3
Courtway Cotts. Corr 180 B3
Coval Ave. Chelm 111 D2
Coval La. Chelm 111 D2
Covenbrook. Brent 159 D4
Coverley Cl. Brent 158 B2
Covert Rd. Chig 153 F2
Coverts The. Brent 147 D1
Coverts The. Writ 110 A1
Cow La. Gt C 2 A1
Cow Watering La. Writ 109 F2
Cowdray Way. Hornc 174 A4
Cowell Ave. Chelm 110 C3
Cowels Farm La. Thax 51 F3
Cowley Rd. Romf 156 A2
Cowper Ave. Tilb 193 D3
Cowper Rd. Rain 174 A1
Cowslip Mead. Basil 171 D3
Cowslip Rd. Woodf 152 A1
Cox Ley. Hat B O 79 D2
Coxes Cl. Corr 179 E2
Coxes Farm Rd. Bill 161 E4
Coxtie Green Rd. Brent 145 E2
Crabb's La. St Pel 45 F3
Crabtree Hill. Widd 37 D2
Craigdale Rd. Hornc 164 C2
Craiston Way. Gt Bad 124 C3
Crammavill St. Grays 185 D3
Crammerville Wlk. Rain 174 A1
Cramphorn Wlk. Chelm 110 C2
Cranborne Gdns. Upm 166 A1
Cranborne Rd. Hod 100 B4
Cranbourne Dri. Hod 87 E1
Cranbrook Dr. Romf 165 E4
Crane Cl. Dag 173 D3
Cranell Green. S Ock 184 A3
Cranes Cl. Basil 162 C1
Cranes Ct. Basil 171 E4
Cranes Farm Rd. Basil 171 D4
Cranes La. Basil 171 E4
Cranfield Ct. Runw 163 E4
Cranfield Park Rd. Wick 163 F2
Cranham Gdns. Upm 166 C2
Cranham Rd. Brox 49 F2
Cranham Rd. Hornc 165 D3
Cranleigh Gdns. Lou 140 C2
Cranmer Cl. Bill 149 D3
Cranmer Gdns. Dag 173 E4
Cranmore Cl. Els 48 B1
Cranston Park Ave. Upm 175 E4
Cranwell Gdns. Bis St 57 E1
Cranworth Cres. Ching 139 E1
Craven Gdns. Romf 155 D3
Craven Gdns. Romf 157 E2
Craven Gdns. Woodf 153 E1
Crawford Ave. Grays 185 D3
Crawford Cl. Bill 149 E3
Crawford Compton Cl. Hornc ... 174 B3
Crawley Cl. Corr 180 A3
Crayfields. Gt Dun 61 F1
Craylands. Basil 171 F4
Craylands La. Swan 191 E1

Craylands Sq. Swan 191 E1
Crays Hill. Bill 162 B3
Crays Hill Rd. Bill 162 B2
Crays View. Bill 161 D4
Creasey Cl. Hornc 165 D1
Credo Way. W Thu 191 D4
Cree Way. Romf 155 F2
Creek The. Grave 192 A1
Creek View. Basil 171 F2
Creekside. Rain 173 F1
Crescent Ave. Grays 192 B4
Crescent Ave. Hornc 164 C1
Crescent Cl. Bill 148 C2
Crescent Dr. Brent 146 C1
Crescent Gdns. Bill 148 C2
Crescent Rd. Ave 183 E2
Crescent Rd. Bill 148 C2
Crescent Rd. Bis St 68 A3
Crescent Rd. Brent 158 A3
Crescent Rd. Ching 139 F1
Crescent Rd. Dag 164 A1
Crescent Rd. Gt Bad 125 D4
Crescent Rd. Woodf 152 B1
Crescent The. Epp 128 C4
Crescent The. Gt Le 85 F3
Crescent The. Harl 90 B3
Crescent The. Lou 140 B2
Crescent The. Ste B 18 A4
Crescent The. Swan 191 E1
Crescent The. Upm 166 C2
Crescent View. Lou 140 B2
Crescent Way. Ave 183 E3
Crescent Wlk. Ave 183 E2
Cress Croft. Brain 66 B1
Cressages Cl. Felst 74 C3
Cressells. Basil 170 C3
Cresset Cl. Sta Ab 87 E2
Cressing Rd. Brain 66 B1
Crest Ave. Basil 172 B3
Crest Ave. Grays 192 A4
Crest The. Saw 77 E4
Cresthill Ave. Grays 185 E1
Crete Hall Rd. Grave 192 C1
Cricketers Cl. Broom 98 B1
Cricketers La. Brent 159 E2
Cricketers Row. Brent 159 E2
Cricketers Way. Wick 163 D1
Cricketfield La. Bis St 67 F4
Cricklade Ave. Romf 156 B2
Crina Wlk. Basil 171 F3
Cripsey Ave. Ch Ong 118 C3
Crittall Dr. Brain 65 E2
Crix Green Villas. Felst 75 E3
Croasdaile Rd. Stan M 57 F4
Croasdale Cl. Stan M 57 F4
Crocus Way. Sprin 111 F4
Croft Cl. Brain 66 A2
Croft Cl. Sprin 111 F1
Croft La. Hav 7 D3
Croft Lodge Cl. Woodf 152 A2
Croft The. Els 48 B1
Croft The. Lou 141 D4
Crofters. Saw 77 F2
Crofters End. Saw 77 F2
Crofton Ave. Corr 179 F2
Crofton Rd. Grays 185 F2
Cromer Ave. Basil 170 A4
Cromer Cl. Basil 170 A4
Cromer Rd. Hornc 165 E2
Cromer Rd. Romf 164 B3
Cromer Rd. Woodf 152 A3
Crompton Cl. Basil 170 C4
Crompton St. Chelm 110 C1
Cromwell Ave. Bill 149 D2
Cromwell Cl. Bis St 67 E4
Cromwell Rd. Brent 158 A3
Cromwell Rd. Grays 185 D1
Cromwell Rd. Saff W 25 F4
Crondon Park La. Stock 136 C2
Crooked La. Grave 193 D1
Crooked Mile. Wa Aby 126 B4
Crooked Way. Lo Naz 100 C1
Croppath Rd. Dag 173 D4
Crosby Rd. Dag 173 D2
Cross Ave. Wick 163 E3
Cross Green. Basil 170 C3
Cross Park Rd. Wick 163 E2
Cross Rd. Basil 172 C4
Cross Rd. Ching 139 F1
Cross Rd. Grave 192 C1
Cross Rd. Romf 164 A4
Cross Rd. Woodf 152 C2
Cross Roads. Wa Aby 140 A4
Cross St. Grave 193 D1
Cross St. Harl 102 B4
Cross St. Saff W 13 E1
Crossbow Rd. Chig 153 F3
Crossfield Rd. Hod 100 A4
Crossfields. Lou 141 D2
Crossing Rd. Epp 129 D3
Crossway. Corr 179 F2
Crossway. Woodf 152 B3
Crossway The. Bill 149 E2
Crossways. Brent 147 D2
Crossways. Chelm 124 B4
Crossways. Romf 165 D3
Crossways Bvd. Stone 190 B2
Crouch Dr. Wick 163 E4

Crouch Rd. Grays 186 A1
Crouch St. Bill 161 F1
Crouch Valley. Upm 166 C2
Crow Green La. Brent 146 A2
Crow Green Rd. Brent 146 A3
Crow Green Rd. Dodd 145 F3
Crow La. Romf 164 A2
Crow St. Hen 48 C3
Crowland Rd. Hav 6 C4
Crowlands Ave. Romf 164 A3
Crown Ave. Basil 172 B4
Crown Cl. Saw 78 B1
Crown Cl. Sheer 91 E4
Crown Ct. Tilb 193 D3
Crown Gate. Harl 102 B4
Crown Hill. Wa Aby 127 F3
Crown Rd. Bill 149 D1
Crown Rd. Grays 192 A4
Crown Rd. Kelv H 145 E4
Crown St. Brent 158 B4
Crown St. Dag 173 E3
Crown St. Gt Ba 42 A1
Crown Terr. Bis St 68 A4
Crownfield. Hod 100 A1
Crownhill Rd. Woodf 152 C2
Crownmead Way. Romf 164 A4
Crows Field Cotts. W Han ... 137 F2
Crows Rd. Epp 115 F1
Crowsheath La. S Han 150 C3
Crowstone Rd. Grays 185 E2
Croxford Way. Romf 164 B2
Cruick Ave. S Ock 184 B3
Crummock Cl. Bl Not 76 B3
Crunch Croft. Stur 7 F3
Crushes Cl. Brent 147 F2
Crystal Ave. Hornc 165 F1
Cuckoo La. T Thu 184 C3
Cuckoos La. Gt Can 71 D2
Culford Rd. Grays 185 E2
Cullen Sq. S Ock 184 B3
Cullings Ct. Wa Aby 126 C3
Culpeper Cl. Woodf 153 D2
Culverdown. Basil 171 D3
Cumberland Ave. Hornc 165 F1
Cumberland Cl. Brain 66 A2
Cumberland Cl. Hornc 165 F1
Cumberland Cres. Chelm ... 111 D4
Cumberland Dr. Basil 170 A3
Cumley Rd. Ch Ong 117 F1
Cumming Rd. S Han 151 D1
Cummings Hall La. Romf ... 156 B4
Cunningham Rise. N W Bas . 117 E3
Cunnington Rd. Brain 66 B2
Cupthall Ct. Gt Ha 68 C2
Curlew Cres. Basil 171 D2
Curling La. Grays 184 C1
Curling Tye. Basil 171 E4
Curling Wlk. Basil 171 E4
Currants Farm Rd. Brain 65 F3
Curtis Mill La. Sta Abb 143 F3
Curtis Rd. Hornc 165 F2
Curzon Dr. Grays 192 A4
Curzon Way. Sprin 112 A1
Curzon Wlk. Basil 172 A3
Cusak Rd. Sprin 111 F1
Cutforth Rd. Saw 77 F2
Cutmore Pl. Chelm 123 F4
Cuton Hall La. Bore 112 A3
Cutty Sark Cl. Stone 191 D1
Cygnet View. W Thu 184 A1
Cypress Cl. Wa Aby 126 B3
Cypress Dr. Chelm 124 B3
Cypress Gr. Chig 153 F2
Cypress Rd. Romf 156 B2

D'Arcy Gdns. Dag 173 D2
Dacre Ave. Ave 183 E3
Dacre Ave. Woodf 153 D1
Dacre Cl. Chig 153 E3
Dacre Cres. Ave 183 E3
Dacre Gdns. Chig 153 E3
Daffodil Ave. Brent 146 A2
Daffodil Way. Sprin 111 F4
Dagenham Rd. Rain 173 F3
Dagenham Rd. Romf 164 B1
Dagmar Rd. Dag 173 E3
Dagnam Park Cl. Romf 157 D3
Dagnam Park Dr. Romf 156 C3
Dagnam Park Gdns. Romf ... 157 D2
Dagnam Park Sq. Romf 157 D2
Dagnets La. Gt Le 76 B1
Dagwood La. Dodd 133 D1
Dahlia Cl. Sprin 111 F3
Daiglen Dr. S Ock 184 A4
Daines Rd. Bill 149 E1
Dairy Rd. Sprin 111 F2
Daisley Rd. Lind 52 A2
Daisleys La. Gt Le 86 A1
Daisy Ct. Bore 112 A3
Daisy Rd. Woodf 152 A1
Dakyn Dr. Stock 136 B2
Dale Cl. S Ock 184 A4
Dale Cl. Saw 77 E1
Dale Gdns. Woodf 152 A3
Dale The. Wa Aby 126 C3
Daleside Gdns. Chig 153 E4
Dalewood Cl. Hornc 165 F2
Dallwood Way. Brain 66 A2
Dalmeney. Basildon 170 A2

Dalroy Cl. S Ock 184 A4
Dalrymple Cl. Sprin 111 E2
Dalton Gdns. Bis St 67 F2
Daltons Fen. Basil 172 B4
Danacre. Basil 170 B4
Danbury Cl. Brent 145 F2
Danbury Down. Basil 171 F4
Danbury Rd. Lou 140 C2
Danbury Rd. Rain 173 F2
Danbury Way. Woodf 152 B2
Dane Acres. Bis St 67 E4
Dane O'Coys Rd. Bis St 56 C1
Dane Park. Bis St 67 E4
Dane Rd. Chelm 110 C1
Dane St. Bis St 68 A4
Danemead. Hod 87 D1
Danes Rd. Romf 164 A2
Danes Way. Brent 146 A2
Daniel Cl. Grays 184 C2
Daniel Cl. Grays 186 A2
Danyon Cl. Rain 174 B2
Darby Dri. Wa Aby 126 B3
Darcy Cl. Brent 147 D1
Darell Way. Bill 149 E1
Darenth La. S Ock 184 A4
Dark La. Brent 158 A2
Dark La. Romf 157 F2
Darlington Ct. Brent 146 A2
Darlington Gdns. Romf 156 B3
Darlington Path. Romf 156 B3
Darnay Rise. Chelm 110 B3
Darnley Rd. Grave 193 D1
Darnley Rd. Grays 192 A4
Darnley Rd. Woodf 152 A1
Darrell Cl. Chelm 111 D3
Dart Cl. Upm 166 B3
Dart Green. S Ock 184 A4
Dartfields. Romf 156 B2
Dartmouth Rd. Sprin 111 F3
Dartview Cl. Grays 185 F1
Darwin Cl. Brain 65 F1
Darwin Rd. Tilb 192 C3
Dashes The. Harl 89 F1
Davenants. Basil 163 D1
Daventry Gdns. Romf 156 B3
Daventry Green. Romf 156 B3
Daventry Rd. Romf 156 B3
David Ave. Runw 151 E1
David Dr. Romf 157 D2
David's Wlk. Chig 153 F2
Davids Way. Chig 153 F2
Davies Cl. Rain 174 B1
Davinia Cl. Woodf 152 C2
Davis Rd. Ave 183 E3
Davis Rd. Grays 186 C2
Daw St. Bird 19 D4
Daw St. Finch 42 C2
Dawes Ave. Hornc 165 F1
Dawley Green. S Ock 184 A4
Daws Cl. Writ 109 F1
Daws Hill. Wa Aby 139 E3
Dawson Cl. Saff W 13 F1
Dawson Dr. Rain 174 A3
Daylop Dr. Chig 154 A4
Days Cl. Chelm 111 D4
Days La. Dodd 146 A4
De Bohun Ct. Saff W 13 F1
De Mandeville Rd. Els 48 B1
De Vigier Ave. Saff W 14 A1
Deacon Way. Woodf 152 C2
Deadman's La. Gt Bad 124 B2
Deal Cl. Brain 65 F3
Dealtree Cl. Dodd 133 D2
Dean Rd. Bart 4 A4
Dean Rogers Pl. Brain 65 F4
Dean Way. Chelm 110 C1
Deanery Gdns. Brain 65 F4
Deanery Hill. Brain 65 F4
Deans Rd. Brent 158 A3
Debden Cl. Woodf 152 B2
Debden Dr. Wim 26 C1
Debden Green. Basil 170 B2
Debden La. Lou 128 B1
Debden Rd. Lou 128 A1
Debden Rd. New 37 E4
Debden Rd. Saff W 25 E4
Debden Rd. Saff W 25 F3
Debden Wlk. Hornc 174 A3
Deben. Grays 187 E2
Deben Rd. Hav 7 D4
Dedham Cl. Bill 149 E1
Dedham Rd. Bill 149 E1
Dee Cl. Upm 166 C3
Dee Way. Romf 155 F1
Deepdene. Basil 171 D3
Deepdene. Ing 135 D2
Deepdene Path. Lou 141 D3
Deepdene Rd. Lou 141 D3
Deer Park. Harl 102 A3
Deerbank Rd. Bill 149 E2
Deere Ave. Rain 174 A3
Deerleap Gr. Ching 139 D2
Deerleap Way. Brain 66 B2
Defoe Par. Grays 186 A2
Defoe Way. Romf 155 D2
Deirdre Ave. Wick 163 D4
Deirdre Cl. Wick 163 D4
Delafield Rd. Grays 185 C1
Delamere Rd. Chelm 110 C1

Delargy Cl. Grays 186 A2
Delhi Rd. Basil 172 B3
Delimands. Basil 170 C3
Delius Way. Corr 179 E2
Dell Cl. Woodf 152 A4
Dell La. Bis St 68 A4
Dell La. L Hal 78 A4
Dell Rd. Grays 185 D1
Dell The. Basil 171 D2
Dell The. Brent 158 A2
Dell The. Gt Bad 124 C3
Dell The. Gt Dun 61 F1
Dell The. Wick 163 F4
Dell The. Woodf 152 A4
Dellfield Ct. Harl 90 B2
Dellows La. Ugl 48 A1
Delis Cl. Ching 139 D2
Dells The. Bis St 67 F4
Delmar Rd. Brent 147 E2
Delmores. Basil 170 B2
Delta Rd. Brent 147 E2
Delvers Mead. Dag 173 E4
Delvins. Basil 172 A4
Denbigh Cl. Hornc 166 A4
Denbigh Rd. Basil 170 A3
Dencourt Cres. Basil 171 F3
Dene Ct. Chelm 110 B3
Dene Path. S Ock 184 A4
Dene Rd. Lou 140 C1
Denecroft Gdns. Grays 185 E2
Denehurst Gdns. Woodf 152 A3
Deneway. Basil 171 E1
Dengayne. Basil 171 E3
Denholme Wlk. Rain 173 F3
Dennis Rd. Ave 176 A2
Dennis Rd. S Ock 176 A2
Dennises La. Upm 175 F3
Denny Ave. Wa Aby 126 B3
Denny Ct. Bis St 57 D1
Dent Cl. S Ock 184 A4
Denver Dr. Basil 163 E1
Denys Dr. Basil 162 C1
Derby Ave. Romf 164 B3
Derby Ave. Upm 166 A1
Derby Cl. Bill 149 E3
Derby Rd. Grays 185 D1
Derby Rd. Roy 100 B2
Derby Road Bridge. Grays 192 A4
Derham Gdns. Upm 166 B1
Deri Ave. Rain 174 A1
Derry Ave. S Ock 184 A4
Derwent Par. S Ock 184 A4
Derwent Way. Bl Not 76 B4
Derwent Way. Chelm 110 B2
Derwent Way. Hornc 174 A4
Detling Ct. Hornc 174 B4
Devereux Rd. Grays 184 C2
Devereux Way. Bill 149 D3
Deveron Gdns. S Ock 184 A4
Deveron Way. Romf 155 F1
Devoils La. Bis St 67 F4
Devon Cl. Lou 152 A4
Devonshire Cl. Basil 170 A4
Devonshire Gdns. Brain 66 A2
Devonshire Gdns. Sta L H 187 D2
Devonshire Rd. Basil 170 A4
Devonshire Rd. Grays 184 C2
Devonshire Rd. Hornc 165 E1
Dewes Green Rd. Berd 46 A4
Dewey Rd. Dag 173 E3
Dewlands. Basil 171 D4
Dewsbury Cl. Romf 156 C2
Dewsbury Gdns. Romf 156 B2
Dewsbury Rd. Romf 156 C2
Dewsgreen. Basil 171 F2
Dexter Cl. Grays 185 D2
Deyncourt Gdns. Upm 166 B1
Deynes Rd. Deb 38 A4
Diamond Cl. Grays 184 C2
Diana Cl. Grays 184 C2
Diana Cl. Woodf 152 A1
Diban Ave. Hornc 174 A4
Dickens Ave. Stone 190 A2
Dickens Ave. Tilb 193 D3
Dickens Dr. Basil 170 B4
Dickens Pl. Chelm 110 B4
Dickens Rise. Chig 153 D4
Dicky Moors. Gt Wal 97 F4
Digby Gdns. Dag 173 D2
Digby Rd. Corr 180 B3
Digby Wlk. Hornc 174 B3
Dimsdale Cres. Bis St 68 A3
Dinant Link Rd. Hod 100 A4
Disney Cl. Ing 135 D2
Ditchfield Rd. Hod 87 D1
Dixon Ave. Chelm 110 C2
Dobb's Weir Rd. Roy 100 B2
Dock Approach Rd. Grays 185 F1
Dock Rd. Grays 185 F1
Dock Rd. Tilb 192 C3
Docklands Ave. Ing 135 E2
Doctor's La. Ashe 9 E1
Doddenhill Cl. Saff W 13 F2
Doddinghurst Rd. Brent 146 B2
Doddinghurst Rd. Dodd 133 E1
Doesgate La. Horn H 169 E1
Doeshill Dr. Wick 163 F4
Dog Chase. Weth 43 E2
Dog Kennel La. Ing 135 E4

Dogden La. Man 46 C1
Doggett's Cnr. Hornc 165 F1
Dolby Rise. Sprin 111 F1
Dolphin App. Romf 164 C4
Dolphin Gdns. Bill 148 C3
Dolphin Way. Bis St 68 A4
Dolphin Yd The. Grave 193 D1
Dombey Cl. Chelm 110 C4
Dominion Dr. Romf 155 D2
Dominion Way. Rain 174 A1
Domsey La. Lit Wal 98 C2
Don Way. Romf 155 F2
Donald Thorn Cl. Wick 163 E3
Donald Way. Chelm 124 B4
Doncaster Way. Upm 165 F1
Donovan's Dr. Brent 159 E2
Dorchester Ave. Hod 100 A4
Dorchester Rd. Bill 149 D3
Dordells. Basil 170 C3
Dorewards Ave. Brain 65 F4
Dorian Rd. Hornc 165 D2
Dorking Rd. Romf 156 B3
Dorking Rise. Romf 156 B3
Dorking Wlk. Romf 156 B3
Dorkins Way. Upm 166 C2
Dorrington Gdns. Hornc 165 E2
Dorset Ave. Gt Bad 124 C3
Dorset Ave. Romf 164 B4
Dorset Cl. Gt Bad 124 C3
Dorset Gdns. Sta L H 187 D2
Dorset Way. Bill 149 D3
Dorvis La. Ash 4 A1
Doubleday Rd. Lou 141 E3
Doublet Mews. Bill 149 E3
Doug Siddons Ct.Greys 192 B4
Douglas Cl. Chelm 124 B2
Douglas Dr. Wick 163 E3
Douglas Rd. Ching 139 F1
Douglas Rd. Hornc 164 C3
Douglas Wlk. Chelm 124 A4
Dove Cl. Bis St 67 F2
Dove Cl. Stan M 57 F4
Dove Crofts. H Rod 81 F4
Dove La. Chelm 124 A3
Dovedale Ave. Woodf 153 D1
Dovedale Cl. Basil 170 A2
Dovehouse Croft. Harl 90 A1
Dovehouse Rd. Hav 7 D4
Dover Cl. Brain 65 F3
Dover Cl. Romf 155 E1
Dover Rd. Grave 192 B1
Doves La. Gt Dun 72 A1
Dowding Ct. Hornc 174 A3
Dowland Cl. Corr 179 E2
Dowland Wlk. Basil 170 B4
Downey Cl. Basil 171 E4
Downhall Rd. Hat B O 92 B3
Downham Rd. Runw 151 E2
Downham Rd. S Han 150 B3
Downham Rd. S Han 150 B4
Downing Rd. Dag 173 D2
Downing Rd. Dag 173 D3
Downlands. Wa Aby 126 C3
Downs Cres. Gt Dun 61 E1
Downs Cres. Hav 6 C4
Downs Gr. Basil 171 F2
Downs Pl. Hav 6 C4
Downs The. Gt Dun 61 E1
Downs The. Harl 102 C4
Downsland Dr. Brent 158 B4
Downsway. Sprin 111 E3
Downton Dr. Hav 6 C4
Dowsett La. S Han 150 B3
Doyle Way. Tilb 193 E3
Drake Cl. Brent 158 B3
Drake Gdns. Brain 66 B2
Drake Rd. Grays 184 B2
Drakes La. Lit Wal 99 D1
Draper's Chase. Feist 75 E4
Draper's Crnr. Ch Ong 118 B1
Drapers La. Hel B 6 A1
Drayson Cl. Wa Aby 126 C4
Drayton Ave. Lou 140 C2
Dreys The. Saff W 26 B4
Driberg Way. Brain 66 A1
Drive The. Brent 158 B2
Drive The. Chelm 111 D3
Drive The. Ching 139 E1
Drive The. Harl 89 F1
Drive The. Hod 100 A4
Drive The. Lou 140 B1
Drive The. Lou 140 C3
Drive The. Romf 155 E2
Drive The. Romf 156 C1
Drive The. Saw 77 F1
Drive The. Thax 39 F2
Drive The. Woodf 152 A4
Drood Cl. Chelm 110 C4
Droveway. Lou 141 D4
Druce The. Clav 35 E2
Drummond Ave. Romf 164 B4
Drummond Rd. Romf 164 B4
Drummonds The. Epp 116 A1
Drummonds The. Lou 152 A4
Drury La. Ay Rod 81 E1
Drury La. Brain 65 F2

Drury La. Ridge 20 A3
Dry St. Basil 170 C1
Dryden Cl. Chig 153 F2
Dryden Pl. Tilb 193 D3
Drysdale Ave. Ching 139 D2
Duarte Pl. Grays 184 C2
Duchess Cl. Bis St 67 E4
Duck La. N W Bas 116 B3
Duck St. Lit Ea 60 C3
Duck St. Wen A 24 C3
Duckend Farm La. Thax 51 F3
Ducketts Mead. Roy 88 A1
Ducking Stool Ct. Romf 164 C4
Duckling La. Saw 77 F1
Dudbrook Rd. Nave H 132 A1
Duddery Hill. Hav 7 D4
Duddery Rd. Hav 7 D4
Dudley Cl. Grays 184 C2
Dudley Gdns. Romf 156 B2
Dudley Rd. Romf 156 B2
Duffield Rd. Gt Bad 124 B3
Duffries Cl. Gt Wal 97 F4
Duggers La. Brain 66 A1
Duke St. Chelm 111 D2
Duke St. Hod 100 A4
Duke's Pl. Brent 146 B1
Dukes Ave. Grays 185 D2
Dukes Ave. The B 128 C2
Dukes Cl. N W Bas 117 D2
Dukes Farm Cl. Bill 149 E3
Dukes Farm Rd. Bill 149 D3
Dukes La. Sprin 111 F2
Dukes La. Will 107 E3
Dukes Orchard. Hat B O 79 B3
Dukes Park Ind Est. Sprin 111 F2
Dukes Rd. Bill 149 E2
Dukes Rd. Brain 65 F3
Dukes Ride. Bis St 67 E4
Dulverton Rd. Romf 156 B2
Dumney La. Gt Le 85 F4
Dunbar Ave. Dag 164 A1
Dunbar Gdns. Dag 173 D4
Duncan Rise. Gt Y 20 C1
Dunedin Rd. Rain 173 F1
Dunfane. Bill 149 E3
Dunkellan Gr. S Ock 184 A4
Dunkellan Way. S Ock 184 A4
Dunkin Rd. Stone 190 A2
Dunlop Rd. Tilb 192 C3
Dunmore Rd. Sprin 112 A2
Dunmow Dr. Rain 173 F2
Dunmow Gdns. Horn H 168 B3
Dunmow Rd. Abb Rod 93 F1
Dunmow Rd. Ay Rod 81 E2
Dunmow Rd. Birhr 68 C4
Dunmow Rd. Bis St 68 A4
Dunmow Rd. Fyf 106 C3
Dunmow Rd. Gt Ba 52 C4
Dunmow Rd. H Rod 81 E2
Dunmow Rd. Hat B O 79 F3
Dunmow Rd. Lit Ba 52 C4
Dunmow Rd. Ray 64 B1
Dunmow Rd. Take 70 C4
Dunning Cl. S Ock 184 A4
Dunningford Cl. Romf 173 F4
Dunnings La. Horn H 168 A1
Dunoon Cl. Brain 66 B2
Dunspring La. Woodf 153 D1
Dunstable Cl. Romf 156 B2
Dunstable Rd. Corr 179 E2
Dunstable Rd. Romf 156 B2
Dunstalls. Harl 102 A2
Dunster Cl. Romf 155 E1
Dunster Cres. Hornc 166 A1
Dunster Dr. Hav 6 C4
Dunton Rd. Basil 160 C1
Dunton Rd. Romf 164 C4
Durants Wlk. Wick 163 E3
Durban Gdns. Dag 173 E3
Durban La. Bill 161 F1
Durdans The. Basil 170 A2
Durham Ave. Romf 165 E4
Durham Ave. Woodf 152 B3
Durham Cl. Gt Ba 42 A1
Durham Cl. Saw 77 E1
Durham Cl. Sta Ab 87 D3
Durham Rd. Basil 169 F3
Durham Rd. Dag 173 E4
Durley Ave. Wick 162 C4
Durnell Way. Lou 141 D3
Durninge Wlk. Grays 185 D3
Durrants Cl. Rain 174 B2
Durrington Cl. Basil 171 E3
Dury Falls Cl. Hornc 166 A2
Duxford Cl. Hornc 174 B3
Duxford Dr. Hinx 1 A4
Dyer's Way. Romf 156 A2
Dyers Way. Stam 19 F1
Dymchurch Cl. Woodf 153 D1
Dymoke. Hornc 164 C2
Dymokes Way. Hod 87 D1
Dytchleys Rd. Nave H 145 D3
Dytchleys Rd. Nave H 144 C3

Eagle Cl. Rain 174 A3
Eagle Cl. Wa Aby 127 D3
Eagle La. Brain 65 F3
Eagle La. Kelv H 132 C1

Eagle Terr. Woodf 152 A2
Eagle Way. Brent 158 B2
Earl Mountbatten Way. Bill 148 C2
Earls Cl. Bis St 67 E3
Earls Path. Lou 140 B3
Earlsfield Dr. Sprin 111 F2
Easedale Dr. Hornc 174 A4
Easington Way. S Ock 184 A4
East Cl. Rain 174 A1
East Crescent Rd. Grave 193 E1
East Dene Dr. Romf 156 B3
East Dri. Saw 77 F1
East Entrance. Dag 173 D2
East Gate. Harl 89 E1
East Hall La. Rain 182 B4
East Kent Ave. Grave 192 B1
East Mayne. Basil 163 D1
East Park. Harl 90 B2
East Park. Saw 77 F1
East Rd. Bis St 68 A4
East Rd. Harl 90 A2
East Rd. Romf 164 B2
East Sq. Basil 171 D3
East St. Brain 66 A2
East St. Grays 191 F4
East St. Grays 192 B4
East St. Saff W 13 F1
East Terr. Grave 193 E1
East Thorpe. Basil 171 E3
East Thurrock Rd. Grays 192 B4
East Tilbury Rd. Sta L H 187 D2
East View. Writ 109 F1
East View Cl. Rad 27 F4
East Wlk. Basil 171 D3
East Wlk. Harl 89 E1
Eastbrook Ave. Dag 173 E4
Eastbrook Dr. Romf 164 C1
Eastbrook Rd. Wa Aby 126 C3
Eastbrooks. Basil 172 A4
Eastbrooks Mews. Basil 172 A4
Eastbrooks Pl. Basil 172 A4
Eastbury Rd. Romf 164 B3
Eastby Cl. Saff W 25 F4
Eastend La. Els 59 E4
Eastern App. Sprin 111 F3
Eastern Ave. Ave 183 E2
Eastern Ave. Hav 6 C4
Eastern Ave E. Romf 155 F1
Eastern Ave W. Romf 164 A4
Eastern Cres. Chelm 110 C3
Eastern Rd. Grays 185 E1
Eastern Rd. Romf 164 C3
Eastern Way. Grays 185 D1
Eastfield Gdns. Dag 173 D4
Eastfield Rd. Bill 161 F1
Eastfield Rd. Brent 158 B4
Eastfield Rd. Dag 173 D4
Eastgate. Basil 171 D3
Eastgate. Gt C 1 B1
Eastham Cres. Brent 159 D4
Easton End. Basil 170 A3
Eastwick Hall La. E Wick 89 D3
Eastwick Rd. East 89 D2
Eastwick Rd. H Wy 89 F3
Eastwood Cl. Woodf 152 A1
Eastwood Dr. Rain 182 A4
Eastwood Rd. Woodf 152 A1
Eaton Cl. Bill 149 D3
Eaton Dr. Romf 155 D2
Eaton Rd. Upm 166 C1
Ebbsfleet Ind Est. Grave 192 A1
Ebbsfleet Wlk. Grave 192 A1
Eccleston Gdns. Bill 149 D3
Echo Hts. Ching 139 D1
Eckersley Rd. Chelm 111 E2
Eddy Cl. Romf 164 A3
Eden Green. S Ock 184 A4
Eden Rd. Hav 7 D4
Eden Way. Chelm 110 B3
Edenhall Cl. Romf 156 B3
Edenhall Glen. Romf 156 B3
Edenhall Rd. Romf 156 B3
Edens Cl. Bis St 68 A4
Edens Mount. Saw 77 F2
Edgecotts. Basil 170 C2
Edgehill Gdns. Dag 173 D4
Edinburgh Ave. Corr 179 F3
Edinburgh Gdns. Brain 66 B3
Edinburgh Mews. Tilb 193 D3
Edinburgh Pl. Harl 90 A2
Edinburgh Way. Harl 89 F2
Edinburgh's Dr. Romf 164 B4
Edison Ave. Hornc 164 C2
Edison Cl. Brain 65 F1
Edison Cl. Hornc 164 C2
Edith Cavell Way. Ste B 18 A3
Edith Way. Corr 180 A3
Edmund Cl. Hav 6 C4
Edmund Rd. Rain 173 F1
Edridge Cl. Hornc 174 B4
Edward Cl. Bill 148 C3
Edward Ct. Wa Aby 126 C3
Edward Dr. Chelm 124 B4
Edward Gdns. Runw 163 E4
Edwards Cl. Brent 147 F2
Edwards Way. Brent 147 F2
Edwin Cl. Rain 173 F1
Edwin St. Grave 193 D1

Egbert Gdns. Runw ...... 151 E
Egg Hall. Epp ...... 116 A
Eggshell La. Ste B ...... 18 C
Eglington Rd. Ching ...... 139 E
Eglinton Rd. Swan ...... 191 F
Ehringshausen Way. Hav ...... 7 D
Eisenhower Rd. Basil ...... 170 A
Elan Rd. S Ock ...... 184 A
Eldeland. Basil ...... 170 C
Elder Ave. Wick ...... 163 E
Elder Way. Rain ...... 174 B
Elder Way. Wick ...... 163 E
Elderberry Cl. Basil ...... 170 A
Elderfield. Harl ...... 90 B
Eldon Rd. Roy ...... 100 B
Eldred Gdns. Upm ...... 166 C
Eleanor Chase. Wick ...... 163 E
Eleanor Way. Brent ...... 158 C
Eleanor Way. Wa Aby ...... 126 A
Eleven Acre Rise. Lou ...... 140 C
Elgar Cl. Basil ...... 170 B
Elgar Cl. Lou ...... 152 B
Elgar Gdns. Tilb ...... 193 D
Elgin Cl. Wick ...... 163 E
Elgin Ave. Romf ...... 157 D
Elham Dr. Basil ...... 172 A
Eliot Cl. Wick ...... 163 E
Eliot Rd. Stone ...... 190 A
Elizabeth Cl. Lo Naz ...... 113 E
Elizabeth Cl. Romf ...... 155 D
Elizabeth Cl. Saff W ...... 13 F
Elizabeth Cl. Tilb ...... 193 D
Elizabeth Ct. Grave ...... 193 D
Elizabeth Dr. The B ...... 128 C
Elizabeth Dr. Wick ...... 163 D
Elizabeth Rd. Bis St ...... 67 F
Elizabeth Rd. Brent ...... 146 A
Elizabeth Rd. Grays ...... 184 C
Elizabeth Rd. Rain ...... 182 A
Elizabeth St. Stone ...... 190 C
Elizabeth Way. Harl ...... 89 D
Elizabeth Way. Saff W ...... 13 F
Elkins The. Romf ...... 155 F
Ellen Way. Bl Not ...... 76 B
Ellenborough Cl. Bis St ...... 67 E
Ellerman Rd. Tilb ...... 192 C
Elliott Gdns. Romf ...... 156 A
Ellis Ave. Rain ...... 182 A
Ellmore Cl. Romf ...... 156 A
Elm Ave. Upm ...... 175 D
Elm Bungalows. Brain ...... 65 E
Elm Cl. Broom ...... 111 D
Elm Cl. Els ...... 48 B
Elm Cl. Ep Gr ...... 115 D
Elm Cl. Gt Bad ...... 124 C
Elm Cl. Hav ...... 6 C
Elm Cl. Lou ...... 152 B
Elm Cl. Romf ...... 155 D
Elm Cl. Take ...... 70 B
Elm Cl. Wa Aby ...... 126 B
Elm Ct. Elm ...... 11 D
Elm Gdns. N W Bas ...... 117 D
Elm Gr. Hornc ...... 165 F
Elm Gr. Saff W ...... 13 E
Elm Gr. Woodf ...... 152 A
Elm Green. Basil ...... 172 A
Elm Green. Bill ...... 149 F
Elm Grove. Bis St ...... 68 A
Elm Park Ave. Hornc ...... 165 D
Elm Rd. Ave ...... 183 E
Elm Rd. Basil ...... 163 F
Elm Rd. Bis St ...... 67 F
Elm Rd. Chelm ...... 124 A
Elm Rd. Grays ...... 192 B
Elm Rd. Hod ...... 100 A
Elm Rd. Romf ...... 155 D
Elm Rd. Runw ...... 163 E
Elm Rd. Stone ...... 190 C
Elm Terr. W Thu ...... 191 D
Elm Way. Bore ...... 99 F
Elm Way. Brent ...... 158 A
Elm Wlk. Ray ...... 64 C
Elm Wlk. Romf ...... 165 D
Elmbridge. Harl ...... 90 C
Elmbridge Rd. Chig ...... 154 A
Elmbrook Cl. Bis St ...... 67 F
Elmdene Ave. Hornc ...... 165 F
Elmer Ave. Hav B ...... 155 F
Elmer Cl. Rain ...... 174 A
Elmer Gdns. Rain ...... 174 A
Elmhurst Cl. Bis St ...... 67 F
Elmhurst Cl. Hav ...... 7 D
Elmhurst Dr. Hornc ...... 165 E
Elmhurst Dr. Woodf ...... 152 A
Elmhurst Way. Lou ...... 140 C
Elmores. Lou ...... 141 D
Elms Dr. Chelm ...... 111 D
Elms Farm Rd. Hornc ...... 174 B
Elms The. Ch Ong ...... 119 D
Elms The. Gt C ...... 1 C
Elmslie Cl. Woodf ...... 152 C
Elmstead Cl. Corr ...... 180 A
Elmtree Ave. Kelv H ...... 132 C
Elmtree Rd. Basil ...... 172 A
Elmway. Grays ...... 185 E
Elmwood. Saw ...... 77 F
Elsenham Cres. Basil ...... 171 F
Elverston Cl. Basil ...... 170 B
Elvet Ave. Romf ...... 165 E

205

wick Rd. S Ock

Freeborne Gdns. Rain

ick Rd. S Ock 184 B4
Gdns. Dag 164 B1
Pl. Chig 153 D3
anuel Rd. Basil 170 A2
berson Ct. Sprin 111 F2
berson Way. N W Bas 117 E3
erald Gdns. Dag 164 A2
erson Dr. Hornc 165 E2
ma's Cres. Sta Ab 87 D2
maus Way. Chig 153 D3
son Cl. Saff W 13 E1
sworth Rd. Woodf 153 D1
borne Green. S Ock 184 A4
dway The. Gt Ea 60 C4
dway The. Ste B 18 B4
gayne Gdns. Upm 166 A2
gland's La. Lou 141 D4
gleric. Chris 10 B2
nerdale Ave. Bl Not 76 B3
nerdale Ave. Hornc 174 A4
erprise Centre The. Basil 162 C1
erprise Ct. Brain 66 A1
terprise Way. Wick 163 F3
ping Cl. Chelm 110 C1
ping Cl. Romf 164 A4
ping Glade. Ching 139 E2
ping La. Sta T 143 E4
ping La. The B 142 A4
ping New Rd. Lou 140 A2
ping New Rd. Wa Aby 140 A2
ping Rd. Bobb 118 B3
ping Rd. Ch Ong 117 E1
ping Rd. Ch Ong 118 B3
ping Rd. Epp 116 B2
ping Rd. Harl 101 E3
ping Rd. Lo Naz 101 E3
ping Rd. N W Bas 117 D2
ping Rd. Roy 101 D4
ping Rd. Sta T 116 B2
ping Rd. Wa Aby 128 A2
ping Way. Ching 139 D2
som Cl. Bill 149 E3
som Way. Hornc 165 F1
c Rd. Basil 172 C3
ck Ave. Chelm 111 D4
dge Cl. Sprin 111 E4
swell Rd. Hav 7 D4
th Cres. Romf 155 E1
th Ct. Pur 183 D1
nan Cl. S Ock 184 A4
nan Rd. S Ock 184 A4
nest Rd. Hornc 165 F3
iff Dr. S Ock 184 A4
ington Cl. Grays 186 A2
roll Rd. Romf 164 C4
dale Gdns. Upm 166 B2
daile La. Hod 100 A3
her Ave. Romf 164 B3
k Way. Romf 155 F2
kley Gdns. S Ock 184 A4
smond Cl. Rain 174 A3
ssex Ave. Chelm 111 D4
sex Cl. Basil 170 A3
sex Cl. Romf 164 A4
ssex Gdns. Hornc 166 A3
ssex Gdns. Sta L H 187 D2
ssex Hill. Elm 11 D1
ssex Rd. Brain 66 A2
ssex Rd. Ching 139 F1
ssex Rd. Dag 173 E4
ssex Rd. Hod 100 B3
ssex Rd. Romf 164 A4
ssex Rd. W Thu 191 D4
ssex Rd. Woodf 152 A1
ssex Regiment Way. Broom 111 E4
ssex Regiment Way. Lit Wal 85 D1
ssex Regiment Way. Lit Wal 98 B3
ssex Way. Brent 158 B2
stella Mead. Chelm 110 C4
helburga Rd. Romf 157 D1
helred Gdns. Runw 151 E1
heridge Green. Lou 141 E3
heridge Rd. Lou 141 E3
ton Cl. Hornc 165 F1
uclid Way. Ave 183 F1
ugene Cl. Hornc 165 E4
vans Cl. Stone 191 D1
vansdale. Rain 173 F1
velyn Rd. Felst 75 E2
velyn Sharp Cl. Romf 165 E4
velyn Wlk. Brent 158 B2
verard Rd. Basil 172 A4
verest Rise. Bill 148 C1
veritt Rd. Saff W 13 F1
versleigh Gdns. Upm 166 B2
versley Rd. Basil 172 B3
ves Cres. Chelm 111 D3
wan Rd. Romf 156 C1
wanrigg Terr. Woodf 152 B2
wellhurst Rd. Woodf 152 C1
xchange St. Romf 164 C3
xchange Way. Chelm 111 D1
xeter Cl. Basil 171 F4
xeter Cl. Brain 66 A3
xeter Rd. Dag 173 D3
xeter Rd. Sprin 111 F3
xley Cl. Ing 135 D2
xmoor Cl. Chelm 110 B1
xmoor Cl. Woodf 153 E1
Exmouth Rd. Grays 192 A4
Eyhurst Ave. Hornc 165 D1
Eynesham Way. Basil 163 D1
Eynsford Rd. Swan 191 E1
Eyre Cl. Romf 165 D4

Factory Rd. Grave 192 B1
Faggoters La. H Lav 105 D4
Faggots Yd. Brain 65 F3
Fagus Ave. Rain 174 B1
Fair Leas. Saff W 13 F2
Fair Mead. Basil 171 E4
Fairbank Cl. Ch Ong 118 C1
Faircross Ave. Romf 155 E2
Fairfax Ave. Basil 172 B4
Fairfax Mead. Sprin 111 F1
Fairfax Rd. Grays 185 D1
Fairfax Rd. Tilb 192 C3
Fairfield. Ing 135 E2
Fairfield Ave. Grays 185 E3
Fairfield Ave. Upm 166 B1
Fairfield Cl. Hornc 165 D2
Fairfield Rd. Brain 65 F1
Fairfield Rd. Brent 158 B4
Fairfield Rd. Ch Ong 118 C1
Fairfield Rd. Chelm 111 D2
Fairfield Rd. Epp 116 A1
Fairfield Rd. Hod 100 A4
Fairfield Rd. Woodf 152 A2
Fairfield Rise. Bill 148 C1
Fairford Cl. Romf 157 D2
Fairford Way. Romf 157 D2
Fairham Ave. S Ock 184 A3
Fairholme Ave. Romf 165 D4
Fairholme Gdns. Upm 166 C2
Fairhouse Ct. Basil 171 E3
Fairkytes Ave. Hornc 165 E2
Fairlands Ave. Lou 152 A4
Fairlawn Dr. Woodf 152 A2
Fairlawns Cl. Hornc 165 F2
Fairleigh Ave. Basil 172 B3
Fairleigh Rd. Basil 172 B3
Fairlight Ave. Woodf 152 A2
Fairlop Cl. Hornc 174 A3
Fairlop Gdns. Basil 171 E3
Fairlop Gdns. Woodf 153 E2
Fairlop Rd. Woodf 153 E1
Fairmead Rd. Wa Aby 140 A3
Fairmeadside. Lou 140 B2
Fairoak Gdns. Romf 155 F1
Fairstead. Basil 171 D3
Fairview. Bill 149 D1
Fairview Ave. Brent 147 F2
Fairview Ave. Rain 174 B1
Fairview Ave. Sta L H 179 E1
Fairview Chase. Sta L H 187 E4
Fairview Cl. Chig 153 F3
Fairview Dr. Chig 153 F3
Fairview Gdns. Woodf 152 A1
Fairview Rd. Basil 171 F3
Fairview Rd. Chig 153 F3
Fairway. Bis St 68 B3
Fairway. Grays 185 D3
Fairway. Gt Bad 124 B4
Fairway. Saw 77 F1
Fairway. Wick 163 E2
Fairway. Woodf 152 B3
Fairway The. Harl 103 D3
Fairway The. Upm 166 B2
Fairways. Wa Aby 126 C3
Fairy Hall La. Ray 65 D1
Fairycroft Rd. Saff W 13 F1
Falcon Ave. Grays 192 B4
Falcon Cl. Hav 7 E4
Falcon Cl. Saw 77 E1
Falcon Cl. Wa Aby 127 D3
Falcon Way. Basil 171 E2
Falcon Way. Chelm 124 A3
Falcon Way. Rain 174 A3
Falconer Rd. Chig 154 A3
Falconer Rd. Hav 7 E3
Falconers Park. Saw 77 E1
Falkenham End. Basil 171 E4
Falkenham Path. Basil 171 E4
Falkenham Rise. Basil 171 E4
Falkenham Row. Basil 171 E4
Falkirk Cl. Hornc 166 A2
Falkland Cl. Bore 112 C4
Falkner Cl. Stock 136 C2
Fallow Cl. Chig 153 F3
Fallowden La. Ash 14 C4
Falmouth Rd. Sprin 111 F3
Falstones. Basil 170 C3
Fambridge Dr. Wick 163 F3
Fambridge Rd. Dag 164 A2
Fanns Rise. Pur 183 D1
Fanshawe Cres. Hornc 165 E3
Fanshawe Rd. Grays 186 A2
Fanton Ave. Wick 163 F2
Faraday Cl. Brain 65 F1
Farm Cl. Brent 147 E1
Farm Cl. Dag 173 E3
Farm Cl. Lou 152 B4
Farm End. Wa Aby 139 F2
Farm Hill Rd. Wa Aby 126 B3
Farm Rd. Grays 185 F2
Farm Rd. Grays 187 E1
Farm Rd. Rain 174 B1
Farm Way. Hornc 174 B4
Farm Way. Lou 152 B3
Farmadine. Saff W 13 F1
Farmadine Gr. Saff W 13 F1
Farmbridge End Rd. G Ea 95 E2
Farmer Ct. Wa Aby 127 D3
Farnaby Way. Corr 179 E2
Farnes Ave. Wick 163 E4
Farnes Dr. Romf 156 B1
Farnham Cl. Saw 77 E1
Farnham Rd. Romf 156 B3
Farnley Rd. Ching 139 F1
Farnol Rd. Stone 190 A2
Farriers. Sta Ab 87 D3
Farriers Dr. Bill 149 D3
Farringdon Ave. Romf 156 B2
Farrow Gdns. Grays 185 E3
Farrow Rd. Chelm 123 F4
Farthing Centre The. Chelm 111 D1
Farthingale La. Wa Aby 127 D3
Fastnet Cl. Hav 7 E4
Fauners. Basil 171 D3
Faversham Ave. Ching 139 F1
Faversham Cl. Chig 154 A4
Fawkner Cl. Sprin 111 F1
Fawkon Wlk. Hod 100 A3
Fawn Rd. Chig 153 F3
Fawters Cl. Brent 147 E2
Faymore Gdns. S Ock 184 A4
Fearns Mead. Brent 158 B3
Feathers Hill. Hat B O 79 F3
Feenan Highway. Tilb 193 D3
Feering Dr. Basil 171 F3
Feering Green. Basil 171 F3
Feering Rd. Bill 149 E1
Feering Row. Basil 171 F3
Felhurst Cres. Dag 173 E4
Felicia Way. Grays 186 A1
Fell Rd. Bird 19 D4
Fellcroft. Basil 172 B3
Felmongers. Harl 90 A1
Felmores. Basil 172 A4
Fels Cl. Dag 164 A1
Fels Farm Ave. Dag 164 B1
Felstead Ave. Woodf 153 D1
Felstead Cl. Brent 147 E2
Felstead Rd. Lou 140 C1
Felstead Rd. Romf 155 E2
Felsted Rd. Bill 149 E1
Fen Cl. Brent 147 E3
Fen Cl. Horn H 177 F4
Fen La. Grays 177 F1
Fen La. Horn H 177 E4
Fen La. Upm 176 C4
Fencepiece Rd. Chig 153 E2
Fencepiece Rd. Woodf 153 E2
Fennels. Harl 102 B2
Fennes Rd. Brain 55 F1
Fentiman Way. Hornc 165 F2
Fenton Rd. Grays 7 D4
Fenton Way. Basil 169 F4
Ferguson Ave. Romf 156 B1
Ferguson Ct. Romf 156 B1
Fern Cl. Bill 149 D2
Fern Gr. Hav 6 C4
Fern Hill. Basil 170 B2
Fern Hill La. Harl 102 C2
Fernbank. Bill 148 C1
Fernbank. Lou 140 A1
Fernbank Ave. Hornc 174 B4
Ferndale Rd. Romf 155 E1
Fernden Way. Romf 164 A3
Ferndown. Hornc 165 F3
Fernhall La. Wa Aby 127 E4
Fernie Cl. Chig 154 A3
Fernie Rd. Brain 65 E1
Fernside. Lou 140 A1
Fernside Cl. Corr 180 A3
Ferro Rd. Rain 174 A1
Ferry La. Rain 182 A4
Ferry Rd. Tilb 193 D2
Feryby Rd. Grays 186 A2
Feryngs Cl. Harl 90 B2
Fesants Croft. Harl 90 A2
Fetherston Rd. Sta L H 179 E1
Field Cl. Abr 142 A3
Field Cl. Lou 152 B4
Field Gate La. Ugl 48 A2
Field Rd. Ave 183 E3
Field Way. Hod 87 E1
Fieldfare. Bill 161 E4
Fielding Ave. Tilb 193 E3
Fielding Way. Brent 147 E2
Fieldway. Basil 172 B2
Fieldway. Grays 185 D3
Fieldway. Sta Ab 87 D2
Fieldway. Wick 163 E2
Fiesta Dr. Rain 173 E1
Fifth Ave. Chelm 111 D3
Fifth Ave. Harl 89 E1
Fifth Ave. W Thu 191 D4
Finches Cl. Corr 180 B3
Finchingfield Ave. Woodf 152 B2
Finchingfield Rd. Stam 31 E4
Finchingfield Rd. Ste B 18 B3
Finchingfield Way. Wick 163 E3
Finchingfields. Kelv H 132 C1
Finchley Ave. Chelm 124 A4
Finchley Cl. Stone 190 A1
Finchley Rd. Grays 192 A4
Finchmoor. Harl 102 B3
Findon Gdns. Rain 182 A4
Fingrith Hall La. Bla 120 C1
Fingrith Hall La. H Ong 120 C3
Finucane Gdns. Rain 174 A3
Fir Park. Harl 102 A3
Fir Tree Cl. Romf 164 B4
Fir Tree Rise. Chelm 124 A3
Fir Tree Wlk. Dag 164 B1
Firbank Rd. Romf 155 D3
Firecrest Rd. Chelm 124 B3
Firecrest Rd. Gt Bad 124 B3
Firham Park Ave. Romf 157 D2
Firlands. Bis St 67 F3
Firle The. Basil 170 B2
Firmans. Basil 170 A2
Firs Dr. Lou 141 D4
Firs Dr. Writ 110 A1
Firs The. Brent 146 A2
Firs The. Grays 185 E3
Firs Wlk. Woodf 152 A3
Firsgrove Cres. Brent 158 A3
Firsgrove Rd. Brent 158 B3
First Ave. Basil 169 F2
First Ave. Bill 160 C4
First Ave. Chelm 111 D3
First Ave. Corr 179 E2
First Ave. Dag 173 D2
First Ave. Dodd 133 E3
First Ave. Harl 89 F1
First Ave. W Thu 191 D4
Fisher Cl. Hav 7 E4
Fisher Way. Brain 66 B2
Fishermen's Hill. Grave 192 A1
Fishers Cl. Ches 126 A3
Fishmarket St. Thax 40 A1
Fitzilian Ave. Romf 156 C1
Fitzpiers. Saff W 13 F1
Fitzroy Cl. Bill 149 D2
Fitzwalter Pl. Chelm 110 C2
Fitzwalter Rd. Bore 112 C4
Fitzwilliams Ct. Harl 90 C2
Five Acres. Harl 102 C3
Five Acres. Stan M 57 F4
Five Oaks La. Hav B 154 C3
Five Oaks La. Romf 154 C3
Flagstaff Rd. Wa Aby 126 A3
Flamingo Wlk. Rain 174 A3
Flanders Cl. Brain 65 F3
Flavian Cl. Hav 7 E4
Fleet Ave. Upm 166 B3
Fleet Cl. Upm 166 B3
Fleethall Gr. Grays 185 D3
Fleetway. Basil 171 F2
Fleming Cl. Brain 65 F1
Fleming Gdns. Romf 156 B1
Fleming Gdns. Tilb 193 E3
Flemings. Brent 158 B2
Fletcher Rd. Chig 153 F3
Fletchers. Basil 170 C2
Flint St. W Thu 191 D4
Flintwich Manor. Chelm 110 C4
Flitch Ind Est The. Gt Dun 72 B4
Flitch La. Gt Dun 72 C4
Florence Cl. Grays 191 F4
Florence Cl. Harl 103 E3
Florence Cl. Hornc 165 F1
Florence Rd. Basil 170 B3
Florence Way. Basil 170 A3
Flux's La. Epp 129 D3
Fobbing Farm Cl. Basil 171 D2
Fobbing Rd. Corr 180 B2
Fodderwick. Basil 171 D3
Fold Croft. Harl 89 D1
Fold The. Basil 171 D3
Folkes La. Upm 166 C4
Folly Mill La. Thax 51 D3
Folly View. Sta Ab 87 D2
Fontayne Ave. Chig 153 E3
Fontayne Ave. Rain 173 F3
Fontayne Ave. Romf 155 F1
Fonteyn Cl. Basil 170 B4
Fonteyne Gdns. Woodf 152 B1
Fontwell Park Gdn. Hornc 174 C4
Forbes Cl. Hornc 165 D2
Ford Cl. Basil 170 A3
Ford Cl. Rain 173 F3
Ford End. Woodf 152 A2
Ford La. Rain 173 F3
Ford Rd. Dag 173 D3
Ford Rd. Grave 192 A1
Fordham Cl. Hornc 166 A2
Fordhams Row. Grays 186 A4
Fordson Rd. Bore 112 A3
Fordwater Cl. Stur 8 A2
Fordyce Cl. Hornc 165 F2
Fore St. Bill 161 F1
Fore St. Harl 90 B2
Forebury Ave. Saw 77 F1
Forebury Cres. Saw 77 F1
Forebury The. Saw 77 F1
Forefield Green. Sprin 111 F4
Forelands Pl. Saw 77 F1
Foremark Cl. Chig 153 F2
Forest App. Ching 139 F1
Forest App. Woodf 152 A2
Forest Ave. Chig 153 D3
Forest Ave. Ching 139 F1
Forest Cl. Wa Aby 127 D1
Forest Cl. Woodf 152 A3
Forest Ct. Ching 139 F1
Forest Dr. Chelm 110 C1
Forest Dr. The B 128 C2
Forest Edge. Lou 152 B4
Forest Glade. Basil 169 F2
Forest Glade. Basil 170 A2
Forest Glade. N W Bas 116 C2
Forest Heights. Lou 152 A4
Forest House Fields. Chig 153 F3
Forest Ind Park. Chig 153 F1
Forest La. Chig 153 D3
Forest Rd. Chig 154 A2
Forest Rd. Lou 140 C3
Forest Rd. Romf 164 A4
Forest Rd. Woodf 152 A4
Forest Rd. Woodf 154 A2
Forest Side. Ching 139 F1
Forest Side. Lou 140 B1
Forest Side. The B 128 B3
Forest View. Ching 139 E1
Forest View Rd. Lou 140 B3
Forest Way. Lou 140 C3
Forest Way. Woodf 152 A3
Forester Ct. Bill 148 C2
Foresthall Rd. Birhr 57 F2
Forge Rd. Rain 173 E1
Forres Cl. Hod 100 A4
Forsythia Cl. Sprin 111 F4
Fort Rd. Tilb 193 E3
Fort William Rd. Basil 171 D1
Forth Rd. Upm 166 B3
Forties Cl. Hav 7 E4
Fortin Cl. S Ock 184 A3
Fortin Path. S Ock 184 A3
Fortin Way. S Ock 184 A3
Fortune Cl. Gt Le 86 A4
Fortunes The. Harl 102 C3
Foster St. Match 103 F3
Fosters Cl. Woodf 152 A1
Fosters Cl. Writ 109 F1
Fountain Farm. Harl 102 C3
Fountain Pl. Wa Aby 126 B3
Fountain Rd. G Ea 95 E2
Fountain Wlk. Grave 192 C1
Four Acres. Gt C 1 C2
Four Acres. Saff W 13 F1
Four Acres The. Saw 78 A1
Four Ash Hill. Bird 8 C1
Four Wants The. Ch Ong 119 D2
Fourth Ave. Basil 169 F2
Fourth Ave. Chelm 111 D3
Fourth Ave. Corr 179 F3
Fourth Ave. Harl 102 A4
Fourth Ave. Romf 164 B2
Fourth Ave. W Thu 191 D4
Fourways. Els 48 B1
Fowlmere Rd. Hey 10 A3
Fox Burrow Rd. Hav B 154 B3
Fox Burrows La. Writ 110 A1
Fox Cl. Romf 155 D3
Fox Cres. Chelm 110 C2
Fox Hatch. Kelv H 132 C1
Fox's Rd. Ashe 9 F1
Foxborough Chase. Stock 137 D3
Foxdells La. Bis St 56 C1
Foxes Gr. Brent 148 B1
Foxes Green. Grays 186 A2
Foxfield Dr. Corr 179 F3
Foxglove Rd. S Ock 184 B4
Foxglove Way. Sprin 111 F3
Foxgloves The. Bill 148 C2
Foxhall Rd. Upm 175 E4
Foxhatch. Wick 163 F3
Foxhills Rd. Grays 185 E3
Foxholes Rd. Gt Bad 124 C3
Foxhunter Wlk. Bill 149 E3
Foxlands Cres. Dag 173 E4
Foxlands Rd. Dag 173 E4
Foxleigh. Bill 161 D4
Foxleigh Cl. Bill 161 D4
Foxley Cl. Lou 141 D4
Foxley Dri. Bis St 68 A4
Foxton Rd. Grays 191 E4
Foxton Rd. Hod 100 A3
Foyle Dr. S Ock 184 A4
Foys Wlk. Bill 161 E4
Frambury La. New 36 C4
Frame The. Basil 170 B4
Frampton Rd. Basil 163 D1
Frampton Rd. Epp 116 C3
Frances Gdns. S Ock 183 F4
Francis Cl. Hav 6 C4
Francis Cl. Horn H 178 C2
Francis Rd. Brain 65 E1
Francombe Gdns. Romf 165 D3
Frankland Cl. Woodf 152 B3
Franklin Rd. Hornc 174 B3
Franklins Way. Wick 163 F4
Franklyn Gdns. Chig 153 E2
Franmil Rd. Hornc 165 D2
Fraser Cl. Basil 169 F3
Fraser Cl. Chelm 124 B4
Fraser Cl. Romf 164 C2
Frating Cres. Woodf 152 A2
Frederica Rd. Ching 139 E1
Frederick Rd. Rain 173 F2
Fredrick Andrews Ct. Grays 192 B4
Freeborne Gdns. Rain 174 A3

Freeman Ct. Corr

Freeman Ct. Corr 179 F2
Freeman Way. Hornc 165 F3
Fremantle Rd. Woodf 153 E1
Freewood La. Elm 11 D2
Fremnells The. Basil 171 E4
French's Cl. Sta Ab 87 D2
Freshfields Ave. Upm 175 E4
Freshwater Dr. Basil 171 F2
Freshwaters. Harl 89 F1
Freshwell Gdns. Horn H 168 B3
Freshwell Gdns. Saff W 13 E1
Freshwell St. Saff W 13 E1
Frettons. Basil 171 F3
Friar's Ave. Brent 147 D1
Friar's Cl. Brent 147 D1
Friars La. Brain 66 A2
Friars La. Hat B O 79 E1
Friars The. Chig 153 F3
Friars Wlk. Chelm 111 D1
Friars Wood. Bis St 68 B4
Friarscroft. Hod 100 A2
Friary La. Woodf 152 A3
Friedburg Ave. Bis St 67 E2
Friends Wlk. Saff W 25 E4
Friern Gdns. Wick 163 D4
Friern Pl. Wick 163 D3
Friern Wlk. Wick 163 D4
Frimley Ave. Hornc 166 A2
Frinton Rd. Romf 155 D2
Friston Path. Chig 153 F3
Frithwood Cl. Bill 160 C4
Frithwood La. Bill 160 C4
Frizlands La. Dag 164 A1
Frobisher Way. Brain 66 B2
Froden Brook. Bill 161 E3
Froden Cl. Bill 161 E4
Froden Ct. Bill 161 E3
Frog St. Kelv H 145 F4
Frogge St. Hinx 1 A1
Frome. Grays 187 E1
Front La. Upm 166 C2
Fry Cl. Romf 155 D2
Fryerning La. Ing 135 D2
Fryth The. Basil 171 F4
Fulbrook La. S Ock 183 F3
Fulfen Way. Saff W 25 E4
Fullarton Cres. S Ock 183 F4
Fuller Ct. Bis St 68 A4
Fuller's La. Romf 155 E2
Fullers Cl. Romf 155 E2
Fullers Cl. Wa Aby 127 C3
Fullers Mead. Harl 103 E4
Fullwell Ave. Woodf 153 D1
Fulmar Rd. Rain 174 A3
Fulton Cres. Bis St 68 B4
Fulwich Rd. Stone 190 A1
Furlong Way. Sta Ab 87 D3
Furlongs. Basil 171 E2
Furlongs The. Ing 135 D2
Furness Cl. Grays 186 A1
Furness Way. Hornc 174 A4
Furrowfelde. Basil 171 D2
Further Meadow. Writ 123 D4
Furze Farm Cl. Romf 154 C1
Furze Glade. Basil 170 A3
Furze La. S Han 150 A4
Furze La. Stock 137 D1
Fusedale Way. S Ock 183 F3
Fyfield Ave. Wick 163 E3
Fyfield Cl. Horn H 168 B3
Fyfield Rd. Ch Ong 119 D3
Fyfield Rd. More 105 F2
Fyfield Rd. Rain 173 F2
Fyfield Rd. Will 107 E2
Fyfield Rd. Woodf 152 B2
Fyfields. Basil 172 B4

Gabion Ave. W Thu 183 E1
Gablefields. Sand 125 E3
Gables The. Basil 172 A4
Gabriel Cl. Romf 155 E2
Gaces Acre. New 25 D1
Gadsden Cl. Upm 166 C3
Gaiger Cl. Sprin 111 E4
Gainsborough Ave. Tilb 193 D3
Gainsborough Cl. Bill 149 D1
Gainsborough Cres. Sprin 111 F2
Gainsborough Rd. Rain 174 A2
Gainsborough Rd. Woodf 152 C2
Gainsford End Rd. Topp 32 A3
Gainsthorpe Rd. Bobb 118 B4
Gales Way. Woodf 152 C2
Galey Green. S Ock 184 A4
Gall End La. Stan M 57 F4
Galleon Bvd. Stone 190 B2
Galleons Hill. Rox 109 E3
Galley Green. Hod 87 D1
Galley Hill Rd. Swan 191 F1
Galley Hill Trad Est. Swan 191 F1
Galleydene Ave. Chelm 124 B2
Galleyhill Rd. Wa Aby 126 C4
Galleywood Cres. Romf 155 E2
Galleywood Rd. Chelm 124 A3
Galleywood Rd. Gt Bad 124 C3
Gallops The. Basil 170 A3
Galloway Cl. Bis St 67 F4
Galloway Rd. Bis St 56 C1
Gallows Green Rd. Lind 51 F1

Gallows Hill. Saff W 25 E4
Galsworthy Rd. Tilb 193 E3
Gambleside. Basil 171 F2
Ganels Cl. Bill 161 E4
Ganels Rd. Bill 161 E4
Gangies Hill. H Wy 77 D2
Ganley Cl. Bill 149 D1
Gannet Cl. Hav 7 E4
Gant Ct. Wa Aby 126 C3
Gap The. Arkes 23 F1
Garbutt Rd. Upm 166 B1
Garden Fields. Sta R 131 F3
Garden Fields. Steb 62 B3
Garden Terrace Rd. Harl 90 B2
Garden Way. Lou 128 A1
Gardeners. Gt Bad 124 B3
Gardens The. Dodd 133 D2
Gardiners Cl. Basil 162 B1
Gardiners La N. Bill 162 C2
Gardiners La S. Basil 162 C1
Gardiners Way. Basil 162 B1
Gardner Ave. Corr 180 A2
Garfield Rd. Ching 139 E1
Garland Way. Hornc 165 F4
Garnetts. Take 70 A4
Garnetts Bungalows. Felst 74 B3
Garnetts La. Felst 74 B3
Garnon Mead. Epp 116 B2
Garrettlands. Sand 125 F3
Garrick St. Grave 193 D1
Garron La. S Ock 183 F4
Garry Cl. Romf 155 F2
Garry Way. Romf 155 F2
Garth Rd. S Ock 176 B1
Gascoigne Way. Bill 149 E1
Gascoyne Cl. Romf 156 B2
Gasson Rd. Swan 191 F1
Gate Lodge Sq. Bill 161 F1
Gate Lodge Way. Bill 161 F1
Gatehope Dr. S Ock 183 F4
Gatehouse Villas. Gt Dun 72 C4
Gateway. Basil 171 D3
Gatwick Cl. Bis St 57 D1
Gatwick View. Bill 161 D4
Gatwick Way. Hornc 174 C4
Gauden Rd. Brain 65 F4
Gavenny Path. S Ock 183 F4
Gawlers. Berd 46 A4
Gay Bowers. Basil 171 E4
Gay Gdns. Dag 173 E4
Gay Links. Basil 171 D4
Gaylor Rd. Tilb 192 C3
Gaynes Ct. Upm 175 D4
Gaynes Hill Rd. Woodf 152 C2
Gaynes Park Rd. Upm 175 D4
Gaynes Rd. Upm 166 A1
Gaynesford. Basil 170 C2
Gaywood. Basil 170 A4
Geary Ct. Brent 158 B4
Geddings Rd. Hod 100 A3
Geerings The. Corr 180 A2
Geisthorp Ct. Wa Aby 127 D3
Gelsthorpe Rd. Romf 155 D2
Generals La. Bore 99 D1
Gentry Cl. Sta L H 179 E1
Geoffrey Ave. Romf 157 D2
George Avey Croft. N W Bas 117 D3
George Gent Cl. Ste B 18 A3
George La. Woodf 152 A1
George Rd. Brain 65 E1
George St. Chelm 111 D1
George St. Grays 192 A4
George St. Romf 164 C3
George St. Saff W 13 E1
George Yd. Brain 65 F2
Georges Dr. Brent 145 F2
Gepps Cl. H Ea 82 B1
Gerard Ave. Bis St 67 F2
Gernon Cl. Broom 98 A2
Gernon Cl. Rain 174 B2
Gernons. Basil 170 C2
Gerpins La. Upm 175 D3
Gerrard Cres. Brent 158 B4
Ghyllgrove. Basil 171 D4
Gibbons Rd. Gt Dun 61 D1
Gibbs Croft. Harl 102 C2
Gibbs Field. Bis St 67 E3
Gibcracks. Basil 171 F3
Gibraltar Cl. Brent 158 B4
Gibson Cl. N W Bas 117 E3
Gibson Cl. Saff W 13 E1
Gibson Gdns. Saff W 13 E1
Gibson Way. Saff W 13 E1
Gidea Ave. Romf 165 D4
Gidea Cl. Romf 165 D4
Gidea Cl. S Ock 176 B1
Gideons Way. Corr 179 F2
Giffins Cl. Brain 65 F1
Gifford Green. Basil 172 A3
Gifford Pl. Brent 158 B3
Giffords Cross Ave. Corr 180 A2
Giffords Cross Rd. Corr 180 A2
Giffordside. Grays 186 A3
Gilbert Cl. Swan 191 E1
Gilbert Dr. Basil 170 A3
Gilbert Rd. Romf 164 C4
Gilbert Way. Brain 66 B3
Gilbey Ave. Bis St 68 A3

Gilbey Cres. Stan M 57 F4
Gilbey Green. New 24 C1
Gilchrist Way. Brain 65 F2
Gilda Terr. Brain 65 D1
Gildbourne Cl. Corr 180 B3
Gilden Cl. Harl 90 C2
Gilden Way. Harl 90 C2
Gilders. Saw 77 E1
Giles Cl. Rain 174 B2
Gillam Way. Rain 174 A3
Gillian Cres. Romf 156 B1
Gilmore Way. Gt Bad 125 D3
Gilmour Rise. Bill 148 C1
Gilpin Way. Bl Not 76 B4
Gilpin's Gallop. Sta Ab 87 D2
Gilroy Cl. Rain 173 F3
Gilsland. Wa Aby 126 C2
Gilson Cl. Sprin 111 F1
Gilwell Cl. Ching 139 D3
Ginns Rd. St Pel 45 E3
Gippeswyck. Basil 171 E4
Gipping Cl. Hav 6 C3
Gipsy La. Grays 192 B4
Gipsy La. Stan M 57 E2
Girton Rd. Hav 7 D4
Gisborne Gdns. Rain 173 F1
Glade The. Basil 171 E2
Glade The. Brent 147 D1
Glade The. Upm 175 E4
Glade The. Woodf 152 A4
Glade The. Woodf 152 C1
Gladeway The. Wa Aby 126 B3
Gladstone Ct. Chelm 111 D1
Gladstone Rd. Hod 100 A4
Gladstone Rd. Lou 140 B1
Gladwyns. Basil 170 C4
Glamis Dr. Hornc 165 F2
Glanmead. Brent 146 C1
Glanmire. Bill 149 E3
Glanthams Cl. Brent 158 C4
Glanthams Rd. Brent 158 C4
Glanville Dr. Hornc 165 F2
Glastonbury Ave. Woodf 152 B2
Glebe Ave. Brain 65 F3
Glebe Ave. Woodf 152 A2
Glebe Cres. Broom 98 A1
Glebe Ct. Bis St 68 A4
Glebe End. Els 48 B1
Glebe Field. Basil 171 E4
Glebe Gdns. Brent 159 E2
Glebe La. Lit Ea 60 C3
Glebe Rd. Ch Ong 118 C1
Glebe Rd. Chelm 111 D2
Glebe Rd. Dag 173 D3
Glebe Rd. Wick 150 C1
Glebe Rd. Wick 163 F4
Glebe The. Mag Lav 104 B3
Glebe The. Saff W 25 F4
Glebe Way. Hornc 165 F2
Glebelands. Chig 154 A4
Glebelands. Harl 89 F2
Glebelands Ave. Woodf 152 A1
Glebeway. Woodf 152 B3
Glen Cres. Woodf 152 A2
Glen Faba Rd. Roy 100 C3
Glen Hazel. Bla 133 E2
Glen Rd. Basil 171 F2
Glen Rise. Woodf 152 A2
Glen The. Corr 179 F2
Glen The. Rain 174 B1
Glencoe Dr. Dag 173 D4
Glencree. Bill 149 E3
Glendale Cl. Brent 146 C1
Glendower Rd. Ching 139 E1
Gleneagles Cl. Romf 156 C2
Glenester Cl. Hod 87 D1
Glenfield Rd. Corr 180 A3
Glengall Rd. Woodf 152 A2
Glenmere. Basil 171 E1
Glenmire Terr. Sta Ab 87 E2
Glenside. Bill 149 E1
Glenside. Chig 153 D2
Glenton Cl. Romf 155 F2
Glenton Way. Romf 155 F2
Glenwood Ave. Rain 174 A1
Glenwood Dr. Romf 165 D4
Globe Cres. Far 56 B3
Globe Rd. Hornc 165 D3
Globe Rd. Woodf 152 B2
Gloucester Ave. Chelm 124 B3
Gloucester Ave. Grays 185 E2
Gloucester Ave. Grays 187 E1
Gloucester Ave. Hornc 166 A4
Gloucester Cl. S Ock 176 B1
Gloucester Cres. Chelm 111 D3
Gloucester Ct. Tilb 192 C3
Gloucester Gdns. Brain 66 A2
Gloucester Pl. Bill 149 D3
Gloucester Rd. Brent 146 A2
Gloucester Rd. Hav 6 C3
Gloucester Rd. Romf 164 C3
Glovers Field. Kelv H 132 C1
Glovers La. N W Bas 103 F2
Goat Hall La. Chelm 124 A2
Goatsmoor La. S Han 149 F3
Gobions. Basil 171 D2
Gobions Ave. Romf 155 E2
Goddard Rd. Grays 185 D3

Goddard Way. Saff W 13 F2
Goddard Way. Sprin 111 F1
Godfrey Way. Gt Dun 61 E1
Godfrey's Mews. Chelm 111 D1
Godlings Way. Brain 65 F1
Godman Rd. Grays 186 A2
Godsafe. Harl 90 C2
Godwin Cl. Wa Aby 139 E4
Gold Cl. Els 48 A1
Gold St. Saff W 13 E1
Goldcrest Dr. Bill 149 E1
Golden La. Rad 16 A1
Goldenacres. Sprin 111 F4
Goldhanger Cross. Basil 171 F4
Goldhaze Cl. Woodf 152 B2
Golding Cres. Corr 179 F2
Golding Thoroughfare. Sprin . 111 F2
Golding's Hill. Lou 127 F1
Goldingham Ave. Lou 141 E4
Goldings. Bis St 68 A4
Goldings Cres. Basil 171 F2
Goldings Rd. Lou 141 D4
Goldings Rise. Lou 141 D4
Goldington Cres. Bill 148 C3
Goldlay Ave. Chelm 111 E1
Goldlay Gdns. Chelm 111 E1
Goldlay Rd. Chelm 111 E1
Goldsmith. Grays 191 F4
Goldsmith Ave. Romf 164 A2
Goldsmiths Ave. Corr 180 A2
Goodliffe Park. Birhr 57 D1
Goodmans La. Gt Le 85 F2
Goodmayes Wlk. Wick 163 E3
Goodview Rd. Bill 162 A1
Goodwin Stile. Bis St 67 E3
Goodwins Cl. Litt 12 C2
Goodwood Ave. Brent 147 F2
Goodwood Ave. Hornc 174 C4
Goodwood Cl. Hod 100 A4
Goose La. Gt Ha 78 C4
Goose La. Lit Hal 79 D4
Gooshays Dr. Romf 156 C2
Gooshays Gdns. Romf 156 C2
Gordon Ave. Hornc 164 C1
Gordon Cl. Bill 148 C2
Gordon Pl. Grave 193 E1
Gordon Rd. Basil 171 E3
Gordon Rd. Brent 147 D1
Gordon Rd. Chelm 124 A3
Gordon Rd. Ching 139 F1
Gordon Rd. Corr 179 F2
Gordon Rd. Grave 192 C1
Gordon Rd. Grays 185 F2
Gordon Rd. Horn H 178 C2
Gordon Rd. Wa Aby 126 A3
Gordon Rd. Woodf 152 A1
Gordons. Basil 172 A3
Gore La. Brain 65 D1
Gore The. Basil 171 D4
Gorfield Rd. Take 59 D2
Goring Cl. Romf 155 E1
Goring Rd. Dag 173 E3
Gorseway. Romf 164 C2
Gosfield Rd. Dag 164 A1
Goshawk Dr. Chelm 124 A3
Gosport Dr. Hornc 174 B3
Gossets The. Mar Rod 94 C2
Gould Cl. More 105 E1
Goulton Rd. Broom 98 A1
Gourney Gr. Grays 185 D3
Government Row. Enf 126 A1
Gowers Ave. Gt Bad 124 C3
Gowers La. Grays 185 F2
Gowers The. Harl 90 A1
Grace Cl. Chig 153 F2
Grace Gdns. Bis St 67 F2
Grafton Pl. Sprin 112 A2
Graham Cl. Bill 149 E3
Graham Cl. Brent 147 E2
Graham Cl. Corr 179 F2
Grailands. Bis St 67 E4
Grampian Gr. Chelm 110 B3
Granary Meadow. Dodd 133 F2
Granary The. Roy 88 A1
Granby Rd. Grave 192 B1
Grandville Cl. Bill 148 C3
Grange Ave. Wick 163 E3
Grange Ave. Woodf 152 A2
Grange Cl. Brent 159 E3
Grange Cl. Woodf 152 A2
Grange Cres. Chig 153 E3
Grange Ct. Lou 140 B2
Grange La. Lit Dun 73 E4
Grange La. Roy 101 E4
Grange Park. Bis St 56 C1
Grange Rd. Ave 183 E3
Grange Rd. Basil 172 C4
Grange Rd. Bill 161 E4
Grange Rd. Bis St 68 A4
Grange Rd. Grays 192 A4
Grange Rd. Hinx 11 D4
Grange Rd. Ple 83 F1
Grange Rd. Romf 156 A2
Grange Rd. Runw 151 E1
Granger Way. Hornc 165 D3
Grangeside. Bis St 57 D1
Grangeway. Woodf 152 B3
Grangewood Ave. Grays 185 F2

Greenfields Cl. B

Grangewood Ave. Rain 174
Grangewood Cl. Brent 159
Granites Chase. Bill 161
Granta Cl. GT C 1
Grantham Way. Grays 185
Granton Ave. Upm 165
Granville Gdns. Hod 87
Granville Rd. Epp 116
Granville Rd. Woodf 152
Grapnells. Basil 171
Grasmere Cl. Bl Not 76
Grasmere Cl. Lou 140
Grassmere Rd. Hornc 165
Gratmore Green. Basil 171
Gravel Cl. Chig 154
Gravel Hill. Wa Aby 127
Gravel La. Chig 142
Gravelly La. Rox 109
Gray Ave. Dag 164
Gray Gdns. Rain 174
Gray's La. Weth 43
Graylands. The B 128
Grays Ave. Basil 170
Grays Ct. Bis St 67
Grays End Cl. Grays 185
Grays Town Centre. Grays .. 192
Grays Wlk. Brent 147
Great Berry Farm Chase. Basil 170
Great Berry La. Basil 170
Great Brays. Harl 103
Great Canfield Rd. Gt Can .. 70
Great Cob. Sprin 111
Great Cullings. Romf 164
Great Eastern Rd. Brent 158
Great Fox Meadow. Kelv H .. 132
Great Gardens Rd. Hornc .. 165
Great Godfreys. Rox 109
Great Gregorie. Basil 170
Great Gregories La. The B .. 128
Great Hadham Rd. Bis St .. 67
Great Knightleys. Basil 170
Great Lawn. Ch Ong 119
Great Leighs Way. Basil 163
Great Leylands. Harl 103
Great Meadow. Lo Naz 100
Great Mistley. Basil 171
Great Nelmes Chase. Hornc . 165
Great Oaks. Basil 171
Great Oaks. Brent 147
Great Oaks. Chig 153
Great Owl Rd. Chig 153
Great Oxcroft. Basil 170
Great Plumtree. Harl 89
Great Ranton. Basil 172
Great Ropers La. Brent 158
Great Spenders. Basil 171
Great Sq. Brain 65
Great Warley St. Brent 158
Great Yeldham Rd. Topp 32
Greathouse Chase. Corr 180
Grebe Cres. W Thu 184
Greding Wlk. Brent 159
Green Cl. Ep Gr 115
Green Cl. Sprin 111
Green Cl. Writ 110
Green Glade. The B 128
Green Glades. Hornc 166
Green La. Bill 161
Green La. Brent 147
Green La. Grays 185
Green La. Kelv H 145
Green La. Lo Naz 113
Green La. Match 104
Green La. Rox 109
Green La. Wa Aby 139
Green Lane. Chig 153
Green Manor Way. Grave .. 191
Green Shaw. Brent 146
Green St. Gt Can 70
Green St. Ing 134
Green The. Bis St 67
Green The. Bla 133
Green The. Chelm 110
Green The. Ching 139
Green The. Cla 9
Green The. Grays 186
Green The. Grays 193
Green The. S Ock 176
Green The. Saff W 13
Green The. Sta L H 179
Green The. The B 128
Green The. Wa Aby 126
Green The. Woodf 152
Green The. Writ 110
Green Trees. Epp 129
Green Wlk. Ch Ong 119
Green Wlk. Woodf 152
Green Wlk The. Ching 139
Greenacre La. Stock 149
Greenacres. Ep Gr 115
Greenacres Cl. Rain 174
Greenbank Cl. Romf 156
Greenbanks. Upm 166
Greenfield St. Wa Aby 126
Greenfields. Bill 161
Greenfields. Chelm 124
Greenfields. Lou 141
Greenfields Cl. Bill 161

207
Greenfields Cl. Lou
Heythrop The. Sprin

eenfields Cl. Lou 141 D3
eenfields Way. Brent 158 B2
eenfields Way. Hav 6 C3
eenhill. Lou 140 B1
eenhill Park. Bis St 67 E3
eenhills. Harl 102 C4
eenleas. Wa Aby 126 C3
eenock Way. Romf 155 F2
eens Cl The. Lou 141 D4
eens Farm La. Bill 161 E4
eenstead. Saw 77 F1
eenstead Ave. Woodf 152 B2
eenstead Cl. Brent 147 F1
eenstead Cl. Woodf 152 B2
eenstead Gdns. Woodf 152 B2
eensted Rd. Ch Ong 118 B1
eensted Rd. Lou 140 C1
eensted The. Basil 171 F3
eenway. Bill 149 E1
eenway. Bis St 68 B3
eenway. Brent 147 D1
eenway. Romf 157 D2
eenway. Woodf 152 B3
eenway Gdns. Bl Not 76 B4
eenway The. Runw 151 E2
eenways. Chelm 111 D3
eenways. Saff W 25 F4
eenwood Ave. Dag 173 D4
eenwood Cl. Hav 6 C4
eenwood Gdns. Woodf 153 E2
eenwood Rd. Chig 154 A3
eenyard. Wa Aby 126 B3
enfell Ave. Hornc 164 C2
ennan Cl. Brent 159 E2
enville Gdns. Woodf 152 B2
enville Rd. Brain 65 F1
esham Ct. Brent 158 B4
esham Rd. Brent 158 B4
rey Hollow. Quen 47 E4
rey Ladys. Chelm 124 A1
rey Towers Ave. Hornc 165 E2
rey Towers Gdns. Hornc 165 E2
reyfriars. Brent 147 D1
reygoose Park. Harl 102 A3
reyhound La. Grays 186 A2
reystone Gdns. Woodf 153 E1
ridiron Pl. Upm 166 A1
riffin Ave. Upm 166 C3
riffin's Wood Cotts. Ep Gr 128 B4
riffins The. Grays 185 D2
rimshaw Way. Romf 164 C3
rimston Rd. Basil 162 C1
rimstone Cl. Romf 155 D2
rinstead La. L Hal 78 B3
rosvenor Cl. Gt Bad 124 B4
rosvenor Cl. Lou 141 D4
rosvenor Dr. Hornc 165 E2
rosvenor Dr. Lou 141 E4
rosvenor Gdns. Bill 149 D2
rosvenor Gdns. Upm 166 B2
rosvenor Gdns. Woodf 152 A2
rosvenor Path. Lou 141 E4
rosvenor Rd. Grays 186 B4
rosvenor Rd. Romf 164 B2
rove Ave. Basil 170 A2
rove Ct. Wa Aby 126 A3
rove Gdns. Dag 164 B1
rove Hill. Stan M 57 F4
rove Hill. Woodf 152 A1
rove La. Chig 153 F4
rove La. Epp 116 A1
rove Park Rd. Rain 174 A2
rove Pl. Bis St 67 F4
rove Rd. Bill 148 C1
rove Rd. Chelm 111 D1
rove Rd. Grave 192 A1
rove Rd. Grays 192 B4
rove Rd. Sta L H 187 E4
rove Rd. Woodf 152 A1
rove The. Bill 149 E2
rove The. Brent 157 F3
rove The. Grave 193 E1
rove The. Gt Ha 68 C2
rove The. Swan 191 F1
rove The. Upm 175 D4
rove Villas. Gt Sal 64 A4
rovelands Rd. Wick 163 E3
rovelands Way. Grays 184 C1
rover Wlk. Corr 179 F2
rovesnor Cl. Bis St 67 E2
rubb's Hill. Wa Aby 113 E1
uardian Cl. Hornc 165 D2
uardsman Cl. Brent 158 B3
ubbins La. Romf 156 C1
uelph's La. Thax 40 A2
uernsey Gdns. Runw 151 E1
uernsey Way. Brain 65 E1
uildford Gdns. Romf 156 C2
uildford Rd. Romf 156 C2
uildhall Way. Ash 14 C4
uilfords. Harl 90 B3
ull Wlk. Rain 174 A3
umley Rd. Grays 191 F4
un Hill. Tilb 193 E4
un Hill Pl. Basil 171 E3
unn Rd. Swan 191 F1
utters La. Chelm 111 D4
uysfield Cl. Rain 174 A2
uysfield Dr. Rain 174 A2
Gwyn Cl. Bore 99 F1
Gwynne Park Ave. Woodf 152 C2

Habgood Rd. Lou 140 C3
Hacton Dr. Hornc 174 C4
Hacton La. Hornc 165 F1
Hadfield Rd. Sta L H 179 E1
Hadham Rd. Bis St 67 E4
Hadleigh Ct. Saff W 13 F1
Hadrian Cl. Hav 7 E4
Haggers Cl. Gt C 1 B1
Haig Ct. Chelm 111 D1
Haig Rd. Grays 186 A2
Hailes Wood. Els 48 B1
Hailey Ave. Hod 87 D1
Hailsham Cl. Romf 156 B3
Hailsham Gdns. Romf 156 B3
Hailsham Rd. Romf 156 B3
Hainault Gr. Chelm 110 C1
Hainault Gr. Chig 153 E3
Hainault Rd. Chig 153 E3
Hainault Rd. Romf 154 A1
Hainault Rd. Romf 164 B4
Halchfields. Gt Wal 97 F4
Halcyon Way. Hornc 165 F2
Haldon Cl. Chig 153 F3
Hale End. Romf 156 A2
Halesworth Cl. Romf 156 C2
Halesworth Rd. Romf 156 C2
Half Acres. Bis St 67 F4
Half Moon La. Epp 128 C4
Halfhides. Wa Aby 126 B3
Halfway Ct. Pur 183 D1
Halidon Rise. Romf 157 D2
Hall Ave. Ave 183 E3
Hall Chase. H Ea 83 F4
Hall Cl. Corr 179 F2
Hall Cl. Gt Bad 125 D3
Hall Cl. Hen 48 C3
Hall Cres. Ave 183 E2
Hall Green La. Brent 147 E1
Hall La. Br Pel 33 D3
Hall La. Brent 146 C2
Hall La. Ing 135 E1
Hall La. Mtssg 184 A4
Hall La. Ridge 20 A3
Hall La. S Ock 176 B2
Hall La. Sand 125 E3
Hall La. Stock 137 E3
Hall La. Upm 166 B3
Hall Park Rd. Upm 175 E4
Hall Rd. Ave 183 E2
Hall Rd. Els 58 C4
Hall Rd. Pan 65 D3
Hall Rd. Romf 165 D4
Hall St. Chelm 111 D1
Hall Terr. Ave 183 E2
Hallam Cl. Dodd 133 D2
Hallam Ct. Bill 148 C2
Halling Hill. Harl 89 F1
Hallingbury Cl. L Hal 68 A1
Hallingbury Rd. Bis St 68 A2
Hallingbury Rd. Saw 78 A2
Hallmores. Hod 100 A2
Hallwood Cres. Brent 146 C1
Halstead Ct. Wick 163 E3
Halstead Way. Brent 147 E2
Halstow Way. Basil 172 B3
Halt Dr. Sta L H 187 D2
Halton Rd. Grays 186 B2
Hamble La. S Ock 183 F4
Hambro Rd. Brent 158 B4
Hamden Cres. Dag 164 A1
Hamel Way. Widd 37 E2
Hamerton Rd. Grave 192 A1
Hamilton Ave. Hod 100 A4
Hamilton Ave. Romf 155 E1
Hamilton Cres. Brent 158 B3
Hamilton Dr. Romf 156 C1
Hamilton Mews. Saff W 13 F1
Hamilton Rd. Basil 172 C4
Hamilton Rd. Romf 165 D3
Hamilton Rd. Take 70 C4
Hamlet Cl. Romf 155 D2
Hamlet Hill. Roy 101 D2
Hamlet Rd. Chelm 111 D1
Hamlet Rd. Hav 7 D4
Hamlet Rd. Romf 155 D2
Hammarskjold Rd. Harl 89 E1
Hammonds La. Bill 161 E4
Hammonds La. Brent 158 A2
Hammonds Rd. Hat B O 80 A3
Hammonds Rd. Lit Bad 112 C2
Hammonds Rd. Sand 112 C2
Hampden Cl. N W Bas 117 D2
Hampden Cres. Brent 158 B3
Hampden Rd. Grays 185 D1
Hampden Rd. Romf 155 D2
Hampit Rd. Arkes 23 E1
Hampshire Gdns. Sta L H 187 D2
Hampshire Rd. Hornc 166 A4
Hampton Mead. Lou 141 D3
Hampton Rd. Gt Bad 124 C3
Hamstel Rd. Harl 89 E1
Hanbury Rd. Chelm 123 F4
Hance La. Ray 64 C1
Hand La. Saw 77 E1
Handel Cres. Tilb 193 D4
Handley Green. Basil 170 B3
Hanford Rd. Ave 183 E3
Hanging Hill. Brent 147 E1
Hanging Hill La. Brent 147 E1
Hannards Way. Chig 154 A3
Hanover Cl. Basil 171 F3
Hanover Ct. Hod 100 A4
Hanover Dr. Basil 171 F3
Hanover Gdns. Woodf 153 E2
Hanover Pl. Saff W 13 E1
Hansells Mead. Roy 101 D4
Hanson Cl. Lou 141 E4
Hanson Dr. Lou 141 E4
Hanson Gr. Lou 141 E4
Harberts Rd. Harl 102 A4
Harbourer Cl. Chig 154 A3
Harbourer Rd. Chig 154 A3
Hardie Rd. Dag 164 B1
Hardie Rd. Sta L H 179 E1
Harding Rd. Grays 186 A2
Harding's Elms Rd. Bill 162 A2
Harding's La. Ing 135 D4
Hardley Cres. Hornc 165 E4
Hardwick Rd. Hav 7 D4
Hardy Gr. Stone 190 A2
Hare Hall La. Romf 165 D4
Hare St. Harl 102 A4
Harebel Way. Romf 156 B2
Harebell Cl. Bill 148 C2
Harefield. Harl 90 A1
Hares Chase. Bill 148 C2
Haresfield Rd. Dag 173 D3
Harewood Dr. Woodf 152 C1
Harewood Hill. The B 128 C2
Harewood Rd. Brent 146 A2
Harewood Rd. Chelm 110 C1
Harford Cl. Ching 139 D1
Harford Rd. Ching 139 D1
Hargrave Cl. Stan M 57 F4
Harkilees Way. Brain 65 F3
Harkness Cl. Romf 156 C3
Harlesden Cl. Romf 156 C2
Harlesden Rd. Romf 156 C2
Harlesden Wlk. Romf 156 C2
Harley Wlk. Basil 172 A3
Harlings Gr. Chelm 111 E2
Harlow Common. Match 103 F3
Harlow Gdns. Romf 155 E2
Harlow Rd. Match 91 E2
Harlow Rd. More 105 E1
Harlow Rd. Rain 173 F2
Harlow Rd. Roy 88 B1
Harlow Rd. Saw 90 B4
Harlow Rd. Sheer 91 D4
Harlton Ct. Wa Aby 126 C3
Harmer Rd. Swan 191 F1
Harmer St. Grave 193 E1
Harness Cl. Sprin 111 F4
Harold Court Rd. Romf 157 D2
Harold Cres. Wa Aby 126 B4
Harold Gdns. Runw 151 F1
Harold Rd. Brain 65 F1
Harold Rd. Woodf 152 A1
Harold View. Romf 156 C1
Harpers La. Dodd 133 E1
Harrap Chase. Grays 184 C1
Harrier Cl. Rain 174 A3
Harriescourt. Wa Aby 127 D4
Harrison Cl. Brent 147 E2
Harrison Dr. Brain 66 A1
Harrison Dr. N W Bas 117 D3
Harrison Rd. Dag 173 D3
Harrisons. Birhr 57 E1
Harrods Ct. Bill 149 F1
Harrow Cres. Romf 156 A2
Harrow Dr. Hornc 165 E2
Harrow Hill. Topp 31 F3
Harrow Way. Gt Bad 125 D3
Hart Cres. Chig 153 F3
Hart Rd. Harl 90 B3
Hart St. Brent 158 B4
Hart St. Chelm 111 D1
Hart Wood Rd. Brent 158 C3
Hartford End. Basil 172 A3
Hartland Rd. Epp 116 A1
Hartland Rd. Hornc 165 D1
Hartley Cl. Sprin 112 A2
Harts Gr. Woodf 152 A3
Hartswood Cl. Brent 158 C3
Harty Cl. Grays 185 D3
Harvard Wlk. Hornc 174 A4
Harvey. Grays 185 D2
Harvey Gdns. Lou 141 D3
Harvey Rd. Basil 163 E1
Harvey Way. Hemp 16 C1
Harvey Way. Saff W 13 F1
Harvey's La. Romf 164 C1
Harveyfields. Wa Aby 126 B3
Harwater Dr. Lou 140 C4
Harwood Ave. Hornc 165 F4
Harwood Hall La. Upm 175 E3
Haselfoot Rd. Bore 112 C4
Haskins. Corr 179 F1
Haslemere Rd. Runw 151 E1
Haslewood Ave. Hod 100 A3
Hassenbrook Rd. Sta L H 179 F1
Hasted Cl. Swan 191 E1
Hastings Rd. Romf 165 D3
Hastings The. Runw 151 E1
Hastingwood Rd. Mag Lav 104 A3
Hastingwood Rd. N W Bas 103 F2
Hatch Green. L Hal 78 A4
Hatch Rd. Brent 146 A2
Hatch Side. Chig 153 D3
Hatches Farm Rd. Bill 160 B3
Hatfield Cl. Brent 147 E1
Hatfield Cl. Hornc 174 B4
Hatfield Cl. Woodf 153 D1
Hatfield Dr. Bill 149 E1
Hatfield Gr. Chelm 110 B1
Hatfields. Lou 141 D3
Hathaway Rd. Grays 185 D1
Hatherleigh Way. Romf 156 B1
Hatherley The. Basil 171 E4
Hatterill. Basil 170 B3
Havana Cl. Romf 164 C3
Haven Cl. Basil 171 F2
Haven Pl. Grays 185 E2
Haven Rise. Bill 161 E3
Haven The. Grays 185 F1
Havengore. Basil 172 B4
Havengore. Sprin 111 F3
Haverhill Rd. Bart 5 F3
Haverhill Rd. Ching 139 E1
Haverhill Rd. Hel B 6 B1
Haverhill Rd. Ste B 7 D1
Havering Dr. Romf 164 C4
Havering Rd. Romf 155 E2
Havers La. Bis St 67 F3
Havis Rd. Corr 179 F2
Havisham Way. Chelm 110 C4
Haward Rd. Hod 100 B4
Hawes La. Wa Aby 126 B1
Hawfinch Wlk. Chelm 124 A3
Hawk Cl. Wa Aby 127 D3
Hawkbush Green. Basil 163 D1
Hawkdene. Ching 139 E2
Hawkenbury. Harl 102 A3
Hawkes Cl. Grays 192 A4
Hawkesbury Bush La. Basil 171 D1
Hawkhurst Cl. Chelm 110 C1
Hawkhurst Gdns. Romf 155 E2
Hawkinge Way. Hornc 174 B3
Hawkins Way. Brain 66 B2
Hawksmoor Green. Brent 147 E2
Hawksmouth. Ching 139 E1
Hawksway. Basil 171 D2
Hawkswood Rd. S Han 151 D3
Hawkwood Cres. Ching 139 D2
Hawsted. Lou 140 A1
Hawthorn Ave. Brent 158 C3
Hawthorn Ave. Rain 174 A1
Hawthorn Cl. Chelm 124 B3
Hawthorn Cl. Take 70 B4
Hawthorn Rd. Hod 100 A4
Hawthorn Rd. Woodf 152 B3
Hawthorn Rise. Thor 67 F2
Hawthorne Rd. Corr 179 F2
Hawthorns. Harl 102 C2
Hawthorns. Harl 103 D2
Hawthorns. Woodf 152 A4
Hawthorns The. Corr 180 B2
Hawthorns The. Lou 141 D3
Hay Green La. Dodd 133 F2
Hay La. Brain 66 B2
Hayburn Way. Hornc 164 C2
Haycroft. Bis St 68 B4
Hayden Way. Romf 155 E1
Haydens Rd. Harl 102 A4
Haydock Cl. Hornc 174 C4
Hayes Cl. Chelm 111 D1
Hayes Cl. Grays 191 E4
Hayes Dr. Rain 174 A3
Hayes Rd. Stone 190 C1
Hayle. Grays 187 E2
Hayley Bell Gdns. Bis St 67 F2
Haymeads La. Bis St 68 B3
Haynes Rd. Hornc 165 E3
Haysoms Cl. Romf 164 C4
Haytor Cl. Brain 66 B1
Haywards Cl. Brent 147 F2
Haywood Ct. Wa Aby 126 C3
Hazel Cl. Hav 6 C4
Hazel Cl. Hornc 165 D1
Hazel Gdns. Grays 185 F2
Hazel Gr. Brain 65 F1
Hazel Rise. Hornc 165 E3
Hazelbrouck Gdns. Chig 153 E2
Hazeldon Cl. Lit Wal 98 B3
Hazeleigh. Brent 159 D4
Hazeleigh Gdns. Woodf 152 C3
Hazelend Rd. Stan M 57 D2
Hazell Cres. Romf 155 D1
Hazelmere. Basil 172 A2
Hazelmere Gdns. Hornc 165 E3
Hazelwood. Lou 140 B2
Hazelwood. Sta L H 187 D1
Hazelwood Gdns. Brent 146 A2
Hazelwood Park Cl. Chig 153 F3
Headcorn Cl. Basil 172 B3
Headingley Cl. Chig 153 F2
Headland Ave. Hav 6 C4
Headley Chase. Brent 158 B3
Headley Rd. Bill 149 E2
Heard's La. Brent 146 C3
Heard's La. Finch 30 B3
Hearn Rd. Romf 164 C3
Hearsall Ave. Chelm 111 D4
Heath Cl. Romf 165 D4
Heath Dr. Chelm 124 A3
Heath Dr. Romf 156 A1
Heath Dr. The B 128 C2
Heath Park Ct. Romf 165 D3
Heath Park Rd. Romf 165 D3
Heath Rd. Grays 186 A2
Heath Rd. S Han 150 A2
Heath Row. Bis St 57 D1
Heath View Gdns. Grays 185 E2
Heath View Rd. Grays 185 E2
Heathcote Ave. Woodf 152 C1
Heather Ave. Romf 155 E1
Heather Bank. Bill 149 E1
Heather Cl. Brent 146 A2
Heather Cl. Romf 155 E1
Heather Ct. Sprin 111 F3
Heather Dr. Romf 155 F1
Heather Gdns. Romf 155 F1
Heather Glen. Romf 155 E1
Heather Way. Romf 155 E1
Heathfield Rd. Chelm 111 D4
Heathleigh Rd. Basil 170 A2
Heathway. Dag 173 D3
Heathway. Woodf 152 B3
Heaton Ave. Romf 156 A2
Heaton Cl. Romf 156 B2
Heaton Grange Rd. Romf 155 F1
Heaton Way. Romf 156 B2
Hedge Place Rd. Stone 190 C1
Hedgerow The. Basil 171 F2
Hedgerows. Bore 112 A3
Hedgerows. Saw 77 F1
Hedingham Rd. Hornc 166 A2
Hedley Ave. W Thu 191 E4
Heideck Gdns. Brent 159 D4
Heighams. Harl 101 F3
Heights The. Lou 140 C4
Helen Rd. Hornc 165 E4
Helford Way. Upm 166 B3
Helions Bumpstead Rd. Hav 7 D3
Helions Park Ave. Hav 7 D4
Helions Park Gdns. Hav 7 D4
Helions Park Gr. Hav 7 D4
Helions Rd. Harl 102 A4
Helions Rd. Ste B 18 A3
Helions Service Rd. Hav 7 D4
Helions Wlk. Hav 7 D4
Helleborine. Grays 184 C1
Helmons La. W Han 138 A2
Helmores. Basil 169 F3
Helmsdale Cl. Romf 155 F2
Helmsdale Rd. Romf 155 F2
Helpeston. Basil 171 E3
Helston Rd. Sprin 111 F3
Hemley Rd. Grays 186 C4
Hemmels. Basil 170 A4
Hemnall St. Epp 116 A1
Hemnall St. Epp 128 C4
Hempstead Cl. Woodf 152 A4
Henbone Path. Romf 156 B2
Henderson Cl. Hornc 165 D1
Henderson Dr. Stone 190 A2
Hendon Cl. Wick 163 E3
Hendon Gdns. Romf 155 E2
Hengist Gdns. Runw 151 E1
Henham Cl. Bill 149 E1
Henham Rd. Deb 38 C2
Henham Rd. Els 48 C1
Henham Rd. Hen 48 C1
Henniker Gate. Sprin 112 A2
Henry Rd. Chelm 111 D2
Henry St. Grays 192 B4
Henry's Wlk. Chig 153 E2
Henwood Side. Lou 152 C2
Herald Cl. Bis St 67 E3
Herbert Rd. Hornc 165 F2
Herbert Rd. Swan 191 F1
Herd La. Corr 180 B2
Hereford Wlk. Basil 171 F4
Hereward Cl. Wa Aby 126 B4
Hereward Gdns. Runw 151 E1
Hereward Green. Lou 141 E4
Hereward Way. Weth 43 E2
Herga Hyll. Grays 186 A4
Herington Gr. Brent 147 D1
Hernshaw. Brent 159 E2
Heron Cl. Lou 140 A1
Heron Cl. Saw 77 E1
Heron Ct. Bis St 68 A4
Heron Dale. Basil 171 E3
Heron Flight Ave. Rain 174 A3
Heron Way. Upm 166 C2
Heron Way. W Thu 184 A1
Herons La. Fyf 106 B1
Herons Wood. Harl 89 D1
Heronsgate Trdng Est. Basil 162 C1
Heronswood. Wa Aby 126 C3
Heronway. Brent 147 D1
Heronway. Woodf 152 B3
Hertford Dr. Basil 171 E1
Hertford La. Elm 10 C3
Hesselyn Dr. Rain 174 A3
Heybridge Dr. Wick 163 F4
Heybridge Dr. Woodf 153 E1
Heybridge Rd. Ing 135 D1
Heycroft Way. Gt Bad 124 C3
Heydon La. Elm 10 C2
Heythrop The. Ing 135 D2
Heythrop The. Sprin 111 E2

Hicks Way. Stur 7 F3
Hickstars La. Bill 161 E4
Hides The. Harl 89 E1
High Ash Cl. Sta L H 187 D1
High Bank. Basil 169 F2
High Barrets. Basil 172 A3
High Beech Rd. Lou 140 C3
High Bridge Rd. Sprin 111 E1
High Chelmer. Chelm 111 D1
High Cl. Hey 10 A3
High Cloister. Bill 149 D1
High Easter Rd. Barn 72 C1
High Easter Rd. Lea Rod 94 B4
High Elms. Chig 153 F3
High Elms. Upm 166 C2
High Elms. Woodf 152 A3
High Fields. Gt Dun 72 B4
High Gables. Lou 140 B2
High House Estate. Harl 90 C2
High House La. Grays 186 B2
High La. Match 91 F3
High La. Stan M 57 F4
High Mead. Chig 153 E4
High Meadow. Bill 149 E1
High Meadow. Gt Dun 72 B4
High Meadows. Chig 153 E3
High Pastures. Sheer 91 E4
High Rd. Basil 170 A3
High Rd. Basil 172 A3
High Rd. Bill 161 E1
High Rd. Chig 153 D4
High Rd. Corr 180 A1
High Rd. Corr 180 B3
High Rd. Ep Gr 128 B3
High Rd. Grays 185 F4
High Rd. Horn H 178 C2
High Rd. Lou 140 B2
High Rd. N W Bas 116 B3
High Rd. N W Bas 117 E3
High Rd. T Thu 184 C3
High Rd. Woodf 152 A1
High Rd Buckhurst Hill. Woodf152 A4
High Rd Knighton. Lou 152 A4
High Rd Knighton. Woodf ... 152 A4
High Rd Woodford Green.
　Woodf......................152 A3
High Silver. Lou 140 B3
High St. Ave 183 E3
High St. Bart 5 F2
High St. Bill 149 D1
High St. Bis St 67 F4
High St. Brain 65 F1
High St. Brent 158 B4
High St. Ch Ong 119 D2
High St. Chelm 111 D1
High St. Chris 10 B2
High St. Clav 35 E2
High St. Deb 38 A4
High St. Els 48 B1
High St. Epp 128 C4
High St. Grave 192 B1
High St. Grave 193 D1
High St. Grays 192 A4
High St. Gt Ba 42 A1
High St. Gt Bad 124 C4
High St. Gt C 1 C1
High St. Gt Dun 72 B4
High St. Harl 90 B2
High St. Hat B O 79 F3
High St. Hav 7 D4
High St. Hemp 16 C1
High St. Hen 48 C3
High St. Hinx 1 A4
High St. Hod 100 A3
High St. Hornc 165 E2
High St. Hun 88 A1
High St. Ing 135 D2
High St. Litt 12 C2
High St. New 37 D4
High St. Pur 183 D1
High St. Romf 164 C3
High St. Saff W 13 E1
High St. Sta Ab 87 E2
High St. Sta L H 179 E1
High St. Steb 62 C3
High St. Stock 136 C2
High St. Swan 191 D2
High St. Swan 191 F1
High St. Weth 43 E2
High St. Wick 163 E4
High St. Widd 37 E2
High St. Woodf 153 E1
High Stile. Gt Dun 72 B4
High View. Birhr 57 E2
High View Ave. Grays 185 E1
High View Cl. Lou 140 B2
High View Rise. Bill 162 B3
High View School La. Chig . 153 F3
High Wych La. Saw 77 D1
High Wych Rd. H Wy 89 F4
High Wych Rd. Saw 77 E1
Higham Rd. Woodf 152 A2
Higham View. N W Bas 117 D3
Highbury Ave. Hod 100 A4
Highcliff Dr. Wick 162 C4
Highcliffe Cl. Wick 163 F4
Highcliffe Rd. Wick 163 F4
Highcliffe Way. Wick 163 F4
Highcross La. Can E 71 E3

Highfield. Harl 103 D4
Highfield App. Bill 161 E4
Highfield Ave. Bis St 68 B3
Highfield Cl. Brain 66 A3
Highfield Cl. Romf 155 E2
Highfield Cres. Hornc 165 F1
Highfield Ct. Bill 161 E4
Highfield Gdns. Grays 185 E3
Highfield Green. Epp 128 C4
Highfield Link. Romf 155 E2
Highfield Pl. Epp 128 C4
Highfield Rd. Bill 161 E4
Highfield Rd. Chelm 110 C2
Highfield Rd. Hornc 165 F1
Highfield Rd. Romf 155 E2
Highfield Rd. Woodf 152 C2
Highfield Stile Rd. Brain 66 A3
Highfield Way. Hornc 165 F1
Highfields. Deb 38 A4
Highfields. Hen 48 C3
Highfields. Langl 22 B1
Highfields. Saff W 13 F1
Highgate Gr. Saw 77 E1
Highland Ave. Brent 146 B1
Highland Ave. Dag 164 B1
Highland Ave. Lou 140 C2
Highland Gr. Bill 149 D1
Highland Rd. Corr 171 D1
Highland Rd. Lo Naz 100 C1
Highland Rd. Thor 67 F2
Highlands Ave. Basil 171 E2
Highlands Cres. Basil 172 C3
Highlands Rd. Basil 172 C3
Highmead. Stan M 57 F4
Hightrees. Stock 136 B1
Highview Cres. Brent 147 E2
Highview Gdns. Upm 166 A1
Highwood Cl. Brent 146 A1
Highwood La. Lou 141 D2
Highwood Rd. Ing 122 A3
Hilary Cl. Hornc 174 B4
Hill Ave. Wick 163 F4
Hill Cres. Chelm 111 E1
Hill Cres. Hornc 165 E3
Hill Crest Rd. Ch Ong 117 F1
Hill Ct. Basil 171 E3
Hill Gr. Romf 164 C4
Hill House Rd. Stone 190 B1
Hill La. Stur 7 F2
Hill Rd. Brent 158 A4
Hill Rd. Chelm 111 E1
Hill Rd. Hemp 28 B4
Hill Rd. The B 128 C1
Hill Rise. Upm 166 A1
Hill St. Saff W 13 E1
Hill Terr. Corr 180 B2
Hill The. Grave 192 B1
Hill The. Harl 90 B2
Hill Top. Lou 141 D3
Hill Top Cl. Lou 141 D3
Hill Top La. Saff W 25 F4
Hill Top View. Lou 152 C2
Hill Way The. Mtssg 147 F4
Hill's Chace. Brent 158 B3
Hillary Cl. Sprin 111 E2
Hillary Mount. Bill 149 D1
Hillcrest Ave. Basil 169 F2
Hillcrest Ave. W Thu 191 D4
Hillcrest Cl. Horn H 178 C2
Hillcrest Dr. Swan 191 D1
Hillcrest Rd. Horn H 178 C2
Hillcrest Rd. Hornc 165 D2
Hillcrest Rd. Lou 140 B2
Hillcrest Rd. Woodf 152 A1
Hillcrest View. Basil 171 E2
Hillcrest Way. Epp 129 D4
Hillcroft. Lou 141 D4
Hilldene Ave. Romf 156 B3
Hilldene Cl. Romf 156 B3
Hillfoot Ave. Romf 155 E1
Hillfoot Rd. Romf 155 E1
Hillhouse. Wa Aby 126 C3
Hillhouse Cl. Bill 149 D2
Hillhouse Dr. Bill 149 D2
Hillington Gdns. Woodf 152 B1
Hillman Cl. Hornc 165 E4
Hillrise Rd. Romf 155 E2
Hills Cl. Brain 65 F2
Hills Rd. Lou 140 A1
Hillside. Grays 185 E1
Hillside. Harl 103 D4
Hillside Ave. Bis St 68 A4
Hillside Ave. Woodf 152 B3
Hillside Cl. Bill 149 D1
Hillside Cl. Woodf 152 B3
Hillside Cres. Sta Ab 87 D2
Hillside Gdns. Brain 65 F1
Hillside Gr. Chelm 124 A4
Hillside La. Sta Ab 87 D2
Hillside Mews. Chelm 124 A4
Hillside Rd. Bill 149 D1
Hillside Rd. Lit Dun 73 F3
Hillside Wlk. Brent 157 F4
Hilltop Rd. Basil 170 C4
Hilltop Rd. W Thu 191 D4
Hillview Ave. Hornc 165 E3
Hillview Gdns. Corr 179 F3
Hillway. Bill 149 E1

Hillwood Cl. Brent 147 D1
Hillwood Gr. Brent 147 D1
Hillwood Gr. Wick 163 F4
Hilly Field. Harl 102 C2
Hilly Rd. Basil 170 B4
Hillyfields. Lou 141 D4
Hind Cl. Chig 153 F3
Hipkins. Bis St 67 F3
Hishbridge St. Wa Aby 126 C4
Hitch Common Rd. New 36 C4
Hitchin Cl. Romf 156 B3
Hitherwood Cl. Hornc 174 B4
Hive La. Grave 192 A1
Hive The. Grave 192 A1
Hobart Cl. Chelm 110 C3
Hobart Rd. Tilb 193 D3
Hobart Rd. Woodf 153 E1
Hobbs Cross Rd. Harl 90 C2
Hobbs Cross Rd. The B 129 E2
Hobhouse Rd. Corr 179 E2
Hoblongs Ind Est. Gt Dun ... 72 C3
Hobtoe Rd. Harl 89 D1
Hockerill St. Bis St 68 A4
Hockley Cl. Basil 171 E3
Hockley Dr. Romf 156 A1
Hockley Green. Basil 171 F3
Hockley Rd. Basil 171 E3
Hoddesdon Rd. Sta Ab 87 E2
Hodings Rd. Harl 89 E1
Hoe La. Abr 142 B2
Hoe La. Gt Wal 97 F3
Hoe La. Lo Naz 101 D1
Hoe St. Rox 109 E2
Hoe The. Bill 161 D2
Hoecroft. Lo Naz 100 C1
Hoestock Rd. Saw 77 E1
Hog Hill Rd. Romf 155 D2
Hog's La. Chris 10 B2
Hogarth Ave. Brent 158 C4
Hogarth Reach. Lou 140 C2
Hogarths Rd. Grays 185 D3
Hogg La. Grays 185 D1
Holbech Rd. Basil 171 F4
Holbrook Cl. Bill 149 E1
Holbrook Rd. Hav 6 C3
Holdbrook Way. Romf 156 C1
Holden Gdns. Basil 162 C1
Holden Gdns. Brent 158 B3
Holden Rd. Basil 162 C1
Holden Way. Upm 166 B2
Holecroft. Wa Aby 126 C3
Holford Rd. Grays 186 C2
Holgate. Basil 172 B4
Holgate Rd. Dag 173 D4
Holiday Hill. W Han 137 F2
Hollands Rd. Hav 7 D3
Hollands Wlk. Basil 171 E1
Holley Gdns. Bill 149 D2
Hollidge Way. Dag 173 D3
Hollies The. Sta L H 179 E1
Hollis Lock. Sprin 112 A2
Hollis Pl. Grays 185 D1
Hollow Cotts. Pur 183 D1
Hollow La. Broom 110 C4
Hollow Rd. Ashe 9 F2
Hollow Rd. Chris 10 B1
Hollow Rd. Elm 11 E2
Hollow Rd. Felst 75 D2
Hollow Rd. Widd 37 D2
Holloway Cres. Lea Rod 94 B4
Hollowfield Ave. Grays 185 E1
Holly Cl. Lou 152 B4
Holly Cl. Bill 149 D1
Holly Dr. Ching 139 D1
Holly Field. Harl 102 B3
Holly Gr. Basil 169 F3
Holly Way. Chelm 124 B4
Hollybank. Basil 169 F2
Hollycross Rd. Ware 87 D4
Hollyford. Bill 149 E3
Hollyhock Rd. Saff W 13 F1
Hollymead. Corr 179 F2
Hollywood Cl. Gt Bad 124 C3
Holme Rd. Hornc 166 A2
Holmes Cl. Horn H 178 C2
Holmes Meadow. Harl 102 A1
Holmwood Ave. Brent 147 D2
Holst Ave. Basil 170 B4
Holst Cl. Corr 179 E2
Holt Cl. Chig 153 F3
Holt The. Chig 153 E2
Holt Way. Chig 153 F3
Holyfield Rd. Wa Aby 113 E2
Holyrood Gdns. Grays 186 B1
Home Cl. Harl 102 C4
Home Cl. Ste B 18 B4
Home Farm Rd. Brent 155 E1
Home Gdns. Dag 164 B1
Home Mead. Basil 170 A4
Home Mead. Chelm 124 B1
Home Mead. Writ 110 A1
Home Meadows. Bill 149 D1
Homebridge. Gt Sam 29 D2
Homecroft Gdns. Lou 141 D3
Homefield. Wa Aby 127 D4
Homefield Cl. Bill 161 E3
Homefield Cl. Chelm 110 B3
Homefield Cl. Epp 116 A1
Homefield Rd. Hav 6 C3

Homelands Gr. S Han 150 B2
Homelye Chase. Gt Dun 62 A1
Homestead. Sprin 111 D4
Homestead Dr. Basil 170 B1
Homestead Rd. Basil 172 C4
Homestead Rd. Wick 162 B4
Homeway. Romf 157 D2
Honey Bourne. Bis St 67 F3
Honey Brook. Wa Aby 126 C3
Honey Cl. Bla 133 E2
Honey Cl. Gt Bad 124 B3
Honey La. Clav 34 C2
Honey La. Wa Aby 126 C3
Honeycroft. Lou 141 D3
Honeyhill. Harl 102 C2
Honeymeade. Saw 90 B4
Honeypot La. Basil 171 D4
Honeypot La. Brent 158 A4
Honeypot La. Stock 136 B1
Honeysuckle Cl. Brent 146 A2
Honeysuckle Cl. Romf 156 B2
Honiley Ave. Wick 163 E2
Honiton Rd. Romf 164 B3
Honywood Rd. Basil 162 C1
Hoo The. Harl 90 B3
Hood Gdns. Brain 66 B2
Hood Rd. Rain 173 F2
Hood Wlk. Romf 155 D1
Hook End La. Dodd 133 E3
Hook End Rd. Dodd 133 E2
Hook Field. Harl 102 C3
Hook La. Sta Abb 143 D2
Hooks Hall Dr. Dag 164 B1
Hookstone Way. Woodf 152 B2
Hoover Dr. Basil 169 F3
Hope Ave. Corr 179 F3
Hope Cl. Mtssg 147 F4
Hope Cl. Woodf 152 B2
Hope Rd. Bill 162 B3
Hope Rd. Swan 191 F1
Hopgrounds The. Finch 42 B3
Hopkins Cl. Romf 165 E4
Hopkins Mead. Sprin 112 A1
Hoppit Mead. Brain 65 F1
Hoppit Rd. Wa Aby 126 A3
Hoppits The. H Lav 105 E2
Horace Ave. Romf 164 B2
Horace Rd. Bill 149 E2
Horkesley Way. Wick 163 F3
Horksley Gdns. Brent 147 E2
Horn La. Woodf 152 A2
Horn Yd. Grave 193 D1
Hornbeam Ave. Upm 175 D4
Hornbeam Cl. Brent 159 D4
Hornbeam Cl. Chelm 124 A3
Hornbeam Cl. Lou 152 B4
Hornbeam Cl. The B 128 C1
Hornbeam La. Wa Aby 139 F2
Hornbeam Rd. Lou 152 B4
Hornbeam Rd. The B 128 B1
Hornbeam Way. Bill 161 E1
Hornbeams The. Harl 89 E1
Hornchurch Rd. Hornc 165 D2
Horndon Cl. Romf 155 E1
Horndon Green. Romf 155 E1
Horndon Rd. Horn H 179 F2
Horndon Rd. Romf 155 E1
Hornford Way. Romf 164 C2
Hornminster Glen. Hornc .. 166 A1
Hornsby La. Grays 186 A3
Hornsby Sq. Basil 169 F4
Hornsby Way. Basil 169 F4
Hornsea Villas. Steb 62 A3
Horse and Groom La. Chelm 124 A2
Horsecroft Pl. Harl 101 F4
Horsecroft Rd. Harl 101 F4
Horseman Ct. Kelv H 132 C1
Horseman Side. Nave H 144 B2
Horses La. Kelv H 145 E3
Horseshoe Cl. Bill 149 D3
Horseshoe Cl. Wa Aby 127 D3
Horseshoe Hill. Wa Aby 127 E4
Horseshoe La. Hav 6 C4
Horsley Cross. Basil 171 D4
Hospital App. Broom 98 A2
Houblon Dr. Chelm 124 B1
Houblons Hill. Epp 116 B1
Houchin Dr. Fyf 106 B1
Hovefields Ave. Wick 163 E2
Hovefields Dr. Wick 163 E2
Howard Chase. Basil 171 D4
Howard Cl. Brain 66 B2
Howard Cl. Wa Aby 126 B3
Howard Cres. Basil 172 B3
Howard Dr. Sprin 112 A1
Howard Lodge Rd. Nave H . 132 B1
Howard Rd. Saff W 13 F1
Howard Rd. Stone 190 A1
Howard Rd. Upm 166 B1
Howard Way. Harl 89 F1
Howards Cl. Bore 112 C4
Howe Cl. Romf 155 D1
Howe La. Gt Sam 29 D3
Howell Rd. Corr 179 F3
Howfield Green. Hod 87 D1
Hows Mead. N W Bas 117 E4
Hoylake Gdns. Romf 157 D2
Hubbard Chase. Hornc 166 A3
Hubbards Cl. Hornc 166 A3

Hubert Rd. Brent .... 158 A
Hubert Rd. Rain .... 173 F
Hucknall Cl. Romf .... 156 C
Hudson Cl. Hav .... 7 E
Hudson's Hill. Weth .... 43 E
Hudsons Cl. Corr .... 179 E
Hughes Rd. Grays .... 186 A
Hugo Gdns. Rain .... 174 A
Hull Gr. Harl .... 102 A
Hull Green. Match .... 92 B
Hull's La. Sand .... 125 F
Hullett's La. Dodd .... 145 F
Hulse Ave. Romf .... 155 D
Hulton Cl. Bore .... 112 C
Humber Ave. S Ock .... 183 F
Humber Dr. Upm .... 166 B
Humber Rd. Sprin .... 111 E
Hume Ave. Tilb .... 193 D
Humphrey Cl. Woodf .... 152 C
Humphrey's Farm La. Gt Wal . 97 E
Hungerdown. Ching .... 139 E
Hunnable Rd. Brain .... 65 F
Hunsdon Rd. Sta Ab .... 88 A
Hunt's Cl. Writ .... 123 D
Hunt's Dr. Writ .... 123 D
Hunter Ave. Brent .... 147 D
Hunter Dr. Hornc .... 174 B
Hunter Rd. Brain .... 66 B
Hunter Sq. Dag .... 173 D
Hunter's Gr. Romf .... 155 D
Hunters Ave. Bill .... 161 D
Hunters Chase. Brent .... 148 B
Hunters Hall Rd. Dag .... 173 C
Hunters Way. Saff W .... 25 E
Hunters Way. Sprin .... 111 F
Huntings Rd. Dag .... 173 D
Huntland Cl. Rain .... 182 A
Huntley Ave. Grave .... 192 B
Hunts La. Hinx .... 1 A
Hunts Mead. Bill .... 149 D
Huntsman Rd. Chig .... 154 A
Huntsmans Dr. Upm .... 175 E
Hurlock Rd. Bill .... 149 D
Hurrell Down. Bore .... 99 F
Hurrells La. Lit Bad .... 112 C
Hurricane Way. N W Bas ... 117 D
Hursley Rd. Chig .... 153 F
Hurst Park Ave. Hornc ...... 174 C
Hurst Rd. Lou .... 140 C
Hurst Way. Sprin .... 111 F
Hurstlands Cl. Hornc .... 165 E
Hurstleigh Gdns. Woodf ... 153 D
Hurstwood Ave. Brent ...... 146 A
Hutchins Cl. Hornc .... 165 F
Hutton Cl. Woodf .... 152 A
Hutton Dr. Brent .... 147 E
Hutton Gate. Brent .... 147 D
Hutton Rd. Brent .... 147 E
Hutton Village. Brent .... 147 F
Hyacinth Ct. Sprin .... 111 F
Hycliffe Gdns. Chig .... 153 E
Hyde Mead. Lo Naz .... 113 F
Hyde The. Basil .... 170 B
Hyde Way. Wick .... 163 E
Hyder Rd. Grays .... 186 B
Hyland Cl. Hornc .... 165 D
Hyland Way. Hornc .... 165 D
Hylands Cl. Barn .... 73 D
Hyll Cl. Gt C .... 1 B
Hythe Cl. Brain .... 65 F

Ian Rd. Bill .... 148 C
Ibbetson Path. Lou .... 141 D
Ibscott Cl. Dag .... 173 E
Ickleton Rd. Elm .... 11 D
Ickleton Rd. Gt C .... 1 B
Ickleton Rd. Hinx .... 1 A
Icknield Cl. Hinx .... 1 A
Ilford Trad Est. Basil .... 162 C
Ilfracombe Ave. Basil .... 172 B
Ilfracombe Cres. Hornc .... 174 B
Ilgars Rd. Runw .... 151 F
Ilmington Dr. Basil .... 169 F
Imperial Bsns Est. Grave ... 192 C
Ingatestone By-Ps. Ing ..... 135 D
Ingatestone Rd. Bla .... 133 F
Ingatestone Rd. Ing .... 121 F
Ingatestone Rd. Stock ...... 136 A
Ingatestone Rd. Woodf ..... 152 A
Ingaway. Basil .... 170 C
Ingels Mead. Epp .... 115 D
Ingham Rd. Hav .... 7 D
Ingleby Gdns. Chig .... 154 A
Ingleby Rd. Dag .... 173 D
Ingleby Rd. Grays .... 186 A
Inglefield Rd. Corr .... 180 A
Ingleglen. Hornc .... 174 B
Ingleside Ct. Saff W .... 13 E
Inglewood Cl. Chig .... 153 F
Inglewood Rd. Hornc .... 174 B
Ingram Rd. Grays .... 185 E
Ingrave Cl. Wick .... 163 F
Ingrave Rd. Brent .... 158 C
Ingrave Rd. Romf .... 164 B
Ingrebourne Gdns. Upm ... 166 B
Ingrebourne Rd. Rain .... 174 A
Ingress Gdns. Swan .... 191 E
Ingreway. Romf .... 157 D
Inkerpole Pl. Sprin .... 111 F

mans Row. Woodf 152 A3
skip Dr. Hornc 165 F2
stitute Rd. Epp 116 B1
verness Dr. Chig 153 F2
ricta Rd. Stone 190 A1
ton Pl. Grays 185 D1
s Cl. Brent 146 A2
s Cl. Sprin 111 F3
s Path. Romf 156 B2
ens Way. Romf 155 E2
ine Gdns. S Ock 183 F4
y Way. Bill 149 D1
ing Cl. Bis St 67 E2
on Hill Rd. Wick 163 E4
ell Gdns. Romf 155 F2
s Dr. Upm 166 C3
er Rd. Brent 146 A2
es Gdns. Romf 164 C4
y Barn La. Marg 122 B1
y Bower Cl. Swan 191 D1
y Chimneys Rd. Epp 128 C4
y Lodge La. Romf 157 D1
y Terr. Hod 100 B4
y Todd Hill. Deb 38 A4
ybridge. Hod 100 A2
worth Rd. Hav 6 C3

acaranda Cl. Sprin 111 F3
ack Evans Ct. S Ock 184 A4
ack Stevens Cl. Harl 103 E3
ck's La. Take 70 B4
acklin Green. Woodf 152 A3
acks Cl. Wick 163 F4
ackson Pl. Gt Bad 124 B3
ackson Sq. Bis St 67 F4
ackson's Cl. La. Gt C 1 B2
ackson's Sq. Gt C 1 B2
acksons Cl. Ch Ong 119 D1
acksons La. Bill 149 E1
acksons Mews. Bill 149 E1
acobs Ave. Romf 156 C1
acqueline Gdns. Bill 149 D3
ames Ave. Dag 164 A2
ames Cl. Romf 165 D3
ames Sq. Bill 149 F1
ames St. Epp 116 C3
anmead. Brent 147 D1
anus Cl. Hav 7 E3
ardine Rd. Basil 172 B4
arvis Way. Romf 156 C1
asmine Cl. Sprin 111 F4
ason Cl. Brent 157 F4
ason Cl. Grays 186 C4
ay Cl. Hav 7 E4
aywick Rd. Hav 7 D4
effcut Rd. Sprin 111 F1
efferies Way. Corr 179 F2
efferson Ave. Basil 170 A3
ekylls La. Finch 30 B2
ellicoe Way. Brain 66 B2
enkins Dr. Els 48 B2
enkins La. Bis St 68 B3
enner Cl. Brain 65 F1
enner Mead. Sprin 112 A2
enningham Dr. Grays 185 D3
enny Path. Romf 156 B2
ericho Pl. Bla 133 F4
ermayns. Basil 170 C3
erningham Ave. Woodf 153 D1
erounds. Harl 102 A3
ersey Cl. Hod 100 A4
ersey Gdns. Runw 163 E4
ersey Rd. Brain 174 A3
ersey Way. Brain 65 E1
ervis Rd. Bis St 67 F3
esmond Rd. Grays 185 E3
essel Dr. Lou 141 E4
etty Wlk. Grays 192 A4
ocelyns. Harl 90 B2
odrell Way. W Thu 183 F1
ohn Clay Gdns. Grays 185 D3
ohn Ct. Hod 87 D1
ohn English Ave. Brain 65 F2
ohn Henry Keene Meml Hms.
    Chelm.......................111 D2
ohn Parker Cl. Dag 173 D3
ohn Ray St. Brain 66 A2
ohn St. Grays 192 B4
ohn Tibauld Ct. Ste B 18 A3
ohns Rd. Bis St 57 D1
ohns The. Ch Ong 119 D2
ohnson Rd. Gt Bad 125 D3
ohnsons Way. Swan 191 E1
ohnston Rd. Woodf 152 A3
ollyboys La S. Felst 74 B2
ordans Cl. Dag 173 D4
ordans Way. Rain 174 B2
oslin Rd. W Thu 183 E1
osselin Ct. Basil 163 E1
osselin Rd. Basil 163 E1
oyce Ct. Wa Aby 126 B3
oyners Field. Harl 102 B2
ubilee Ave. Broom 98 A1
ubilee Ave. Romf 164 B3
ubilee Cl. Romf 164 A3
ubilee Cl. Swan 191 E1

Jubilee Ct. Gt Dun 61 E1
Jubilee Ct. Wa Aby 126 C3
Jubilee Dr. Runw 163 E4
Jubilee Rd. Bill 162 B2
Jubilee Rd. W Thu 191 D4
Judith Ave. Romf 155 D2
Julian Cl. Broom 98 A1
Julian Cl. Hav 7 E4
Julien Court Rd. Brain 66 A2
Juliet Way. Pur 182 C2
Junction Rd. Basil 172 A2
Junction Rd. Brent 158 B3
Junction Rd. Romf 164 C4
Juniper Cl. Bill 149 E2
Juniper Cl. Chelm 124 A3
Juniper Dr. Bore 112 C4
Juniper Way. Romf 156 C1
Jupiter Rd. Hav 7 E3
Jury St. Grave 193 D1
Justinian Cl. Hav 7 E3
Jutsums Ave. Romf 164 A3
Jutsums La. Romf 164 A3

Kandlewood. Brent 147 D1
Kangels The. Langl 22 B1
Karen Cl. Brent 146 B1
Karen Cl. Rain 173 F2
Karen Cl. Sta L H 179 E1
Karen Cl. Wick 163 E3
Kate's La. Ash 15 E4
Katherine Gdns. Woodf 153 E2
Katherine Rd. Basil 172 C4
Katherine's Way. Harl 102 A3
Kathleen Cl. Corr 179 F2
Kathleen Ferrier Cres. Basil .. 170 B4
Kavanaghs Rd. Brent 158 A4
Kavanaghs Terr. Brent 158 A4
Kay Cl. Gt Le 86 A4
Keary Rd. Swan 191 F1
Keats Ave. Brain 76 C4
Keats Ave. Romf 156 A2
Keats Cl. Chig 153 E2
Keats Gdns. Tilb 193 D3
Keats Way. Wick 163 E4
Keats Wlk. Brent 147 E1
Kecksy's. Saw 77 F2
Keefield. Harl 102 A2
Keene Way. Chelm 124 A2
Keighley Rd. Romf 156 C2
Keith Ave. Runw 151 E1
Keith Way. Hornc 165 F2
Kelburn Way. Rain 174 A1
Kelly Rd. Basil 172 C3
Kelsie Way. Chig 153 F2
Kelston Rd. Woodf 153 D1
Kelvedon Cl. Bill 149 E1
Kelvedon Cl. Brent 147 F2
Kelvedon Cl. Chelm 111 D3
Kelvedon Green. Kelv H ... 132 C1
Kelvedon Hall La. Kelv H .. 132 A2
Kelvedon Rd. Bill 149 E1
Kelvedon Way. Woodf 152 C2
Kelvedon Wlk. Rain 173 F2
Kelvin Rd. Tilb 193 D3
Kelvinside. Corr 179 F2
Kempe Rd. Finch 42 B3
Kempley Ct. Grays 192 B4
Kempton Ave. Hornc 165 F1
Kemsley Cl. Swan 191 D1
Kendal Ave. Epp 129 D4
Kendal Croft. Hornc 174 A4
Kendale. Grays 186 A2
Kenilworth Ave. Romf 157 D2
Kenilworth Cl. Bill 148 C1
Kenilworth Gdns. Hornc .. 165 E1
Kenilworth Gdns. Lou 140 C2
Kenilworth Pl. Bill 161 F1
Kenley Gdns. Hornc 165 F1
Kennedy Ave. Basil 169 F3
Kennel La. Bill 161 E4
Kennet Cl. Upm 166 C3
Kennet Green. S Ock 184 A3
Kennet Way. Chelm 110 B3
Kenneth Gdns. Corr 179 F3
Kenneth Rd. Basil 172 B4
Kenning Rd. Hod 100 A4
Kensington Dr. Woodf 152 B1
Kensington Gdns. Bill 149 D2
Kensington Rd. Brent 146 A2
Kensington Rd. Romf 164 B3
Kent Ave. Dag 173 D1
Kent Cl. Basil 170 A3
Kent Cres. Bis St 67 F2
Kent Dr. Hornc 174 B4
Kent Gdns. Brain 66 A2
Kent Kraft Ind Est. Grave .. 191 F1
Kent Rd. Dag 173 D4
Kent Rd. Grays 185 E1
Kent View. Ave 183 E2
Kent View Rd. Basil 171 F2
Kentings The. Brain 65 F1
Kenton Way. Basil 169 F3
Kents La. Mag Lav 104 B1
Kents Yd. Litt 12 C2
Kenway. Rain 174 B1
Kenway. Romf 155 E1
Kenway Cl. Rain 174 B1
Kenway Wlk. Rain 174 B1
Kenwood Rd. Corr 180 A3

Kenworthy Rd. Brain 65 F1
Kerby Rise. Sprin 111 F1
Kernow Cl. Hornc 165 F1
Kerril Croft. Harl 89 D1
Kerry Ave. Pur 182 C2
Kerry Cl. Upm 166 C2
Kerry Dr. Upm 166 C2
Kerry Rd. Grays 185 E3
Kersbrooke Way. Corr 180 A3
Kersey Gdns. Romf 156 C2
Kershaw Rd. Dag 164 A1
Kesteven Cl. Chig 153 F2
Kestrel Cl. Chig 154 B3
Kestrel Cl. Rain 174 A3
Kestrel Rd. Wa Aby 127 D3
Kestrel Wlk. Chelm 124 A2
Keswick Ave. Hornc 165 E2
Ketleys. Chelm 124 B2
Ketleys View. Pan 65 D4
Kettering Rd. Romf 156 C2
Kettlebury Way. Ch Ong ... 118 C1
Kevin Cl. Bill 161 E4
Keyes Rd. Stone 190 A2
Keyes Way. Brain 66 B2
Keys The. Brent 158 B2
Keysers Rd. Lo Naz 100 A1
Kibcaps. Basil 170 C2
Kidder Rd. Ray 64 C1
Kielder Cl. Chig 153 F2
Kilbarry Wlk. Bill 149 E3
Kilmartin Way. Hornc 174 A4
Kilmington Cl. Brent 159 D4
Kiln Field. Bla 133 E2
Kiln La. Harl 103 E4
Kiln Rd. N W Bas 117 D2
Kiln Shaw. Basil 170 B2
Kiln Way. Grays 184 C1
Kilnfield. Ch Ong 118 C1
Kilworth Ave. Brent 147 D2
Kimberley Ave. Romf 164 B3
Kimberley Cl. Bis St 68 A3
Kimberley Rd. Ching 139 F1
Kimberley Way. Ching 139 F1
Kimberly Dr. Bill 161 F1
Kimpton Ave. Brent 146 B1
Kimpton's Cl. Ch Ong 118 C3
Kinfauns Ave. Hornc 165 E3
King Alfred Rd. Romf 156 C1
King Edward Dr. Grays 185 F2
King Edward Rd. Basil 170 A4
King Edward Rd. Brent 158 B4
King Edward Rd. Romf 164 C3
King Edward Rd. Stone 191 D1
King Edward's Rd. Sta L H .. 187 E4
King George Cl. Romf 164 B4
King George Rd. Wa Aby .. 126 B3
King George VI Ave. Grays .. 187 D1
King George's Rd. Brent ... 146 A2
King Henry's Mews. Enf ... 126 A1
King St. Bis St 67 F4
King St. Grave 193 D1
King St. H Ong 120 A2
King St. Saff W 13 E1
King St. Sta L H 179 E1
King Street Mews. Bis St ... 67 F4
King's Ave. Lou 152 B4
King's Ave. Woodf 152 B3
King's Chase. Brent 158 B4
King's Green. Lou 140 C3
King's Hill. Lou 140 C4
King's La. Elm 11 D2
King's Rd. Brain 65 F3
King's Rd. Ching 139 E1
King's Rd. Romf 165 D3
Kingaby Gdns. Rain 174 A3
Kingfisher Cl. Brent 147 D1
Kingfisher Cl. Hav 7 E4
Kingfisher Cl. Sta Ab 87 E2
Kingfisher Rd. Upm 166 C2
Kingfisher Way. Bis St 68 A4
Kingfishers. Basil 171 E2
Kingfishers. Ing 135 E2
Kingley Cl. Wick 163 D4
Kingley Dr. Wick 163 D4
Kings Cres. Bill 161 D1
Kings Ct. Bis St 68 A4
Kings Ct. Lou 152 B4
Kings Gdns. Upm 166 C2
Kings Gr. Romf 155 D3
Kings Head Hill. Ching 139 D1
Kings La. Stis 66 C2
Kings Lynn Dr. Romf 156 B2
Kings Mews. Chig 153 E4
Kings Pl. Lou 152 B4
Kings Rd. Bill 161 D1
Kings Rd. Brent 158 B4
Kings Rd. Chelm 110 C2
Kings Way. Bill 161 E3
Kings Wlk. Grays 192 A4
Kingsbridge Cir. Romf 156 C2
Kingsbridge Cl. Brain 65 F4
Kingsbridge Cl. Romf 156 C2
Kingsbridge Rd. Bis St 68 A4
Kingsbridge Rd. Romf 156 C2
Kingsdon La. Harl 103 E4
Kingsdown Cl. Basil 172 B3
Kingsfield. Hod 100 A4
Kingshill Ave. Romf 155 E3

Kingsland. Harl 102 B3
Kingsley Ave. Stone 190 A1
Kingsley Cl. Dag 173 D4
Kingsley Gdns. Hornc 165 E4
Kingsley Rd. Brent 147 E1
Kingsley Rd. Lou 141 E3
Kingsley Rd. Woodf 153 E1
Kingsley Wlk. Grays 186 A1
Kingsman Dr. Corr 185 D3
Kingsman Rd. Sta L H 179 D1
Kingsmead. Saw 77 F1
Kingsmead Ave. Romf 164 C3
Kingsmead Cl. Roy 101 D4
Kingsmead Hill. Roy 101 D4
Kingsmead Rd. Bis St 68 A4
Kingsmoor Rd. Harl 102 A3
Kingston Ave. Sprin 111 F2
Kingston Cres. Sprin 111 F2
Kingston Ct. Grave 192 A1
Kingston Hill Ave. Romf ... 154 C1
Kingston Rd. Romf 164 C4
Kingsway. Woodf 152 B3
Kingswood Cl. Bill 149 E1
Kingswood Cl. Basil 171 F3
Kingswood Rd. Basil 171 E3
Kinnaird Way. Woodf 152 C2
Kipling Ave. Tilb 193 E3
Kipling Cl. Chelm 111 D3
Kipling Rd. Stone 190 A1
Kirby Cl. Chig 153 F2
Kirby Cl. Lou 140 C1
Kirby Cl. Romf 157 D3
Kirby Rd. Basil 171 F3
Kirk Pl. Sprin 111 F2
Kirkham Ave. Horn N 178 C4
Kirkham Rd. Horn H 178 C4
Kirkham Shaw. Horn H 178 C4
Kirkland Ave. Woodf 153 D1
Kirklees. Chelm 111 D2
Kirkmans Rd. Chelm 124 B2
Kirton Cl. Hornc 174 B3
Kitchener Rd. Dag 173 D3
Kitson Way. Harl 89 E1
Knapton Cl. Sprin 111 E4
Knares The. Basil 170 C2
Knebworth Ct. Bis St 67 E3
Knight St. Saw 77 F1
Knight's Way. Brent 159 D4
Knightbridge Wlk. Bill 149 D2
Knighton Cl. Romf 164 B3
Knighton Cl. Woodf 152 A3
Knighton Dr. Woodf 152 A3
Knighton La. Lou 152 A4
Knighton Rd. Romf 164 B3
Knights. Basil 170 B4
Knights Manor Way. Stone .. 190 A1
Knights Rd. Brain 66 B1
Knights Way. Gt Dun 61 E1
Knights Way. Woodf 153 E2
Knights Wlk. Abr 142 A3
Knightsbridge Gdns. Romf .. 164 B3
Knockhall Chase. Swan 191 E1
Knockhall Rd. Swan 191 E1
Knole La. Elm 23 D4
Knoll The. Bill 149 D2
Knowle The. Basil 171 E2
Knowle The. Hod 100 A3
Kyme Rd. Hornc 164 C3
Kynance Cl. Romf 156 B4
Kynaston Rd. Pan 65 D4

La Plata Gr. Brent 158 A4
Laburnam Cl. Upm 167 D2
Laburnam Wlk. Hornc 174 B4
Laburnham Gdns. Upm 166 C2
Laburnum Ave. Hornc 165 D1
Laburnum Ave. Wick 163 E4
Laburnum Dr. Chelm 124 B3
Laburnum Dr. Corr 180 A2
Laburnum Rd. Epp 116 B1
Laburnum Rd. Hod 100 A4
Lady La. Chelm 124 B4
Ladyfields. Lou 141 E3
Ladyfields Cl. Lou 141 E3
Ladygate Centre. Wick 163 E4
Ladys Hill. Nave H 131 F1
Ladyshot. Harl 90 A1
Ladywell Prospect. Saw 78 A1
Lagonda Ave. Chig 153 F2
Laindon Common Rd. Bill .. 161 D3
Laindon Link. Basil 170 B3
Laing Cl. Chig 153 E2
Laird Ave. Grays 185 E2
Lake Ave. Bill 149 D2
Lake Ave. Rain 174 B2
Lake Gdns. Dag 173 D4
Lake Rd. Dag 173 D1
Lake Rd. Lo Naz 100 C1
Lake Rise. Romf 164 C4
Lake Rise. W Thu 184 A1
Lake View. Basil 169 F2
Lakefields Cl. Rain 174 B2
Lakeland Cl. Chig 154 A3
Lakeside. Bill 149 D2
Lakeside. Rain 174 C3
Lakeside Cres. Brent 158 B4
Lakin Cl. Sprin 112 A2
Lamb Cl. Tilb 193 E3

Lamb's La. Rain 174 B1
Lambert Cross. Saff W 25 E3
Lambourne. Grays 187 E1
Lambourne Cres. Basil 171 F3
Lambourne Cres. Chig 154 A4
Lambourne Dr. Brent 147 F2
Lambourne Gdns. Hornc .. 165 E1
Lambourne Rd. Chig 154 A4
Lambs Meadow. Woodf 152 B1
Lamerton Rd. Woodf 153 D1
Lamlighters Cl. Wa Aby ... 127 D3
Lampits. Hod 100 A3
Lampits Hill. Corr 180 A3
Lampits Hill Ave. Corr 180 A3
Lampits La. Corr 180 A3
Lamson Rd. Rain 173 F1
Lancaster Cl. Brent 146 A2
Lancaster Dr. Hornc 174 B4
Lancaster Rd. N W Bas 117 D3
Lancaster Way. Bis St 67 E4
Lancaster Way. Brain 65 F2
Lancelot Rd. Chig 153 F2
Lancer Way. Bill 148 C2
Lancing Rd. Romf 156 C2
Lander Rd. Grays 185 E1
Landermere. Basil 171 D4
Landscape Rd. Woodf 152 A2
Landscape Way. Saff W 25 E3
Landseer Rd. Hornc 165 D2
Landview Gdns. Ch Ong ... 118 C1
Lane Ave. Swan 191 E1
Langdale. Bl Not 76 B4
Langdale Gdns. Chelm 124 B4
Langdale Gdns. Hornc 174 A4
Langdon Way. Corr 180 A3
Langemore Way. Bill 149 D1
Langenhoe. Wick 163 F3
Langfield Cl. Lo Naz 100 C1
Langford Gr. Basil 172 B4
Langford Green. Brent 147 E2
Langford Rd. Woodf 152 B2
Langfords. Lou 152 B4
Langham Cres. Bill 161 D4
Langham Ct. Hornc 165 E2
Langhorne Rd. Dag 173 D3
Langland Cl. Corr 180 A2
Langley Ave. Finch 43 E4
Langley Cl. Romf 156 B2
Langley Dr. Brent 158 A4
Langley Meadow. Lou 141 E4
Langleys. Basil 171 D2
Langston Rd. Lou 141 E2
Langthorne Cres. Grays ... 185 E1
Langton Ave. Chelm 110 C3
Langton Way. Grays 186 B1
Lanhams. Basil 172 B4
Lansbury Cres. Stone 190 A1
Lansbury Gdns. Tilb 193 D3
Lansdowne Rd. Tilb 192 C3
Lansdowne Rd. Woodf 152 A1
Lansdowne Sq. Grave 192 C1
Lapwing Rd. Runw 151 E1
Larch Cl. Bill 161 E1
Larch Gr. Chelm 124 B3
Larches The. Bore 112 C4
Larchwood. Bis St 67 E3
Larchwood Ave. Romf 155 D2
Larchwood Cl. Romf 155 E2
Larchwood Gdns. Brent 146 A2
Lark's La. Gt Wal 97 F3
Larkfield. Corr 180 A3
Larkin Cl. Brent 147 E1
Larkshall Rd. Ching 139 E1
Larkspur Cl. S Ock 176 B1
Larkswood. Harl 103 E3
Larkswood Rd. Corr 180 A2
Larkswood Wlk. Wick 163 E3
Larsen Dri. Wa Aby 126 B3
Lascelles Cl. Brent 146 A2
Latchett Rd. Woodf 152 A1
Latchetts Shaw. Basil 171 D2
Latchford Pl. Chig 154 A3
Latching Cl. Romf 156 B3
Latchingdon Gdns. Woodf .. 152 C2
Latchmore Bank. L Hal 68 A1
Lathcoates Cres. Gt Bad .. 124 C4
Latimer Dr. Bill 161 D1
Latimer Dr. Hornc 165 E1
Latton Green. Harl 102 C2
Launceston Cl. Romf 156 B1
Launder's La. Rain 174 C1
Laundry La. Lo Naz 113 F3
Laundry La. Mtssg 147 E4
Laurel Ave. Wick 163 E4
Laurel Cl. Brent 147 D2
Laurel Cl. Chig 153 E2
Laurel Cres. Romf 164 C2
Laurel Gdns. Ching 139 D1
Laurel Gr. Chelm 124 A4
Laurence Croft. Writ 110 A1
Laurie Wlk. Romf 164 C3
Lavender Ave. Brent 146 A2
Lavender Cl. Romf 156 B2
Lavender Ct. Sprin 111 F3
Lavender Way. Wick 163 E4
Lawford Cl. Hornc 174 B4
Lawford La. Writ 110 B1
Lawn La. Sprin 111 E3
Lawn Rd. Grave 192 B1

Lawn The. Harl

Lawn The. Harl 90 A2
Lawns Cres. Grays 192 B4
Lawns The. Sprin 111 E3
Lawns Way. Romf 155 E2
Lawrence Ave. Saw 77 F2
Lawrence Ave. Sta Ab 87 E2
Lawrence Cres. Dag 164 A1
Lawrence Gdns. Bla 133 F4
Lawrence Gdns. Tilb 193 D4
Lawrence Hill. Ching 139 D1
Lawrence Moorings. Saw ... 77 F1
Lawrence Rd. Basil 172 C4
Lawrence Rd. Romf 165 D3
Laws Cl. Saff W 25 E4
Lawton Dr. Lou 141 D3
Laxtons. Corr 179 E2
Layer Rd. Hav 6 C4
Lea Cl. Bis St 57 D1
Lea Cl. Brain 66 B1
Lea Gr. Bis St 57 D1
Lea Rd. Grays 186 A1
Lea Rd. Hod 100 B4
Lea Rd. Wa Aby 126 A3
Lea Valley Rd. Ching 139 D2
Leach Cl. Gt Bad 125 D4
Leaden Cl. Lea Rod 94 B4
Leafy Way. Brent 147 E1
Leamington Cl. Romf 157 D2
Leamington Rd. Romf 157 D3
Leapingwell Cl. Sprin 112 A2
Leas The. Ing 135 D1
Leas The. Upm 166 B2
Leasway. Brent 158 B4
Leasway. Grays 185 E3
Leasway. Upm 175 E4
Leasway. Wick 163 D3
Leat Cl. Saw 77 F2
Leathart Cl. Hornc 174 A3
Leather La. Brain 65 F2
Leather La. Hav 6 C4
Leather La. Hornc 165 E2
Leatherbottle Hill. Stock ... 137 D1
Leaview. Wa Aby 126 A3
Leaway. Bill 161 D4
Lechmere App. Woodf 152 B1
Lechmere Ave. Chig 153 E3
Lechmere Ave. Woodf 152 B1
Leconfield Wlk. Hornc 174 B3
Lee Chapel La. Basil 170 B2
Lee Cl. Sta Ab 87 E2
Lee Gardens Ave. Hornc ... 166 A2
Lee Gr. Chig 153 D4
Lee Rd. Basil 172 C3
Lee Wlk. Basil 170 C3
Lee Woottens La. Basil 171 D2
Leez La. Felst 74 C1
Legg St. Chelm 111 D2
Legions Way. Bis St 68 A4
Legon Ave. Romf 164 B2
Leicester Rd. Tilb 192 C3
Leigh Dr. Els 48 B1
Leigh Dr. Romf 156 B3
Leigh Fells. Basil 172 B3
Leighs Rd. Lit Wal 98 C4
Leighs Rifleman. Bill 148 C2
Leighton Gdns. Tilb 193 D4
Leinster Rd. Basil 170 B3
Leiston Rd. Hav 6 C4
Lenham Way. Basil 172 B3
Lenmore Ave. Grays 185 E2
Lennard Row. Ave 183 E3
Lennox Ave. Grave 193 D1
Lennox Cl. Romf 164 C3
Lennox Rd. Grave 192 C1
Lenthall Ave. Grays 185 D2
Lenthall Rd. Lou 141 E3
Leon Dr. Basil 171 E2
Leonard Ave. Romf 164 B2
Leonard Rd. Basil 171 D1
Leonard Way. Brent 157 F3
Lessington Ave. Romf 164 B3
Leston Cl. Rain 174 A1
Leveller Row. Bill 148 C2
Levens Way. Bl Not 76 B3
Lever Sq. Grays 186 A1
Leverton Way. Wa Aby 126 B3
Leveson Rd. Grays 186 A2
Levett Rd. Sta L H 179 F1
Lewes Rd. Romf 156 B3
Lewis Cl. Brent 146 C1
Lewis Dr. Chelm 124 A3
Lewis Rd. Hornc 165 E3
Lewis Rd. Swan 191 F1
Lexington Way. Upm 166 C3
Ley Field. Take 70 B4
Ley The. Brain 66 B1
Leybourne Dr. Sprin 111 F4
Leyburn Cres. Romf 156 C2
Leyburn Rd. Romf 156 C2
Leycroft Cl. Lou 141 D2
Leyfields. Ray 64 C1
Leyland Gdns. Woodf 152 B3
Leys Ave. Dag 173 E3
Leys Cl. Dag 173 E3
Leys The. Basil 171 E2
Leys The. Sprin 111 F3
Leyside. Ray 64 C1
Leysings. Basil 170 C2
Leywood Cl. Brain 66 B1

Liberty The. Romf 164 C3
Library Hill. Brent 158 B4
Lichfield Cl. Chelm 110 C2
Lichfield Terr. Upm 166 C1
Lichfields The. Basil 171 F4
Lilac Ave. Wick 163 E4
Lilac Cl. Brent 146 A2
Lilac Cl. Chelm 124 B3
Lilac Gdns. Romf 164 C2
Lilac Rd. Hod 100 A4
Lilford Rd. Bill 149 E2
Lilian Cres. Brent 159 E4
Lilian Gdns. Woodf 152 A1
Lilley Cl. Brent 157 F3
Lilliard Cl. Hod 87 D1
Lilliput Rd. Romf 164 B2
Lily Cl. Sprin 111 F3
Lilystone Cl. Stock 136 B1
Lime Ave. Brent 158 C4
Lime Ave. Upm 175 D4
Lime Cl. Lou 152 B4
Lime Cl. Romf 164 B4
Lime Cl. S Ock 176 B1
Lime Gr. Chig 153 F2
Lime Gr. Dodd 133 E1
Lime Meadow. Saff W 14 B1
Lime Pl. Bill 161 E1
Lime Wlk. Chelm 124 B3
Limefields.Saff W 13 F2
Limekiln La. Stan M 57 E3
Limerick Gdns. Upm 166 C2
Limes Ave. Chig 153 E2
Limes Cl. Bis St 68 A4
Limes The. Brent 158 C4
Limes The. Chelm 124 A1
Limes The. Ing 135 E2
Limes The. Pur 183 D1
Limeslade Cl. Corr 180 A2
Lincefield. Basil 170 A2
Lincoln Ave. Romf 164 C2
Lincoln Cl. Bis St 67 E3
Lincoln Cl. Hornc 166 A3
Lincoln Hill. Anst 33 D3
Lincoln Rd. Basil 171 F4
Lincoln Rd. Woodf 152 A1
Lincolns Fields. Epp 115 F1
Lincolns La. Brent 145 E2
Linda Gdns. Bill 148 C2
Linden Cl. Chelm 124 B4
Linden Cl. Pur 190 B4
Linden Cres. Woodf 152 A2
Linden Rise. Brent 158 B3
Linden St. Romf 164 B4
Lindens The. Basil 170 A3
Lindens The. Bis St 67 F3
Lindens The. Brain 66 A1
Lindens The. Lou 140 C2
Lindens The. Stock 136 C1
Lindfield Rd. Romf 156 C3
Lindford Dr. Basil 171 F3
Lindhurst Dr. S Han 150 B2
Lindon Rd. Runw 151 E2
Lindsell Green. Basil 171 F3
Lindsell La. Basil 171 F3
Lindsey Cl. Bis St 56 C1
Lindsey Cl. Brent 158 A3
Lindsey Rd. Bis St 56 C1
Lindsey St. Ep Gr 115 F2
Lindsey Way. Hornc 165 E3
Linford Cl. Harl 102 B3
Linford End. Harl 102 B3
Linford Rd. Grays 186 B1
Lingcroft. Basil 171 D2
Lingfield Ave. Upm 166 A1
Lingmere Cl. Chig 153 E4
Lingrove Gdns. Woodf 152 A4
Link Rd. Corr 179 E2
Link Rd. Dag 173 D2
Link Way. Bis St 67 F3
Link Way. Hornc 165 F2
Linkdale. Bill 161 D4
Links Ave. Romf 156 A1
Links Dr. Chelm 123 F4
Links Rd. Woodf 152 A3
Links The. Bill 148 C2
Linkside. Chig 153 E3
Linkside Rd. Bis St 68 B3
Linkway. Basil 171 D3
Linkway Rd. Brent 157 F4
Linley Cl. Grays 194 B4
Linley Cres. Romf 164 B4
Linnet Dr. Chelm 124 A3
Linnet Way. Pur 183 D1
Linnets. Basil 171 D2
Linnets La. Stur 8 A2
Linton Cl. Saff W 25 E4
Linton Ct. Romf 155 F1
Linton Rd. Had 3 D4
Linwood. Saw 77 F1
Lion Hill. Corr 180 B2
Lion La. Bill 149 D1
Lion Meadow. Ste B 18 A4
Lionfield Terr. Sprin 111 E2
Liphook Cl. Hornc 173 F4
Lippitts Hill. Basil 170 B2
Lippitts Hill. Wa Aby 139 F4
Lisa Cl. Bill 149 D3
Lisle Pl. Grays 185 D2

Lister Rd. Brain 76 C4
Lister Rd. Tilb 193 D3
Listowel Rd. Dag 164 A1
Littell Tweed. Sprin 112 A2
Little and Great Sir Hughes La.
  W Han............. 125 D1
Little Aston Rd. Romf 157 D2
Little Belhus Cl. S Ock ... 176 A1
Little Bentley. Basil 171 D4
Little Berry La. Basil 170 A2
Little Brays. Harl 103 D4
Little Cattins. Harl 101 F2
Little Charlton. Basil 172 B3
Little Chishill Rd. Lit Chis ... 21 E4
Little Chittock. Basil 171 F3
Little Dodden. Basil 170 C2
Little Dorrit. Chelm 110 C4
Little Dragons. Lou 140 B3
Little Garth. Basil 172 A3
Little Gaynes Gdns. Upm ... 175 D4
Little Gaynes La. Upm 175 D4
Little Gerpins La. Upm 174 C2
Little Gregories La. The B ... 128 B3
Little Grove Field. Harl ... 102 B4
Little Heath. L Hal 78 C2
Little Hyde La. Ing 135 D3
Little Larchmount. Saff W ... 25 E4
Little Laver Rd. Lit Lav ... 105 F3
Little Laver Rd. More 105 F3
Little London Hill. Finch ... 42 B4
Little Lullaway. Basil 170 C4
Little Meadow. Writ 110 A1
Little Nell. Chelm 110 C4
Little Norsey Rd. Bill 149 E2
Little Oaks. Basil 171 D3
Little Oxcroft. Basil 170 A3
Little Pluckett's Way. Lou ... 140 B1
Little Pynchons. Harl 102 C3
Little Russets. Brent 147 F1
Little Searles. Basil 172 A4
Little Spenders. Basil 171 E2
Little Sq. Brain 65 F2
Little Stile. Writ 123 D4
Little Walden Rd. Saff W ... 13 F3
Little Waltham Rd. Broom ... 98 B1
Little Warley Hall La. Brent ... 167 F3
Little Warley Hall La. Horn H ... 167 F3
Little Wlk. Harl 102 B4
Littlebrook Manor Way. Stone ... 190 A1
Littlebury Ct. Basil 172 A4
Littlebury Ct. Kelv H 132 C1
Littlebury Green. Basil ... 172 A4
Littlebury Green Rd. Litt ... 12 B2
Littlehurst La. Bill 161 F1
Littlethorpe. Basil 171 F2
Littleton Ave. Ching 139 F1
Livingstone Cl. Ch Ong ... 119 D1
Livingstone Terr. Rain 173 F2
Llewellyn Cl. Sprin 111 E2
Loates Pasture. Stan M 57 E4
Lobelia Cl. Brain 112 A3
Locarno Ave. Runw 151 F1
Locke Cl. Corr 179 E2
Locke Cl. Rain 173 F3
Lockwood Wlk. Romf 164 C3
Lockyer Rd. Pur 190 B4
Lodge Ave. Gt Bad 124 C4
Lodge Ave. Romf 165 D4
Lodge Cl. Chig 154 A4
Lodge Cres. Bore 112 C4
Lodge Ct. Hornc 165 F2
Lodge Hall. Harl 102 C2
Lodge La. Basil 185 D2
Lodge La. Hav B 155 D2
Lodge La. Romf 155 D2
Lodge La. Wa Aby 126 B2
Lodge Rd. Brain 65 F1
Lodge Rd. Wa Aby 128 A3
Lodge Rd. Writ 123 D4
Loewen Rd. Grays 186 A2
Loftin Way. Gt Bad 124 B4
Loman Path. S Ock 188 F4
Lombards Chase.. Horn H ... 168 B3
Lombards The. Hornc 165 F2
Lombardy Cl. Basil 172 B3
Lombardy Pl. Chelm 111 D2
London Hill. Chelm 123 F1
London Rd. Abr 142 A3
London Rd. Basil 171 E2
London Rd. Bill 148 C1
London Rd. Bill 163 D4
London Rd. Bis St 68 A3
London Rd. Bl Not 76 B3
London Rd. Brain 65 F1
London Rd. Brent 158 A4
London Rd. Chelm 123 F4
London Rd. Grave 192 C1
London Rd. Grays 191 F4
London Rd. Gt C 1 B1
London Rd. Gt Le 76 B3
London Rd. Harl 90 B1
London Rd. Litt 12 C1
London Rd. N W Bas 103 E1
London Rd. New 24 C2
London Rd. New 37 D3
London Rd. Pur 183 D1
London Rd. Romf 164 A3
London Rd. Saff W 25 E4
London Rd. Saw 77 F1

London Rd. Sta L H 179 D1
London Rd. Sta R 131 D1
London Rd. Sta T 130 C1
London Rd. Stone 190 C1
London Rd. Swan 191 E1
London Rd. Tilb 193 D3
London Rd. Wen A 24 C4
London Rd. Wick 163 D4
London Rd. Widd 37 D3
London Rd Purfleet. Pur ... 190 B4
London Rd W Thurrock. W Thu ... 191 D4
Londons Cl. Upm 175 E4
Long Acre. Harl 90 A2
Long Banks. Harl 102 B2
Long Border Rd. Take 58 C1
Long Brandocks. Writ 110 A1
Long Croft. Stan M 57 E4
Long Croft Dri. Ches 126 A3
Long Ct. Pur 183 D1
Long Deacon Rd. Ching ... 139 F1
Long Fields. Ch Ong 119 D1
Long Gages. Basil 171 D4
Long Green. Chig 153 F3
Long Green La. Ba Sai 53 E1
Long Horse Croft. Saff W ... 25 F4
Long La. Arkes 23 F3
Long La. Grays 185 E3
Long La. Ray 75 F4
Long Ley. Harl 102 C4
Long Ley. Langl 22 B1
Long Lynderswood. Basil ... 170 C3
Long Meadow. Bis St 67 E3
Long Meadow. Brent 159 E4
Long Meadow Dr. Wick 163 F4
Long Riding. Basil 171 E3
Long Ridings Ave. Brent ... 147 D2
Long St. Wa Aby 127 F4
Long Wlk. Wa Aby 126 A4
Long Wood. Harl 102 B2
Longacre. Basil 171 E4
Longacre. Chelm 123 E4
Longacres. Brain 66 A1
Longaford Way. Brent 147 E1
Longborough Cl. Basil 163 D1
Longcroft. Take 70 B4
Longcroft Rise. Lou 141 D2
Longcrofts. Wa Aby 126 C3
Longfellow Dr. Brent 147 E1
Longfield. Harl 103 D3
Longfield. Lou 140 B2
Longfield Ave. Hornc 164 C2
Longfield Rd. Gt Bad 124 C4
Longhedges. Saff W 13 F1
Longhouse Rd. Grays 186 A2
Longland Bridge. Sheer 91 E4
Longleaf Dr. Brain 76 C4
Longleat Cl. Chelm 110 C4
Longmead Ave. Gt Bad ... 124 C4
Longmead Cl. Brent 146 C1
Longmeads Cl. Writ 110 A1
Longmore Ave. Gt Bad ... 124 C4
Longport Cl. Chig 154 A2
Longrise. Bill 161 D4
Longshots Cl. Broom 98 A1
Longstomps Ave. Chelm ... 124 A4
Longtail. Harl 149 E3
Longtown Cl. Romf 156 B3
Longtown Rd. Romf 156 B3
Longview Way. Romf 155 E1
Longwick. Basil 170 B2
Longwood Cl. Upm 175 E4
Lonsdale Ave. Brent 147 E2
Lonsdale Ave. Romf 164 B3
Looe Gdns. Woodf 153 D1
Loompits Way. Saff W 25 E4
Loop Rd. Wa Aby 126 A4
Lord's Ave. Bis St 67 D4
Lord's Croft La. Hav 7 D4
Lordship Cl. Brent 147 E1
Lordship Rd. Writ 110 A1
Lordswood View. Lea Rod ... 94 B4
Lorne Rd. Brent 158 B3
Lorraine Cl. Bill 161 E3
Lorrimore Cl. Bill 148 C3
Loughton La. The B 128 B1
Loughton Way. Lou 140 C1
Louise Gdns. Rain 173 F1
Louvaine Ave. Wick 163 D4
Love La. Ave 183 E2
Love La. Ch Ong 119 D2
Love La. Lou 152 C2
Lovell Wlk. Rain 173 F1
Lover's La. Swan 191 E2
Loves Wlk. Gt Bad 124 C4
Loves Wlk. Writ 123 D4
Lovet Rd. Harl 102 A4
Lovibond Pl. Sprin 111 F2
Low Cl. Stone 190 D1
Low Hall Cl. Ching 139 D1
Low Hill Rd. Roy 101 D3
Low Street La. Grays 186 C1
Lowe Cl. Chig 154 A3
Lowe The. Chig 154 A3
Lowen Rd. Rain 173 E2
Lower Alderton Hall La. Lou ... 141 D2
Lower Anchor St. Chelm ... 111 D1
Lower Ave. Basil 172 C4
Lower Bedfords Rd. Romf ... 156 A2
Lower Broad St. Dag 173 D2

Magpie La. Brei

Lower Bury La. Epp ...... 128 ?
Lower Cloister. Bill ...... 149 ?
Lower Cres. Sta L H ...... 187 ?
Lower Downs Slade. Hav ... 7 ?
Lower Dunton Rd. Basil ... 169 ?
Lower Dunton Rd. Horn H ... 169 ?
Lower Green. Chelm ...... 124 ?
Lower Island Way. Wa Aby ... 126 ?
Lower Mardyke Ave. Rain ... 173 ?
Lower Meadow. Harl ..... 102 ?
Lower Mill Field. Gt Dun ... 72 ?
Lower Park Cres. Bi St ..... 67 ?
Lower Park Rd. Lou ...... 141 ?
Lower Park Rd. Wick ..... 163 ?
Lower Queen's Rd. Lou ... 152 ?
Lower Rd. Grave .... 191 ?
Lower Rd. L Hal .... 78 ?
Lower Rd. Lou .... 141 ?
Lower Rd. Mtssg .... 147 ?
Lower Rd. Sta Ab .... 87 ?
Lower Southend Rd. Wick ... 163 ?
Lower St. Bill .... 161 ?
Lower St. Stan M .... 57 ?
Lower Stock Rd. Stock .... 137 ?
Lower Stock Rd. W Han ... 137 ?
Lower Swaines. Epp ...... 115 ?
Lowfield. Saw .... 77 ?
Lowfield La. Hod .... 100 ?
Lowland Gdns. Romf ..... 164 ?
Lowlands Rd. Ave .... 183 ?
Lowshoe La. Romf .... 155 ?
Loxford. Basil .... 172 ?
Lucas Ave. Chelm .... 124 ?
Lucas Ct. Wa Aby .... 126 ?
Lucas Rd. Grays .... 185 ?
Lucerne Way. Romf ...... 156 ?
Luck's La. Gt Wal .... 84 ?
Lucksfield Way. Gt Bad ... 124 ?
Luckyn La. Basil .... 170 ?
Luctons Ave. Lou .... 140 ?
Ludham Hall La. Bl Not .... 76 ?
Ludlow Pl. Grays .... 185 ?
Lukin's Dr. Gt Dun .... 72 ?
Lulworth Cl. Sta L H ...... 187 ?
Lulworth Dr. Hav .... 6 ?
Lulworth Dr. Romf .... 155 ?
Luncies Rd. Basil .... 171 ?
Lundy Cl. Hav .... 7 ?
Lupin Dr. Sprin .... 111 ?
Lupin Mews. Sprin ...... 111 ?
Luppits Cl. Brent .... 147 ?
Lushes Rd. Lou .... 141 ?
Luther King Rd. Harl ..... 102 ?
Luthers Cl. Kelv H .... 132 ?
Luxborough La. Woodf .... 152 ?
Lynbrook Cl. Rain .... 173 ?
Lynceley Grange. Epp ..... 116 ?
Lynch The. Hod .... 100 ?
Lyndale. Kelv H .... 132 ?
Lyndhurst Dr. Hornc ..... 165 ?
Lyndhurst Rd. Corr ...... 179 ?
Lyndhurst Rise. Chig ..... 153 ?
Lyndhurst Way. Brent .... 147 ?
Lynfords Dr. Runw .... 151 ?
Lynge The. Basil .... 170 ?
Lynmouth Ave. Chelm .... 124 ?
Lynmouth Gdns. Chelm ... 111 ?
Lynross Cl. Romf .... 156 ?
Lynstede. Basil .... 172 ?
Lynton Ave. Romf .... 155 ?
Lynton Dr. Sprin .... 111 ?
Lynwood Cl. Romf .... 155 ?
Lynwood Cl. Woodf ...... 152 ?
Lynwood Dr. Romf .... 155 ?
Lyon Cl. Chelm .... 124 ?
Lyon Rd. Hornc .... 164 ?
Lyons Hall Rd. Brain ...... 66 ?
Lyster Ave. Gt Bad ...... 125 ?
Lytton Cl. Lou .... 141 ?
Lytton Rd. Grays .... 186 ?
Lytton Rd. Romf .... 155 ?
Lyttons Way. Hod .... 87 ?

Maberly Ct. Saff W 13 E1
Mabey's Wlk. H Wy 77 D1
Macaulay Rd. Basil 170 A3
Macdonald Ave. Dag 164 A1
Macdonald Ave. Hornc ... 165 F4
Macdonald Way. Horne ... 165 F4
Mace Ct. Grays 192 C4
Mackley Dr. Corr 179 F3
Maclennan Ave. Rain 174 B1
Macleod Cl. Grays 185 E1
Macmillan Gdns. Stone ... 190 A2
Macon Way. Upm 166 C3
Madden Cl. Swan 191 F1
Maddox Rd. Harl 102 C4
Madeira Gr. Woodf 152 B2
Madeline Pl. Chelm 110 C3
Madells. Epp 128 C4
Madles La. Stock 136 C1
Magdalen Gdns. Brent 147 F1
Magdalen Gdns. Thax 40 A1
Magnaville Rd. Bis St 67 F2
Magnolia Cl. Chelm 124 A3
Magnolia Way. Brent 146 A2
Magnolias. Bill 161 E3
Magnum Cl. Rain 174 B1
Magpie La. Brent 158 C1

Magpies. Ep Gr 115 D4
Magwitch Cl. Chelm 110 C4
Mahonia Dr. Basil 169 F3
Maida Ave. Ching 139 D1
Maida Way. Ching 139 D1
Maidstone Ave. Romf 155 E1
Maidstone Rd. Grays 192 A4
Mailers La. Man 46 C1
Main Rd. Bore 112 B4
Main Rd. Broom 98 A1
Main Rd. Felst 75 F2
Main Rd. Gt Le 85 F4
Main Rd. Romf 165 D4
Main St. Bart 5 D3
Maitland Rd. Stan M 57 F3
Maizey Ct. Brent 146 A2
Makemores. Ray 64 C1
Malan Sq. Rain 174 A3
Maldon Rd. Gt Bad 125 E4
Maldon Rd. Marg 123 E1
Maldon Rd. Romf 164 B2
Maldon Rd. Sand 125 E4
Maldon Wlk. Woodf 152 B2
Malford Gr. Woodf 152 A1
Malgraves. Basil 172 A4
Malgraves Pl. Basil 172 A4
Malin Cl. Hav 7 E4
Mall The. Dag 173 D3
Mallard Cl. Upm 166 C2
Mallard Rd. Chelm 124 A3
Mallard Way. Brent 147 D1
Mallards Rd. Woodf 152 A2
Mallards Rise. Harl 103 E4
Mallinson Cl. Hornc 174 B4
Mallion Ct. Wa Aby 126 C3
Mallories. Harl 89 F1
Mallory Way. Bill 149 D1
Mallow Ct. Grays 192 B4
Mallow Gdns. Bill 148 C3
Mallows Green. Harl 102 A2
Mallows Green Rd. Man 46 C1
Malpas Rd. Grays 186 B2
Malta Rd. Tilb 192 C3
Maltese Rd. Chelm 111 D2
Malting La. Epp 116 A1
Malting La. Grays 178 A1
Maltings Dr. Epp 116 A1
Maltings Hill. More 105 F2
Maltings Rd. Gt Bad 125 D3
Maltings The. Gt Dun 61 E2
Maltings The. Ray 65 D1
Maltings The. Thax 40 A1
Malvern Cl. Chelm 110 B3
Malvern Dr. Woodf 152 B3
Malvern Gdns. Lou 140 C2
Malvern Rd. Grays 185 F1
Malvern Rd. Hornc 165 D3
Malyons. Basil 172 A4
Malyons Cl. Basil 172 A4
Malyons Green. Basil 172 A4
Malyons Mews. Basil 172 A4
Malyons Pl. Basil 172 A4
Manchester Way. Dag 173 D4
Mandela Ave. Harl 89 F1
Mandeville Cl. Harl 103 E3
Mandeville Rd. Saff W 25 E4
Mandeville Way. Basil 169 F3
Mandeville Way. Basil 170 A3
Mandeville Way. Broom 98 A2
Manford Cross. Chig 154 A3
Manford Way. Chig 153 F3
Manning Gr. Basil 170 B2
Manning Rd. Dag 173 D3
Manning St. Ave 183 E3
Mannings Cl. Saff W 25 F4
Mannock Dr. Lou 141 E4
Manor Ave. Basil 172 B3
Manor Ave. Hornc 165 E3
Manor Cl. Ave 183 E3
Manor Cl. Dag 173 E3
Manor Cl. Romf 165 D3
Manor Cl. S Han 150 B2
Manor Cl. S. Ave 183 E3
Manor Cres. Hornc 165 E3
Manor Cres. Lit Wal 98 A3
Manor Ct. Wa Aby 126 B3
Manor Dr. Gt Bad 124 C4
Manor Hatch Cl. Harl 103 D4
Manor La. Gt C 1 B1
Manor Links Dr. Bis St 68 B4
Manor Rd. Abr 142 C1
Manor Rd. Bis St 68 A4
Manor Rd. Chelm 111 E1
Manor Rd. Chig 153 E3
Manor Rd. Dag 173 E3
Manor Rd. Grave 193 D1
Manor Rd. Grays 192 B4
Manor Rd. Harl 90 B3
Manor Rd. Hav 7 D4
Manor Rd. Hod 100 A4
Manor Rd. Lit Ea 60 C3
Manor Rd. Lou 140 B2
Manor Rd. Romf 165 D3
Manor Rd. Sta L H 179 E1
Manor Rd. Stan M 57 F3
Manor Rd. Swan 191 E1
Manor Rd. Tilb 193 D3
Manor Rd. W Thu 191 E4
Manor Rd. Wa Aby 126 B3

Manor Rd. Wa Aby 127 D1
Manor St. Brain 66 A2
Manor Way. Brent 158 A4
Manor Way. Grave 192 A2
Manor Way. Grays 192 A4
Manor Way. Rain 173 F1
Manor Way. Sta L H 180 A1
Manor Way. Swan 191 F2
Manorway. Woodf 152 B3
Manorway The. Sta L H 180 B1
Mansard Cl. Hornc 165 D1
Manser Rd. Rain 173 F2
Mansfield. H Wy 77 D1
Mansfield Gdns. Hornc 165 E1
Mansfield Hill. Ching 139 D1
Mansfields. Writ 109 F1
Manstead Gdns. Rain 182 A4
Manston Dri. Bis St 57 D1
Manston Rd. Harl 102 C4
Manston Way. Hornc 174 A3
Maple Ave. Bis St 67 E4
Maple Ave. Brain 65 E1
Maple Ave. Upm 175 D4
Maple Cl. Bis St 67 E4
Maple Cl. Brent 158 C4
Maple Cl. Chig 153 F3
Maple Cl. Hornc 165 D1
Maple Cl. Lou 152 B4
Maple Cl. Sta Ab 87 E2
Maple Dr. Chelm 124 A3
Maple Gate. Lou 141 D4
Maple Gr. Bis St 67 E4
Maple La. Wim 27 E3
Maple Mead. Bill 161 E4
Maple Rd. Grays 192 B4
Maple Spring. Bis St 67 E4
Maple St. Romf 164 B4
Maple Tree La. Basil 169 F3
Maplecroft La. Lo Naz 100 C1
Mapleford Sweep. Basil 171 E2
Mapleleaf Gdns. Wick 163 D3
Maples. Corr 179 F1
Maples The. Harl 102 A2
Maples The. Wick 163 E3
Maplestead. Basil 171 E4
Mapletree La. Ing 134 C4
Maplin Gdns. Basil 171 F3
Mar Rd.S Ock 176 B1
Marchmant Cl. Hornc 165 E1
Marconi Rd. Chelm 111 D2
Marcus Cl. Hav 7 E4
Marden Ash. Basil 170 A3
Marden Rd. Romf 164 C3
Mardyke Rd. Harl 90 A1
Mardyke Wlk. Grays 185 D3
Margaret Ave. Brent 147 D2
Margaret Ave. Ching 139 D2
Margaret Cl. Romf 165 D3
Margaret Cl. Wa Aby 126 B3
Margaret Dr. Hornc 165 F2
Margaret Rd. Epp 116 A1
Margaret Rd. Romf 165 D3
Margaret St. Thax 40 A2
Margaret Way. Saff W 13 E1
Margaretting Rd. Chelm 123 F1
Margaretting Rd. Writ 123 D3
Margarite Way. Wick 163 D4
Margeth Rd. Bill 161 E2
Mariam Gdns. Hornc 165 F1
Marian Cl. T Thu 184 C3
Marigold Cl. Sprin 111 F3
Marigold Pl. Harl 90 A2
Marina Dr. Grave 192 C1
Marina Gdns. Romf 164 B3
Marion Cl. Chig 153 E2
Marisco Cl. Grays 186 A1
Mariskals. Basil 172 A3
Marjorams Ave. Lou 141 D4
Mark Ave. Ching 139 D2
Mark Hall Moors. Harl 90 A2
Mark La. Grave 193 F1
Mark's Ave. Ch Ong 119 D2
Market Alley. Grave 193 D1
Market Ave. Runw 163 E4
Market Hill. Hav 7 D4
Market Hill. Saff W 13 E1
Market Link. Romf 164 C4
Market Pavement. Basil 171 D3
Market Pl. Abr 142 A3
Market Pl. Brain 65 F2
Market Pl. Gt Dun 61 E1
Market Pl. Ing 135 D2
Market Pl. Romf 164 C3
Market Rd. Chelm 111 D1
Market Rd. Wick 163 E4
Market Row. Saff W 13 E1
Market Sq. Basil 171 D3
Market Sq. Bis St 67 F4
Market Sq. Wa Aby 126 B3
Market St. Bis St 67 F4
Market St. Brain 65 F2
Market St. Harl 90 B2
Market St. Saff W 13 E1
Markfield Gdns. Ching 139 D1
Markhams. Corr 179 F2
Markhams Chase. Basil 170 B4
Marking's Field. Saff W 13 F1
Markland Cl. Chelm 124 B2

Marks Cl. Bill 148 C2
Marks Cl. Ing 134 C1
Marks Gdns. Brain 66 B1
Marks Hall La. Mar Rod 94 C2
Marks La. Rett 151 F4
Marks Rd. Romf 164 B3
Markwell Wood. Harl 102 A1
Markwells. Els 48 B1
Marlands. Saw 77 F2
Marlands Rd. Woodf 152 C1
Marlborough Cl. Bis St 67 F3
Marlborough Cl. Grays 185 E2
Marlborough Cl. Upm 166 C2
Marlborough Gdns. Upm .. 166 C2
Marlborough Rd. Brain 66 A2
Marlborough Rd. Brent 146 A2
Marlborough Rd. Chelm ... 111 D1
Marlborough Rd. Romf 164 A4
Marlborough Rd. Woodf ... 152 A1
Marlborough Way. Bill 149 D3
Marlescroft Way. Lou 141 D2
Marlow Ave. Pur 183 D1
Marlowe Cl. Bill 149 D3
Marlowe Cl. Woodf 153 E1
Marney Cl. Gt Bad 124 C4
Marney Dr. Basil 171 F3
Marple Gdns. Wa Aby 126 B4
Marram Ct. Grays 192 C4
Marsh Green Rd. Dag 173 D2
Marsh Hill. Wa Aby 113 F2
Marsh La. Corr 180 B3
Marsh La. Harl 90 C3
Marsh La. Sta Ab 87 E2
Marsh St. Stone 190 A3
Marshalls Dr. Romf 164 C4
Marshalls Rd. Brain 65 F1
Marshalls Rd. Romf 164 B4
Marshbarnes. Bis St 67 E4
Marshfoot Rd. Grays 185 F1
Marston Ave. Dag 164 A1
Marston Beck. Sprin 112 A1
Marston Cl. Dag 164 A1
Marston Dr. Bis St 57 D1
Marston Rd. Hod 100 A4
Marston Rd. Woodf 152 C1
Martin Cl. Bill 149 D1
Martin Dr. Rain 174 A1
Martin Dr. Stone 190 B1
Martin Rd. Ave 183 E3
Martindale Ave. Bill 161 E1
Martingale Cl. Bill 149 E3
Martingale Dr. Sprin 111 F4
Martingale Rd. Bill 149 E3
Martins Cl. Corr 179 E2
Martlesham Cl. Hornc 174 B4
Marvens. Chelm 124 B2
Marwell Cl. Romf 156 D3
Mary McArthur Pl. Stan M .. 57 F4
Mary Park Gdns. Bis St 67 F2
Marylon Rd. Chig 154 A3
Mascalls Gdns. Brent 157 F3
Mascalls La. Brent 158 A2
Mascalls The. Gt Bad 124 C4
Mascalls Way. Gt Bad 124 C4
Masefield Cl. Romf 156 B1
Masefield Cres. Romf 156 B1
Masefield Dr. Upm 166 B2
Masefield Rd. Grays 185 F2
Masefield Rd. Stone 190 A1
Mashbury Rd. G Ea 96 B3
Mashbury Rd. Gt Wal 97 D4
Mashiters Hill. Romf 155 E1
Mashiters Wlk. Romf 164 C4
Mason Way. Wa Aby 126 C3
Masthead Cl. Stone 190 B2
Matching Field. Kelv H 132 C1
Matching Green. Basil 171 E4
Matching La. Bis St 67 E4
Matching Rd. Hat B O 79 D1
Matching Rd. Match 91 D2
Matfield Cl. Sprin 111 E4
Mathams Dr. Bis St 67 E3
Matlock Gdns. Hornc 165 F1
Matthews Cl. Romf 156 C1
Maugham Cl. Wick 163 E3
Mavis Gr. Hornc 165 F1
Mawney Cl. Romf 155 D1
Mawney Rd. Romf 164 A4
May Ct. Grays 192 C4
May Wlk. Chelm 124 B4
Maybank Ave. Hornc 174 B4
Maybank Ave. Woodf 152 A1
Maybrick Rd. Hornc 165 F2
Maybush Rd. Hornc 165 F2
Maycroft Ave. Grays 185 E1
Maycroft Gdns. Grays 185 E1
Maydells. Basil 172 A3
Mayes Cl. Bis St 68 B4
Mayes La. Sand 125 F3
Mayes Pl. Thax 51 D3
Mayfair Ave. Basil 172 B4
Mayfair Gdns. Woodf 152 A2
Mayfield. Wa Aby 126 B3
Mayfield Ave. Woodf 152 A2
Mayfield Cl. Harl 90 C2
Mayfield Gdns. Brent 146 B1
Mayfield Park. Bis St 67 E2
Mayfield Rd. Writ 110 A1

Mayfields. Grays 185 E2
Mayflower Cl. Lo Naz 100 C1
Mayflower Cl. S Ock 176 B1
Mayflower Rd. Bill 149 D1
Mayflower Way. Ch Ong ... 119 D2
Maygreen Cres. Hornc 165 D2
Maylands Ave. Hornc 174 A4
Maylands Dr. Bl Not 76 B4
Maylands Way. Romf 157 E2
Mayling Rd. Brain 65 E1
Maynard Cl. Gt Dun 61 E1
Maynard Ct. Wa Aby 126 C3
Maynards. Hornc 165 F2
Mayne Crest. Sprin 111 F3
Maypole Cl. Saff W 25 E4
Maypole Cres. Chig 153 E2
Maypole Dr. Chig 154 A4
Maypole The. Thax 39 F2
Maysent Ave. Brain 65 F3
Mayswood Gdns. Dag 173 E3
Maytree Cl. Rain 173 F2
Maytree Gdns. Ugl 48 A2
Maywin Dr. Hornc 165 F2
Maze Green Rd. Bis St 67 E4
Mazoe Cl. Bis St 67 F3
Mazoe Rd. Bis St 67 F3
Mc Adam Cl. Hod 100 A4
McIntosh Cl. Romf 164 C4
McIntosh Rd. Romf 164 C4
Mckenzie Rd. Hod 100 A2
Mead Cl. Grays 185 D2
Mead Cl. Romf 156 A1
Mead Ct. Stan M 57 E4
Mead Ct. Wa Aby 126 A3
Mead Path. Chelm 123 F4
Mead The. Abr 142 A3
Mead The. Basil 170 A4
Mead The. Thax 40 A2
Mead View. St Pel 45 F3
Mead Wlk. Ch Ong 118 C1
Meade Cl. Bill 149 E3
Meade Rd. Bill 149 E3
Meadgate. Basil 172 B4
Meadgate. Lo Naz 100 B2
Meadgate Ave. Gt Bad 124 C4
Meadgate Ave. Woodf 152 C3
Meadow Cl. Ching 139 D1
Meadow Cl. Pan 65 D4
Meadow Cl. Sta L H 187 D2
Meadow Cl. Wick 163 F4
Meadow La. Runw 151 F2
Meadow Rd. Epp 115 F1
Meadow Rd. Grays 185 E3
Meadow Rd. Gt C 1 B2
Meadow Rd. Lou 140 C2
Meadow Rd. Romf 164 B2
Meadow Rise. Bill 149 E1
Meadow Rise. Bla 133 F4
Meadow Side. Chelm 111 D2
Meadow Way. Chig 153 E4
Meadow Way. Saw 78 A1
Meadow Way. Upm 166 B1
Meadow Way. Wick 163 F4
Meadow Way The. Bill 149 E1
Meadowcroft. Stan M 57 F4
Meadowcross. Wa Aby 126 C3
Meadowford. New 24 C1
Meadowgate. Stock 136 C1
Meadowlands. Bis St 57 D1
Meadowlands. Hornc 165 F2
Meadows La. Brent 159 E2
Meadows The. Brent 159 E2
Meadows The. Saw 78 A1
Meadowside. Brain 65 F3
Meadowside Rd. Upm 175 E4
Meadowside.. Chelm 111 E2
Meads Cl. Ing 135 D2
Meads The. Basil 172 A2
Meads The. Ing 135 D2
Meads The. Upm 166 C1
Meads The. Wic Bon 36 A4
Meadside. Weth 43 D2
Meadsway. Brent 158 B2
Meadway. Grays 185 E1
Meadway. Hod 100 A2
Meadway. Romf 156 A1
Meadway. Woodf 152 B3
Meadway The. Lou 140 B1
Meadway The. Lou 140 C2
Mearns Pl. Sprin 111 F2
Medebridge Rd. Grays 184 C3
Medic Ct. Grays 192 C4
Medina Rd. Grays 185 E1
Medlar Rd. Grays 192 C4
Medlar's Mead. Hat B O 79 F3
Medley Rd. Ray 64 C1
Medoc Cl. Basil 172 B4
Medora Rd. Romf 164 B4
Medway Cl. Chelm 110 B2
Meeson's La. Grays 184 C1
Meeting La. Ridge 20 A4
Melba Cl. Writ 110 B1
Melba Gdns. Tilb 193 D4
Melbourne Ave. Chelm 110 C3
Melbourne Rd. Tilb 192 C3
Melksham Cl. Romf 156 C2
Melksham Dr. Romf 156 C2
Melksham Gdns. Romf 156 C2

Mellish Gdns. Woodf 152 A3
Mellor Cl. Ing 135 D2
Mellow Purgess. Basil 170 B3
Mellow Purgess Cl. Basil .. 170 B3
Mellow Purgess End. Basil 170 B3
Melstock Ave. Upm 175 E4
Melton Gdns. Hornc 164 C2
Melville Rd. Rain 174 A1
Melville Rd. Romf 155 D2
Mendip Rd. Chelm 110 B3
Mendip Rd. Hornc 165 D2
Mendoza Cl. Hornc 165 F3
Menish Way. Sprin 112 A2
Mentmore. Basil 170 A2
Menzies Ave. Basil 169 F3
Meon Cl. Sprin 111 E3
Mercer Rd. Bill 149 E3
Mercia Cl. Gt Bad 125 D3
Mercury Cl. Wick 163 F4
Mercury Gdns. Romf 164 C3
Meredene. Basil 171 F3
Meredith Rd. Grays 186 A1
Merefield. Saw 77 F1
Meriden Cl. Woodf 153 E1
Meridian Way. Sta Ab 87 D3
Merlin Cl. Chig 154 A3
Merlin Cl. Romf 155 E2
Merlin Cl. Wa Aby 127 D3
Merlin Gdns. Romf 155 E2
Merlin Gr. Woodf 153 E2
Merlin Pl. Chelm 110 C3
Merlin Rd. Romf 155 E2
Merlin Way. N W Bas 117 D3
Merlin Way. Runw 151 E1
Mermagen Dr. Rain 174 A3
Merricks La. Basil 171 F1
Merrielands Cres. Dag 173 D2
Merring Way. Harl 101 F4
Merryhill Cl. Ching 139 D1
Merrylands. Basil 170 A4
Merrylands Chase. Basil ... 169 E4
Mersey Ave. Upm 166 B3
Mersey Fleet Way. Brain 66 B1
Mersey Way. Chelm 110 B3
Merton Pl. Grays 186 A1
Merton Pl. Litt 12 C2
Messant Cl. Romf 156 C1
Methersgate. Basil 171 E4
Mews Cl. Chelm 111 D1
Mews Pl. Woodf 152 A3
Mews The. Romf 164 C4
Mews The. Stan M 57 F4
Meynell Rd. Romf 156 A2
Micawber Way. Chelm 110 B4
Michael Gdns. Hornc 165 E4
Michaels Rd. Bis St 57 D1
Mid Colne. Basil 171 E2
Middle Boy. Abr 142 B3
Middle Cloister. Bill 149 D1
Middle Crockerford. Basil . 171 F2
Middle Dr. Corr 180 A4
Middle Green. Dodd 133 E1
Middle King. Brain 66 B1
Middle Mead. Wick 163 F4
Middle Mead Cl. W Han ... 137 F2
Middle Rd. Brent 159 E3
Middle Rd. Wa Aby 126 A4
Middle Row. Bis St 67 F3
Middle St. Clav 35 E2
Middle St. Lo Naz 114 A4
Middlefield Ave. Hod 100 A4
Middlefield Rd. Hod 100 A4
Middlemead. S Han 138 B2
Middlemead. W Han 138 B2
Middleton Hall La. Brent .. 158 C4
Middleton Rd. Brent 146 C1
Midhurst Cl. Hornc 174 A4
Milburn Cres. Chelm 110 B1
Milch La. Felst 75 F3
Mildmay Rd. Chelm 111 D1
Mildmay Rd. Romf 164 B3
Mildmayes. Basil 170 B2
Mildred Cl. Stone 190 A1
Mile Cl. Wa Aby 126 B3
Mile Stone Rd. Stone 190 A1
Miles Cl. Harl 102 A4
Miles Gray Rd. Basil 161 F1
Milford Rd. Grays 185 E3
Milkwell Gdns. Woodf 152 A2
Mill Causeway. Chris 10 B3
Mill Chase. Ste B 18 B3
Mill Cl. Els 48 B1
Mill Cl. Gt Ba 42 A1
Mill Cl. Rox 109 D3
Mill Ct. Can E 71 D4
Mill End. Thax 40 A1
Mill Field. Barn 73 D2
Mill Field. Harl 90 B2
Mill Green. Basil 172 A4
Mill Green Ct. Basil 172 A4
Mill Green Pl. Basil 172 A4
Mill Green Rd. Ing 134 C4
Mill Hill. Brain 66 A1
Mill Hill. Brent 146 C1
Mill Hill. Chelm 123 F1
Mill Hill. Far 56 C3
Mill Hill. Hav 7 D4
Mill La. Bla 133 E2
Mill La. Broom 98 B1

Mill La. Corr ... 180 B3
Mill La. Felst ... 84 B4
Mill La. Finch ... 30 C2
Mill La. Grays ... 184 B1
Mill La. Grays ... 186 A4
Mill La. Gt Dun ... 61 E1
Mill La. Gt Le ... 86 A4
Mill La. H Lav ... 105 E3
Mill La. H Ong ... 119 E1
Mill La. Harl ... 90 C2
Mill La. Hinx ... 1 A2
Mill La. Hinx ... 1 A4
Mill La. Horn H ... 178 C2
Mill La. Ing ... 135 D3
Mill La. Kelv H ... 132 C1
Mill La. L Hal ... 78 C2
Mill La. Litt ... 12 C2
Mill La. Mee ... 34 A3
Mill La. Nave H ... 144 A4
Mill La. Ray ... 75 F4
Mill La. S Han ... 150 A3
Mill La. Saff W ... 13 F1
Mill La. Saw ... 77 F2
Mill La. Steb ... 62 C3
Mill La. Stock ... 136 C1
Mill La. Wen A ... 25 D3
Mill La. Woodf ... 152 A3
Mill Park Ave. Hornc ... 165 F1
Mill Rd. Ave ... 183 E3
Mill Rd. Bill ... 161 E3
Mill Rd. Cla ... 8 C1
Mill Rd. Deb ... 38 A4
Mill Rd. Felst ... 74 A2
Mill Rd. Finch ... 42 B3
Mill Rd. G Ea ... 82 B3
Mill Rd. Gt Ba ... 42 A1
Mill Rd. Hav ... 7 D4
Mill Rd. Hel B ... 17 E4
Mill Rd. Hen ... 48 C2
Mill Rd. Pur ... 190 A4
Mill Rd. Ridge ... 20 A3
Mill Rd. Stam ... 19 E2
Mill Rd. Stock ... 136 C1
Mill Rd. Wim ... 27 D2
Mill Side. Stan M ... 57 F3
Mill St. Bis St ... 68 A3
Mill St. N W Bas ... 103 F3
Mill Vue Rd. Sprin ... 111 F1
Millais Pl. Tilb ... 193 D4
Millard Terr. Dag ... 173 D3
Millbank Ave. Ch Ong ... 118 C3
Millbrook Gdns. Romf ... 155 F1
Millcroft. Bis St ... 57 D1
Miller's Cl. Barn ... 73 D2
Miller's La. Chig ... 142 A1
Millers Cl. Brain ... 66 A4
Millers Cl. Chig ... 154 A4
Millers Croft. Bad ... 124 C3
Millers Croft. Gt Dun ... 61 F1
Millers Green Rd. Will ... 107 D2
Millers La. Sta Ab ... 87 E2
Millers Row. Finch ... 30 B3
Millersdale. Harl ... 102 A4
Millfield. H Ong ... 119 E2
Millfields. Saw ... 77 F2
Millfields. Stan M ... 57 F3
Millfields. Writ ... 110 A1
Millfields Way. Hav ... 7 D4
Millhoo Ct. Wa Aby ... 126 C3
Milligans Chase. Chelm ... 124 A1
Mills Way. Brent ... 147 E1
Millsmead Way. Lou ... 140 C4
Millson Bank. Sprin ... 112 A2
Millwell Cres. Chig ... 153 E3
Milner Pl. Bill ... 148 C3
Milton Ave. Hornc ... 164 C1
Milton Ct. Wa Aby ... 126 B3
Milton Gdns. Tilb ... 193 D3
Milton Pl. Chelm ... 111 D3
Milton Rd. Brent ... 158 B3
Milton Rd. Corr ... 179 F2
Milton Rd. Grave ... 193 E1
Milton Rd. Grays ... 185 D1
Milton Rd. Romf ... 165 D3
Milton Rd. Swan ... 191 F1
Milton St. Swan ... 191 E1
Milton St. Wa Aby ... 126 B3
Milwards. Harl ... 102 A2
Mimosa Cl. Brent ... 146 A2
Mimosa Cl. Romf ... 156 B2
Mimosa Cl. Sprin ... 111 F3
Minchen Rd. Harl ... 90 A1
Minerva Cl. Hav ... 7 E3
Minster Way. Hornc ... 166 A1
Miramar Way. Hornc ... 174 B4
Mistley End. Basil ... 171 E3
Mistley Path. Basil ... 171 E3
Mistley Rd. Harl ... 90 A1
Mistley Side. Basil ... 171 E3
Mitchell Circ. Finch ... 43 E3
Mitton Vale. Sprin ... 111 F1
Moat Cl. Dodd ... 133 E2
Moat Cl. S Han ... 150 B2
Moat Edge Gdns. Bill ... 149 D2
Moat Farm. Bird ... 19 D4
Moat Field. Basil ... 171 E4
Moat Rd. Bird ... 19 E4

Moatside. Anst ... 33 D4
Mole Hall La. Widd ... 37 F2
Molesworth. Hod ... 87 D1
Molineaux Ct. Bill ... 149 D2
Mollands. Basil ... 171 F2
Mollands Ct. S Ock ... 176 C1
Mollands La. S Ock ... 176 B1
Mollison Ave. Enf ... 126 A2
Molrams La. Gt Bad ... 125 D3
Momples Rd. Harl ... 90 A1
Monarch Cl. Tilb ... 193 D3
Monkchester Cl. Lou ... 141 D4
Monkham's Ave. Woodf ... 152 A3
Monkham's Dr. Woodf ... 152 A3
Monkham's La. Woodf ... 152 B3
Monks Chase. Brent ... 159 E3
Monks Cl. Hod ... 100 A2
Monks Haven. Corr ... 179 F1
Monks Hill. Saff W ... 25 F4
Monksbury. Harl ... 103 D3
Monksgrove. Lou ... 141 D2
Monkside. Basil ... 171 E4
Monkswick Rd. Harl ... 89 F1
Monkswood Ave. Wa Aby ... 126 B3
Monnow Green. Ave ... 183 E3
Monnow Rd. Ave ... 183 E3
Monoux Cl. Bill ... 149 E1
Mons Ave. Bill ... 149 E1
Montague Way. Bill ... 149 D2
Montfort Ave. Corr ... 180 A2
Montfort Gdns. Woodf ... 153 E2
Montgomery Cl. Grays ... 185 E2
Montgomery Cl. Sprin ... 111 F4
Montgomery Cres. Romf ... 156 B3
Montpelier Cl. Bill ... 149 D3
Montreal Rd. Tilb ... 193 D3
Montrose Ave. Romf ... 156 B1
Montrose Cl. Woodf ... 152 A3
Montrose Rd. Sprin ... 111 F2
Montsale. Basil ... 172 B4
Moon Hall La. Hav ... 7 D3
Moor Hall Rd. Harl ... 90 C2
Moor Hall Rd. Match ... 91 D2
Moor La. Upm ... 166 C2
Moor's La. Ray ... 64 B2
Moore Ave. Grays ... 184 C1
Moore Ave. Tilb ... 193 D3
Moore Cl. Bill ... 149 E3
Moore Rd. Swan ... 191 F1
Moore's Pl. Brent ... 158 B4
Moores Ave. Basil ... 171 E1
Moorefields. Harl ... 102 B2
Moorland Cl. Romf ... 155 D2
Moors La. Lit Dun ... 73 E4
Moran Ave. Chelm ... 111 D4
Morant Gdns. Romf ... 155 D3
Morant Rd. Grays ... 186 A2
Moray Cl. Romf ... 155 F2
Moray Way. Romf ... 155 F2
Morecambe Cl. Hornc ... 174 A4
Moreland Rd. Runw ... 151 E1
Morelands Ave. Grays ... 185 E2
Moremead. Wa Aby ... 126 B3
Mores La. Kelv H ... 145 E3
Moreton Bridge. Bobb ... 105 E1
Moreton Bridge. More ... 105 E1
Moreton Gdns. Woodf ... 152 C3
Moreton Rd. Bobb ... 118 A4
Moreton Rd. Ch Ong ... 118 C3
Moreton Rd. Fyf ... 106 A2
Moreton Rd. More ... 106 A2
Moreton Rd. More ... 118 C3
Moretons. Basil ... 172 A3
Moretons. Chelm ... 124 A1
Morgan Cl. Dag ... 173 D3
Morgan Cres. The B ... 128 C2
Morgan Way. Rain ... 174 B1
Morgan Way. Woodf ... 152 C2
Morland Rd. Dag ... 173 D3
Morley Gr. Harl ... 89 E1
Morley Hill. Corr ... 179 F3
Morley Link. Corr ... 179 F3
Morley Sq. Grays ... 186 A1
Mornington Rd. Ching ... 139 E1
Mornington Rd. Lou ... 141 E3
Mornington Rd. Woodf ... 152 A3
Morningtons. Harl ... 102 B2
Morrells. Basil ... 170 C2
Morris Ave. Bill ... 149 E1
Morris Ct. Wa Aby ... 126 C3
Morris Gdns. Stone ... 190 A1
Morris Harp. Saff W ... 13 E1
Morris Rd. Chelm ... 111 E1
Morris Rd. Romf ... 156 A2
Mosbach Gdns. Brent ... 159 D4
Moss Bank. Grays ... 184 C1
Moss Cl. Basil ... 171 F2
Moss Dr. Basil ... 171 F2
Moss La. Romf ... 164 C3
Moss La. Romf ... 165 D3
Moss Path. Chelm ... 124 B2
Moss Rd. Dag ... 173 D3
Moss Rd. S Ock ... 184 B4
Moss Wlk. Chelm ... 124 A3
Mossford La. Woodf ... 153 E1
Motehill. Basil ... 170 B2
Motherwell Way. W Thu ... 184 A1
Mott St. Wa Aby ... 139 F4

Motts Yd. Steb ... 62 C3
Moules La. Had ... 3 E3
Moulsham Chase. Chelm ... 124 B4
Moulsham Dr. Chelm ... 124 A4
Moulsham Hall La. Gt Le ... 75 F1
Moulsham St. Chelm ... 111 D1
Moulsham Thrift. Chelm ... 124 A3
Mount Ave. Brent ... 147 D1
Mount Ave. Romf ... 157 E2
Mount Cl. Wick ... 163 F4
Mount Cres. Brent ... 158 B3
Mount Dr. Stan M ... 57 F3
Mount Echo Ave. Ching ... 139 D1
Mount Echo Dr. Ching ... 139 D1
Mount Pleasant Ave. Brent ... 147 F2
Mount Pleasant Cotts. Saff W ... 25 E4
Mount Pleasant Rd. Chig ... 153 E4
Mount Pleasant Rd. Romf ... 155 E2
Mount Pleasant Rd. Saff W ... 25 F4
Mount Rd. Brain ... 66 A2
Mount Rd. Dag ... 164 A2
Mount Rd. Hav ... 7 D4
Mount Rd. Sta T ... 129 F4
Mount Rd. Wick ... 163 F4
Mount The. Bill ... 149 F2
Mount The. Brent ... 158 B4
Mount The. Corr ... 179 F2
Mount The. Romf ... 156 B4
Mount View. Bill ... 149 F1
Mount View Rd. Ching ... 139 E1
Mount Way. Wick ... 163 F4
Mountain's Farm Rd. Gt Dun ... 72 B2
Mountbatten Ct. Lou ... 152 B4
Mountbatten Rd. Brain ... 66 B3
Mountbatten Way. Sprin ... 111 F4
Mountfield Cl. Corr ... 179 F2
Mountfields. Basil ... 172 B2
Mountfitchet Rd. Stan M ... 57 F3
Mounthill Ave. Sprin ... 111 E2
Mountnessing Cl. Dodd ... 133 F1
Mountnessing La. Mtssg ... 148 B3
Mountnessing Rd. Bill ... 148 C2
Mountnessing Rd. Dodd ... 134 A2
Mountney Cl. Ing ... 134 C1
Mounts Rd. Swan ... 191 D1
Mowbray Rd. Harl ... 90 A2
Mowbrays Cl. Romf ... 155 E1
Mowbrays Rd. Romf ... 155 E1
Mowbrey Gdns. Lou ... 141 E3
Mucking Wharf Rd. Sta L H ... 187 E4
Muckingford Rd. Grays ... 186 C1
Muckingford Rd. Sta L H ... 187 D1
Muggeridge Rd. Dag ... 173 D4
Mulberry Cl. Romf ... 165 E4
Mulberry Ct. Bis St ... 68 A3
Mulberry Dr. Pur ... 182 C1
Mulberry Green. Harl ... 90 B2
Mulberry Hill. Brent ... 146 C1
Mulberry Terr. Harl ... 90 A2
Mulberry Way. Sprin ... 111 E3
Mulberry Way. Woodf ... 152 A1
Mullberry Gdns. Basil ... 170 A3
Mullien Ct. Grays ... 192 B4
Mullins Rd. Brain ... 65 F3
Mullions The. Bill ... 148 C2
Mundon Rd. Brain ... 66 B1
Mungo Park Rd. Rain ... 174 A3
Murchison Cl. Chelm ... 110 C3
Murchison Rd. Hod ... 87 D1
Murfitt Way. Upm ... 175 D4
Murray Cl. Brain ... 65 F3
Murrell Lock. Sprin ... 112 A2
Murthering La. Nave ... 144 A3
Murtwell Dr. Chig ... 153 E2
Museum St. Saff W ... 13 E1
Muskham Rd. Harl ... 90 A2
Mutlow Cl. Wen A ... 24 C3
Mutlow Hill. Wen A ... 24 C3
Mutton Row. Sta R ... 131 E4
Myddylton Pl. Saff W ... 13 E1
Mygrove Cl. Rain ... 174 B2
Mygrove Gdns. Rain ... 174 B2
Mygrove Rd. Rain ... 174 B2
Myln Meadow. Stock ... 136 C1
Mynchens. Basil ... 170 C3
Myrtle Gr. Ave ... 183 E2
Myrtle Rd. Brent ... 158 B3
Myrtle Rd. Romf ... 156 B2

Nabbott Rd. Chelm ... 110 C1
Nags Head La. Brent ... 157 E2
Nails La. Bis St ... 67 F4
Nairn Ct. Tilb ... 192 C3
Nalla Gdns. Chelm ... 111 D4
Napier Ct. Chelm ... 110 C3
Narboro Ct. Romf ... 165 D3
Nare Rd. Ave ... 183 E3
Naseby Rd. Dag ... 164 A1
Naseby Rd. Woodf ... 152 C1
Nash Dr. Broom ... 98 A2
Nathan Cl. Upm ... 166 C2
Nathan's La. Writ ... 122 C3
Nation Way. Ching ... 139 E1
Nats La. Wen A ... 24 C3
Naunton Way. Hornc ... 165 E1
Navarre Gdns. Romf ... 155 D3
Navestock Cres. Woodf ... 152 B1
Navestock Side. Kelv H ... 145 E4

Navigation Rd. Chelm ... 111 E1
Nayland Cl. Wick ... 163 F4
Nayland Rd. Hav ... 6 C3
Nayling Rd. Brain ... 65 E1
Nazeing Common. Lo Naz ... 114 B4
Nazeing New Rd. Hod ... 100 A1
Nazeing Rd. Lo Naz ... 100 B1
Nazeing The. Basil ... 171 F3
Nazeing Wlk. Rain ... 173 F3
Neal Ct. Wa Aby ... 126 C3
Neave Cres. Romf ... 156 B1
Nelmes Cl. Hornc ... 165 F3
Nelmes Cres. Hornc ... 165 F3
Nelmes Rd. Hornc ... 165 F3
Nelmes Way. Hornc ... 165 F4
Nelson Cl. Brent ... 158 B3
Nelson Cl. Romf ... 155 D1
Nelson Gdns. Brain ... 66 B2
Nelson Rd. Basil ... 171 F3
Nelson Rd. Bis St ... 68 A3
Nelson Rd. Grays ... 186 B4
Nelson Rd. Rain ... 173 F2
Nelson Rd. S Ock ... 176 B2
Nelwyn Ave. Hornc ... 165 F1
Nethan Dr. Ave ... 183 E3
Nether Mayne. Basil ... 171 D2
Nether Priors. Basil ... 171 E3
Netherfield La. Sta Ab ... 87 E2
Netherhall Rd. Roy ... 100 C3
Netherpark Dr. Romf ... 155 F1
Netteswell Cross. Harl ... 89 F1
Netteswell Rd. Harl ... 89 F2
Nevell Rd. Grays ... 186 A2
Nevendon Rd. Basil ... 163 D1
Nevendon Rd. Wick ... 163 E3
Nevill Way. Lou ... 140 C2
Neville Rd. Saff W ... 13 F1
Neville Rd. Woodf ... 153 E1
Neville Shaw. Basil ... 171 D3
Nevin Dr. Ching ... 139 E1
Nevis Cl. Romf ... 155 F2
New Ave. Basil ... 170 A2
New Barn La. Gt Ha ... 68 B1
New Barn La. L Hal ... 68 A1
New Barns Way. Chig ... 153 D4
New Bowers Way. Sprin ... 111 F3
New Century Rd. Basil ... 170 A3
New Dukes Way. Sprin ... 111 F3
New Farm Dr. Abr ... 142 B3
New Forest La. Chig ... 153 D2
New Hall Dr. Romf ... 156 C1
New House La. Ash ... 15 E2
New London Rd. Chelm ... 111 D1
New Maltings. Ave ... 183 E3
New Meadgate Terr. Gt Bad ... 124 B4
New Nabbots Way. Sprin ... 111 F4
New North Rd. Chig ... 153 F2
New Path. Bis St ... 67 F3
New Place Gdns. Upm ... 166 B1
New Pond La. Saff W ... 13 E1
New Rd. Abr ... 142 B2
New Rd. Bart ... 5 E4
New Rd. Bill ... 161 E2
New Rd. Brent ... 158 B4
New Rd. Broom ... 98 A1
New Rd. Dag ... 173 D2
New Rd. Els ... 48 B1
New Rd. Grave ... 193 D1
New Rd. Grays ... 192 A4
New Rd. Gt Bad ... 125 D3
New Rd. Harl ... 90 B2
New Rd. Hinx ... 1 A4
New Rd. Hod ... 100 A2
New Rd. Ing ... 135 E2
New Rd. Ing ... 135 E3
New Rd. Rain ... 174 B1
New Rd. Ray ... 64 C1
New Rd. Saff W ... 13 F1
New River Ave. Sta Ab ... 87 D2
New River Cl. Hod ... 100 A4
New St. Brain ... 65 F1
New St. Chelm ... 111 D2
New St. Gt Dun ... 72 B4
New St. Saw ... 77 F2
New Street Fields. Gt Dun ... 72 B4
New Street Pas. Gt Dun ... 72 B4
New Waverley Rd. Bill ... 161 F1
New Writtle St. Chelm ... 111 D1
New Zealand Way. Rain ... 173 F1
Newberry Side. Basil ... 170 B3
Newbiggen St. Thax ... 39 F2
Newbury Cl. Bis St ... 67 F4
Newbury Cl. Romf ... 156 B3
Newbury Gdns. Romf ... 156 B3
Newbury Gdns. Upm ... 165 F1
Newbury Rd. Romf ... 156 B3
Newbury Wlk. Romf ... 156 B3
Newcastle Ave. Chig ... 154 A2
Newcourt Rd. Sprin ... 111 E2
Newcroft. Saff W ... 13 F1
Newhall Ct. Wa Aby ... 126 C3
Newhouse Ave. Wick ... 162 C4
Newhouse La. Bobb ... 105 E1
Newland Ave. Gt Ba ... 42 A1
Newlands Cl. Bill ... 149 D2
Newlands Cl. Brent ... 147 E1
Newlands End. Basil ... 170 A4
Newlands Rd. Bill ... 149 D2
Newlands Rd. Wick ... 163 E2

Newlands Rd. Woodf ... 152 A4
Newman Cl. Hornc ... 165 F3
Newmans Cl. Lou ... 141 D3
Newmans Dr. Brent ... 147 E1
Newmans La. Lou ... 141 D3
Newmarket Rd. Gt C ... 1 B2
Newmarket Way. Hornc ... 174 C4
Newnham Cl. Brain ... 65 F1
Newnham Cl. Lou ... 140 B2
Newnham Pl. Grays ... 186 A1
Newpasture La. Steb ... 63 E3
Newpiece. Lou ... 141 D3
Newport Cl. Gt Bad ... 125 D3
Newport Dr. Quen ... 36 C2
Newport Rd. Saff W ... 25 E3
Newports. Saw ... 77 E1
Newteswell Dr. Wa Aby ... 126 B4
Newton Cl. Brain ... 65 F1
Newton Cl. Corr ... 180 A3
Newton Cl. Hod ... 87 D1
Newton Dr. Saw ... 77 E1
Newton Green. Gt Dun ... 61 E1
Newton Rd. Chig ... 154 A3
Newton Rd. Tilb ... 193 D3
Newtons Cl. Rain ... 173 F3
Newtown Rd. Bis St ... 67 F3
Nicholas Cl. S Ock ... 176 B1
Nicholas Cl. Writ ... 110 A1
Nicholas Ct. Chelm ... 110 C3
Nicholl Rd. Basil ... 170 B4
Nicholl Rd. Epp ... 128 C4
Nicholls Field. Harl ... 103 D4
Nickleby Rd. Chelm ... 110 B3
Nicola Mews. Woodf ... 153 D2
Nicolas Wlk. Grays ... 186 A2
Nightingale Ave. Upm ... 166 C2
Nightingale Gr. Stone ... 190 A2
Nightingale La. Brent ... 169 E4
Nightingale Mews. Saff W ... 13 F1
Nightingales. Basil ... 169 F3
Nightingales. Wa Aby ... 126 C3
Nine Ashes Rd. Bla ... 120 B1
Nine Ashes Rd. H Ong ... 120 B1
Nine Ashes Rd. Sto M ... 133 D3
Nineacres. Brain ... 66 A1
Ninefields. Wa Aby ... 126 C3
Nita Rd. Brent ... 158 B3
Noak Hill. Bill ... 161 E2
Noak Hill Rd. Bill ... 161 E2
Noak Hill Rd. Romf ... 156 B4
Noakes Ave. Gt Bad ... 124 C3
Nobel Sq. Basil ... 163 E1
Nobles The. Bis St ... 67 E3
Nonsuch Cl. Woodf ... 153 D2
Norfolk Cl. Basil ... 170 A3
Norfolk Dr. Chelm ... 111 D4
Norfolk Gdns. Brain ... 66 A2
Norfolk Rd. Dag ... 173 D4
Norfolk Rd. Grave ... 193 F1
Norfolk Rd. Romf ... 164 B3
Norfolk Rd. Upm ... 166 A1
Norfolk Way. Bis St ... 67 F3
Norman Ave. Bis St ... 67 E3
Norman Cl. Romf ... 155 D1
Norman Cl. Wa Aby ... 126 B3
Norman Cres. Brent ... 159 D4
Norman Cres. Stan M ... 57 F4
Norman Ct. Woodf ... 152 A3
Norman Rd. Hornc ... 165 D2
Norman's Way. Stan M ... 57 F4
Normanhurst. Brent ... 147 E2
Normansfield. Gt Dun ... 72 C4
Norris Cl. Bis St ... 68 B4
Norris Cl. Brain ... 66 B3
Norris Rd. Hod ... 100 A3
Norsey Cl. Bill ... 149 D2
Norsey Dr. Bill ... 149 E2
Norsey Rd. Bill ... 149 E2
Norsey View Dr. Bill ... 149 D3
North Ave. Chelm ... 110 C3
North Barn. Lo Naz ... 100 A1
North Benfleet Hall Rd. Wick ... 163 F1
North Circular Rd. Woodf ... 152 B1
North Cl. Chig ... 154 A3
North Cl. Dag ... 173 D2
North Colne. Basil ... 171 E2
North Cres. Ste B ... 18 A4
North Cres. Wick ... 163 E4
North Crockerford. Basil ... 171 F2
North Dell. Sprin ... 111 F4
North Dr. Brent ... 148 B1
North Dr. Gt Bad ... 124 C4
North Dr. Romf ... 165 E4
North End. Lou ... 140 B1
North End Rd. Hinx ... 1 A4
North Gate. Harl ... 89 E1
North Gr. Harl ... 103 D4
North Gunnels. Basil ... 171 D3
North Hall Rd. Hen ... 37 D1
North Hill. Horn H ... 178 C3
North Hill Dr. Romf ... 156 B3
North Hill Green. Romf ... 156 B3
North Kent Ave. Grave ... 192 B1
North Pl. Harl ... 90 A3
North Pl. Wa Aby ... 126 A3
North Rd. Bill ... 162 B3
North Rd. Brent ... 146 B1

North Rd. Hav B 155 F4
North Rd. Hod 100 A4
North Rd. S Ock 176 B2
North Rd. Take 70 B4
North Rd. W Thu 183 E1
North Road Ave. Brent 158 A4
North Service Rd. Brent 158 B4
North St. Bis St 67 F4
North St. Gt Dun 61 E1
North St. Hornc 165 E2
North St. Lo Naz 100 C1
North St. Romf 164 B4
North St. Ste B 18 A4
North Terr. Bis St 67 F4
North View Rd. Tilb 193 D3
Northallerton Way. Romf ... 156 B3
Northampton Meadow. Gt Ba . 42 A1
Northbrooks. Harl 102 B4
Northdene. Chig 153 E3
Northdown Rd. Hornc 165 D2
Northend. Brent 158 B3
Northey. Basil 170 B4
Northfield. Finch 42 B3
Northfield. Lou 140 B3
Northfield Cl. Bill 149 E1
Northfield Rd. Saff W 25 F4
Northfield Rd. Saw 77 F2
Northfields. Grays 185 E1
Northgate End. Bis St 67 F4
Northolt Ave. Bis St 57 D1
Northlands App. Basil 170 B1
Northlands Cl. Corr 179 F3
Northlands Pavement. Basil . 172 A3
Northolme Cl. Grays 185 E2
Northolt Way. Hornc 174 B4
Northumberland Ave. Basil . 170 B3
Northumberland Ave. Hornc . 165 E4
Northumberland Cl. Brain .. 66 A2
Northumberland Ct. Sprin .. 111 F2
Northumberland Rd. Sta L H . 187 D2
Northview Dr. Woodf 152 B1
Northwood. Grays 186 A2
Northwood Ave. Hornc 174 A4
Norton Cl. Corr 180 A2
Norton Heath Rd. Will 120 C4
Norton La. H Ong 120 B3
Norton Rd. Chelm 111 D2
Norton Rd. Dag 173 E3
Norton Rd. Hav 6 C3
Norton Rd. Ing 135 D2
Norway Wlk. Rain 174 B1
Norwich Wlk. Basil 171 F4
Norwood Ave. Romf 164 C2
Norwood End. Basil 171 E4
Norwood End. Fyf 106 B3
Notley Rd. Brain 65 F1
Nottage Cl. Corr 179 F2
Nunns Way. Grays 185 E1
Nursery Cl. Bis St 67 F3
Nursery Cl. S Ock 176 B1
Nursery Cl. Woodf 152 A3
Nursery Dr. Brain 66 A3
Nursery Fields. Saw 77 E1
Nursery Gdns. Basil 170 B4
Nursery Rd. Bis St 67 F3
Nursery Rd. Chelm 124 A4
Nursery Rd. Corr 179 F2
Nursery Rd. Dodd 133 E3
Nursery Rd. Hod 87 D1
Nursery Rd. Lo Naz 100 B1
Nursery Rd. Lou 140 B3
Nursery Rise. Gt Dun 72 B4
Nursery Wlk. Romf 164 B3
Nutberry Ave. Grays 185 D2
Nutbrowne Rd. Dag 173 D2
Nuthatch Cl. Bill 161 E4
Nyssa Cl. Woodf 152 C2
Nyth Cl. Upm 166 B3

Oak Ave. Bill 162 B2
Oak Ave. Uph 175 D4
Oak Bungalows. Brain 65 F2
Oak Chase. Wick 163 D4
Oak Cl. Wa Aby 126 B3
Oak Dene Cl. Hornc 165 D4
Oak Dri. Saw 90 B4
Oak End. Harl 102 C3
Oak Glade. Epp 116 B1
Oak Glen. Hornc 165 F4
Oak Hill. Weth 55 D4
Oak Hill Rd. Sta Abb 143 F1
Oak Ind Park. Gt Dun 72 C3
Oak La. Bill 162 B2
Oak Lodge Ave. Chig 153 E3
Oak Lodge Tye. Bore 112 A3
Oak Piece. N W Bas 117 E3
Oak Rd. Bill 162 B2
Oak Rd. Epp 115 F1
Oak Rd. Grays 192 B4
Oak Rd. Romf 156 C1
Oak Rd. S Han 150 B3
Oak Rd. Stone 190 C1
Oak Rise. Lou 152 B4
Oak St. Bis St 67 F3
Oak St. Romf 164 B3
Oak Wood Gr. Basil 172 A3
Oakbank. Brent 147 F2
Oakdale Rd. Woodf 152 A1
Oakdene Rd. Basil 172 B4

Oakfield. Steb 63 D2
Oakhill Rd. Pur 183 D1
Oakhurst Cl. Wick 163 E3
Oakhurst Cl. Woodf 153 E1
Oakhurst Dr. Wick 163 E3
Oakhurst Gdns. Ching 139 F1
Oakland Gdns. Brent 147 E2
Oaklands Ave. Romf 164 C4
Oaklands Cl. Bis St 57 D1
Oaklands Cl. Bl Not 76 B4
Oaklands Cres. Chelm 124 A4
Oaklands Dr. Bis St 57 D1
Oaklands Dr. Harl 103 E4
Oaklands Dr. S Ock 184 B4
Oaklands Park. Bis St 57 D1
Oaklea Ave. Sprin 111 F2
Oakleigh Ct. Bis St 67 E4
Oakleigh Rise. Epp 129 D4
Oakley Cl. W Thu 191 E4
Oakley Dr. Bill 148 C3
Oakley Dr. Romf 157 D3
Oakley Rd. Brain 65 F4
Oakmoor Way. Chig 153 F3
Oakroyd Ave. Gt Dun 72 C4
Oaks Ave. Romf 155 E1
Oaks The. Bill 161 E3
Oaktree Cl. Brent 158 C4
Oakway. Grays 185 E3
Oakwood. Wa Aby 126 C3
Oakwood Ave. Brent 147 E2
Oakwood Chase. Hornc 165 F3
Oakwood Cl. Woodf 152 C2
Oakwood Hill. Lou 141 D2
Oakwood Hill Ind Est. Lou ... 141 D2
Oakwood Rd. Corr 180 A2
Oasthouse Ct. Saff W 13 E1
Oates Rd. Romf 155 D3
Ockelford Ave. Chelm 110 C3
Ockendon Rd. S Ock 176 B3
Ockendon Rd. Upm 175 F3
Ogard Rd. Hav 100 B4
Oglethorpe Rd. Dag 164 A1
Okehampton Rd. Romf 156 B2
Okehampton Sq. Romf 156 B2
Old Barns La. Ing 121 E2
Old Church Hill. Corr 170 A1
Old Church Rd. Mtssg 147 F3
Old Church Rd. Basil 172 C3
Old Church Rd. Mtssg 147 F4
Old Clements La. Hav 6 C4
Old Court Rd. Chelm 111 E2
Old Croft Cl. G Ea 95 E3
Old Crown La. Keiv H 145 E4
Old Farm Ct. Bill 149 D2
Old Forge Rd. Bore 112 C4
Old Hall La. Brent 168 B4
Old Highway. Hod 100 B4
Old Hill Ave. Corr 179 D4
Old House La. Harl 101 F3
Old House La. Lo Naz 113 F4
Old Jenkins Cl. Sta L H 179 D1
Old Mead La. Hen 48 B2
Old Mead Rd. Els 48 B2
Old Mead Rd. Hen 48 B2
Old Mill La. L Hal 78 A3
Old Mill Rd. Saff W 25 F4
Old Nazeing Rd. Lo Naz 100 A1
Old Oaks. Wa Aby 126 C4
Old Orchard. Harl 102 B3
Old Rd. Harl 90 B3
Old Rd. Nave H 144 C3
Old Rectory Rd. Sta R 131 D3
Old Rope Wlk. Hav 6 C4
Old Shire La. Wa Aby 127 D2
Old Southend Rd. Sand 138 B4
Old Station Rd. Lou 140 C2
Old Street Hill. Hat B O 79 E3
Old Vicarage The. Finch 42 B3
Oldbury Ave. Gt Bad 124 C4
Oldchurch Gdns. Romf 164 B2
Oldchurch Rd. Romf 164 C3
Oldchurch Rise. Romf 164 C2
Oldhouse Croft. Harl 89 F1
Oldwyk. Basil 171 F2
Olive St. Romf 164 B3
Oliver Cl. W Thu 190 C4
Oliver Rd. Brent 147 D2
Oliver Rd. Rain 173 F2
Oliver Rd. W Thu 191 D4
Oliver Way. Chelm 110 C4
Ollard's Gr. Lou 140 B3
Olympic Bsns Centre. Basil . 162 C1
One Tree Hill. Corr 170 C1
Ongar,Rd. Abr 142 B4
Ongar Rd. Brent 146 A1
Ongar Rd. Ch Ong 119 D4
Ongar Rd. Dodd 132 B2
Ongar Rd. Fyf 106 B1
Ongar Rd. Gt Dun 72 B3
Ongar Rd. Kelv H 132 B2
Ongar Rd. Mar Rod 94 B2
Ongar Rd. Sto M 132 C4
Ongar Rd. Writ 122 A4
Ongar Way. Rain 173 F2
Onslow Gdns. Ch Ong 119 D2
Orange St. Thax 40 A1
Orange Tree Cl. Chelm 124 B3
Orange Tree Hill. Hav B 155 F3
Orchard Ave. Bill 149 E3

Orchard Ave. Brent 158 C4
Orchard Ave. Rain 174 B1
Orchard Ave. Wick 150 C1
Orchard Cl. Gt Bad 124 B3
Orchard Cl. Hav 6 C4
Orchard Cl. New 36 C4
Orchard Cl. Ridge 20 A3
Orchard Cl. S Ock 176 B1
Orchard Cl. Saff W 25 E4
Orchard Cl. Sheer 91 E4
Orchard Cl. Sta Ab 87 E2
Orchard Cl. Writ 110 A1
Orchard Croft. Harl 90 A1
Orchard Dr. Grays 185 D2
Orchard Dr. The B 128 C2
Orchard Gdns. Wa Aby 126 B3
Orchard La. Brent 145 F2
Orchard La. Lou 152 B3
Orchard La. Saw 77 E1
Orchard Piece. Bla 133 F4
Orchard Pightle. Had 3 E3
Orchard Rd. Bis St 57 D1
Orchard Rd. Dag 173 D2
Orchard Rd. Romf 155 D1
Orchard Rd. S Ock 184 B4
Orchard Rd. Swan 191 F1
Orchard St. Chelm 111 D1
Orchard The. Wick 163 D4
Orchard Way. Chig 154 A4
Orchards N The. Epp 129 D4
Orchards S The. Epp 129 D4
Orchards The. Saw 77 F2
Orchis Gr. Grays 184 C1
Orchis Way. Romf 156 C2
Ordnance Rd. Enf 126 A1
Ordnance Rd. Grave 193 E1
Oreston Rd. Rain 174 B1
Orford Cres. Sprin 111 E3
Orford Rd. Hav 6 C3
Organ La. Ching 139 E1
Orion Ct. Basil 163 D1
Orion Way. Brain 66 A2
Orkney Cl. Hav 7 E4
Orlando Dr. Basil 163 E1
Ormonde Rise. Lou 140 B1
Orsett End. Basil 171 E4
Orsett Heath Cres. Grays ... 186 A2
Orsett Rd. Grays 185 D1
Orsett Rd. Horn H 178 C1
Orsett Terr. Woodf 152 B2
Orton Cl. Marg 136 A4
Orwell. Grays 187 E1
Osborne Cl. Hornc 165 D3
Osborne Rd. Basil 171 E3
Osborne Rd. Basil 172 C4
Osborne Rd. Brent 146 A2
Osborne Rd. Hod 100 A2
Osborne Rd. Hornc 165 E3
Osborne Rd. Lou 140 A1
Osea Way. Sprin 111 F3
Osprey Way. Chelm 124 A3
Osterley Dr. Basil 169 F3
Ottawa Gdns. Dag 173 E3
Ottawa Rd. Tilb 193 D3
Outing's Cl. Dodd 133 D2
Outwood Common Rd. Bill . 149 F1
Outwood Farm Cl. Bill 149 F1
Outwood Farm Rd. Bill 149 F1
Oval Gdns. Grays 185 E2
Oval Rd N. Dag 173 D2
Oval Rd S. Dag 173 D2
Over Hall La. Ash 4 B1
Overcliff Rd. Grays 185 E1
Overcliffe. Grave 193 D1
Ovington Gdns. Bill 149 D3
Owen Gdns. Woodf 152 C2
Owlets Hall La. Horne 165 F4
Oxcroft. Bis St 67 F2
Oxcroft Cl. Basil 170 A3
Oxendon Dri. Hod 100 A3
Oxford Ave. Grays 186 A1
Oxford Ave. Hornc 166 A4
Oxford Cl. Brent 158 B3
Oxford Cl. Sprin 111 F3
Oxford Rd. Horn H 178 C2
Oxford Rd. Romf 156 C2
Oxford Rd. Sta L H 179 D1
Oxford Rd. Woodf 152 B3
Oxley Cl. Romf 156 B1
Oxley Gdns. Corr 179 F3
Oxleys Rd. Wa Aby 127 D4
Oxleys The. Harl 90 C2
Oxlow La. Dag 173 D4
Oxney Mead. Writ 122 C4
Oxney Villas. Felst 74 B3
Oxwich Ct. Corr 180 A2
Oyster Pl. Sprin 111 F2
Ozier Ct. Saff W 25 F4
Oziers. Els 48 B1
Ozonia Ave. Wick 163 E3
Ozonia Cl. Wick 163 D3
Ozonia Way. Wick 163 E3
Ozonia Wlk. Wick 163 E3

Paceheath Cl. Romf 155 E2
Paddock Cl. Bill 161 E4
Paddock Cl. Grays 186 A4
Paddock Dr. Sprin 111 F4

Paddock Mead. Harl 102 B2
Paddock The. Bis St 67 E2
Paddock The. Hod 100 A2
Paddock The. Stock 136 C2
Paddocks The. H Rod 81 F4
Paddocks The. Ing 135 D2
Padgets The. Wa Aby 126 C3
Padham's Green Rd. Mtssg . 148 B3
Page Rd. Basil 172 C4
Pageant Cl. Tilb 193 E3
Pagel Mead. Basil 171 D3
Pages Cl. Bis St 67 E3
Pages La. Romf 157 D1
Paget Ct. Els 48 B1
Paget Dr. Bill 149 D3
Pagette Way. Grays 185 D1
Paglesfield. Brent 147 E2
Paignton Ave. Sprin 111 E3
Paines Brook Rd. Romf 156 C2
Paines Brook Way. Romf ... 156 C2
Painsford Way. Hornc 165 D2
Painswick Ave. Corr 179 F3
Pakes Way. The B 128 C1
Palace Gdns. Lou 140 B1
Palatine Park. Basil 169 F3
Paley Gdns. Lou 141 E3
Paling Way. Grays 185 D3
Palm Cl. Chelm 124 B3
Palm Rd. Corr 171 D1
Palm Rd. Romf 164 B3
Palmer's Ave. Grays 185 E1
Palmers. Corr 179 F2
Palmers Croft. Sprin 112 A1
Palmers Dr. Grays 185 E1
Palmers Gr. Lo Naz 100 C1
Palmers Hill. Epp 116 A1
Palmers La. Chris 10 B2
Palmers La. Bis St 67 F4
Palmerston Gdns. Grays 184 B1
Palmerston Rd. Grays 184 B1
Palmerston Rd. Lou 140 B1
Palmerston Rd. Rain 174 B2
Pamela Gdns. Bis St 67 F2
Pamplins. Basil 170 C3
Pan La. E Han 138 C3
Pan Wlk. Chelm 110 B3
Panadown. Basil 170 C3
Pancroft. Abr 142 A3
Panfield La. Brain 65 F3
Panfields. Basil 170 A3
Paprills. Basil 170 C3
Parade The. Brent 158 B4
Paradise Rd. Wa Aby 126 B3
Paradise Rd. Writ 123 D4
Paringdon Rd. Harl 102 B2
Parish Cl. Hornc 165 D1
Park Ave. Bis St 67 F2
Park Ave. Brent 147 E1
Park Ave. Chelm 110 C2
Park Ave. Harl 103 E3
Park Ave. Upm 166 C2
Park Ave. W Thu 191 D4
Park Ave. Woodf 152 A3
Park Bvd. Romf 155 F1
Park Cl. N W Bas 117 D2
Park Cl. Wick 163 E3
Park Cres. Hornc 165 D2
Park Ct. Harl 89 E1
Park Dr. Dag 164 B1
Park Dr. Hat B O 79 D1
Park Dr. Ing 135 E2
Park Dr. Romf 164 C4
Park Dr. Upm 175 E4
Park Dr. Wick 163 E3
Park End Rd. Romf 164 C4
Park Farm La. Nut 21 E1
Park Farm Rd. Upm 175 D3
Park Fields. Roy 101 D4
Park Gate Rd. Corr 180 A4
Park Hill. Harl 90 A2
Park Hill. Lou 140 B2
Park La. Ave 183 E3
Park La. Bart 5 F2
Park La. Bis St 67 F2
Park La. Brent 159 E2
Park La. Harl 89 E1
Park La. Hornc 165 D2
Park La. Hornc 174 A3
Park La. Langl 22 A2
Park La. Ple 83 F2
Park La. S Han 150 B2
Park La. Saff W 13 E1
Park La. Topp 32 A4
Park Mead. Harl 89 D1
Park Meadow. Dodd 133 F1
Park Pl. Grave 193 E1
Park Rd. Brent 158 A4
Park Rd. Chelm 111 D1
Park Rd. Corr 180 A2
Park Rd. Els 48 B1
Park Rd. Grays 185 D1
Park Rd. Gt C 1 C3
Park Rd. Hav 6 B4
Park Rd. Hod 100 A3
Park Rd. Lit Ea 60 C2
Park Rd. Ple 83 F2
Park Rd. Sta L H 179 D1
Park Rd. Stan M 57 F3
Park Rd. Swan 191 F1

Park Side. Basil 172 A4
Park Side. Bill 149 E1
Park Side. Lou 152 A4
Park Side. Steb 62 B3
Park St. Thax 40 A1
Park Terr. Swan 191 E1
Park View. Ave 183 E3
Park View. Hod 100 A3
Park View Cres. Gt Bad 124 C3
Park View Gdns. Grays 185 D1
Park Way. Brent 146 C1
Parker Ave. Tilb 193 E3
Parker Cl. Chelm 111 E1
Parker Rd. Grays 184 C1
Parker's Farm Rd. Horn H .. 177 F3
Parkes Rd. Chig 153 F3
Parkhall Rd. Gos 55 F4
Parkhill Cl. Hornc 165 E1
Parkhill Rd. Ching 139 E1
Parkhurst Rd. Basil 172 A3
Parkland Ave. Romf 155 F1
Parkland Ave. Upm 175 D4
Parkland Cl. Hod 87 D1
Parkland Rd. Woodf 152 A2
Parkland Way. Ch Ong 118 C1
Parklands. Bill 149 D2
Parklands. Chig 153 E4
Parklands. Epp 116 B1
Parklands. Wa Aby 126 B3
Parklands Cl. Chig 153 E4
Parklands Dr. Sprin 111 E2
Parklards Way. Chelm 124 B1
Parkmead. Lou 141 D2
Parkmill Cl. Corr 180 A2
Parkmore Cl. Woodf 152 A3
Parkside. Grays 185 F2
Parkside Ave. Romf 155 F1
Parkside Ave. Tilb 193 D3
Parkstone Ave. Hornc 165 E3
Parkstone Ave. Wick 162 C4
Parkway. Bart 5 E3
Parkway. Chelm 111 D1
Parkway. Corr 180 B3
Parkway. Grays 186 A4
Parkway. Romf 155 F1
Parkway. Saw 77 F1
Parkway. Woodf 152 B3
Parnall Rd. Harl 102 B2
Parndon Mill La. Harl 89 D3
Parndon Wood Rd. Harl 102 B2
Parrock St. Grave 193 D1
Parrotts Field. Hod 100 A4
Parry Cl. Corr 179 E2
Parsloe Rd. Harl 102 A2
Parsloes Ave. Dag 173 D3
Parsonage Cl. Broom 98 A1
Parsonage Farm La. Gt Sam . 29 D2
Parsonage Field. Dodd 133 E1
Parsonage La. Barn 73 E2
Parsonage La. Birhr 57 F2
Parsonage La. Bis St 68 B4
Parsonage La. Clav 35 D2
Parsonage La. Gt Wal 84 C1
Parsonage La. Marg 136 A4
Parsonage Leys. Harl 102 C4
Parsonage Rd. Rain 174 B1
Parsonage Rd. Take 70 B4
Parsonage Rd. W Thu 191 E4
Partridge Ave. Chelm 110 C3
Partridge Green. Basil 172 A3
Partridge Rd. Harl 102 C3
Parvills. Wa Aby 126 B3
Paschal Way. Gt Bad 124 C4
Pasfield. Wa Aby 126 B3
Paske Ave. Hav 6 C4
Paslowes. Basil 171 F2
Passingham Ave. Bill 161 E3
Passingham Cl. Bill 161 E3
Patching Hall La. Chelm 111 D4
Paternoster Cl. Basil 126 C3
Paternoster Hill. Wa Aby ... 126 C4
Paternoster Row. Hav B 144 B1
Pathways. Basil 171 F3
Patmore Cl. Bis St 67 E4
Patmore Fields. Ugl 47 F3
Patmore Rd. Wa Aby 126 C3
Patmore Way. Romf 155 D3
Patricia Dr. Corr 180 B4
Patricia Dr. Hornc 165 E2
Patricia Gdns. Bill 161 E4
Patricia Gdns. Bis St 67 F3
Pattiswick Cnr. Basil 171 F4
Pattiswick Sq. Basil 171 F4
Pattocks. Basil 171 F3
Paul's Rd. Basil 170 B4
Pauline Gdns. Bill 148 C2
Pauls La. Hod 100 A3
Pavet Cl. Dag 173 D3
Pavilion La. Marg 7 D4
Pawle Cl. Gt Bad 125 D4
Paxfords. Basil 169 F3
Paycock Rd. Harl 102 A3
Paycocke Cl. Basil 162 C1
Paycocke Rd. Basil 162 C1
Paynes La. Lo Naz 113 E4
Paynters Hill. Basil 171 F2
Paynters Mead. Basil 171 F2
Pea La. Upm 176 A3
Peacock Cl. Hornc 165 F4

Peacock St. Grave 193 E1
Peacocks. Harl 101 F3
Peal Rd. Saff W 25 F4
Pear Tree Mead. Harl 103 D3
Pearmain Cl. Runw 151 E1
Pearsons. Corr 179 F2
Peartree Cl. Dodd 133 E1
Peartree Cl. S Ock 176 B2
Peartree Cl.. Brain 66 A1
Peartree Gdns. Romf 155 D1
Peartree La. Dodd 133 E1
Peartree La. Horn H 168 C1
Peartrees. Brent 159 E2
Pease Cl. Hornc 174 A3
Peaslands Rd. Saff W 25 F4
Pebmarsh Dr. Wick 163 F3
Peck's Hill. Lo Naz 100 C1
Pedlars End. More 105 E1
Peel Cres. Brain 65 F2
Peel Dr. Woodf 152 C1
Peel Pl. Woodf 152 C1
Peel Rd. Sprin 111 F2
Peel Way. Romf 156 C1
Peerage Way. Hornc 165 F2
Pegasus Way. Brain 65 F3
Pegelm Gdns. Hornc 165 F2
Peggotty Cl. Chelm 110 C3
Peggy's Wlk. Litt 12 C2
Peldon Pavement. Basil 171 E4
Pelham Pl. Corr 179 F2
Pelham Rd. Clav 35 E2
Pemberton Ave. Ing 135 D2
Pemberton Ave. Romf 165 D4
Pembrey Way. Hornc 174 B3
Pembroke Ave. Corr 180 A2
Pembroke Cl. Bill 149 D3
Pembroke Cl. Hornc 166 A4
Pembroke Gdns. Dag 164 A1
Pembroke Mews. Basil 172 B4
Pembroke Pl. Chelm 111 D4
Pendine. Corr 180 A2
Pendle Cl. Basil 163 D1
Pendle Dr. Basil 162 C1
Penerley Rd. Rain 182 A4
Penhurst Rd. Woodf 153 D2
Peniston Wlk. Romf 156 B2
Penlow Rd. Harl 102 B3
Penn Cl. Grays 178 A1
Penn Gdns. Romf 155 D2
Pennine Rd. Chelm 110 B3
Pennington Cl. Romf 155 D3
Pennington La. Stan M 47 E1
Penningtons. Bis St 67 E3
Penny Cl. Rain 174 A1
Penny La. Corr 179 F2
Penny's La. Marg 135 F4
Pennyfields. Brent 158 B3
Pennymead. Harl 90 A1
Pennystone Rd. Saff W 25 F4
Penrith Cres. Hornc 174 A4
Penrith Rd. Chig 153 F2
Penrith Rd. Romf 157 D2
Penshurst. Harl 90 B2
Penticton Rd. Brain 65 E1
Pentire Cl. Upm 166 C3
Pentland Ave. Chelm 111 D3
Pentlow Hawke Cl. Hav 7 D4
Pentlow Way. Lou 140 C1
Pentney Rd. Ching 139 E1
Penwood Cl. Bill 149 E3
Penzance Cl. Sprin 111 F3
Penzance Gdns. Romf 157 D2
Penzance Rd. Romf 157 D2
Peony Cl. Brent 146 A2
Pepper Hill. Gt Am 87 D2
Pepples La. Wim 27 D1
Pepys Cl. Stone 190 A2
Pepys Cl. Tilb 193 E3
Percival Rd. Hornc 165 E3
Percy Rd. Romf 164 B4
Percy St. Grays 192 B4
Percys. Basil 172 A3
Peregrine Rd. Wa Aby 127 D3
Peregrine Cl. Basil 171 D2
Peregrine Cl. Bis St 67 E3
Peregrine Dr. Chelm 124 A2
Peregrine Rd. Chig 154 A3
Peregrine Wlk. Rain 174 A3
Perriclose. Sprin 111 E4
Perrin Pl. Chelm 111 D1
Perry Cl. Rain 173 E2
Perry Gr. Stone 190 A2
Perry Green. Basil 171 D4
Perry Hill. Lo Naz 113 F4
Perry Hill. Sprin 111 E2
Perry Rd. Harl 102 B2
Perry Spring. Basil 171 E3
Perry Spring. Harl 103 E3
Perry St. Bill 149 E3
Perry Way. Ave 183 E3
Perryfield. Match 92 B1
Pertwee Dr. Gt Bad 124 C3
Peter St. Stock 136 C1
Peterborough Ave. Upm 166 C2
Peterborough Way. Basil 171 F4
Petersfield. Chelm 111 D4
Petersfield Ave. Romf 156 C3
Petersfield Cl. Romf 157 D2

Peterswood. Harl 102 B2
Petlands. Saff W 13 F4
Petre Cl. Horn H 168 B3
Petre Cl. Ing 135 D1
Petrebrook. Sprin 112 A2
Petrel Way. Chelm 124 B3
Petresfield Way. Horn H 168 B3
Pettit's Pl. Dag 173 D4
Pettit's Rd. Dag 173 D4
Pettits Bvd. Romf 155 F1
Pettits Cl. Romf 155 F1
Pettits La. Romf 164 C4
Pettits La N. Romf 155 F1
Pettley Gdns. Romf 164 B3
Petts La. Saff W 13 F4
Petunia Cres. Sprin 111 F3
Petworth Way. Hornc 173 F4
Peverells. Wim 26 B1
Phelips Rd. Harl 102 A2
Philan Way. Romf 155 E2
Philip Ave. Romf 164 B2
Philip Cl. Brent 146 A2
Philip Rd. Rain 173 F1
Philippa Way. Grays 186 A1
Philips Cl. Ray 64 C1
Philips Rd. Ray 64 C1
Phillida Rd. Romf 157 D1
Phillips Chase. Brain 66 A3
Philpot End La. Gt Dun 72 A2
Phoenix Gr. Chelm 124 A4
Pick Hill. Wa Aby 127 D4
Pickwick Ave. Chelm 110 B3
Pickwick Close. Basil 170 B4
Pier Rd. Grave 192 C1
Piercing Hill. The B 128 B2
Pierrefitte Way. Brain 65 F2
Pig La. Bis St 68 A2
Piggotts Way. Bis St 67 F3
Pightle The. Finch 42 B3
Pightle The. Hav 7 D4
Pigstye Green Rd. Will 121 D4
Pike La. Upm 175 F4
Pike Way. N W Bas 117 D2
Pilgrim Cl. Brain 65 F3
Pilgrim's La. Dodd 145 E3
Pilgrims Cl. Bill 149 D1
Pilgrims Cl. Brent 145 F2
Pilgrims Cl. Gt C 1 B1
Pilgrims La. Grays 184 B2
Pilgrims Wlk. Bill 149 D1
Pilgrims' Rd. Swan 191 F2
Pimpernel Way. Romf 156 B2
Pincey Rd. Take 58 C1
Pinchpools Rd. Man 47 D2
Pindar Rd. Hod 100 B4
Pine Cl. Ing 135 E2
Pine Cl. Wick 163 E3
Pine Cres. Brent 147 E2
Pine Dr. Ing 135 E2
Pine Gr. Bis St 68 A3
Pinecourt. Upm 175 D4
Pinecroft. Romf 147 D1
Pinelands. Bis St 56 C1
Pines Hill. Stan M 57 E3
Pines Rd. Chelm 110 B3
Pines The. Bill 161 E1
Pines The. Grays 185 D3
Pines The. Woodf 152 A4
Pinewood Ave. Rain 174 A1
Pinewood Cl. Harl 103 E4
Pinewood Cl. Sta L H 187 D2
Pinewood Rd. Hav B 155 E3
Pinewood Way. Brent 147 E2
Pinkeneys. Hey 10 B3
Pinkney Cl. Brain 66 A2
Pinmill. Basil 171 E3
Pinnacles. Wa Aby 126 C3
Pintail Rd. Woodf 152 A2
Pintails. Basil 172 B3
Pipchin Rd. Chelm 110 C3
Piper's Tye. Chelm 124 B2
Piperell Way. Hav 7 D3
Pipers Cl. Hav 7 E4
Pipps Hill Cl. Basil 162 A1
Pipps Hill Rd. Basil 162 A1
Pipps Hill Rd N. Bill 162 A1
Pishiobury Dri. Saw 90 B4
Pitcairn Cl. Romf 164 A4
Pitsea Rd. Basil 172 A3
Pitsea View Rd. Bill 162 B2
Pitseaville Gr. Basil 171 F3
Pitt Chase. Gt Bad 124 C3
Pittfields. Basil 170 A3
Pittman Cl. Brent 159 E3
Pittman's Field. Harl 89 F1
Place Farm La. Kelv H 133 D1
Plain The. Epp 116 A1
Plains Field. Brain 66 B1
Plaistow Cl. Corr 179 E1
Plane Tree Cl. Chelm 124 A3
Plantation Cl. Saff W 25 F3
Plantation Rd. Bore 99 F1
Plashet Cl. Corr 179 E1
Plashet Gdns. Brent 159 D3
Plashets. Saw 78 B1
Plashetts. Basil 171 E4
Platford Green. Hornc 165 F4

Plaw Hatch Cl. Bis St 68 A4
Playfield Ave. Romf 155 E1
Playhouse Sq. Harl 102 B4
Pleasant Rd. Bis St 67 F4
Pleasant Valley. Saff W 25 E4
Pleshey Cl. Wick 163 F3
Pleshey Rd. Gt Wal 84 A3
Plough Rise. Upm 166 C2
Plover Gdns. Upm 166 C2
Plover Wlk. Chelm 124 A2
Plovers Barron. Bla 133 E2
Plovers Mead. Bla 133 E2
Ployters Rd. Harl 102 B2
Plumberow. Basil 170 C3
Plumleys. Basil 172 A4
Plumpton Ave. Hornc 165 F1
Plumpton Rd. Hod 100 B4
Plums La. Ba Sal 53 F2
Plumtree Ave. Gt Bad 124 C3
Plumtree Mead. Lou 141 D3
Plymouth Rd. Sprin 111 F3
Pocklington Cl. Sprin 112 A2
Pods La. Ray 64 B1
Pole Hill Rd. Ching 139 E1
Poley Rd. Sta L H 179 E1
Pollard Cl. Chig 154 A3
Pollard Hatch. Harl 102 A3
Pollards Cl. Lou 140 B2
Pollards Green. Sprin 111 F1
Pollards Villas. Ba Sal 53 E1
Polsteads. Basil 171 F2
Pomfret Mead. Basil 171 D3
Pompadour Cl. Brent 158 B3
Pond Cross Farm. New 37 D4
Pond Cross Way. New 37 D4
Pond Wlk. Upm 166 C1
Pondfield La. Brent 159 D4
Pondfield Rd. Dag 173 D4
Ponds Rd. Chelm 124 A1
Pontypool Wlk. Romf 156 B2
Pool's La. Hav 121 F2
Poole Rd. Hornc 165 F2
Poore St. Arkes 36 A4
Poore Rd. Wic Bon 36 A4
Popes Cres. Basil 172 A3
Poplar Cl. Bla 133 F4
Poplar Cl. Chelm 124 B3
Poplar Cl. Ing 135 D1
Poplar Dr. Brent 147 E2
Poplar Row. The B 128 C1
Poplar Shaw. Wa Aby 126 C3
Poplar St. Romf 164 B4
Poplars The. Abr 142 A3
Poppy Cl. Brent 146 A2
Poppy Green. Bore 112 A3
Porchester Cl. Hornc 165 F3
Porchester Rd. Bill 149 D3
Pork Hall La. Gt Le 86 A3
Port Ave. Swan 191 D1
Port La. L Hal 68 A1
Porter Cl. Grays 191 E4
Porters. Basil 172 B4
Porters Cl. Brent 146 A1
Portland Cl. Brain 66 A2
Portland Pl. Bis St 67 F4
Portland Rd. Bis St 67 F4
Portland Rd. Grave 192 B1
Portman Dr. Bill 149 D3
Portman Dr. Woodf 152 B1
Portmore Gdns. Romf 155 D3
Portnoi Cl. Romf 155 E1
Portreath Pl. Chelm 111 D4
Portsea Rd. Tilb 193 E3
Post Meadow. Bill 161 E3
Post Office Rd. Chelm 111 D4
Post Office Rd. Harl 89 E1
Post Office Rd. Ing 135 D2
Potash Rd. Bill 149 E3
Potash Rd. Match 92 B2
Potter St. Bis St 67 F4
Potter St. Harl 103 E3
Potters Cl. Lou 140 C4
Potters Field. Harl 103 E3
Pottery La. Chelm 111 D3
Poulteney Rd. Stan M 57 F4
Pound Cl. Lo Naz 113 F4
Pound Fields. Writ 123 D4
Pound Gate. Steb 62 B3
Pound La. Basil 170 B4
Pound La. Basil 172 C4
Pound La Cent. Bill 161 E1
Pound La. Grays 178 A1
Pound La N. Bill 161 E1
Pound Wlk. Saff W 13 F1
Poundfield Rd. Lou 141 D2
Powdermill La. Wa Aby 126 A3
Powdermill Way. Wa Aby 126 A3
Powell Gdns. Dag 173 D4
Powell Rd. Basil 170 A4
Powell Rd. Lou 140 B1
Poynder Rd. Tilb 193 D3
Poynings Way. Romf 156 C1
Pratts Farm La. Lit Wal 98 B2
Precinct The. Sta L H 179 E1
Premier Ave. Grays 185 E2
Prentice Pl. Harl 103 E3
Prescott. Basil 170 B2
Prescott Cl. Hornc 165 D2
Prescott Green. Lou 141 E3

Preston Rd. Romf 156 B3
Prestwick Dr. Bis St 57 D1
Prestwood Dr. Romf 155 E3
Pretoria Cres. Ching 139 E1
Pretoria Rd. Ching 139 E1
Pretoria Rd. Romf 164 B3
Priest's La. Brent 158 C4
Priestley Ct. Grays 185 E1
Priests Ave. Romf 155 E1
Priests Field. Brent 159 E3
Primary La. Saw 78 B1
Primrose Cl. Basil 170 A2
Primrose Field. Harl 102 C3
Primrose Glen. Hornc 165 F4
Primrose Hill. Brent 158 B4
Primrose Hill. Chelm 110 C2
Primrose Hill. Hav 6 C4
Primrose Rd. Woodf 152 A1
Primula Way. Bore 112 A3
Prince Charles Ave. Grays .. 178 A1
Prince Edward Rd. Bill 149 E1
Prince Philip Ave. Grays 185 D3
Prince's Rd. Nave H 145 D4
Princes Ave. Corr 180 A2
Princes Ave. Woodf 152 B3
Princes Cl. Bill 149 E3
Princes Cl. N W Bas 117 E3
Princes Cl. Bill 149 E3
Princes Gate. Bis St 67 E4
Princes Mews. Bill 149 E3
Princes Park. Rain 174 A3
Princes Rd. Chelm 124 A4
Princes Rd. Lou 152 B4
Princes Rd. Romf 165 D3
Princes St. Grave 193 D1
Princes Way. Brent 147 D1
Princes Way. Lou 152 B4
Princesfield Rd. Wa Aby 127 D3
Princess Ave. Grays 187 E1
Princess Margaret Rd. Grays 187 D1
Princess Way. Hav 6 C4
Printers Way. Harl 90 A3
Prior Chase. Grays 184 C1
Priors Cl. Basil 171 E3
Priors East. Basil 171 E3
Priors Pk. Hornc 165 E1
Priors Wood Rd. Take 70 B4
Priory Ave. Harl 90 B3
Priory Ave. Hav 6 C4
Priory Cl. Brent 146 A2
Priory Cl. Chelm 110 C1
Priory Cl. Hinx 1 A2
Priory Cl. Hod 100 A3
Priory Cl. Woodf 152 A1
Priory Ct. Harl 103 D3
Priory Dr. Stan M 57 F3
Priory Gr. Romf 156 C4
Priory Mead. Dodd 133 E2
Priory Path. Romf 156 C4
Priory Rd. Corr 179 F2
Priory Rd. Lou 140 C3
Priory Rd. Romf 156 C4
Priory The. Bill 149 E3
Priory The. Writ 110 A1
Proctors Way. Bis St 68 A2
Progress Ct. Brain 65 F2
Prospect Ave. Sta L H 187 E4
Prospect Pl. Grave 193 E1
Prospect Pl. Grays 192 A4
Prospect Pl. Romf 155 E1
Prospect Pl. Saff W 13 F1
Prospect Rd. Horne 165 F4
Prospect Rd. Woodf 152 B3
Prospect Way. Brent 147 F3
Providence St. Stone 191 D1
Provident Sq. Chelm 111 E1
Prower Cl. Bill 149 D1
Prykes Dr. Chelm 111 D1
Pryors Cl. Bis St 68 A3
Pryors Rd. Chelm 124 B1
Puckleside. Basil 170 B2
Pudding La. Chig 141 F1
Pugh Pl. Corr 179 E2
Pump Hill. Gt Bad 124 C4
Pump Hill. Lou 140 C4
Pump La. Ep Gr 115 D4
Pump La. Ple 83 F1
Pump La. Sprin 111 F3
Pump St. Corr 179 D1
Purbeck Ct. Gt Bad 124 C3
Purbeck Rd. Hornc 165 D2
Purcell Cl. Basil 170 B4
Purcell Cl. Corr 179 E2
Purcell Cole. Writ 110 A1
Purcell Way. Corr 179 E2
Purfleet By-Ps. W Thu 183 C1
Purfleet Rd. Ave 183 D3
Purford Green. Harl 103 D4
Purleigh Ave. Woodf 152 C2
Purleigh Cl. Basil 163 E1
Purley Cl. Woodf 153 D1
Purlieu Way. The B 128 C2
Pyenest Rd. Harl 102 A3
Pygot Pl. Brain 65 F2
Pym Pl. Grays 185 D1
Pyms Rd. Chelm 124 A2
Pynchbek. Bis St 67 F2
Pynchon Paddocks. L Hal 78 B4

Pyne Gate. Chelm 124 A1
Pynest Green La. Wa Aby ... 127 D1
Pyrles La. Lou 141 D4
Pytt Field. Harl 103 D4

Quadrant The. W Thu 183 E1
Quaker La. Wa Aby 126 B3
Quaker's La. Hav 7 D4
Quarles Cl. Romf 155 D2
Quarry Hill. Grays 185 D1
Quarry Mews. Pur 183 D1
Quarry Spring. Harl 103 D4
Quarry Way. W Thu 190 C4
Quebec Rd. Tilb 193 D3
Queen Edith Dr. Ste B 18 A3
Queen Elizabeth Ave. Grays 187 E1
Queen Elizabeth Dr. Corr ... 179 F2
Queen Elizabeth Rd. Tilb 193 D2
Queen Mary Ave. Grays 187 E1
Queen Mary Cl. Romf 164 C3
Queen St. Brent 158 B3
Queen St. Chelm 111 D1
Queen St. Fyf 106 C1
Queen St. Grave 193 D1
Queen St. Romf 164 B3
Queen's Alley. Epp 128 C4
Queen's Ave. Woodf 152 A3
Queen's Cl. Saw 77 F2
Queen's Cl. Stan M 57 F4
Queen's Dri. Cres 126 A3
Queen's Gdns. Pan 65 D4
Queen's Grove Rd. Ching ... 139 E1
Queen's Rd. Brent 158 B4
Queen's Rd. Chelm 111 E1
Queen's Rd. Lou 152 B4
Queenborough La. Brain 76 B4
Queens Cres. Bis St 67 E3
Queens Gate Mews. Bill 148 C3
Queens Gdns. Rain 173 E2
Queens Gdns. Upm 166 C3
Queens Park Ave. Bill 149 D3
Queens Park Rd. Romf 157 D1
Queens Rd. Bill 161 E1
Queens Rd. Bill 162 A2
Queens Rd. Brain 65 F3
Queens Rd. Lou 140 C3
Queens Rd. N W Bas 117 D3
Queens St. Hav 7 D4
Queens Wlk. Ching 139 E1
Queensland Cres. Chelm 110 C3
Queenstown Gdns. Rain 173 F1
Queensway. Ch Ong 118 C3
Queensway. Hav 6 C4
Queenswood Ave. Brent 147 E2
Quendon Dri. Wa Aby 126 B3
Quendon Rd. Basil 171 F4
Quennell Way. Brent 147 E1
Quickset Rd. Elm 11 E3
Quickside Hill. Arkes 23 F1
Quilp Dr. Chelm 110 C4
Quilters Cl. Basil 171 E4
Quilters Straight. Basil 171 E4
Quince Tree. S Ock 176 B1
Quinion Cl. Chelm 110 B4
Quinton Way. Wa Aby 126 B2
Quorn The. Ing 135 D2

Rachael Clarke Cl. Corr 179 F2
Radburn Cl. Harl 103 D2
Radburn Pl. Swan 191 F1
Radford Cres. Bill 149 D2
Radford Ct. Bill 149 D2
Radford Way. Bill 149 D2
Radley Green Rd. Rox 121 E4
Radley Green Rd. Will 121 E4
Radley's La. Woodf 152 A1
Radleys Mead. Dag 173 D3
Radwinter Ave. Wick 163 E3
Radwinter Rd. Ash 15 D4
Radwinter Rd. Saff W 14 A1
Radwinter Rd. Saff W 14 C1
Rahn Rd. Epp 129 D4
Raider Cl. Romf 155 D1
Railey Rd. Saff W 25 F4
Railway App. Basil 170 A3
Railway Cotts. Wen A 24 C3
Railway Sq. Chelm 111 D2
Railway St. Brain 66 A2
Railway St. Chelm 111 D2
Railway St. Grays 192 A4
Rainbow La. Sta L H 179 F1
Rainbow Rd. Match 91 F2
Rainham Rd. Dag 173 F3
Rainham Rd. Dag 164 A1
Rainham Rd S. Dag 173 E4
Rainsford Ave. Chelm 110 C2
Rainsford La. Chelm 110 C1
Rainsford Rd. Chelm 110 C2
Rainsford Rd. Stan M 57 F4
Ram Gorse. Harl 89 D1
Ramsay Dr. Basil 171 F2
Ramsden Dr. Romf 155 D2
Ramsden Park Rd. Wick 150 B1
Ramsden View Rd. Wick 162 C3
Ramsey Gdns. Romf 156 B1
Ramshaw Dr. Sprin 111 F2
Rana Ct. Brain 65 F2
Rana Dr. Brain 65 F2

Randall Cl. Gt Dun 61 E1
Randall Dr. Hornc 165 E1
Randalls Dr. Brent 147 F2
Randolph Ave. Finch 43 E3
Rands Rd. H Rod 81 F4
Randulph Terr. Sprin 111 E2
Ranger's Rd. Ching 140 A1
Ranger's Rd. Lou 140 A1
Rantree Fold. Basil 170 C2
Ranworth Ave. Hod 87 D1
Raphael Ave. Tilb 193 D4
Raphael Dr. Sprin 111 F4
Raphael.Ave. Romf 164 C4
Raphaels. Basil 170 C3
Rapier Cl. Pur 183 D1
Rathmore Rd. Grave 193 D1
Ratty's La. Hod 100 B3
Ravel Gdns. Ave 183 E4
Ravel Rd. Ave 183 E4
Raven Cl. Bill 148 C2
Raven Cres. Bill 148 C2
Raven La. Bill 148 C2
Raven Rd. Woodf 152 B1
Ravencroft. Grays 186 A2
Ravens Cres. Felst 74 C3
Ravensbourne Cres. Romf ... 165 F4
Ravensbourne Dr. Chelm 110 C1
Ravensbourne Gdns. Woodf . 153 D1
Ravenscourt Dr. Basil 171 F3
Ravenscourt Dr. Hornc 165 F1
Ravenscourt Gr. Hornc 165 F1
Ravensdale. Basil 171 D2
Ravensfield. Basil 171 F3
Ravensmere. Epp 116 A1
Ravenswood Cl. Romf 155 D3
Rawdon Dri. Hod 100 A3
Ray Lodge Rd. Woodf 152 B2
Ray Mead. Gt Wal 97 F4
Ray Rd. Romf 155 D3
Ray The. Sprin 111 F3
Rayburn Rd. Hornc 166 A2
Rayfield. Epp 116 A1
Rayfield Cl. Barn 73 D2
Rayleigh Cl. Brain 66 B2
Rayleigh Cl. Brent 147 E2
Rayleigh Rd. Brent 147 E2
Rayleigh Rd. Sta L H 179 D1
Rayleigh Rd. Woodf 152 B2
Rayley La. N W Bas 117 D4
Raymond Gdns. Chig 154 A4
Rayne Rd. Brain 65 E2
Raynham Rd. Bis St 68 B4
Rayside. Basil 171 E3
Read Ct. Wa Aby 127 D3
Readers Ct. Gt Bad 124 C3
Readings The. Harl 102 C3
Rebecca Meade. Gt Ea 60 C4
Recreation Ave. Corr 180 B2
Recreation Ave. Romf 156 C1
Recreation Ave. Romf 164 B3
Recreation Ave. Romf 165 F4
Recreation Ground. Stan M ... 57 F3
Recreation Rd. Hav 6 C4
Recreation Wlk. S Han 150 B3
Rectory Chase. Brent 167 F4
Rectory Chase. Dodd 133 E1
Rectory Cl. Hun 88 B4
Rectory Cl. Ing 135 D2
Rectory Cl. Lit Wal 98 B3
Rectory Cl. Litt 12 C2
Rectory Cl. Stock 136 B1
Rectory Cl. Thor 67 E2
Rectory Ct. Basil 172 B4
Rectory Field. Harl 102 A3
Rectory Gdns. Basil 172 B3
Rectory Gdns. Upm 166 C1
Rectory Gr. Wick 163 F4
Rectory La. Ash 4 A1
Rectory La. Chelm 111 D2
Rectory La. Far 56 B3
Rectory La. Gt Le 85 E4
Rectory La. Harl 102 A3
Rectory La. Lou 141 D3
Rectory Park Dr. Basil 172 A3
Rectory Rd. Basil 172 B3
Rectory Rd. Bill 160 C2
Rectory Rd. Dag 173 D3
Rectory Rd. Grays 185 E1
Rectory Rd. Grays 186 A4
Rectory Rd. Grays 186 B1
Rectory Rd. Sta L H 179 E1
Rectory Rd. Writ 123 D4
Rectory Wood. Harl 89 E1
Red Lion Cres. Harl 103 E3
Red Lion Ct. Bis St 68 A4
Red Lion La. Harl 103 E3
Red Oaks Mead. The B 128 B1
Red Rd. Brent 158 A3
Red White and Blue Rd. Bis St 57 D1
Red Willow. Harl 101 F3
Redbury Cl. Rain 174 A1
Redcar Rd. Romf 156 C3
Redcliff Rd. Chelm 111 D1
Redden Court Rd. Romf .. 165 F4
Reddings Cl. Saff W 25 F4
Redfern Gdns. Romf 156 B1
Redgates La. Saff W 14 C2
Redgates Pl. Sprin 111 F2

Redgrave Rd. Basil 171 F2
Redinge The. Bill 161 E4
Redings The. Upm 166 B3
Redlei Cl. Corr 179 E2
Redmayne Dr. Chelm 124 A4
Redrick La. H Wy 89 F3
Redricks La. Saw 90 C4
Redriff Rd. Romf 155 D1
Redrose La. Bla 120 C1
Redruth Cl. Sprin 111 F3
Redruth Gdns. Romf 156 C3
Redruth Rd. Romf 156 C3
Redruth Wlk. Romf 156 C3
Redvers Cl. Bis St 57 D1
Redwing Dr. Bill 161 E4
Redwood Cl. Woodf 152 A4
Redwood Dr. Writ 109 F1
Redwood Gdns. Chig 154 A3
Reed Pond Wlk. Basil 170 A2
Reed Pond Wlk. Romf 156 A1
Reede Gdns. Dag 173 D4
Reede Rd. Dag 173 D3
Reede Way. Dag 173 D3
Reedings Way. Saw 77 F2
Reeds La. Hav 7 D4
Reeds Way. Wick 163 E4
Reeves Cl. Sto M 133 D3
Reeves La. Roy 101 E3
Regan Cl. Corr 179 F2
Regarder Rd. Romf 154 A3
Regarth Ave. Romf 164 C3
Regency Cl. Bis St 67 F4
Regency Cl. Chig 153 E3
Regency Cl. Runw 151 E1
Regency Cl. Sprin 111 E2
Regency Ct. Brent 158 B4
Regency Ct. Harl 103 D3
Regency Gdns. Hornc 165 E2
Regent Cl. Grays 185 E2
Regent Rd. Epp 115 F1
Regina Rd. Chelm 111 E2
Reginald Rd. Romf 157 D1
Rembrandt Gr. Sprin 111 F3
Renacres. Basil 170 C2
Rennie Rd. Chelm 111 E1
Renoir Pl. Sprin 111 F4
Renown Cl. Romf 155 D1
Repton Ave. Romf 165 D4
Repton Cl. Basil 163 D1
Repton Dr. Romf 165 D4
Repton Gdns. Romf 165 D4
Repton Gr. Woodf 152 C1
Repulse Cl. Romf 155 D1
Retford Cl. Romf 157 D2
Retford Path. Romf 157 D2
Retford Rd. Romf 157 D2
Retreat The. Brent 146 A1
Retreat The. Brent 147 D2
Retreat The. Grays 192 A4
Retreat Way. Chig 154 A4
Rettendon Gdns. Runw 151 F1
Rettendon View. Wick 163 F4
Reubens Rd. Brent 147 D2
Review Rd. Dag 173 D2
Reynard Ct. Gt Bad 124 C3
Rhodes Ave. Bis St 67 F3
Ribble Cl. Woodf 152 B2
Rich Cl. Gt Le 85 F4
Richards Ave. Romf 164 B3
Richmond Cl. Bis St 67 E4
Richmond Rd. Ching 139 E1
Richmond Rd. Grays 185 E1
Richmond Rd. Romf 164 C3
Richmond Rd. Runw 151 E1
Richmond Rd. Sprin 112 A2
Ricketts Dr. Bill 148 C2
Rickling. Basil 171 F2
Rickling Green Rd. Quen 36 C1
Rickling Rd. Wic Bon 36 A3
Riddings La. Harl 103 D2
Ridgeway. Bill 161 D4
Ridgeway. Brent 147 D1
Ridgeway. Grays 185 F1
Ridgeway. Ing 135 D1
Ridgeway. Woodf 152 B3
Ridgeway The. Brain 66 A1
Ridgeway The. Ching 139 E1
Ridgeway The. Romf 156 C1
Ridgeway The. Romf 165 D4
Ridgewell Ave. Grays 178 A1
Ridgewell Cl. Dag 173 D2
Ridgewell Rd. Bird 8 C1
Ridgewell Rd. Gt Y 20 C2
Ridings The. Bis St 67 E2
Ridings The. Gt Bad 124 B4
Ridley Cl. Romf 156 A1
Ridley Gdns. Els 48 B1
Ridley Rd. Basil 163 E1
Ridley Rd. Chelm 111 D4
Riffams Ct. Basil 172 B4
Riffams Dr. Basil 172 B4
Riffhams. Brent 159 D4
Riffhams Dr. Gt Bad 125 D4
Rifle Hill. Brain 65 F1
Rigby Gdns. Grays 186 A1
Rignals La. Chelm 124 B2
Ringwood Ave. Horne 165 E1
Ripley View. Lou 128 A1
Ripple Rd. Dag 173 D2

Rippleside. Basil 171 F3
Risdens. Harl 102 B3
Rise Park. Basil 170 C3
Rise Park Bvd. Romf 155 F1
Rise Park Par. Romf 155 F1
Rise The. Lou 140 B1
Rising Gr. Basil 170 B3
Rising The. Bill 149 E1
River Ave. Hod 100 A4
River Cl. Ches 126 A3
River Cl. Rain 182 A4
River Cotts. Bore 112 C4
River Dr. Upm 166 B3
River Meads. Stan 87 E2
River Rd. Brent 157 F3
River Rd. Lou 140 C1
River View. Brain 65 F1
River View. Grays 186 A1
River Way. Harl 90 A3
River Way. Lou 141 D2
Riverfield La. Saw 77 F2
Rivermead. Chelm 111 D2
Rivermill. Harl 89 E1
Riversdale Rd. Romf 155 D2
Riverside. Bis St 67 F4
Riverside. Gt Dun 61 F1
Riverside Ave. Lo Naz 100 A1
Riverside Cotts. Sta Ab 87 E2
Riverside Ct. Ching 139 D2
Riverside Wlk. Bis St 67 F4
Riverside Wlk. Wick 163 D4
Riversmead. Hod 100 A3
Rivertons. Basil 171 F2
Riverview. Basil 172 A2
Riverview Cl. Basil 171 F2
Riverview Rd. Swan 191 D1
Rivington Ave. Woodf 152 B1
Roach. Grays 187 E1
Roach Cl. Bill 148 C1
Robert Cl. Chig 153 E3
Robert Suckling Ct. Ste B 18 A3
Robert Wallace Cl. Bis St 56 C1
Robert Way. Wick 163 F3
Roberts Cl. Romf 156 A1
Roberts Rd. Basil 170 A4
Robin Cl. Bill 149 E3
Robin Cl. Bill 161 E1
Robin Cl. Romf 155 E2
Robin Hood Rd. Brent 146 B1
Robin Hood Rd. Els 48 B1
Robin Way. Chelm 124 A3
Robinia Cl. Chig 153 F2
Robins The. Bla 133 E2
Robinson Cl. Bis St 67 F3
Robinson Cl. Hornc 174 A3
Robinson Rd. Dag 173 D4
Robinson Rd. Horn H 178 C2
Robinsway. Wa Aby 126 C3
Robjohns Rd. Chelm 123 F4
Roborough Wlk. Hornc 174 B3
Rochelle Cl. Thax 40 A2
Rochester Way. Basil 171 F4
Rochford Ave. Brent 147 D2
Rochford Ave. Lou 141 E3
Rochford Ave. Wa Aby 126 B3
Rochford Cl. Hornc 174 A3
Rochford Cl. Wick 163 F3
Rochford Green. Lou 141 E3
Rochford Rd. Bis St 57 D1
Rochford Rd. Chelm 111 E1
Rock Gdns. Dag 173 D4
Rockall Cl. Hav 7 E4
Rockchase Gdns. Hornc 165 F3
Rockingham Ave. Hornc 165 D3
Rockwell Rd. Dag 173 D4
Roden Cl. Harl 90 C2
Roding Ave. Woodf 152 C2
Roding Cl. Fyf 106 B1
Roding Dr. Kelv H 132 C1
Roding La. Chig 153 D4
Roding La. Lov 153 D4
Roding La N. Woodf 152 C1
Roding Rd. Lou 140 C2
Roding View. Ch Ong 119 D2
Roding View. Lou 140 B1
Roding Way. Rain 174 B2
Roding Way. Wick 163 F3
Rodings Ave. Corr 179 E2
Rodings The. Woodf 152 B2
Rodney Cres. Hod 100 A4
Rodney Gdns. Brain 66 B2
Rodney Rd. Ch Ong 118 C1
Rodney Way. Chelm 123 F4
Rodney Way. Romf 155 D1
Roebuck La. Lou 140 B1
Roebuck Rd. Chig 154 A2
Roger Reede's Almshouses.
  Romf 164 C4
Rogers Gdns. Dag 173 D4
Rogers Rd. Dag 173 D4
Rogers Rd. Grays 185 E1
Rokeby Gdns. Woodf 152 A1
Rokells. Basil 171 D4
Rokescroft. Basil 172 A4
Rolands Cl. Chelm 111 D4
Rollestons. Writ 122 C4

Rom Cres. Romf 164 C2
Rom Valley Way. Romf 164 C2
Roman. Grays 187 E1
Roman Cl. Rain 173 E2
Roman Rd. Chelm 111 D1
Roman Rd. Lit Wal 98 A3
Roman St. Hod 100 A4
Roman Vale. Harl 90 B3
Roman Way. Bill 161 D4
Roman Way. Hav 7 E4
Roman Way. Litt 12 C2
Romans Pl. Writ 110 A1
Romans Way. Writ 110 A1
Romeland. Wa Aby 126 B3
Romford Rd. Ave 183 E4
Romford Rd. Chig 154 B3
Romford Rd. Romf 154 B3
Romford Rd. Sta R 131 F4
Romney Chase. Hornc 166 A3
Romney Cl. Brain 65 F3
Romney Rd. Bill 148 C1
Romsey Cl. Sta L H 179 D1
Ronald Rd. Romf 157 D1
Roneo Cnr. Hornc 164 C2
Roneo Link. Hornc 164 C2
Roodegate. Basil 171 D3
Rook Cl. Rain 174 A3
Rook End La. Deb 38 A3
Rookery Cl. C 1 B2
Rookery Cres. Dag 173 D3
Rookery Ct. W Thu 191 D4
Rookery Hill. Corr 180 B2
Rookery La. Wen A 24 C2
Rookery La. H Ong 120 B2
Rookery Rd. Grays 185 E1
Rookery The. Stan M 57 F4
Rookery The. W Thu 191 D4
Rookery View. Grays 185 E1
Rookes. Saff W 13 E2
Rookwood Ave. Lou 141 E3
Rookwood Cl. Grays 185 D1
Rookwood Gdns. Lou 141 E3
Rookwood Way. Hav 7 D3
Rookyards. Basil 171 F3
Roos Hill. Saff W 25 F3
Roosevelt Rd. Basil 170 A3
Roosevelt Way. Dag 173 E3
Roper's Chase. Writ 123 D4
Rose Ave. Woodf 152 A1
Rose Bank. Brent 158 B4
Rose Glen. Chelm 124 B4
Rose Glen. Romf 164 C2
Rose Hill. Brain 66 A1
Rose La. Bill 149 D1
Rose La. Gt C 1 C1
Rose St. Grave 192 A1
Rose Vale. Hod 100 A3
Rose Valley. Brent 158 B4
Rose Valley Cres. Corr 179 F2
Roseacre Cl. Hornc 165 F2
Roseacres. Saw 77 E2
Roseacres. Take 70 B4
Rosebank. Wa Aby 126 C3
Rosebank Ave. Hornc 174 B4
Rosebay Ave. Bill 148 C3
Roseberry Ave. Basil 170 A2
Roseberry Cl. Upm 166 C3
Roseberry Gdns. Upm 166 C3
Roseberry Rd. Grays 191 F4
Rosebery. Bis St 68 B3
Rosebery Rd. Chelm 124 A4
Rosecroft Cl. Basil 170 A2
Rosedale Rd. Grays 185 E1
Rosedale Rd. Romf 164 B4
Rosefinch Cl. Hav 7 E4
Roselaine. Basil 171 D4
Rosemary Ave. Brain 65 F2
Rosemary Ave. Romf 164 C4
Rosemary Cl. Gt Dun 61 E1
Rosemary Cl. Harl 90 B2
Rosemary Cl. S Ock 176 B1
Rosemary Cres. Gt Dun 61 E1
Rosemary La. Gt Dun 61 E1
Rosemary La. Steb 62 B4
Rosemead Gdns. Brent 147 E3
Rosemount. Harl 102 A3
Rosemount Cl. Woodf 152 C2
Rosewood Ave. Hornc 174 A4
Roslings Cl. Chelm 110 B3
Roslyn Gdns. Romf 155 F1
Roslyn Ave. Dag 164 A2
Rosslyn Ave. Romf 156 C1
Rosslyn Rd. Bill 148 C1
Roth Dr. Brent 159 D4
Rothbury Ave. Rain 182 A4
Rothbury Rd. Chelm 110 B1
Rothesay Ave. Chelm 124 A4
Rothmans Ave. Gt Bad 124 C3
Roughtallys. N W Bas 116 C2
Roughtons. Chelm 124 A4
Round Coppice Rd. Stan M ... 69 D4
Round Coppice Rd. Take 58 A1
Roundacre. Basil 171 D3

Roundaway Rd. Woodf 152 C1
Roundhills. Wa Aby 126 C3
Roundmead Ave. Lou 141 D4
Roundmead Cl. Lou 141 D4
Roundwood Ave. Brent 147 D1
Roundwood Gr. Brent 147 D1
Rounton Rd. Wa Aby 126 C3
Rous Chase. Chelm 124 A1
Rous Rd. Lou 140 C1
Rover Ave. Chig 153 F2
Row The. Hen 48 C3
Rowan Green E. Brent 158 C4
Rowan Green W. Brent 158 C4
Rowan Wlk. Hornc 165 E4
Rowans The. Ave 183 E3
Rowans The. Bill 161 E4
Rowans Way. Lou 140 C3
Rowenhall. Basil 169 F3
Rowhedge. Brent 159 D4
Rowhedge Cl. Basil 163 E1
Rowland Cres. Chig 153 F3
Rowley Hill. Stur 7 F3
Rowley Mead. N W Bas 116 B3
Rowley Rd. Grays 186 A4
Rowney Ave. Wim 26 C1
Rowney Gdns. Saw 90 B4
Rowney Wood. Saw 77 E1
Rowntree Way. Saff W 25 E4
Roxburgh Ave. Upm 166 B1
Roxwell Ave. Chelm 110 B2
Roxwell Gdns. Brent 147 E2
Roxwell Rd. Chelm 110 B2
Roxwell Rd. Writ 110 B2
Roxwell Way. Woodf 152 B2
Royal Pier Rd. Grave 193 E1
Roycroft Cl. Woodf 152 A1
Roydon Bridge. Basil 171 E4
Roydon Cl. Lou 140 C1
Roydon Lodge Chalet Est. Roy 88 B1
Roydon Rd. Harl 88 C1
Roydon Rd. Sta Ab 87 F2
Royle Cl. Romf 165 D3
Royston Ave. Bill 161 E1
Royston La. Hinx 1 D4
Royston Rd. Romf 157 D2
Royston Rd. Wen A 24 C3
Rubens Gate. Sprin 111 F4
Rubicon Ave. Wick 163 F4
Rue De St Lawrence. Wa Aby 126 A3
Rumbold Rd. Hod 100 B4
Rumbullion Dr. Bill 148 C2
Rundells. Harl 103 D2
Rundells Wlk. Basil 171 F4
Running Mare La. Chelm 124 A2
Running Waters. Brent 159 D3
Runnymede Ct. Sta L H 179 E1
Runnymede Rd. Sta L H 179 E1
Runwell Gdns. Runw 151 E1
Runwell Rd. Runw 151 F1
Rural Cl. Hornc 165 D2
Rural Vale. Grave 192 C1
Rush Cl. Sta Ab 87 E2
Rush Green Gdns. Romf 164 B2
Rush Green Rd. Romf 164 B2
Rushden Gdns. Woodf 153 D1
Rushdene Rd. Bill 148 C1
Rushdene Rd. Brent 146 B1
Rushdon Cl. Grays 185 D2
Rushdon Cl. Romf 165 D3
Rushes Ct. Bis St 68 A3
Rushes Mead. Harl 102 C3
Rushfield. Saw 77 F1
Rushleigh Green. Bis St 67 E2
Rushley. Basil 163 E1
Rushley Cl. Grays 185 E3
Rushleydale. Sprin 111 F3
Rushmere Ave. Upm 166 B1
Rusholme Ave. Dag 164 A1
Ruskin Ave. Upm 166 B2
Ruskin Ave. Wa Aby 126 C3
Ruskin Gdns. Romf 156 A2
Ruskin Gr. Stone 190 A1
Ruskin Path. Wick 163 E3
Ruskin Rd. Chelm 111 F1
Ruskin Rd. Grays 186 A1
Ruskin Rd. Sta L H 179 E1
Ruskins The. Ray 64 C1
Russel Rd. Grays 185 D1
Russell Cl. Basil 170 A4
Russell Cl. Brent 146 A1
Russell Gdns. Chelm 124 A2
Russell Gdns. Wick 163 F4
Russell Rd. Grave 193 E1
Russell Rd. Lou 140 B1
Russell Rd. Tilb 192 C3
Russell Way. Chelm 123 F4
Russet Cl. Brain 66 A1
Russet Cl. Corr 179 E2
Russets. Chelm 124 B2
Russetts. Basil 170 A3
Russetts. Hornc 165 F4
Rustic Cl. Upm 166 C2
Rutherford Cl. Bill 149 D3
Rutherford St. Broom 98 A1
Rutland App. Hornc 166 A3
Rutland Cl. Basil 170 A3
Rutland Dr. Hornc 166 A3
Rutland Gdns. Brain 66 A2
Rutland Rd. Chelm 111 D4

Rydal Way. Bl Not 76 B3
Ryde Dr. Sta L H 187 E4
Ryder Gdns. Rain 173 F3
Ryder Way. Basil 163 E1
Rye Cl. Hornc 174 B4
Rye Hill Rd. Ep Gr 102 C1
Rye Hill Rd. Harl 102 C1
Rye Hill Rd. N W Bas 102 C1
Rye Mead. Basil 170 B2
Rye Rd. Hod 100 B4
Rye Rd. Sta Ab 87 E1
Rye St. Bis St 56 C1
Rye Wlk. ing 135 D1
Ryecroft. Harl 102 A4
Ryecroft Ave. Woodf 153 D1
Ryedene. Basil 171 F2
Ryedene Cl. Basil 171 F2
Ryedene Pl. Basil 171 F2
Ryefeld Cl. Hod 87 D1
Ryes La. Hat B O 79 D4
Rykhill. Grays 186 A2
Ryle The. Writ 123 D4
Rylstone Way. Saff W 25 F4

Sabina Rd. Grays 186 B1
Sabines Rd. Nave H 144 C3
Sable Way. Basil 169 F4
Sackville Cl. Chelm 110 C2
Sackville Cres. Romf 156 C1
Saddle Rise. Sprin 111 F4
Saddleworth Rd. Romf 156 B2
Saddleworth Sq. Romf 156 B2
Sadlers Cl. Bill 149 E3
Sadlers Mead. Harl 103 D4
Saffro Ct. Basil 169 F3
Saffron Cl. Grays 179 D2
Saffron Cl. Horn H 168 B3
Saffron Cl. Weth 43 E2
Saffron Gdns. Weth 43 E2
Saffron Rd. Romf 155 E1
Saffron Wlk. Bill 149 D1
Sages. Hen 48 C3
Sages End Rd. Hel B 17 D4
Sailing Green. Bill 161 F1
Sains. Basil 170 B4
St Agnes Rd. Bill 161 E2
St Alban's Cres. Woodf 152 A1
St Alban's Rd. Epp 116 B1
St Alban's Rd. Woodf 152 A2
St Albans Ave. Upm 166 C1
St Andrew's Rd. Tilb 192 C3
St Andrews Ave. Hornc 174 A4
St Andrews Cl. N W Bas 117 E4
St Andrews Pl. Brent 158 C4
St Andrews Rd. Bore 99 F1
St Andrews Rd. Romf 164 B3
St Anne's Rd. Mtssg 147 E4
St Annes Cl. Grays 185 D3
St Anthony's Ave. Woodf 152 B2
St Anthony's Dr. Chelm 124 B4
St Augustine Rd. Grays 186 A1
St Barnabas Rd. Woodf 152 B2
St Botolph's Way. Hav 6 C4
St Catherine's Ct. Hod 100 A2
St Catherine's Rd. Chelm ... 110 C1
St Catherines Cl. Wick 163 F4
St Cecilia Rd. Grays 186 A1
St Cedds Ct. Grays 185 D3
St Chad's Rd. Tilb 193 D4
St Charles Dr. Wick 163 F4
St Charles Rd. Brent 146 A1
St Clair Cl. Woodf 152 C1
St Clement's Ave. W Thu ... 191 D4
St Clement's Rd. W Thu 191 E4
St Clements. Thax 40 A1
St Clements Ct. Pur 183 D1
St Cleres Cres. Wick 163 F4
St Cross Cl. Hod 100 A2
St Cuthbert's Rd. Hod 87 E1
St David's Rd. Basil 170 A2
St David's Way. Wick 163 F4
St Dunstan's Rd. Hun 88 B4
St Ediths Ct. Bill 149 D1
St Ediths La. Bill 149 D1
St Edmund's Way. Harl 90 B2
St Edmunds Fields. Gt Dun .. 61 F1
St Edmunds La. Gt Dun 61 F1
St Edmunds Rd. Stone 190 A2
St Edwards Way. Romf 164 C4
St Egberts Way. Ching 139 E1
St Fabian's Dr. Chelm 110 C2
St Gabriels Ct. Basil 172 A3
St George's Ave. Grays 185 E1
St George's Ave. Hornc 165 F2
St George's Centre. Grave .. 193 D1
St Georges Cl. Dodd 133 D2
St Gile's Ave. Dag 173 D3
St Giles Cl. Dag 173 D3
St Giles Cl. Grays 178 A1
St Helens Rd. Rain 174 A1
St Helens Wlk. Bill 148 C2
St Ivians Dr. Romf 165 D4
St James Ave. Ch Ong 119 D1
St James Ave E. Corr 179 F2
St James Ave W. Corr 179 F2
St James La. Stone 190 C1
St James Park. Chelm 110 B2
St James Rd. Basil 171 E3
St James Rd. Brain 65 F3

St James's Ct. Hav 6 C4
St James's Ave. Grave 193 D1
St James's Rd. Brent 158 B4
St James's Rd. Grave 193 D1
St James's St. Grave 193 D1
St John Ave. Brain 65 F1
St John's Ave. Brent 158 B3
St John's Ave. Chelm 124 A4
St John's Ave. Harl 90 B2
St John's Cres. Stan M 57 F4
St John's Ct. Lou 140 A1
St John's Green. Writ 110 A1
St John's La. Stan M 57 F4
St John's Mews. Corr 179 F2
St John's Rd. Bill 149 D2
St John's Rd. Chelm 124 A4
St John's Rd. Epp 115 F1
St John's Rd. Lou 140 C4
St John's Rd. Stan M 57 F4
St John's Rd. Stone 190 B1
St John's Way. Corr 179 F2
St Johns Cl. Gt C 1 B1
St Johns Cl. Rain 174 A3
St Johns Rd. Grays 186 A1
St Johns Rd. Romf 155 E3
St Johns Wlk. Harl 90 B2
St Kilda's Rd. Brent 146 B1
St Lawrence Rd. Upm 166 B1
St Leonards Cl. Saff W 25 D1
St Leonards Rd. Lo Naz 113 F4
St Leonards Way. Hornc 165 D2
St Margaret's Ave. Sta L H .. 187 E4
St Margaret's Rd. Hod 87 D1
St Margaret's Rd. Sprin 111 F2
St Margaret's Rd. Sta L H ... 187 E4
St Mark's Ave. Grave 192 C1
St Martin's Mews. Ch Ong .. 119 D1
St Martins Cl. Wh Rot 93 E4
St Mary's Ave. Bill 149 D1
St Mary's Ave. Brent 147 D2
St Mary's Cl. Gt Bad 124 C3
St Mary's Cl. Pan 65 D4
St Mary's Cres. Basil 172 B3
St Mary's Ct. Grays 192 B4
St Mary's Dr. Stan M 57 F3
St Mary's La. Horn H 167 E2
St Mary's La. Upm 167 E2
St Mary's Mead. Broom 98 A2
St Mary's Path. Basil 172 B4
St Mary's Pl. Lit Dun 73 E4
St Mary's Rd. Brain 66 A2
St Mary's Rd. Grays 186 A1
St Mary's Wlk. Ste B 18 A3
St Marys Rd. Stone 190 C2
St Marys Way. Chig 153 D3
St Matthew's Cl. Rain 174 A3
St Michael's Cl. Harl 89 F1
St Michael's Dr. Rox 109 D3
St Michael's Rd. Brain 65 F1
St Michael's Rd. Chelm 124 A4
St Michael's Rd. Hod 100 A4
St Michaels Ave. Basil 172 B2
St Michaels Cl. Ave 183 E3
St Michaels Rd. Grays 186 A1
St Michaels Wlk. Chelm 124 B1
St Mildreds Rd. Chelm 124 A4
St Nazaire Rd. Chelm 110 C3
St Neots Rd. Romf 156 C2
St Nicholas Ave. Hornc 165 D1
St Nicholas Field. Berd 46 A4
St Nicholas Gr. Brent 159 E3
St Nicholas La. Basil 170 B4
St Patrick's Pl. Grays 186 B1
St Paul's Cl. Ave 183 E3
St Paul's Pl. Ave 183 E3
St Pauls Gdns. Bill 149 D2
St Pauls Way. Wa Aby 126 B3
St Peter's Ave. Ch Ong 118 C3
St Peter's Cl. Brain 65 F2
St Peter's Pavement. Basil .. 162 C1
St Peter's Rd. Brain 65 F2
St Peter's Rd. Brent 158 A3
St Peter's Rd. Chelm 110 C1
St Peter's Terr. Wick 163 E4
St Peters Rd. Grays 186 A1
St Peters Wlk. Bill 148 C2
St Peters-s-in-the-Fields. Brain 65 F2
St Ronans Cres. Woodf 152 A2
St Stephen's Cres. Brent 159 D3
St Teresa Rd. Grays 186 A1
St Thomas' Rd. Brent 158 B4
St Thomas's Cl. Wa Aby 127 D3
St Thomas's Pl. Grays 192 B4
St Valerie. Take 70 B4
St Vincent Chase. Brain 66 A3
St Vincents Ave. Stone 190 A1
St Vincents Rd. Chelm 124 A4
St Vincents Rd. Stone 190 A1
St Winifred's Cl. Chig 153 E3
Saint Francis Way. Grays ... 186 B2
Saint's Wlk. Grays 186 B1
Sakins Croft. Harl 102 C3
Saladin Dr. Pur 183 D1
Salcombe Rd. Brain 66 B1
Salcott Cres. Wick 163 F3

Salerno Way. Chelm 110 C3
Salesbury Dr. Bill 149 E1
Salisbury Ave. Basil 170 B3
Salisbury Ave. Sta L H 179 E1
Salisbury Cl. Bis St 67 F3
Salisbury Gdns. Lou 152 B4
Salisbury Rd. Dag 173 D3
Salisbury Rd. Grays 185 E1
Salisbury Rd. Hod 100 B4
Salisbury Rd. Romf 165 D3
Salix Rd. Grays 192 B4
Salmond's Gr. Brent 159 E3
Saltash Cl. Chig 153 E2
Salter Pl. Sprin 111 F1
Salway Cl. Woodf 152 A2
Samantha Mews. Hav B 155 F4
Samphire Ct. Grays 192 C4
Samuel Manor. Sprin 111 F2
Samuel Rd. Basil 170 A2
Sanctuary Gdn. Corr 179 F1
Sanderson Cl. Horn H 168 B3
Sandford Ave. Lou 141 E3
Sandford Mill Rd. Sprin 112 A1
Sandford Rd. Chelm 111 F2
Sandgate Cl. Romf 164 B2
Sandhurst Rd. Tilb 193 E3
Sandle Rd. Bis St 68 A4
Sandon Hill. Gt Wal 84 A3
Sandon Pl. Ch Ong 119 D1
Sandon Rd. Basil 171 F3
Sandown Ave. Dag 173 E3
Sandown Ave. Hornc 165 E1
Sandown Ct. Dag 173 E3
Sandown Rd. Grays 186 C4
Sandpiper Cl. Hav 7 D4
Sandpiper Wlk. Chelm 124 B3
Sandpit La. Brent 145 F1
Sandpit Rd. Brain 65 F3
Sandringham Cl. Corr 179 F2
Sandringham Rd. Brent 146 A2
Sandwich Cl. Brain 65 F3
Sandy La. Ave 183 D3
Sandy La. Grays 186 B1
Sandy La. Rain 183 D3
Sandy La. W Thu 191 D4
Sappers Cl. Saw 77 F1
Sarre Ave. Hornc 174 B3
Saunders Ave. Brain 65 F2
Saunton Rd. Hornc 165 D1
Savill Row. Woodf 152 A3
Saville Cl. Clav 35 D2
Savoy Wood. Harl 102 A2
Sawbridgeworth Rd. Saw 78 C2
Sawkins Ave. Gt Bad 124 B3
Sawkins Cl. Gt Bad 124 B3
Sawkins Gdns. Gt Bad 124 B3
Sawney Brook. Writ 110 A1
Sawpit La. Berd 46 B4
Sawyer's Chase. Abr 142 A3
Sawyer's Hall La. Brent 146 B1
Saxon Cl. Brent 159 D4
Saxon Cl. Romf 156 C1
Saxon Cl. Runw 151 F1
Saxon Way. Chelm 111 D4
Saxon Way. Saff W 13 E1
Saxon Way. Wa Aby 126 B3
Sayes Gdns. Saw 77 F1
Sayesbury Ave. Saw 77 F2
Sayesbury Rd. Saw 77 F1
Saywell Brook. Sprin 112 A1
Scaldhurst. Basil 172 B4
Scarletts. Basil 171 E4
Scholars Rd. Ching 139 E1
School Green La. N W Bas .. 117 E3
School La. Abb Rod 93 F1
School La. Abb Rod 107 D4
School La. Brent 159 E2
School La. Broom 98 A1
School La. Brox 59 E3
School La. Elm 23 D4
School La. Grays 186 A4
School La. Gt Le 85 F4
School La. H Ea 82 A2
School La. Harl 89 F1
School La. Hav 6 C4
School La. Hen 48 C3
School La. Mag Lav 104 B3
School La. New 24 C1
School La. Stock 136 B1
School Rd. Bill 149 D1
School Rd. Dag 173 D2
School Rd. G Ea 95 E3
School Rd. Kelv H 132 C1
School Rd. Ray 75 F4
School Rd. S Han 150 C3
School Rd. Sta R 131 D4
School St. Gt C 1 B1
School View Rd. Chelm 110 C2
School Villas. Brox 49 F1
School Wlk. Brain 65 F2
Schoolfield Rd. W Thu 191 D4
Schooner Ct. Stone 190 B2
Scilla Ct. Grays 192 B4
Scoter Ct. Woodf 152 A2
Scotland Rd. Lou 140 B1
Scotney Walk. Hornc 174 B4
Scott Ave. Finch 43 E3
Scott Ave. Sta Ab 87 D2

Scott Rd. Bis St 67 F3
Scott Rd. Grays 186 A1
Scotts Cl. Hornc 174 B4
Scotts Wlk. Chelm 110 B3
Scratton Rd. Sta L H 179 E1
Scrub Rise. Bill 160 C4
Scurvy Hall La. Lit Wal 85 D1
Seaborough Rd. Grays 186 B1
Seabrook Gdns. Bore 99 F1
Seabrook Rd. Gt Bad 125 D3
Seabrooke Rise. Grays 192 A4
Seaburn Cl. Rain 173 F1
Seaforth Cl. Romf 155 F2
Seaforth Gdns. Woodf 152 B3
Seamans La. Stock 137 E1
Seaview Ave. Basil 171 E2
Seax Ct. Basil 169 F4
Seax Way. Basil 169 F4
Sebastian Ave. Brent 147 D2
Sebert Cl. Bill 161 E4
Second Ave. Basil 169 F2
Second Ave. Bill 160 C4
Second Ave. Chelm 111 D3
Second Ave. Corr 179 E2
Second Ave. Dag 173 D2
Second Ave. Dodd 133 E3
Second Ave. Harl 102 C4
Second Ave. W Thu 191 D4
Sedge Ct. Grays 192 C4
Sedge Green. Lo Naz 100 C3
Sedge Green. Roy 100 C2
Sedgefield Cl. Romf 156 C3
Sedgefield Cres. Romf 156 C3
Sedgemoor Dr. Dag 173 D4
Sedley Rise. Lou 140 C4
Sedop Cl. Saff W 25 E4
Seeleys. Harl 90 B2
Selsdon Cl. Romf 155 E1
Selwood Rd. Brent 157 F4
Selworthy Cl. Bill 161 E4
Selwyn Rd. Tilb 192 C3
Semper Rd. Grays 186 B2
Semples. Corr 179 F1
Settle Rd. Brent 157 D3
Seven Acres. Wick 163 F4
Seven Arches Rd. Brent 158 C4
Seven Ash Green. Sprin 111 E3
Sevenoaks Cl. Romf 156 B3
Seventh Ave. Chelm 111 D3
Severn. Grays 187 D2
Severn Ave. Romf 165 D4
Severn Dr. Upm 166 C3
Severn Rd. Ave 183 E4
Severns Field. Epp 116 A1
Sewards End. Wick 163 F3
Sewardstone Gdns. Ching .. 139 D2
Sewardstone Rd. Ching 139 D3
Sewardstone Rd. Wa Aby .. 139 D2
Sewardstone Way. Wa Aby .. 126 B2
Sewell Harris Cl. Harl 90 A1
Sexton Cl. Rain 173 F2
Sexton Rd. Tilb 192 C3
Seymer Rd. Romf 164 B4
Seymour Rd. Ching 139 D1
Seymour Rd. Tilb 192 C3
Seymour St. Chelm 111 D1
Seymours. Harl 101 F3
Seymours. Harl 102 A3
Seymours. Lou 141 D4
Shaftenhoe End Rd. Nut 21 D4
Shafter Rd. Dag 173 E3
Shaftesbury La. Stone 190 A2
Shaftesbury Rd. Ching 139 E1
Shaftesbury Rd. Epp 116 A1
Shaftesbury Rd. Romf 164 C3
Shaftsbury. Lou 140 B3
Shakespeare Ave. Basil 170 A3
Shakespeare Ave. Bill 149 E1
Shakespeare Ave. Tilb 193 D3
Shakespeare Rd. Romf 164 C3
Shakespeare Rd. Stone 190 A2
Shakespeare Sq. Woodf 153 E2
Shakeston Cl. Writ 123 D4
Shakletons. Ch Ong 119 D2
Shalford Rd. Bill 149 E1
Shalford Rd. Ray 64 C2
Shangani Rd. Bis St 67 F3
Shanklin Ave. Bill 149 D1
Shannon Cl. Hav 7 E4
Shannon Way. Ave 183 E4
Sharlands Cl. Wick 163 F4
Sharpecroft. Harl 102 B4
Sharpington Cl. Chelm 124 B2
Shaw Cl. Hornc 165 D2
Shaw Cres. Brent 147 E3
Shaw Cres. Tilb 193 D3
Shaw Dr. Finch 43 E4
Shawbridge. Harl 102 B3
Shearers Way. Bore 99 F1
Sheds La. Saff W 13 F1
Sheepcote La. Man 46 C2
Sheepcotes La. Lit Wal 98 B3
Sheering Dri. Harl 90 C2
Sheering Lower Rd. Harl 90 C4
Sheering Lower Rd. Saw 78 A1
Sheering Mill La. Saw 77 F1
Sheering Rd. Harl 90 C3
Sheering Rd. Sheer 91 D3

Sheffield Dr. Romf 157 D3
Sheffield Gdns. Romf 157 D3
Sheila Cl. Romf 155 D2
Sheila Rd. Romf 155 D2
Sheilings The. Hornc 165 F3
Sheldon Ave. Woodf 153 D1
Sheldon Cl. Corr 180 A3
Shelley Ave. Basil 170 A3
Shelley Ave. Hornc 164 C1
Shelley Cl. Ch Ong 118 C3
Shelley Gr. Lou 140 C3
Shelley Pl. Tilb 193 D3
Shelley Rd. Brent 147 E1
Shelley Rd. Chelm 111 E1
Shellow Rd. Will 107 E2
Shelsley Dr. Basil 170 B2
Shenfield Cres. Brent 158 C4
Shenfield Gdns. Brent 147 D2
Shenfield Green. Brent 147 D1
Shenfield Pl. Brent 146 C1
Shenfield Rd. Brent 146 C1
Shenfield Rd. Woodf 152 A2
Shenley Rd. Stone 190 A1
Shenstone Gdns. Romf 156 B1
Shepeshall. Basil 170 C3
Shepherds Hill. Romf 157 D1
Shepherds Way. Saff W 13 F1
Shepley Cl. Hornc 174 B4
Shepley Mews. Enf 126 A1
Sheppard Dr. Sprin 112 A2
Sheppards. Harl 101 F3
Sherborne Gdns. Romf 155 D3
Sherborne Rd. Sprin 111 E3
Sherbourne Dr. Basil 163 D1
Sherfield Rd. Grays 192 A4
Sheridan Cl. Romf 156 B2
Sheridan Cl. Stone 190 A2
Sheringham Ave. Romf 164 B3
Sheringham Cl. Corr 179 F2
Shernbroke Rd. Wa Aby 126 C3
Sherwood. T Thu 184 C3
Sherwood Dr. Chelm 110 B1
Shetland Rd. Hav 7 E4
Shevon Way. Brent 157 F3
Shillibeer Wlk. Chig 153 F4
Shingle Cl. Wa Aby 127 D3
Ship La. Ave 183 E2
Ship Rd. Stock 137 E3
Ship Rd. W Han 137 E3
Shire Cl. Bill 149 E3
Shire Cl. Sprin 111 F4
Shire Hill. Saff W 13 F4
Shire Hill La. Saff W 25 F4
Shirley Gdns. Basil 172 B4
Shirley Gdns. Hornc 165 E1
Shonks Mill Rd. Nave H 131 E1
Shooters Dr. Lo Naz 100 C1
Shore The. Grave 192 B1
Short Croft. Kelv H 132 C1
Short La. S Han 150 B2
Shortace. Basil 171 E3
Shortcroft. Bis St 68 B4
Shorter Ave. Brent 146 C1
Shortlands. Basil 171 D3
Shortlands Ave. Ch Ong 118 C3
Shrubberies The. Chig 153 E3
Shrubberies The. Woodf 152 A1
Shrubberies The. Writ 122 C4
Shrubbery Cl. Basil 170 B4
Shrubbery The. Upm 166 B1
Shrublands. Saff W 13 F2
Shrublands Cl. Chelm 111 E1
Shrublands Cl. Chig 153 E2
Sibneys Green. Harl 102 C2
Siddons Cl. Sta L H 187 D2
Sidmouth Rd. Sprin 111 F3
Sidney Rd. The B 128 B2
Sidney Terr. Bis St 67 F3
Silver Birch Way. N W Bas .. 116 C2
Silver Birches. Brent 147 D1
Silver La. Will 108 A1
Silver St. Abr 142 A3
Silver St. Anst 33 D3
Silver St. Stan M 57 E3
Silver St. Wa Aby 126 B3
Silver St. Weth 43 D2
Silver Way. Romf 164 A4
Silver Way. Runw 163 E4
Silverdale. Corr 179 E2
Silverdale Dr. Hornc 174 A4
Silverdale East. Corr 179 E2
Silverlocke Rd. Grays 192 B4
Silvermead. Woodf 152 A1
Silvermere. Basil 170 A3
Silvermere Ave.. Romf 155 D3
Silvertown Ave. Corr 179 E2
Silverwood Cl. Grays 185 D3
Simmons Pl. Grays 192 B4
Simpson Rd. Rain 173 F3
Sims Cl. Romf 164 C4
Singleton Cl. Hornc 173 F4
Sir Francis Way. Brent 158 A4
Siviter Way. Dag 173 E4
Six Bells Ct. Brain 65 F3
Sixth Ave. Chelm 111 D3
Skarnings Ct. Wa Aby 127 D3
Skeins Way. Clav 35 E2
Skerry Rise. Chelm 111 D4
Skiddaw Cl. Bl Not 76 B4

Skinner's La. Chelm 124 A2
Skitts Hill. Brain 66 A1
Skreens Ct. Chelm 110 B2
Skreens Park Rd. Rox 108 C3
Skylark Cl. Bill 149 E1
Skylark Wlk. Chelm 124 A3
Slade's La. Chelm 124 A2
Slades The. Basil 171 F2
Slaney Rd. Romf 164 C3
Sleepers Farm Rd. Grays 186 A2
Slewins Cl. Hornc 165 E3
Slewins La. Hornc 165 E3
Sloane Mews. Bill 148 C3
Slough Rd. H Ea 82 A1
Smallgains La. Stock 149 F4
Smart Cl. Romf 156 A1
Smart's La. Lou 140 C3
Smeaton Cl. Wa Aby 126 C4
Smeaton Rd. Chig 152 C3
Smith's End La. Nut 21 D4
Smithers Dr. Gt Bad 125 D3
Smiths Field. Ray 64 C1
Smiths Green. Deb 38 B4
Smythe Cl. Bill 149 E3
Smythe Rd. Bill 149 E3
Snake's La E. Woodf 152 B3
Snake's La W. Woodf 152 A2
Snakes Hill. Kelv H 145 E3
Snakes La. Stan M 48 A1
Snelling Gr. Gt Bad 124 C3
Snowdonia Cl. Basil 172 B4
Snowdrop Cl. Sprin 111 F4
Snowdrop Path. Romf 156 B2
Soames Mead. Sto M 133 D3
Soane St. Basil 163 D1
Solid La. Dodd 145 F4
Solway. Grays 187 E2
Somerby Cl. Hod 100 A1
Somercoates. Basil 170 B3
Somercoates Ct. Basil 170 B3
Somerdean. Basil 172 B3
Somerset Cl. Woodf 152 A1
Somerset Gdns. Basil 172 A3
Somerset Gdns. Hornc 166 A2
Somerset Pl. Chelm 111 D4
Somerset Rd. Basil 170 A3
Somerset Rd. Enf 126 A1
Somerset Rd. Sta L H 187 D2
Sorrel Ct. Grays 192 B4
Sorrel Wlk. Romf 164 C4
Sorrell Cl. Lit Wal 98 A3
Sorrells The. Corr 179 F2
South Ave. Ching 139 E1
South Ave. Corr 179 D4
South Beech Ave. Wick 163 E4
South Cl. Dag 173 D2
South Colne. Basil 171 E2
South Crockerford. Basil 171 F2
South Dr. Brent 158 B3
South Dr. Romf 165 E4
South End Rd. Hornc 174 A3
South End Rd. Rain 174 A3
South Gate. Harl 102 B4
South Gate. W Thu 183 E1
South Gunnels. Basil 171 D3
South Hall Dr. Rain 182 A4
South Hanningfield Rd. Rett . 151 E4
South Hanningfield Rd. S Han151 E4
South Hanningfield Way. Runw151 E2
South Hill. Horn H 179 D4
South Hill Cres. Grays 179 D2
South Kent Ave. Grave 192 B1
South Mayne. Basil 172 A3
South Par. Wa Aby 126 B3
South Pl. Harl 90 A2
South Primrose Hill. Chelm ... 110 C2
South Rd. Bill 162 B3
South Rd. Bis St 68 A4
South Rd. Harl 90 A2
South Rd. S Ock 184 B4
South Rd. Saff W 25 F4
South Rd. Take 70 B4
South Ridge. Bill 149 E1
South Riding. Basil 171 F3
South St. Bis St 67 F3
South St. Brain 65 F1
South St. Brent 158 B4
South St. Gt C 1 B1
South St. Gt Wal 97 F4
South St. Rain 173 E2
South St. Romf 164 C2
South St. Sta Ab 87 E2
South View. Grays 186 A4
South View. Gt Dun 72 B4
South View Dr. Upm 166 A1
South View Rd. Lou 140 C2
South View Rd. Tilb 193 D3
South View Rd. W Thu 191 E4
South Wash Rd. Bill 161 F1
South Way. Wa Aby 126 B2
South Weald Dri. Wa Aby 126 B3
South Weald Rd. Brent 158 A4
South Wlk. Basil 171 D3
Southall Way. Brent 157 F3
Southborough Rd. Chelm 124 A4
Southbourne Gr. Wick 163 D4
Southbrook. Saw 77 F1
Southbury Cl. Hornc 174 B4
Southcote Cres. Basil 171 F4

Southcote Row. Basil 171 F4
Southcote Sq. Basil 171 F4
Southdale. Chig 153 E2
Southdown Rd. Hornc 165 D2
Southend Arterial Rd. Basil 162 B1
Southend Arterial Rd. Brent .. 167 E3
Southend Arterial Rd. Hornc . 165 F4
Southend Arterial Rd. Romf .. 156 B1
Southend Arterial Rd. Upm 166 B3
Southend La. Wa Aby 127 D3
Southend Rd. Bill 161 E3
Southend Rd. Corr 179 F2
Southend Rd. Grays 185 E1
Southend Rd. Gt Bad 125 E2
Southend Rd. Sand 125 E2
Southend Rd. W Han 125 E2
Southend Rd. Woodf 152 A1
Souther Cross Rd. G Ea 95 E3
Southern Dr. Lou 140 C2
Southern Lodge. Harl 102 B3
Southern Way. Harl 102 B3
Southern Way. Romf 164 A3
Southernhay. Basil 171 D3
Southernhay. Lou 140 B2
Southey Wlk. Tilb 193 D3
Southfield. Hinx 1 A2
Southfield Chase. Basil 160 C1
Southfield Rd. Hod 100 A4
Southfleet Rd. Swan 191 F1
Southlands Chase. Sand 125 F1
Southlands Rd. Bill 162 C3
Southmill Rd. Bis St 68 A3
Southview Rd. Basil 171 F3
Southway. Basil 170 B1
Southway. W Thu 183 F2
Sovereign Ct. Harl 102 A3
Sowerberry Cl. Chelm 110 C4
Sowrey Ave. Rain 174 A3
Spains Hall Pl. Basil 171 E3
Spains Hall Rd. Will 107 F1
Spalding Ave. Chelm 110 C3
Spalding Way. Gt Bad 124 C4
Spalt Cl. Brent 159 D4
Spareleaze Hill. Lou 140 C3
Sparepenny La N. Gt Sam 29 D2
Sparepenny La S. Gt Sam 29 D2
Sparkbridge. Basil 170 A3
Sparks La. Ridge 20 A3
Sparrow Gr. Dag 164 A1
Sparrow's La. Hat B O 79 F1
Sparrows Herne. Basil 171 D2
Sparrowsend Hill. Saff W 25 D3
Speedwell Ct. Grays 192 C4
Spellbrook La E. Spel 77 F4
Spellbrook La W. Spel 77 F4
Spencer Cl. Els 48 B2
Spencer Cl. Stan M 57 F3
Spencer Cl. Woodf 152 B3
Spencer Rd. Gt C 1 B2
Spencer Rd. Rain 173 E2
Spencer Sq. Brain 65 F4
Spencer Wlk. Tilb 193 D3
Spencers Croft. Harl 103 D3
Spenders Cl. Basil 171 E4
Spenlow Dr. Chelm 110 B4
Spenser Cres. Upm 166 B2
Spey Way. Romf 155 F2
Spicers La. Harl 90 B2
Spilbutters. Dodd 133 D2
Spilsby Rd. Hav 6 B4
Spindle Rd. Hav 6 B4
Spindles. Tilb 193 D4
Spinney Cl. Rain 173 F2
Spinney Cl. Wick 163 F4
Spinney The. Bill 149 D2
Spinney The. Brain 66 B1
Spinney The. Brent 147 E2
Spinney The. Ch Ong 119 D1
Spinney The. Grays 178 A1
Spinning Wheel Mead. Harl ... 103 D3
Spires The. Gt Bad 124 C3
Spital La. Brent 157 F4
Sporhams. Basil 170 C2
Spots Wlk. Chelm 124 B2
Spriggs La. Bla 121 D1
Spring Gdns. Hornc 174 A4
Spring Gdns. Romf 164 B3
Spring Gdns. Woodf 152 B2
Spring Gr. Lou 140 B2
Spring Hill. Saff W 13 D1
Spring Hills. Harl 89 D1
Spring Pond Cl. Gt Bad 124 C4
Spring Pond Meadow. Dodd . 133 E3
Spring Rise. Chelm 124 B3
Spring Vale. Swan 191 E1
Springbank Ave. Hornc 174 B4
Springfield. Epp 128 C4
Springfield Ave. Brent 147 F1
Springfield Cl. Ch Ong 118 C3
Springfield Cl. Rain 174 B1
Springfield Gdns. Upm 166 B1
Springfield Gdns. Woodf 152 B2
Springfield Green. Sprin 111 F2
Springfield Park Ave. Chelm .. 111 E1
Springfield Park Hill. Chelm .. 111 E1
Springfield Park La. Chelm ... 111 F1
Springfield Park Par. Chelm .. 111 E1

Springfield Park Rd. Chelm ... 111 E1
Springfield Pl. Sprin 111 E3
Springfield Rd. Bill 149 D3
Springfield Rd. Chelm 111 E2
Springfield Rd. Ching 139 F1
Springfield Rd. Grays 185 F2
Springfield Rd. Sprin 111 E2
Springfield Rd. Wick 163 F4
Springfields. Basil 171 F2
Springfields. Gt Dun 72 B4
Springfields. Wa Aby 126 C3
Springhall La. Saw 77 F1
Springhall Rd. Saw 77 F1
Springhead Rd. Grave 192 B1
Springhill Rd. Saff W 25 E4
Springhouse La. Sta L H 180 A2
Springhouse Rd. Corr 179 F2
Springmead. Bl Not 76 B4
Springwell Rd. Lit C 13 D3
Springwood Ct. Brain 65 E2
Springwood Dr. Brain 65 E2
Springwood Way. Romf 165 D3
Spruce Cl. Bill 161 E1
Spruce Hill. Harl 102 C2
Spur Cl. Abr 142 A3
Spurriers. Basil 170 B3
Squadrons App. Hornc 174 B3
Square The. Horn H 178 C2
Square The. Saw 77 F1
Square The. Stock 136 C1
Square The. Woodf 152 A3
Squirrel's Chase. Grays 186 A2
Squirrel's Heath Ave. Romf ... 165 D4
Squirrells Ct. Chelm 110 C3
Squirrells. Basil 170 A2
Squirrels Cl. Bis St 67 F4
Squirrels Heath La. Hornc 165 E4
Squirrels Heath Rd. Romf 156 C1
Stablecroft. Sprin 111 F4
Stables The. Lou 140 B1
Stacey Dr. Basil 170 B1
Stacey's Mount. Bill 162 B3
Stackfield. Harl 90 A2
Stafford Ave. Hornc 165 E4
Stafford Cl. Sta L H 187 D2
Stafford Dr. Hod 100 A2
Stafford Green. Basil 169 F2
Staffords. Harl 90 C2
Stag La. Lou 152 A4
Stagden Cross. Basil 171 F3
Staggart Green. Chig 154 A2
Stambourne Rd. Gt Y 20 B2
Stambourne Rd. Ridge 19 F3
Stambourne Rd. Topp 32 A4
Standen Ave. Hornc 165 F1
Standfield Gdns. Dag 173 D3
Standfield Rd. Dag 173 D4
Standingford. Harl 102 A2
Standrums. Gt Dun 72 B4
Stane Cl. Bis St 56 C1
Stanes Rd. Brain 65 F3
Staneway. Basil 170 B2
Stanford Cl. Romf 164 A3
Stanford Cl. Woodf 152 C3
Stanford Ct. Wa Aby 127 D3
Stanford Gdns. Ave 183 F3
Stanford Rd. Grays 186 C4
Stanford Rd. Sta L H 179 D1
Stanford Rivers Rd. Ch Ong . 132 A4
Stanford-Le-Hope By-Ps. Corr179 E3
Stanhope Rd. Rain 174 A2
Stanhope Rd. Swan 191 F1
Stanley Ave. Dag 164 A2
Stanley Ave. Romf 165 D4
Stanley Cl. Hornc 165 E1
Stanley Cl. Romf 165 D4
Stanley Pl. Ch Ong 119 D1
Stanley Pl. Stan M 57 F3
Stanley Rd. Ching 139 E1
Stanley Rd. Grays 192 A4
Stanley Rd. Gt C 1 C2
Stanley Rd. Horn H 177 F4
Stanley Rd. Hornc 165 E1
Stanley Rd. Romf 173 F2
Stanley Rd. Swan 191 F1
Stanley Rd N. Rain 173 F2
Stanley Rise. Sprin 111 F2
Stanleys Farm Rd. Saff W 25 F4
Stanmore Way. Lou 141 D4
Stannetts. Basil 170 A4
Stansgate Rd. Dag 164 A1
Stanstead Abbots By-Ps. Sta Ab87 E1
Stanstead Dr. Hod 100 A4
Stanstead Rd. Hod 87 D1
Stansted Cl. Bill 149 E1
Stansted Cl. Chelm 110 C1
Stansted Cl. Hornc 174 B3
Stansted Rd. Bis St 57 D2
Stansted Rd. Els 48 B1
Stanway Cl. Chig 153 F3
Stanway Way. Wa Aby 127 D3
Stanwyck Dr. Chig 153 E3
Stanwyck Gdns. Romf 156 A3
Staple Tye. Harl 102 B3
Staple's Rd. Lou 140 C3
Stapleford Gdns. Romf 155 D2
Stapleford Rd. Sta Abb 143 D3

Stapleford Tawney. Sta T 130 B2
Stapleford Tawney. Sta T 143 E4
Stapleton Cres. Rain 174 A3
Star La. Epp 116 A1
Star La. Gt Dun 61 E1
Star La. Ing 135 E2
Star Mead. Thax 40 A1
Starboard Ave. Swan 191 D1
Starch House La. Woodf 153 E1
Starling Cl. Lou 140 A1
Starr Rd. Hen 48 C3
Station App. Basil 170 B3
Station App. Basil 172 A2
Station App. Brain 66 A1
Station App. Grays 192 A4
Station App. Runw 163 E4
Station App. Woodf 152 A1
Station Approach Rd. Tilb 193 D2
Station Ave. Basil 172 A2
Station La. Basil 172 A2
Station La. Hornc 165 F1
Station La. Ing 135 D2
Station Par. Hornc 174 A4
Station Pass. Woodf 152 A1
Station Rd. Bill 148 C1
Station Rd. Bis St 68 A4
Station Rd. Brain 65 F1
Station Rd. Chig 153 D4
Station Rd. Ching 139 E1
Station Rd. Cla 8 B1
Station Rd. Els 48 B1
Station Rd. Epp 129 D4
Station Rd. Felst 73 F3
Station Rd. Grave 192 A1
Station Rd. Grays 194 A3
Station Rd. Gt Dun 72 C4
Station Rd. Harl 90 B2
Station Rd. Hav 7 D4
Station Rd. Hod 100 A2
Station Rd. Horn H 168 B3
Station Rd. Lit Bur 73 F3
Station Rd. Lou 140 C2
Station Rd. N W Bas 117 D2
Station Rd. New 37 D4
Station Rd. Ray 64 C1
Station Rd. Romf 165 E4
Station Rd. Runw 151 E1
Station Rd. Saff W 25 E4
Station Rd. Saw 77 F2
Station Rd. Sta Ab 87 E2
Station Rd. Stan M 57 F3
Station Rd. Swan 191 D1
Station Rd. Take 70 B4
Station Rd. Upm 166 B1
Station Rd. Wen A 24 C3
Station Rd Ind Est. Gt Dun 72 C4
Station St. Saff W 13 E1
Station Way. Basil 171 D3
Station Way. Woodf 152 B3
Staverton Rd. Hornc 165 E3
Stebbing Rd. Felst 74 A4
Stebbings. Basil 170 B2
Steeds Way. Lou 140 C3
Steele Ave. Stone 191 D1
Steen Cl. Ing 135 D2
Steeple Bumpstead Rd. Hel B 17 E4
Steeple View. Bis St 67 F4
Steeple Way. Dodd 133 D1
Steeplehall. Basil 172 A3
Steerforth Cl. Chelm 110 B4
Stenning Ave. Sta L H 187 D1
Stephen Ave. Rain 174 A3
Stephen Cl. Hav 6 C4
Stephen Marshall Ave. Finch .. 42 B3
Stephens Cl. Romf 156 B3
Stephens Cres. Horn H 178 C2
Stephenson Ave. Tilb 193 D3
Stephenson Rd. Brain 66 A1
Sterry Cres. Dag 173 D4
Sterry Gdns. Dag 173 D3
Sterry Rd. Dag 173 D4
Stevens La. Felst 74 C3
Stevens Way. Chig 153 F3
Stevenson Way. Wick 163 E3
Stewards Cl. Epp 129 D3
Stewards Green Rd. Epp 129 D3
Stewards Wlk. Romf 164 C3
Stewardstone St. Wa Aby 126 B3
Stewart Ave. Upm 166 A1
Stewart Rd. Chelm 124 A4
Stewarts The. Bis St 67 F3
Stewarts Way. Man 46 C1
Stifford Clays Rd. Grays 185 D4
Stifford Hill. S Ock 184 B3
Stifford Hill. W Thu 184 B3
Stifford Rd. S Ock 184 A3
Stile Croft. Harl 103 D3
Stilemans. Wick 163 E4
Stirling Cl. Rain 174 A1
Stirling Dr. Hav 6 C4
Stirling Pl. Basil 172 A4
Stirrup Cl. Sprin 111 F4
Stock Hill. Stock 149 E4
Stock La. Ing 135 E2
Stock Rd. Bill 149 E3
Stock Rd. Bill 149 E3
Stock Rd. Chelm 137 D4
Stock Rd. Stock 137 D4
Stockfield Ave. Hod 100 A4

Stockland Rd. Romf 164 B3
Stocks La. Kelv H 132 C1
Stocksfield. Harl 132 C1
Stockwell Cl. Bill 161 E4
Stoke Ave. Chig 154 A2
Stoke Rd. Rain 174 B1
Stokefelde. Basil 172 A4
Stonards Hill. Epp 129 E4
Stonards Hill. Lou 140 C2
Stondon Rd. Ch Ong 119 D1
Stone Cross. Harl 89 E1
Stone Ness Rd. W Thu 191 D4
Stone Place Rd. Stone 190 C1
Stone St. Grave 193 D1
Stonebridge Rd. Grave 192 A1
Stonebridge Wlk. Chelm 111 D1
Stonechat Rd. Bill 161 E4
Stonehill Rd. Rox 108 C2
Stonehouse La. W Thu 183 F1
Stoneleigh. Saw 77 E2
Stoney Common. Stan M 57 F3
Stoney Common Rd. Stan M .. 57 E3
Stoneycroft Rd. Woodf 152 C2
Stoneyfield Dri. Stan M 57 F3
Stonleigh Dri. Hod 87 D1
Stony Hills. S Han 150 A3
Stony La. Bobb 118 B4
Stony La. Thax 40 A1
Stony Path. Lou 140 C4
Stony Wood. Harl 102 C4
Stonyshotts. Wa Aby 126 C3
Stormonts Way. Basil 170 B1
Storr Gdns. Brent 147 E2
Stort Lodge. Bis St 67 E4
Stort Mill. Harl 90 A3
Stort Rd. Bis St 67 F3
Stortford Hall Park. Bis St 68 A4
Stortford Rd. Can E 71 E4
Stortford Rd. Clav 35 E2
Stortford Rd. Gt Dun 72 A4
Stortford Rd. Hod 100 B4
Stortford Rd. L Hal 78 C2
Stortford Rd. Lea Rod 94 A3
Stour Rd. Dag 164 A1
Stour Rd. Grays 186 A1
Stour Vale. Cla 8 B2
Stour Vale. Cla 8 B2
Stour Valley Rd. Hav 7 D4
Stour Way. Upm 166 C3
Stow The. Harl 89 F1
Stradbroke Dr. Chig 153 D2
Stradbroke Gr. Lou 140 B1
Stradbroke Park. Chig 153 D2
Strafford Ave. Woodf 153 D1
Straight Rd. Romf 156 B2
Straits The. Wa Aby 126 A4
Stratford Cl. Dag 173 E3
Stratford Gdns. Corr 179 E2
Strathmore. Grays 187 E1
Strathmore Gdns. Hornc 164 C2
Stratton Rd. Romf 157 D3
Stratton Wlk. Romf 157 D3
Strawberry Cl. Brain 66 A1
Strawbrook Hill. Gt Le 85 F2
Street The. Ashe 9 E1
Street The. Berd 46 A4
Street The. Bird 19 D4
Street The. Chelm 124 A1
Street The. Cla 9 E2
Street The. Fu Pel 45 D2
Street The. Gt Ha 69 D2
Street The. Gt Hal 69 D2
Street The. H Ea 82 B1
Street The. H Ong 119 E2
Street The. Lit Dun 73 E4
Street The. Lit Wal 98 A3
Street The. Man 46 C1
Street The. Ple 83 F1
Street The. Ray 64 C1
Street The. Rox 109 D3
Street The. Saw 78 C1
Street The. Sheer 91 E4
Street The. Topp 32 A4
Strethall Rd. Litt 12 B2
Strood Ave. Romf 164 B2
Struan Ave. Corr 179 F3
Strudwick Cl. Brain 65 F1
Stuart Cl. Brent 146 A2
Stuart Cl. Gt Bad 125 D4
Stuart Rd. Grave 193 D1
Stuart Rd. Grays 185 D1
Stuart Way. Bill 149 F1
Stuarts Way. Brain 66 A1
Stubbers La. Upm 175 F3
Stubbs La. Brain 66 B1
Stublands. Basil 171 F3
Studland Ave. Wick 162 C4
Stump La. Sprin 111 E2
Sturmer End Ind Est. Hav 7 E3
Sturmer Rd. Hav 7 E3
Sturrocks. Basil 171 F2
Styles. Lit Ba 41 E1
Sudbrook Cl. Wick 163 E3
Sudbury Rd. S Han 151 D3
Sudburys Farm Rd. Bill 160 B3
Sudicamps Ct. Wa Aby 127 D3
Suffolk Dr. Basil 170 A3
Suffolk Dr. Sprin 112 A2
Suffolk Rd. Dag 173 E4

Suffolk Rd. Grave 193 E1
Suffolk Way. Hornc 166 A4
Sugar La. Si Hed 44 C4
Sugden Ave. Wick 163 D4
Sullivan Rd. Tilb 193 D3
Summerdale. Bill 149 D1
Summerfield Rd. Lou 140 B2
Summerlields. Ing 135 E2
Summerhill Rd. Saff W 25 E4
Summit Dr. Woodf 152 B1
Summit The. Lou 140 C4
Sun Ray Ave. Brent 147 F2
Sun Rd. Swan 191 F1
Sun St. Bill 149 D1
Sun St. Saw 78 A1
Sun St. Wa Aby 126 B3
Sunbank. Gt Dun 72 C4
Sundew Ct. Grays 192 B4
Sundridge Cl. Stone 190 A1
Sunflower Cl. Sprin 111 F3
Sunflower Way. Romf 156 B1
Sunnedon. Basil 171 E3
Sunningdale. Bis St 67 F3
Sunningdale Ave. Rain 174 A1
Sunningdale Rd. Chelm 110 C2
Sunningdale Rd. Rain 174 A3
Sunnings La. Upm 175 E3
Sunnycroft Gdns. Upm 166 C2
Sunnydene Cl. Romf 156 C2
Sunnymede. Chig 154 A4
Sunnyside. Basil 169 F2
Sunnyside. Brain 65 F2
Sunnyside. Stan M 57 F3
Sunnyside Ave. Basil 172 B2
Sunnyside Dr. Ching 139 E1
Sunnyside Gdns. Upm 166 B1
Sunnyside Rd. Epp 129 D4
Sunrise Ave. Chelm 111 D3
Sunrise Ave. Hornc 165 E1
Sunset Ave. Ching 139 D1
Sunset Ave. Woodf 152 A3
Surman Cres. Brent 147 E1
Surrey Dr. Hornc 166 A4
Surrey Rd. Dag 173 D4
Surrey Way. Basil 170 A3
Surridge Cl. Rain 174 B1
Susan Cl. Romf 164 B4
Sussex Ave. Romf 156 C2
Sussex Cl. Basil 170 A3
Sussex Cl. Bore 112 C4
Sussex Cl. Hod 100 A4
Sussex Rd. Brent 158 A3
Sutcliffe Cl. Wick 163 E3
Sutherland Pl. Wick 163 E3
Sutton Acres. L Hal 78 B4
Sutton Cl. Lou 140 C1
Sutton Mead. Sprin 112 A2
Suttons Ave. Hornc 165 E1
Suttons Gdns. Hornc 165 E1
Suttons La. Hornc 174 B4
Swale Cl. Ave 183 E4
Swallow Dale. Basil 171 E2
Swallow Path. Chelm 124 A2
Swallow Rd. Runw 151 E1
Swallow Wlk. Rain 174 A3
Swallows. Harl 90 B2
Swallows The. Bill 161 E4
Swan Ave. Upm 166 C2
Swan La. Hav 7 D4
Swan La. Kelv H 132 C1
Swan La. Runw 151 E1
Swan La. Stock 136 B3
Swan Mead. Basil 171 E2
Swan Paddock. Brent 158 B4
Swan Pike Rd. Enf 126 A1
Swan Side. Brain 65 F2
Swan Wlk. Romf 164 C3
Swan Yd. Grave 193 D1
Swanbourne Dr. Hornc 174 B4
Swanscombe St. Swan 191 F1
Swanshope. Lou 141 D4
Swanstead. Basil 171 F2
Sweet Mead. Saff W 13 F2
Sweyne Rd. Swan 191 F1
Sweyns. Harl 103 E3
Swift Cl. Upm 166 C2
Swinborne Ct. Basil 163 D1
Swinborne Rd. Basil 163 E1
Swinbourne Dr. Brain 65 E2
Swinbourne Gdns. Tilb 193 D3
Swindon Cl. Romf 156 C3
Swindon Gdns. Romf 156 C3
Swindon La. Romf 156 C3
Swiss Ave. Chelm 111 D2
Sycamore Ave. Upm 175 D4
Sycamore Dr. Brent 146 B1
Sycamore Field. Harl 102 A3
Sycamore Gr. Brain 65 E1
Sycamore Way. Chelm 124 B3
Sycamores The. Basil 172 B3
Sycamores The. Ave 183 E3
Sycamores The. Bis St 68 A3
Sydenham Cl. Romf 164 C4
Sydner Cl. Gt Bad 125 D3
Sydney Rd. Tilb 193 D3
Sydney Rd. Woodf 152 A3
Sydney Rd. Woodf 153 E1
Syers Field. Weth 44 A1
Sylvan Ave. Hornc 165 F3

Sylvan Cl. Chelm 124 A3
Sylvan Cl. Grays 184 C1
Sylvan Tryst. Bill 149 D2
Sylvan Way. Basil 169 F4
Sylvan Way. Chig 154 A4
Sylvester Gdns. Chig 154 A3
Sylvesters. Harl 101 F3
Sylvia Ave. Brent 159 E4
Symmons Cl. Ray 64 C1
Syracuse Ave. Rain 174 C1
Syringa Ct. Grays 192 B4

Tabor Ave. Brain 65 F2
Tabor's Hill. Gt Bad 124 C4
Tabors Ave. Gt Bad 124 C4
Tabrums Way. Upm 166 C2
Tadlows Cl. Upm 175 D4
Tadworth Par. Hornc 174 A4
Taits. Corr 179 F1
Takeley Cl. Romf 155 E1
Takeley Cl. Wa Aby 126 B3
Takely End. Basil 171 D3
Takely Ride. Basil 171 D3
Talbrook. Brent 157 F4
Talisman Wlk. Bill 149 E3
Tall Trees Cl. Hornc 165 F3
Tallis Cl. Corr 179 E2
Tallis Rd. Basil 170 B4
Tallon Rd. Brent 147 F2
Tally-Ho Dr. Brent 148 B1
Talus Cl. W Thu 183 E1
Tamar Cl. Upm 166 C3
Tamar Dr. Ave 183 E4
Tamar Rise. Sprin 111 E3
Tamar Sq. Woodf 152 A2
Tamarisk Rd. S Ock 176 B1
Tan House La. Nave H 145 D3
Tanfield Dr. Bill 149 D1
Tangent Rd. Romf 156 B1
Tangmere Cres. Hornc 174 A3
Tank Hill Rd. W Thu 183 D1
Tank La. Pur 183 D1
Tanners Way. Hun 88 B4
Tanners Way. Saff W 13 F1
Tannery Cl. Dag 164 A1
Tanswell Ave. Basil 172 A3
Tanswell Cl. Basil 172 A3
Tansy Cl. Romf 156 C2
Tany's Dell. Harl 90 A2
Tanyard The. Thax 40 A1
Tapley Rd. Chelm 110 C4
Tarnworth Rd. Romf 157 D2
Tasker Rd. Grays 186 A2
Tasman Cl. Corr 179 F2
Tasman Cl. Chelm 110 C3
Tasman Rd. Hav 7 E4
Tatsfield Ave. Lo Naz 113 E4
Tattenham Rd. Basil 170 A4
Tattersall Way. Chelm 123 F4
Taunton Cl. Chig 153 F2
Taunton Rd. Romf 156 B3
Taunton Rd. Sprin 111 F3
Taunton Rd. Swan 192 A1
Taverners Green Cl. Wick 163 F3
Taverners Way. Ching 139 F1
Taverners Way. Hornc 100 A3
Tavistock Cl. Romf 156 B1
Tavistock Dr. Bill 148 C3
Tavistock Rd. Basil 170 B4
Tavistock Rd. Sprin 111 F3
Tawney Comm. Sta T 130 B4
Tawneys Rd. Harl 102 C3
Tawny Ave. Upm 175 D4
Tay Way. Romf 155 F1
Taylifers. Harl 102 A2
Taylor Ave. Chelm 110 C3
Taylor Cl. Romf 155 D2
Taylors Ave. Hod 100 A3
Taylors End Rd. Take 58 C1
Teagles. Basil 170 C3
Tees Cl. Upm 166 B3
Tees Dr. Romf 156 B4
Tees Rd. Sprin 111 E3
Telford Rd. Brain 66 A1
Tempest Way. Rain 174 A3
Templar's Ct. Hav 6 C4
Temple Cl. Bill 148 C3
Temple Bank. Harl 90 A3
Temple Mead. Roy 88 A1
Templer Ave. Grays 186 A2
Templewood Rd. Basil 172 A3
Tendring Rd. Harl 102 C3
Tennyson Ave. Grays 185 E2
Tennyson Ave. Wa Aby 126 C3
Tennyson Cl. Brain 76 C4
Tennyson Dr. Basil 172 A3
Tennyson Rd. Brent 147 E1
Tennyson Rd. Chelm 110 C3
Tennyson Rd. Romf 156 B2
Tennyson Rd. Stone 190 A1
Tennyson Way. Hornc 164 C1
Tennyson Wlk. Tilb 193 D3
Tensing Gdns. Bill 149 D1
Tenterfields. Basil 172 B4
Tenterfields. Gt Dun 72 C4
Tenterfields. New 24 C1
Tercel Path. Chig 154 A3
Terling. Basil 171 D3

Terling Rd. Dag 164 A1
Terlings The. Brent 158 A4
Terminal Rd N. Take 59 D2
Terminal Rd S. Take 59 E2
Terminus Dr. Basil 172 A2
Terminus St. Harl 102 B4
Tern Cl. Hav 7 E4
Tern Gdns. Upm 166 C2
Tern Way. Brent 157 F3
Terrace St. Grave 193 D1
Terrace The. Grave 193 E1
Teviot Ave. Ave 183 E4
Thackeray Ave. Tilb 193 D3
Thackeray Row. Wick 163 E3
Thalmassing Cl. Brent 159 D4
Thames Ave. Chelm 110 B2
Thames Cl. Brain 66 B1
Thames Cl. Corr 180 A2
Thames Cl. Rain 182 A4
Thames Cres. Corr 180 B3
Thames Dr. Grays 186 A1
Thames Haven Rd. Corr 180 A2
Thames Rd. Grays 192 A4
Thames View. Basil 170 B1
Thames View. Grays 186 A1
Thames Way. Grave 192 C1
Thameshill Ave. Romf 155 E1
Thamley. Pur 183 D1
Thane Ave. Dag 173 E1
Thatchers Cl. Lou 141 E4
Thaxted Rd. Deb 38 B3
Thaxted Rd. Lou 140 C1
Thaxted Rd. Saff W 25 F4
Thaxted Rd. Wim 26 B2
Thaxted Way. Wa Aby 126 B3
Thaxted Wlk. Rain 173 F3
Thele Ave. Sta Ab 87 E2
Thele Estate. Sta Ab 87 F2
Theobalds Ave. Grays 185 E1
Thetford Pl. Bill 161 E1
Theydon Cres. Basil 162 C1
Theydon Ct. Wa Aby 127 D3
Theydon Gdns. Rain 173 F3
Theydon Gr. Epp 116 A1
Theydon Gr. Woodf 152 B2
Theydon Park Rd. The B 128 C1
Theydon Pl. Epp 128 C4
Theydon Rd. Epp 128 B3
Theydon Rd. The B 128 B3
Third Ave. Basil 169 F2
Third Ave. Chelm 111 D3
Third Ave. Corr 179 F2
Third Ave. Dag 173 D2
Third Ave. Harl 102 B4
Third Ave. W Thu 191 D4
Thirlmere Cl. Bl Not 76 B4
Thirtieth St. Take 58 C2
Thistle Mead. Lou 141 D3
Thistledene Ave. Hav B 155 D3
Thistledown. Basil 171 E3
Thistledown. Pan 65 D4
Thistledown St. Basil 171 E3
Thistley Cres. Quen 36 C1
Thistley Green Rd. Brain 66 A4
Thoby La. Mtssg 134 B1
Thomas Bata Ave. Grays 187 D1
Thomas Cl. Brent 158 C4
Thomas Rd. Basil 172 C4
Thomasin Rd. Basil 163 E1
Thomley High. Thor 67 F1
Thorley Hill. Bis St 67 F3
Thorley La. Bis St 67 F2
Thorley La. Thor 67 E2
Thorley Park Rd. Bis St 67 F2
Thorley Rd. Grays 185 D3
Thorn Gr. Bis St 68 A3
Thorn La. Rain 174 B2
Thornbera Cl. Bis St 67 F2
Thornbera Gdns. Bis St 67 F2
Thornbera Rd. Bis St 67 F2
Thornbury Cl. Hod 87 D1
Thornbush. Basil 170 C4
Thorncroft. Hornc 165 D3
Thorncroft. Saff W 13 F1
Thorndales. Brent 158 B3
Thornden Gate. Brent 159 E3
Thorndon App. Brent 159 E2
Thorndon Ave. Horn H 168 B3
Thornfield Rd. Bis St 67 F4
Thornhill. N W Bas 117 E3
Thornridge. Brent 146 A1
Thornton Pl. Stock 136 C1
Thornton Rd. Take 70 C4
Thornton Way. Basil 170 A3
Thorntons. Brent 159 E2
Thorntons Farm Ave. Romf .. 164 B1
Thornwood Cl. Woodf 152 A1
Thornwood Rd. N W Bas 116 B3
Thorogood Way. Rain 173 F2
Thorolds. Basil 171 F2
Thorrington Cross. Basil 171 E3
Thors Oak. Corr 179 F1
Three Horseshoes Rd. Harl .. 102 A3
Three Mile Hill. Chelm 123 E1
Thremhall Ave. Birhr 68 C4
Thremhall Ave. Stan M 69 E4
Thremhall Ave. Take 58 C1
Threshelford. Basil 170 C2
Thrift Green. Brent 159 D4

Thrifts Mead. The B 128 C1
Throwley Cl. Basil 172 B3
Thurgood Rd. Hod 100 A4
Thurlby Cl. Woodf 152 C3
Thurloe Gdns. Romf 164 C3
Thurloe Wlk. Grays 185 D2
Thurlow Gdns. Chig 153 E2
Thurrock Park Way. Grays 192 B4
Thurso Cl. Romf 157 D2
Thurstans. Harl 102 B2
Thynne Rd. Bill 149 E1
Tiberius Cl. Hav 7 E4
Tickenhall Dr. Harl 103 E4
Tidworth Ave. Runw 151 F1
Tidy's La. Epp 116 A1
Tilbury Gdns. Tilb 193 D2
Tilbury Hotel Rd. Tilb 193 D2
Tilbury Mead. Harl 103 D3
Tilbury Rd. Horn H 168 C3
Tilbury Rd. Ridge 20 B2
Tilegate Rd. Harl 102 C3
Tilegate Rd. Mag Lav 104 C3
Tillingham Ct. Wa Aby 127 D3
Tillingham Green. Basil 170 A3
Tillwicks Rd. Harl 102 C4
Tilney Dr. Lou 152 A4
Tilney Turn. Basil 171 F2
Timberdene Ave. Woodf 153 E1
Timberlog Cl. Basil 171 F3
Timberlog La. Basil 171 F3
Timbermans View. Basil 171 F2
Timpsons La. Sprin 111 F2
Tindal Sq. Chelm 111 D1
Tindal St. Chelm 111 D1
Tindall Cl. Romf 156 C1
Tindon End Rd. Lit Sam 28 B1
Tine Rd. Chig 153 F3
Tinker Ave. Finch 43 E3
Tinkler Side. Basil 171 D3
Tiplers Bridge. S Han 150 A3
Tipps Cross La. Dodd 133 D2
Tips Cross Mead. Dodd 133 D2
Tiptree Cl. Hornc 166 A2
Tiptree Cres. Woodf 153 D1
Tiptree Gr. Wick 163 E4
Titan Rd. Grays 185 D1
Tithe The. Wick 163 D3
Tithelands. Harl 101 F3
Tithelands. Harl 102 A3
Tiverton Ave. Woodf 153 D1
Tiverton Gr. Romf 157 D3
Tobruk Rd. Chelm 110 C3
Toddbrook. Harl 102 A4
Toft Ave. Grays 185 E1
Tolbut Ct. Romf 164 C3
Tollesbury Cl. Wick 163 F3
Tollgate Rd. Stone 190 B1
Tom's La. Finch 42 A3
Tomkins Cl. Corr 179 E2
Tomkyns La. Upm 166 B4
Tomlyns Cl. Brent 147 F2
Tomswood Hill. Woodf 153 D2
Tomswood Rd. Chig 153 D2
Tonbridge Rd. Romf 156 B2
Toot Hill Rd. Ch Ong 117 F1
Top House Rise. Ching 139 E1
Top Rd. Wim 27 F2
Toplands Ave. Ave 183 E3
Toppesfield Ave. Wick 163 E3
Toppesfield Rd. Gt Y 32 C4
Tor Bryan. Ing 135 D1
Toronto Cl. Tilb 193 D3
Torquay Rd. Sprin 111 E3
Torrance Cl. Hornc 165 E2
Torridge. Grays 187 E1
Torrington Cl. Sprin 111 F3
Torrington Dr. Lou 141 E3
Torrington Gdns. Lou 141 E3
Torrington Rd. Dag 164 A2
Torver Cl. Bl Not 76 B3
Tot La. Birhr 57 E2
Totnes Wlk. Sprin 111 F3
Toucan Way. Basil 171 D2
Tovey Ave. Hod 100 A4
Tovey Cl. Lo Naz 113 F4
Tower Ave. Chelm 110 C2
Tower Cl. N W Bas 117 E4
Tower Cl. Woodf 153 D2
Tower Ct. Brent 158 B4
Tower Ct. Ch Ong 119 D1
Tower Hill. Brent 158 B4
Tower Rd. Epp 115 F1
Tower Rd. Writ 109 F1
Towers Rd. Grays 185 E1
Town Croft. Chelm 111 D3
Town Mead Rd. Wa Aby 126 B3
Town Pier. Grave 193 D1
Town Sq. Basil 171 D3
Town St. Thax 40 A1
Townfield St. Chelm 111 D2
Towngate. Basil 171 D3
Tracyes Rd. Harl 103 D3
Traddles Ct. Chelm 110 C3
Trafalgar Rd. Rain 173 F2
Trafalgar Way. Bill 149 D3
Trafalgar Way. Brain 66 A2
Trafford Cl. Chig 153 F2
Trap's Hill. Lou 140 C3
Travers Way. Basil 172 A3

Trebble Rd. Swan 191 F1
Tredgetts. Ash 4 A1
Tree Tops. Brent 146 B1
Trefgarne Rd. Dag 164 A1
Tregelles Rd. Hod 100 A4
Trehearn Rd. Chig 153 E2
Trelawney Rd. Chig 153 E2
Trenchard Cres. Sprin 111 E4
Trenham Ave. Basil 172 B4
Trent. Grays 187 E1
Trent Ave. Upm 166 B3
Trent Cl. Wick 163 E3
Trent Rd. Chelm 110 B3
Trent Rd. Lou 140 A1
Trentbridge Cl. Chig 153 F2
Trescoe Gdns. Romf 155 E3
Trevor Cl. Bill 160 C4
Trevor Rd. Woodf 152 A2
Trimble Cl. Ing 135 D2
Trimley Cl. Basil 171 E4
Trindehay. Basil 170 C3
Trinder Way. Wick 163 D3
Tring Cl. Romf 156 C3
Tring Gdns. Romf 156 C3
Tring Green. Romf 156 C3
Tring Wlk. Romf 156 C3
Trinidad Gdns. Dag 173 E3
Trinity Cl. Bill 161 E3
Trinity Cl. Bis St 67 F3
Trinity Cl. Chelm 111 E3
Trinity Rd. Bill 161 E3
Trinity Rd. Chelm 111 E1
Trinity Rd. Woodf 153 E1
Trinity St. Bis St 67 F3
Trinity Way. Bis St 67 F3
Tripat Cl. Corr 180 B3
Tripton Rd. Harl 102 C4
Troopers Dr. Romf 156 B3
Trotter's Gap. Sta Ab 87 F2
Trotters Field. Brain 66 A2
Trotters Rd. Harl 103 D3
Trotwood. Chig 153 E2
Trotwood Cl. Chelm 110 C4
Trowbridge Rd. Romf 156 C3
Trueloves La. Ing 134 C2
Trueman Cl. Basil 170 A3
Trumpeter Ct. Bill 148 C2
Truro Wlk. Romf 156 B2
Trustons Gdns. Hornc 165 D2
Tuck Rd. Rain 174 A3
Tucker's Row. Bis St 67 F3
Tudor Ave. Corr 179 F2
Tudor Ave. Romf 165 D4
Tudor Cl. Brent 146 C2
Tudor Cl. Chig 153 D3
Tudor Cl. Hun 88 B4
Tudor Cl. Ing 135 D1
Tudor Cl. Woodf 152 A3
Tudor Cres. Woodf 153 D2
Tudor Ct. Bill 161 F1
Tudor Dr. Romf 156 D4
Tudor Gdns. Romf 165 D4
Tudor Gdns. Upm 166 B3
Tudor Way. Wa Aby 126 B3
Tudor Way. Wick 163 D4
Tufter Rd. Chig 153 F3
Tugby Pl. Chelm 110 C3
Tukes Way. Saff W 25 E4
Tulip Cl. Brent 146 A2
Tulip Cl. Romf 156 B2
Tulip Cl. Sprin 111 F4
Tumbler Rd. Harl 103 D4
Tunnmeade. Harl 90 A1
Tunstall Ave. Chig 154 A2
Tunstall Cl. Basil 172 B3
Tupman Cl. Chelm 110 B3
Turkey Oaks. Chelm 111 E2
Turners Cl. Ch Ong 118 C1
Turnpike La. Grays 186 B1
Turold Rd. Corr 179 F2
Turp Ave. Grays 185 E2
Turpin Ave. Romf 155 D2
Turpin's La. Chig 152 C3
Turpins The. Basil 171 E4
Tusser Ct. Gt Bad 124 B4
Tuttlebee La. Lou 152 A4
Twain Terr. Wick 163 E3
Tweed. Grays 187 E1
Tweed Glen. Romf 155 E2
Tweed Green. Romf 155 E2
Tweed Way. Romf 155 E2
Twentieth St. Take 58 C2
Twentyfirst St. Take 58 C2
Twentyman Cl. Woodf 152 A3
Twitten La. Chelm 124 A1
Twyford Bury La. Bis St 68 A3
Twyford Cl. Bis St 68 A3
Twyford Gdns. Bis St 67 F2
Twyford Rd. Bis St 68 A3
Tyburns The. Brent 159 D4
Tycehurst Hill. Lou 140 C3
Tye Common Rd. Bill 160 B4
Tye Green Rd. Els 58 B3
Tye Green Village. Harl 102 C3
Tyefields. Basil 172 B4
Tyelands. Bill 160 C4
Tyle Green. Hornc 165 F4
Tyler Ave. Basil 170 B3
Tylers. Saff W 14 C1

...ers Ave. Bill 149 E3
...ers Cl. Chelm 124 A3
...ers Cl. Lou 140 C1
...ers Rd. Roy 101 E2
...ney Croft. Harl 102 B3
...ne. Grays 187 E1
...ne Cl. Upm 166 B3
...ne Ave. Basil 183 E3
...ne Way. Chelm 110 B3
...nfield Rd. Hod 87 D1
...rell Rise. Brent 158 B3
...rells Cl. Sprin 111 F2
...rells Cl. Upm 166 A1
...rells The. Corr 180 A2
...rells Way. Gt Bad 124 C4
...rone Cl. Bill 161 E3
...rone Rd. Bill 161 E3
...rell Ct. Basil 172 B3
...rells Hall Cl. Grays 185 E1
...rells Rd. Bill 161 E3
...sea Cl. Harl 102 C3
...sea Hill. Nave H 143 F1
...sea Hill. Sta Abb 143 F1
...sea Rd. Harl 102 C3
...ssen Pl. S Ock 176 B2
...the Cl. Sprin 111 F4

...all Gdns. Romf 155 D2
...swater Rd. Bl Not 76 B3
...swater Way. Hornc 174 A4
...a Rd. Basil 172 C3
...nderwood Rd. Woodf 152 B2
...win Pl. Stock 136 C1
...t Cl. Bill 148 C2
...land Court Rd. Romf 156 C1
...land Croft Rd. Romf 156 C1
...land Dr. Bill 148 C2
...land Rd. Bill 148 C2
...land Rd. Ep Gr 115 F3
...lands Dr. Sprin 111 E4
...lands Rd. Woodf 152 C2
...lands The. Lou 140 C3
...minster Rd. Hornc 165 F1
...minster Rd N. Rain 174 B1
...minster Rd S. Rain 174 A1
...minster Trad Pk. Brent . 167 E2
...pper Ave. Basil 172 C4
...pper Brentwood Rd. Romf .. 165 E4
...pper Bridge Rd. Chelm .. 111 D1
...pper Chase. Chelm 124 A4
...pper Cornsland. Brent .. 158 B4
...pper Farm Rd. Ashe 20 B4
...pper Hook. Harl 102 C3
...pper Market Rd. Runw .. 163 E4
...pper Marsh La. Hod 100 A3
...pper Mayne. Basil 170 C4
...pper Mealines. Harl 103 D3
...pper Mill Field. Gt Dun ... 72 C4
...pper Moors. Gt Wal 97 F4
...pper Park. Harl 89 D1
...pper Park. Lou 140 B2
...pper Park Rd. Wick 163 E2
...pper Rainham Rd. Hornc .. 164 C1
...pper Rd. Bill 162 B3
...pper Roman Rd. Chelm .. 111 D1
...pper Ryle. Brent 146 A1
...pper Stonyfield. Harl 102 A4
...pper Swaines. Epp 115 F1
...psheres. Saff W 25 F4
...shire Rd. Wa Aby 127 D3
...ton Cl. Corr 179 E1
...oway The. Basil 171 E4
...rban Ave. Hornc 165 E1
...rban Rd. Bis St 68 A4
...sk Rd. Ave 183 E4
...sterdale Rd. Saff W 13 F2
...vedale Rd. Dag 164 A1
...xbridge Cl. Wick 163 F3

...alance Ave. Ching 139 F1
...alance Rd. Clav 35 D4
...ale Cl. Brent 145 F2
...ale End. Chelm 124 B2
...ale The. Basil 171 E2
...ale The. Bill 149 E4
...ale The. Brent 146 B1
...ale The. Woodf 152 A2
...alence Way. Basil 170 B2
...alentines. Stock 136 C1
...alentines. Wick 163 E3
...alentines Way. Romf 164 C1
...aliant Cl. Romf 155 D1
...alletta Cl. Chelm 111 D2
...alley Bridge. Chelm 111 D3
...alley Cl. Lou 140 C2
...alley Cl. Wa Aby 126 B4
...alley Hill. Lou 140 C2
...alley Rd. Bill 149 E1
...alley Rd. Brain 66 A2
...alley Side. Ching 139 D1
...alley View. Swan 191 D1
...almar Ave. Sta L H 179 D1
...andenbury Circ. Finch 43 E3
...ange Corner Dr. Corr 171 D1
...ange Hill Dr. Basil 171 F2
...ange Park Rd. Basil 171 D1
...anguard Cl. Romf 155 D1

Vanguard Way. Brain 66 A2
Vantorts Cl. Saw 77 F1
Vantorts Rd. Saw 77 F1
Varden Cl. Chelm 110 C3
Vaughan Ave. Hornc 174 B4
Vaughan Cl. Ray 64 C1
Vaughan Willaims Rd. Basil .. 170 B4
Vauxhall Dr. Brain 65 E1
Velizy Ave. Harl 102 B4
Vellacotts. Chelm 111 D4
Venette Cl. Rain 182 A4
Venmore Dr. Gt Dun 72 C4
Venue Rd. Brent 158 B3
Veny Cres. Hornc 174 B4
Vera Rd. S Han 151 D1
Verbena Cl. S Ock 184 B4
Verderers Rd. Chig 154 A3
Vere Rd. Lou 141 E3
Vermeer Ride. Sprin 111 F4
Vermont Cl. Basil 172 B4
Vernon Ave. Woodf 152 A2
Vernon Cnr. Stock 136 B1
Vernon Cres. Brent 159 D4
Vernon Rd. Romf 155 D2
Vernon Rd. Swan 191 F1
Vernon Way. Brain 66 B3
Vernon's Cl. Hen 48 C2
Vernons Wlk. Basil 163 D1
Veronica Cl. Romf 156 B2
Vexil Cl. W Thu 183 F1
Veysey Gdns. Dag 164 A1
Viaduct Rd. Chelm 111 D1
Viaduct The. Woodf 152 A1
Vicarage Cl. Brent 157 F3
Vicarage Cl. Gt Sal 64 A4
Vicarage Cl. Rox 109 D3
Vicarage Dr. Grave 192 B1
Vicarage La. Berd 46 A4
Vicarage La. Chig 153 E4
Vicarage La. Gt Bad 124 C3
Vicarage La. N W Bas 117 D4
Vicarage La. Thax 40 A2
Vicarage La. Ugl 47 F3
Vicarage Mews. Gt Bad 124 C3
Vicarage Rd. Chelm 124 A4
Vicarage Rd. Dag 173 D3
Vicarage Rd. Epp 116 B1
Vicarage Rd. Finch 42 B3
Vicarage Rd. Hornc 165 D2
Vicarage Rd. Ple 83 F1
Vicarage Rd. Rox 109 E3
Vicarage Rd. Woodf 152 C2
Vicarage Sq. Grays 192 A4
Vicarage Wood. Harl 90 A1
Victor App. Hornc 165 E2
Victor Ave. Basil 172 B3
Victor Cl. Hornc 165 E2
Victor Gdns. Hornc 165 E2
Victor Wlk. Hornc 165 E2
Victor's Cres. Brent 159 D4
Victoria Ave. Basil 170 B2
Victoria Ave. Grays 185 E2
Victoria Ave. Romf 155 D2
Victoria Ave. Saff W 13 F1
Victoria Ave. Wick 163 E4
Victoria Cl. Basil 170 A4
Victoria Cl. Grays 185 E2
Victoria Cres. Basil 170 B4
Victoria Cres. Chelm 111 D2
Victoria Cres. Wick 163 D4
Victoria Gdns. Saff W 25 F4
Victoria Rd. Basil 170 A4
Victoria Rd. Basil 171 E1
Victoria Rd. Brent 158 B4
Victoria Rd. Brent 158 B4
Victoria Rd. Chelm 111 E2
Victoria Rd. Ching 139 F1
Victoria Rd. Dag 173 E4
Victoria Rd. Horn H 177 F4
Victoria Rd. Horn H 178 C2
Victoria Rd. Lou 152 B4
Victoria Rd. Romf 164 C3
Victoria Rd. Sta L H 179 E1
Victoria Rd. Wa Aby 126 B3
Victoria Rd. Woodf 152 A1
Victoria Rd. Writ 109 F1
Victoria Rd S. Chelm 111 D1
Victoria St. Brain 66 A1
Victory Rd. Rain 174 A2
Victory Way. Romf 155 D1
Vienna Cl. Woodf 152 C1
View Cl. Chig 153 E3
Vigerons Way. Grays 186 A1
Vignoles Rd. Romf 164 A2
Viking Way. Brent 146 A2
Viking Way. Runw 151 E1
Village Gate. Sprin 112 A2
Village The. Will 107 E2
Villiers Pl. Bore 99 F1
Villiers-Sur-Marne Ave. Bis St . 67 E3
Vincent Ave. Horn H 178 C2
Vincent Cl. Chig 153 E2
Vincent Cl. Corr 180 A2
Vincent Rd. Rain 174 B1
Vincent Way. Bill 149 D3
Vine Gr. H Wy 89 F3
Vine St. Gt Ba 42 A1
Vine St. Romf 164 B4
Vineries Cl. Dag 173 D3

Vineway. Brent 146 B1
Vineyards The. Gt Bad 124 C4
Viola Cl. S Ock 176 B1
Violet Cl. Sprin 111 F4
Violet Rd. Woodf 152 A1
Violets La. Fu Pel 45 D2
Virginia Gdns. Woodf 153 E1
Vista Rd. Wick 163 F4
Vowler Rd. Basil 170 A2
Voysey Gdns. Basil 163 D1

Wadham Cl. Ing 135 D2
Wagon Mead. Hat B O 79 D2
Wainfleet Ave. Romf 155 E1
Wainsfield Villas. Thax 40 A1
Wainwright Ave. Brent 147 E2
Wakefield Ave. Bill 149 D1
Wakefield Cl. Gt C 1 B2
Wakefield Cl. Hornc 165 F3
Wakelin Chase. Ing 135 D2
Waldeck Rd. Stone 190 A1
Waldegrave. Basil 171 D2
Waldegrave Gdns. Upm ... 166 A2
Walden Ave. Rain 173 E2
Walden Ave. Wim 26 C1
Walden Rd. Ash 14 C3
Walden Rd. Gt C 1 C1
Walden Rd. Had 3 D3
Walden Rd. Hornc 165 E3
Walden Rd. Lit C 12 C4
Walden Rd. Litt 12 C2
Walden Rd. Rad 27 E4
Walden Rd. Saff W 14 B1
Walden Rd. Thax 39 F3
Walden Rd. Wen A 24 C3
Walden Way. Chig 153 F2
Walden Way. Hornc 165 E3
Waldgrooms. Gt Dun 61 E1
Waldon. Grays 187 E2
Waldringfield. Basil 171 D4
Walford Pl. Sprin 111 F1
Walfords Cl. Harl 90 B2
Walk The. Gt Ba 42 A1
Walk The. Hornc 165 F1
Walker Ave. Fyf 106 B1
Walker's Hoppet. Lou 140 C4
Walkers Cl. Sprin 111 E4
Wall Chase. St Wal 83 F4
Wallace Cres. Chelm 124 B4
Wallace Gdns. Swan 191 F1
Wallace Rd. Grays 185 D1
Wallace's La. Bore 99 F2
Wallasea Gdns. Sprin 111 F3
Wallenger Ave. Romf 165 D4
Wallers Cl. Woodf 152 C2
Wallers Way. Hod 87 D1
Wallflower Cl. Sprin 111 F3
Wallis Cl. Hornc 165 D2
Wallis Park. Grave 192 A1
Walmer Cl. Romf 155 D1
Walnut Dri. Bis St 67 E2
Walnut Gr. Brain 65 F1
Walnut Tree Ave. Saw 77 F1
Walnut Tree Cl. Hod 100 A3
Walnut Tree Cres. Saw 77 F2
Walnut Way. Lou 152 B4
Walpole Cl. Grays 185 E1
Walsingham Way. Bill 149 D3
Walters Cl. Chelm 124 B2
Waltham Cl. Brent 147 E2
Waltham Glen. Chelm 124 B4
Waltham Rd. Bore 99 F3
Waltham Rd. Lo Naz 113 F3
Waltham Rd. Lo Naz 114 A3
Waltham Rd. Terl 86 C1
Waltham Rd. Woodf 152 C2
Waltham Way. Ching 139 D1
Walthams. Basil 172 A4
Walthams Pl. Basil 172 A4
Walton Cl. Brent 170 B4
Walton Gdns. Brent 147 E2
Walton Gdns. Wa Aby 126 A3
Walton Rd. Hod 100 B4
Walton Rd. Romf 154 C2
Walton's Hall Rd. Sta L H .. 187 D3
Wambrook Cl. Brent 147 E1
Wannock Gdns. Woodf 153 D2
Wansford Cl. Brent 157 F4
Wansford Rd. Woodf 152 B1
Wantz La. Rain 174 A1
Wantz Rd. Dag 173 D4
Wantz Rd. Marg 136 A4
Warburtons. Corr 180 A2
Ward Ave. Grays 185 D1
Ward Cres. Bis St 67 F3
Warden Ave. Romf 155 E3
Ware Rd. Gt Am 87 D1
Ware Rd. Hod 100 A4
Warehouse Rd. Steb 62 C2
Warehouse Villas. Steb 63 D2
Wares Rd. G Ea 95 F3
Warescot Cl. Brent 146 A1
Warescot Rd. Brent 146 A1
Warley Gap. Brent 158 B2
Warley Hall La. Horn H 167 F2
Warley Hill. Brent 158 B3
Warley Mount. Brent 158 B3
Warley Rd. Brent 157 F1
Warley Rd. Upm 157 F1

Warley Rd. Woodf 152 A2
Warley Rd. Woodf 153 D1
Warley St. Brent 167 E3
Warleywoods Cres. Brent .. 158 A3
Warner Cl. Bill 149 E1
Warner Dr. Brain 65 E2
Warners. Gt Dun 72 B4
Warners Cl. Woodf 152 A3
Warren Cl. Broom 98 A2
Warren Cl. Take 70 B4
Warren Ct. Chig 153 E3
Warren Dr. Hornc 165 D1
Warren Field. Epp 129 D4
Warren Hill. Lou 140 B2
Warren La. Grays 184 B1
Warren La. Kelv H 146 A4
Warren La. Writ 110 B2
Warren Pond Rd. Ching ... 139 F1
Warren Rd. Brain 66 B3
Warren Rd. Ching 139 E1
Warren Rd. S Han 151 E4
Warren Terr. Grays 184 B2
Warren The. Bill 148 C2
Warrene Cl. Sta L H 179 E1
Warriner Ave. Horne 165 E1
Warrington Gdns. Hornc .. 165 E3
Warrington Sq. Bill 148 C2
Warwick Cl. Brain 66 A2
Warwick Gdns. Romf 165 E4
Warwick La. Upm 175 D2
Warwick Pl. Basil 169 F2
Warwick Pl. Grave 192 A1
Warwick Pl. Kelv H 145 E3
Warwick Rd. Bis St 68 A3
Warwick Rd. Rain 174 B1
Warwick Rd. Take 70 C4
Warwick Sq. Chelm 110 C2
Wash Rd. Bill 161 F1
Wash Rd. Brent 147 E2
Wash The. St Pel 45 E3
Washington Ave. Basil 170 A3
Wat Tyler Way. Basil 172 A1
Watch House Rd. Bill 62 C3
Watchouse Rd. Chelm 124 B2
Water Hall La. Shal 54 C4
Water La. Bis St 67 F4
Water La. Brox 60 B4
Water La. Deb 26 A1
Water La. Hel B 17 E4
Water La. New 25 D1
Water La. Pur 183 D1
Water La. Rad 27 F4
Water La. Roy 101 F2
Water La. Shal 54 C2
Water La. Ste B 18 A3
Water La. Stur 7 F3
Waterhouse La. Chelm 110 C1
Waterhouse Moor. Harl 102 C4
Waterhouse St. Chelm 110 C1
Waterloo Gdns. Romf 164 B3
Waterloo La. Chelm 111 E1
Waterloo Rd. Brent 146 B1
Waterloo Rd. Romf 164 C3
Waterloo Rd. Woodf 153 E1
Watermans Way. N W Bas .. 117 D2
Waters Gdns. Dag 173 D4
Waterside. Stan M 57 F3
Watersmeet. Harl 102 A2
Waterson Rd. Grays 186 B1
Waterville Rd. Basil 172 A2
Waterworks La. Corr 180 B3
Watery La. Gt Dun 72 A1
Watery La. Lit Lav 105 E4
Watery La. Man 46 B1
Wates Way. Brent 146 B1
Watling La. Thax 39 F2
Watling St. Thax 40 A2
Watlington Rd. Harl 90 B2
Watson Cl. Grays 191 D3
Watson Gdns. Romf 156 B1
Watts Cl. Barn 73 D2
Watts Cres. W Thu 183 E1
Wavell Cl. Sprin 111 E4
Waveney Dr. Sprin 111 E3
Waveney Terr. Hav 7 D4
Waverley Cl. Woodf 152 B1
Waverley Cres. Romf 156 B2
Waverley Cres. Runw 151 E2
Waverley Gdns. Grays 185 D2
Waverley Gdns. Woodf 153 E1
Waverley Rd. Bill 161 F1
Waverley Rd. Rain 174 A1
Waverley Rd. Woodf 152 B1
Way Bank La. Cla 8 C4
Wayback The. Saff W 13 F1
Waycross Rd. Upm 166 C3
Wayfaring Green. Grays ... 184 C1
Wayletts. Basil 170 A4
Wayre St. Harl 90 B2
Wayre The. Harl 90 B2
Wayside Ave. Hornc 165 E1
Wayside Cl. Romf 164 C4
Wayside Gdns. Dag 173 D4
Waytemore Rd. Bis St 67 F3
Weald Bridge Rd. Mag Lav .. 104 C1
Weald Bridge Rd. N W Bas .. 104 C1
Weald Cl. Brent 158 A4
Weald Hall La. N W Bas ... 116 C3

Weald Park Way. Brent 157 F4
Weald Rd. Brent 145 F1
Weald Way. Romf 164 A3
Wear Dr. Sprin 111 E3
Weaverhead Cl. Thax 40 A2
Weaverhead La. Thax 40 A2
Weavers. Basil 171 F2
Weavers Cl. Bill 149 D1
Webster Cl. Hornc 165 E1
Webster Cl. Wa Aby 127 D3
Webster Pl. Stock 136 C1
Webster Rd. Sta L H 179 F1
Weddell Rd. Hav 7 E3
Wedgewood Cl. Epp 116 A1
Wedhey. Harl 102 B4
Wedlake Cl. Hornc 165 F2
Wedmore Ave. Woodf 153 D1
Wednesbury Gdns. Romf .. 156 C2
Wednesbury Green. Romf .. 156 C2
Wednesbury Rd. Romf 156 C2
Wedow Rd. Thax 40 A2
Weelkes Cl. Corr 179 E2
Weight Rd. Chelm 111 E1
Weind The. The B 128 C2
Weir Wynd. Bill 149 D1
Welbeck Dr. Basil 170 A2
Welbeck Rise. Basil 170 A2
Well Field. Writ 110 A1
Well La. Chelm 124 A1
Well La. Dodd 145 F3
Well La. Harl 89 D1
Well La. Harl 102 A4
Well La. Stock 136 C1
Well La. T Thu 184 C3
Well Mead. Bill 161 E4
Well's St. Chelm 111 D2
Well-Green Cl. Saff W 25 F4
Welland. Grays 187 E1
Welland Ave. Chelm 110 B3
Weller Gr. Chelm 110 C4
Wellesley. Harl 102 A2
Wellesley Rd. Brent 146 B1
Wellfields. Lou 141 D3
Welling Rd. Grays 186 B4
Wellington Cl. Brain 66 B2
Wellington Cl. Chelm 110 B3
Wellington Cl. Dag 173 E3
Wellington Ct. Grays 185 D3
Wellington Dr. Dag 173 E3
Wellington Hill. Wa Aby ... 127 D1
Wellington Mews. Bill 149 D2
Wellington Pl. Brent 158 B3
Wellington Rd. N W Bas ... 117 D2
Wellington Rd. Tilb 193 D3
Wellingtonia Ave. Hav B ... 155 F4
Wellmeads. Chelm 124 A4
Wells Ct. Sprin 111 E3
Wells Gdns. Basil 171 F4
Wells Gdns. Dag 173 D4
Wells Gdns. Rain 173 F3
Wellstye Green. Basil 171 F4
Wenden Rd. Saff W 25 D4
Wendene. Basil 171 F2
Wendover Gdns. Brent 159 D4
Wendover Way. Hornc 174 B4
Wenham Gdns. Brent 147 E2
Wenlocks La. Bla 133 F3
Wennington Green. Rain .. 182 C3
Wennington Rd. Rain 182 B4
Wensley Ave. Woodf 152 A2
Wensley Cl. Romf 155 D3
Wensleydale Ave. Woodf .. 152 C1
Wentworth Cres. Brain 65 F3
Wentworth Dri. Bis St 67 E3
Wentworth Way. Rain 174 A1
Wesley End Rd. Stam 19 E2
Wesley Gdns. Bill 148 C3
West Ave. Chelm 110 C3
West Beech Ave. Wick 163 F4
West Beech Cl. Wick 163 F4
West Cl. Hod 100 A4
West Cl. Rain 174 A1
West Cloister. Bill 149 D1
West Crescent Rd. Grave .. 193 E1
West Croft. Bill 149 E1
West Dene Dr. Romf 156 B3
West Dr. Weth 43 E2
West Fields. Saff W 25 F4
West Gate. Harl 102 B4
West Gr. Woodf 152 B3
West Hanningfield Rd. Sand . 124 C1
West Hanningfield Rd. W Han 124 A1
West Hill Rd. Hod 100 A4
West Hook. Basil 169 F2
West Kent Ave. Grave 192 B1
West Lawn. Chelm 124 B1
West Malling Way. Hornc .. 174 B4
West Mayne. Basil 169 F3
West Park Ave. Bill 149 D2
West Park Cres. Bill 149 D1
West Park Dr. Bill 149 D1
West Park Hill. Brent 158 A4
West Rd. Bis St 67 F3
West Rd. Harl 90 A2
West Rd. Romf 164 B2
West Rd. S Ock 176 A1
West Rd. Saff W 25 E4
West Rd. Saw 77 E2
West Rd. Stan M 57 F3

West Ridge. Bill 149 D1
West Sq. Chelm 111 D1
West Sq. Harl 89 E1
West St. Grave 193 D1
West St. Grays 192 A4
West Thorpe. Basil 171 E3
West Thurrock Way. W Thu .. 183 F1
West Thurrock Way. W Thu .. 184 A1
West View. Lou 140 C3
West Way. Brent 158 A4
West Way. Wa Aby 126 A1
West Wlk. Harl 102 B4
Westall Rd. Lou 141 E3
Westbourne Ct. Hav 7 D4
Westbourne Dr. Brent 157 F3
Westbourne Gdns. Bill 149 D3
Westbourne Gr. Gt Bad 124 B4
Westbury Dr. Brent 158 B4
Westbury La. Lou 152 B4
Westbury Rd. Brent 158 B4
Westbury Rd. Lou 140 B1
Westbury Terr. Upm 166 C1
Westcroft Ct. Hod 100 A2
Westerdale. Sprin 111 E4
Westergreen Meadow. Brain .. 65 F1
Westerings The. Gt Bad ... 124 C3
Western Ave. Brent 146 B1
Western Ave. Dag 173 E3
Western Ave. Epp 128 C4
Western Ave. Romf 156 B1
Western Ave. W Thu 183 F1
Western Cross Cl. Swan 191 E1
Western Gdns. Brent 158 B4
Western Mews. Bill 149 D1
Western Rd. Bill 149 D1
Western Rd. Lo Naz 100 C1
Western Rd. Romf 164 C3
Westfield. Basil 170 A4
Westfield. Harl 102 C4
Westfield. Lou 140 B2
Westfield Ave. Chelm 111 D2
Westfield Cl. Bis St 67 F4
Westfield Cl. Wick 163 F4
Westfield Rd. Bis St 67 F4
Westlake Ave. Basil 172 C3
Westland Ave. Hornc 165 F2
Westland View. Grays 185 D3
Westley La. Saff W 13 E3
Westley Rd. Basil 170 B1
Westlyn Cl. Rain 174 B1
Westmede. Basil 170 B3
Westmede. Chig 153 E2
Westminster Cl. Woodf 153 E1
Westminster Gdns. Brain 66 A2
Westminster Gdns. Ching ... 139 F1
Westminster Gdns. Woodf ... 153 E1
Westmoreland Ave. Hornc .. 165 E4
Weston Ave. W Thu 183 F1
Weston Cl. Brent 147 E1
Westview Dr. Woodf 152 B1
Westway. Chelm 123 F4
Westwood Ave. Brent 158 A3
Wetherfield. Stan M 57 E4
Wetherland. Basil 170 C3
Weydale. Corr 180 A3
Weymarks. Basil 170 B4
Weymouth Rd. Sprin 111 F3
Whadden Chase. Ing 135 D2
Whalebone La N. Romf 154 C1
Wharf Cl. Sta L H 179 E1
Wharf Rd. Bis St 67 F3
Wharf Rd. Brent 158 B4
Wharf Rd. Chelm 111 E1
Wharf Rd. Corr 180 B2
Wharf Rd. Grave 193 F1
Wharf Rd. Grays 191 F4
Wharf Rd. Sta L H 187 E4
Wharf Rd S. Grays 191 F4
Wharley Hook. Harl 102 C3
Wheat Croft. Bis St 67 F2
Wheatear Pl. Bill 149 E1
Wheatfield Way. Basil 170 A2
Wheatfield Way. Chelm 110 C2
Wheatley Ave. Brain 66 B2
Wheatley Cl. Saw 77 E1
Wheatley Rd. Corr 180 A3
Wheatsheaf Rd. Corr 164 C3
Wheel Farm Dr. Dag 164 B1
Wheeler's Hill. Lit Wal 98 C3
Wheelers. Epp 115 F1
Wheelers Cl. Lo Naz 100 C1
Wheelers Fm Gdns. N W Bas 117 D3
Wheelers La. Corr 180 B3
Wheelers La. Nave H 145 D3
Whinhams Way. Bill 148 C2
Whist Ave. Runw 151 F1
Whitakers Way. Lou 140 C4
Whitby Ave. Brent 159 E2
Whitchurch Rd. Romf 156 C3
Whitcroft. Basil 170 B2
White Bear. Stan M 57 F4
White Cotts. Fair 86 B2
White Gdns. Dag 173 D3
White Hall. Abr 142 A3
White Hart La. Brent 158 A4
White Hart La. Romf 155 D1
White Hart La. Sprin 111 F4
White Horse La. New 25 D1

White Lyons Rd. Brent 158 B4
White Post Field. Saw 77 E1
White St. Gt Dun 72 B4
Whitebarn La. Dag 173 D2
Whitebarns. Fu Pel 45 D3
Whitebarns La. Fu Pel 45 D3
Whiteditch La. New 24 C1
Whitehall Cl. Chig 154 A4
Whitehall Cl. Lo Naz 100 C1
Whitehall Gdns. Ching 139 E1
Whitehall La. Bis St 56 C1
Whitehall La. Corr 180 B4
Whitehall La. Grays 185 E1
Whitehall La. Woodf 152 A4
Whitehall Rd. Bis St 56 C1
Whitehall Rd. Ching 139 F1
Whitehall Rd. Grays 185 E1
Whitehall Rd. Woodf 152 A4
Whitehills Rd. Lou 141 D3
Whitehouse Cres. Gt Bad ... 124 B4
Whitehouse Rd. Steb 62 C3
Whitelands. Bla 133 E2
Whitelands Cl. Runw 151 F1
Whitelands Way. Romf 156 B1
Whitemead. Broom 98 A1
Whites Cl. Swan 191 E1
Whites Hill. Stock 150 A4
Whites La. Gt Le 85 F3
Whiteshot Way. Saff W 13 F1
Whiteshott. Basil 171 D2
Whitethorn Gdns. Chelm .. 124 B4
Whitethorn Gdns. Hornc .. 165 E3
Whitewaites. Harl 89 F1
Whiteways. Bill 149 F2
Whiteways. Gt C 1 B1
Whitfields. Sta L H 179 F1
Whitley Rd. Hod 100 A4
Whitley's Chase. Finch 30 B3
Whitmore Ave. Grays 185 D3
Whitmore Ct. Basil 171 F4
Whitmore Way. Basil 171 E4
Whittingstall Rd. Hod 100 A4
Whittington Rd. Brent 147 E2
Whittington Way. Bis St 67 F2
Whybrews. Corr 179 F1
Whybridge Cl. Rain 173 F2
Whytewaters. Basil 171 F2
Whyverne Cl. Sprin 111 F3
Wick Beech Ave. Wick 163 F4
Wick Cres. Wick 163 F3
Wick Dr. Wick 163 E4
Wick Dr. Wick 163 F3
Wick Glen. Bill 148 C2
Wick La. Wick 163 F4
Wicken Rd. New 36 C4
Wickets Way. Chig 153 F2
Wickfield Ash. Chelm 110 B3
Wickford Ave. Basil 172 A3
Wickford Cl. Romf 156 C3
Wickford Dr. Romf 156 C3
Wickham Pl. Basil 171 E3
Wickham Rd. Grays 186 B2
Wickhay. Basil 170 C3
Wicklands Rd. Hun 88 B4
Wicklow Ave. Chelm 110 B3
Wicklow Cl. Brain 65 E2
Wid Cl. Brent 147 E2
Widecombe Cl. Romf 156 B1
Widford Chase. Chelm 123 F4
Widford Cl. Chelm 123 F4
Widford Gr. Chelm 123 F4
Widford Park Pl. Chelm 123 F4
Widford Rd. Chelm 123 F4
Widgeons. Basil 172 B3
Widworthy Hayes. Brent ... 147 D1
Wiggin's La. Bill 160 C4
Wigley Bush La. Brent 157 F4
Wigton Rd. Romf 156 C3
Wigton Way. Romf 156 C3
Wilde Cl. Tilb 193 E3
Wilfred Ave. Rain 182 A4
Wilfred St. Grave 193 D1
Wilkes Rd. Brent 147 E2
Wilkinson Cl. Stone 190 A2
Wilkinsons Mead. Sprin ... 112 A2
Will's Ayley La. Saff W 14 C1
William Cl. Romf 155 E1
William Rd. Basil 172 C3
William St. Grays 192 B4
Williams Rd. Broom 98 A1
Williamsons Way. Corr 179 F3
Willingale Cl. Brent 147 F2
Willingale Cl. Lou 141 E4
Willingale Cl. Woodf 152 B2
Willingale Rd. Fyf 106 C1
Willingale Rd. H Ong 120 C3
Willingale Rd. Lou 141 E4
Willingales The. Basil 170 A3
Willinghall Cl. Wa Aby 126 B4
Willoughby Dr. Rain 173 F3
Willoughby Dr. Sprin 111 F1
Willoughby's La. Brain 66 B4
Willow Cl. Bis St 67 F4
Willow Cl. Brent 147 D2
Willow Cl. Broom 98 A1
Willow Cl. Dodd 133 E1
Willow Cl. Hornc 165 D1
Willow Cl. Lou 152 B4
Willow Green. Ing 135 D2

Willow Mead. Saw 77 F1
Willow Path. Wa Aby 126 C3
Willow St. Ching 139 E1
Willow St. Romf 164 B4
Willow Walk. Upm 166 C2
Willow Way. Romf 157 D2
Willowbank. Chelm 124 A2
Willowdale Centre. Runw .. 163 E4
Willowdene. Brent 145 F2
Willowdene Ct. Brent 158 B3
Willowfield. Basil 170 B4
Willowfield. Bill 161 E1
Willowfield. Harl 102 B3
Willowherb Wlk. Romf 156 B2
Willowhill. Corr 179 F3
Willowmead. Chig 154 A4
Willowmead. S Han 150 B2
Willows The. Basil 172 B3
Willows The. Bill 161 E4
Willows The. Bore 112 C4
Willows The. Grays 192 B4
Willows The. Gt C 1 B2
Wills Hill. Corr 179 E2
Wilmot Green. Brent 158 B2
Wilshire Ave. Sprin 111 F2
Wilsman Rd. S Ock 176 B2
Wilsner. Basil 172 B4
Wilson Cl. Sta L H 187 E4
Wilthorne Gdns. Dag 173 D3
Wilton Cl. Bis St 68 A4
Wilton Dr. Romf 155 E2
Wiltshire Ave. Hornc 165 F4
Wimbish Wlk. Wim 26 C1
Wimborne Cl. Lou 152 B4
Wimborne Cl. Saw 77 E1
Wimbourne. Basil 170 A4
Wimbourne Ct. Basil 172 A4
Wimbush End. Basil 172 A3
Wimbush Mews. Basil 172 A4
Wincanton Gdns. Woodf ... 153 D1
Wincanton Rd. Romf 156 B4
Wincelow Hall Rd. Hemp ... 16 B1
Winchelsea Dr. Gt Bad 124 C4
Winchester Ave. Upm 166 C1
Winchester Cl. Bis St 67 E2
Winchester Gdns. Bill 161 E1
Wind Hill. Mag Lav 105 D2
Windermere Ave. Hornc ... 174 A4
Windermere Dr. Bl Not 76 B3
Windhill. Bis St 67 F4
Windhill Fields. Bis St 67 F4
Windhill Old Rd. Bis St 67 F4
Windmill Cl. Gt Dun 61 F1
Windmill Cl. Upm 166 A1
Windmill Cl. Wa Aby 126 C3
Windmill Fields. Harl 90 A2
Windmill Gdns. Brain 66 A4
Windmill Heights. Bill 161 D4
Windmill Hill. Saff W 13 E2
Windmill Meadows. Ay Rod .. 81 E1
Windmill St. Grave 193 D1
Windmill Way. Kelv H 132 C1
Windmills The. Broom 98 A2
Windrush Dr. Sprin 111 E3
Windsor Ave. Corr 180 A3
Windsor Ave. Grays 185 D2
Windsor Gdns. Bis St 67 D4
Windsor Gdns. Brain 66 A2
Windsor Gdns. Runw 151 E1
Windsor Rd. Basil 172 A4
Windsor Rd. Brent 146 A2
Windsor Rd. Hornc 165 E2
Windsor Rd. S Han 150 B2
Windsor Way. Chelm 110 C1
Windsors The. Lou 152 C4
Windy Hill. Brent 147 E1
Winfields. Basil 172 B4
Wingate Cl. Brain 65 F2
Wingfield. Grays 184 C1
Wingfield Cl. Brent 159 D4
Wingfield Gdns. Upm 166 A2
Wingletye La. Hornc 166 A2
Wingrave Cres. Brent 157 F3
Wingway. Brent 146 B1
Winifred Ave. Hornc 174 C4
Winifred Rd. Basil 172 A3
Winsey Chase. Finch 42 B3
Winstanley Rd. Saff W 25 F4
Winstead Gdns. Dag 173 E4
Winston Cl. Romf 164 A4
Winstree. Basil 172 A4
Winters Way. Wa Aby 127 D3
Winton Ave. Wick 163 D4
Wiscombe Hill. Basil 170 B2
Wisdons Cl. Dag 164 A2
Wisemans Gdns. Saw 77 E1
Wissants. Harl 102 A2
Witchards. Basil 171 D3
Witchtree La. Hemp 16 C2
Witham Cl. Lou 140 C2
Witham Gdns. Horn H 168 B3
Witham Rd. Dag 173 D4
Witham Rd. Romf 165 D3
Witherings The. Hornc 165 F3
Withersfield Rd. Hav 6 C4
Wittering Wlk. Hornc 174 B3
Woburn Ave . Bis St 67 E4
Woburn Ave. Hornc 174 A4
Woburn Ave. The B 128 C1

Woburn Pl. Bill 148 C3
Wokingdon Rd. Grays 186 A2
Wollaston Cres. Basil 163 E1
Wollaston Way. Basil 163 E1
Wolmers Hey. Gt Wal 97 F4
Wolseley Rd. Chelm 111 D1
Wolseley Rd. Romf 164 B2
Wolsey Gdns. Woodf 153 E2
Wood Ave. W Thu 183 E1
Wood Dale. Gt Bad 124 C3
Wood End. Widd 37 E2
Wood Green. Basil 163 D1
Wood La. Dag 164 A1
Wood La. Hornc 174 A4
Wood La. Mee 34 A3
Wood La. Will 107 F2
Wood Meads. Epp 116 A1
Wood St. Chelm 124 A4
Wood St. Grays 192 B4
Wood View. Grays 185 F1
Woodberry Down. Epp 116 C3
Woodberry Way. Ching 139 E1
Woodbine Cl. Harl 102 B3
Woodbridge Cl. Romf 156 B4
Woodbridge La. Romf 156 B4
Woodbrook Cres. Bill 148 C2
Woodbrook Gdns. Wa Aby . 126 C3
Woodbrooke Way. Corr 180 A3
Woodbury Hill. Lou 140 C4
Woodcock Cl. Hav 7 E4
Woodcote Ave. Hornc 174 A4
Woodcote Cres. Basil 172 B3
Woodcroft. Harl 102 B3
Woodcroft Ave. Sta Ab 87 E2
Woodcutters Ave. Grays ... 185 E2
Woodedge Cl. Ching 139 F1
Woodfield. Wick 163 E3
Woodfield Cl. Stan M 57 F3
Woodfield Cl. Romf 165 D4
Woodfield Rd. Brain 66 A2
Woodfield Terr. Stan M 57 F3
Woodfield Way. Hornc 165 E2
Woodfields. Stan M 57 F3
Woodfines The. Hornc 165 E3
Woodford Ct. Wa Aby 127 D3
Woodford Rd. Woodf 152 A1
Woodford Trad Est. Woodf .. 152 B1
Woodgreen Rd. Wa Aby 127 E3
Woodhall Cres. Hornc 165 F2
Woodhall Gr. Bis St 67 E3
Woodhall Hill. Broom 97 E1
Woodhall Rd. Chelm 111 D4
Woodham Way. Sta Ab 87 E2
Woodhays. Basil 172 B4
Woodhill. Harl 102 C3
Woodhouse La. Broom 98 A2
Wooding Gr. Harl 102 A4
Woodland Ave. Brent 147 E2
Woodland Cl. Brent 147 E2
Woodland Cl. Woodf 152 A4
Woodland Rd. Chelm 111 D2
Woodland Rd. Ching 139 E1
Woodland Rd. Lou 140 C3
Woodland Way. Ch Ong ... 118 C1
Woodland Way. The B 128 C2
Woodland Way. Woodf 152 A4
Woodlands. Bis St 68 B4
Woodlands. Brain 66 B2
Woodlands. Epp 129 D4
Woodlands Ave. Hornc 165 F3
Woodlands Cl. Basil 171 F2
Woodlands Cl. Grays 185 F2
Woodlands Cl. Hod 100 A3
Woodlands Cl. Ing 135 E2
Woodlands Dr. Basil 171 E1
Woodlands Dr. Hod 100 A2
Woodlands Rd. Romf 157 D1
Woodlands Rd. Romf 164 C4
Woodlands Rd. Wick 163 E4
Woodman La. Wa Aby 139 F2
Woodman Path. Chig 153 F2
Woodman Rd. Brent 158 B3
Woodman Rd. Chig 153 F3
Woodmanhurst Rd. Corr ... 179 F3
Woodmill Mews. Hod 100 A4
Woodredon Cl. Roy 101 D4
Woodredon Farm La. Wa Aby 127 E2
Woodridden Hill. Wa Aby .. 127 E2
Woodroffe Cl. Sprin 112 A2
Woods Rd. Gt Wal 84 A3
Woodshire Rd. Dag 164 A1
Woodside. Birhr 68 B4
Woodside. Lou 152 B4
Woodside. N W Bas 116 B2
Woodside Cl. Brent 147 E2
Woodside Cl. Rain 174 B1
Woodside Rd. Woodf 152 A3
Woodstock Ave. Romf 157 D2
Woodstock Cres. Basil 169 F3
Woodstock Gdns. Basil 169 F3
Woodview Dr. Gt Le 86 A4
Woodview Rd. Gt Dun 72 B4
Woodville Rd. Woodf 152 A1
Woodward Cl. Grays 185 D1
Woodward Hts. Grays 185 D1
Woodward Terr. Stone 190 C1
Woodwards. Harl 102 B3
Woodway. Brent 147 D1
Woolf Wlk. Tilb 193 E3

Woolhampton Way. Chig .. 154 A4
Woolifers Ave. Corr .... 180 A
Woollard St. Wa Aby .... 126 B
Woollard Way. Bla .... 133 F
Woolmergreen. Basil ...... 170 C
Woolmers Mead. Ple .... 83 F
Woolmongers La. H Ong .. 133 D
Woolnough Cl. Ste B .... 18 A
Woolpack La. Brain .... 65 F
Woolpits Rd. Ba Sal .... 53 F
Woolshots Rd. Wick .... 162 C
Wootton Cl. Hornc .... 165 E
Worcester Ave. Upm .... 166 C
Worcester Cl. Brain .... 66 A
Worcester Cl. Corr .... 179 E
Worcester Cl. Swan .... 191 E
Worcester Cres. Woodf .... 152 B
Worcester Ct. Gt Bad ...... 125 D
Wordsworth Cl. Romf ...... 156 B
Wordsworth Cl. Tilb .... 193 E
Wordsworth Ct. Chelm .... 111 D
Wordsworth Rd. Brain ...... 65 F
Wordsworth Way. Stone ... 190 A
Wormley Ct. Wa Aby ...... 127 D
Wormyngford Ct. Wa Aby .. 127 D
Worrin Cl. Brent .... 146 C
Worrin Rd. Brent .... 146 C
Wortham Pl. Hav .... 7 D
Worthing Rd. Basil .... 170 A
Wouldham Rd. Grays ...... 191 F
Wraglins The. Bis St .... 68 A
Wrangley Ct. Wa Aby ...... 127 D
Wratting Rd. Hav .... 7 D
Wray Cl. Hornc .... 165 E
Wraysbury Dr. Bill .... 161 E
Wren Cl. Bill .... 149 E
Wren Gdns. Hornc .... 164 C
Wren Pl. Brent .... 158 B
Wren Wlk. Tilb .... 193 D
Wrenbrook Rd. Bis St .... 67 F
Wrens The. Harl .... 102 A
Wrexham Rd. Basil .... 170 A
Wrexham Rd. Romf .... 156 B
Wright Cl. Swan .... 191 E
Wright's Green La. L Hal .... 78 A
Wright's Piece. Hen .... 49 D
Wrights La. Bla .... 133 E
Wrightsbridge Rd. Romf ... 156 C
Writtle Rd. Chelm .... 123 F
Writtle Rd. Marg .... 122 C
Writtle Walk. Rain .... 173 F
Writtle Wlk. Basil .... 171 F
Wroths Path. Lou .... 140 C
Wyatt's Green Rd. Dodd ... 133 F
Wyatts Green La. Bla ...... 133 E
Wych Elm. Harl .... 89 E
Wych Elm Cl. Hornc .... 166 A
Wych Elm Rd. Hornc ...... 166 A
Wychford Dri. Saw .... 77 E
Wyes's Rd. Ing .... 122 A
Wyfields. Woodf .... 153 D
Wykeham Ave. Hornc ...... 165 E
Wykeham Rd. Writ .... 110 A
Wykes Green. Basil .... 171 E
Wyldwood Cl. Harl .... 90 B
Wynndale Rd. Woodf ...... 152 A
Wynters. Basil .... 171 D
Wynyard Rd. Saff W .... 13 F
Wythams. Basil .... 172 B
Wythefield. Basil .... 172 A
Wythenshawe Rd. Dag .... 164 A

Yale Way. Hornc 174 A4
Yardeley. Basil 170 C3
Yardley Cl. Ching 139 D2
Yardley Hall La. Thax 39 E3
Yardley La. Ching 139 D2
Yarmouth Pl. Hav 7 D4
Yarwood Rd. Chelm 111 F4
Yeldham Lock. Sprin 112 A1
Yeldham Pl. Hav 7 D4
Yellowpine Way. Chig 154 A3
Yelverton Cl. Romf 156 B1
Yeoman Way. Woodf 153 E2
Yevele Way. Hornc 165 F2
Yew Cl. Lou 152 B4
Yew Tree Cl. Brent 147 D2
Yew Tree Gdns. Chelm 124 B3
Yew Tree Gdns. Romf 164 B3
Yew Wlk. Hod 100 A3
Yewlands. Hod 100 A3
Yewlands. Saw 77 F1
York Ave. Corr 180 A3
York Cl. Brent 146 C1
York Cres. Lou 140 C3
York Gdns. Brain 66 A2
York Hill. Lou 140 C3
York Pl. Grays 192 A4
York Rd. Bill 149 D3
York Rd. Brent 146 C1
York Rd. Chelm 124 A4
York Rd. Dag 173 E3
York Rd. Hav 6 C4
York Rd. Hornc 178 C2
York Rd. N W Bas 117 D2
Yorkes. Harl 102 C3

Zambesi Rd. Bis St 67 F3

STREET ATLASES ORDER FORM

All Street Atlases contain Ordnance Survey mapping and provide the perfect solution for the driver who needs comprehensive, detailed regional mapping in a choice of compact and easy-to-use formats. They are indispensable and are ideal for use in the car, the home or the office.

The series is available from all good bookshops or by mail order direct from the publisher. Before placing your order, please check by telephone that the complete range of titles are available. Payment can be made in the following ways:

By phone Phone your order through on our special Credit Card Hotline on 01733 371999 (Fax: 01733 370585). Speak to our customer service team during office hours (9am to 5pm) or leave a message on the answering machine, quoting your full credit card number plus expiry date and your full name and address.

By post Simply fill out the order form (you may photocopy it) and send it to: Reed Books Direct, 43 Stapledon Road, Orton Southgate, Peterborough PE2 6TD.

NEW COLOUR EDITIONS

	HARDBACK	SPIRAL	POCKET	£ Total
	Quantity @ £10.99 each	Quantity @ £8.99 each	Quantity @ £4.99 each	
BERKSHIRE	☐ 0 540 06170 0	☐ 0 540 06172 7	☐ 0 540 06173 5	➤ ☐
	Quantity @ £10.99 each	Quantity @ £8.99 each	Quantity @ £3.99 each	
MERSEYSIDE	☐ 0 540 06480 7	☐ 0 540 06481 5	☐ 0 540 06482 3	➤ ☐
	Quantity @ £12.99 each	Quantity @ £8.99 each	Quantity @ £4.99 each	
SURREY	☐ 0 540 06435 1	☐ 0 540 06436 X	☐ 0 540 06438 6	➤ ☐
	Quantity @ £12.99 each	Quantity @ £9.99 each	Quantity @ £4.99 each	
DURHAM	☐ 0 540 06365 7	☐ 0 540 06366 5	☐ 0 540 06367 3	➤ ☐
GREATER MANCHESTER	☐ 0 540 06485 8	☐ 0 540 06486 6	☐ 0 540 06487 4	➤ ☐
HERTFORDSHIRE	☐ 0 540 06174 3	☐ 0 540 06175 1	☐ 0 540 06176 X	➤ ☐
TYNE AND WEAR	☐ 0 540 06370 3	☐ 0 540 06371 1	☐ 0 540 06372 X	➤ ☐
SOUTH YORKSHIRE	☐ 0 540 06330 4	☐ 0 540 06331 2	☐ 0 540 06332 0	➤ ☐
WEST YORKSHIRE	☐ 0 540 06329 0	☐ 0 540 06327 4	☐ 0 540 06328 2	➤ ☐
	Quantity @ £14.99 each	Quantity @ £9.99 each	Quantity @ £4.99 each	
LANCASHIRE	☐ 0 540 06440 8	☐ 0 540 06441 6	☐ 0 540 06443 2	➤ ☐

BLACK AND WHITE EDITIONS

	HARDBACK	SOFTBACK	POCKET	£ Total
	Quantity @ £12.99 each	Quantity @ £9.99 each	Quantity @ £4.99 each	
BRISTOL AND AVON	☐ 0 540 06140 9	☐ 0 540 06141 7	☐ 0 540 06142 5	➤ ☐
BUCKINGHAMSHIRE	☐ 0 540 05989 7	☐ 0 540 05990 0	☐ 0 540 05991 9	➤ ☐
CARDIFF, SWANSEA & GLAMORGAN	☐ 0 540 06186 7	☐ 0 540 06187 5	☐ 0 540 06207 3	➤ ☐

STREET ATLASES ORDER FORM

BLACK AND WHITE EDITIONS

	HARDBACK	SOFTBACK	POCKET	£ Total
	Quantity @ £12.99 each	Quantity @ £9.99 each	Quantity @ £4.99 each	
CHESHIRE	☐ 0 540 06143 3	☐ 0 540 06144 1	☐ 0 540 06145 X	➤ ☐
DERBYSHIRE	☐ 0 540 06137 9	☐ 0 540 06138 7	☐ 0 540 06139 5	➤ ☐
EDINBURGH & East Central Scotland	☐ 0 540 06180 8	☐ 0 540 06181 6	☐ 0 540 06182 4	➤ ☐
GLASGOW & West Central Scotland	☐ 0 540 06183 2	☐ 0 540 06184 0	☐ 0 540 06185 9	➤ ☐
SOUTH HAMPSHIRE	☐ 0 540 05855 6	☐ 0 540 05856 4	☐ 0 540 05857 2	➤ ☐
WEST KENT	☐ 0 540 06029 1	☐ 0 540 06031 3	☐ 0 540 06030 5	➤ ☐
NOTTINGHAMSHIRE	☐ 0 540 05858 0	☐ 0 540 05859 9	☐ 0 540 05860 2	➤ ☐
OXFORDSHIRE	☐ 0 540 05986 2	☐ 0 540 05987 0	☐ 0 540 05988 9	➤ ☐
STAFFORDSHIRE	☐ 0 540 06134 4	☐ 0 540 06135 2	☐ 0 540 06136 0	➤ ☐
WEST SUSSEX	☐ 0 540 05876 9	☐ 0 540 05877 7	☐ 0 540 05878 5	➤ ☐
	Quantity @ £10.99 each	Quantity @ £8.99 each	Quantity @ £4.99 each	£ Total
WARWICKSHIRE	☐ 0 540 05642 1	—	—	➤ ☐
	Quantity @ £12.99 each	Quantity @ £8.99 each	Quantity @ £4.99 each	£ Total
EAST ESSEX	☐ 0 540 05848 3	☐ 0 540 05866 1	☐ 0 540 05850 5	➤ ☐
WEST ESSEX	☐ 0 540 05849 1	☐ 0 540 05867 X	☐ 0 540 05851 3	➤ ☐
NORTH HAMPSHIRE	☐ 0 540 05852 1	☐ 0 540 05853 X	☐ 0 540 05854 8	➤ ☐
EAST KENT	☐ 0 540 06026 7	☐ 0 540 06027 5	☐ 0 540 06028 3	➤ ☐
EAST SUSSEX	☐ 0 540 05875 0	☐ 0 540 05874 2	☐ 0 540 05873 4	➤ ☐

Post to: Reed Books Direct, 43 Stapledon Road, Orton Southgate, Peterborough PE2 6TD

◆ Free postage and packing

◆ All available titles will normally be dispatched within 5 working days of receipt of order but please allow up to 28 days for delivery

☐ Please tick this box if you do not wish your name to be used by other carefully selected organisations that may wish to send you information about other products and services

Registered Office: Michelin House, 81 Fulham Road, London SW3 6RB. Registered in England number:1974080

I enclose a cheque / postal order, for a **total** of ☐

made payable to *Reed Book Services,* or please debit my

☐ Access ☐ American Express ☐ Visa ☐ Diners

account by ☐

Account no ☐☐☐☐ ☐☐☐☐ ☐☐☐☐ ☐☐☐☐

Expiry date ☐☐ ☐☐

Signature..

Name...

Address...

....

....

....POSTCODE